Game
Programming
Gems 4

Game Programming Gems 4

Edited by Andrew Kirmse

CHARLES RIVER MEDIA, INC.

Hingham, Massachusetts

Publisher: Jenifer Niles
Series Editor: Mark DeLoura
Production: Publishers' Design and Production Services, Inc.
Cover Design: The Printed Image
Cover Image: "Delivering the Goods" from *MechAssaultII* © Day 1 Studios 2003. © Microsoft ® 2003.

CHARLES RIVER MEDIA, INC.
10 Downer Avenue
Hingham, Massachusetts 02043
781-740-0400
781-740-8816 (FAX)
info@charlesriver.com
www.charlesriver.com

This book is printed on acid-free paper.

Andrew Kirmse. *Game Programming Gems 4*.
ISBN: 1-58450-295-9

Library of Congress Cataloging-in-Publication Data
Game programming gems 4 / edited by Andrew Kirmse.
    p.   cm.
  ISBN 1-58450-295-9 (Hardback with CD-ROM : alk. paper)
  1. Computer games—Programming. I. Kirmse, Andrew.
  QA76.76.C672G364 2004
  794.8'0285—dc22
                  2003023519
Printed in the United States of America
04 7 6 5 4 3 2 First Edition

Contents

Foreword

Mark DeLoura

madsax@satori.org

Welcome to *Game Programming Gems 4*! This latest volume of the *Game Programming Gems* series continues to explore the vast array of problems you face as a game programmer. Someone, somewhere out there, has likely solved the technical challenge you're facing right now. Why re-invent the wheel? If you can stand on the shoulders of giants (by using their solution), you get the opportunity to be a giant for someone else. Extend the algorithms of others and then share your results—that's how our industry grows, and how you can remain excited about the programming tasks in front of you each day.

In this volume we've further refined the material presented to you to reflect the challenges you're facing today by adding a section on game physics. As game platforms have grown more powerful, the popularity of implementing real-time physics has increased. Upcoming titles are beginning to add physics in a transparent way; many objects just react physically as you would expect them to. Consequently, emergent gameplay is becoming much more possible, and interesting. So, you don't have a weapon? Well, throw a chair at that zombie!

The material in this book has been lovingly crafted by Andrew Kirmse, a developer of the first 3D massively multiplayer online role-playing game, *Meridian 59* (in 1996!). Andrew is currently a lead programmer at LucasArts, where he has worked on titles such as *Star Wars: Starfighter*. He was also the network and multiplayer section editor for *Game Programming Gems 3*, and a contributor to both the original *Game Programming Gems* and *Game Programming Gems 2*!

State of the Industry

As this book goes to print, we're all waiting for information about the next generation of video game consoles. We have suspicions about the techniques we'll need to learn to work on them effectively, but the new capabilities they'll provide us remain a mystery.

More immediate at this time is the upsurge of interest in portable game devices. Nintendo® GameBoy® has been around for over a decade in various forms, but it's been just during this past year that other companies have stepped forward with competitive platforms. From Nokia's N-Gage™ to Tapwave's Zodiac™ to Sony's PSP and whatever Microsoft might have up its sleeves, the handheld gaming market is about ready to explode.

And this is good timing. Console titles have gotten quite expensive to produce, and they're very risky, so having an alternate platform that is less expensive to develop for is definitely a plus. If you're a garage developer, it's especially welcome news. Who can afford the $15 million it takes to produce a quality game now, except for the biggest publishers?

The rising cost of producing games has led to a number of unsavory problems in the industry, not the least of which is an increasing lack of innovation. Who can blame the publishers for not being willing to take a risk? If you had $15 million riding on the line, wouldn't you be tempted to play it safe too? We now see many more sequels, clones of existing games, and licensed products. It's understandable, but it isn't very satisfying. If you're a game player, it's doubtful you'll be excited about playing the same kinds of games repeatedly.

So, what's the solution? How do we free everyone up so that we can innovate more? I don't have the answer, but I do have an idea that will help.

Contributing

People have asked me why people contribute to the *Gems* series. Aren't they all just giving away their technical expertise to their competitors? You certainly don't see this happening in other fields—Coca-Cola® doesn't share its secret recipe with Pepsi™! So, why would you want to share your algorithms with other publishers and developers who are creating games that you compete with?

Consider it from this angle. If you started with a new code base each time you wrote a game, you'd have to rewrite your save game library each time, right? Do you really want to do that? Wouldn't you rather find a way to save time and potentially save your sanity as well? What if you gave that library to your friend after you wrote it? I know, why would you do that, after spending so much time creating it? You would do it because your friend has the exact same problem. He's been writing memory defragmentation routines over and over again, and he's bored to death with it, too. However, if the two of you were to share your libraries, you'd both have to spend half as much time writing them all. Wouldn't that be worthwhile?

At a higher level, let's say you work at a publisher, and you're working with two development studios that are both creating all their code from scratch. They're rewriting all the same sets of low-level libraries. Wouldn't you be interested in consolidating that development to save money? The basic routines of a game don't have much of an impact on the game itself, so why pay for both studios to write them independently? Now, if you work at one of those studios, this idea will save you time and let you concentrate on adding features to your game, which will make it stand out from the others. And, by the way, since your publisher receives the majority of your game's revenue in trade for the services it provides you, wouldn't it be great if you could get some useful code out of it as part of the deal?

Let's take this one more step higher. We're a big industry. There are easily over 1,000 development studios working on games. One thousand studios recreating the same libraries, over and over and over. Why bother? Isn't this why libraries like the STL have been written, to save everyone time, and ultimately, money? Wouldn't it be better if these studios could collaborate on an abstract level, so that each one could spend more of its time working on the parts of its game that make it unique? It's no wonder no one has time to create innovative games—everyone is spending so much time writing their own low-level code (which only gets more complex over time) that they don't have the time in their schedules to be creative.

Share and Share Alike

Okay, you might say, that's great. So I'll let everyone else write code and share it, and I'll just use what they produce. That way, I'll benefit from them, but I won't have to share anything at all. But that breaks the system. If everyone did that, there would be no conferences, no books, no magazines, no sharing of any information whatsoever. For the economy to work properly, everyone needs to contribute.

You can make a similar argument about taxes. If everyone stopped paying his or her taxes, government would fall apart. The roads would decay, bridges would fall down, and the snow would pile up in the street without anyone cutting a path through it. Now, you could just take care of all these things yourself, maintaining the area around where you live. But it's far more efficient to contribute some money and let the experts of each need take care of it properly for everyone. It's just like that with software. If you contribute some of your resources, especially what you're an expert at, you'll be able to take advantage of what all the other experts in the industry create as well.

In a tax-paying society, each person who holds back their resources, who doesn't pay taxes, robs the rest of the community just a little bit. Each other person will need to pay more taxes to make up for those who are delinquent. Consider that it's just like that with your technical expertise. By not contributing to our community, you withhold your wisdom from each person in it. Those people get a little bit of their time stolen away—they have to try writing that amazing memory card library that you could simply have contributed. Do you then have any right to complain about the lack of innovation in our industry? You're forcing these people to write their own memory card library! No wonder they didn't have time to innovate!

So, at a simple level this is how a sharing economy can work, and why it's such an important facet of our development community. In addition to getting the benefit of everyone else's ideas, each person who contributes to the community also gets positive feedback, in terms of improvements to his or her code from the community, and perhaps a little fame, or even money.

Now, certainly at some level there are probably trade secrets that you don't want to share with others, and this is understandable. If you've developed an incredible new pixel shader, it's understandable that you might want to ship a game using your technique before you share it with the world. However, at the point that you ship your game, the technique is turned loose to anyone who cares to analyze your title. So, why not share it openly with the community? As time goes on, developers who do this increase the amount of information available, as well as its complexity. This leads to books like this one, the fourth volume of the *Game Programming Gems* series. It is because of a huge number of people around the world that the *Gems* books exist. Nearly 200 people have written for the *Gems* series so far, from countries like the United States, Canada, England, France, Germany, Switzerland, Australia, and Brazil. Clearly, the sharing economy works for many folks.

Consider what you can contribute back to the game development community, whether it be by submitting an article for the *Gems* series, writing a magazine article, writing a book, publishing some articles on your own Web site, or turning loose the source code from your latest game. You'll get more by giving your information away than just sitting on it. Reading other people's ideas is how we all learned computer science, and it is how future game developers will learn the techniques that work so that they too can avoid reinventing the wheel. This frees them up to innovate and create new experiences for us all to enjoy. And isn't that really what we all want as game players anyway?

Preface

Andrew Kirmse, LucasArts Entertainment Company

ark@alum.mit.edu

Practical books on game development have been proliferating in the past few years, and a big reason is the success of the *Game Programming Gems* series. The series, including the current volume, is one of the few places where professional game developers share their secrets in detail with people outside their companies. We hope that you will enjoy this look behind the screen of many of today's most advanced and best-selling games, and that you will apply their techniques in your own work.

Putting together a practical book is a balancing act between cutting-edge knowledge that you can use immediately, and insight that will have you returning years from now. Because game development has become so specialized, we recruited industry experts to select and edit articles in each of seven subject areas:

- **General Programming:** Chris Corry, LucasArts Entertainment Company
- **Mathematics:** Jonathan Blow
- **Physics:** Graham Rhodes, Applied Research Associates, Inc.
- **Artificial Intelligence:** Paul Tozour, Retro Studios/Nintendo
- **Graphics:** Alex Vlachos, ATI Research, Inc.
- **Network and Multiplayer:** Pete Isensee, Microsoft
- **Audio:** Eddie Edwards, Sony Computer Entertainment Europe

The Physics section is new to this volume, and reflects the growing importance of real-time simulation and dynamics in many games. Once restricted solely to flight simulators and racing games, physics is now a major component of most games involving vehicles or articulated characters. The articles in this section cover everything from "Physics for Game Programmers 101" to the latest advances in real-time deformation.

There are other firsts in this volume: the first female authors (congratulations!), a greater contribution from academia, and in graphics, the debut of techniques that rely on the pixel and vertex shaders in modern hardware. Comparing the color plates in this volume with the original *Game Programming Gems* from just three years ago shows just how rapidly the field is progressing. Shadows in particular are an active area of research, and new shadow techniques are well represented in the Graphics section.

Even with all the focus on hardware features, though, some of the most visually arresting new effects require nothing more than a little cleverness.

How to Use This Book

ON THE CD

We tried to build a book that you will keep on your desk, as opposed to in your bookcase. When you encounter a new problem, see if it has already been solved; in many cases, you might be able to adapt the code on the companion CD-ROM, or use it directly. If you are a specialist in a subject area, you will of course want to read that section first, but the other sections (especially General Programming) might contain the solution to an annoying problem that has haunted your game. You might take on a different role on your next project and return to read other sections of the book.

Within each section, articles are generally arranged in increasing order of complexity. Veterans will still benefit from earlier articles, and beginners will find applications in later ones; as you proceed through each chapter, articles will assume a greater familiarity with the subject, and more mathematical sophistication. Linear algebra is particularly useful in the Mathematics and Physics sections, and a few articles use basic calculus, differential equations, and numerical methods.

As the scope of books in this series has expanded, so has the use of alternative languages and third-party APIs. Most code is written in C++, although several interpreted languages (Java and Python) are also represented. Graphics articles make free use of OpenGL, DirectX, and the various available shader languages. We have made an effort to describe the techniques in a way that is not tied to any particular API.

Coming Full Circle

Many who began in the industry some years ago can remember a single moment that ignited our interest in making games. For me, it began when I learned in sixth grade that it was possible to draw a circle on a computer screen using a type of magic called "trigonometry." Later, we taught ourselves from now-battered books, perhaps Knuth's *The Art of Computer Programming*, Sedgwick's *Algorithms*, the *Graphics Gems* series, or maybe the Bresenham circle-drawing description in Foley and van Dam's *Computer Graphics*. When, years ago, I was asked to derive that algorithm in an interview, I thought fondly of tracing out circles on an Atari 800 back in sixth grade.

If you are a gaming professional, I hope that this book will reawaken that sense of wonder. If you are just getting started, I hope you will find an idea that inspires a lifetime of tinkering and discovery.

Acknowledgments

I am grateful to *Game Programming Gems 3* editor Dante Treglia and series editor Mark DeLoura for offering me the opportunity to work on this book. Dante's templates and advice from the previous volume were extremely helpful in getting me started. Mark built and ran the Web-based application the section editors used while selecting articles, and later provided me with continual feedback during the editing process.

The staff at Charles River Media were uniformly responsive and a joy to work with. Most of my contact was with the book's publisher, Jenifer Niles, who has been instrumental in the entire series. David Pallai, Meg Dunkerley, and Jennifer Blaney also helped field my many questions.

Most of the work, of course, was done by the seven section editors and the dozens of authors. Contributing to a book of this kind is a very time-consuming labor of love. Many authors and editors went beyond the call of duty to provide extra figures, color illustrations, and impressive working demos and test programs. Their spirit of sharing knowledge, so rare in cutting-edge industries, is what keeps these books alive.

I would also like to thank Jennifer Sloan for her editorial assistance, her moral support, and her inexhaustible laughter.

About the Cover Image

TJ Wagner, Day 1 Studios

The cover is a scene from *MechAssault II*, a game developed by Day 1 Studios™, LLC and Microsoft® Game Studios for the Xbox® video game system.

All in-game geometry is built and mapped via custom material and texture plugins from within 3ds max™. From there, game assets are exported and placed in the level using in-house world building tools.

The *MechAssault II* rendering engine is an entirely shader-driven engine using a custom shader compiler and linker to assemble vertex shaders on the fly. The engine employs a wide range of rendering techniques, incorporating per-vertex lighting with multipass normal-mapped lighting and light mapping. *MechAssault II* also performs post-processing to simulate variable depth of field and high dynamic range lighting.

All of the buildings in the game are constructed so that they can be dynamically damaged by the player. Damage is done by deforming the building geometry on the fly. Buildings can be significantly damaged and then collapsed in the game. The building collapse sequences are scripted by designers using in-house effects tools.

In the cover scene, the player controlling the BattleArmor has just hooked onto a VTOL and is being taken quickly to an enemy location. A tow cable is pulling along the gem. Let's hope that the AI or player piloting the VTOL doesn't scrape the BattleArmor off on a building!

Contributor Bios

Marwan Y. Ansari

mansari@ati.com

Marwan Y. Ansari is a member of the 3D Application Research group at ATI Research. He received a master's degree in computer science from the University of Illinois at Chicago and a bachelor of science in computer science and mathematics from DePaul University. Prior to moving to ATI's 3D Application Research group, he worked on OpenGL drivers for Number Nine Visual Technology before joining ATI's Digital TV group. In addition to his Gem on sepia tone conversion in this book, Marwan has also contributed to *ShaderX2* and spoken about real-time video processing using shaders at the Game Developers Conference.

Jonathan Blow

jon@number-none.com

Jonathan Blow is a game technology consultant living in New York City. He writes the monthly technical column, "The Inner Product," for *Game Developer Magazine*. He also organizes the annual Experimental Gameplay Workshop, an event that show-cases and encourages risky new kinds of gameplay.

James Boer

james.boer@gte.net

James Boer started his career by creating *Deer Hunter*, and has endured good-natured ribbing from his coworkers ever since. Other game credits include *Rocky Mountain Trophy Hunter*, *Deer Hunter II*, *Microsoft Baseball 2000*, and *Tex Atomic's Big Bot Battles* (online game). In addition to his professional programming credits, James has also contributed prolifically to the game industry's print media, including several articles in *Game Developer Magazine*, co-authoring *DirectX Complete*, contributing to *Game Programming Gems I & II*, and his latest book *Game Audio Programming*. James is currently employed at Amaze Entertainment's Black Ship studio, developing cross-platform games for current and next-generation consoles.

Paul Bragiel

paul@paragon5.com

Paul Bragiel has served as CEO of Paragon Five since 2000. He has brokered over 25 music deals on various handheld platforms. He also holds executive producer credits on 3 GBC, 3 GBA, and a slew of mobile phone titles. In the past, he has held presentations at the GDC and Assembly conferences.

Warrick Buchanan

warrick@chimeric.co.uk

Warrick Buchanan is development director at Chimeric Ltd, working on the Maxinima and ScreenSaverMax products. Amongst working for various game development companies over the years, he also did a stint in graphics card driver development for Imagination Technologies Ltd. He enjoys playing with toys that range from cutting-edge graphics cards to trampolines.

Bill Budge

billbudge@hotmail.com

Bill Budge knew at age three that building things would be his life's work. Since then he has moved from blocks to template metaprogramming in C++, but amazingly is still having lots of fun playing with interesting new forms of construction. When not coding, he spends time with his family, drinks Peet's Mocha Fredos, and reads computer books.

Waldemar Celes

celes@inf.puc-rio.br

Waldemar Celes is an assistant professor in the computer science department at PUC-Rio, Brazil. He is a researcher and senior project manager associated with Tecgraf/PUC-Rio (Computer Graphics Technology group at PUC-Rio) and a former postdoctoral associate at the program of computer graphics, Cornell University. Waldemar is also one of the authors of the Lua programming language. His current research interests in computer graphics include real-time rendering, scientific visualization, physical simulation, and distributed graphics applications.

Chris Corry

chris@thecorrys.com

Chris Corry is a lead engineer at LucasArts, a division of Lucasfilm Ltd. He has been authoring, co-authoring, or editing technical books for more than a decade—*Game Programming Gems 4* is his ninth collaborative effort.

Carsten Dachsbacher

dachsbacher@cs.fau.de

Carsten Dachsbacher is a Ph.D. student in computer graphics at the university of Erlangen-Nuremberg. His research focuses on interactive, hardware-assisted computer graphics; in particular, shadowing techniques, point-based rendering, and procedural models. He is author of a series of more than 50 articles on computer graphics in a German PC magazine. Furthermore, he is working as a freelancer on 3D game engines for different game companies.

Mark DeLoura

madsax@satori.org

Mark is the creator of the *Game Programming Gems* series of books. In his role as the manager of developer relations at Sony Computer Entertainment America, he gets the opportunity to share information, both technical and nontechnical, with game developers around the world. Mark is fascinated with the concept of creating shared, entertaining experiences that educate people and encourage them to communicate with each other. He has been pursuing ways to broaden the concept of what an "entertaining experience" is, through a variety of roles, including former positions as editor-in-chief of *Game Developer* magazine, and lead software engineer of Nintendo of America's Developer Support group.

Shekhar Dhupelia

sdhupelia@midwaygames.com

Shekhar works for Midway Games, LLC, focusing on online gameplay design and engineering. Previously, Shekhar served as lead engineer for Sony Computer Entertainment America (SCEA), spending two years on the buildup and launch of Sony's PlayStation® 2 online technology and backend systems, as a core member of the SCE-RT group. This technology was the backbone for *SOCOM: US Navy Seals*, *NFL Gameday 2003*, *Frequency*, and many other titles. Shekhar served a stint with High Voltage Software, working on their Xbox™ Live initiative for Microsoft's *NBA Inside Drive 2004*. He has a B.S. in computer science from DePaul University. Shekhar's current project with Midway is *NBA Ballers*, to be released in Q1 2004.

Thomas Di Giacomo

thomas@miralab.unige.ch

Thomas Di Giacomo completed a master's degree on multiresolution methods for animation with iMAGIS lab and Atari ex-Infogrames R&D department. He is now a research assistant and a Ph.D. candidate at MIRALab, University of Geneva. His work focuses on level of detail for animation and physically based animation.

Michael Dougherty

mdougher@hotmail.com

Michael Dougherty currently works in the Xbox Advanced Technology group at Microsoft. He specializes in graphics techniques and system performance. Michael holds a computer engineering degree from the University of Washington. He would like to thank his wife Jessica and his daughter Elyse for their infinite support and patience through all of his endeavors.

George Drettakis

George.Drettakis@sophia.inria.fr

George Drettakis received a Ptychion (B.Sc.) in 1988 from the C.S. Department in Crete, Greece. He completed an M.Sc. (1990) and a Ph.D. (1994) at the Dept. of C.S. at the University of Toronto, Canada, under the supervision of Eugene Fiume. After an ERCIM post-doc (1994–1995) at iMAGIS, Grenoble, France, UPC/LiSi graphics Barcelona, and VMSD-GMD Germany, he was appointed permanent INRIA researcher at iMAGIS in 1995, and obtained the Habilitation degree (Grenoble, 1999). In July 2000, he moved to INRIA Sophia-Antipolis, where he founded and leads the REVES research group. Recent research work includes shadows, lighting, reconstruction from images, and interactive rendering.

Eddie Edwards

eddie@tinyted.net

Eddie cut his gaming teeth doing the official Archimedes conversion of *Wolfenstein 3D* and then *DOOM*. Since then he has worked at Cranberry Source, Argonaut, Mucky Foot, and Naughty Dog (SCEA), where he worked on *Jak & Daxter* as a general low-level coder (among other things, he wrote the audio engine for that game). Eddie is now based back in England and leads the Graphics group at Psygnosis (SCEE).

David Etherton

etherton@rockstarsandiego.com

David joined Rockstar San Diego back in 1996 when they were still Angel Studios. He has done rendering and low-level optimization work on many of the games the studio has shipped, but was most involved in *Midtown Madness*, *Midtown Madness 2*, *Midnight Club*, and *Midnight Club 2*. David is the technical lead on the studio's cross-platform game library that has been the foundation of all titles shipped since 2000, and is currently the director of research and development.

Glenn Fiedler

gaffer@gaffer.org

Glenn Fiedler knows way too much about heightfields and is currently putting this knowledge to good use on *Tribes: Vengeance* at Irrational Games. His previous accomplishments include totally rewriting the pathfinder and physics systems of *Freedom Force* to use, you guessed it, a heightfield. One day, Glenn hopes to extend his formidable programming skills to include techniques that support overhangs.

Peter Freese

pfreese@ncaustin.com

Peter has been active in the game industry since the early 1990s, when he decided he'd rather make games than graphics tools for database programmers. After developing several award-winning educational games, Peter founded Q Studios in 1994 with former Edmark colleague Nick Newhard and led development on the campy 3D shooter *Blood*, which launched publisher Monolith into the spotlight. After developing the graphics engine behind Sierra Studio's final adventure game, *Gabriel Knight 3*, Peter joined the *Ultima Online 2* team at Origin Systems to learn all the joys and trials of MMP game development. In 2001, Peter established a Core Technology group for NCsoft in Austin, TX, where he directs development on the state-of-the-art graphics engine technology behind many of NCsoft's new online games.

Bert Freudenberg

bert@isg.cs.uni-magdeburg.de

Bert Freudenberg is developing nonphotorealistic real-time rendering techniques at the University of Magdeburg, Germany, which hopefully will award him a Ph.D. for his efforts. Besides writing research papers and presenting at conferences including EuroGraphics and SIGGRAPH, he contributed to the OpenGL Shading Language specification and book (Addison-Wesley, 2003). Bert enjoys teaching tricky stuff and working with children, in particular hacking on the cross-platform Squeak environment. His newest interest is in the OpenCroquet operating system experiment, mostly out of frustration that nothing has really changed in computing since he began programming in the 1980s.

Paul Glinker

paul@glinker.com

Initially inspired by the Atari 2600, Paul began programming at age seven on a TRS-80 Co-Co-2 with 16K RAM. At age 13, his need for power turned him to C on an 8086. In high school, inspiration and encouragement from his favorite computer studies teacher lead him to write an arcade-style game, which was sold at a local computer store. Taking Honors Computer Science at Laurentian University, his professors were a strong influence in his life, always willing to discuss how the principles of computer science can be applied to game development. In 2000, he was hired by Rockstar Games as a programmer and is still there today.

Mario Grimani

mariogrimani@yahoo.com

Mario Grimani is an industry veteran who joined the gaming industry almost two decades ago. He has worked at big name studios such as Ion Storm, Ensemble Studios, Verant Interactive, and Sony Online Entertainment. While at Ensemble Studios, he was a dedicated AI specialist in charge of improving the computer player competitiveness. He has developed a scripting system and a computer player AI for *Age of Empires II: The Age of Kings*, and *Age of Empires II: The Conquerors*. During the early stages of *Age of Mythology* development, Mario served as AI lead in charge of AI architecture. After joining Verant Interactive, in an attempt to help create a new MMO RTS genre, he took over as lead programmer on *Sovereign*. Currently, he is working for Sony Online Entertainment and implementing various game systems for *Everquest II*. Mario has a bachelor's degree in electrical engineering from the University of Zagreb, Croatia and a master's degree in computer science from Southwest Texas State University.

John Hancock

jhancock93@post.harvard.edu

John Hancock received his Ph.D. in robotics in 1999 from Carnegie Mellon University (CMU). While at CMU, he worked on vision and navigation algorithms for robotic cars. After receiving his doctorate, John began his game industry career at Activision, where he was co-lead programmer and AI developer for *Star Trek™: Armada* (shipped March 2000). He joined LucasArts in May 2000, where he has worked on *Star Wars: Obi-Wan*, and *Star Wars: Bounty Hunter*. He is currently working on the squad AI for *Star Wars: Republic Commando*.

Søren Hannibal

sorenhan@yahoo.com

Søren Hannibal has been programming almost continually since 1985, taking short breaks to sleep, eat, and study when it has been absolutely necessary. Søren recently wrote the animation system for *Enter the Matrix,* and is currently having fun cracking the whip as lead programmer at Shiny Entertainment.

Matthew Harmon

matt@matthewharmon.com

Matthew Harmon has been developing games since college, working on *Microsoft Flight Simulator* for subLogic Corporation while earning his degree in film theory and criticism. Since then, he has served as lead programmer and director of development at Mission Studios Corp. and Velocity Development. Recently, he co-founded eV Interactive Corporation to continue developing games and use game technology in the military training and simulation arena. In his spare time, Matt chases his sons Alex and Greg around the house.

Oliver Heim

Oliver.Heim@intel.com

Oliver Heim is a senior software engineer in the Graphics Core Engineering group at Intel working on Direct3D device drivers for integrated chipsets. Previously, Oliver worked for Intel's Graphics and 3D Technologies group, where he worked on real-time collision detection and physics algorithms for the Shockwave3D game engine and investigated real-time global illumination algorithms including radiosity, ray-tracing, and photon mapping. Before joining Intel in 1999, Oliver worked for three years as the director of Clemson University's virtual reality laboratory. Oliver received a B.S. in computer science from the University of Georgia, and an M.S. in computer science from Clemson University. In his spare time, Oliver can be found playing guitar on his back porch or kayaking off some waterfall in northern California.

Jim Hejl

jhejl@ea.com

Jim Hejl is a senior software engineer for Electronic Arts, and is a member of the Research and Development group at the Tiburon studio. Previously, Jim worked on *John Madden Football* (2000–2003). He loves his job more then he loves taffy—and he's a man who loves taffy.

Pete Isensee

pkisensee@msn.com

Pete Isensee is the lead engineer of the Xbox Advanced Technology group at Microsoft. He specializes in networking, performance, and security issues. Pete holds a degree in computer engineering. In his spare time, he throws few exceptions, but catches just about everything.

Toby Jones

tjones@humanhead.com

Thobias Jones is a programmer for Human Head Studios working on games for the Xbox and PC. He has a B.S. in computer science from the University of Wisconsin, Platteville. Thobias has been programming since the PC was introduced, and studies 3D graphics and computer architecture for fun. When not programming or watching anime, Thobias publishes shareware through his company, Genkisoft. His work is made possible with the support of the love of his life, Jess.

Andrew Kirmse

ark@alum.mit.edu

Andrew was the co-inventor and director of *Meridian 59* (1996), and the graphics programmer on *Star Wars: Starfighter* (2001). He has degrees in physics, mathematics, and computer science from the Massachusetts Institute of Technology (MIT). Andrew has contributed to each of the *Game Programming Gems* books. He now works at LucasArts.

Adam Lake

adam.t.lake@intel.com

Adam Lake is a senior software engineer in the Intel Microprocessor Research Labs (MRL) in Hillsboro, Oregon, specializing in next-generation computer graphics architectures and programming models. He has several publications and over 20 patent applications in the area of computer graphics, virtual reality, geometry compression, e-commerce, and nonphotorealistic rendering. Previous to working at Intel, he obtained a master's degree in computer science at the University of North Carolina at Chapel Hill studying computer graphics and virtual reality. Before studying at UNC-Chapel Hill, he worked at Los Alamos National Laboratory in the Applied Theoretical Physics and Computational Science Methods (XCM) group. There, he worked on a computer-aided design application for physicists called Justine. More information is available at *www.cs.unc.edu/~lake/vitae.html*. In his spare time, he is a mountain biker, road cyclist, hiker, camper, avid reader, snowboarder, and Sunday driver.

Jay Lee

jlee@ncaustin.com

Jay Lee came into the games industry after a 10-year career with EDS, serving clients such as General Motors, Exxon, and Sprint in their information technology needs. He started as a programmer with Sierra and contributed to titles such as *Gabriel Knight 2*, *Betrayal at Antara*, *Colliers Encyclopedia*, and *SWAT 2*. He entered the world of online multiplayer games when he joined Origin Systems, working as the database programmer and scripting lead on *Ultima Online 2*. In his current assignment, Jay serves as a technical lead and database programmer on *Tabula Rasa* for NCsoft Corporation in Austin, TX.

Noel Llopis

llopis@convexhull.com

Noel Llopis is the author of the book *C++ for Game Programmers*. He has also contributed several articles to earlier *Game Programming Gems* volumes. For his last project, he worked on the technology behind *MechAssault* at Day 1 Studios. He is now busy researching and implementing the technology for their next game. He focuses on all aspects of game engines, from the overall architecture, to graphics and collision detection. He obtained his undergraduate degree in computer engineering from the University of Massachusetts Amherst, and his master's degree in computer science from the University of North Carolina at Chapel Hill.

Thomas Lowe

tomlowe@kromestudios.com

Building on an honors degree in computer science from Warwick University in the UK and a firm interest in creating computer games, Tom became a game programmer with Krome Studios in Brisbane, Australia. While there, he has worked on a variety of genres over the last four years, including surfing, action, and platform games that have been released on all main consoles and the PC. Tom specializes in dynamic simulation, special effects, mathematics, and character control.

Frank Luchs

gameprogramminggems@visiomedia.com

In 1983, Frank Luchs wrote his first music program for the Atari computer and started his dual music/programming career. His projects have ranged from producing and composing scores for movies and TV, to sound design and programming of custom applications and multimedia software. He has produced and composed hundreds of songs, jingles, and movie scores (including Germany's most-known crime serial, *Tatort*). He is the founder of Visiomedia Software Corporation, a company specializing in virtual instruments. At Visiomedia, he designed the Sphinx Modular Media System, which is the base for the software synthesizers Saccara™, Chephren™, and Cheops™. Frank currently works in the movie business in Munich, Germany. When he's not programming, he enjoys making a lot of noise with his synthesizer gear and composing electronic symphonies.

Nadia Magnenat-Thalmann

thalmann@miralab.unige.ch

Nadia Magnenat-Thalmann has pioneered research into virtual humans over the last 20 years. She obtained several bachelor's and master's degrees in various disciplines, and a Ph.D. in quantum physics from the University of Geneva. From 1977 to 1989, she was a professor at the University of Montreal in Canada. In 1989, she founded MIRALab at the University of Geneva.

Carl S. Marshall

Carl.S.Marshall@intel.com

Carl S. Marshall is a senior software engineer in the Future Platform Labs of Intel Corporation. He has an M.S. in computer science from Clemson University, where he conducted research in the area of virtual reality. He has authored chapters for both *Game Programming Gems 2* and *3*. Previously, he worked on the NPR and other aspects of the Shockwave3D graphics engine. Currently, Carl is pursuing research interests in real-time photorealistic graphics engines and future hardware architectures.

Adam Martin

gpg@grexengine.com

For more than a decade, Adam has been fascinated by virtual worlds and the technology—the graphics, processing, and distributed systems—needed to achieve them. He has a computer science degree from Cambridge University, has twice worked in IBM's research labs, and co-founded an IT consultancy. He used to co-run the Cambridge £50,000 business plan competition, and is always eager to share his experiences and advice for startups. In 2001, he founded Grex Games to commercialize his prior research into MMOG development and middleware, and gives conference talks on the GrexEngine architecture.

Maic Masuch

masuch@isg.cs.uni-magdeburg.de

Maic Masuch works at the University of Magdeburg and is Germany's first professor for computer games. He started teaching computer game development courses in 1996. Since then, many student game projects have been developed under his supervision, ranging from simple adventures to nonviolent multiplayer FPS to interactive VR installations. His research focuses on methods and tools for game development and innovative user interfaces. Currently, he is conducting research on intelligent development tools, cinematographic storytelling, nonphotorealistic rendering, and automatic gameplay analysis. Maic also is co-founder of Impara, a company developing educational media authoring and edutainment systems for children.

Dave McCoy

david.mccoy@comcast.net

Dave McCoy is a graphic artist working for Microsoft's Xbox Advanced Technology group. He has served as art director, designer, and producer on games since 1991. His work has appeared in various books and periodicals on game graphics, and he holds two patents for graphics techniques.

Ádám Moravánszky

adam.moravanszky@novodex.com

Ádám Moravánszky is responsible for the core technology group of NovodeX AG, a physics middleware company he co-founded. He received a graduate degree in computer science from the Swiss Federal Institute of Technology (ETH) in Zurich after studying at schools in Hungary, Germany, and the United States.

Frederic My

fmy@fairyengine.com

In 1985, at the age of 14, Frederic started programming and wrote a couple of games as a hobby on a TO7-70 and an Amstrad CPC. In the mid-1990s, he spent most of his spare time programming demos on the PC with his talented friend Alexis Vaginay. After completing his education, he began a career in the game industry, coding 3D engines and tools in assembler and C++. When his computer is off, Frederic is probably running, cycling, or watching *Buffy* again.

James F. O'Brien

job@eecs.Berkeley.edu

Dr. James F. O'Brien is a professor of computer science at U.C. Berkeley. He has written more than 30 journal and conference papers, including eight papers in the prestigious ACM SIGGRAPH conference. In addition to his experience teaching at U.C. Berkeley, he has delivered numerous technical talks and short courses, including several courses at the Game Developers Conference and SIGGRAPH. His research interests focus primarily on physically based simulation for both offline and interactive animation.

Chris Oat

Coat@ati.com

Christopher Oat is a software engineer in the 3D Application Research group at ATI, where he develops novel rendering techniques for real-time 3D graphics applications. His focus is on pixel and vertex shader development for current and future graphics platforms. Chris has contributed as an original member of the RenderMonkey development team and more recently as a shader programmer for ATI's demos and screen savers. He regularly publishes articles on advanced rendering techniques in books such as *Game Programming Gems 3*, *Game Programming Gems 4*, *ShaderX*, and *ShaderX2*. Chris is a graduate of Boston University.

John M. Olsen

infix@xmission.com

John M. Olsen started working on graphics software of various types long before graduating from the University of Utah in 1989, and is now working for Microsoft on Xbox game projects. He has contributed to several books on computer graphics and game development, including the *Game Programming Gems* and *Massively Multiplayer Game Development* series, and has spoken at the Game Developers Conference. His interests include autonomous AI, stereographic image production, networking, and the organization and analysis of data.

Marcin Pancewicz

highway@idreams.com.pl

Marcin Pancewicz is a full-time programmer at Infinite Dreams in Poland. He works on 2D game engines and tools required for game development. He lives in Gliwice, Poland, and when not writing code, he tries to keep his 14-year old Trans Am running.

Kurt Pelzer

kurt.pelzer@gmx.net

Kurt Pelzer is a software engineer at Piranha Bytes, where he worked on the PC game *Gothic*, the top-selling *Gothic II* (both awarded "RPG of the year," 2001 and 2002, in Germany), and the add-on *Gothic II: The Night of the Raven*. Earlier he was a senior programmer at Codecult and developed several real-time simulations and technology demos built on their high-end 3D engine Codecreatures (e.g., a simulation of the Shanghai TRANSRAPID track for SIEMENS AG, and the well-known *Codecreatures Benchmark Pro*). He has published in *ShaderX2* and *GPU Gems*.

Borut Pfeifer

borut_p@yahoo.com

Borut Pfeifer graduated from Georgia Tech in 1998, and after working in various software development positions, he co-founded White Knuckle Games in May 2001. Up until April 2003, Borut worked there as lead designer and gameplay/AI programmer. He currently works at Radical Entertainment, and is the author of various articles on game development.

Karén Pivazyan

pivazyan@stanford.edu

Karén Pivazyan is a game AI architect with nine years of consulting experience. His expertise is in solving challenging problems in game AI by leveraging hitherto undiscovered techniques from academic research. He started playing computer games at the age of 6 and writing them at the age of 10. Now, he holds degrees from MIT and Stanford University. His Ph.D. contributed to the development of multi-agent systems learning. His other passion is modeling human behavior using state-of-the-art psychology. He envisions teaching courses and writing a fundamental book on game AI.

Nick Porcino

nporcino@lucasarts.com

Nick Porcino is the lead of the R2 graphics group at LucasArts. Nick published his first computer game in 1981, for the Apple][, and his first console game in 1984, for the Colecovision™. He tried escaping the games industry a few times in the past, once to create AI for autonomous submersibles at Royal Roads Military College in Canada, once to do VR architectural previsualization, and once to design toys, cool giant robots, and linear accelerators for Bandai in Japan. Somehow, he always got dragged back into games, and there he stays! Nick is now content to be happy building shared core technologies for next-generation platforms.

Mark T. Price

mark@suddenpresence.com

Mark has been working on games for as long as there have been personal computers, starting way back in 1979 with an old CP/M system, through the years of Apple and Atari, then on to PCs, and now on the GameBoy Advance. Sadly, very little of this work was for marketed games. When he graduated from college in 1987, the prospects of a career in game development seemed bleak, so Mark opted instead for a "regular" job. For many years he worked for Reuters Ltd. where he wrote real-time networked stock market information systems that are used by more than 60,000 retail stock brokers across the United States and Canada. In 2001, sensing that the time was right to re-enter the game industry, Mark co-founded Sudden Presence, a game and multimedia contracting firm where he currently serves as chief scientist.

Matt Pritchard

mpritchard@ensemblestudios.com

Matt Pritchard is a senior developer at Ensemble Studios, where among other things he helped launched the *Age of Empires* game series. These days, when he's not working on an unannounced game or battling those who cheat at online games, he can be found at home raising his children, keeping house, and explaining why a station wagon that goes 175 MPH makes perfect sense.

Justin Quimby

justin@turbinegames.com

Justin Quimby is a lead engineer at Turbine Entertainment Software. Over the past five years, the Brown University graduate has worked on each of the award-winning video games in the *Asheron's Call* franchise and *The Lord of the Rings: Middle-Earth Online*. Currently, he is realizing his childhood dreams of working on *Dungeons & Dragons Online*. When not contributing to Turbine's quest to rule the MMP world, Quimby enjoys reading about Zeppelins, fighting Orc hordes in the name of the Emperor, and striking up conversations with strangers on the T.

Steve Rabin

steve@aiwisdom.com

Steve Rabin has been in the game industry for more than a decade and currently works at Nintendo of America. He has written AI for three published games and was a contributor to *Game Programming Gems 1*, *2*, *3*, and *4*. He served as the AI section editor for *Game Programming Gems 2* and was also the founder and chief editor of *AI Game Programming Wisdom 1* and *2*. He has spoken on AI at the Game Developers Conference and holds a degree in computer engineering from the University of Washington, where he specialized in robotics. In addition to working full time, Steve is currently pursuing a master's degree in computer science at the University of Washington.

Graham Rhodes

grhodes@nc.rr.com

Graham has 20 years of experience in various aspects of game programming, including computational geometry, real-time 3D graphics, and physics. He is currently a principal scientist at Applied Research Associates, Inc. While at ARA, Graham developed the game engine that powers several educational mini-games in the *WorldBook Multimedia Encyclopedia* (Windows-based version on CD-ROM). Among the mini-games are realistic real-time physics simulations of toy gliders and flying discs that teach readers about controlled flight. For a few years, Graham led the development of NASA's Next Generation Revolutionary Analysis and Design Environment Smart Assembly Modeler (NextGRADE SAM). Graham contributed an article for *Game Programming Gems 2*, and has presented at the GDC and XGDC game developer conferences. Recently, Graham has been the lead developer of a first-person safety training game for offshore oil-rig crewmembers.

Thomas Rolfes

tr@circensis.com

Thomas Rolfes worked on the game and technology teams of Criterion and Kuju and as lead technology programmer at Lionhead on engines and titles including *Redline Racer Dreamcast*, *Microsoft Train Simulator*, *Lotus Challenge PS2/Xbox*, and *Black & White 2*. He holds degrees in physics and computer science from the University of Münster and the University of Hagen, Germany. Thomas has contributed to a book on planet orbits and builds telescopes when not writing shader programs.

Greg Seegert

gseegert@alum.wpi.edu

Greg Seegert is the graphics programmer at Stainless Steel Studios, where he worked on *Empires: Dawn of the Modern World* and *Empire Earth*. When he's not special casing code, modifying globals in other threads, and writing goto's, Greg can be found trying to convince the Stainless Steel Studios upper management to allow him to implement the latest and greatest Nvidia or ATI tech demo. He is contemplating starting a used PC charity in hopes that one day he will not be shackled by the mainstream CPUs and GPUs of five years ago, which are inexplicably owned by the majority of RTS gamers.

Jake Simpson

jmsimpson@maxis.com

Jake Simpson tells people that he's been making games far longer than it's possible for him to have actually been doing so. There's no way he was working on Eliza in the 1960s, when he wasn't born until 1968, and don't let him tell you otherwise. However, he did work for Midway Chicago for six years on arcade games (trying to get his name into the credits of games like *Revolution X, WWF Wrestlemania, NBA-JAM (Nani Edition)*, and *Mortal Kombat III* by paying people off periodically), and at Raven Software for almost four years on such titles as *Heretic II, Soldier of Fortune I & II, Star Trek Voyager: Elite Force* and *Jedi Knight II*. He's currently working at Maxis doing his best to get a shotgun object into *The Sims 2.0* and not having much success.

Roger Smith

roger@fingersofdeath.com

Roger Smith is a group chief technology officer with Titan Corporation and the president of Modelbenders LLC. He develops simulation systems for the military, creates commercial courses on simulation and virtual world technologies, and writes a constant stream of technical papers for conferences, journals, and books. He has presented a tutorial at the Game Developers Conference for four years running and regularly teaches courses at several universities. The concepts behind Fingers of Death have become a minor hobby and obsession that he and Don Stoner are venting through their Web site of the same name.

Russ Smith

russ@q12.org

Russ Smith is the author of the Open Dynamics Engine, an open-source library for simulating articulated rigid body dynamics. Russ's other simulator work includes the core of MathEngine's game industry products, control research for simulated walking biped robots, and simulation of virtual characters for movie production.

Marco Spoerl

mspoerl@gmx.de

Marco started his professional career in the field of computer graphics as an engine programmer at Codecult Software, working on the Codecreatures Game Development System and Codecreatures Benchmark Pro. After receiving his diploma in computer science and a short walk on the wild side as a freelance software developer, he's now working at Munich-based Krauss-Maffei Wegmann's training and simulation department.

Marc Stamminger

stamminger@cs.fau.de

Marc Stamminger received a Ph.D. in computer graphics at the University of Erlangen-Nuremberg. The topic of his thesis was finite element methods for global illumination computations. After that, he was a post-doc at the Max-Planck-Institute for Computer Science in Saarbrücken, Germany, and at the INRIA Sophia-Antipolis, France. His research focus moved to interactive computer graphics, where he worked on shadow algorithms and point-based rendering. In 2002, he was a lecturer on computer-based gaming at the Bauhaus University in Weimar, Germany, and since October 2002, he has been a professor for computer graphics and visualization at the University of Erlangen-Nuremberg.

Jonathan Stone

jon@doublefine.com

Jonathan Stone wrote his first video games in Atari 800 Basic, and has been a professional game programmer since 1992. His most recent published title was Blizzard North's *Diablo II*, and he's currently working with Double Fine Productions to develop *Psychonauts* for the Xbox.

Don Stoner

don@fingersofdeath.com

Don Stoner is a software engineer for the Titan Corporation. He develops simulation systems for the military, has developed tools for visualizing simulation events, for networking multiple simulations, and is currently working with speech recognition technology in the development of Radio Systems Trainers. He is a former member of Army Military Intelligence and Special Forces with experience in combat operation, signals interception, reconnaissance, and surveillance. He was recruited by Dr. Roger Smith to work on the Fingers of Death and has gradually been drawn into the same obsession.

Thomas Strothotte

tstr@isg.cs.uni-magdeburg.de

Thomas Strothotte is professor at the University of Magdeburg, where he has been the chair of graphics and interactive systems since 1993. His research interests include smart graphics, image-text coherence, rendering illustrations, nonphotorealistic rendering, and virtual communities, with applications to medical illustrations, technical documentation, and computer games. Thomas received a Ph.D. in computer science from McGill University.

Natalya Tatarchuk

natashat35@yahoo.com

Natalya Tatarchuk is a senior software engineer working in the 3D Application Research group at ATI Research, Inc. where she is working on developing tools for efficient real-time shader development as the team lead for the RenderMonkey IDE project. She has been in the graphics industry for over six years, working on 3D modeling applications and scientific visualization prior to her employment at ATI. Natalya has published articles in the *ShaderX2* books. She has presented at Microsoft Meltdown Seattle, GDC, and GDC Europe. Natalya is a graduate of Boston University.

Pierre Terdiman

pierre.terdiman@novodex.com

Pierre Terdiman has been programming computers for more than 15 years, but his serious coding life started in the demoscene on Atari ST, where he learned the joy (and earned the scars) of full-screen programming. At RAYflect (now EOVIA), Pierre was in charge of the scanline renderer and A-buffer anti-aliasing. Some of Pierre's personal projects, including Flexporter and Opcode, are now used by various game and graphics companies. More recently, he implemented a physics engine for Elsewhere Entertainment's upcoming game, *Symbiosis*. In 2001, he created his own company, Synthetic3, dedicated to 3D technologies for the Web. Recently, Pierre joined NovodeX, where he is now working on advanced collision detection and physics libraries.

Jerry Tessendorf

jerryt@rhythm.com

Jerry Tessendorf is an effects technical director and software developer at Rhythm & Hues Studios. He has developed and applied water simulation software for 20 years and was responsible for the water effects software for many feature films, including *Titanic*, *Waterworld*, and *X2: X-Men United*. His real-time water simulations have been used in game and defense simulation applications. In addition to water, he also develops custom algorithms and software for rendering clouds, particles, and hair. Other interests include beam tracing, differential geometry in graphics, and loop quantum gravity. Jerry has a Ph.D. in physics from Brown University.

Paul Tozour

ptozour@austin.rr.com

Paul Tozour has been in the game industry since 1994 and has previously worked with Red Orb Entertainment, Gas Powered Games, Microsoft Game Studios, and Ion Storm. He is currently one of several AI developers working on the sequel to *Metroid Prime* at Retro Studios in Austin, Texas. Paul has also written numerous AI articles for the *Game Programming Gems* and *AI Game Programming Wisdom* series.

Joe Valenzuela

jvalenzu@infinite-monkeys.org

Joe Valenzuela is a programmer at Treyarch, a subsidiary of Activision. He is also the primary author and maintainer of the Linux implementation of OpenAL.

Jim Van Verth

jimvv@redstorm.com

Jim Van Verth is one of the founding members of Red Storm Entertainment, where he has worked for the past seven years. During most of that time, he has been a lead engineer, particularly on such projects as Tom Clancy's *Politika* and *Force 21*. Jim holds a master's degree in computer science from UNC Chapel Hill, where he studied scientific visualization and computer graphics. He lives in a haunted house located on a windswept, rocky outcropping, with his wife and daughter and 500 hungry dogs. He also has been known to exaggerate on occasion: there's only one dog.

Scott Velasquez

scottv@gearboxsoftware.com

Scott Velasquez is an audio and game programmer for Gearbox Software and has worked on *Counterstrike: Condition Zero*, *Nightfire*, and is currently wrapping up *Halo* for the PC. Scott holds a bachelor's degree in software engineering. Before joining Gearbox, Scott worked at Cinematix Studios helping develop their PS2/PC engine. While at Cinematix, he was responsible for creating their audio engine, multiple perspective cameras, and even dabbled a bit in their rendering system. When not at work, Scott can be found spending time with his wife and daughter.

Alex Vlachos

Alex@Vlachos.com

Alex Vlachos is a staff engineer in the 3D Application Research group at ATI where he has worked since 1998, focusing on 3D engine development as the lead programmer for ATI's Demo Team. He developed N-Patches (a curved surface representation introduced in Microsoft's DirectX 8), also known as PN Triangles and TRUFORM. He has published in *Game Programming Gems 1, 2, 3*, and *4*, ACM Symposium on Interactive 3D Graphics (I3DG), ShaderX, and ShaderX2. He has presented at several GDCs, GDC Europe, Microsoft Meltdown Seattle & UK, WWDC, and I3DG. Alex is a graduate of Boston University. He can be contacted at *http://alex.vlachos.com*.

Tao Zhang

zhangtao@cc.gatech.edu

Tao Zhang graduated with a bachelor's degree in computer science from Peking University in China. He is currently a Ph.D. student at the Georgia Institute of Technology, where he has been doing extensive research in compilers, architecture, and security. Once obsessed with computer games, he is always willing to contribute to the game community.

GENERAL PROGRAMMING

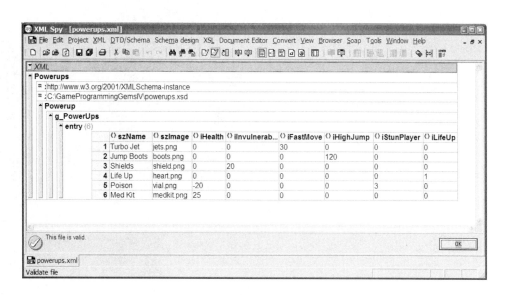

Introduction

Chris Corry, LucasArts

Take any two game developers, throw them in a room together, and you're likely to find that they disagree about many things. Programmers in our industry tend to have a strong dose of maverick in their personalities, and that often manifests itself as a rebellious streak of self-confidence. Yet, if there's anything that game programmers will agree on, it's the somewhat obvious observation that computer and video games are not getting any easier to build. Quite the contrary, they'll tell you; games are becoming more complicated and technically intricate with each passing holiday season. Indeed, managing the complexity of our games is one of the biggest challenges facing programmers today. It's no wonder, then, that so many of us are starting to adopt innovations in software development that originated outside the entertainment industry. And it's no wonder that we see this reflected in the programming articles that appear in this book.

The most obvious and widespread example of this trend can be found in the use of C++ for the development of both console and PC titles. It was only a few years ago that the idea of writing a console game in C++ would have been met with skepticism and derision—but no longer. More and more programmers use C++ not simply as "a better C," but as a full-blown object-oriented programming language that profoundly impacts every facet of our games' architecture and technical design. Sure, our single-minded fixation on performance will never stop us from needing to dip down into straight C, assembly language, or even microcode, but there is a growing awareness that solid object-oriented design in C++ is not incompatible with good performance. Certainly, it's a dictum that most of the authors in this section appear to live by.

It doesn't stop with object-oriented programming in C++ either. Template meta-programming, the STL, UML, XML, design patterns—all of these "nongaming" technologies and methodologies are starting to make inroads into even the most old-school of development houses. You'll find many of these tools and techniques referenced by the following articles, and as we become more comfortable and conversant with these new technologies they might eventually become permanent fixtures in your programming toolbox.

There's so much about our industry that's exciting and new and unique. The fact that we're making entertainment products certainly has a lot to do with it, but games development is rich with opportunities to gain exposure to hardware and software that you simply will not find anywhere else. In an industry like this, with so much technical innovation, it's not surprising that we can sometimes become insular and suspicious of "outside" technologies that have never been vetted by the game development community.

However, let's make a point of fighting these tendencies. Software developers outside the games industry are often faced with the very same problems that we grapple with on a daily basis. How do we create flexible file formats that can easily evolve over the course of a two- or three-year project? How can we quickly and efficiently load large quantities of data into memory? How can we maximize the decoupling of design decisions from programming decisions, enabling us to build tools that are user-friendly and ultimately focused on nothing but quality content generation? The games industry hasn't cornered the market on these problems and there's a lot to be gained by broadening our horizons a bit. Go ahead, do something crazy. Buy a magazine devoted to corporate software development. Pick up a journal dedicated to the use of UML or Java or SQL databases—you might be surprised.

1.1

The Science of Debugging Games

Steve Rabin, Nintendo of America Inc.

steve@aiwisdom.com

Debugging a game, or any other piece of software, can be an arduous task. For the most part an experienced programmer can quickly identify and correct even the most difficult bug, but for the novice, it can become a frustrating and insurmountable task. To make matters worse, when you start looking for the source of a bug, you never know how long it will take to find. The trick is not to panic and to instead be disciplined and remain focused on the bug-finding process. Once you are armed with the techniques and knowledge presented in this article, you will be able to beat back even the toughest bugs and regain control of your game.

The difficult chore of debugging can be made simpler by using the *Five-Step Debugging Process* described in this article. The disciplined use of such a process will ensure that you spend a minimal amount of time searching for and identifying each bug. It is also important to have some expert tricks up your sleeve when approaching an especially tough bug, so this article includes some valuable time-tested tips. We will also present a list of tough debugging scenarios explaining what to do when dealing with particular bug patterns. Since good tools are essential to debugging any game, we will discuss specific tools that you can embed within your game to help debug situations that are unique to game programming. Finally, we will review some simple techniques for preventing bugs in the first place.

The Five-Step Debugging Process

Expert programmers have the uncanny ability to quickly and masterfully track down even the toughest bugs. The magical way in which they instinctively know where to find the flaw can be awe-inspiring. While experience plays a significant role in this apparent talent, they have also internalized a disciplined method for investigating and narrowing down possible causes. The following five-step process aims to reproduce that discipline and will help you track down bugs in a methodical and focused manner.

Step 1: Reproduce the Problem Consistently

No matter what the bug, it is important that you know how to reproduce it consistently. Trying to fix a bug that shows up randomly is frustrating and usually a waste of time. The fact is, almost all bugs will consistently occur given the right circumstances, so it is the job of either you or your testing department to discover those circumstances.

Given a fictional game bug, a tester might report, "Sometimes the game crashes when the player kills an enemy." Unfortunately, this type of bug report is too vague, especially since the problem doesn't seem to happen consistently. The player might regularly blast away enemies, so there must be some other correlation to when the game crashes.

For bugs that are nontrivial to reproduce, the ideal situation is to create a set of "repro steps" that show how to reproduce the bug every time. For example, the following steps greatly improve on the previous bug report:

Repro steps:

1. Start a single-player game.
2. Choose Skirmish on map 44.
3. Find the enemy camp.
4. From a distance, use projectile weapons to attack the enemies at the camp.
5. Result: 90 percent of the time the game crashes.

Obviously, repro steps are a great way for a tester to help others reproduce a bug; however, the process of narrowing down the chain of events that lead to a bug is also critical for three other reasons. First, it provides valuable clues as to why the bug is happening in the first place. Second, it provides a systematic way to test that the bug has been fixed. Third, it can be used in regression testing to ensure that the bug doesn't reappear.

While this information doesn't tell us the direct cause of the bug, it does let us reproduce it consistently. Once you are sure of the circumstances that cause the bug to occur, you can comfortably move forward to the next step and begin to gather useful clues.

Step 2: Collect Clues

Now that you can reliably force the bug to occur, the next step is to put on your detective hat and collect clues. Each clue is a chance to rule out a possible cause and narrow the list of suspects. With enough clues, the source of the bug will be obvious, so it's worth the effort to keep track of every clue and understand its implications.

One word of caution—in the back of your mind you should always consider that a gathered clue might be misleading or incorrect. For example, maybe we were told that a particular bug always followed an explosion. While it might be a vital clue, it could be a false lead. Be prepared to discard clues that end up conflicting with other information you gather.

Continuing with the example bug report, we now know that the game crashes during a projectile attack on a particular enemy camp. What is so special about projectiles or fighting from a distance? These are important points to ponder, but don't spend too much time doing so. Get in there and observe exactly how it fails. We need more hard evidence, and mulling over superficial clues is the least efficient way to get it.

In the example, when we get into the game and actually watch the failure, we will notice that the crash occurs in an arrow object when it references a bad pointer. Further inspection shows that the pointer should point to the character that shot the arrow. In this case, the arrow was trying to report back that it hit an enemy and that the shooter should receive experience points for the successful attack. While it might appear that we found the cause, the real underlying cause is still unknown. We must discover what made the pointer bad in the first place.

Step 3: Pinpoint the Error

When you think you have enough clues, it's time to focus your search and pinpoint the error. There are two main ways to do this. The first is to propose a hypothesis for what is causing the bug and try to prove or disprove that hypothesis. The second, more methodical way is to use the divide-and-conquer method.

Method 1: Propose a Hypothesis

With enough clues, you will begin to suspect what is causing the bug. This is your hypothesis. Once it is clearly stated in your mind, you can begin to design tests that will either prove it or disprove it.

In the game example, our detective work has produced the following clues and information about the game design:

- When an arrow is shot, it is given a pointer to the character who shot it.
- When an arrow hits an enemy, it gives credit back to the shooter.
- The crash occurs when an arrow tries to use a bad pointer to give credit back to the shooter.

Our first hypothesis might be that the pointer becomes corrupted sometime during the arrow's flight. Armed with this hypothesis, we now need to design tests and collect data to prove or disprove this cause. One method might involve having every arrow register the shooter's pointer in a backup location. When we catch the crash again, we can check the backup data to see if the pointer is different from when it was originally given to the arrow.

Unfortunately in this particular game example, this hypothesis turned out not to be correct. The backup pointer was equal to the pointer that caused the game to crash. Thus, we have to make a decision. Do we want to come up with another hypothesis and test it, or revert to looking for more clues? Let's try one more hypothesis.

If the arrow's shooter pointer never became corrupted (our new clue), perhaps the shooter was deleted after the arrow was shot but before the arrow hit an enemy. To check for this, let's record the pointer of every character who dies in the enemy camp. When the crash occurs, we can compare the bad pointer to the list of enemies who died and were deleted from memory. With a little work, it turns out that this was the cause. The shooter died while his arrow was in mid-flight!

Method 2: Divide and Conquer

The two hypotheses that led to finding the bug also demonstrate the concept of divide and conquer. We knew the pointer was bad, but we didn't know if it actually changed values as a result of being corrupted, or if the pointer became invalid at some earlier point. By testing the first hypothesis, we were able to rule out one of the two possibilities. As Sherlock Holmes once said, ". . . when you have eliminated the impossible, whatever remains, however improbable, must be the truth."

Some people might describe the divide-and-conquer method as simply identifying the point of failure and backtracking through the inputs to discover the error. Given a noncrashing bug, there is a certain point at which an initial error cascaded and eventually caused the failure. Identifying the initial error is usually accomplished through setting breakpoints (conditional or not) at all of the input paths until you find the input that breaks the output, thus causing the bug.

When backtracking from the point of failure, you are looking for any anomalies in local variables or in functions higher in the stack. With a crash bug, you should be looking for NULL values or values with extremely high numbers. If it's a bug with floating-point numbers, look for NANs or really large numbers further up on the stack.

Whether you make educated guesses at the problem, test a hypothesis, or hunt down the culprit through a methodical search, eventually you *will* find the problem. Trust yourself and keep your wits about you during this stage. Further sections in this article elaborate on specific techniques that can be used during this step.

Step 4: Repair the Problem

Once the true cause of the bug has been identified, a solution must be proposed and implemented. However, the fix must also be appropriate for the particular stage of the project. For example, in the latter stages of development, it's generally not reasonable to change the underlying data structures or architecture in order to fix a bug. Depending on the stage of development, the lead or system architect should make the decision about what type of fix should be implemented. At critical times, individual engineers (junior or mid-level) often make poor decisions because they aren't looking at the big picture.

Another important issue is that the programmer who wrote the code should ideally fix the bug. When this is not possible, try to discuss the fix with the original author before implementing any remedies. This will give you insight into what might have been done in the past about similar problems and what might break as a result of your proposed solution. It is dangerous to change other people's code without thoroughly understanding the context.

Continuing along in our game example, the source of the crash was a bad pointer to an object that didn't exist anymore. A good solution for this type of game pattern is to use a level of indirection so that this type of crash can't happen. Often, games use handles to objects instead of direct pointers for this very reason. This would be a reasonable fix.

However, if the game must be ready for a milestone or an important demo, you might be tempted to implement a more direct fix for this special situation (like having the shooter invalidate his pointer in the arrow when he is deleted). If this kind of quick hack is made, be sure to make a note of it so that it can be re-evaluated after the deadline. It's a common problem to see quick fixes forgotten, only to cause trouble months later.

While it seems that we've found the bug and identified a fix (using handles instead of pointers), it is crucial to explore other ways that might make the same problem occur. This can take extra time, but it's worth the effort to make sure that the underlying bug was fixed, and not just one particular manifestation. In our game example, it's probably the case that other types of projectiles will also cause the game to crash, but other nonweapons or even character relationships might also be vulnerable to the same design flaw. Find these related cases so that your solution addresses the core problem and not just one symptom.

Step 5: Test the Solution

Once the solution has been implemented, it must be tested to verify that it actually repaired the bug. The first step is to make sure that the original repro steps no longer cause the bug. It is also a good idea to have someone else, like a tester, independently confirm that the bug is fixed.

The second step in fixing the bug is making sure that no other bugs were introduced. You should run the game for a reasonable amount of time and ensure that nothing else was affected by the fix. This is very important since many times a bug fix, especially toward the end of the development cycle, will cause other systems to break. At the very end of a project, you'll also want every bug fix to be reviewed by the lead or another developer as an additional sanity check that it won't adversely affect the build.

Expert Debugging Tips

If you follow the basic debugging steps, you should be able to find and repair most bugs. However, when you attempt to come up with a hypothesis, prove/disprove a cause, or try to find the point of failure, you might want to consider the following tips.

Question Your Assumptions

It is important to keep an open mind when debugging and not make too many assumptions. If you assume that the simple stuff works, you could be prematurely narrowing your search and missing the cause completely. For example, don't always assume that you are running with the most up-to-date software or libraries. It often pays to make sure your assumptions are valid.

Minimize Interactions and Interference

Sometimes, systems interact with each other in ways that complicate debugging. Try to minimize this interaction by disabling subsystems that you believe are not related to the problem (for example, disable the sound system). Sometimes this will help identify the problem since the cause might be in the system that you disable, indicating that you should look there next.

Minimize Randomness

Often, bugs are hard to reproduce because of variability introduced by the frame rate or from actual random numbers. If your game has a variable frame rate, try locking the "time elapsed per frame" to a constant. For random numbers, either disable your random number generator or seed it with a constant so that it always produces the same sequence. Unfortunately, the player introduces a significant source of randomness that you can't control. If player randomness must be controlled, consider recording player input so that it can be fed back into your game in a predictable manner [Dawson01].

Break Complex Calculations into Steps

If a particular line of code combines many calculations, perhaps breaking the line up into multiple steps will help identify the problem. For example, maybe one piece of the calculation is being cast badly, a function doesn't return what you thought it did, or the order of operations is different from what you expected. This also allows you to examine the calculation at each of the intermediate steps.

Check Boundary Conditions

The classic off-by-one problem has bitten all of us at one time or another. Check algorithms for these boundary conditions, especially in loops.

Disrupt Parallel Computations

If you suspect a race condition, serialize the code to check if the bug disappears. In threads, add extra delays to see if the problem shifts. The problem can be narrowed down if you can identify it as a race condition and use experiments to isolate it.

Exploit Tools in the Debugger

Understand and know how to use conditional breakpoints, memory watches, register watches, stack, and assembly/mixed debugging. Tools help you to find clues and the hard evidence that is key to identifying the bug.

Check Code That Has Recently Changed

It's amazing the debugging that can be done with source control. If you know a date when it worked and the date when it stopped working, you can look at which files changed and quickly find the offending code. This will at least narrow your search to particular subsystems or files.

Another way to exploit source control is to create a build of the game before the bug was introduced. This is helpful if you can't eyeball the problem. Running the old and new versions through a debugger and comparing values might be the key to finding the problem.

Explain the Bug to Someone Else

Often, when explaining a bug to someone else, you'll retrace your steps and realize something you missed or forgot to check. Other programmers are also great for suggesting alternate hypotheses that can be explored. Don't underestimate the power of talking to other people, and never be embarrassed to seek advice. The people on your team are your allies and one of your best weapons against truly difficult bugs.

Debug with a Partner

This usually pays off since each person carries different experiences and tactics for dealing with bugs. You'll often learn new techniques and attack the bug from an angle you might not have tried. Having someone looking over your shoulder can be one of the very best ways to track down a bug.

Take a Break from the Problem

Sometimes, you're so close to the problem that you can't look at it clearly any longer. Try removing yourself from the situation and take a stroll outside of your environment. When you relax and come back to the situation, you will have a fresh perspective. Once you've given yourself permission to take a break, sometimes your subconscious mind will work on the problem and the solution will simply dawn on you.

Get Outside Help

There are many great resources for getting assistance. If you are making a game for a console, each console manufacturer has a full team of people ready to assist you when you run into trouble. Know their contact information. The big three console makers all provide telephone support, e-mail support, and newsgroups where developers can help each other.

Tough Debugging Scenarios and Patterns

Bugs often follow patterns in which they give themselves away. In tough debugging scenarios, the patterns are the key. This is where experience pays off. If you've seen the pattern before, you have a good chance of quickly finding the bug. The following scenarios and patterns will give you some guidance.

The Bug Exists in Release But Not Debug

A bug that only exists in a release build usually points toward uninitialized data or a bug in optimized code. Often, debug builds will initialize variables to zero even though you wrote no code to do so. Since this invisible initialization doesn't happen in release builds, the bug shows up.

Another tactic for tracking down the cause is to take your debug build and slowly turn on optimizations one by one. By testing with each optimization, you can sometimes find the culprit. For example, in debug builds, functions are usually not inlined. When they become inlined for optimized builds, sometimes a bug will show up.

It is also important to note that debug symbols can be turned on in release builds. This allows limited (albeit often frustrating) debugging of optimized code and even allows you to keep some debugging systems enabled. For example, you could have your exception handlers perform a full-blown stack trace (which requires symbols) to the crash site. This can be especially helpful when testers must run an optimized version of the game, yet you want to be able to trace crashes.

The Bug Disappears When Changing Something Innocuous

If a bug goes away by changing something completely unrelated, like adding a harmless line of code, then it is likely a timing problem or a memory overwrite problem. Even if it looks like the bug has disappeared, it probably has just moved to a different part of your code. Don't lose this opportunity to find the bug. It's still there and it will most certainly bite you in the future in a subtle or nearly undetectable way.

Truly Intermittent Problems

As mentioned previously, most problems will occur reliably given the correct circumstances. If you truly can't control the circumstances, then you must catch the problem when it rears its ugly head. The key here is to record as much information as you can when you do catch the problem so that you can examine the data later, if needed. You won't get many chances, so make the most of each failure. Another helpful tip is to compare the data collected from the single failure case to data collected from when it worked properly and then identify the differences.

Unexplainable Behavior

There are cases when you will step through code and variables will change without anything touching them. Truly bizarre behavior such as this usually points towards the system or debugger becoming out of sync. The solution is to try to resync the system with "increasing levels of cache flushing."

The following four Rs of cache flushing are courtesy of Scott Bilas:

- **Retry** (flush the current state of the game and run again)
- **Rebuild** (flush the intermediate compiled objects and do a full rebuild)
- **Reboot** (flush the memory of your machine with a hard reset)
- **Reinstall** (flush the files and settings of your tools/OS by reinstalling)

Of these four Rs, the most important is rebuild. Sometimes, compilers don't properly track dependencies and will fail to recompile affected code. The symptoms are usually general weirdness. A complete rebuild often fixes the problem.

When dealing with unexplainable behavior, it is important to second-guess the debugger. Verify the real value of variables with `printf`s since sometimes the debugger becomes confused and won't accurately reflect the true values.

Internal Compiler Errors

Every once in a while you'll run into a situation where the compiler itself has given up on your code and complains of an internal compiler error. These errors could signal a legitimate problem in your code or they could be entirely the fault of the compiler software (for example, if it exceeded its memory limit or can't deal with your fancy templates). When faced with an internal compiler error, here's a good series of first steps to follow:

1. Perform a full rebuild.
2. Reboot your machine, and then perform a full rebuild.
3. Check that you have the latest version of the compiler.
4. Check that you have the latest version of any libraries you're using.
5. See if the same code compiles on other machines.

If these steps don't fix the problem, attempt to identify what piece of code is causing the error. If possible, use the divide-and-conquer technique to pare down the code until the internal compiler error goes away. Once it's identified, examine the code visually and ensure that it looks correct (it might help to have several different people look at it). If the code looks reasonable, the next step is to try rearranging the code to see if you can get a more meaningful error message from the compiler. One last step you might want to try is compiling with older versions of the compiler. It's quite possible that a bug was introduced into the newest compiler version, and an older compiler will compile the code correctly.

If none of these solutions helps, search Web sites for similar problems. If nothing turns up, contact the compiler maker for additional assistance.

When You Suspect It's Not Your Code

Shame on you—you should always suspect your own code! However, if you're convinced that it's not your code, the best course of action is to check Web sites for patches to libraries or compilers that you're using. Study the readme files or search

Web sites for known bugs with your libraries or compiler. Often, other people have run into similar problems and workarounds or fixes exist.

However, there is always a remote possibility that your bug is a result of someone else's library or even faulty hardware (and you happen to be the first person to find it). While this is usually not the case, it certainly happens. The fastest way to deal with this is to make a tiny sample program that isolates the problem. You can then e-mail that program to the makers of the libraries or the hardware vendor so that they can investigate the problem further. If it really is someone else's bug, then you can get it fixed the fastest by helping these other people identify and reproduce the problem.

Understanding the Underlying System

To find really tough bugs, you must understand the underlying system. Thoroughly knowing C or C++ simply isn't enough. To be a really good programmer, you must understand how the compiler implements higher-level concepts, you must understand assembly, and you must know the details of your hardware (especially for console development). It's nice to think that high-level languages mask all of these complexities, but the truth is that when something *really* breaks, you'll be clueless unless you understand what lies beneath the abstractions. For more discussion on how high-level abstractions can *leak*, please see "The Law of Leaky Abstractions" [Spolsky02].

So, what underlying details should you know? For games, you should understand the following:

- **Know how a compiler implements code.** Be familiar with how inheritance, virtual function calls, calling conventions, and exceptions are implemented. Know how the compiler allocates memory and deals with alignment.
- **Know the details of your hardware.** For example, understand a particular hardware's caching issues (when memory in the cache might differ from main memory), address alignment constraints, endianness, stack size, and type sizes (such as int, long, and bool).
- **Know how assembly works and be able to read it.** This can help track down problems with optimized builds where the debugger has trouble tracing through the source.

Without a firm grasp of these issues, you will have an Achilles heel when it comes down to fighting the really tough bugs. You must understand the underlying system and know its rules intimately.

Adding Infrastructure to Assist in Debugging

Debugging in a vacuum without the right tools can be very frustrating. The solution is to swing the pendulum in the other direction and build great debugging tools directly into your game. The following tools will help greatly when tracking down bugs.

Alter Game Variables During Gameplay

A valuable tool in debugging and reproducing bugs is the ability to change game variables at runtime. The classic interface for doing this is to use a keyboard to alter variables through a debug command-line interface (CLI) in your game. With the press of a button, debug text is overlaid onto your game screen and a prompt lets you enter input via the keyboard. For example, if you want to change the weather in your game to stormy, you might type "weather stormy" at the prompt. This kind of interface is also great for tuning and checking the value of variables or particular game states.

Visual AI Diagnostics

Good tools are invaluable to debugging and standard debuggers are simply inefficient for diagnosing AI problems. Debuggers give great depth at a moment in time, but they are lousy at showing how an AI system evolves during gameplay. They are also poor at showing spatial relationships in the game world. The solution is to build visualization diagnostics directly into the game that can monitor any given character. By using a combination of text and 3D lines, important AI systems like pathfinding, awareness boundaries, and current targets can be easily tracked and checked for errors [Tozour02], [Laming03].

Logging Capability

Often, in games, we make dozens of characters interact and communicate with each other, resulting in very complex behavior. When these interactions break down and a bug arises, it becomes crucial to be able to log the individual states and events from each character that led to the bug. By creating separate logs for each character, with key events time-stamped, it becomes possible to track down the failure by examining the logs [Rabin00a], [Rabin02].

Recording and Playback Capability

As mentioned before, the key to tracking down bugs is reproducibility. The ultimate in reproducibility would entail recording and playing back player input [Dawson01]. For very rare crashes, this can be a key tool in pinpointing the exact cause. However, to support this capability, you must make your game predictable so that an initial state coupled with player input produces the same result each time. That doesn't mean your game is predictable to players, it just means that you have to carefully deal with random number generation [Lecky-Thompson00], [Freeman-Hargis03], initial state, input, and be able to save the input when a crash happens [Dawson99].

Track Memory Allocation

Create memory allocators that can perform a full stack trace on every allocation. By keeping records of exactly who is requesting memory, you'll never again have to chase down memory leaks.

Print as Much Information as Possible on a Crash

Postmortem debugging is very important. In a crash situation, ideally you'll want to capture the call stack, registers, and any other state information that might be relevant. This information can be printed to the screen, written to a file, or automatically e-mailed to a developer's mailbox. This kind of tool will help you find the source of the crash in a couple of minutes instead of a few hours. This is especially true if the crash happens on an artist or designer's machine and they don't remember how they triggered the crash.

Educate Your Entire Team

While this is not infrastructure that you can program, it's mental infrastructure that must be in place so that your team uses the tools you've created. Train them to not ignore error dialogs, and make sure they know how to gather information so that a found bug is not lost. Spending the time to educate testers, artists, and designers is well worth the investment.

Prevention of Bugs

A discussion of debugging wouldn't be complete without a short guide on how to avoid bugs in the first place. By following these guidelines, you'll either avoid writing some bugs, or stumble upon bugs you didn't know you had. Either way, this will help you eliminate bugs in the long run.

Set your compiler to the highest warning level and enable warnings as errors.
Try to fix as many of the warnings as possible, and then #pragma the rest away. Sometimes, automatic casts and other warning level issues will cause subtle bugs.

Make your game compile on multiple compilers. If you make sure your game builds with multiple compilers and for multiple platforms, the differences between the warnings and errors of both compilers will usually ensure better code all around. For example, people writing Nintendo GameCube™ games can also make sure a crippled version runs in Win32. This can also allow you to see if a bug is platform-specific or not.

Write your own memory manager. This is crucial for console games. You must understand what memory you're using and shield against memory overruns. Since memory overruns cause some of the toughest bugs to track down, it is important to make sure they never happen in the first place. Using overrun and underrun guard blocks in debug builds can make bugs show up before they can manifest themselves. For PC developers, writing your own memory manager is not really necessary, since the memory system in VC++ is quite powerful, and good tools like SmartHeap can be exploited to identify errors with memory.

Use asserts to verify your assumptions. Add asserts to the beginning of functions to verify assumptions about arguments (such as non-NULL pointers or ranges). In addition, if the default case of a switch statement should never be reached, add an assertion for that case. Additionally, the standard assert can be expanded to give you much more debugging power [Rabin00b]. For example, it can be extremely helpful if your assertions print out a call stack.

Always initialize variables when they are declared. If you can't assign a variable a meaningful value when it's declared, then assign it something recognizable so that you can spot that it was never properly set. Some ideas for values are 0xDEADBEEF, 0xCDCDCDCD, or simply zero.

Always bracket your loops and if statements. This keeps you honest by making you explicitly wrap the intended code, making it more obvious what was intended.

Use variable names that are cognitively different. For example, m_objectITime and m_objectJTime look almost the same. The typical example of this problem is the use of "i" and "j" as loop counters. The characters "i" and "j" are very similar looking and you could easily mistake one for the other. As an alternative, you could use "i" and "k" or simply use names that are more descriptive. More information on cognitive differences in variable naming can be found in [McConnell93].

Avoid having identical code in multiple places. Having the same code in several different places is a liability. If the code is changed in one place, it is unlikely it will also get changed in the other locations. If it seems necessary to duplicate code, then rethink the core functionality and try to centralize a majority of the code in one place.

Avoid magic (hardcoded) numbers. When a unique number appears in code, its meaning and significance can be completely lost. If there is no comment, then it is unclear why that particular value was chosen and what it represents. If you must use magic numbers, declare them as constants or defines that give a meaningful label to the number.

Verify code coverage when testing. When you write a piece of code, verify that it executes correctly down every branch. If you have never seen it execute a particular branch, there's a good chance it contains a bug. One possible bug that you might catch from this process is discovering that it's impossible to take a particular branch. The sooner this is discovered, the better.

Conclusion

This article has given you the tools you need to effectively debug games. Debugging is sometimes described as an art, but that's only because people get better at it with experience. As you internalize the *Five-Step Debugging Process*, learn to spot bug patterns, integrate your own debugging tools into your game, and build up your repertoire of debugging techniques, you'll quickly become adept at methodically tracking down and squashing tough bugs. With an ounce of prevention, hopefully your game will be smooth sailing and nary a bug will bite you.

Acknowledgments

Thanks go out to Scott Bilas and Jack Matthews for making great suggestions and lending some of their own personal experience and wisdom to this article. There are many different viewpoints with regard to debugging, and their opinions were invaluable in tempering the advice presented.

References

[Dawson99] Dawson, Bruce, "Structured Exception Handling," *Game Developer Magazine* (Jan 1999), pp. 52–54.

[Dawson01] Dawson, Bruce, "Game Input Recording and Playback," *Game Programming Gems 2*, Charles River Media, 2001.

[Freeman-Hargis03] Freeman-Hargis, James, "The Statistics of Random Numbers," *AI Game Programming Wisdom 2*, Charles River Media, 2003.

[Laming03] Laming, Brett, "The Art of Surviving a Simulation Title," *AI Game Programming Wisdom 2*, Charles River Media, 2003.

[Lecky-Thompson00] Lecky-Thompson, Guy, "Predictable Random Numbers," *Game Programming Gems*, Charles River Media, 2000.

[McConnell93] McConnell, Steve, *Code Complete: A Practical Handbook of Software Construction*, Microsoft Press, 1993.

[Rabin00a] Rabin, Steve, "Designing a General Robust AI Engine," *Game Programming Gems*, Charles River Media, 2000.

[Rabin00b] Rabin, Steve, "Squeezing More Out of Assert," *Game Programming Gems*, Charles River Media, 2000.

[Rabin02] Rabin, Steve, "Implementing a State Machine Language," *AI Game Programming Wisdom*, Charles River Media, 2000.

[Spolsky02] Spolsky, Joel, "The Law of Leaky Abstractions," *Joel on Software*, 2002, available online at *www.joelonsoftware.com/articles/LeakyAbstractions.html*.

[Tozour02] Tozour, Paul, "Building an AI Diagnostic Toolset," *AI Game Programming Wisdom*, Charles River Media, 2002.

1.2

An HTML-Based Logging and Debugging System

James Boer

james.boer@gte.net

Debugging games is often much more challenging than working with traditional applications due to the chaotic, real-time nature of the input conditions. In many applications, it is often trivial to exactly reproduce the steps that lead to a bug. Games, however, typically have the additional disadvantages of unpredictable user input, a complex real-time game environment, and a random sprinkling of nondeterministic factors like AI. Often, by the time a bug is spotted, the moment at which the data or variables responsible for the faulty event can be analyzed has long since passed. Additionally, bugs are often found by testers who might be running a release build or running the game without a debugger on the system. How, then, can developers hope to track down the cause of these elusive bugs? One potential answer lies in event logging.

The Benefits of a Logging System

We've all heard these types of bugs from a tester: "At the very end of level six of Kaptain Keeno, I got to the big group of Zarbovian Firebots. If I kill the very last robot with the KaBlaminator Ray Gun while at the same time doing a super-leap, then the robots all start dancing the macarena." These types of bugs are among the trickiest type to find and fix. Not only is the reproduction extremely difficult or tedious, even if you reproduce the bug, you're often left wondering what put the code into such a bizarre state to begin with.

This is exactly the kind of detective work at which a logging system excels. By dumping a continuous report of key events, variables, and statistics into a formatted text file, a programmer can get an idea of what was happening in the code *leading up to a bug*. A logging system gives you the ability to watch data over time without having to manually step through huge amounts of code.

What Exactly Is Event Logging?

By "event logging," we mean the task of capturing real-time events and messages for later retrieval and analysis. In the simplest case, logging can simply mean using basic disk functions to store information from the game, such as variable contents and descriptions of messages in real-time. This allows a developer to see, for example, the history of a variable's content over time, instead of just seeing the contents of that variable at a single moment in time via a debugger. In truth, although events are captured and logged in real-time, we might characterize what this system does as a form of "post-mortem debugging" because the system excels at tracking events that have already occurred. However, unlike most post-mortem debuggers that are designed to track down the immediate cause of an application crash, this type of system is adept at tracking behavioral bugs, as long as enough relevant data about the code is logged.

So, what happens if you're not logging any data from a section of code that goes haywire and needs debugging? Simply add the logging information you require and wait for an opportunity to reproduce the problem. Event logging isn't a magic bullet—it's just another wrench in the debugging toolkit, and it requires active planning and participation by the programmer. However, the beauty of a log file is that it is generally unobtrusive, and so it is practical to leave quite a bit of active logging going on at any given time. Once you've added an informative log message to the system, there generally isn't much reason to remove that message, and so future logs have more information about the game state the more you use the system.

How should a logging system work? While no one design can be considered perfect for all situations, we'll demonstrate one method of efficiently sorting through the clutter of debugging data.

HTML and Call-Stack Tracking to the Rescue

Frankly, it's not too hard to create a logging system that dutifully records data into a text file. Unfortunately, this type of raw data dump can be difficult to decipher due to the sheer amount of data logged, so we'll want a method of differentiating certain messages from others using formatting cues. Additionally, the relative time of each event must also be tracked to give the event a frame of reference within the sequence of logged messages. Finally, it would be helpful to provide a context for the log events, which allows for simplified tracing of logic through the game code. Developers typically use a call stack in their debugger as the first means of identifying how any particular code was reached. In our logging system, we'll also use a call stack to identify the location and origin of every message. The last area of technical concern is that, like all debugging tools, the logging system should be able to completely compile out of the final executable (or any interim build) with little effort.

Besides these technical requirements, it should be also noted that the logging system should be simple to integrate and to use. Experience has taught that a highly functional but complex system, while perhaps a marvel of software engineering, will likely sit unused. "Simple and practical" is the key to debugging tools.

We will attempt to solve the data analysis problem by using three key mechanisms. The first and most visible of the solutions is to format the data using Hyper-Text Markup Language (HTML). HTML has several advantages: it is an established, text-based standard, the basic formatting rules are very simple, it is flexible enough to provide nearly any type of formatting we want, and all modern computer systems come equipped with an HTML reader—a Web browser. Using HTML, we can accomplish several formatting tasks with relative ease. Perhaps most importantly, we can easily represent the logged events' call stack using basic indentation, as represented in Listing 1.2.1. This listing shows a sample of log output that we might see generated from a baseball game.

Listing 1.2.1 An example of log output.

```
HittingBrain::updateSwing()
    HittingBrain::updatePitchData()
        HittingBrain::calculateSwingTimingAndPosition()
        Expected pitch time: 0.857448
        Expected pitch location: (-8.150428, -8.516977)
        Actual pitch time: 1.244251
        Actual pitch location: (8.695169, 7.850054)
Update = 38185, Game Time = 00:10:36.41
```

With some context, you can see what's actually going on at this point in the game (about $10\frac{1}{2}$ minutes into the game, actually). You can see that the class function `HittingBrain::updateSwing()` has called the `updatePitchData()` function, which has called the `calculateSwingTimingAndPosition()` function. This is where the logged message is originating; the AI is attempting to hit the ball. You can surmise that the AI is looking for a fastball up and inside, and the actual pitch ended up as more of a low and away changeup. From this data, one might imagine that the AI batter should most likely swing early and miss the ball. Using this kind of detailed historical data, we can essentially rewind the game and review what was actually occurring in the game before we knew there was a problem.

Additionally, although this is not represented in Listing 1.2.1, the text can be color-coded and uniquely formatted for any given log message. One reasonable approach is to define categories, and assign unique colors and styles to each, so that any message of interest in that particular category can be easily spotted among the many messages in the log file.

How It Works

ON THE CD

Although the logging system code is provided in its entirety on the companion CD-ROM, there are a few interesting components worth discussing in detail. The event logger is quite simple to use. There are essentially three steps involved in using it: housekeeping, function tracking, and logging messages. We'll first show you the housekeeping procedures, demonstrating initializing, updating, and shutting down the system. Listing 1.2.2 shows what this code looks like.

Listing 1.2.2   Starting up and shutting down the logging system.

```
// At program startup
LOG_INIT("gamelog.html");

//...

// This is called once per update loop.
// m_GameTickDelta is a floating-point representation
// in seconds of how much time has elapsed since the
// last game tick.
LOG_UPDATE(m_GameTickDelta);

//...

// At program termination
LOG_TERM();
```

Next, you must insert function markers at the beginning of every function body you want to track. This typically involves placing macros in most major game loop update functions. Listing 1.2.3 shows what this looks like, along with a basic logged message.

Listing 1.2.3   Placing logging macros.

```
SomeClass::DoSomething(int value)
{
    FN("SomeClass::DoSomething()");
    LOG("A value of %d was passed to this function",
        value);
}
```

Although it might seem a bit tedious to have to type an FN macro in every single function, this bit of extra work provides a great deal of service later when tracking down exactly where a log message came from. By adding the macro we see here, as well as to the functions that call this function, we will see a log message that looks similar to the results shown in Listing 1.2.1—you can trace who called which functions by simply traversing back up the tree of function names.

You might notice that we're using macros to hide some of the implementation details. This makes the code easier to type and read, and allows us to ensure that the entire logging system can easily be compiled out of the final build, similar to the way a standard assert macro works.

The call-stack tracking system uses a small temporary object to track the scope of the function. Listing 1.2.4 shows how the FN macro actually creates a small object each time it is placed.

Listing 1.2.4   The implementation of the FN macro.

```
#define FN(var_1)    EventLogFN obj__scope(var_1)

// Helper function designed to push and pop
class EventLogFN
{
public:
    EventLogFN(const char* szFunction);
    ~EventLogFN();
};

EventLogFN::EventLogFN(const char* szFunction)
{
    g_Log.pushFunction(szFunction);
}

EventLogFN::~EventLogFN()
{
    g_Log.popFunction();
}
```

Because the object is so lightweight, has no data of its own, and is being created on the stack, we are assured that a minimal amount of overhead is generated by these macros. To further guarantee a lightweight operation, we are restricting the string to a constant character pointer. By using only constant character strings in this portion of the code, we allow the logging system to avoid memory allocations and string copies, reducing the system overhead to pushing and popping a single pointer. Because we're dealing with constant strings, we can get away with this optimization. It's important, therefore, to remember *not* to pass in temporary string data, such as what would be output from a standard string object's c_str() function.

Because we're outputting our log entries in HTML format, it would be a shame not to take advantage of the color and formatting capabilities of this standard. One way color-coded output can be extremely helpful is in differentiating between different types of messages, perhaps divided by logical code separation. Listing 1.2.5 shows our logging system's set of formatting flags that can be applied to any message.

Listing 1.2.5   Logging format flags.

```
#define LOG_COLOR_RED        0x00000001
#define LOG_COLOR_DK_RED     0x00000002
#define LOG_COLOR_GREEN      0x00000004
#define LOG_COLOR_DK_GREEN   0x00000008
#define LOG_COLOR_BLUE       0x00000010
```

```
#define LOG_COLOR_DK_BLUE    0x00000020
#define LOG_BOLD             0x00000040
#define LOG_ITALICS          0x00000080
#define LOG_UNDERLINE        0x00000100
#define LOG_PRINTF           0x00000200
#define LOG_DEBUG_OUT        0x00000400
#define LOG_DISABLE          0x00000800
```

Some of the flags alter the color or appearance of message text, while others might redirect the text to alternative debugging locations, such as stdout or a debug window. By OR-ing several of these flags into a single #define, you can easily create categories of messages that all have a unique appearance in the output stream.

These category #defines can be passed as the first argument to an overloaded LOG function call. You'll notice that we've opted for a simple printf-style system to handle data formatting and multiple arguments. Listing 1.2.6 demonstrates what typical logged messages look like in the code when used with predefined formatting flags.

Listing 1.2.6   Examples of different log calls.

```
#define LOG_AI    LOG_DEBUG_OUT|LOG_BOLD|LOG_COLOR_RED
#define LOG_AUDIO LOG_ITALICS|LOG_COLOR_BLUE

LOG(LOG_AI, "Test AI message");
LOG(LOG_AUDIO, "Test Audio message");
```

The output of these two messages will result in two differently colored and formatted messages, making them very easy to distinguish from each other.

The actual HTML output is quite simple to generate. Formatting commands in HTML are delimited with less-than and greater-than symbols, like this: <command>. Generally speaking, commands that can be abbreviated are shortened to a single letter as well. For example, starting a new paragraph is done with the HTML command <p>. In HTML, every command must have a closing pair that ends the formatting command. These terminating commands are identical to the initial command, except they contain a forward slash just before the command identifier, like this: </p>. We've used a very basic set of commands including *paragraph, font, unsorted list*, and of course, the basic text modifiers such as *bold, italic*, and *underline*.

Each of these commands (as well as their equivalent terminators) is encapsulated as a member function of the logging class. This makes it simple to string together a set of HTML formatting commands, as shown in Listing 1.2.7. This sample code, taken from the EventLogger::logOutput() function, demonstrates how to write a formatted line of text using the formatting flags passed into a standard log message.

Listing 1.2.7   Breaking a single line of log text into multiple formatting calls.

```
// Write formatted HTML to the output buffer
writeIndent();
writeStartListItem();
writeStartFont("Arial", 2, r, g, b);
writeText(nFlags, m_szLogBuffer);
writeEndFont();
writeEndListItem();
writeEndLine();
```

ON THE CD

One important optimization that we've made to prevent the output buffer from filling up with useless data is to only display the data relevant to the messages that are actually being output. In other words, the logging system does not write output on every frame, only frames in which a logged message has occurred. Likewise, we don't track and print the code path for the entire frame; we limit the stack print to only that which is required to correctly show the positioning of messages that were actually logged. These two optimizations help cut down the clutter in the final log file considerably, and make the end result much more readable. You can dig into the code found on the companion CD-ROM to see exactly how this was done, but it mostly involves tracking positions within the function stack.

Some Helpful Hints

Like any tool, it is important to understand this system's strengths and weaknesses so that you can use it most effectively. Here are a few hints and suggestions for your consideration:

- This system is not thread-safe. To be made thread-safe, the stack calls would require a per-thread context, or a separate object to track data coming from each thread.
- Be careful when adding logging message or function markers to constructors or destructors of global objects. It's a good bet that these will be called before the logging system is initialized, which will cause the logging routines to fail.
- It is not an ideal use of the system to track variables every single frame (although it certainly is capable of doing this). Rather, the system shines when tracking periodic events, such as logging state changes in an AI entity. One problem with writing out variables on every frame is that the size of the log will tend to grow huge as the game runs for a long time.
- The system (as currently implemented) is not particularly well suited to catching crash bugs. Rather, it is more helpful when used to catch abhorrent behavior.
- As with any debugging tool, it is up to the programmer to intelligently use this system. It requires a fair investment of time to place all the function identification macros and to intelligently log relevant data.

- In addition to its obvious uses as a debugging tool, this logging system is also a great way to assist a programmer in understanding the basic flow of execution through a large section of code in a project.

Conclusion

Event logging is certainly not the last word in real-time debugging techniques, but it can be a powerful tool in your debugging arsenal. It's especially valuable in helping to track down events that occurred in your program before the problem manifested itself—something traditional debuggers cannot easily do. Best of all, because we're using a standard file format, you can get even more creative with the data output and the reader will still be able to handle the data display. For example, you might want to use cascading style sheets to define the properties of the various categories of messages, allowing different programmers to highlight different portions of the output, or perhaps even switch to using XML to more efficiently navigate large amounts of data output. You might even want to avoid the use of a browser as a reader, instead outputting in a format like a tab- or comma-delimited text file table that a spreadsheet program like Excel can understand.

Each project has different requirements, and you should think carefully about how to best capture runtime data from your project that can be used to figure out when things go wrong. When used carefully, a logging system like the one described in this article can provide you with an effective shortcut to tracking down and fixing some of the most difficult types of bugs.

1.3

The Clock: Keeping Your Finger on the Pulse of the Game

Noel Llopis, Day 1 Studios

llopis@convexhull.com

In a game, the clock drives everything. The clock moves time forward, and the passage of time is what makes it possible for objects in the world to move, for the camera to follow the player, and even for the credits to scroll by at the end of the game. Unfortunately, the naive approach of simply querying some system timer whenever the game needs to know the current time is fraught with problems. To name just a few:

- Querying the time at different points within one frame can return different values (causing strange warping artifacts when screen objects are updated).
- Pausing the game but allowing some parts to continue executing is problematic (for example, user interface animations, or a spinning camera while the game is paused).
- Frame rate variations can cause very noticeable jitter in the animations and camera movement.

Time Basics

Once upon a time, in the dark ages of game development, most programmers didn't bother using clocks. They just did as many things as they could in one frame (which was determined by how much work the CPU could perform, or by the amount of time between the vertical sync signals of the monitor). That worked fine as long as the game only ran on a comparably configured machine. As soon as somebody with a faster CPU tried to run it, the entire game was faster. Not only did the game run at a faster frame rate, everything actually moved faster on the screen, usually causing the game to become unplayable.

Today, things are different. Most contemporary games use some form of clock to drive the game and make it independent of the speed of the system on which they are run. Even console games that can always count on running on the same hardware usually benefit from using a clock to deal with updating the game at different video frequencies on PAL and NTSC video systems.

Most games are organized around a main game loop. That loop gets executed once per frame, over and over, while the game is running. Everything that happens during a frame must happen in that loop. The following are some of the major events that typically happen during a frame:

- Check for any input from the user.
- Run AI.
- Get network packets.
- Update all the objects in the world.
- Render everything visible on the screen.

The preceding can happen in any order. Some games have a much more complex organization in which the AI or simulation part of the game runs only every few frames to keep the rendering as decoupled from the rest of the game as possible. Some will have multiple update passes, or a special messaging step. It doesn't matter; in the end, they are all very similar to our basic main loop.

The type of computations performed in the loop typically involve determining how long it has been since an object was last updated, computing what changes are necessary since that time, and updating it to reflect its correct state. Since those computations often occur every frame, the time since an object was updated is approximately the duration of the last frame.

Games typically choose one of two approaches to handling time: variable frame duration or fixed frame duration. Most games on PCs, as well as many console games, use variable frame duration. That means that frames can be of any duration, and that duration can vary depending on what is displayed on the screen.

Fixed frame duration games are most commonly found on consoles, where the hardware is known, and frames can always be assumed to be of the same duration (which will usually coincide with a multiple of the vertical sync signal on the display). Even if your game uses a fixed frame time approach, which alleviates many of the problems discussed later, it can still benefit from the clean organization and some of the features presented in this article.

Clock System Organization

We want to develop a clock system that allows us to:

- Reliably get the current time and duration of a frame.
- Pause and scale gameplay time values independent of other parts of the program.
- Reset the time, or even feed the clock our own values.
- Work with both variable and fixed frame duration.
- Avoid artifacts caused by consecutive frames with very different durations.
- Avoid precision problems.

A good starting point is to use two separate concepts: *clocks* and *timers*.

There is a single clock in the game, which is used to drive all the different timers. A clock reports the current time, which is always monotonically increasing. The clock cannot be paused or manipulated directly, much as we don't have control over real time.

Unlike the single clock, there might exist many timers, each created for a different use within the game. A timer is driven by the clock, but it can be manipulated by the user: it can be paused, reset, or even scaled to make its time move faster or slower than the central clock. The game can create one timer to keep track of world time, another timer for the GUI, another for playing movies, and so forth. Clearly, each timer could have a different view of what the current time is, and possibly even of the duration of the frame.

Where exactly does the clock get its time values? Normally, it gets the time from some type of high-resolution system timer, which is usually platform dependent. However, in our case it helps to abstract the service of generating time values into the logical idea of a *time source*. A time source might use different platform-dependent timers, read values from a file, or even calculate the time based on the number of vertical sync signals. In any case, our clock will always function the same way, independent of the specific time source.

Conveniently, the three concepts we have presented—clock, timers, and time sources—can each be represented with a C++ class. Figure 1.3.1 is a UML diagram that shows the relation between the classes.

The full implementation for those classes, along with the rest of the features presented in this article and a set of unit tests, is found on the companion CD-ROM.

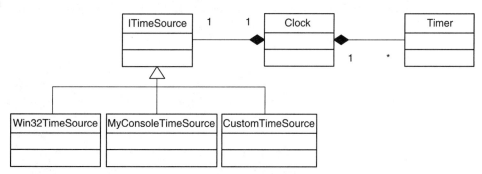

FIGURE 1.3.1 *UML class diagram for the classes involved in the clock system.*

ON THE CD

At the beginning of each frame, the clock member function FrameStep() is called. It causes the clock to get an updated time reading from the time source, update its internal time values, and update all the timers that depend on that clock. Once that function has been called, the current time and the duration of the last frame will remain constant until FrameStep() is called again at the beginning of the next frame. Not only is this efficient, since there are no calculations to do whenever we query a timer, but it allows us to have a stable frame of reference to update all objects this frame. This solves the challenge of getting a stable time measurement within the same frame.

Because timers are independent of each other, we can freely operate on them without fear of affecting the central clock or any other timer. We can pause the game timer, which will cause all the action in the game to stop, but all our user interface controls will continue to animate correctly, because they're using the GUI timer. We can even explore the possibility of speeding up or slowing down a timer to create striking visual effects, such as slow-motion explosions, subjective viewpoints, or even high-speed camera movement while the action is almost stopped.

Another feature this system provides us is the ability to feed our own values into the clock system. This is trivial to do, by applying a new time source that contains the values we want, but why exactly would we want to do that? We might, for example, want to feed the exact clock values that were used to record a cut scene so the playback will be exact (this assumes that the original clock values are available as part of the cut scene data).

Finally, if our game uses a fixed frame duration approach, we could use a very simple time source that always indicates our desired frame duration, while still retaining the ability to have multiple timers.

Avoiding Artifacts

So far, we have addressed many of the issues related to clocks that we had set out to solve at the beginning of the article. There is one thorny problem we have yet to address, though, and that is the issue of time artifacts. There are three main causes of time artifacts that we need to look at separately.

Spikes

Let's go back for a moment to think again about what exactly we're measuring. Specifically, what do we mean when we get the frame duration? We really want to know the amount of time that has passed since the beginning of the last frame (which is when we last updated the objects).

Figure 1.3.2 shows a plot of the possible durations of several consecutive frames. In particular, notice the two spikes on an otherwise relatively even plot. Spikes like that are not all that uncommon, especially in PC games, as there is often hard disk access, or a large amount of textures being shipped across to the video card.

If an object—for example, a car—is moving at a constant speed across the screen when one of those spikes hits, what is going to happen? Once we take the hit and a frame takes a long time to complete, there's nothing we can do about it, so there will be a hitch in the perceived motion of the object. However, in the next frame, the car should continue moving at a constant speed.

If we use the duration of the last frame to determine how much to update the objects in the world, the car will jump to catch up with the time lost during the spike. That's the correct behavior, but is it really what we want? First, the user gets hit with a long frame, and then with a jumpy frame. That's not going to look good, not to

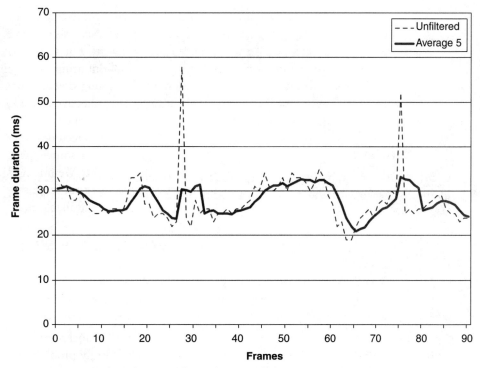

FIGURE 1.3.2 *Frame duration for some part of the game. One series shows the unfiltered frame duration, and the other shows the frame duration averaged over the last five frames.*

mention the potential problems of updating the world with a large time step (physics and collision problems, or just the simulation feedback loop).

Most of the time, we end up with better results if we prevent our time delta from changing so quickly. A simple way to accomplish that is to average out the duration of the last n frames instead of just relying on the duration of the last frame alone. A value for n between 5 and 10 is small enough to allow the frame duration to change quickly in response to frame rate variability, but large enough to avoid major spikes. Figure 1.3.2 shows the same time values smoothed out by averaging the last five frames.

What about big spikes: a 10-second spike, or a 5-minute spike? Even if we average those out over 10 normal frames, the frame duration is still going to be huge.

How can such a spike occur? The most common case is when we break in the middle of the game loop with our debugger. We examine a few variables, step into a few places, and five minutes later, we're ready to resume execution of the game. Unless we have taken some precautions, the next time step is going to be huge. Most likely, all the objects will travel so far and so fast that they'll go straight out of the world, and unless you have a fixed-step physics simulation, you're virtually guaranteed to blow up all your computations.

A useful safeguard is to simply put a cap on the maximum frame duration. If our game is supposed to run at 30 frames per second, which is about 33 ms per frame, we should never, under normal circumstances, have a frame that is over 250 ms. That would be four frames a second! Therefore, by setting a limit of about 250 ms, the next time we break in with the debugger and we resume, the next time step will be 250 ms (averaged out over a few frames, so it will end up being smaller), and we'll be able to continue playing the game as usual.

Vertical Sync

Often, we want to wait for the next vertical sync before displaying the next frame. Doing so avoids any tearing caused by the monitor or TV updating at a rate different from our game. When waiting for vertical sync, the usual mode of operation is to do everything we need to do for one frame, and then block, waiting for the vertical sync to occur. As soon as it happens, we display the back buffer and move to the next frame.

That is fine until we run up against the highly parallel graphics systems of today's PCs and consoles. More often than not, all the commands we send to the graphics processor are queued to be processed as soon as the hardware can, and execution returns to the game immediately. This means that, if we are not careful, we can get into a very annoying situation where the frame duration varies wildly from frame to frame. Not even our simple averaging is going to save us here.

Consider the following situation. We are trying to wait for every other vertical sync on a 60 Hz display in the hope of maintaining a constant 30 frames per second. However, the player is looking at a very simple part of the world where rendering and the updating take very little time. That means that we'll do all the updating for the frame in a few milliseconds, and then tell the graphics processor to flip buffers when the correct vertical sync happens. Because that command was queued, execution returns to us right away, which allows us to start the next frame.

A problem occurs because the real duration of the last frame was only a few milliseconds. This small time delta is the value we use to update the state of objects in this frame, yet visually, we're displaying our scene at 30 frames per second. After several frames, we will probably fill the graphics queue, and then we'll have a long frame until most of the queue is emptied, resulting in a particularly long frame duration.

This problem will manifest itself with jerking, unstable animations. Even though the frame rate will be a solid 30 frames per second, the movement of objects in the world will stutter noticeably.

If your platform has this problem, a good solution is to put some platform-specific blocks around the code that flip the back buffers to prevent the game from getting more than one frame ahead of the graphics processor. That way, time steps will be regular, yet we still get all the parallelism we can out of the hardware.

Precision

One thorny issue when dealing with clocks and timers is precision. How should we represent time, and what types of errors can we expect?

Even if your platform of choice has a super-high resolution timer that returns the number of nanoseconds since the Paleozoic era, we still need to deal with how we're going to represent discrete time values within the game. Do we want to use a float with the number of seconds since the level started, should we use a large integer containing the number of milliseconds instead, or should we use something completely different? The answer is that it depends on your game and on your platform, so it is best to understand the tradeoffs for the different possibilities.

Storing the time in an integer as the number of milliseconds elapsed should be familiar to those who have dabbled in systems programming. This is the familiar "tick" interface, where a tick is a millisecond. This approach has constant precision, but it is always rather coarse. The smallest unit of time that can be represented is 1 ms. Considering that one frame at 60 Hz is 16.6667 ms, we're always going to be almost half a millisecond off. The other major drawback is that we can only represent about 49 days in one 32-bit integer. If our game is supposed to run for longer than that continuously, then we need to use a different scheme or come up with a wrap-around scheme. The last disadvantage of this representation is that an integer number of milliseconds is not the most convenient way of working with time when we're doing physics calculations or even simple position updates. Chances are we'll want to convert it into a floating-point number before we do anything with it.

Using a float containing the number of seconds is much more natural for most computations. However, floats have their own share of precision problems. Unlike an integer, a float will have higher precision with small numbers, and slowly lose precision as the number gets larger. With a 32-bit float, after just four hours, our resolution is limited to roughly 1 ms, and after about three days, we're down to a resolution of 15 ms, which is hardly enough to represent one frame at 60 Hz. Clearly, it only gets worse from there.

A double, which is a floating-point number with 64 bits, is a much more reliable representation. It has enough bits to last us for a long time, yet it's stored in a convenient form for mathematical computations. The drawback is that on 32-bit platforms, 64-bit floating-point operations can be significantly more expensive.

Until 64-bit platforms become available, it will probably be wise to keep 64 bits of accuracy internally, and expose whatever representation you prefer to the game. It particularly makes sense to use floats for the frame duration, since those are all small numbers, and a float will have more than enough precision for that range of values.

Figure 1.3.3 shows the precision of a 32-bit integer, a float, and a double for a given period of time. Notice that the y-axis (precision) is represented with a logarithmic scale. While the integer stays at a constant precision of 1 ms for the entire range,

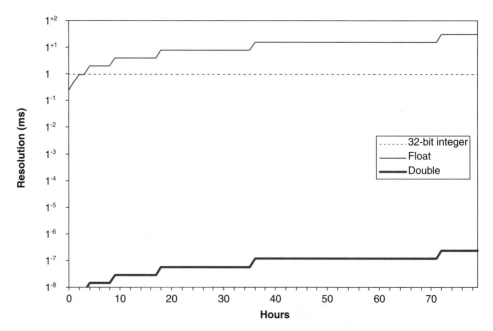

FIGURE 1.3.3 *Precision for three different time representations.*

a float "quickly" loses precision, although it manages to stay below 5 ms for over 16 hours. Moreover, for the first four to five hours, a float has better precision than an int. A double has so much precision that it's the reason why the plot had to be represented in a logarithmic scale: after 80 hours, its sub-second accuracy is an amazing 0.00000023 ms!

Conclusion

ON THE CD

There is more to the game clock than meets the eye. This article presented a clean organization for a clock/timer system and explained some of the major pitfalls and how to avoid them. The code on the companion CD-ROM provides a working implementation along with a full set of unit tests.

An interesting extension of this system would be to be able to make timers dependent on other timers, creating a hierarchical dependency tree. It would then be possible to manipulate entire groups of timers by just changing the parameters of a common parent. This could be particularly useful if your game contains a lot of variation on time scales such as *Matrix*-style shots or slow-motion explosions.

1.4

Designing and Maintaining Large Cross-Platform Libraries

David Etherton, Rockstar San Diego

etherton@rockstarsandiego.com

In today's game market, with project budgets continuing to creep skyward, publishers often hope to get a better return on their investment by releasing the same title on multiple platforms. While there is always the option of outsourcing ports to separate development studios, the final product risks being compromised; the end result will nearly always be superior if the port is planned from the beginning. Publishers often balk at having to spend too much extra to get multiple platform ports, so it's better for the developer to do the port development in parallel as much as possible.

The Design

Before you write a single line of code, you need to plan the basic structure of your libraries. An average project from a large studio can contain dozens of different libraries, divided between shared engine and project-specific code. Some subsystems are more complex than others are, so don't hesitate to layer functionality across several related modules. For example, separate collision detection and collision response into separate modules for your physics library.

Always keep interface and implementation as separated as possible. Try to avoid having your interfaces depend on other interfaces directly.

```
// Class.h
#include "object1.h"
#include "object2.h"

class Object3
{
```

```
private:
    Object1 m_Obj1;
    Object2 m_Obj2;
};
```

is nearly always better as:

```
// Class.h
class Object1;
class Object2;

class Object3
{
private:
    Object1 *m_Obj1;
    Object2 *m_Obj2;
};
```

Sometimes, the latter form is not appropriate because of performance requirements—you need to own the subobject directly so that you can inline more computations.

If you're coding in C++, you should never have public member variables; always provide accessors for everything. This allows you to change your mind on the implementation side without breaking the interface. Consider using class factories where possible. Their major drawback is that nearly every entry point is a virtual function, which does incur an additional performance penalty, particularly on platforms with smaller data caches.

As your code grows over time, you need to aggressively prune unused classes and squash the cyclic dependencies that inevitably arise. For example, if two different classes both need data from each other, consider moving that shared data into a separate class that they can both depend on directly. If low-level code needs to call back up to higher-level code, use function pointers or virtual class factories to resolve the dependency. More detail can be found in [Lakos96].

To avoid duplicate symbol names and provide a basic level of documentation, partition your modules into namespaces with short prefixes; gfx for graphics, ph for physics, and so forth. Equivalently, consider using C++ namespaces and fully qualified names, like gfx::Texture instead of gfxTexture.

Important Abstractions

Abstract all of your file operations; stdio is broken on some platforms, and a clean abstraction allows you to add compression or archive support to your engine. You really need to reduce the total number of disk files as much as possible if you want to have reasonable load times on any console without a hard drive. Furthermore, don't get in the habit of keeping multiple files open simultaneously, because disk seek times are significant. A quick fix is to read entire files into memory before parsing their contents.

Supply your own random number generator and use it everywhere. Make sure you support multiple random number streams and clearly separate simulation-dependent random numbers from camera-dependent random numbers if you want your replay modes to be deterministic. You'll also get results that are more consistent across platforms.

Add a level of indirection to your input devices; never allow high-level code to explicitly check the "R" key or the left analog stick. Use a manager of some kind to allow higher-level code to check for a reset event or the brake pedal reading. This makes your life much simpler when your designers decide late in the project to remap several controls, or when you have to add support for a new platform whose controller does not have as many shoulder buttons.

Consider replacing the memory manager supplied with your platform with your own versions of `malloc` and `free`. There are robust, freely available versions available on the Internet [Lea00]. By keeping memory management consistent, you can guarantee that your newly allocated memory is always initialized to the same known state.

The Build System

Whatever build system you choose, make sure it is easy to configure and allows you to reliably make sweeping build changes to all of your modules simultaneously. This is where makefiles are typically much simpler to manage; every major IDE or sophisticated text editor supports invoking a command-line *make* and allows you to step through the resulting errors. You should centralize as many of your rules as possible in a common makefile; the only information that should be present in the local module-specific makefile is the name of the module, the list of files that form the library for the module, and zero or more use-case tests. Most compilers can generate automatic dependency lists, or you can use a freely available version of the *makedepend* utility to help jump-start the process.

There are many good versions of *make* floating around on the Internet; GNU make [GNU02] is probably the most widely used. Newer tools like *jam* [Jam02] can be considerably less cryptic in practice.

Build Configurations

Most development tools offer just Debug and Release build configurations for your projects, but a wider selection of configurations is critical for finding certain classes of bugs. Having configuration sets for each of the following broad categories can be invaluable; each configured build type should be independent of the others:

- Debug information present or not
- Optimizations enabled or not
- Assertions enabled or compiled out
- Trace statements enabled or compiled out
- In-game development and tuning tools enabled or compiled out

In many cases, generating debug information can considerably slow compilation and linking, so you don't always want it enabled. The optimizer can interfere with debugging, but obviously, you want it on for general use. Being able to independently control assertions, particularly while still leaving lots of other debug information enabled, is important for tracking down bugs where you accidentally added an assertion with a critical side effect.

It's not always sensible to have every permutation listed previously available as a build configuration; some combinations make more sense than others do. Keep a per-configuration forced-include file that allows you to make quick customizations as needed.

You should always configure your tools to generate as many warnings as you can practically tolerate, and make sure that you do this for every platform you target (/W4 under Developer Studio, -Wall under gcc, etc.). Some compilers are pickier than others; compiling your code on as many targets as possible increases your chances of finding bugs before you even execute your code. Always enable your compiler's "treat warnings as errors" option, because this forces you to keep your code clean and helps prevent you from distributing code to the rest of the team that might produce errors and warnings on other platforms.

Every project in your studio should have a dedicated build machine. When a programmer checks in code and makes it available to other team members, they should log into the build machine, update the code, and build the project's core configurations. This will quickly identify any files that were not checked back in or that might be missing, protecting other programmers from potential downtime. Every night the same central build machine should rebuild all possible configurations and forward any error logs to the team. For very large programming teams, you might want to perform continuously rolling builds instead.

Consider using external source code validation tools like *PC-lint*™ [Gimpel03]. A strong lint tool will often perform more static semantic analysis of your code than your compiler will and can spot serious logic errors at build time.

The Details

Writing portable code has been covered in numerous places before, so we'll just cover the issues that crop up most commonly with games. Whether you use middleware or the native APIs available on your target machine, it's nearly always beneficial to add your own layer of abstraction, in case a new platform or new middleware comes along in the future.

Scalar Type Sizes

Don't count on scalar types being a particular size, or certain types being the same size as other scalar types. Use typedefs for signed and unsigned 8-, 16-, 32-, and 64-bit integers and place their definitions into your forced-include files so that they are always available.

Endianness

Byte endianness isn't really that difficult to deal with; the biggest issue lies with reading and writing binary data that might have been written on a different platform. One option is to use Read/WriteInt, Read/WriteShort, Read/WriteFloat routines consistently in your code that manage any byte swapping for you. Another option is to avoid binary files altogether unless they were created on their target platform.

Structure Field Order

Where possible, try to sort your structure fields by size; if you declare a char, an int, and then another char, the compiler is likely to either insert extra padding bytes or reorder the fields entirely. In C++, don't forget about data owned by parent classes and remember that polymorphic object instances also include a pointer to the class virtual function table (v-table). All modern game consoles support some type of SIMD instruction set, which typically require stricter alignment than a single word; don't forget to account for these alignment requirements when padding your structures. When in doubt, print out the size of critical heavily instanced objects at runtime and make sure you understand where every byte is going. Use the ANSI-standard offsetof macro where necessary to track down any discrepancies.

The Virtual Function Table Pointer

Different compilers will place an object's v-table pointer in different parts of the structure. If keeping the v-table pointer in a consistent place is important, consider deriving from an empty class containing only a virtual destructor; this will force the v-table pointer to appear first on all platforms.

```
class Base
{
    virtual ~Base() { }
};
```

On some platforms, virtual function tables take more than four bytes per function by default. Older versions of gcc suffer from this problem; consider using -fvtable-thunks=3 on those versions.

Assertions

The value of assertions has been covered elsewhere [Rabin00]. They are particularly important in cross-platform libraries because your code is more likely to be re-used in the future by people who do not fully understand it. Consider using templated array classes for all of your constant-sized arrays; the overhead will compile out completely, but they can save hours of debugging time when they trigger out-of-bound checks, instead of trashing memory. They are an absolute necessity for your asset pipeline tools, which must be as friendly and robust as possible.

Conditional Compilation

Conditional compilation is used for two broad reasons: to differentiate between build configurations on the same platform, and to differentiate between code intended for different platforms. The former is generally a necessary evil, while the latter can be avoided somewhat with class factories. Keep conditional compilation to a minimum because it becomes unreadable quickly; you're best off using it sparingly in the interface, and separating out platform-dependent interfaces from each other entirely. When you do use conditional compilation, consider using `#if  SYMBOL` instead of `#ifdef SYMBOL`. All gcc-based platforms support `-Wundef`, which displays a warning if you've tried to evaluate an undefined preprocessor symbol. This can help prevent a nasty class of bugs where you accidentally render a block of code useless.

```
#ifdef XBOOX   // Typo, code will be silently removed
   ...
#endif
```

Precompiled Headers

Precompiled headers are nearly always a win, but you need to carefully consider how you use them. On some platforms, you're encouraged to place an "`Everything.h`" file at the top of every source module. You'll end up with a single large precompiled header that can be processed very quickly and your build times will benefit greatly. The problem with this approach is that not all compilers on all platforms support precompiled headers, and a monolithic include file is just about the worst thing you can do for your build times. In practice, this approach makes the fast platforms build faster, but the slower platforms build *much* slower. One option is simply to not use precompiled headers; with proper forward declarations, you can minimize dependencies in your interface. If you do decide to use precompiled headers, consider structuring your code as follows to get the best of both worlds.

```
// Class.h
#if !__PCH
#include "subclass1.h"
#include "subclass2.h"

class Subclass3 ...

// Class.cpp
#if !__PCH
#include "class.h"
#include "subclass4.h"
#else
#include "Everything.h"
#endif
```

If you're not using precompiled headers, always include your code's matching header file first. This ensures that your class interface doesn't have any hidden dependencies inherited from previously included files.

Testers

Every library should have use-case tests, simple test cases that exercise the functionality of the library. They are valuable as both a form of documentation and as a means to validate consistent functionality across multiple platforms and subsequent releases of the library. Consider capturing output or screenshots and comparing them to known-good versions as a way to allow the code to self-validate during your library release process.

Conclusion

Creating and developing large cross-platform libraries is a crucial endeavor in the current game production market, regardless of the amount of middleware you adopt. No platform has ever totally dominated the market enough to warrant ignoring the additional effort necessary to support its competitors; the more you plan up front and are diligent with maintenance of all platforms, the fewer problems you will have along the way.

References

[Gimpel03] Gimpel Software, "PC-Lint," available online at *www.gimpel.com/*, March 2003.

[GNU02] Free Software Foundation, "GNU Make," available online at *www.gnu.org/ software/make/make.html*, April 20, 2002.

[Jam02] Perforce Software Inc., "Jam," available online at *www.perforce.com/jam/jam .html*, March 2002.

[Lakos96] Lakos, John, *Large-Scale C++ Software Design*, Addison-Wesley Publishing Co., 1996.

[Lea00] Lea, Doug, "A Memory Allocator," available online at *http://g.oswego.edu/dl/html/ malloc.html*, April 4, 2000.

[Rabin00] Rabin, Steve, "Squeezing More Out of Assert," *Game Programming Gems*, Charles River Media, 2000.

1.5

Fight Memory Fragmentation with Templated Freelists

Paul Glinker, Rockstar Games Toronto

paul@glinker.com

In the world of games, dynamic memory allocation and deletion at runtime is a no-no. While it might seem very convenient (and even appropriate) under certain circumstances, you almost always take a speed hit, cause memory fragmentation, and end up with poor locality of reference. Yet, there is hope. This article will introduce you to the templated freelist and show you how to use this technique to gain the convenience of runtime allocation and deletion without the associated penalties.

What Is That Grinding?

Frequent allocation and deletion can cause excessive *memory fragmentation*. This can lead to a situation where there is at least as much free memory available as is requested by the application, but there is no contiguous block large enough to fulfill the request [Ravenbrook03]. When we end up in such a situation on a typical PC, our frame rate will momentarily plunge while the operating system hits virtual memory in order to honor the request. Things are even worse on a console, where fragmentation will almost certainly cause our game to crash, as there is no swap file to bail us out (see Figure 1.5.1).

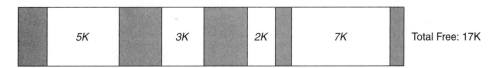

| 5K | 3K | 2K | 7K | Total Free: 17K |

FIGURE 1.5.1 *The fragmented heap presented here has 17K free, but an attempt to allocate anything more than 7K at once would fail because there is no contiguous block large enough to fulfill such a request.*

Another unfortunate side effect of frequent allocation and deletion is poor *locality of reference*. Locality of reference refers to the way in which an application references nearby memory locations. An application that consecutively references memory locations scattered throughout the heap is said to have poor locality of reference. This type of behavior causes cache misses, a source of serious performance degradation on any system architecture, but particularly so on consoles that have small data and instruction caches. An application that consecutively references nearby memory locations is said to have good locality of reference [Ravenbrook03]. This type of behavior reduces the number of cache misses, thereby improving the application's performance. Frequent allocation and deletion make this ideal difficult to achieve.

Contributing further to performance degradation is the default memory manager. General-purpose memory managers have to deal with a lot of issues behind the scenes on our behalf. Every time we request a block, the memory manager might have to search through a list of available blocks for the best fit, and failing that, might end up splitting a larger existing block into smaller ones to avoid wasting too much space in one allocation. When we free a block, the memory manager might attempt to merge it with neighboring free blocks [Flynn97], in an attempt to cut down on fragmentation. Certainly, we want a general-purpose memory manager to take care of these things for us, but usually not at the expense of runtime CPU cycles.

The Solution

One way to gain the convenience of runtime allocation and deletion without the associated penalties is to use freelists.

In short, a freelist is a list of memory blocks available for allocation; freelists are most frequently found within memory managers. When an application allocates memory, the memory manager searches the freelist for an available block with at least as much space as was requested. Memory deleted by an application is returned to the freelist.

As alluded to previously, the freelist employed by a full-blown memory manager might have to deal with variable-sized blocks and other time-consuming issues that can burn precious CPU cycles. To keep things under control, we're going to create our own freelist external to the default memory manager. In fact, we will create a separate freelist for each data type that we want to allocate and delete in large quantities at runtime. Then we will allocate and delete our data directly to and from these freelists. For example, allocating and deleting tree nodes might normally look something like this:

```
CTreeNode *pNode = new CTreeNode;
delete pNode;
```

but now becomes

```
TFreeList<CTreeNode> TreeNodePool(1024);
CTreeNode *pNode = TreeNodePool.NewInstance();
TreeNodePool.FreeInstance(pNode);
```

We have only a few requirements for our freelist implementation. It must eliminate memory fragmentation, it must improve locality of reference, it must be fast, it must have a simple interface, it must be reusable, and it must be type-safe. Meeting all of these requirements will make our minimal up-front effort worthwhile.

Implementation Details

The snappy title of our article and the previous example clearly indicate that our freelist is to be a template. Reusability aside, there are other good reasons for this design decision that will soon become obvious. We will declare our template as

```
template <class FLDataType>
```

When we instantiate our TFreeList, the first thing we will do is allocate an array of FLDataType objects and an array of FLDataType pointers. We will then store a pointer to each of the FLDataType objects by using our pointer array as a fixed-sized stack.

```
TFreeList(int iNumObjects)
{
    ASSERT(iNumObjects > 0);

    m_pObjectData = new FLDataType[iNumObjects];
    m_ppFreeObjects = new FLDataType*[iNumObjects];

    ASSERT(m_pObjectData);
    ASSERT(m_ppFreeObjects);

    m_iNumObjects = iNumObjects;
    m_bFreeOnDestroy = true;

    FreeAll();
}

void FreeAll(void)
{
    int iIndex = (m_iNumObjects-1);

    for (m_iTop = 0; m_iTop < m_iNumObjects; m_iTop++)
    {
        m_ppFreeObjects[m_iTop] =
                &(m_pObjectData[iIndex--]);
    }
}
```

The FreeAll() member function is responsible for populating the pointer stack. This functionality is kept separate from the constructor because it is sometimes handy for us to be able to free everything at once.

At this point, our TFreeList constructor might concern you because it requires the FLDataType to have a default constructor, which might not always be convenient. For this reason, we have an additional constructor that accepts pre-allocated data.

```
TFreeList(FLDataType   *pObjectData,
          FLDataType  **ppFreeObjects,
          int           iNumObjects)
{
    ASSERT(iNumObjects > 0);

    m_pObjectData = pObjectData;
    m_ppFreeObjects = ppFreeObjects;

    ASSERT(m_pObjectData);
    ASSERT(m_ppFreeObjects);

    m_iNumObjects = iNumObjects;
    m_bFreeOnDestroy = false;

    FreeAll();
}
```

When we request an instance, our TFreeList will pop the first pointer off the pointer stack and return it to us.

```
FLDataType *NewInstance(void)
{
    ASSERT(m_iTop);
    return m_ppFreeObjects[--m_iTop];
}
```

When we free an instance, our TFreeList will return the instance pointer to the pointer stack.

```
void FreeInstance(FLDataType *pInstance)
{
    ASSERT( (pInstance >= &(m_pObjectData[0])) &&
            (pInstance <=
             m_pObjectData[m_iNumObjects-1])));
    ASSERT(m_iTop < m_iNumObjects);
    m_ppFreeObjects[m_iTop++] = pInstance;
}
```

Why This Is All So Great

Our implementation meets all of our initial requirements. It prevents fragmentation, improves locality of reference, is faster than our default memory manager, has a simple interface, is reusable, and is type-safe.

Fragmentation is completely eliminated by the way in which we have stored our objects. We pre-allocate all data of a specific type in one contiguous block, and then we do all of our allocations from within that block. Since all of the individual blocks are the same size, fragmentation cannot occur within the contiguous block from which we frequently allocate and delete instances (see Figure 1.5.2).

FIGURE 1.5.2 *Even though the free portions of this contiguous memory block are somewhat scattered, fragmentation cannot occur because every allocation and deletion is of fixed size.*

This leads us right into locality of reference. Pre-allocating our objects in one contiguous block will confine groups of memory accesses to one area of memory. By definition, this is an improvement in locality of reference and will help to reduce the number of cache misses experienced by applications doing a number of successive accesses to objects of the same type. Unfortunately, this benefit can still be thwarted by applications that exhibit poor memory access patterns.

Improvement in speed comes partially from improved locality of reference, but also because our `NewInstance()` function takes advantage of something that our default memory manager cannot: the fact that all blocks are the same size. This obviously gives us a huge speed advantage by avoiding the need to search for the best-sized block of memory. We know we will always get a proper-sized memory block because we know that every block in our freelist is of an appropriate size.

It is true that one could implement a freelist class without using templates (using raw data), but templates give us two distinct advantages in this case. Having the class templated forces the compiler to make sure that data is properly aligned in memory. Proper alignment is important on a PC, and is crucial on a console. The other advantage is compile-time error checking. The compiler will easily be able to detect erroneous situations in which we have mistakenly tried to delete or allocate data of one type to or from a `TFreeList` containing data of a different type.

Effective Use of Our Freelist

The fact that the default constructor of our `TFreeList` requires the `FLDataType` to have a default constructor can be used to our advantage. Any one-time initialization required by `FLDataType` objects can be put into the default constructor. We can then add a `Reset` function to do whatever small amount of re-initialization is required after allocation from a `TFreeList` and use it like this:

```
CParticle *pParticle = ParticlePool.NewInstance();
pParticle->Reset(SMOKE01, orientation, vel);
```

Things to Watch Out For

When using TFreeList in conjunction with a container class—like a binary tree for example—it is important to make the TFreeList a member of each tree instance. If we were to create just one global tree node pool:

```
TFreeList<CTreeNode> g_TreeNodes(MAX_TREENODES);
```

an application that generates many trees might still end up with poor locality of reference. It would be better to use our TFreeList as an internal member of the tree class so that allocations are physically closer together in memory.

```
m_pNodePool = new TFreeList<CTreeNode>(iMaxTreeSize);
```

Obviously, our TFreeList has the added memory overhead of the pointer stack. This was done to make the code fast, simple, and easy to digest. It is possible to implement a freelist class without using extra data to store the pointer stack. In that case, you would overwrite the first four bytes of each free instance with a pointer to the next free instance. Be forewarned that in so doing you might destroy the instance's pointer to the virtual function table (if one exists, and depending on your compiler's implementation), in which case you will have to perform a *placement new* on the object to make it valid again. Also be aware that this method would not be possible with data elements less than sizeof(FLDataType*) in size.

Conclusion

Now that we have a good handle on the freelist concept and our very own implementation in TFreeList, you should apply this programming technique in as many places as you can.

Most container classes, including dynamically linked lists, stacks, queues, and various kinds of trees can benefit from freelists [Headington94]. Task managers [Harvey02], particle systems, and player managers could all benefit. Freelists can also be used to store game state objects to speed classical search algorithms for applications in artificial intelligence [Russell95]. They could even be used as a mechanism for resource control in networked applications, or any other situation where resources need to be strictly regulated.

Throughout the course of this article you learned why dynamic memory allocation and deletion at runtime can cause problems. There is an effective way to avoid those problems through the use of freelists.

If you are looking for ways to improve upon this idea and you have already written a custom memory manager for your game, you might consider incorporating an external freelist class into your memory management system and setting it up so that your freelists automatically send statistical tracking information back to the main memory manager.

References

[Flynn97] Flynn, Ida M., and Ann McIver McHoes, *Understanding Operating Systems, Second Edition*, PWS Publishing Company, 1997.

[Harvey02] Harvey, Michael, and Carl S. Marshall, "Scheduling Game Events," *Game Programming Gems 3*, Charles River Media, 2002.

[Headington94] Headington, Mark R., and David D. Riley, *Data Abstraction and Structures Using C++*, D.C. Heath and Company, 1994.

[Ravenbrook03] Ravenbrook Limited, "The Memory Management Reference," available online at *www.memorymanagement.org*, June 2003.

[Russell95] Russell, Stuart, and Peter Norvig, *Artificial Intelligence, A Modern Approach*, Prentice Hall, 1995.

1.6

A Generic Tree Container in C++

Bill Budge, Electronic Arts

billbudge@hotmail.com

After arrays and lists, trees are the most important data structures in game programming. Trees can represent character skeletons, scene graphs, spatial partitions, and hierarchical bounding volumes. In asset processing tools, trees can also be used to represent shaders and parsed script code.

Implementing trees that use memory efficiently and that can be traversed and modified rapidly is not easy. Where performance is critical—for example, in character skeletons and hierarchical collision detection—many games avoid trees altogether, pre-baking them into special arrays. Such representations are fast and efficient but very difficult to modify. That's too bad, because dynamic trees make it easy to add attachments to characters and to update objects during the game. As gamers demand more interactive environments, flexible tree structures will be very desirable.

The only readily available C++ implementations of trees have been too slow or waste too much memory to be suitable for game runtime use [Kovachev02], [Peeters03]. However, it is possible to create a fast and efficient tree library. This article describes the design of such a library.

Reusable Libraries

There are several ways to design a reusable tree container. The simplest is the "C" way—define a tree that can hold void pointers. This is the technique of choice if we are building a C library. It has the obvious problems of type safety, lots of casting, and the overhead of allocating both the tree and its contents as separate objects on the heap.

The "classic" C++ way relies on inheritance—we define a node class and a tree class to contain nodes. The client derives node types from the base node class, which can be added to the tree. Again, we have problems with type safety and the need for a lot of downcasting. Furthermore, clients must define a new node class for each new type of tree.

The "modern" C++ way is to implement containers generically. A template class is created for a tree of objects of type T. The C++ Standard Template Library (STL) is the best example of this approach. Generic libraries can be very flexible and efficient. We will follow the example of the STL to create a generic tree library.

A Quick Review of Trees

A tree is a collection of nodes that are linked together in a branching pattern like trees in nature. By convention, trees are drawn upside down (Figure 1.6.1). A tree node contains zero or more child nodes that are themselves trees, so a tree is a recursive structure. A node with children is called an interior or branch node, while a node without children is called a leaf node. The top node of a tree is called the root. For an excellent overview of trees, see *The Art of Computer Programming: Fundamental Algorithms* [Knuth73].

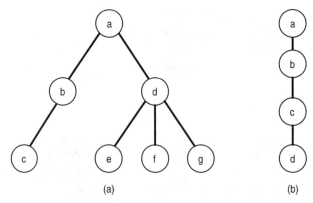

FIGURE 1.6.1   *Examples of trees.*

There are several different ways in which the contents of a tree can be traversed. A pre-order traversal visits each node first, followed by its children (a-b-c-d-e-f-g in Figure 1.6.1a). A post-order traversal visits the children first, then the node (c-b-e-f-g-d-a). Finally, a level-order traversal visits the root, then its children, then its grandchildren, and so on (a-b-d-c-e-f-g). The most important traversal order in game runtime code is pre-order. This is the natural order for calculating transforms in a skeletal animation system, for culling scene graphs to the view frustum, and for finding intersections of hierarchical bounding volumes. Post-order traversal is useful when interpreting scripts and shaders, where we can't evaluate a parent until all its children are evaluated. Level-order is least useful. One of our design principles is to make pre-order traversal very fast.

In most of our tree applications, the order in which we visit the children is unimportant. Such trees are said to be oriented or unordered, and we can simulate a post-order traversal by performing a pre-order traversal in reverse. If node order is important, the tree is said to be ordered. In that case, we could get the effect of post-order by adding children to the tree in reverse order. In this article, we will only implement forward and backward pre-order traversal.

Implementing Trees

A very simple way to implement a tree node is to use a list or dynamic vector to hold its child nodes. This makes it easy to perform modifying operations, such as adding or removing nodes. Traversal is also easy. The following code sample shows how we might write the contents of a tree to a stream in pre-order.

```
struct tree
{
    T _value;
    std::vector<tree> _children;
};

void OutputTree(tree& t, Stream& output)
{
    output << t._value;
    int childCount = t._children.size();
    for (int i = 0; i < childCount; i++)
        OutputTree(t._children[i], output);
}
```

A big problem with this approach is that it wastes memory. An efficient dynamic vector implementation will on average waste 25- to 33-percent of the memory it allocates. While it's possible to substitute a linked list for the vector, lists are often implemented with a dummy node. Either way, there is wasted memory at each node in the tree.

Another problem with this design is that we have to write a recursive function to traverse the tree. Recursion is elegant but inefficient. Although we can reduce the function overhead by replacing the recursion with an explicit stack and a loop, it is still costly to traverse the tree. Whatever the traversal method, this code must be duplicated in every additional operation on our tree. This is tedious and a potential maintenance headache. What if we decided to change from using a vector to a list in our implementation? It would be a significant editing chore to change all of the for loops in the processing functions. A better design would isolate the traversal logic in the library.

Fortunately, we can make trees more efficient. The following node structure with just two pointers can be used to represent a tree.

```
struct node
{
    T _value;
    node* _first_child;
    node* _next_sibling;
};
```

To visit a node's children, we follow its _first_child link, and then the children's _next_sibling links, until a NULL is encountered. We haven't solved the speed problem, though. We still need a stack to traverse the tree, and there will be serious difficulties implementing tree modification functions. We can fix all of these problems simply by adding more pointers. With just four pointers per node, we get efficient pre-order traversal, and efficient tree modification.

```
struct node
{
    T _value;
    node* _parent;          // NULL for root
    node* _prev_sibling;    // previous sibling
    node* _next;            // next in pre-order
    node* _last_descendant; // leaf points to itself
};
```

The _next pointer makes pre-order traversal lightning fast, just a single indirection, but what about in reverse? There is no _prev pointer, and in fact, we don't need one. The following node member function will calculate prev() in constant time, regardless of tree size.

```
node* prev() const
{
    node* prev = NULL;
    if (_parent)  // root of entire tree has no prev
    {
        if (_parent->_next == this)  // first child?
            prev = _parent;
        else
            prev = _prev_sibling->_last_descendant;
    }
    return prev;
}
```

The following navigation functions also can be performed in constant time.

```
node* first_child() const
{
    node* child = NULL;
    if (_next && (_next->_parent == this))
        child = _next;
    return child;
}

node* last_child() const
{
    node* child = first_child();
    if (child)
        child = child->_prev_sibling;
    return child;
}
```

```
node* next_sibling() const
{
    node* sib = _last_descendant->_next;
    if (sib && (sib->_parent != _parent))
        sib = NULL;
    return sib;
}

node* prev_sibling() const
{
    node* sib = NULL;
    if (_parent && (_parent->_next != this))
        sib = _prev_sibling;
    return sib;
}
```

One wrinkle in this design is that the _prev_sibling pointer points to the previous sibling for all child nodes except the first, where it wraps back to the last child to form a circular, singly linked list. This "hack" is necessary in order to get the last child of a node in constant time (see Figure 1.6.2).

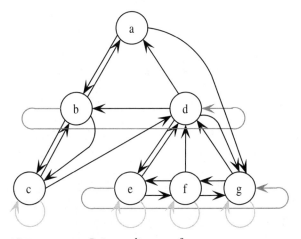

FIGURE 1.6.2 *Pointer diagram for tree.*

Given these tree navigation functions, it's possible to implement functions to modify the tree. We'll implement all of our tree modifications in terms of the following member functions of our tree.

```
void insert_subtree(TreeT& child, TreeT* next);
void remove_subtree(TreeT& child);
```

An important consequence of having the _last_descendant pointer is that adding a node to a tree might require updates all the way back up to the root node. In fact, this is what happens if the tree is built in the usual way by appending new children in pre-order. In the worst case (Figure 1.6.1b), the cost is quadratic in the number of elements in the tree. In practice, this is not a problem, because the worst case is rare and because trees are usually built at initialization time and then modified infrequently. In any case, if it's a problem, the client can insert children in reverse order.

Playing Well with the STL

Now that we know how to implement our tree, it's time to design the interface. We would like to pattern it after the STL for familiarity and to allow us to leverage as much STL code as possible. Can we make a tree look like an STL container?

The STL containers provide iterators to access their contents in sequence without exposing the underlying representation. This concept is what allows the STL to decouple algorithms from containers. An algorithm works for any container that can provide iterators. If we package our tree in the same way, so that our nodes are hidden and our iterators reference the T objects, then we can write the following:

```
tree<T> t;
tree<T>::iterator it;
for (it = t.begin(); it != t.end() ++it) {}

// use <algorithm>
void MyTFunction(const T& t);
for_each(t.begin(), t.end(), MyTFunction);
```

Unfortunately, we've also hidden the tree's hierarchical structure, since iterators only expose the T objects. That's very inconvenient. When processing a tree, it is often necessary to reference a node's parent or child nodes. In our previous examples, we have no way to access these relatives. Why not add member functions to iterators to get neighboring nodes? That solves the problem in the first example, but not the second. Anyway, it's a bad idea—iterators should look as much like pointers as possible, which means no member functions [Alexandrescu02].

The problem is that the STL container concept is wrong for trees. A tree is not a linear sequence of T objects; it's a hierarchical structure that contains T objects. We now boldly depart from the STL container concept, and actually emphasize the tree's internal structure. A tree is a linear sequence of trees, and tree iterators expose subtrees.

How do we get to the T object? We simply expose it as a public data member of tree named value. It would be silly to encapsulate it, since it belongs to the client. Now we can write code like this:

```
tree<T> t;
for (tree<T>::iterator it=t.begin(); it!=t.end() ++it)
{
    tree<T> subtree& child = *it;
    if (!child.is_root())
        child.value *= child.parent()->value;
}
```

```
void MyTreeFunction(tree<T>& t);
for_each(t.begin(), t.end(), MyTreeFunction);
```

It turns out that it's also useful to be able to iterate over the children of a tree, without descending into the sub-trees. For this purpose, it's easy to provide a child_iterator. We can implement it efficiently (constant time increment and decrement) with the next_sibling() and prev_sibling() functions. Both iterator and child_iterator are bidirectional, defining increment and decrement operators. Finally, we can leverage some STL machinery to provide reverse iterators and reverse child iterators with just a few lines of boilerplate code.

Given our tree traversal functions, the only difficulty in implementing iterators is handling the end value so that we can iterate backwards from it. Dummy nodes that are linked on to the end work well for STL containers like std::list, but not for trees. We'd need one per tree node, which is clearly impractical. Instead, our iterators store two pointers, one to the current tree and one to the root tree that produced it. The end position is represented by setting the current pointer to NULL. The decrement operator checks for NULL, and if so sets current to the last descendant of the root tree. In all other ways, our iterators are similar to list iterators, remaining valid until the sub-trees they point to are erased.

Now we know what our tree interface should look like. We define some simple constructors and a destructor. We also define the copy constructor and the assignment operator to give our tree full value semantics. These two functions perform "deep" copies and provide powerful tree-building capabilities.

```
tree();
tree(const T& t);
tree(const TreeT& copy);
~tree();
const tree& operator=(const TreeT& rhs);
```

Because our tree is a linear sequence of trees, it looks and feels a lot like a list. Thus, it's natural to mimic the interface of std::list.

```
void push_back(const TreeT& subtree);
void push_front(const TreeT& subtree);
void pop_back();
void pop_front();
iterator insert(iterator it, const TreeT& subtree);
iterator erase(iterator it);
void clear();
iterator splice(iterator it,
    iterator first, iterator last);
iterator splice(iterator it,
    child_iterator first, child_iterator last);
```

The splice functions move tree nodes around by manipulating internal pointers. This is much more efficient than copying subtrees and then deleting the originals.

Note that any function that takes a `tree` argument can also take a `T` argument because we defined the constructor `tree(const T& t)` and did not make it explicit. Since there is a natural one-to-one mapping between a `tree<T>` and a `T`, this is one of those rare occasions where allowing the implicit conversion doesn't cause problems.

Finally, we define some tree-specific operations.

```
bool is_root() const;
bool is_leaf() const;
bool is_descendant_of(const TreeT& ancestor);
size_t size() const;   // number of descendants
size_t degree() const; // number of children
size_t level() const;  // depth in tree
```

The STL has a policy of exception safety, which means that containers are guaranteed to remain unchanged when the underlying `T` objects throw certain kinds of exceptions. While most games avoid using exceptions, it doesn't take much work to provide exception safety. This tree container matches the STL guarantees using techniques described in [Sutter00], but throws no exceptions itself.

Memory allocation is always a touchy subject for game programmers. For a library to be suitable for use in game code, it should allow the client to control how memory is allocated. The STL container templates satisfy this requirement. They accept an allocator as an optional argument so that client code can provide custom memory allocation when necessary. We will provide this flexibility as well, although it presents a problem. Our elegant concept of a tree recursively containing trees leaves us no convenient place to store an allocator object. One solution would be to make tree and node separate concepts and store the allocator in the tree. However, the tree would become cumbersome to use, since we couldn't operate on a tree node without the tree object.

If we are less ambitious, we can get most of the benefit of allocators without abandoning our elegant tree concept. We simply make the allocator a static member of our tree class. That limits us to a single allocator per template instantiation of tree, noting that the STL standard makes it hard for implementers to provide much more than this anyway [Plauger01]. Now, with the right custom allocator [Isensee02], `tree` is eminently usable in runtime code.

Conclusion

The tree library we created can generate a tree containing any object type. If we fear template code bloat, we can instantiate just `tree<void*>` and privately derive type-safe tree-of-pointer interfaces from that to get a C style tree that is type-safe [Meyers98]. Template containers are both powerful and flexible.

The tree library provides powerful facilities for building trees. We can add `T` objects to a tree with a simple interface patterned after `std::list`. Because `tree` has value semantics (a copy constructor and assignment operator), we can copy entire trees in a single assignment. For efficiency, the `splice` functions allow trees to be "glued" together from existing pieces.

Once we've built a tree, we can iterate rapidly in pre-order, forward and backward. We can even perform recursive traversal using child iterators.

```
// preorder traversal, using recursion
void DoSomething(tree<T>& t)
{
    t.value.DoSomething();
    tree<T>::child_iterator it;
    for (it=t.begin_child(); i!=t.end_child() ++i)
        DoSomething(*it);
}

// postorder traversal, using recursion
void DoSomething(tree<T>& t)
{
    tree<T>::reverse_child_iterator it;
    for (it=t.rbegin_child(); i!=t.rend_child() ++i)
        DoSomething(*it);
    t.value.DoSomething();
}
```

ON THE CD

See the source code on the companion CD-ROM for example code that uses tree<T>.

References

[Alexandrescu01] Alexandrescu, Andrei, *Modern C++ Design*, Addison-Wesley, 2001.

[Isensee02] Isensee, Pete, "Custom STL Allocators," *Game Programming Gems 3*, Charles River Media, 2002.

[Knuth73] Knuth, Donald, *The Art of Computer Programming: Fundamental Algorithms*, Addison-Wesley, 1973.

[Kovachev02] Kovachev, Alexander, "Tree data class for C++," available online at *www.codeproject.com/cpp/treedata_class.asp*, January 13, 2002.

[Meyers98] Meyers, Scott, *Effective C++*, Addison-Wesley, 1998.

[Peeters03] Peeters, Kasper, "tree.hh: An STL-like C++ Tree Class," available online at *www.damtp.cam.ac.uk/user/kp229/tree/*, April 17, 2003.

[Plauger01] Plauger, P. J., et al., *The C++ Standard Template Library*, Prentice Hall, 2001.

[Sutter00] Sutter, Herb, *Exceptional C++*, Addison-Wesley, 2000.

The Beauty of Weak References and Null Objects

Noel Llopis, Day 1 Studios

llopis@convexhull.com

Programmers often have a love-hate relationship with pointers. They're small, they're efficient, and they let you manipulate memory in just about any way you can imagine. However, the smallest mistake tends to cause memory leaks, dangling pointers, or, in the worst of cases, program crashes and unhappy users.

This article looks into the problems caused by moving objects around in memory, something we commonly want to do with game resources. Some of the techniques discussed here also have relevance to the problem of loading and unloading objects in and out of memory. We will look at how weak references are a good alternative to straight C++ pointers. To complement that idea, we will put *null objects* to work, which will allow us to finally stop checking whether a pointer is NULL or not before we use it, as well as having a few other useful side effects.

Using Pointers

Even though they are very convenient, and we have many years of experience using them, pointers are sometimes not the best approach for certain tasks. Let's look specifically at how to deal with dynamic resources in a game. By resources, we mean everything that is loaded from the disk: textures, geometry, sounds, and so forth.

One of the fundamental problems we encounter when dealing with pointers is determining the lifetime of the resource. If you load a large texture, and two models use that same texture, they should both be pointing to the same location in memory. What should we do when one of the models is destroyed? We can't delete the texture because the other model is using it, but how do we know that? Moreover, we can't just leave it in memory, because when we delete both models we'll have a large memory leak.

In situations like these, we're forced to come up with our own solutions. A common approach is to use reference counting. Every time a model gets a pointer to a texture, it increases the reference count of the texture. Whenever the model is deleted, it decreases the texture's reference count. Whenever the reference count reaches zero, the texture is automatically deleted. This sounds great in theory, but it can make for cumbersome code and is frequently the source of programming errors.

Related to that problem is the issue of moving the resource around in memory, or even temporarily swapping it out and loading it later. If that texture is only used in a small section of the world, wouldn't it be great to be able to remove it from memory whenever the player is in a different area, and then load it on the fly as the player approaches that area again? The potential memory savings are substantial, and doing so would allow us to break free of the memory limitations of the machine and the constraints of small levels.

How would we go about swapping out a texture? One way would be to notify the parts of the program that are holding a pointer to the texture so they could invalidate it. Otherwise, if they tried to use the texture, the program would likely crash. Even if the program never had a need to access the texture because it never came into view, by the time we reload the texture, it will probably end up residing in a different memory location. To avoid these problems, we need a way to update the pointer value of all the objects that use it.

If we had a good solution, it would even allow us to load intermediate textures containing just a few mipmaps when the models are far away, and only load the most detailed and memory-intensive versions when the camera is very close to the model.

As is the case with many computer science dilemmas, this problem can be solved by adding a level of indirection. One possible solution is the use of handles. Every resource is identified with a unique ID (probably assigned at load time by the resource management system), which is called a *handle*. The game promises never to keep a pointer to a resource, and keeps the handle instead. Every frame, whenever the game wants to display a model or do any computation that requires accessing the texture, it asks the resource manager to give us the pointer to the texture that corresponds to that handle. We check whether the returned pointer is NULL, and if it isn't, we can proceed as usual.

This gives us the freedom to unload resources or move them around in memory, because the resource manager can keep track of those changes, and the rest of the program always goes through the indirection of the handle before getting a pointer. Unfortunately, this is very cumbersome; having to do the translation between handle and pointer every time, and even having to check whether it's NULL, becomes tedious very quickly. There is also the problem of what happens if we decide to store a pointer "just for a few frames" and then the resource is unloaded out from underneath us.

The rest of this article presents a solution that provides the feel and convenience of working with straight pointers, but addresses most of the problems discussed here.

Weak References

For the purposes of this article, a *weak reference* is a reference that has at least one level of indirection between itself and the object it points to. A handle, as discussed earlier, is a good example of a weak reference, since it uses a mapping scheme as a level of indirection. A plain C pointer, however, is a strong reference, because its reference mode is immediate (the pointer contains the actual memory address of the object it is referring to).

Be warned that the term *weak reference* is often used in memory management literature to mean something different. In that context, objects that have no strong references to them are freed by the system, while weak references do not force an object to stay alive.

Our objective is to make a weak reference as convenient to use as a regular pointer. These types of references are usually called *smart pointers*, because they behave like a pointer, but have logic embedded in them that controls the nature of the indirection.

It is possible to build a smart pointer around a handle-based system [Hawkins02], but here we're going to use a slightly different approach. In the interest of simplicity, ease of debugging, and efficiency, we'll use a smart pointer that ultimately wraps a raw C++ pointer, but we'll also enlist the services of some intermediate objects to help us achieve our objective.

Figure 1.7.1 is a UML diagram that shows how the system is going to be organized. Our smart pointer (`ResourcePtr`) is not going to point directly to the resource; instead, it is going to point to an intermediate object (`ResPtrHolder`) that contains a regular pointer to the resource. The resource manager uses a map container to associate resource names with resource pointer holders, so whenever a resource needs to be updated or invalidated, the contents of the holder are changed, and all the smart pointers in the game will automatically use the correct values.

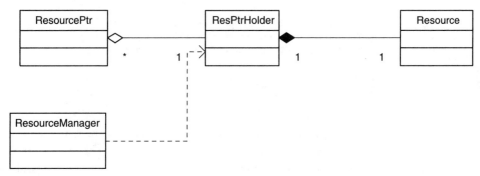

FIGURE 1.7.1 *Class organization of the resource system.*

The Smart Pointer

How can we create this smart pointer that looks like a pointer and behaves like a pointer, but has all this extra logic built in? It's fairly easy, especially if we don't have to deal with some of the headaches introduced by object lifetime determination or copy-on-write semantics. We just need to override certain operators that make it look like a pointer, such as operator-> and operator*. It also makes sense to make it a templated class so it can be type-safe with respect to the type of object it accesses. You can find more information on smart pointers in [Meyers96] and [Alexandrescu01].

ON THE CD

Here are some of the most interesting parts of our smart pointer's interface. The code on the companion CD-ROM includes the full source code along with some unit tests. Notice how the operators to access the data go through the indirection of a pointer holder instead of accessing it directly.

```
template <class ResType>
class ResourcePtr
{
public:
    ResourcePtr(const ResourcePtr<ResType> & ResourcePtr);
    explicit ResourcePtr(ResType * pRes);
    ResourcePtr(ResPtrHolder * pHolder = NULL);
    ~ResourcePtr();

    ResourcePtr<ResType> & operator= (
        const ResourcePtr<ResType> & ResourcePtr);

    ResType * operator->() const
    {
        return static_cast<ResType *>
                    (m_pResHolder->pRes);
    }

    ResType & operator*() const
    {
        return *(static_cast<ResType *>(
                    (m_pResHolder->pRes)));
    }

    bool operator==(ResourcePtr<ResType> res) const;
    bool operator!=(ResourcePtr<ResType> res) const;
    bool operator< (ResourcePtr<ResType> res) const;

private:
    ResPtrHolder * m_pResHolder;
};
```

One important aspect of our smart pointer is that it is the same size as a normal pointer (which is currently 32 bits on most platforms). That means that we can efficiently copy it, pass it as a parameter, or do anything with it that we would do with a regular pointer. Moreover, because the smart pointer is pointer-based instead of handle-based, there is very little extra performance overhead. There is no need to perform a handle lookup every time the resource is accessed. Instead, the only cost is an extra pointer dereferencing. It's not free, but it's very cheap, and certainly worth the minor performance cost for what it gets us.

The Resource Pointer Holder

The resource pointer holder class looks very simple. All it needs to do is to hold a pointer to the resource itself. Each holder object will have to be dynamically allocated whenever we need to create one. We can't really put them as part of an array or a vector because we want to be able to create and delete them without ever changing the memory location of other holders, so they have to be dynamically allocated. Doing many small dynamic memory allocations can potentially waste a lot of memory. The best way to deal with that is to override the new and delete operators for the holder class and make sure they're efficiently allocated out of a memory pool [Llopis03], [Glinker04]. That will result in no memory overhead and very good run-time performance.

It's also worth noting that the ResPtrHolder class is not itself a template, even though you might expect it to be. Although it would be nice to make ResPtr-Holder a template parameterized on ResType, and therefore alleviate the need for those ugly static casts in the ResourcePtr class, doing so simply moves those same casts into the resource manager class. In fact, pushing these casts into the resource manager class causes a whole series of additional complications, particularly if you want to have a single global resource manager responsible for managing all of your active resources.

ON THE CD

Now that we have the extra level of indirection hidden behind the mechanics of a regular pointer, we can solve the resource lifetime problem by adding reference counting to the resource pointer holders. The creation and destruction of smart pointers controls the number of references in a holder, and whenever there are no references left, the holder destroys the resource and then destroys itself (and makes sure to notify the resource manager as well). The companion CD-ROM contains an alternate version of the smart pointer system that uses reference counting in this way.

The Resource Manager

The resource manager is simply a big map that stores the relation between resource names and the resource pointer holders. It's important that it points to the holders, not the resources themselves; that way, all operations are done on the holder, which prevents us from breaking all the smart pointers in the rest of the game.

Depending on your game's architecture, you could organize a single global resource manager for all the resources in the game, or each type of resource could have a separate manager that keeps track of them. The advantage of the latter approach is that it is easier to implement different algorithms for resource eviction and swapping knowing what type of resource it is and having more information about each.

This map can be implemented in many different ways. A straightforward approach uses a std::map of strings and resource pointer holders. On real production code you probably want to make this mapping as efficient as possible, so you would either override the mapping function, or try to use integers as keys. (You can generate these integers at load time from a hash or CRC of the resource's name, or by simply branding your resources with a unique resource ID.) If you're willing to sacrifice a small amount of memory for better performance, you could use a std::hash_map and reduce the element access to constant time.

Null Objects

Weak references are great. They allow us to unload resources or move them around in memory with impunity. There is, however, one aspect we haven't addressed: having to check whether our pointers are NULL.

The Concept

We're so used to checking for NULL pointers (either through a conditional or the use of an assert) that we might not think much of it. Still, it leads to bloated code, where the intent of the program might be diluted or even overwhelmed by the volume of conditional statements scattered throughout your source files. In addition, while it's an admittedly minor concern, technically you're absorbing a slight performance hit for each of these conditional evaluations.

Wouldn't it be great if we could assume that resource pointers are always valid? The program would never have to check if they are NULL. That might be simple to do if the resources are simply loaded once and then stay permanently in memory, but it becomes harder to do if they are being dynamically loaded.

This is where *null objects* come in. A null object is just a resource, but one that doesn't contain any data, or the minimum amount of data to still function as a correct resource. For example, in the case of texture resources, the null resource could be a small, 4 x 4 fully transparent texture. This concept can be applied to any type of resource: geometry (a mesh with one vertex), sounds (a short sample with silence), animations (nothing moves), and so forth.

Whenever we decide that we want to evict a resource from memory, we free it, and, instead of setting the pointer inside the resource pointer holder to NULL, we set it to point to the null object for that type of resource. At this point, the program can freely access any resource and never worry about whether it is null. Every resource is guaranteed to be in memory, even if it is a null resource.

The reason to keep null objects as invisible as possible is to avoid artifacts if the program ever tries to display them. For example, if the player rushes into a new area, we might not be done loading the textures for a faraway street sign by the time we display it on the screen. A null object would ensure that the sign is simply transparent until we get a chance to load it, at which point it is likely to pop in. We hope the sign will still be far enough away that the popping won't be too objectionable, but in most cases you also have the option of building out the system so that it can smoothly blend between the depiction of the null object and the loaded resource.

For null objects to work correctly, we need one null resource for every type of resource. That way, the null resource can behave in every way like any other resource of its type. If the program accesses a texture, it will probably try to call texture-specific functions on that resource, which the null texture resource will provide.

Potential Problems

There are just a few issues we need to be aware of when dealing with null objects.

The first is that if the program expects to find some specific data in the resource, the final behavior is unlikely to be correct. For example, if the program tries to access a particular terrain texture that was evicted, it will get the tiny null texture object. However, the program might assume that the texture is 128 x 128, because that's the size of all terrain textures in our game, and try to access a pixel that doesn't exist in the null texture object. Ideally, the program should never try to access a resource that was evicted; doing so probably indicates a bug (more on that later). Even if it does, it is best not to make any assumptions about each resource when working with a system that can freely swap resources around.

The other issue is that of a program that attempts to modify its resources. Fortunately, this is not a very common situation; most resources are treated as read-only because they can be shared. However, this does happen on occasion and we need to be prepared. Perhaps we want to perform some special stamping effect on a texture or modify geometry on the fly. Trying to do that operation on a null resource could have unfortunate consequences, such as causing all of our null transparent textures to become bright red all of a sudden. To avoid this, it would be useful to flag null resources as read-only. Even better, if we want to maintain total transparency, we can allow the program to call functions to modify null resources, but make sure that all those functions have no effect on the resource itself.

Extensions

Now that we have null objects integrated into our resource management system, we can take them one step further and make them even more useful. For example, we can decide that trying to display a null object is something that should never happen, and should be treated as a bug. In that case, we want to make null objects as noticeable as possible. The null texture could become bright pink, the sound an annoying, loud, square wave, and the geometry one big sphere: anything that will catch people's attention right away. Additionally, null objects could even write an entry to the game log indicating which resource the game attempted to display.

In release mode, however, we probably want to revert to the previous behavior and make them as invisible as possible just in case the player ever accesses them in the final shipped game.

Conclusion

This article presented a flexible alternative to using pointers to keep track of game resources. It allows us to have more control over a resource's lifetime, as well as allowing us to move it around. We can even unload it from memory while the game is running. These new abilities might allow us to have larger game levels or to create a continuous world.

The article also presented the idea of null objects, which are special resources that are put in place of missing resources. These resources behave like any resource of their type, which frees the game code from having to check whether resources are loaded every time one is used. These null resources are often invisible to avoid causing any artifacts if they are displayed, but they can be alternately made very noticeable for debugging purposes.

References

[Alexandrescu01] Alexandrescu, Andrei, *Modern C++ Design*, Addison-Wesley, 2001.
[Glinker04] Glinker, Paul, "Fight Memory Fragmentation with a Templated Freelist," *Game Programming Gems 4*, Charles River Media, 2004.
[Hawkins02] Hawkins, Brian, "Handle-Based Smart Pointers," *Game Programming Gems 3*, Charles River Media, 2002.
[Llopis03] Llopis, Noel, *C++ for Game Programmers*, Charles River Media, 2003.
[Meyers96] Meyers, Scott, *More Effective C++*, Addison-Wesley, 1996.

1.8

A System for Managing Game Entities

Matthew Harmon, eV Interactive Corporation

matt@matthewharmon.com

New game developers are often enamored with the "output" side of their work: developing a new shader, creating a particle system, or playing 3D sounds. While these facets of development are essential, and certainly fun, it is frequently the less sexy tasks that turn a loose collection of code into a fully functional game. This article focuses on one of these elements: the management of game entities.

To promote the philosophy of entity management, rather than explore a specific implementation, this article presents a solution in C. While converting to C++, Java, or C# is a straightforward task, even in C the system is object-based, featuring polymorphism and well-encapsulated implementations.

Overview

Modern games are teeming with a variety of entities. Players, enemies, and projectiles buzz around the game world. Terrain, structures, sky, and clouds define the environment. Waypoints, triggers, and scripts guide the player's experience. Scoring, damage, and physics form the logic and rules of the game's universe.

Instead of treating all of these differently, as special-purpose elements, it is convenient to bind them together into a system that provides a common structure and method of communication. A message-based approach to managing entities can solve many problems and provides a method of unifying most of these critical game elements.

Everything Happens via Messages

In a message-based system, everything entities do is in response to messages. To draw an entity, you send it a message. To let an entity move itself through the world, you send it a message. If they don't get any messages, entities sit around and do nothing.

A good metaphor for this is the Win32 windowing API. Everything the Windows GUI does is in response to messages that can come from the application, other windows, or the operating system. Entities, like windows, have no knowledge of each other's internal data or implementation. They simply send and respond to a set of well-defined messages. Entities are also free to ignore any message that they don't care about or don't understand.

A Short Example

It is helpful to dive into the system with a simple example. Let's take the case of the player firing a missile. Since both the player and the missile are entities, this operation is a simple matter of messaging. In fact, this code can be used to fire any type of projectile from any type of entity.

```
ENTITY* FireProjectile(
        char*   className, // type of projectile
                           // to create
        ENTITY* shooter,   // shooter/owner of
                           // projectile
        ENTITY* parent)    // scene graph parent
{
    ENTITY*    entProj;  // projectile entity
    VECTOR3    pos;      // position of
                         // shooter/projectile
    VECTOR3    dir;      // direction vector of
                         // shooter
    VECTOR3    velocity; // velocity vector of
                         // shooter

    // create the projectile as a scene-graph
    // child of 'parent'
    entProj = EntCreate(className, parent, 0, 0);
    if (entProj)
    {
        // get position, direction and velocity
        // from the shooter
        EntSendMessage(entShooter, EM_GETPOS,
                    (int)&pos, 0);
        EntSendMessage(entShooter, EM_GETDIR,
                    (int)&dir, 0);
        EntSendMessage(entShooter, EM_GETVELOCITY,
                    (int)&vel, 0);

        // setup the new projectile
        EntSendMessage(entProj, EM_SETPOS,
                    (int)&pos, 0);
        EntSendMessage(entProj, EM_SETDIR,
                    (int)&dir, 0);
        EntSendMessage(entProj, EM_SETVELOCITY,
                    (int)&vel, 0);
        EntSendMessage(entProj, EM_SETOWNER,
                    (int)entShooter, 0);
        EntSendMessage(entProj, EM_START, 0, 0);
    }

    return(entProj);
}
```

Everything Is an Entity

A key aspect to building an entity management system is to try to think of everything as an entity that can be controlled via messages. It might seem counterintuitive to try to unify elements as diverse as projectiles, terrain, and game scripts, but it is from this unification that the power and simplicity of the system is derived.

A bullet, for example, needs to update its position, check for collisions, and be drawn. Terrain needs to be drawn and respond to collision tests. A script that tests a level's "win condition" needs to be executed each frame, but it doesn't respond to any other messages. From this simple example, we can start to unify our entities via messages. Table 1.8.1 shows how three different entity types would handle various messages.

Table 1.8.1 How Bullet, Terrain, and Script Entities Respond to Various Messages

	Bullet	Terrain	Script
Update	Process	Ignore	Process
Draw	Process	Process	Ignore
Check for collisions	Process	Ignore	Ignore
Respond to collision test	Ignore	Process	Ignore

In this scheme, even a logic script that doesn't "physically" exist in the world can be treated like any other entity. The entity mechanism can act as a simple but powerful wrapper around more complex game code.

Elements of the System

The entity management system consists of four principal components:

- **Entity messages:** Define how entities communicate.
- **Entity code:** The code and data that implements an entity class.
- **The class list:** Maintains a list of registered entity classes.
- **The entity manager:** Creates entities, manages the entity tree, and supports sending messages to one or more entities.

Entity Messages

A message should be seen as a function call—a request (or demand) for an entity to do something. Most entities need to respond to only a small subset of the messages you define. Therefore, entities must be able to safely ignore messages that they don't need or understand.

Some messages, like DESTROY, are simple and require no extra data. Other messages, like SETPOSITION, require parameters. Following the example of Win32, we support two generic parameters called var1 and var2. They are declared as integers, but their actual type is defined by the message being sent. In the case of SETPOS, the var1 parameter is used to pass the address of a 3D vector. Given this, the prototype for our standard entity message processing function is defined as follows:

```
// message processing function type
typedef int(ENT_PROC)(
    ENTITY* ent,      // pointer to _this_ entity
                      // container
    EM      message,  // EM_... entity message
    int     var1,     // generic parameter 1
    int     var2);    // generic parameter 2
```

In a C++ implementation, the casting of parameters var1 and var2 disappears in favor of virtual functions that take correctly typed parameters. The return value of the function signals whether recursion should continue through the entity tree. This allows the entity tree to act as a scene graph if desired.

The messages you create form the conventions within which all game entities operate. The message list should be well published and documented.

```
typedef enum entMessageTag
{
    // CLASS OPERATIONS
    EM_CLSINIT,       // initialize class,
                      // var1=char* data path
    EM_CLSFREE,       // free up class
    EM_CLSNAME,       // copy class name to var1

    // CREATION AND DESTRUCTION
    EM_CREATE,        // create entity
    EM_START,         // turn the entity 'on'
    EM_SHUTDOWN,      // destroy entity gracefully
    EM_DESTROY,       // destroy entity immediately

    // STANDARD ACTIONS
    EM_UPDATE,        // var1 = int elapsed seconds
    EM_DRAW,          // _normal_ rendering

    // DATA ACCESS
    EM_SETPOS,        // var1 = VECTOR3* position
    EM_GETPOS,        // copy VECTOR3 position to
                      // var1
    ...
} EM;
```

Adding a new message is as simple as appending another value to this enumeration. Since old entities will simply ignore new messages, the system can be extended without breaking existing code.

Entity Code

In C, an entity is essentially a data structure and a single function that processes messages. In addition, there might be static class data, such as resource handles, game-play tuning values, and the like. A skeleton module for a missile entity (with functional contents omitted) could look something like this:

```c
// missile class
typedef struct missileTag structure
{
    char        name[MAX_NAME];
    VECTOR3     velocity;       // velocity vector
    VECTOR3     position;       // world-space position
    VECTOR3     forceAccum;     // force accumulator
    MATRIX4     matModel;       // orientation matrix
} MISSILE;

// resources and class-wide variables
// loaded during CLSINIT and released
// during CLSFREE
static MODEL    mdlMissile;
static SOUND    launchSound;
static float    thrust = 10000.0f;

// message processor
int MissileProc(
    ENTITY*     entity,     // this entity's container
    EM          message,    // message to process
    int         var1,       // general purpose
                            // parameter 1
    int         var2)       // general purpose
                            // parameter 2
{
    MISSILE* e;  // pointer to actual entity data

    // get the entity's class data from the container
    e = ((MISSILE*)entity->data);

    // process any messages that concern a
    // Missile entity
    switch(message)
    {
        // class operations
        case EM_CLSNAME:
            strcpy((char*)var1, "MISSILE");
            return(TRUE);
        case EM_CLSINIT:
            return( ClsInit((char*)var1) );
        case EM_CLSFREE:
            return( ClsFree() );

        // creation and destruction
        case EM_CREATE:
            return( Create(ent) );
        case EM_SHUTDOWN:  // for a missile, same
                           // as destroy
        case EM_DESTROY:
            return( Destroy(e) );
        case EM_START:
            return( Start(e, var1, var2) );
```

```
                // standard actions
                case EM_UPDATE:
                    return( Update(e, var1) );
                case EM_DRAW:
                    return( Draw(e) );

                // data access
                case EM_SETPOS:
                    V3Copy(&e->position, (VECTOR3*)var1);
                    return(TRUE);
                case EM_SETVEL:
                    V3Copy(&e->velocity, (VECTOR3*)var1);
                    return(TRUE);
                case EM_SETDIR:
                    return(SetDirection(e,(VECTOR3*)var1));
                default:
                    return(DefEntityProc(message, var1,
                                        var2));
            }
            return(TRUE);
        }
```

The first parameter to the message handler is a generic entity container that is used to reference any type of entity in the system. This is described in more detail later in this article. After extracting the container's private data, the handler vectors messages off to their processing functions. A `default` case can be provided to support a crude form of inheritance, much like the `DefWindowProc` in Win32.

The Class List

To the outside world, an entity class exposes only its message processing function, much like a window class in Win32. The class list maintains a linked list or vector of these message handlers that allows classes to be referenced and created via a textual name. The class structure is quite simple.

```
typedef struct entityClass
{
    char                name[64];  // unique class name
    ENT_PROC*           clsProc;   // class's message
                                   // handler
    struct entityClass* next;      // next class in
                                   // list
} ENTCLASS;
```

Registration is done with the `EntCreateClass` function. This adds an entry to the class list and sends an `EM_CLSNAME` message to `clsProc` in order to retrieve the textual name to be associated with the class. It then sends the `EM_CLSINIT` message to `clsProc`, giving the class an opportunity to do one-time initialization, such as load resources, and so forth. Initialization of the various classes used by a game can be done at startup with code similar to this:

```
void GameInitClasses(
    char*   dataPath) // path where entities find
                      // their data
{
    EntCreateClass(PlayerProc,  dataPath, 0);
    EntCreateClass(MissileProc, dataPath, 0);
    ...
}
```

There are also `EntDestroyClass` and `EntDestroyAllClasses` functions that send `EM_CLSFREE` messages to one or all registered classes, facilitating cleanup.

The Entity Manager

The entity manager creates and destroys individual entities, and manages the list or tree that contains them. Entities are referenced by a simple, generic "container" structure with pointers to the entity's message processing function and its private data. It is this common container structure that allows the system to treat all entities the same. There are also fields to support a tree or list, as well as a unique id (the `guid` data member) that is used for synchronizing entities over a network.

```
typedef struct entityTag
{
    ENT_PROC*       Proc;           // message
                                    // processor fn
    void*           data;           // entity's custom
                                    // data
    int             guid;           // unique id for
                                    // net sync
    struct entityTag *parent;       // parent or NULL
    struct entityTag *prevSibling;  // prev sibling or
                                    // NULL
    struct entityTag *nextSibling;  // next sibling or
                                    // NULL
    struct entityTag *child;        // first child
} ENTITY;
```

The key operations of the entity manager are:

```
ENTITY* EntCreateEntity(char    *className,
                        ENTITY *parent,
                        int    var1,
                         int     var2);
```

This function looks up `className` in the class list, and if found, creates a new `ENTITY` structure, hooking it into the entity tree as a child of `parent`. It then saves a pointer to the class's message `Proc`, and immediately sends that `Proc` an `EM_CREATE` message with parameters `var1` and `var2`. In the `CREATE` handler, entities allocate space for their class data and point `data` to it.

```
int EntDestroyEntity(ENTITY* ent);
```

Called internally by entities in response to the DESTROY message, this frees up the ENTITY container structure and unhooks it from the tree. To actually destroy an entity, simply send it an EM_DESTROY message.

```
int EntSendMessage(ENTITY *ent,
                   EM      message,
                   int     var1,
                   int     var2);
```

Sends a message to an individual entity with the given parameters.

```
int EntSendMessageGuid(int guid,
                       EM  message,
                       int var1,
                       int var2);
```

Sends a message to an individual entity via its guid instead of its entity pointer. This is useful for network synchronization where pointers have no meaning.

```
void EntSendMessagePre(ENTITY *ent,
                       EM      message,
                       int     var1,
                       int     var2);
```

Sends a message to an entity and all its children, in pre-order traversal. Recursion is aborted when any entity returns FALSE after processing a message. This supports hierarchical culling should the entity tree also be used as a scene graph or collision tree. A similar function that doesn't abort might be useful as well.

A robust entity manager will also support functions to find entities by name, re-arrange the entity tree, and iterate through the entities issuing a callback at each node.

The Message-Based Game Loop

While entities can and will communicate with each other, the main loop is responsible for sending the critical messages that actually make the game happen. Since almost all of the "game code" ends up residing in the entities themselves, the loop becomes primarily a message dispatcher.

```
void GameProcessInput()
{
    GetInputEvents(&inputEvent);
    MapInputEventsToGameEvents(&inputEvent,
                        &gameEvent);
    EntSendMessage(entPlayer, EM_USERINPUT,
                (int)&gameEvent, 0);
}

void GameUpdateWorld()
{
    EntSendMessagePre(entWorld, EM_UPDATE,
                    elapsedMs, 0);
    EntSendMessagePre(entWorld, EM_POSTUPDATE, 0, 0);
```

```
    }

    void GameDraw()
    {
        // let all entities render themselves, and
        // then overlays
        EntSendMessagePre(entWorld, EM_DRAW, 0, 0);
        EntSendMessagePre(entWorld, EM_DRAWSHADOW, 0, 0);
        EntSendMessagePre(entWorld, EM_DRAWOVERLAY, 0, 0);

        // if in debug mode, draw extra info for entities
        if (debugMode)
            EntSendMessagePre(entWorld, EM_DRAWDEBUG,
                              0, 0);

        // draw editing visualization for currently
        // selected entity
        if (editMode)
            EntSendMessage(entBeingEdited, EM_DRAWEDIT,
                           0, 0);
    }
```

Getting Started: The Class Messages

Each class of entity needs to be initialized and shut down. These messages are sent to an entity procedure only once, as they apply to the entire class, and not an individual instance of an entity. Classes can be initialized when the game is started or upon loading of each level, depending on what is most appropriate for the specific game.

EM_CLSINIT

This message is sent once to every entity class in the game. Upon receiving it, classes can load their resources from disk, set up class-wide "static" variables, and perhaps create a symbol table of parameters available for in-game editing. A common argument to CLASS_CREATE might be a path to the application's data directory.

EM_CLSFREE

This gives a class the opportunity to release any resources it loaded and free any memory it allocated. Classes can be destroyed upon game shutdown or level exit as required.

EM_CLSNAME

Returns the name of the class. This provides the class list with the class' name and supports the rare case that an entity might need to know the class of another entity with which it is communicating.

Starting Simple: The Basic Entity Messages

In the simplest of games, entities will need to be created, destroyed, updated, and drawn.

EM_CREATE

An entity receives the CREATE message immediately after its container has been created by the entity manager. In response to this, an entity allocates the memory it needs for its internal data and initializes any default values. This is analogous to invoking an object's constructor and could certainly be implemented that way.

EM_SET/GET_POS, _DIR, _VELOCITY, _YAW, _COLOR, etc.

These "accessor" messages are used to set and retrieve entity data. Once created, an entity is typically sent several such messages to position and orient it in the world.

EM_START

After an entity is created, positioned, and otherwise set up, it is sent the START message. In response, an entity can play an initial sound or trigger an initial animation state that couldn't otherwise be done when responding to CREATE.

EM_DESTROY

This message demands the immediate destruction of an entity. Like an object's destructor, DESTROY gives an entity the opportunity to clean itself up. This includes freeing memory, and destroying any child entities it has created. DESTROY is typically used only when the player exits a level or otherwise shuts down the game. For graceful destruction of entities, SHUTDOWN should be used instead.

EM_SHUTDOWN

Sometimes an entity needs to be "turned off," but not immediately destroyed. For example, a burning fire might need to be shut down, but the remaining smoke puffs should be allowed to dissipate naturally over time. In this case, SHUTDOWN tells the entity "stop making any new smoke puffs, and DESTROY yourself when the last smoke puff dissipates." In the normal course of a game, calling SHUTDOWN is preferable to DESTROY. Of course, for many entity types, SHUTDOWN and DESTROY will execute the same code.

EM_DRAW

Entities respond to this message by rendering themselves in the world. This is "normal" game-mode rendering. Other types of rendering are discussed later.

EM_UPDATE

This message gives an entity the chance to update its position in the world. In games using variable time updates, the elapsed time since the last frame would be passed as a parameter to this message. Fixed frame rate games could issue the UPDATE message at the appropriate interrupt frequency.

EM_POSTUPDATE

Certain operations, like collision detection and some AI, need to know the "new" state of the world after all entities have been updated. A message like POSTUPDATE is typically sent to the world just after all entities have processed UPDATE.

EM_USERINPUT

This message is used to send input device events or state updates to the entities currently controlled by the players. In debug mode, this makes it easy to quickly change which entity is receiving user input data.

Gameplay and Environment Messages

Messages can also be used to communicate information about the game environment, as well as implement important game play constructs.

EM_FORCE

An explosion entity could broadcast a FORCE message to the entire world. Entities respond by calculating the effect of the FORCE described in the message and accumulating the result into their force vector.

EM_DAMAGE

When a projectile entity strikes a target, it sends a DAMAGE message telling the recipient how many hit points of damage it wants to impart.

EM_GIVEPOINTS

When an entity is destroyed, it can give points to the owner of the projectile that destroyed it, thus implementing a scoring system totally within the entities themselves.

Growing the System: Some Advanced Messages

These messages show how higher-level functionality becomes easy to add. Advanced features can be added to new entities without breaking any old entities; they simply ignore the new messages.

EM_DRAWOVERLAY

Certain entities might need to perform drawing operations after all "normal" rendering has taken place. For example, a sun entity might handle drawing glare or halos when the player is looking at it. The game loop can send DRAWOVERLAY to all entities after the "normal" DRAW message has been sent.

EM_DRAWSHADOW

Similarly, many shadow algorithms are performed after primary rendering. DRAW-SHADOW gives entities the opportunity to render their shadow effects.

EM_SETOWNER

If the entity tree is used as a scene graph, then SETOWNER can be used to establish ownership relationships between entities. For example, when the player entity fires a rocket, it sends SETOWNER to the new rocket, letting the rocket know who fired it.

EM_IMDEAD

It is often important to announce the imminent destruction of an entity. Say, for example, two elves are tracking the same orc. One elf attacks and destroys the orc while the other is still tracking it. The target orc, in its DESTROY handler, sends an IMDEAD message to the entire world. This tells the second elf that it is time to find a new target. This avoids continuous checking for null entity pointers.

The following example shows how a combination of the messages just discussed are used to support damage, scoring, and "death notifications." It takes place in the DAMAGE handler.

```
// processes an EM_DAMAGE message
static DamageHandler(
    ENTITY* me,        // this entity
    ENTITY* sender,    // var1 = entity doing the damage
    int     hitVal)    // var2 = hitpoints
{
    // owner of sender (if a projectile)
    ENTITY* owner=NULL;

    // reduce my hitpoints and determine if I'm dead
    me->hitPoints -= hitVal;
    if (me->hitPoints < 0)
    {
        // I'm dead! Get the sender's
        // owner (if any)
        EntSendMessage(sender, EM_GETOWNER,
                    (int)&owner, 0);

        // If he is owned, he must be a projectile, so
        // give his owner the points.  Otherwise, give
        // sender the points.
        if (owner)
            EntSendMessage(owner, EM_GIVEPOINTS,
                        me->points, 0);
        else
            EntSendMessage(sender, EM_GIVEPOINTS,
                        me->points, 0);

        // tell the world I'm dead
        EntSendMessagePre(world, EM_IMDEAD, 0, 0);

        // destroy myself
        EntSendMessage(me, EM_SHUTDOWN, 0, 0);
    }
}
```

Handling Collisions

Dealing with collisions can be one of the most complex tasks in a game. In the absence of a unified collision system, messages can again come to the rescue. The following examples are somewhat simplified, but show how messages can grow to support complex interactions.

EM_TESTHIT

This message requests that the recipient perform a "hit test." Because many types of collisions might need to be queried, it is typically necessary to pass a collision-test structure that describes the type of test to perform. For example, it might be sufficient for a bullet to perform ray versus polygon tests against potential collidees. A huge vehicle, however, might need to request a volume versus volume test.

In any case, the recipient is responsible for performing the test and returning the results of the test to the caller. This allows each entity class to deal with collisions in a custom manner, if required. Along with actual physical collisions, this message can be used to support 3D picking and line-of-sight tests.

EM_IHITYOU

When an entity determines, via one or more EM_TESTHIT messages, that it has actually collided with an object, the EM_IHITYOU message is sent back to the collidee with information concerning the collision, and how to respond to it.

Extending to Multiplayer

With a few extra messages, the entity architecture can be extended to handle the requirements of networked games as well. In this system, entities can synchronize themselves across the network with little need of assistance from higher-level game code. Using this system, entities can be totally insulated from the actual network transport mechanism. They simply send and receive messages.

EM_SERVERUPDATE

Server nodes send SERVERUPDATE to handle AI, decision-making, and position updating. Additionally, entities on the server can transmit network packets to synchronize themselves across nodes.

EM_CLIENTUPDATE

This message is used instead of the standard EM_UPDATE to allow client nodes to only dead-reckon their entities, without performing any AI or dynamics.

EM_NETPROCESS

As the game loop receives network traffic, it distributes packets destined for individual entities via NETPROCESS. This allows each entity class to use its own most efficient means of network synchronization. In a sense, this establishes direct communication between an entity on a server and the remote versions of itself.

Development and Debugging Messages

It is often helpful to support special messages that are used only during development, debugging, or game editing. The following are some common examples.

EM_DEBUGDRAW

Entities respond to this message by drawing additional debugging information. This can be as simple as drawing the name of the entity on top of its in-game 3D representation.

EM_EDITDRAW

This message gives an entity the ability to draw additional information that might be useful when a game is in "edit" mode. Suppose, for example, that a combat simulator has radar installations that can detect the player. The radar station responds to EDIT-DRAW by rendering a wireframe sphere that represents the range at which the radar can acquire targets.

EM_GETVARTABLE

Using this message, entities can expose a table of internal variables to an editing dialog box, allowing the game to create a custom editing facility for each class.

Benefits

The practical benefits of a message-based entity system are numerous:

- **Homogeneity:** A disparate variety of game entities can be managed and controlled using the same system, even if that simply means hiding more complex code in a thin entity wrapper.
- **Functional separation:** Helps enforce the separation of rendering, dynamics, logic, and even client versus server tasks. This becomes critical for large projects.
- **Single access point:** All control of entities is through a single access point, the EntSendMessage command. Thus, message logging, DLL interfacing, and binding the system to a scripting language become easy.
- **Total abstraction:** The process of firing a bullet is the same as launching a missile. Just change the class name and send the same messages. Simpler entities will ignore messages required by more advanced cousins.
- **Extensibility:** Adding new features is often as simple as creating new messages. Because older entities can ignore the new commands, adding features breaks nothing. Old code can be brought up to speed later.
- **Limited dependencies:** In a pure-message driven system, only the message list (or base class) needs to be included with each entity module.

- **As-is reuse:** Correctly structured, entities can be reused in new games with no changes. This facilitates rapid prototyping of new concepts. The sky entity from a first-person shooter can work properly in a flight simulator as long as the correct messages are supported.

On the Companion CD-ROM

ON THE CD

The code included on the companion CD-ROM outlines a skeleton entity management system in C. It is not meant to be operational, but rather provide a framework on which a complete package can be built, and a design to which a C++, C#, or Java implementation can be crafted. The typecasting, switch statements, and function pointers in this C implementation look a little dated, but they should serve as an example of how a powerful entity system can be created in any language.

Moving to C++

A message-based entity system becomes simpler and easier to maintain when programmed in a language with support for classes and virtual functions. Entity classes implement the necessary functions derived from a robust base class. Sending a direct message is a simple matter of calling a member function. Sending a message to the entire entity tree is somewhat more complex, but manageable.

While creating an entity could be as simple as using the new operator on the derived class, it is still useful to maintain a class registry/entity factory so entities can be created by textual name. This reduces source-file dependencies and allows entities to create and manipulate each other without any knowledge of their class definition.

Conclusion

Creating a robust entity management system is one of the most valuable tasks a game programmer can undertake. It provides a global framework into which the rest of a game can fit. Most importantly, it establishes a set of standards and conventions that facilitate rapid prototyping and development. Implementing the system and retrofitting old code to it takes time, but it is an investment that will pay off tenfold as new features are added.

1.9

Address-Space Managed Dynamic Arrays for Windows and the Xbox

Matt Pritchard, Ensemble Studios

mpritchard@ensemblestudios.com

Most game programmers have frequently encountered the task of managing a dynamically growing or shrinking array. We've handled these chores using the same straightforward algorithmic approach that hasn't changed much over the years. These days, most programmers write classes or templates to automate this basic array management process. However, in this article you will learn about a relatively new variation on this old and basic process that can provide some nonobvious, but substantial performance benefits for very large or highly active arrays.

Typical Dynamic Array Management

The standard approach to array management usually takes some variation on the following form:

1. In private variables, track the following for each array:
   - The size of an individual array element, in bytes.
   - The maximum number of array elements currently allowed.
   - The number of array elements actually in use by the game.
   - A pointer to a block of dynamically allocated memory sized to hold the maximum number of array elements.
2. When the program needs to add an element to the array, it performs the following steps:
   - If the number of elements in use is less than the maximum currently allowed, a pointer to the n-th element is returned, where n is the number of elements currently in use plus one. Otherwise, the array has to be grown, and this step is repeated afterward.
3. To grow the array, the following steps are performed:

> a. The maximum number of array elements is increased either by a specified amount, or by an algorithmically derived amount (such as doubling the current size).
>
> b. A new memory allocation large enough to hold the new maximum number of elements is made.
>
> c. The array elements already used by the game are copied into the new buffer.
>
> d. The old array buffer is deallocated and the array's base pointer is set to the new allocation.
>
> 4. When elements are individually deleted from the array, there is usually no buffer shrinking process. When the entire array is explicitly cleared, the array buffer is often deallocated and optionally reinitialized.

These techniques should be familiar to most experienced programmers. From a performance optimization standpoint, the only interesting part of the algorithm relates to the mechanics of growing the array. Of particular importance is the array growth value, the amount by which the array is extended to accommodate new elements. By using specific knowledge of the bigger picture, this value can be adjusted to minimize the number of times the array is grown.

ON THE CD

The CArrayManager class appears on the companion CD-ROM in the Array-Manager.h and ArrayManager.cpp files, and presents a typical C++ implementation of these techniques. As implemented, the CArrayManager manages a dynamic array of CArrayItem elements. The Initialization() and AddItem() methods show a straightforward implementation of the previously described operations. Note that the CArrayManager class is presented here simply to illustrate the basic mechanisms and framework behind this article and has been stripped of any nonessential functionality to avoid confusion. The CArrayItem elements are meant to be stand-ins for a struct or class instance that is allocated by the caller and passed by reference into the CArrayManager class, which makes a copy of its data. A more sophisticated implementation would likely choose to forgo the use of the CArrayItem class and instead rely on a templated data type.

Taking a Look Beneath the Surface

The techniques described in the preceding section are about as straightforward as you can imagine, and it doesn't seem as if there's much room here for improvement. That might indeed be true as long as we simply consider the algorithms and the language in which they are implemented. However, if we pull back and look at the bigger picture, another factor directly impacts performance: the operating system. The operating system is responsible for providing platform memory services to the compiled code, usually through a specific implementation in the language's runtime library.

Contemporary Windows operating systems, as well as the Xbox console, provide programs with two things: a *private address space* (so it appears to the program as if it is the only program loaded into memory), and *virtual memory*, which—when backed by a paging file on a hard disk—allows a program to use more memory than is physically available in RAM. Even if there is no paging file, as is the case with the Xbox, virtual memory allows programs to successfully request and use memory in a contiguous range of addresses, even if there is no unused region of physical RAM memory large enough to satisfy the request. These modern memory management capabilities enable specialized practices that allow for the improved performance of our tried-and-true array management algorithms.

Keep in mind that the techniques discussed in the remainder of this article are coded specifically for the 32-bit Windows platform API as provided on the PC and Xbox. Many gaming hardware platforms, most notably the PlayStation 2 and Gamecube, do not have memory management hardware capable of supporting virtual memory or do not run an operating system that exposes address space control to the application. Therefore, for now, this technique should be considered Win32 specific.

Address Space Management ! = Memory Management

When a PC or Xbox program allocates memory using services such as `new` or `malloc`, the language's runtime library first attempts to satisfy the request with memory from a private heap that it maintains. If the block requested is too large, or the heap too fragmented, it will request more memory from the operating system. When the memory allocation is passed to the operating system, it performs two main tasks.

The first thing the OS does is scan the list it maintains of address ranges that it has already provided to the program, looking for a range of unused addresses large enough to hold the requested block size. Under Windows, the total address space range available to a program is a little under two gigabytes, as addresses near 0x00000000 are reserved to catch null pointer faults, and the addresses from two gigabytes (0x7FFFFFFF) to four gigabytes (0xFFFFFFFF), the maximum 32-bit value, are reserved for use by the operating system.

Once a suitable address range is located, the OS then sets about the task of finding physical RAM to assign to those addresses. RAM comes in page-sized chunks, which are 4K in size under Win32. These chunks are located by looking for unassigned memory pages in physical RAM or, on the PC, if there is no free physical memory to be found, it will attempt to reclaim physical memory from other running programs. This is accomplished by paging some of the contents of their virtualized address space out to the swap file. The process of allocating storage in physical RAM or the swap file is called *committing* memory.

It's important to note that not all memory addresses accessible by a program actually have memory committed to them. Unless the OS has been asked to provide memory to a range of addresses, any attempt to access them will be caught by the memory controller and trigger a program fault. There is no requirement that the pages of memory backing a range of addresses be in any sort of order in physical RAM, as the memory controller takes care of mapping physical and virtual memory pages into each program's address space. Thanks to the OS, all your programs ever see is a contiguous block of memory.

Rethinking the Growth Process

Several events can cause performance to suffer whenever a dynamic array has to grow.

The first occurs when the application needs to grow the size of an existing array, and must therefore allocate a new memory block larger than the array's current size. The OS must find room for the new block in the program's address space, locate free pages of memory to back it up, and reprogram the memory controller to make the pages appear as a contiguous block of memory for the program. Since we must perform a memory copy, two memory buffers have to be active at the same time: the existing array data and a larger buffer for the expanded array. This means that the peak allocation will be at least two times the size of the array data, and possibly much more depending on the reallocation strategy being employed by the runtime memory manager. As dynamic arrays become larger, this increases the likelihood that other memory will be paged out to disk in order to provide the memory for the copy, even though a third to half of it will be released as soon as the copy is completed. On platforms where there is no swap file, such as the Xbox, a program will be unable to grow an array if there is not enough free memory to hold both buffers, even though it might have enough free memory for the expanded array.

The rest of the performance hit is due to the copying of the array's contents. All the array elements have to be read, even though nothing is done with them, and CPU caches are likely to be cleared of data that are more important. As a side effect of the copy operation, the application heap might become further fragmented when the original buffer is deleted. Since the address of the array's data might change, other parts of the program can't take advantage of pointers to individual array elements. Instead, the program needs to save the element's array index and recompute the pointer each time it needs to access it.

Finally, as a dynamic array grows, there is the issue of "slack space"—memory that is allocated but not yet used to hold anything and therefore not available for other needs. Choosing larger growth sizes to minimize the number of times an array must be reallocated has the unfortunate consequence of increasing the amount of the average array's slack space.

A Better Way to Grow

The key to this article is understanding that a program's address space can be assigned and managed independently of physical memory. Since the operating system allows our programs to do this if we choose, we can manage the memory of a dynamic array more efficiently.

The main difference with address-space managed dynamic arrays is that upon array initialization, a range of address space large enough to hold the maximum anticipated array size is allocated, but no physical memory is committed to back up those addresses. Then, as the array grows, pages of memory are dynamically committed to the addresses needed for the new array elements. This might sound simple enough, but it gives us several advantages:

- It eliminates the need to perform a memory copy of the entire array's data each time the array grows! No time is wasted copying, and the CPU's caches are not thrashed.
- The amount of work the operating system's memory manager has to do when the array grows is significantly less. The OS only needs to find enough memory pages to back the new extension to the array, as opposed to finding enough memory to hold the entire newly grown array. It also does not have to do any new address space management.
- By having the OS doing significantly less work when the array grows, it becomes more practical to grow the array more frequently but by smaller amounts, reducing the amount of slack space at any given time.
- By not having to allocate a buffer for holding a copy of the array, and by reducing slack space in arrays, the amount of pressure on the virtual memory system is reduced and less page file activity will take place. In an environment without a paging file, such as the Xbox console, an array can be grown even when there is not enough free memory to grow an array the traditional way.
- Since the address used for the array's data never changes, direct pointers to individual elements can be saved and used by the program without having to recompute a pointer each time.
- Shrinking the memory used by the array as elements are removed or deleted becomes practical. As the array manager sees that there are unused memory pages at the end of the committed area, it can release them. Typically, when a page is released, the operating system doesn't do anything with it until it needs to satisfy another memory allocation request.

Using Address-Space Managed Arrays

ON THE CD

The `ArrayManager2.h` and `ArrayManager2.cpp` files on the companion CD-ROM present a `CAddressSpaceArrayManager` class that exposes an interface identical to that of `CarrayManager`, but implements its services using the address-space managed dynamic array technique you've been reading about.

The `Initialization()` method has a bit more work to do in this case. It tracks the array maximum and the current "in-use" sizes in two forms: the number of array elements and number of memory pages. First, an address space needed to accommodate the maximum array size is reserved with a call to `VirtualAlloc()` using the `MEM_RESERVE` parameter. Then, a second call to `VirtualAlloc()` is made using the `MEM_COMMIT` parameter. This provides actual memory to store the initial number of array elements that we expect we will need. The number of array elements we actually have committed memory for is stored in the `m_Num_Elements_Committable` variable.

Note that we round this amount up from the `Initial_Size` variable that is passed in to reflect how many array elements can actually be held by the committed memory pages. When elements are added, this value is checked to determine if additional memory pages need to be committed; we don't want to do that until absolutely necessary.

```
void CAddressSpaceArrayManager::Initalize
            (int Maximum_Size, int Initial_Size)
{
    // Initialize the Array to the specified capacity
    // (This could be moved into the constructor)
    m_Element_Size = sizeof (CArrayItem);

    // Calculate number of pages we want to reserve
    m_Maximum_Pages_Commitable =
       (( m_Element_Size * m_Maxiumum_Num_Elements )
          + OS_Page_Size - 1) / OS_Page_Size;

    // Note: We could round this up to next page size
    m_Maximum_Num_Elements = Maximum_Size;

    // Reserve address space for this array instance
    m_Array_Data = VirtualAlloc(NULL,
        m_Element_Size * m_Maxiumum_Num_Elements,
        MEM_RESERVE, PAGE_READWRITE);

    if (!m_Array_Data)
        assert("address allocation failed");

    // Commit Memory for an initial # of array elements

    // Calculate amount of memory to commit
    m_Num_Pages_Committed =
       ((Initial_Size * m_Element_Size)
          + OS_Page_Size - 1) / OS_Page_Size;

    // Round up commitable array element count
    // to the next page size
    m_Num_Elements_Committable =
       (m_Num_Pages_Committed * OS_Page_Size) /
        m_Element_Size;

    // Commit the memory
    void* result = VirtualAlloc(m_Array_Data,
        m_Num_Pages_Committed * OS_Page_Size,
        MEM_COMMIT, PAGE_READWRITE);

    if (!result)
        assert("memory commit failed");

    m_Num_Elements_Used = 0; // No elements added yet
}
```

In 32-bit Windows, `VirtualAlloc()` is the API function that lets us both reserve a range of addresses, and commit memory to a previously reserved address range. The minimum page size is 4K bytes and is indicated by the `OS_Page_Size` variable.

The `AddItem()` method is the workhorse of the class. It takes a pointer to a `CArrayItem` structure and appends a copy of its data to the end of the array. The first check it performs is to see if the array has reached its maximum possible size. Should the array reach this size, the programmer is faced with either generating an error, or falling back to the traditional array growth technique. Assuming success, the class performs a second array size check to see if additional memory pages need to be committed. If additional committed memory is needed, we have a choice as to how many new pages we want to commit at one time. Here we just add one page at a time, which keeps slack space to a minimum, but your own variations of this class might want to provide a tuning interface that allows applications to indicate how many memory pages should be committed at a time. To commit additional pages we call `VirtualAlloc()` again with the `MEM_COMMIT` parameter and specify the size and address where we want to place the newly committed pages. Note that we cast our pointer to a byte type to avoid the problem of having the compiler scale the address offset by the size of the array element. Then the memory tracking variables are updated and the element data is copied to the end of the array.

```
void CAddressSpaceArrayManager::AddItem
                    (CArrayItem* the_Element)
{
  if (m_Num_Elements_Used >= m_Maximum_Num_Elements)
  {
    // Must decide what to do here
    assert("Array exceeded maximum size");
      }

  // Committed memory Full?
  if (m_Num_Elements_Used==m_Num_Elements_Committable)
  {
    // Add more committed to memory to
    // the Array's address range

    // Many ways we could calculate this...
    int  Num_Pages_To_Grow = 1;

    void* result = VirtualAlloc(
        (byte*)m_Array_Data +
        m_Num_Pages_Committed * OS_Page_Size,
        Num_Pages_To_Grow * OS_Page_Size,
        MEM_COMMIT, PAGE_READWRITE);

    m_Num_Pages_Committed = m_Num_Pages_Committed +
                        Num_Pages_To_Grow;

    // Update number of elements we have memory for
```

```
      m_Num_Elements_Committable =
        (m_Num_Pages_Committed * OS_Page_Size)
          / m_Element_Size;
  }

  // Add element to the Array
  m_Array_Data[m_Num_Elements_Used] = *the_Element;

  // Update number of elements in use
  m_Num_Elements_Used++;
}
```

Some thought also needs to go into choosing the maximum possible array size. It should be large enough that it will never be encountered in any realistic situation, but not so large as to wantonly waste address space. In 32-bit Windows, a program has a little less than two gigabytes of total address space available to it. While this is far more than most programs presently use, if we just chose an arbitrarily large maximum array size, it would not take too many managed arrays to risk running out of address space.

An additional caveat to be aware of is that when reserving a range of addresses, the VirtualAlloc() API function will return a memory address that starts on a 64K boundary.

The RemoveItem() method does just what its name implies; it removes an element from the array and fills in the gap by shifting the last array element down into the deleted element's position. What the CAddressSpaceArrayManager version adds is a check to see if it can free up, or *decommit*, a page of unused memory and return it to the program. To do that it uses the Windows API function VirtualFree(). On Windows, there is no requirement that memory be decommitted in the same size or order in which it was committed, as the OS coalesces and subdivides memory blocks as needed. Once the determination is made that there is a committed memory page at the end of the array that is presently unused, VirtualFree() is called with the MEM_DECOMMIT parameter, and the address and size of the memory pages to release.

```
    void CAddressSpaceArrayManager::RemoveItem
                        (int the_Element_Index)
    {
      if (the_Element_Index < 0 ||
          the_Element_Index >= m_Num_Elements_Used)
      {
        assert("Bad Array Element Index");
      }

      // Remove requested item, and fill in gap
      // with the last array element
      m_Num_Elements_Used--;
      if (the_Element_Index < m_Num_Elements_Used)
      {
        m_Array_Data[the_Element_Index] =
          m_Array_Data[m_Num_Elements_Used];
      }
```

```
// See if we want to release any committed pages
int Unused_Memory = (m_Num_Elements_Committable -
    m_Num_Elements_Used) * OS_Page_Size;
if (Unused_Memory > OS_Page_Size)
{
  // Free the last page of committed memory
  m_Num_Pages_Committed--;
  VirtualFree((byte*)m_Array_Data +
          m_Num_Pages_Committed * OS_Page_Size,
          OS_Page_Size, MEM_DECOMMIT);

  // Recalculate the number of items we
  // have committed memory for
  m_Num_Elements_Committable =
          (m_Num_Pages_Committed * OS_Page_Size) /
          m_Element_Size;
}
}
```

Conclusion

Address-space managed dynamic arrays can provide performance benefits by taking advantage of memory management capabilities provided to programs by modern operating systems. You should consider using this technique when the number of elements in your array will be changing frequently and dramatically over the lifespan of the container, or if the array is likely to become very large at some point. For small data sets or arrays that never change size, there is little to no benefit to be had by using this technique. For large or volatile amounts of data, address-space managed arrays provide a new twist on a traditional technique and an opportunity to gain efficiency and performance while reducing memory consumption.

1.10

Critically Damped Ease-In/Ease-Out Smoothing

Thomas Lowe, Krome Studios

tomlowe@kromestudios.com

Smoothing is an enormously useful concept and can be of great service to the quality of every part of a game. Its use can make the difference between a game that looks rushed, jerky, and rough around the edges, and one that looks slick, polished, and natural.

By *smoothing*, we are referring to a method of gradually changing a value over time toward a desired goal. We can smooth almost any value that changes over time, whether represented by scalars, vectors, colors, or angles, and therefore the technique described here is widely applicable. Here are some examples:

- **Camera motion:** A camera that follows an object can exhibit jerky motion, especially when the object itself has jerky motion or when the camera collides with world geometry. Smoothing the camera gives a more natural look, and is much easier on the eyes of the player.
- **Flexible path following:** One can "smooth" toward a point that follows a path rather than following the path exactly. This will allow for deflection off objects en route. The technique will smooth sharp changes in the path's direction and can provide a smooth speedup and slowdown at the start and end of the path.
- **State changes:** When implementing a complex object's behavior, undesired and sudden changes in position or velocity can often arise, especially when moving from one state to another. Smoothing removes such glitches so that they no longer draw the player's attention.
- **Front end:** Moving text or an item from one part of the screen to another, changing its size or its color can all be done by smoothing toward a desired value.

This article describes a method of ease-in/ease-out smoothing based on a critically damped spring model. The model is implemented as an easy-to-use function, providing a robust and powerful smoothing tool.

Alternative Techniques

Given that smoothing has such widespread uses, it's worthwhile to consider several different methods. Let's start with a short comparison.

S Curve

When one simply needs to smooth from one static value to another over a specified time period, then an S curve gives a smooth ease-in/ease-out motion. Part of a sine wave or two parabolas can be used and provide C^1 continuity, although a C^2 curve (continuous acceleration) can be generated at little extra cost (see Figure 1.10.1).

Exponential Decay

Exponential decay is a common method and often looks something like:

```
y = y + (desiredY - y) * 0.1f * timeDelta
```

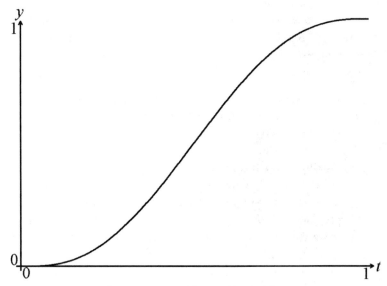

FIGURE 1.10.1 C^2 S curve: $y = 6t^5 + 15t^4 - 10t^3$.

where *timeDelta* is the time step between updates of the specified code, in seconds.

The value in this type of smoothing is that you can smooth toward a changing target; additionally, there is no need to retain the "time from start" data. This method can be described as "ease-out," but notice that the initial motion is sudden (see Figure 1.10.2).

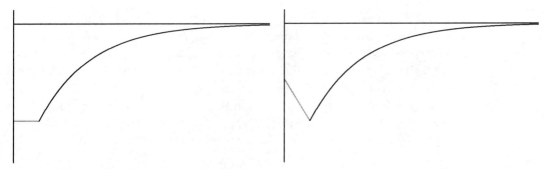

FIGURE 1.10.2 *Exponential decay, initially static and initially moving.*

Critically Damped Spring

This model combines the robustness of the exponential decay with the ease-in property of the S curve; one can smooth toward a changing target while maintaining a continuous velocity. Unlike the exponential decay technique, a velocity variable must be maintained (see Figure 1.10.3).

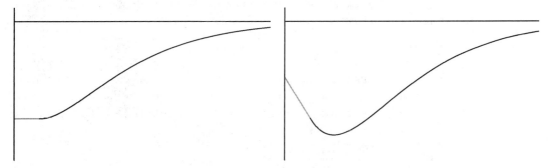

FIGURE 1.10.3 *Critically damped spring, no sudden change in velocity.*

Damped Springs and Critical Damping

How does the last method work? The technique is based on a damped spring (a spring with drag). A point at the end of a spring (y) has a force on it proportional to the extension from the spring's natural length (the desired position y_d); this is Hooke's law. A damped spring additionally has a force acting against the point's velocity. Therefore, the motion of a point y on a damped spring can be modeled by the differential equation:

$$m \frac{d^2y}{dt^2} = k(y_d - y) - b \frac{dy}{dt} \qquad (1.10.1)$$

where m is the point's mass, k is the spring constant (or spring strength), and b is the damping constant (or amount of drag).

The constants affect how the spring recoils toward y_d, or in the context of our smoothing function, how our value approaches the desired value. A small value for b produces overshoot and oscillations, while large values for b give us a slow convergence. Critical damping occurs when b falls between these two extremes such that it produces no oscillations and approaches y_d at an optimal convergence rate. This can be shown to occur when $b^2 = 4mk$. Therefore, we can simplify Equation 1.10.1:

$$\frac{d^2y}{dt^2} = \omega^2(y_d - y) - 2\omega\frac{dy}{dt} \text{ where } \omega = \sqrt{\frac{k}{m}} \qquad (1.10.2)$$

ω (omega) is the spring's natural frequency, or less formally a measure of the stiffness or strength of the spring.

In Practice

We will now show how to implement this model. Our goal is to write a function that will update a position and velocity given a desired position, a time period, and some type of smoothness factor—something like this:

```
y = SmoothCD(y, desiredY, velY, smoothness);
```

The critically damped spring model (Equation 1.10.2) can be approximated using standard numerical integration techniques, but there is really no need because an exact closed form (analytical) solution exists (see [Stone99]). It can be shown to be:

$$y(t) = y_d + ((y_0 - y_d) + (\dot{y}_0 + \omega(y_0 - y_d))t)e^{-\omega t} \qquad (1.10.3)$$

where y_0 is the initial position and $\dot{y}_0$ is the initial gradient or velocity.

Applying this equation incrementally and differentiating, we get:

$$y_1 = y_d + ((y_0 - y_d) + (\dot{y}_0 + \omega(y_0 - y_d))\Delta t)e^{-\omega\Delta t} \qquad (1.10.4)$$

$$\dot{y}_1 = (\dot{y}_0 - (\dot{y}_0 + \omega(y_0 - y_d))\omega\Delta t)e^{-\omega\Delta t} \qquad (1.10.5)$$

These two equations give us (exactly) a new position and velocity after a time step Δt, precisely what we want.

Regarding our smoothness factor, note that we could use ω but it is usually more intuitive to control a smooth function with some type of *smooth time* rather than a spring strength. A good definition for our smooth time is "the expected time to reach the target when at maximum velocity" (see Figure 1.10.4). This definition is useful for two reasons. First, it is equivalent to the lag time (due to drag) when smoothing toward a moving target, making lag calculations easy. Second, it provides us with this simple conversion: $\omega = 2\ /\ smooth\ time$, which can be derived from Equation 1.10.2.

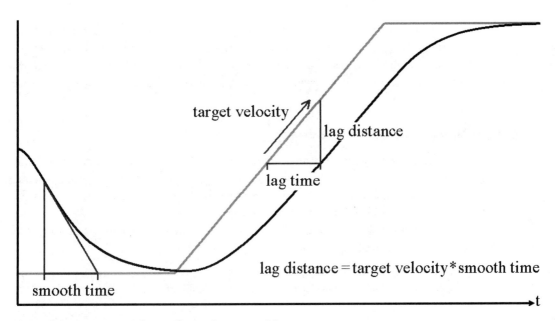

FIGURE 1.10.4   *Equivalence of smooth time and lag time.*

The one remaining problem is that exponential function call, which is computationally expensive. Fortunately, it can be approximated precisely for the range that we'll use. This results in our completed function.

```
float SmoothCD(float from,
               float to,
               float &vel,
               float smoothTime)
{
  float omega = 2.f/smoothTime;
  float x = omega*timeDelta;
  float exp = 1.f/(1.f+x+0.48f*x*x+0.235f*x*x*x);
  float change = from - to;
  float temp = (vel+omega*change)*timeDelta;
  vel = (vel - omega*temp)*exp;  // Equation 5
  return to + (change+temp)*exp; // Equation 4
}
```

A good basis for approximating e^x is to take a truncated Taylor expansion (shown below). Our exponential $e^{-w\Delta t}$ can then be calculated as $1/e^x$ where x is $w\Delta t$

$$e^x \approx \sum_{i=0}^{n} \frac{x^i}{i!} \tag{1.10.6}$$

The coefficients can be tweaked to better approximate within the most commonly used range. For our function, this range is roughly $0 < x < 1$ and here the approximation *exp* used above has less than 0.1% error. It is also roughly 80 times faster than the function exp() on PC! An even better approximation could be achieved by using higher order polynomials.

Adding a Maximum Smooth Speed

We will finish with a brief examination of a handy extension: how to add a maximum smooth speed. Since a source and target moving at speed s will have a lag distance equal to $s*smoothTime$, if our distance to target is clamped to be no longer than this lag distance, then s becomes the maximum speed.

This idea can be implemented by modifying *change* after it is set, leading to a smoothly approached top speed.

```
float maxChange = maxSpeed*smoothTime;
change = min(max(-maxChange, change), maxChange);
```

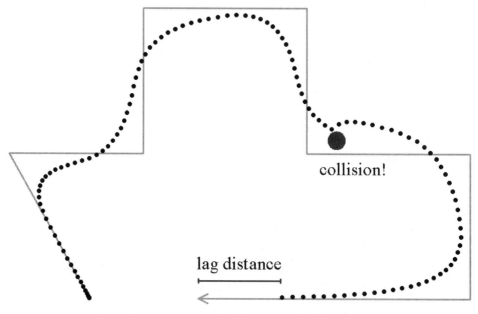

FIGURE 1.10.5   *Smoothing a vector, path following with deflection en route.*

Conclusion

ON THE CD

Critically damped spring smoothing can be achieved with a simple algorithm. The implementation shown here is a precise approximation to the exact solution and is always stable no matter how large the time step or small the smooth time. Since smoothing can be performed on floats, colors, vectors, and so on, it is an ideal candidate for a template function, and just such a version has been provided for you on the companion CD-ROM.

References

[Stone99] Stone, B. J., "A Summary of Basic Vibration Theory," available online at *www.mech.uwa.edu.au/bjs/Vibration/OneDOF/1DOF.pdf.*

1.11

A Flexible, On-the-Fly Object Manager

Natalya Tatarchuk, ATI Research, Inc.

natashat35@yahoo.com

At the heart of many contemporary games is a database. This database is used to manage all of the runtime game objects and to provide relevant lifecycle services. This includes operations like creation, destruction, caching, querying, saving, and loading. All of these operations must often be performed on objects of varying types within the same data management system. Thus, the crucial requirements for any programmer developing the database component of a game are flexibility, convenience, and efficiency.

In the past, this problem has been solved using straightforward template implementations for object allocation and management, as well as other related techniques that allow for the flexible creation of objects of different types. See [Bilas00] for an example of how to implement a handle-based resource manager using templates, and [Hawkins02] for a discussion of an object management mechanism using handle-based smart pointers. However, most of these approaches exhibit constraints that can cause developers to get stuck during the development of their object management systems. For example, there are cases when the game programmer does not know about all of the possible object types planned for use in the game, or perhaps the technical staff wants to allow for the addition of new object types at some arbitrary time in the project timeline. This is especially relevant if the game object manager is to be wrapped into a stand-alone library and more object types are added to the system after the library has been completed. Without flexible object management, it is very hard to use the previously mentioned techniques without causing a recompile of the entire project, or at least the entire object manager component. This article describes how to approach the problem of dynamic object management by using custom classes for object creation and destruction, and a custom object management system that allows evaluating type information at runtime.

Object Management the "Old Way"

One approach to implementing object management subsystems is to rely on a common technique favored by many programming projects: good old inheritance abuse.

With this approach, the developer creates a base class for an object and provides an object manager that uses the base class representation as the type that it actually manages. New classes are created by deriving subclasses from the base object class. The object manager can be used to manage all derived class objects as well, provided that all objects share common functionality via virtual functions and implement virtual destructors correctly. This approach has two main limitations. First, it enforces a common starting point for all objects in the system. This can be undesirably limiting and implies that all object classes are known at compile time. If the developer wants to add new object classes, he or she must have information about the base class in order to add support for new classes. Second, all object classes are forced to implement the same set of low-level functions, which can be very inconvenient in the case where we would like to use the same object manager to manage a variety of different, completely unrelated types.

A second approach for solving the object database problem consists of using a manager class that has templated data storage and templated object accessor functions. In this approach, you create a container class that is templated for any data type that you might want to use in your project. Then the class allows you to access and manipulate that stored data via template member functions. There are several issues with this approach as well. Anyone who has used templates knows that they must be correctly instantiated prior to being used. This, again, requires that all possible object type combinations be known at compile time by the developer. The addition of new class types requires recompilation of the system.

Another common approach is to simply store objects in the object manager using void pointers and to move the memory management for each object outside of the object manager; while this practice is rather abhorrent, you might be surprised to learn how widespread it is. This technique actually undermines the reason for having the object manager in the first place, since the manager becomes little more than a temporary storage bin for objects.

A Flexible, On-the-Fly Object Manager

Keeping the preceding discussion in mind, let's now introduce the design of an object management system that allows a great amount of runtime flexibility in a data-driven game subsystem. A key advantage of this particular implementation is the ability to manage objects in a type-safe fashion without knowing the object types prior to running the game system—there is no requirement to explicitly define all object classes at compile time. New object types can be automatically added to the system at runtime without penalty. Additionally, this approach does not require the users of the system to have any common base object classes upon which all game entities are based. The system presented in this article also provides a mechanism for correct memory deallocation of each individual object using a customized destruction mechanism. This particular approach uses templates and polymorphism in the implementation. The implementation presented in this chapter requires a compiler that supports member templates, such as the Microsoft Visual Studio C++ compiler.

Runtime Type Information

To use the approach described in this chapter, Runtime Type Identification (RTTI) must be enabled for your project. Runtime Type Information is a mechanism that allows the type of an object to be determined during program execution, and is supported at the language level in all contemporary C++ compilers. Typically, the runtime type information mechanism is implemented by placing an additional pointer in the virtual function table, and thus it follows that enabling RTTI incurs some modest program size overhead. The RTTI vtable pointer references the `typeinfo` structure for that particular data type, and only one instance of the `typeinfo` structure is created for each new class. Thus, the additional program size overhead is small, and for a program that uses polymorphism heavily, the RTTI facility can provide a significant advantage. Note that the compiler automatically generates the type information for all of the classes used by your project if RTTI is enabled.

Another common concern about the use of RTTI is execution speed overhead. There are two main mechanisms for retrieving type information at runtime in C++: the `typeid` operator and the `dynamic_cast` operator. The effect of a `typeid` expression is quite simple: the pointer in the vtable is used to fetch the `typeinfo` pointer, which produces a reference to the resulting `typeinfo` structure. Thus, the `typeid` operator operates in constant time and is a completely deterministic process. In the case of the `dynamic_cast` operator, the runtime type information is first retrieved for the source object type and then the RTTI data is fetched for the destination data type. The C++ runtime then determines whether the destination data type is compatible with that of the source data type. Since the internal routines used to implement `dynamic_cast` must walk a list of base classes, the overhead for `dynamic_cast` is a bit higher than that of a `typeid` call. Also note that the time taken by a given `dynamic_cast` operation is related to the complexity of the inheritance chain for the classes involved, since it will take more time for the runtime to walk complicated inheritance structures (particularly when multiple inheritance is involved). However, the cost of this overhead is usually very modest, and the advantages of having dynamic runtime identification significantly outweigh these concerns in all but the most performance-critical parts of your code. See [Eckel03] for more in-depth discussion of runtime type information usage. You can also find out how to implement your own dynamic runtime type identification system in the [Wakeling01] article.

Some programmers argue that because RTTI allows programs to discover type information from an anonymous polymorphic pointer, RTTI is ripe for misuse by the novice programmer. For many people coming from a procedural background, it is very tempting to organize their programs into sets of switch statements that make heavy use of RTTI services. In doing so, however, they lose many of the benefits of polymorphism and encapsulation. This is a valid concern, and new C++ programmers should be quickly taught that good object-oriented design relies on the thoughtful construction of polymorphic object hierarchies and templates, with RTTI to be used only when absolutely necessary. The approach described in this article presents a case of RTTI usage that can benefit the programmer without encouraging poor programming practices.

Object Manager Class Implementation

The system for storing and managing the objects is implemented in the `ObjectMan-ager` class. `ObjectManager.h` provided on the companion CD-ROM contains sample code implementing this system. The object manager class is the entry point for the entire system—it stores all objects as entries in its internal object database, manages each object entry's data, maintains type-safe checks for all operations on existing object entries, and controls deallocations of object entries and their data. Each object entry is used to store an individual object in the database. For the sake of simplicity, we used an STL `map` within the object manager to store all object entries in the system. In this implementation, we use object names as the unique object identifiers in the system; however, this can be a limiting and inefficient approach in a real-time production environment. More sophisticated and convenient schemes can easily be designed for actual object storage and identification assignment. For example, each object could be assigned an opaque object ID at creation time by registering the object with the object manager, which would provide the ID used to identify the object for all subsequent operations.

The object manager internally stores all object entries in object containers. Each container stores a single object and is used to provide memory management services for the entire lifespan of the object. The object manager provides a mechanism for adding new objects via the `AddObjectEntry()` method, which takes the object name as the unique object identifier in the database and the actual object that will be stored in an object container. We use a member template to discern the data type of the specified object being added to the database. During addition of the object entry to the database, the object manager creates a new object container to store the object. Using this member template, the object container determines the data type of the object at runtime and provides type-safe checks thereon for all manipulations of that specific object entry. We will discuss how the object container discerns the data type of the object shortly.

There are two entry points for the removal of objects from the system: the `RemoveObjectEntry()` and `DeleteObjectEntry()` calls. The first method simply removes the object from the object manager without actually destroying the object, while the second method deallocates object memory by correctly invoking the appropriate destructor for the object. The object manager provides the mechanism for type-safe data assignment of an existing object via the `SetObjectEntryData()` call, which accepts an object identifier (in our case, this is the name of the object) and the new object. Since we are implementing a truly type-safe object manager system, the new data type must match the type for data already stored in the object container with the given identifier. The object manager will always check whether the new data type matches the data type of the data stored in the container and will fail to reset the object container's data if the types do not match. For example, if you added an object of type `SorcererCharacter` named "Merlin" to the database, and later wanted to replace the data in the "Merlin" entry with an instance of class `MedusaCharacter`, the object manager will fail on the assignment, since the newly supplied object doesn't match the data type of the object already stored in the object container.

For convenience, the object manager also provides methods to retrieve object entry data types in two ways: the GetObjectEntryType() method takes only the identifier of the object entry and returns the actual type_info pointer for the data that is stored in the object entry, and the CheckObjectEntryType() method automatically checks the data type at runtime using the specified data and the identifier of the object entry to be checked. This method might be useful for your system if you want to add serialization support to save out objects to a file containing the data for many different instances. You can also use this method to find all objects of the specified data type and store them first. In the interest of simplicity and clarity, the classes described in this article and provided on the companion CD-ROM only provide a bare-bones implementation, but it should be reasonably clear to see how these classes can be extended to perform more complicated object management operations.

Object Container Implementation

At the heart of the system lives the ObjectContainer class. This class is used to manage the actual object within the object manager. The fact that we are using a concrete class with member template function instead of a fully templated class is what allows this particular implementation to add new data types without requiring recompilation of the manager class. When we add a new object to the object manager, the manager creates an object container instance that is used to wrap the object and manage its resources. For the purposes of this article, we will only provide examples of how to perform type checking, data assignment and replacement, and data deallocation for object containers. Let's look at the object container implementation in more detail. Each object container stores the following values:

```
void*       m_pData;
IDestroyer* m_pDestroyer;
type_info*  m_pTypeName;
```

Upon creation of each object container instance, all of the member data are set to null. However, during the first data assignment to the object container entry, the m_pData field is filled with the actual object presented as the parameter to the Set-Data() method (see Listing 1.11.1). Upon assignment of the data, the object container determines the type information for the assigned data and creates the storage for the data value. Instead of simply retrieving the name of the data type, to avoid possible collisions, we actually use the type_info pointer for that particular class and access the type information directly every time we want to match the type of data. This is done in lines 9 through 13 of the SetData() method. The type identifier for the newly assigned data is also stored (lines 16 through 17)—this data member is necessary for providing type-safe assignment of data.

Listing 1.11.1   `SetData` method used for object assignment.

```
1. template<class DataType>
2. bool SetData( DataType& const dataValue )
3. {
4.     // First make sure to delete any data previously
5.     // stored in this object:
6.     if ( m_pData )
7.         delete_ptr ( m_pDestroyer );
8.
9.     // Create new storage for the data value:
10.    DataType* pData = new DataType (dataValue);
11.
12.    // Assign the data:
13.    m_pData = pData;
14.
15.    // Save the type information for this object:
16.    m_pTypeName = const_cast <type_info *>
17.                           (&(typeid(DataType)));
18.
19.    // Create a destroyer for the data for
20.    // this data object:
21.    m_pDestroyer = new Destroyer<DataType> ( pData );
22.
23.    return true;
24.}
```

The object container provides an interface for retrieval of type information belonging to the stored object (through the `GetTypeID()` method), while the `CheckType()` method allows the caller to verify whether the input object matches the object type already stored in this object container instance. The `IsEmpty()` method checks whether this object container instance is empty or filled with an object.

Destroyer Implementation

In line 21 of Listing 1.11.1, we see the creation of the `Destroyer` object by the container instance. This is necessary to ensure accurate deallocation of the owned instance upon deletion of the container. Let's examine the mechanism for memory deallocation in more detail. Remember that one of the goals of our implementation is to avoid having to recompile manager code every time the database needs to support a new stored class type. A widespread solution for storing polymorphic objects in a database is to use a common base class with a virtual destructor, so that stored objects can be correctly destroyed when operator `delete` is used on them. Provided that all objects managed by this database have a common base class, this ensures that all object memory is correctly deallocated. However, if we want to implement a system that does not require a common base class for all objects, we are left with storing the object as a `void` pointer. This decision, however, does not present an obvious solution for how to handle object destruction. This design problem is overcome with the creation of a `Destroyer` object that is used by each object container.

ON THE CD

The object container stores an interface pointer to a Destroyer object. Listing 1.11.2 provides code for the Destroyer implementation (you can also find it in the Destroyer.h source file on the companion CD-ROM). The interface simply provides allocation and destruction entry points; it is not templated, which allows us to use it directly in the object container class without having to specify a templated data type at runtime. The implementation of the Destroyer interface is the converse of the oft-encountered class factory pattern [Gamma95], which destroys an object by knowing only its data type at runtime.

We implement the Destroyer mechanism in two stages. When the SetData() method of the ObjectContainer instance is invoked to store the actual object, the container creates a concrete instance of the Destroyer templated for that object's type. Because the Destroyer instance is templated by the data type of the object, it can correctly deallocate the stored object's memory.

Listing 1.11.2 The Destroyer pattern used by the object manager.

```
class IDestroyer
{
public:
    IDestroyer () {};
    virtual ~IDestroyer () {};
};

template <class T> class Destroyer : public IDestroyer
{
public:
    Destroyer()
    {
        m_pData = NULL;
    }

    Destroyer ( T* pValue )
    {
        m_pData = pValue;
    }

    virtual ~Destroyer()
    {
        if ( m_pData )
            delete ( m_pData );
    }
private:
    T* m_pData;
};
```

Although templates are used heavily in our implementation of the object database, the crucial difference between the generalized templated object management previously described in the *Object Management the "Old Way"* section of this article and this new approach lies in the fact that none of the classes created here is implemented as full-on templated classes. Instead, we use concrete classes with template member functions for implementation of object containers. This seemingly subtle distinction allows the object manager to remain decoupled from the stored data classes at compile time. Thus, we allow for the easy addition of new data types at any point in the project without requiring recompilation or modification of the object manager code.

Conclusion

In this article, we presented an approach for implementing a flexible object manager that manages objects without complete compile-time type identification. This method represents a clear improvement over the more standard approaches using templated data storage and monolithic inheritance schemes, as it allows for the addition of new game classes at any point in the game development cycle without demanding a recompilation of the core object management game system.

References

[Bilas00] Bilas, Scott, "A Generic Handle-Based Resource Manager," *Game Programming Gems*, Charles River Media, 2000.

[Eckel03] Eckel, Bruce, *Thinking in C++: Practical Programming, Second Edition*, Prentice Hall, 2003.

[Gamma95] Gamma, Erich, et al., *Design Patterns: Elements of Reusable Object-Oriented Software*, Addison-Wesley, 1995.

[Hawkins02] Hawkins, Brian, "Handle-Based Smart Pointers," *Game Programming Gems 3*, Charles River Media, 2002.

[Wakeling01] Wakeling, Scott, "Dynamic Type Information," *Game Programming Gems 2*, Charles River Media, 2001.

1.12

Using Custom RTTI Properties to Stream and Edit Objects

Frederic My

fmy@fairyengine.com

Loading or saving levels is not a trivial task, and it becomes even more difficult when the tools used to manipulate level data continue to evolve while a game is still under construction. The purpose of the technique presented in this article is to automate, as much as possible, the process of streaming and editing variables that make up your levels, and to simplify or even remove compatibility problems with old data files. The method discussed here is based on three simple elements working together: an extended Runtime Type Information (RTTI) system, properties associated with each type of variable, and an object factory.

Extended RTTI

RTTI is a system for storing metadata about the classes used by your program. In the implementation described in [Wakeling01], for example, the class metadata includes an ID (for example, the name of the class) and a pointer to the metadata of its parent class (multiple inheritance is not supported). From the address of an object, it is possible to access the metadata of the class to which it belongs, and then walk the metadata tree of its associated class hierarchy. This is most often used to check at runtime if a C++ object is an instance of a given class or of a derived one, in order to safely cast from a base class to a derived class (downcast) when polymorphism is involved.

The C++ language has built-in support for RTTI metadata, and every contemporary compiler is able to generate the runtime type information for us. For example, to leverage C++ RTTI to enable safe typecasting we use the `dynamic_cast` operator.

```
// pBase points to an object of class 'Base'
// 'Derived' inherits from 'Base'
Derived* pDerived = dynamic_cast<Derived*>(pBase);
```

If `pBase` really points to an object of the `Derived` class, then `pDerived` contains the address of this object after the cast; otherwise, it contains `NULL`.

It is also conceivable to design our own RTTI system, as in [Wakeling01] or [Eberly00]. The advantage to this approach is that we are no longer dependent on a particular compiler's RTTI implementation, and we are not forced to capture RTTI metadata for every class (some small classes don't benefit from it). Finally, with a custom system we can arbitrarily extend the information captured in metadata beyond that specified by the C++ standard.

This is exactly what the following code, available on the companion CD-ROM, does. In addition to capturing standard metadata, the CRTTI class we use to store this information supports an m_pExtraData member, enabling us to store arbitrary application data side by side with the standard metadata information (this might remind you of similar techniques used throughout the MFC class library).

```cpp
class CRTTI
{
public:
    CRTTI(const CStdString& strClassName,const CRTTI*
        pBase,CExtraData* pExtra=NULL) :
        m_strClassName(strClassName),
        m_pBaseRTTI(pBase), m_pExtraData(pExtra) {}
    virtual ~CRTTI() {}

    const CStdString& GetClassName() const
        { return m_strClassName; }
    const CRTTI* GetBaseRTTI() const
        { return m_pBaseRTTI; }
    CExtraData* GetExtraData() const
        { return m_pExtraData; }

protected:
    const CStdString  m_strClassName;
    const CRTTI*      m_pBaseRTTI;
    CExtraData*       m_pExtraData;
};
```

Four macros are available to help you integrate custom runtime type information into your classes:

- DECLARE_RTTI adds a static CRTTI member to the declaration of a class, and defines the virtual method GetRTTI() used to access this member.
- DECLARE_ROOT_RTTI is placed in the declaration of a root class in an inheritance tree. In addition to the elements included in DECLARE_RTTI, this macro inserts the methods needed by the RTTI system.
- IMPLEMENT_ROOT_RTTI is used in the implementation file of a root class to initialize the static metadata declared with DECLARE_ROOT_RTTI. This macro takes a single argument: the name of the class.
- IMPLEMENT_RTTI is very similar to IMPLEMENT_ROOT_RTTI, but is intended to be used in a derived class and takes an additional argument: the name of the parent class. As in [Wakeling01], this implementation does not support multiple inheritance.

Here is an example of the RTTI macros in action:

```
// RootClass.h
#include "RTTI.h"
class CRootClass
{
    DECLARE_ROOT_RTTI;
    ...
};

// RootClass.cpp
#include "RootClass.h"
IMPLEMENT_ROOT_RTTI(CRootClass);
...

// Derived.h
#include "RootClass.h"
class CDerived : public CRootClass
{
    DECLARE_RTTI;
    ...
};

// Derived.cpp
#include "Derived.h"
IMPLEMENT_RTTI(CDerived,CRootClass);
...
```

ON THE CD

Once the system is in place, the following code shows how to use a few straight-forward macros (see RTTI.h on the companion CD-ROM) and methods to access standard RTTI functionality.

```
// this one replaces the C++ dynamic_cast instruction
Derived* pDerived = DYNAMIC_CAST(Derived,pBase);

// we verify that pBase points to an instance of
// the Derived class
if (IS_EXACT_CLASS(Derived,pBase)) { ... }

// we verify that pDerived points to an object of
// the Base class or one of its derived classes
if (IS_KIND_OF(Base,pDerived)) { ... }

// this code snippet gets a pointer to the metadata of
// the class pDerived belongs to, and walks the
// metadata tree of its associated class hierarchy
const CRTTI* pRTTI = pDerived->GetRTTI();
while (pRTTI)
{
    pRTTI = pRTTI->GetBaseRTTI();
}
```

In the next section, we will see how the m_pExtraData member is used to add other metadata information to support class properties.

Properties

A property, created to represent a variable within a class [Cafrelli01], consists of a name, a type (implying the size of the variable's footprint in memory), the variable's offset from the beginning of the class definition, an optional textual description, and some flags. The flags capture information about whether the variable is editable or read-only, if it needs to be saved or not, and so forth. It is important to understand that a property is defined only once for a given class, and that it is used by all instances of this class; this explains why it does not contain a pointer to a specific variable, but an offset that will be added to the address of an object instance to access the variable's value.

Before defining properties in existing classes, we must tell the framework that we want the properties to be stored in the class metadata. For a given object, this will enable us to retrieve the properties of the class it belongs to, and those of the inherited classes; this is exactly what we will need when editing or streaming the object instance.

Two macros are defined in the `ExtraProp.h` file to help simplify this task: `DECLARE_PROPERTIES` and `IMPLEMENT_PROPERTIES`. The former is used in the following way:

```
class CMyClass : public CPersistent
{
    DECLARE_RTTI;
    DECLARE_PROPERTIES(CMyClass,CExtraProp);
public:
    // ... your usual interface ...
protected:
    bool m_boSelected;  // an example variable
};
```

Every class that wants to use our RTTI edit/save system must be derived from the `CPersistent` class; we will see later that this class is responsible for the streaming process. Of course, if a class requires RTTI support but does not need to declare any properties, only the `DECLARE_RTTI` macro is added to its declaration.

The `DECLARE_PROPERTIES` macro takes two arguments: the name of the class that contains it, and the name of another class called `CExtraProp`. The latter is derived from the empty `CExtraData` class used in `CRTTI` to store additional metadata, and it owns a property list. `DECLARE_PROPERTIES` adds a static `CExtraProp` member to `CMyClass`; this static instance is where the properties of `CMyClass` will be kept. A static `GetPropList()` accessor is also inserted, and finally the macro declares a static method named `DefineProperties()`, which has to be implemented in the cpp file.

```
#include "MyClass.h"
#include "Properties.h"

IMPLEMENT_RTTI_PROP (CMyClass,CPersistent);
IMPLEMENT_PROPERTIES(CMyClass,CExtraProp);

bool CMyClass::DefineProperties()
```

```
    {                                        // static
        REGISTER_PROP(Bool,CMyClass,
                        m_boSelected, "Selected",
                        CProperty::EXPOSE|CProperty::STREAM,
                        "help or comment");
        return true;
    }
```

IMPLEMENT_RTTI_PROP is a variant of IMPLEMENT_RTTI (these two macros are mutually exclusive) that initializes the class RTTI data member so that it points to the CExtraProp object instance defined by DECLARE_PROPERTIES. An IMPLEMENT_ROOT_RTTI_PROP macro is also available to replace IMPLEMENT_ROOT_RTTI in root classes where property support is needed. With these new macros, we establish the link between our RTTI system and the properties of a class.

IMPLEMENT_PROPERTIES takes the same arguments as DECLARE_PROPERTIES; its role is to implement the static CExtraProp member and to pass it the address of Define-Properties() as a constructor parameter.

As its name implies, DefineProperties() is called to initialize the properties of the class to which it pertains. This is done only once, automatically, when the CEx-traProp instance intended to store the properties is constructed.

Finally, REGISTER_PROP is used to add a new property to the class. Here a Boolean property (Bool), named "Selected", is associated with the m_boSelected variable of class CMyClass. This property is editable (CProperty::EXPOSE flag) with a "help or comment" note, and allowed to persist to external files (CProperty::STREAM flag). The various types of properties are indicated with values—like Bool in the previous example—coming from an enumeration defined in the Properties.h file.

This example is deliberately straightforward: DefineProperties() can contain elements other than a list of macros, as we will see later. Table 1.12.1 shows the properties available in the sample program.

Table 1.12.1 Properties Implemented in the Demonstration Program

Variable Type	Name in REGISTER_PROP	Property Class
bool	Bool	CPropBool
float	Float	CPropFloat
unsigned long	U32	CPropU32
string (CStdString)	String	CPropString
2d / 3d / 4d vector	Vect2D / 3D / 4D	CPropVect2D/3D/4D
pointer, smart pointer	Ptr, SP	CPropPtr, CPropSP
special cases	Fct	CPropFct

Here is a summary of the steps required to add properties to an existing class:

1. If the class does not support our RTTI system, add it first.

2. Use the DECLARE_PROPERTIES and IMPLEMENT_PROPERTIES macros with the CExtraProp class as a second argument. This will add a property list to the class's metadata information block.

3. Make the connection between the RTTI system and the properties by replacing IMPLEMENT_RTTI with IMPLEMENT_RTTI_PROP (or their counterparts for root classes).

4. Create properties associated to the variables you want to edit or stream by implementing DefineProperties() and calling REGISTER_PROP to create your property definitions.

Using the Properties for Editing

Once we have defined some properties for our classes, we want to use them to display and modify the contents of object instances located in memory.

Displaying Values

To display the values of an object instance's variables, we need to access the metadata information of the class, retrieve the properties that are stored in the metadata, and ask each property to return the value of the variable it represents for the given instance. This is exactly what the following code does.

```
// pObj points to an object instance of a class
// derived from CPersistent
const CRTTI* pRTTI = pObj->GetRTTI();
while (pRTTI)
{
    CExtraData* pData  = pRTTI->GetExtraData();
    CExtraProp* pExtra =
                DYNAMIC_CAST(CExtraProp,pData);
    if (pExtra)
    {
        CPropList* pList = pExtra->GetPropList();
        if (pList)
        {
            CProperty* pProp = pList->GetFirstProp();
            while (pProp)
            {
                // do what you want, for example:
                Display(pProp->GetValue(pObj));
                    // ...
                pProp = pList->GetNextProp();
            }
        }
    }
    pRTTI = pRTTI->GetBaseRTTI();
}
```

In the preceding code, we see that properties have a virtual GetValue() method that takes the address of an object as a parameter and returns the value of the corresponding variable as a string. This is exactly what we need to display the value in a console window or an edit control, for example. However, it is also possible to retrieve the value as its native type, like in this code snippet:

```
// pProp is a CProperty* variable
CPropFloat* pFloat = DYNAMIC_CAST(CPropFloat,pProp);
if (pFloat)
{
    float fValue = pFloat->Get(pObj);
    ...
}
```

The difference is that in this case we must know the exact type of the property before we can perform the appropriate cast. Because property classes use our custom RTTI system, verifying their type is straightforward, as demonstrated here.

Other methods are available in CProperty to retrieve the various pieces of data (name, type, help text, flags) defined when the properties were originally registered. In the sample program on the companion CD-ROM, these methods are used to populate an MFC grid control [Maunder02] with this property data. The use of a grid to represent any class avoids having to code a large number of custom dialog boxes, thus cutting back on code maintenance and enabling us to display a uniform interface to the user.

Modifying Values

In most cases, modifying values associated with properties is as simple as displaying them:

- If the new value is text coming from a console window or an edit control, we just have to pass it to the SetValue() method of the CProperty class: if the text does not match the type of the property (for example, "a00" is entered for a float), the variable is left untouched, and SetValue() returns false to indicate a problem; otherwise, the value is converted and the variable is modified.
- If we know the real type of the property, we can cast it and use the specific accessor of its class to set the new value.

However, some properties require special editing considerations, a frequent case being that of pointers to other persistable object instances. These editing considerations fall into two main categories:

- We do not want to display a hexadecimal address, which has no meaning to the user. Instead, we want to display the logical name of the referenced object.
- The user should be able to choose the object to be referenced from a list of existing objects of the corresponding type.

Other types of properties can benefit from custom processing, from selecting a color in a palette to entering a quaternion in the form of Euler angles. To handle these particular needs, the sample's framework calls several virtual methods of CPersistent to allow classes to override the default display and modification behaviors:

- `SpecialGetValue()` is responsible for providing the text to be displayed; for example, in the case of a pointer property we can return the name of a referenced object instead of its address.
- `SpecialEditing()` is in charge of handling the user's input when special editing considerations are required; this usually consists of opening an appropriate dialog box, and processing its results. For example, this enables the user to choose an object from a list.
- `ModifyProp()` is called before `SetValue()` when the user has entered a new value; this method allows the programmer to perform some additional processing on the property input for those cases where simply calling `SetValue()` would not be enough.

ON THE CD

Refer to the code on the companion CD-ROM for further implementation details.

Saving

ON THE CD

The example program found on the companion CD-ROM supports saving objects to an XML format and to a binary format. In this article, we focus our attention on the human-readable XML format, which is made up of tags delimiting data blocks.

Each object data definition is preceded by a `<data class=... ID=...>` tag and followed by a `</data>` tag. The `class` parameter is used to identify the object's type, which will be needed to recreate the instance when loading; the `ID` is used to represent the object instance when it is pointed to by other objects. Of course these IDs must be unique, so how are they generated? In this implementation, we simply use the memory address of the object [Eberly00]. The primary drawback of this approach is that if a given level is loaded and saved several times without modification, it is unlikely to result in strictly identical files, because the addresses of object instances are likely to differ from one run of the program to the next.

The service of persisting an object and writing out all of its properties to disk is provided by the `CPersistent` class, from which every streamable object derives. This process is very similar to what we saw earlier when we wanted to display the values of an instance's variables; however, in this case, the topic of pointers requires special treatment.

When an object being saved contains a pointer property that references another persistable object, the following steps are performed:

1. The property writes its value to the file like any other property. For a pointer property, this value is the address of the pointed to object. As stated before, memory addresses are used as object IDs in the file, so no conversion is needed.
2. If the pointer is not `NULL`, the address of the pointed to object is added to an internally maintained references list.
3. Once the streaming of the current object is completed, addresses are popped off the references list and each referred object is then persisted.

4. Another class tracks the addresses of objects that have already been saved, thus preventing a single object instance from being saved multiple times in the same file and allowing for the support of cyclic data.

This is how a whole scene can be recursively persisted simply by saving its scene root.

Loading

When loading, it is necessary to create objects corresponding to the class IDs encountered in the save file. This is exactly the scenario for which object factories are designed [Alexandrescu01]. Once the object instance is created, its data must be read. The persisted properties are traversed, with each property reading in its value and assigning it to the corresponding variable as if the user had entered this value.

We still need to address the special case of pointers. The problem is that not only is it likely that our new object instances will have different addresses from when they were initially saved, but the objects we want to point to might not have even been created yet. We know that a mapping between the persisted instance ID and the real object address needs to be established, so a second stage is required: linking.

Linking

Linking consists of replacing the value of pointer properties with the real memory addresses of referenced instances once all objects have been loaded. For that purpose, an STL map is filled as objects are created: the collection key is the object's ID in the file, and the associated value is the new address returned by the class factory. When a pointer property is asked by the loading routine to read in its value from a file, it performs the following steps:

1. The property sets its corresponding pointer to NULL. This is to ensure that every pointer is initialized to a value that we can test.
2. The ID of an object is simply its memory address when it was persisted, so if the ID loaded by the property equals zero, we know that the persisted object legitimately had a NULL pointer when it was saved. Since the property has already set the pointer to NULL, the other steps are unnecessary and will not be executed.
3. If the ID does not equal zero, the property creates a CLinkLoad object and adds it to a list that contains the links to be restored once the loading is finished. The CLinkLoad instance stores the address of the object owning the pointer property, the address of this property, and the ID of the pointed to object.

After all objects have been created and loaded, linking is processed in the following manner:

1. For each CLinkLoad instance in the list, the ID of the referenced object is looked up in the map of created objects, and the corresponding memory address is retrieved.

2. The Link() method of the property referenced by the CLinkLoad object is called with this address as a parameter.

This method just has to assign the address to its associated pointer variable.

If the linking of a pointer fails—for example, because an ID is not found in the map—the owning object will not contain an invalid address, but the NULL value set by the property when loading. This solution might not be perfect, but it does avoid creating dangling pointers. In any case, linking should not fail; if it does, it probably means that the file is corrupted or malformed.

Finally, the PostRead() method in CPersistent is called for each loaded object by traversing the map used during the linking process. This map contains every object returned by the factory, allowing each class to perform class-specific initialization [Brownlow02].

Compatibility with Old Files: Class Descriptions

With the streaming system in place, we now turn our attention to what happens when somebody modifies the properties of a class, such as adding new ones. In this case, the properties registered in the executable no longer correspond to the ones persisted in a previously created file, and the program is unable to retrieve values from this file any longer.

We solve this by saving, either in the persistence file itself, or perhaps in a separate associated file, a description of the metadata data it contains; that is to say, for each class, we write out the list of its properties (names and types) at the time the file was written, as well as the property data for the class from which it derives. For example, a game engine can save out a sphere instance into a definition that looks like this:

```
<class name="CRefCount" base="">
</class>

<class name="CPersistent" base="CRefCount">
    <prop name="Name" type="String"/>
</class>

<class name="CEngineObj" base="CPersistent">
</class>

<class name="CEngineNode" base="CEngineObj">
    <prop name="Subnodes" type="Fct"/>
    <prop name="Rotation" type="Vect4D"/>
    <prop name="Position" type="Vect3D"/>
    <prop name="Draw Node" type="Bool"/>
    <prop name="Collide" type="Bool"/>
</class>

<class name="CEngineSphere" base="CEngineNode">
    <prop name="Radius" type="Float"/>
    <prop name="Section Pts" type="U32"/>
    <prop name="Material" type="Fct"/>
</class>
```

```
<data class="CEngineSphere" id="0xD7E7C0">
    sphere0001
    0
    0; 0; 0; 1
    10; -0.5; 0
    true
    true
    1
    8
    0x0
</data>
```

You can see here that the CPersistent class is derived from another class, namely CRefCount, which is a reference counting class [Meyers96]. Also notice that the CEngineObj class description does not contain any property definitions; this does not mean that the class has no variable members, only that the class has no member variables that need to be persisted.

In the previous example, the saved object was at memory address 0xD7E7C0, its name is "sphere0001", it is located at position (10; –0.5; 0), and so forth. If another instance of the CEngineSphere class—or one of its parent classes (e.g., CEngineNode)—is saved in the same file, the definition of the class is not repeated, and only a new <data ...> block is written. Several types (bool, float, 32 bits integer, string, vectors) of properties are used here; we will discuss shortly the special case of a "functions" type ("Fct").

Compatibility with Old Files: Matching

Suppose that the descriptions of our classes have been saved into one file and our object instances have been persisted into a separate file. Our loading routine begins by retrieving the (possibly outdated) descriptions, to compare them with those in memory that correspond to the current version of the software. We call this stage "matching," because it tries to establish a link between the properties of a class in the file and those currently in memory. Three cases can occur:

• For a given class, there is a property in the executable that has the same name and type as in the external file. In this case, the property will receive the file's data. As you can see, the mapping is not established according to the order of the properties in the description, but by comparing the names and types of the properties. This enables us to change their order, to swap, remove, and insert properties, or even to move them about in the class hierarchy (in the previous example, we could decide that the Collide flag should be a member of the CEngineObj class instead of the CEngineNode class and the previously saved file could still be loaded). A limitation of our system also becomes evident: there cannot be two properties with the same type and name in the property list of a class or its parents. A test could be added when properties are registered to enforce this rule.

- A file's property has no equivalent in the executable. In this case, the property is obsolete (it has been removed or renamed) and its data will be ignored. More precisely, a virtual method called `ReadUnmatched()` will be called, allowing applications to provide some custom behavior (e.g., writing a warning to a log file).
- An executable's property does not exist in the persistence file. In this case, the property will not receive any data, and the corresponding variable will keep the default value set by its class constructor. This is the case for every property created since the file has been saved. Saving the file again will of course have the effect of adding these new properties in both the descriptions and data.

The property matching code is found primarily in the `RecursiveMatch()` and `MatchProperty()` methods of `CPersistent`. It associates each property of the file with one from the executable, if possible. When loading, object data is directed to the executable's properties corresponding to those found within the persistence file. The matching is therefore only done once per class, no matter how many objects have been persisted to the file.

"Functions" Properties

The implementation so far handles some basic types (bool, unsigned long, float), classes (string, vectors), and pointers. Each property corresponds to a variable member of a class, with a known size, but what do we do about saving the contents of a collection, such as a list of pointers? In such a case, we are faced with several fundamental problems. We don't know in advance how many objects the collection is going to hold, and the type of objects can vary greatly from one collection to another, as well as the manner in which the collections are accessed. These special cases are managed by the `CPropFct` class.

The "functions" property allows you to specify the addresses of functions to call whenever the framework wants to perform a `Get` (conversion of a property's variable to a string), `Set` (conversion of a string to a property's variable type), `Write` (writing to a file), `Read` (loading from a file), or `Link` operation. Here is an example extracted from `CEngineNode::DefineProperties()`:

```
CProperty* pProp = REGISTER_PROP(Fct,...);
CPropFct*  pFn   = DYNAMIC_CAST(CPropFct,pProp);
pFn->SetFct(NULL,NULL,WriteNodes,ReadNodes,LinkNodes);
```

Some pointers can be `NULL`. In the preceding example, only the streaming and linking operations are supported for the registered "Subnodes" property. The three functions passed as parameters execute the following operations to handle the saving, loading, and linking of an STL list of node pointers:

- `WriteNodes()` writes the number of pointers stored in the collection, and then writes out the value of each one [Beardsley02].
- `ReadNodes()` reads the number of saved pointers, and then creates a `CLinkLoad` object for each that will be used by the linking stage.

- `LinkNodes()` is called for each object created by `ReadNodes()`. It inserts the referenced address into the nodes list of the loaded object.

Of course, this is only an example; a class can support as many "functions" properties as needed.

Tips and Tricks

The current implementation of the properties and RTTI system presented here supports some interesting tricks:

- Several properties can map onto the same variable. For example, this would allow you to define one property that streams an angle in radians—presumably because this is the unit used by the game engine—and another property that displays the same variable in degrees.
- The properties of a class are stored in the extra data of its RTTI, by the `CExtraProp` class. It is, of course, possible to derive from `CExtraProp` without obstructing the previously described mechanics, in order to add other data relevant to your classes. Notice that it is only necessary to add data to a `CExtraProp` subclass if this data needs to respect the class hierarchy; otherwise, keeping this same data in simple static variables can probably do the job.
- When you register a property, you indicate if it is going to be displayed in the user interface, and whether it is read-only. Sometimes, however, you might want to show a value for the instances of one class but hide it for instances of a derived class. Moreover, you might want a property to be editable only for specific object instances. For example, in an editing tool, some cameras are likely to be fixed (their position is read-only) whereas others are permitted to be free-roaming. You can accomplish this by overriding the `IsPropExposed()` and `IsPropReadOnly()` methods in the affected classes to handle these special cases.

Going Further

Here are some additional features that could be added to the RTTI system that would make it even more useful:

- File compatibility problems only need to be addressed during the development of a game. When the title is complete, all files can (and should) be saved in their "final version." Therefore, the descriptions of properties could be removed: if the loading routine does not find them, it must trust the application, and retrieve data according to the executable's format.
- The current system does not support aggregation, where a class of one type has a variable of another class among its members. When an instance of the owning class is saved, all properties of the owned instance must be written with those of the owner. A new property type should be enough to add this feature to the system; to date, this feature has not been necessary because pointer properties to object instances can be used as a reasonable workaround.

- When the value of a property is changed (through `ModifyProp()` or `SetValue()`), the operation can be tracked by a manager singleton. With this architectural change, it is then straightforward to implement an undo command for many of the most common cases.

Conclusion

This article presented a method that automates the editing, loading, and saving of C++ objects by adding specific properties to custom runtime type information maintained for each class. Links between objects (i.e., pointers) are taken into account and recreated at load time. The description of properties at the moment of persistence is also recorded, which enables us to compare them later with the metadata compiled into the current executable and to handle potential file incompatibility problems cleanly.

The overhead of this method is not very high: properties are static objects that do not take a lot of memory. The most time-consuming operation involves comparing the properties found within a persistence file with those in the native executable when loading; even so, this process is only performed once for each class. Finally, the binary format implemented in the demonstration program removes the many string conversions required by the human-readable XML format.

References

[Alexandrescu01] Alexandrescu, Andrei, *Modern C++ Design*, Addison-Wesley, 2001.

[Beardsley02] Beardsley, Jason, "Template-Based Object Serialization," *Game Programming Gems 3*, Charles River Media, 2002.

[Brownlow02] Brownlow, Martin, "Save Me Now!" *Game Programming Gems 3*, Charles River Media, 2002.

[Cafrelli01] Cafrelli, Charles, "A Property Class for Generic C++ Member Access," *Game Programming Gems 2*, Charles River Media, 2001.

[Eberly00] Eberly, David H., *3D Game Engine Design*, Morgan Kauffman, 2000.

[Maunder02] Maunder, Chris, "MFC Grid Control 2.24," available online at *www.codeproject.com/miscctrl/gridctrl.asp*, July 14, 2002.

[Meyers96] Meyers, Scott, *More Effective C++*, Addison-Wesley, 1996.

[Wakeling01] Wakeling, Scott, "Dynamic Type Information," *Game Programming Gems 2*, Charles River Media, 2001.

1.13

Using XML Without Sacrificing Speed

Mark T. Price,
Sudden Presence/phobia lab
mark@suddenpresence.com

One of the biggest challenges in creating a new game is generating the massive amounts of data that goes into it. A standardized data meta-format such as XML helps in this regard by allowing reuse of existing tools to create and edit the data. However, using XML also has several disadvantages, most notably its larger data size and slower load and parse times.

In this article, we present a new binary file/stream format called XDS (for eXtensible Data Stream) that, while roughly equivalent in representational power to XML, does not suffer from these drawbacks. We also present a toolkit that supports both XML and XDS data, which allows for a smooth transition between the two during your game's production cycle.

Why Use XML?

XML has been around for several years [W3C100], and in that time it has proven itself invaluable in the areas of openness and interoperability, two things that aren't normally high on the priority list when creating a new game. In that same time, the hype surrounding XML has mostly continued unabated. It seems that everywhere you look, someone is touting XML as the solution to a problem you didn't even know you had. So, is it all hype? Is any of it even relevant to games anyway?

The Good Stuff

XML matters. It is an important tool in modern software development and the benefits of using it outweigh many of its drawbacks. While it might not be the solution for every problem, it certainly does have its place in your development shop.

While there are many alternative storage techniques [Olsen00], [Boer01], the single biggest advantage that XML has over any proprietary data format is that it is a well-established standard with a fairly large industry behind it. There are literally hundreds of off-the-shelf tools that you can immediately put to work for your project, ranging from editors to presentation tools to transformation tools. By using XML for your game data, you make it possible to take maximum advantage of these tools. For example, if you take an XML editor and add an XML schema [W3C301] describing your game data, you will get a simple level editor for your game without having to write a single line of code. This means your design team can start generating game data sooner.

If your game's data needs change during development, you won't have to throw away all of your already generated data or write a one-off program to transform it to the new data format. Instead, you can simply write an XSL transformation and use it to convert your data into the new format [W3C299].

Using XML allows your designers to make changes and immediately see them in the game. Conversely, if they see something strange in the game, they can open the XML file and examine it in their editor or Web browser to identify and correct the problem.

Trouble in Paradise

All is not well in the XML world, however. To start with, it is much more complex to read XML than it is to read an application-specific binary file format. Because of this, general-purpose XML libraries are typically large and complex. It is not uncommon for a fully featured XML library to weigh in at more than a megabyte of compiled code. Try squeezing that into your already overcrowded memory footprint. XML's overhead also extends to the amount of space the data files take on disk and to the amount of time it takes to read them.

Finally, the same feature that allows your designers to inspect the game data in a browser lets your end users do it too. While this might be good in helping to foster the generation of a MOD community for your game, it also gives away the farm with respect to any in-game secrets you might want to keep from your players.

It is clear that most of the advantages of XML come in the design and development phases, while most of the advantages of binary data come in the release phase. We'd like to take advantage of the benefits that XML can give us, but we don't want to pay the price of slower code and a larger memory and disk footprint. The XDS meta-format was designed to address just this problem.

A Brief Introduction to the XDS Meta-Format

XDS was originally designed as a comprehensive 3D model format but was quickly put to use for all kinds of data. XDS is a binary data meta-format that is roughly equivalent to XML in expressive power. However, while XDS is XML-like, it is not just tokenized XML. Where XML was designed primarily for readability and portability, XDS was designed primarily for parsing speed and minimal size. In fact, it achieves both of these goals while retaining the portability and internationalization capabilities of XML.

Like XML, all data in XDS is tagged. Unlike XML, XDS tags are tokenized into two-byte identifiers that are usually the only overhead for a block of data. All data elements in XDS are strongly typed and are stored in the same layout as the equivalent C/C++ type in memory. XDS supports nearly every conceivable C/C++ data type, including integral and enumerated integral types, strings, fixed-point and floating-point types, arrays, structures, all the way up to arbitrary graphs of data structures.

XDS files are made up of a short header followed by any number of records. There are records to define the name of the stream, to specify character encodings, to define data types, attributes, elements, and additional data records, to carry data payloads, to carry comments, and to terminate the stream.

Data records in XDS are made up of a short header followed by any number of attributes, elements, or subrecords. The XDS format is optimized to enable reading an entire record in a single read call.

The key to the flexibility of XDS lies in the XDS Data Stream Definition, or DSD. A DSD is a regular XDS file that only contains records to define a content stream—that is, it doesn't contain any data records. In many ways, a DSD is very similar to an XML schema. For one, just as XML schemas define the content of an XML file, a DSD defines the types, records, attributes, and elements that exist in an XDS stream. For another, just as an XML schema is an XML document; a DSD is a regular XDS stream. Unlike XML, data in an XDS file cannot be parsed without its data stream definition.

The DSD can be *explicit*, in which case it is included within the XDS stream; *referenced*, in which case it is specified separately from the XDS stream but a reference to it is included in the stream; *implied*, in which case it is specified separately from the XDS stream and there is no reference in the stream; or *implicit*, in which case it is coded into the structure of the program that reads the XDS file.

The XDS Toolkit

ON THE CD

To help you to get up and running quickly using XML and XDS in your project's pipeline, we have provided a development toolkit consisting of two tools and a library, along with a full specification of the XDS meta-format. These can be found both on the *Game Programming Gems 4* companion CD-ROM and on the Web [SP03]. Full source to the entire toolkit is included. While the tools were written for the Windows platform, care has been taken to make it a simple matter to port them to run on other platforms.

The two tools in the XDS Toolkit are xdsMakeSchema and xdsConvert. They:

- Parse your C/C++ source to gather the data types and variables used in your program.
- Use the gathered data to generate XML schema definitions, XDS DSDs, and C header files containing DSDs and supporting #defines.
- Convert XML instance documents that are compliant with the XDS DSD into XDS data files.

The XDS Lite API library included in the XDS Toolkit is used to:

- Read XML instance documents
- Read XDS data files
- Write XDS data files

Figure 1.13.1 shows how the two tools, the library, and the files they generate fit together.

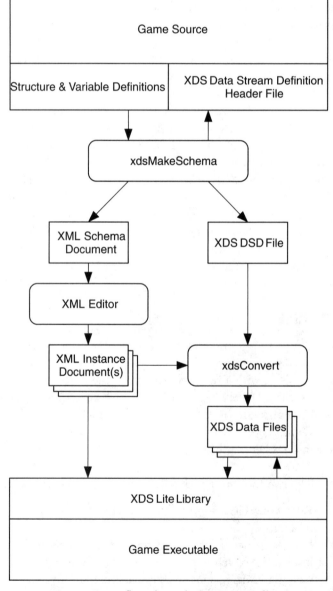

FIGURE 1.13.1 *Data flow through the XDS Toolkit.*

The XDS Toolkit in Action

To illustrate the simplicity of implementing a system using XDS, we will now go step by step through the production process of an elementary XDS data stream. For this example, we will be generating and then loading a data file containing power-up definitions for a simple game. We have placed the data structure we will be using for this purpose along with an instance variable to contain the data in a header file named, appropriately enough, "powerups.h." Here are the contents of that file:

```
struct PowerUp_t
{
    char szName[10];        // display name
    char szImage[16];       // image file name

    // health increase/decrease (-128 to 127)
    signed char iHealth;

    // temporary abilities/penalties
    // (value is duration in seconds)
    unsigned char iInvulnerability;
    unsigned char iFastMove;
    unsigned char iHighJump;
    unsigned char iStunPlayer;

    // extra life (count)
    unsigned char iLifeUp;
};

// global power-up definition cache
extern struct PowerUp_t *g_PowerUps;
```

Step 1: Extracting Type Data from Source

Before we can start writing XML data files, we need an XML schema definition document. This document will describe the data types and variables in your program and how they fit together. For example, here's the portion of a schema that defines our power-up structure:

```
<xs:complexType name="PowerUp_t" final="#all">
    <xs:sequence>
        <xs:element name="szName">
            <xs:simpleType>
                <xs:restriction base="xs:string">
                    <xs:maxLength value="10"/>
                </xs:restriction>
            </xs:simpleType>
        </xs:element>
        <xs:element name="szImage">
            <xs:simpleType>
                <xs:restriction base="xs:string">
                    <xs:maxLength value="16"/>
                </xs:restriction>
            </xs:simpleType>
```

```
            </xs:element>
            <xs:element name="iHealth" type="xs:byte"/>
            <xs:element name="iInvulnerability"
              type="xs:unsignedByte"/>
            <xs:element name="iFastMove"
              type="xs:unsignedByte"/>
            <xs:element name="iHighJump"
              type="xs:unsignedByte"/>
            <xs:element name="iStunPlayer"
              type="xs:unsignedByte"/>
            <xs:element name="iLifeUp"
              type="xs:unsignedByte"/>
        </xs:sequence>
    </xs:complexType>
```

As you can see, XML schema documents can get big pretty fast, and it sometimes requires a lot of work to define a simple piece of data. Luckily, we don't have to worry about this since we won't be hand-writing the schema. Instead, we'll use the `xds-MakeSchema` tool to extract the type information directly from our C/C++ source.

While the `xdsMakeSchema` tool is effective, it isn't too bright. It indiscriminately grabs all of the global type and variable definitions in the source you feed it. Because of this, you might want to prepare your C/C++ source for parsing before using the tool. The source you pass to the tool should contain only those types and variables that you want to use as the basis for your data files.

`xdsMakeSchema` is driven by a command-line interface.

```
xdsMakeSchema [-C] [-m macroFile]
    [-D name [= definition ]] [-U name ]
    [-s streamName] [-r recordName [: lengthSize ]]
    [-o outFile] input-files
```

If the `-s` and `-r` options aren't provided, the stream name will default to "xdsStream" and there will be a single record type called "xdsDataRecord". It is possible, and frequently desirable, to have multiple record types. To define additional record types, just add additional `-r` options to the `xdsMakeSchema` command line.

To extract the type data and create the XML schema document (`powerups.xsd`), XDS DSD (`powerups.dsd`), and XDS DSD header file (`powerups_dsd.h`), we use this command (entered on a single line):

```
xdsMakeSchema -s Powerups -r Powerup:2 -o powerups.xsd
    -o powerups.dsd -o powerups_dsd.h powerups.h
```

Step 2: Creating XML Instance Documents

With the XML schema in hand, we can now put it to use. As mentioned earlier, XML editors use XML schema documents to create conforming XML instance documents. This is fancy talk for an XML document that contains just the data we want in the format we want.

If the data we were editing were a bit more complex, it might be worth investing some time to create a document template for the data. This is a feature present in many of the more advanced XML editors that allows you to create an attractive fill-in-the-blanks form. In some cases, these forms can even offer some level of interactivity.

Since our power-up data is pretty straightforward, we'll just edit it directly. To do so, we simply open our XML editor and create a new XML instance document based on the generated XML schema. Of course, the precise means of accomplishing this will vary depending on what XML editor you use; Figure 1.13.2 shows what this might look like when using XML Spy.

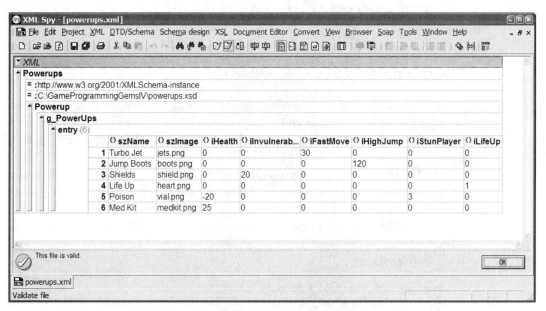

FIGURE 1.13.2 *Using the XML Spy editor to edit game data.*

Step 3: Integrating the XDS Lite API with Your Game

To read the XML data you generate into your game, you'll have to compile the XDS Lite library and the previously generated XDS DSD header file with your game and make calls into the library. Before you do that, however, you'll need to perform a little customization.

To make the library flexible, much of its contents are driven by the use of "#ifdef"ed code. In addition, to simplify the task of integrating the library with a host program, the library makes use of several callback functions. Thus, to use the library, you must configure it and provide implementations of the callback functions.

All of the library's configuration options are isolated into a single header file named "XDSconfig.h", but if you look you'll see that there is no such file in the toolkit. Instead, there is a sample configuration header file named "XDSconfig_sample.h". Just copy this file to "XDSconfig.h" and modify it to suit your needs. The specific items you'll want to pay attention to are addressed next.

Configuration Options

XDS_SUPPORT_XML—must be defined to allow reading XML files.

XDS_SUPPORT_WRITING—must be defined to allow writing of XDS files.

Callback Function Declarations

```
int XDS_READ(void *hFile, void *buf, int iSize);
int XDS_WRITE(void *hFile, void *buf, int iSize);
void *XDS_ALLOC(void *buf, int iSize, int iMemType);
void XDS_FREE(void *buf);
void XDS_PROCESSNODE(unsigned short nodeType, void *nodeData,
    unsigned long nodeSize);
void XDS_ERROR(const char *errText);
```

The comments in the "XDSconfig_sample.h" file go into some detail as to what each of these items is used for and its expected behavior. Most of the callback functions are fairly simple to understand, but the XDS_PROCESSNODE function deserves a little more attention.

The XDS_PROCESSNODE function is called whenever a complete block of data is read from an input stream. Data passed to this function is allocated using the XDS_ALLOC callback function and it is up to the host program to free it. The values for XDS_PROCESSNODE's nodeType argument are defined in the XDS DSD header file. In our example, this is the "powerups_dsd.h" file we generated earlier. Here are the relevant lines from the file:

```
#define XDS_Powerups_Powerup    0x0100  // Record
#define XDS_Powerups_PowerUp_t  0x0101  // Type
#define XDS_Powerups__xdsType1  0x0102  // Type
#define XDS_Powerups_g_PowerUps 0x0103  // Element
```

These #define names were created based on the stream name, the record names, and the type and variable names in "powerups.h". The "_xdsType1" in this example is an automatically generated anonymous type that holds arrays of PowerUp_t objects. This was needed since g_PowerUps was defined as a pointer to PowerUp_t.

The implementation of XDS_PROCESSNODE is usually just a switch statement with code to handle each data type. Here's the implementation for the power-up sample:

```
#include "powerups.h"
#include "powerups_dsd.h"

extern int g_iPowerUpCount;
```

```
void XDS_PROCESSNODE(unsigned short  nodeType,
                     void            *nodeData,
                     unsigned long   nodeSize)
{
    switch(nodeType)
    {
    case XDS_Powerups_Powerup:
        // record start -- do nothing
        break;

    case XDS_Powerups_g_PowerUps:
        // powerup data -- save it
        g_PowerUps = (struct PowerUp_t *)nodeData;
        g_iPowerUpCount = nodeSize /
          sizeof(struct PowerUp_t);
        break;
    }
}
```

Step 4: Reading the Data into Your Game

With the library configured, the next step is to actually read the data. After all the work done to this point, loading the data is thankfully very simple.

```
#define DEFINE_DSD
#include "powerups_dsd.h"

FILE *fp = fopen("powerups.xml", "rb");

struct xdsHandle *h = xdsInit(fp, "Powerups",
                              &XDSDSD_Powerups[0]);

while (xdsReadRecord(h))
    ;

xdsFini(h);
```

The POSIX `fopen()` call is used here for illustration purposes only. The actual I/O system is up to you—this is one of the reasons for the `XDS_READ` and `XDS_WRITE` callback functions.

The `XDSDSD_Powerups` argument to `xdsInit()` contains the XDS DSD. It is defined in the "powerups_dsd.h" header file generated earlier by `xdsMakeSchema`. The library uses it to drive the conversion of XML data into C/C++ structures.

Step 5: Making It Faster

Our power-up sample is quite small, so reading the data from an XML file isn't too bad. However, if you scale it up to an entire level's worth of game data, you'll notice the speed hit. The next step is to use `xdsConvert` to convert our XML data to XDS so that it doesn't have to be converted while reading.

The `xdsConvert` tool is driven by a command-line interface.

```
xdsConvert [ -d DSD-file ] [ -x DSD | Comments |
    Signature | Name ] [ -o output-file ] input-files
```

The `-x` option is used to exclude various types of data from being written to the output stream. Multiple `-x` options can be specified. The output file name cannot also be used as an input file name. As you might notice from the command syntax, xdsConvert can combine multiple input files into a single output file.

To convert our XML file containing power-up information, we use this command (entered on a single line):

```
xdsConvert -d powerups.dsd -x Name -x Comments
    -o powerups.xds powerups.xml
```

Using the converted XDS data file with the game is as simple as updating the file-name passed to `fopen()`. The XDS Lite library determines the type of the data file by examining the file contents.

Step 6: Making It Smaller

There are several configuration options in the "XDSconfig.h" header file, and all of them will affect the size and speed of the library. The three that have the most significant impact are described in this section.

Once your game has advanced far enough, you might want to remove XML support from the copy of the XDS Lite library that your game uses. This can be accomplished by commenting out the line "`#define XDS_SUPPORT_XML`". Doing this will significantly reduce both the library's code size and memory requirements.

If you don't plan on using the library to read and write your game save files, you can also reduce its size by removing all support for writing files by commenting out the line "`#define XDS_SUPPORT_WRITING`". This will also reduce the library's code size and memory requirements, though not by as much as removing XML support.

Finally, if you want the library to be the smallest and fastest it can be, then you can try uncommenting the line "`#define  XDS_SUPPORT_COMPACTDSD`". While this does work in conjunction with writing support, it should be noted that it is not compatible with all of the available configuration options. If it isn't compatible with the options you have chosen, you will get an error when attempting to recompile the library.

Putting It All Together

The guidelines in Table 1.13.1 represent a best-case use of XML and XDS in a game development project. By following these guidelines, your project will get the most out of both XML and XDS by leveraging each in the area in which it excels.

Table 1.13.1 Migration of Data from XML to XDS by Project Phase

Development Phase	Data Format and Library
Project start/prototype	Use XML for all data. Load using a dual-purpose version of the XDS Lite library. Initially use standard XML editor until special-purpose level editor is ready.
Level design/tuning /tweaking	Use XML for data that is being actively modified, XDS for stable resources. Load using a dual-purpose version of the XDS Lite library.
Integration testing	Use XDS for all data. Load using an XDS-only version of the XDS Lite library.
Acceptance testing/beta/release	Use XDS for all data. Load using either an XDS-only version of the XDS Lite library or with an optimized hard-coded XDS reader.

Conclusion

ON THE CD

The XDS meta-format is both fast and flexible. By leveraging the tools and library included on the companion CD-ROM, taking advantage of XDS is simple. Used as a group, the tools will allow your project to get to a fast start with highly flexible and readable XML data written using an off-the-shelf editor, and ship with blazing fast XDS data loaded directly into your in-game data structures.

However, the provided tools and library only use a small subset of the full functionality of the XDS meta-format. A fully generalized XDS reader would be especially attractive for network games where the content continues to evolve after the first release. Such a reader, used as part of a carefully designed communication layer, would allow the types of data being sent over the network to be changed while maintaining both forward and backward compatibility with earlier versions.

References

[Boer01] Boer, James, "A Flexible Text Parsing System," *Game Programming Gems 2*, Charles River Media, 2001.

[Olsen00] Olsen, John, "Fast Data Load Trick," *Game Programming Gems*, Charles River Media, 2000.

[SP03] "XDS Resources" Web page, available online at *www.suddenpresence.com/xds*.

[W3C100] W3C, "Extensible Markup Language (XML) 1.0 (Second Edition)," available online at *www.w3.org/TR/REC-xml*, October 6, 2000.

[W3C299] W3C, "XSL Transformations (XSLT) 1.0," available online at *www.w3.org/TR/xslt*, November 16, 1999.

[W3C301] W3C, "XML Schema Part 0: Primer," available online at *www.w3.org/TR/xmlschema-0/*, May 2, 2001.

MATHEMATICS

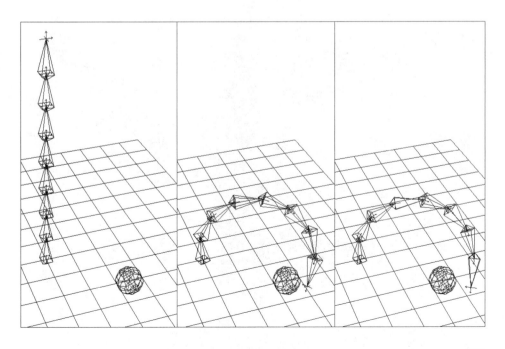

Introduction

Jonathan Blow

jon@number-none.com

In past years, an introduction such as this would say "game programmers need to learn a lot of math in order to do a good job," and then proceed with examples to justify this point. For a pertinent and clear set of such examples, see John Byrd's preamble to the math section of *Game Programming Gems 3*. I won't continue in this tradition, as it seems the idea is no longer controversial. Game programmers now expect to learn mathematics. As an example, this year, one of the hottest mailing-list topics has been the use of spherical harmonics.

We now understand that nonobvious mathematics is necessary to solve certain engineering problems we happen upon. However, I would like to press a stronger position than that: mathematics is absolutely central to what we do, for reasons strange and deep. To become masters of our discipline, we will need to come to grips with this, developing a math-centric way of thinking about our systems.

We can view game creation as the construction of a simulated world. Sometimes the simulated world is abstract and discrete, like a chessboard. These days (due to the increase in available computing power), we are building more concrete and continuous, heavily interactional systems. We invariably manipulate concepts that we know from the physical world: time, space, and number.

We are attempting to build small worlds that are analogous to, and often imitative of, the world we inhabit. This very fact calls to mind an important observation about the physical world, which has been dubbed "The Unreasonable Effectiveness of Mathematics." For background, see R.W. Hamming's discussion [Hamming80], and Eugene Wigner's earlier essay [Wigner60]. I will not attempt to remake these authors' arguments, but the gist is this: mathematics seems to be the "correct" language for describing our world, and nobody really understands why. As Hamming puts it, "We must begin somewhere and sometime to explain the phenomenon that the world seems to be organized in a logical pattern that parallels much of mathematics, that mathematics is the language of science and engineering."

Hamming and Wigner provide a host of examples wherein some mathematical concept—say, the system of complex numbers—is first created to flesh out some area of math, in the absence of a physically applied purpose. But lo, eventually the concept turns out to be exactly the right description of some aspect of physics. In some cases, mathematics has predicted physical phenomena before those phenomena were empirically detected.

Since we were born deep within the age of science we tend to take for granted this correspondence between mathematics and the world, but when we sit back and question our fundamentals, we can see how remarkable it really is. What implications does this have for the act of game creation? To recast the Unreasonable Effectiveness concept in a brief and foolishly bold fashion, I would say there is a strong sense in which we can view the physical world as being comprised of math (and perhaps some other things).

We are attempting to build work-alikes of the real world, this thing that is comprised of math. How can we expect to do this but by constructing our replicas out of math, themselves? To the extent that the physical world embodies certain mathematical concepts (such as derivatives or the hypercomplex numbers), we must expect to master those concepts, sooner or later, before we can deeply impersonate the world.

This viewpoint would seem to offer that mathematics is more fundamental than the algorithms and data structures we spend most of our time fussing with. The math is somehow the same as the thing we want to create; algorithms and data structures are just implementation details.

Imagine that many years go by, and the art of game creation becomes much more advanced, and the pursuit of physics advances as well. We might be creating games that are nearly indistinguishable from small parts of the physical world. In this situation, one might view the advanced physicist as an "empirical ontologist," and the advanced creator of game engines as a "constructive ontologist." At present, it might seem batty to place the game programmer parallel with the physicist. However, I think if we work hard, given time, we will get there.

Game programming is still in its infancy, but I would not be surprised if, someday, the advanced simulation techniques we devise will teach us things about the low-level of behavior of our own world. Articles like those in this section of this book are baby steps; through taking these steps, we will grow into something bigger.

Or, if you prefer the shorter-term view: these articles will help you to solve certain engineering problems that confront us today.

References

[Hamming80] Hamming, R.W., "The Unreasonable Effectiveness of Mathematics," *American Mathematical Monthly*, Vol. 87, No. 2 (February 1980), available online at *www.lecb.ncifcrf.gov/~toms/Hamming.unreasonable.html*.

[Wigner60] Wigner, Eugene, "The Unreasonable Effectiveness of Mathematics in the Natural Sciences," *Communications in Pure and Applied Mathematics*, Vol. 13, No. 1 (February 1960). New York: John Wiley & Sons, Inc, available online at *www.dartmouth.edu/~matc/MathDrama/reading/Wigner.html*.

2.1

Zobrist Hash Using the Mersenne Twister

Toby Jones, Human Head Studios, Inc.

tjones@humanhead.com

In many games, deep and wide searches of game states are used to make decisions. Once a game state is calculated, an evaluation function determines the pros and cons of the state. This has been a popular technique used in games such as chess [Moreland01], go [Huima00], and reversi, and many of the leading chess games use some variation of it. Strategy games are especially well suited, especially if they are turn-based. High-level character AIs can use these techniques to some degree if their set of discrete states can be bounded.

A good searching technique will generate a large number of game states to be evaluated. Because of the nature of strategy games, game states can repeat, and the same state can result from many different sets of moves. Because running the evaluation function of a game state is often a critical performance factor, we want to minimize the use of this function.

In the case of chess, we can cache the contents of every board state that has previously been evaluated. Before evaluating any new board, the board can be compared against the list of cached boards, and the evaluation can be avoided if the board is already in the list. Searching the list is a linear operation, but the performance can be improved to around constant-time by using a hash.

The Zobrist Hash

The Zobrist hash is a way of rapidly calculating the hash key of a game state from the hash key of a previous game state [Zobrist70]. The Zobrist hash is not a specific type of hash function, but a way to generate keys based on the game state that are incredibly good for hashing. A few of the key points of the Zobrist hash include:

- It is implemented with simple, fast operations.
- Operations can be undone without recalculating the entire hash.
- Collisions are reduced because similar game states result in very different keys.

The exact details of implementing a Zobrist hash tend to vary from application to application, but the concept is the same. Take the game state and combine together random numbers representing parameters of that game state. The combination should be done using a fast math operation. The operation should be associative and commutative, so that operations can be undone in an arbitrary order. Random numbers are used so that similar states will generally have several bits of difference in the hash key.

For example, to generate the Zobrist key for the set of pawns on a chessboard, assign a random number to each square on the chessboard, and then add together the values of all of the positions where pawns sit.

Now consider the act of moving one of those pawns. The beauty of the Zobrist hash is that it allows a new key to be created without much work. Simply subtract the current pawn position value from the current key, and add in the new position's value. Because of the properties of addition, this generates the same key as if the full hash key had been computed. This saves a great deal of time when building search trees.

Implementation of the Zobrist Hash

In chess, a 64-bit key is generally used. Although there are more than 2^{64} valid positions on a chessboard, the number of searchable positions is far smaller, so a 64-bit key gives enough room with which to work.

An n-dimensional *Zobrist table* is constructed and filled with 64-bit random numbers. The number of dimensions depends on the number of game state parameters that are under consideration. The parameters usually considered for chess are piece position, piece type, and piece color. The color to move next could also be a dimension of the table, but since it is a state of the game board, and not a state of each game piece, an added dimension is not warranted. That can be better handled elsewhere.

```
uint64_t m_aZobristTable[BOARD_SIZE]
                        [NUM_PIECES]
                        [NUM_COLORS];
```

An exclusive-or function is used to combine the piece parameters together. Exclusive-or has the advantage of being reversible using the same inputs. Iterate over all of the pieces on the board, and exclusive-or together values from the Zobrist table using the position, piece type, and color as indices.

```
uZobristKey ^= m_aZobristTable[pos][piece][color];
```

Since the piece values are exclusive-ored together, a fast way to move a game piece is to exclusive-or the value of the old position into the key, and then exclusive-or the value of the new position into the key.

Once the key is created, a 64-bit constant should be exclusive-ored into the key if the current player is black. Alternatively, the constant could always be exclusive-ored in to change the current player. While the side to move could be encoded as a dimension in the Zobrist table, as piece color is, using a constant allows the side to move to be quickly toggled without calculating a complete hash key.

Once the Zobrist key is calculated, the easiest way to use it as a hash key is as an address modulo the size of the hash table. Collisions are rare enough that they are sometimes ignored in practice, which trades off some robustness to gain a speed advantage. In general, when using a Zobrist hash, the primary cause of collisions is that the hash table is too small. The hash table should be as large as physical memory permits without overrunning into virtual memory.

The reason for the minimal number of hash table collisions has to deal with the choice of numbers in the Zobrist table. Because of the use of random numbers, moving a single game piece results in a radically different Zobrist key. These numbers can be carefully chosen, but it is just as valid to use highly random numbers. The C rand() function has often been used for generating Zobrist table values. However, the rand() function is not actually very random, and it only generates 15-bit numbers. We would prefer a fast, 64-bit, "more random" function.

Mersenne Twister

The Mersenne Twister is a fast pseudorandom number generator that has an extremely long period and high order of equidistribution. While there is no mathematical definition of pseudorandom, the Mersenne Twister does satisfy a number of tests, including the k-distribution test, which is commonly considered a strong pseudorandomness test.

The Mersenne Twister has several nice properties:

- Implementations are easily adapted to generation of 64-bit numbers.
- A 623 dimensional equidistribution property ensures that all bits of a generated number are fairly random.
- It has a huge period of $2^{19937} - 1$, which is the length before repetitions occur.
- It is implemented with simple, fast operations, with consideration to caching, and many implementations are far faster than rand().

These are all great properties for any general-purpose random number generator, but for use with the Zobrist hash, only the first two properties are critical.

Previous generators were flawed in various ways, and the Mersenne Twister was specifically designed to address some of these flaws. It is based on the linear recurrence:

$$x_{k+n} = x_{k+m} \oplus (x_k^u \mid x_{k+1}^\lambda)A \tag{2.1.1}$$

x is a w-bit word. x_k^u represents the upper w-r bits of x_k, and x_{k+1}^λ represents the lower r bits of x_{k+1}. Exclusive-or and concatenation correspond to $\oplus$ and $|$, respectively. w, r, m, n, and A are all constant parameters.

A is a *w* x *w* matrix of the form:

$$\begin{pmatrix} 0 & I_{w-1} \\ a_{w-1} & a \end{pmatrix}$$

$(2.1.2)$

I_{w-1} is an identity matrix and a is a vector representing $a_{w-2} \ldots a_0$. While all of the Mersenne Twister parameters affect the properties of the generated numbers, this matrix form was chosen because it allows the implementation to be done with fast bit operations.

Each generated word is tempered with transformations to improve the k-distribution:

$$y = x \oplus (x >> u)$$

$$y = y \oplus ((y << s) \cap b)$$

$$y = y \oplus ((y << t) \cap c)$$ $(2.1.3)$

$$y = y \oplus (y >> l)$$

u, s, t, l, b, and c are all constant parameters of the Mersenne Twister implementation. $<<$ and $>>$ are left and right shifts, and $\cap$ is a bitwise AND.

The Mersenne Twister is a parameterized algorithm, and how the parameters are specified will determine the properties of the random numbers. The recommended implementation is MT19937, which defines the parameters as:

$$w = 32, n = 624, m = 397, r = 31,$$

$$u = 11, s = 7, t = 15, l = 18,$$

$$A = 0x9908B0DF,$$ $(2.1.4)$

$$b = 0x9D2C5680,$$

$$c = 0xEFC60000$$

Implementation of the Mersenne Twister

To start, a 624-element array, s_aMT, is seeded with 32-bit numbers. Any numbers are valid for this array except for all zeros. The reference implementation in [Matsumoto98] uses a seeded random number generator, but this author likes to statically initialize the array with prime numbers. All seeds have the same period, so it does not matter.

Using m_ix as an index into s_aMT, a 32-bit random number is calculated like this:

```
static const int        MT_W = 32;
static const int        MT_N = 624;
```

```
static const int        MT_M = 397;
static const int        MT_R = 31;
static const uint32_t   MT_A = 0x9908b0df;
static const int        MT_U = 11;
static const int        MT_S = 7;
static const uint32_t   MT_B = 0x9d2c5680;
static const int        MT_T = 15;
static const uint32_t   MT_C = 0xefc60000;
static const int        MT_L = 18;
static const uint32_t   MT_LLMASK = 0x7fffffff;
static const uint32_t   MT_UMASK = 0x80000000;

uint32_t y;
y = s_aMT[m_ix++];
y ^= y >> MT_U;
y ^= y << MT_S & MT_B;
y ^= y << MT_T & MT_C;
y ^= y >> MT_L;
```

After exhausting all 624 numbers in the array, the array needs to be reloaded. This is perhaps the most complex part of the Mersenne Twister.

```
for(int kk = 0; kk < MT_N; kk++)
{
    uint32_t ui = (s_aMT[kk] & MT_UMASK) |
        (s_aMT[(kk + 1) % MT_N] & MT_LLMASK);
    s_aMT[kk] = s_aMT[(kk + MT_M) % MT_N] ^
        (ui >> 1) ^ ((ui & 0x00000001) ? MT_A : 0);
}
```

In practical implementations, the loop is usually unwound to eliminate the modulus operators.

By default, the Mersenne Twister generates 32-bit numbers, but [Matsumoto98] suggests that concatenating two successive 32-bit numbers together to create a 64-bit number is valid.

The Mersenne Twister is not cryptographically strong, although it has a number of good uses, including noise generation or as a fast replacement for rand(). Because of its high order of equidistribution, it can be a good choice for populating the Zobrist table, which requires highly random numbers.

Conclusion

The use of a Zobrist hash is a good way to trim the amount of repeated evaluations of a game state. This opens the door to more complex evaluation functions and smarter AI. The Mersenne Twister is a great replacement for rand() because it is fast and robust. The algorithm is great when partnered with the Zobrist hash, but it also stands alone for use in other applications.

References

[Huima00] Huima, Antti, "A Group-Theoretic Zobrist Hash Function," available online at *http://persoweb.francenet.fr/~fgrieu/zobrist.pdf*, December 31, 2000.

[Matsumoto98] Matsumoto, Nishimura, "Mersenne Twister: A 623-dimensionally equidistributed uniform pseudorandom number generator," available online at *www.math.keio.ac.jp/~matumoto/emt.html*, January 1998.

[Moreland01] Moreland, Bruce, "Computer Chess," available online at *www.seanet .com/~brucemo/chess.htm*, 2001.

[Zobrist70] Zobrist, A. L., "A New Hashing Method with Application for Game Playing," Technical Report 88, University of Wisconsin, April 1970.

Extracting Frustum and Camera Information

Waldemar Celes,

Computer Science Department,

PUC-Rio

celes@inf.puc-rio.br

For the implementation of several graphics algorithms, we need information related to the view frustum and camera parameters in object space. For example, a culling algorithm needs to compute the intersection between bounding volumes and frustum planes. A multiresolution algorithm requires access to camera parameters to compute the appropriate level of detail. Even a simple algorithm to position a billboard depends on viewing parameters (the view and up directions might be required). If we attempt to design such algorithms to be independent from any particular graphics engine, we face the problem of not being able to track camera position and orientation, thus making the task of extracting viewing information difficult. Fortunately, however, there is a simple and straightforward way to extract frustum and camera information based uniquely on the transformation (modeling, viewing, and projection) matrices.

In this article, we detail how viewing information can be easily extracted. This discussion varies slightly depending on the underlying graphics Application Programming Interface (API). Here, we first adopt the OpenGL convention. We then adapt the discussion to other APIs and extend it to arbitrary projective transformations.

Plane Transformation

On its way through the geometry stage of the rendering pipeline, a vertex is transformed into different spaces or coordinate systems, from object space to clip space [Akenine-Möller02]. Figure 2.2.1 illustrates the sequence of spaces of a typical rendering pipeline, with their corresponding transformation matrices. The view frustum is transformed into an axis-aligned box that represents the canonical view volume in clip space.

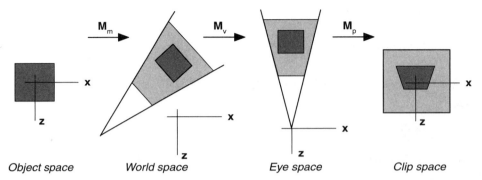

Object space   *World space*   *Eye space*   *Clip space*

FIGURE 2.2.1   *Spaces and transformation matrices along the rendering pipeline. In OpenGL, for performance reasons, the model, **Mm**, and view, **Mv**, transformations are represented by a single, already accumulated, modelview matrix, **Mmv**.*

A vertex **V** migrates to each different space by being multiplied by the corresponding matrix, **M**, thus resulting in the transformed vertex $\mathbf{V'} = \mathbf{MV}$. The same matrix is used to transform the polygons; indeed, the transformed polygons are obtained by transforming all their incident vertices.

However, this matrix **M** cannot always be used to transform planes (and thus normal vectors). Let us consider a simple example, illustrated in Figure 2.2.2, where a unit cube is subjected to a shear transformation. If we used the shear matrix to transform the right plane of the cube, we would get an incorrect result (Figure 2.2.2b). The resulting normal vector would no longer be perpendicular to its corresponding surface. Which matrix should then be used to transform planes (and normal vectors)?

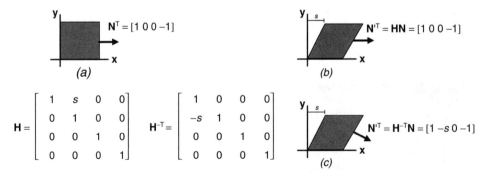

FIGURE 2.2.2   *The effect of a shear transformation, **H**, on planes: (a) the original model; (b) the incorrect plane transformation; (c) the correct plane transformation.*

It can be shown that planes have to be transformed by the corresponding inverse-transpose matrices. This is demonstrated in [Foley96]. A plane equation is given by:

$$ax + by + cz + d = 0 \qquad (2.2.1)$$

If we represent the coefficients of the plane equation in a four-dimension column vector, $\mathbf{N}^\mathrm{T} = [a \quad b \quad c \quad d]$, and use homogeneous coordinates to express points on that plane, $\mathbf{P}^\mathrm{T} = [x \quad y \quad z \quad 1]$, we can rewrite the plane equation in the following vector form:

$$\mathbf{N}^\mathrm{T}\mathbf{P} = 0 \qquad (2.2.2)$$

Let us now consider that the points $\mathbf{P}$ are transformed by a matrix $\mathbf{M}$, and we want to find the corresponding matrix, $\mathbf{Q}$, that should transform the plane so that the equation also holds after the transformation.

$$\mathbf{N}'^\mathrm{T}\mathbf{P}' = \left(\mathbf{QN}\right)^\mathrm{T}\left(\mathbf{MP}\right) = 0 \qquad (2.2.3)$$

Working out this equation, we have:

$$\left(\mathbf{QN}\right)^\mathrm{T}\left(\mathbf{MP}\right) = \mathbf{N}^\mathrm{T}\mathbf{Q}^\mathrm{T}\mathbf{MP} = \mathbf{N}^\mathrm{T}\left(\mathbf{Q}^\mathrm{T}\mathbf{M}\right)\mathbf{P} \qquad (2.2.4)$$

Thus, if $\mathbf{Q}^\mathrm{T}\mathbf{M} = \mathbf{I}$, then we have $\mathbf{N}^\mathrm{T}(\mathbf{Q}^\mathrm{T}\mathbf{M})\,\mathbf{P} = \mathbf{N}^\mathrm{T}\mathbf{I}\,\mathbf{P} = \mathbf{N}^\mathrm{T}\mathbf{P} = 0$, and so we can take $\mathbf{Q} = (\mathbf{M}^{-1})^\mathrm{T} = \mathbf{M}^{-\mathrm{T}}$. Therefore, if a matrix includes arbitrary transformations, as long as it is invertible (that is, nonsingular), the planes should be transformed by the inverse-transpose matrix. Figure 2.2.2c shows the correct transformed plane by applying the inverse-transpose of the shear matrix.

If only the normal vectors are of interest, we have $\mathbf{N}^\mathrm{T} = [a \quad b \quad c \quad 0]$, and only the matrix's upper left 3×3 needs to be considered [Turkowski90]. In this case, the matrix can include transformations that do not preserve angles, such as shears and nonuniform scales, but cannot include perspective transformations. Moreover, if the vertex matrix is composed uniquely of rigid-body transformations and uniform scales, no special care needs to be taken, as the same vertex matrix applies to planes.

Transforming planes by the inverse-transpose matrix can, in fact, help us to extract the original plane based on the transformed one. If the plane migrates to a space by being transformed by the matrix $\mathbf{Q}$, we should use the inverse matrix, $\mathbf{Q}^{-1}$, to bring the plane back to its original space. Therefore, having access to the matrix used to transform the vertices, $\mathbf{M}$, we can use its transpose to invert the plane transformation ($\mathbf{Q}^{-1} = \mathbf{M}^\mathrm{T}$).

Extracting Frustum Information

The view frustum is defined by six planes: left, right, bottom, top, near, and far. A two-dimensional view of such planes is illustrated in Figure 2.2.3. If we have these planes in clip space, we can easily bring them back to object space by applying the transpose of the matrix used to transform the vertices.

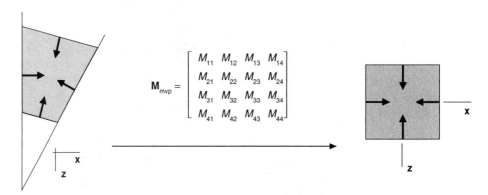

$$\mathbf{M}_{\text{mvp}} = \begin{bmatrix} M_{11} & M_{12} & M_{13} & M_{14} \\ M_{21} & M_{22} & M_{23} & M_{24} \\ M_{31} & M_{32} & M_{33} & M_{34} \\ M_{41} & M_{42} & M_{43} & M_{44} \end{bmatrix}$$

FIGURE 2.2.3   *Frustum planes in object and clip spaces together with the vertex transformation matrix.*

Using OpenGL parlance, let us consider the modelview matrix $\mathbf{M}_{\text{mv}}$, and the projection matrix $\mathbf{M}_{\text{p}}$. If we concatenate both, we end up with a single matrix, the modelview-projection matrix, $\mathbf{M}_{\text{mvp}} = \mathbf{M}_{\text{p}}\mathbf{M}_{\text{mv}}$, which transforms vertices from object to clip space (Figure 2.2.3). Conversely, the transpose matrix, $\mathbf{M}_{\text{mvp}}^{\text{T}}$, transforms planes from clip to object space.

The canonical view volume in clip space represents the transformed view frustum. Therefore, the view frustum planes in object space can be obtained from the corresponding canonical volume planes. It suffices to multiply the coefficient vector of the plane equation by the transpose of the modelview-projection matrix. Moreover, we do not even need to compute a full matrix-vector multiplication. As the canonical view volume is represented by an axis-aligned box, the plane equations in clip space are rather simple, allowing us to express the planes in object space directly from the matrix entries.

Let us consider the left plane. In OpenGL, the canonical volume is given by a cube with diagonal vertices at $(-1, -1, -1)$ and $(1, 1, 1)$. Therefore, in clip space, the left plane's normal vector is given by $(a', b', c') = (1, 0, 0)$. The independent plane's coefficient can be obtained by knowing that the point $(-1, 0, 0)$ belongs to the plane. Substituting in the plane equation, we have: $1(-1) + d' = 0$, that is, $d' = 1$. The left plane in clip space is then $\mathbf{N}'^{\text{T}} = [1 \quad 0 \quad 0 \quad 1]$, which, transformed by the transpose matrix, yields:

$$\mathbf{N} = \mathbf{M}_{mvp}^{\text{T}}\mathbf{N}' = \begin{bmatrix} M_{11} + M_{41} & M_{12} + M_{42} & M_{13} + M_{43} & M_{14} + M_{44} \end{bmatrix}^{\text{T}} \quad (2.2.5)$$

The other planes can be obtained in a similar way. The six frustum planes in object space are expressed by the coefficients presented next. In [Gribb01, Akenine-Möller02], the same results are obtained in a different way.

$$
\begin{aligned}
\mathbf{N}_{left} &= \begin{bmatrix} M_{41} + M_{11} & M_{42} + M_{12} & M_{43} + M_{13} & M_{44} + M_{14} \end{bmatrix}^{\mathrm{T}} \\
\mathbf{N}_{right} &= \begin{bmatrix} M_{41} - M_{11} & M_{42} - M_{12} & M_{43} - M_{13} & M_{44} - M_{14} \end{bmatrix}^{\mathrm{T}} \\
\mathbf{N}_{bottom} &= \begin{bmatrix} M_{41} + M_{21} & M_{42} + M_{22} & M_{43} + M_{23} & M_{44} + M_{24} \end{bmatrix}^{\mathrm{T}} \\
\mathbf{N}_{top} &= \begin{bmatrix} M_{41} - M_{21} & M_{42} - M_{22} & M_{43} - M_{23} & M_{44} - M_{24} \end{bmatrix}^{\mathrm{T}} \\
\mathbf{N}_{near} &= \begin{bmatrix} M_{41} + M_{31} & M_{42} + M_{32} & M_{43} + M_{33} & M_{44} + M_{34} \end{bmatrix}^{\mathrm{T}} \\
\mathbf{N}_{far} &= \begin{bmatrix} M_{41} - M_{31} & M_{42} - M_{32} & M_{43} - M_{33} & M_{44} - M_{34} \end{bmatrix}^{\mathrm{T}}
\end{aligned}
\tag{2.2.6}
$$

Extracting Camera Information

Once we have access to the frustum planes, all essential camera parameters can be readily obtained by computing cross products and plane intersections. We can also use the modelview matrix to extract information from eye to object space.

View and Up Directions

Once we have the near plane, the view direction is directly given by its normal vector: $\mathbf{V}_{\mathrm{dir}}^{\mathrm{T}} = [a_{near} \quad b_{near} \quad c_{near}]$. As the modelview matrix does not include perspective transformations, the same view direction can also be obtained by taking its value in eye space and bringing it back to object space. In eye space, the view direction is given by $\mathbf{V}_{\mathrm{dir}}'^{\mathrm{T}} = [0 \quad 0 \quad -1]$, resulting in $\mathbf{V}_{\mathrm{dir}}^{\mathrm{T}} = -[M_{31} \quad M_{32} \quad M_{33}]$, with $\mathbf{M}$ representing the modelview matrix.

The up direction can also be extracted in two ways. We can compute it by evaluating the cross product between the normal vectors of the left and right frustum planes, $\mathbf{V}_{\mathrm{up}}^{\mathrm{T}} = [a_{left} \quad b_{left} \quad c_{left}] \times [a_{right} \quad b_{right} \quad c_{right}]$, or, similarly to the view direction, we can use the modelview to compute the up direction in object space as it is given by $\mathbf{V}_{\mathrm{up}}'^{\mathrm{T}} = [0 \quad 1 \quad 0]$ in eye space. Therefore, it can be expressed in object space by $\mathbf{V}_{\mathrm{up}}^{\mathrm{T}} = [M_{21} \quad M_{22} \quad M_{23}]$, again with $\mathbf{M}$ representing the modelview matrix.

If we need both view and up direction vectors normalized, we should be careful. If the view direction is extracted from normalized frustum plane, the obtained vector is already normalized; otherwise, explicit normalization is required. For the up direction, normalization is always required.

Camera Position

Several algorithms need to know the position of the observer to perform their computation. Unfortunately, it is the most expensive information to be extracted from the transformation matrices. Again, we can extract it in two ways: via frustum planes or via the modelview matrix. Note that this information makes sense only for perspective projection, because for orthographic projection, the observer is placed at infinity and the view direction is the only information that matters.

Based on the frustum planes, we can extract camera position by computing the intersection of three planes, left, right, and top, for example. We then have a system of linear equations, $\mathbf{AP} = \mathbf{B}$, to be solved, where:

$$\mathbf{A} = \begin{bmatrix} a_{left} & b_{left} & c_{left} \\ a_{right} & b_{right} & c_{right} \\ a_{top} & b_{top} & c_{top} \end{bmatrix}, \quad \mathbf{P} = \begin{bmatrix} x \\ y \\ z \end{bmatrix}, \text{ and } \mathbf{B} = \begin{bmatrix} -d_{left} \\ -d_{right} \\ -d_{top} \end{bmatrix} \quad (2.2.7)$$

Using Cramer's rule, we end up having to compute a few matrix determinants.

$$\mathbf{P} = \begin{bmatrix} \det \mathbf{A}_a / \det \mathbf{A} \\ \det \mathbf{A}_b / \det \mathbf{A} \\ \det \mathbf{A}_c / \det \mathbf{A} \end{bmatrix} \quad (2.2.8)$$

Here, $\mathbf{A}_i$ is the matrix $\mathbf{A}$ with the i-column replaced by $\mathbf{B}$. If det $\mathbf{A}$ equals zero, it means that the observer is at infinity (orthographic projection).

The camera position can also be obtained from the modelview matrix. As we know the camera position in eye space, we can apply the inverse of the modelview matrix to get it back in object space (here, we need the inverse because we are transforming a point). However, we do not need to compute the full inverse matrix. In eye space, the camera is at the origin, being represented in homogeneous coordinates by $\mathbf{P'}_T = [0 \quad 0 \quad 0 \quad 1]$. Therefore, it suffices to find the fourth column of the inverse matrix for $\mathbf{P}^T = [M_{14}^{-1} \quad M_{24}^{-1} \quad M_{34}^{-1}]$, with $\mathbf{M}^{-1}$ representing the inverse of the modelview matrix.

Near and Far Distances

It might be necessary to know the near and far plane distances in object space. Once we have, in object space, the camera position and the near and far planes already normalized, the distances are computed by evaluating the plane equations.

$$\begin{aligned} D_{near} &= -a_{near} P_x - b_{near} P_y - c_{near} P_z - d_{near} \\ D_{far} &= a_{far} P_x + b_{far} P_y + c_{far} P_z + d_{far} \end{aligned} \quad (2.2.9)$$

If the modelview matrix does not include nonrigid body transformations, we can compute these distances in eye space. In that case, we could bring the near and far planes from clip to eye space, using the projection matrix. The distance would be given by $D_{near} = -d_{near}$ and $D_{far} = d_{far}$, with d representing the independent component of the normalized plane equation in eye space.

Angles of the Field of View

The vertical and horizontal angles of the field of view, θ_v and θ_h, can also be computed from the frustum planes. If we have the planes normalized in object space, the angles are extracted simply by evaluating dot products.

$$\cos(\pi - \theta_v) = \begin{bmatrix} a_{bottom} & b_{bottom} & c_{bottom} \end{bmatrix} \cdot \begin{bmatrix} a_{top} & b_{top} & c_{top} \end{bmatrix}$$

$$\cos(\pi - \theta_h) = \begin{bmatrix} a_{right} & b_{right} & c_{right} \end{bmatrix} \cdot \begin{bmatrix} a_{left} & b_{left} & c_{left} \end{bmatrix}$$

(2.2.10)

If the frustum is not symmetrical (which is common in virtual reality applications), we might have to compute two angles in each direction. In this case, we can use the normal vector of the near plane in the computation. For example, the horizontal left angle of view would be computed by the dot product between the normal vectors of the near and left frustum planes.

Arbitrary Projective Transformations

The same results could also be achieved with other graphics APIs. It suffices to consider the appropriate plane equations in clip space. In DirectX, for example, the near and far planes are given by $z = 0$ and $z = 1$, respectively. All other derived information can be extracted similarly.

We can go further and generalize the discussion to arbitrary projective transformations. It is known that all three-dimensional projective transformations are represented by 4 x 4 nonsingular matrices (and every 4 x 4 nonsingular matrix is a projective transformation) [Penna86], [Davis01]. Moreover, if we can transform a point back and forth into different spaces, we can also transform the planes, since points and planes are dual objects in three-dimensional projective space.

Therefore, we can bring any plane back to its original space as long as we have the corresponding vertex transformation matrix. For example, if we had accumulated the screen mapping into the transformation matrix, we would be able to extract view frustum information from screen space.

Of course, we have to adapt the semantics of the extracted information according to the meaning of the corresponding transformation. The "camera position" is, in fact, the apex of the perspective frustum. To illustrate other uses, let us consider the projective transformation used to compute shadows introduced by Heckbert and Herf [Heckbert97] and described in [Akenine-Möller02]. The proposed projective transformation maps a pyramid with parallelogram base into an axis-aligned box. The pyramid's apex corresponds to the light position and the parallelogram base to the shadow receptor. The left and right sides of the pyramid transform into the planes $x = 0$ and $x = 1$, while the top and bottom transform into $y = 0$ and $y = 1$, respectively. The pyramid base plane transforms to $z = 1$, and a plane parallel to it through the apex transforms to $z = \infty$ (Figure 2.2.4).

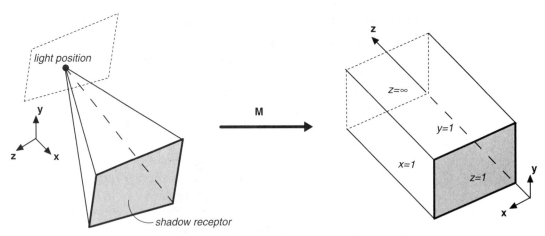

FIGURE 2.2.4   *Projective transformation of a pyramid with parallelogram base.*

Based on a projective matrix of this type, we can recover useful information such as the light position and receptor boundary. To extract such information, we first bring the planes back to object space, remembering that the plane at infinity is expressed in projective geometry as $\begin{bmatrix} 0001 \end{bmatrix}^T$. Then, the light position can be achieved by computing the intersection of the left, right, and top planes. The receptor boundary vertices can be obtained similarly as they represent the intersection of the near (base) plane and the pyramid side planes.

Implementation

The companion CD-ROM includes C++ code to extract frustum and camera information based on the OpenGL transformation matrices. For this implementation, in order to keep the code general, we opted for extracting camera information based uniquely on the frustum planes. For specific applications, it might be more efficient to compute the desired information using other alternatives, such as the ones discussed in the previous sections. The code also provides base classes for extracting information from arbitrary projective transformations.

Class Constructors

The code implements a VglFrustum class that provides methods for querying frustum and camera information from OpenGL matrices. We can create an object of that class by passing the corresponding transformation matrices to be used in extracting the viewing information. It offers three different constructors:

```
VglFrustum (float* Mmv, float* Mp);
VglFrustum (float* Mmvp);
VglFrustum ();
```

The matrices are represented in vectors, column by column, as in OpenGL. The first constructor should be preferred if we have both modelview and projection matrices on hand. These two matrices are then accumulated in a single modelview-projection matrix, which is used to extract information from clip to object space. If we already have the accumulated matrix, it is better to use the second constructor. This constructor is also useful if we want to extract the information in eye space; in that case, we only need to provide the projection matrix. The last constructor extracts the matrices by querying the current state of the graphics API. Its use within the rendering pipeline should be avoided whenever possible, as it forces synchronization between the central and graphics processors.

Querying Methods

Once we have created a `VglFrustum` object, we can extract frustum and camera information. For querying frustum information, methods such as `GetPlane()`, which returns the corresponding plane coefficients in object space, are provided. The returned plane equations are not automatically normalized—normalization should be explicitly requested whenever it is necessary. For extracting camera information, methods such as `GetViewDir()` and `GetEyePos()` are available.

Base Classes

The `VglFrustum` class is built on top of the `AlgFrustum` class, which is used to extract plane equations from arbitrary projective transformations. This class provides a static method `SetCanonicalPlane()` used to inform the corresponding plane equation in transformed space. Again, the `GetPlane()` method allows us to recover such planes in object space. Once we have the plane equations, we can use utility methods of the `AlgPlane` and `AlgVector` classes, such as `Intersect()` and `Cross()`, to extract positions and directions. It is straightforward to derive a `Frustum` class suitable to the DirectX API.

Conclusion

Several graphics algorithms need to extract frustum and camera information to perform their computations. This article showed how such information can be extracted in an efficient and practical manner. It also discussed how information can be extracted from general projective transformations. A good understanding of such transformations is valuable to game programmers, because they can judge the best space in which to perform specific computations.

References

[Akenine-Möller02] Akenine-Möller, Tomas and Eric Haines, *Real-Time Rendering, Second Edition*, A. K. Peters, 2002.

[Davis01] Davis, Tom, "Homogeneous Coordinates and Computer Graphics," *Mathematical Circles*, available online at *www.geometer.org/mathcircles*, November 20, 2001.

[Foley96] Foley, James, Andries van Dam, et al., *Computer Graphics, Principles and Practice, Second Edition*, Addison-Wesley, 1996.

[Gribb01] Gribb, Gil and Klaus Hartmann, "Fast Extraction of Viewing Frustum Planes from World-View-Projection Matrix," available online at *www2.raven-soft.com/users/ggribb/plane%20extraction.pdf*, June 15, 2001.

[Heckbert97] Heckbert, Paul S. and Michael Herf, "Simulating Soft Shadows with Graphics Hardware," Technical Report CMU-CS-97-104, Carnegie Mellon University, available online at *www.cs.cmu.edu/~ph/shadow.html*, January 1997.

[Penna86] Penna, Michael A. and Richard R. Patterson, *Projective Geometry and its Applications to Computer Graphics*, Prentice-Hall, 1986.

[Turkowski90] Turkowski, Ken, "Properties of Surface Normal Transformations," in Glassner, Andrew, *Graphics Gems*, Academic Press, available online at *www.worldserver.com/turk/computergraphics/index.html*, 1990.

2.3

Solving Accuracy Problems in Large World Coordinates

Peter Freese, NCsoft Core Technology Group

pfreese@ncaustin.com

Developers creating extremely large continuous worlds will ultimately run into problems due to floating-point accuracy. Nearly every gaming platform uses 32-bit floating-point numbers for coordinates, yet floats cannot represent areas larger than the typical first-person shooter level without significant accuracy errors at larger coordinate values. This article presents a technique for dealing with large coordinates that is fast, efficient, and does not require switching to double precision numbers.

In this technique, world space positions, which normally consist of three floating-point components, are extended to contain an integer *segment*, which allows the *offset*, or traditional position, to be normalized within a desired accuracy range. The names "segment" and "offset" are borrowed from segmented processor address space notation, and many of the concepts, such as renormalization, are similar.

Problem Description

The IEEE 754 standard for binary floating-point arithmetic defines what is commonly referred to as *IEEE floating point* [Goldberg91]. In single-precision 32-bit IEEE format, one bit is designated as the sign bit, the next 8 bits are the exponent field, and the last 23 bits are the fractional parts of the normalized number (see Table 2.3.1).

Table 2.3.1   IEEE Floating-Point Bit Layout

Sign	Exponent	Fraction (Mantissa)
S	EEEEEEEE	FFFFFFFFFFFFFFFFFFFFFFF

The accuracy for any given 32-bit floating-point number is equivalent to half the place value, or granularity, of the least significant bit (LSB) of the mantissa for a particular exponent. Since the place value of the leading 1 is 2^E (ignoring the exponent bias) and there are 23 bits of fraction, the place value for the LSB is 2^{E-24}. Very near 1, for example, the granularity is 2^{-24}, or approximately 0.0000001192. At values near 1,000, granularity increases to 0.000061 (2^{-13}), and at values near 100,000, granularity is 0.0078125 (2^{-7}). To put it in practical terms: if units represent meters and our world is 100km square, at the farthest corner of our world, 32-bit floating point will only allow us to represent space with 7.8mm granularity. The larger the coordinates we need to represent, the less will be our accuracy at its farthest extents. To represent an area the size of the continental United States (approximately 4,500 kilometers east to west), you would be limited to half-meter granularity at the coast farthest from the origin (see Figure 2.3.1).

32-bit Floating Point Granularity

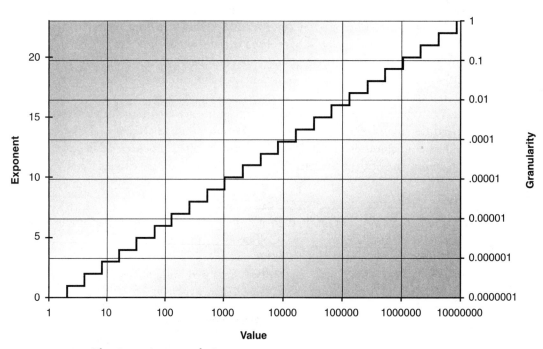

FIGURE 2.3.1   *Floating point granularity.*

Symptoms of Accuracy Errors

Does this mean you don't have to worry about accuracy if you're creating an outdoor area only a few kilometers across? Unfortunately, symptoms of accuracy errors can manifest themselves even with numbers that are ostensibly within range to provide more than adequate accuracy. The primary reason for this is that we are most often not simply using numbers to describe positions, but using them in calculations where errors can become amplified. Hierarchical object graphs, such as model skeletons, often rely on a chain of matrix multiplies to determine the position and orientation of a mesh in camera space. After concatenating several matrix multiplies, an accuracy error that would normally be insignificant might have increased to the point at which it introduces visual discontinuities or changes the behavior of a physics simulation.

While it is possible to precisely calculate the amount of error introduced at each step in a set of mathematical operations [Wilkinson94], and thereby determine the maximal error introduced in order to decide whether it is a problem worth solving, it is a rigorous and laborious process. It is far more straightforward to simply deal with the problem of accuracy if and when it becomes apparent. Here are some telltale symptoms of accuracy errors:

- **Inability to align adjacent objects.** This is a symptom of the grossest errors, in that you are actually prevented from setting objects at desired positions or orientations due to numeric granularity. This will be more likely to occur on objects at odd angles.
- **Cracks in mesh seams.** This is a more subtle variation of the first problem, but one in which very slight errors can be visible. Adjacent terrain meshes might exhibit cracks on seams that use coincident geometry, showing sky or fill color through the seams. Character models composed of multiple wearable meshes might fail to completely close, showing ugly gaps.
- **Jittering animations.** Models with skeletal animation might appear to quiver or shake; this will be particularly noticeable when the animations are subtle and don't involve large-scale movement, such as idle animations. The jittering will be more pronounced on bones farther from the skeletal root, such as hands and feet. Foot bones might fail to track properly to ground movement.
- **Collision errors.** All physics systems are subject to numeric instability, but problems can be greatly exaggerated at large coordinates. Similarly, transforms involve matrix inversions, which can cause coordinate accuracy errors to greatly increase in magnitude. Intersection tests can produce large errors that are highly dependent on order of operations. Object A might report that it is penetrating object B, but the reverse test might indicate that B is still some distance from A.

All of these errors can be identified with large numerical values if they are manifest at bigger coordinates, but nonexistent near the world coordinate origin. If you see jittering characters at coordinates (15356, 9436) but animations all look perfect at (0, 0), you can be almost certain your renderer is suffering from floating-point accuracy issues.

Many of the rendering errors described previously can be greatly exaggerated by graphics hardware. To achieve maximum performance, most GPUs perform math in reduced precision modes, such as 24-bit or 16-bit floating-point formats. The s16e7 24-bit format uses a 16-bit mantissa, which is 7 fewer bits than single precision floats. This means that accuracy granularity is 2^7, or 128 times larger. Granularity is yet another 64 times larger for the s10e5 16-bit format.

Table 2.3.2   Granularity at Some Common Multiples of Ten

Value	E	23-bit Mantissa	16-bit Mantissa	10-bit Mantissa
1	0	0.00000012	0.00001526	0.00097656
10	3	0.00000095	0.00012207	0.00781250
100	6	0.00000763	0.00097656	0.06250000
1000	9	0.00006104	0.00781250	0.50000000
10000	13	0.00097656	0.12500000	8.00000000
100000	16	0.00781250	1.00000000	64.00000000
1000000	19	0.06250000	8.00000000	512.00000000

It is important to note that the choice of unit has no impact on accuracy errors. In other words, whether you choose a unit measure of one kilometer, one meter, or one millimeter makes no difference as to the scale at which accuracy errors become problematic. As shown in Table 2.3.2, accuracy errors are measured in the same units as the values they are associated with, depending only on the scale of the numbers. If you measure your world in meters, you'll experience the same errors at 10,000 meters as you would at 10 kilometers had you chosen kilometers as your units instead.

Potential Solutions

An ideal solution to floating-point accuracy issues should exhibit the following properties:

- **Improved coordinate precision.** Object placement should not suffer from accuracy granularity dependent on location.
- **Reduction in arithmetic errors.** Numeric manipulation, such as rotational transformation or computation of distance vectors should not suffer from additional accuracy loss.
- **Minimal performance impact.** Performance overhead should not significantly impact typical operations, such as rendering, collision detection, and picking.
- **Compatibility with graphics pipelines.** We'd like to be able to hand the results of calculations to graphics hardware in a friendly manner, preferably retaining native numerical format.

There are several alternate ways of dealing with accuracy issues that deserve mentioning before we proceed to the solution that is the focus of this article. In some circumstances, they might be appropriate solutions that have minimal code impact.

Larger Float Types

The most tempting solution to accuracy issues is to simply adopt larger float types. IEEE double precision 64-bit floats use a 52-bit mantissa, more than twice the 23 bits of precision in single precision floats. The extra 29 bits increase relative accuracy by a factor of 536,870,912. Whether switching to double precision floats is feasible depends entirely on your platform. Modern consumer CPUs are capable of performing floating-point calculations in single and double precision modes. However, there is a significant performance benefit for calculating in lower precision, which is why most games switch the FPU state to single precision mode and leave it there for the duration of execution. Single precision floats also have half the storage overhead of doubles, which can be significant for highly detailed geometry. Finally, most graphics APIs deal exclusively with single precision floats, and graphics hardware might internally operate at even lower precisions. Even if you could successfully switch your engine to use double precision floats, accuracy issues will still crop up if the graphics hardware does transformations with lower precision.

Eliminating the World Space Transformation

Most graphics pipelines involve a sequential set of transformations applied to vertices similar to the following:

$$M_{world} \rightarrow M_{view} \rightarrow M_{projection}$$

The world transformation (M_{world}) changes coordinates from model space, where vertices are defined relative to a model's local origin, to world space, where vertices are defined relative to an origin common to all the objects in a scene. In essence, the world transformation places a model into the world, hence its name. The view transformation (M_{view}) locates the viewer in world space, transforming vertices into camera space. The view matrix relocates the objects in the world around a camera's position—the origin of camera space—and orientation. At large coordinates, both M_{world} and M_{view} can contain accuracy errors.

Many engines will submit M_{world}, M_{view}, and $M_{projection}$ independently to their rendering pipeline, or M_{world} and a concatenation of $M_{viewprojection}$. By concatenating M_{world} and M_{view} as early as possible, however, and then submitting $M_{worldview}$ and $M_{projection}$, many accuracy issues can be bypassed. This is particularly applicable to solving animation jitter.

For example, in a skeletal hierarchy, vertices go through the following transformations:

$$[M_{bone} \times M_{parentbone} \times \ldots \times M_{rootbone}] \rightarrow M_{view} \rightarrow M_{projection}$$

Normally, all the bone transformations are concatenated left to right, up the hierarchy, resulting in a set of matrices that transform vertices into world space where they can be blended, lit, and so forth. If the root bone matrix $M_{rootbone}$ is combined with the view matrix M_{view} before being concatenated to the child bone transformations, rendering accuracy errors can be isolated to a single operation, combining the root bone and view matrix.

$$[M_{bone} \times M_{parentbone} \times \ldots \times (M_{rootbone} \times M_{view})] \rightarrow M_{projection}$$

For pipelines that require a discrete view matrix to be submitted, the geometry can be submitted with an identity view matrix. All vertex blending, lighting, and primitive calculations are then done in view space, with no additional accuracy errors.

While this can mitigate some of the more conspicuous visual problems in animations, and serves well as an eleventh hour solution for accuracy issues, it fails to solve the basic problem, which is that there simply isn't enough accuracy to represent positions in the world. Furthermore, it introduces an additional CPU level transformation on every mesh whenever the view matrix changes—essentially every time the camera moves.

Far Positions

ON THE CD

The solution presented in this article addresses all the requirements outlined previously, and essentially involves a hybrid between fixed-point and floating-point numbers. Position vectors, normally consisting of three floating-point numbers, are extended with an additional integer component representing a floating origin. Because of the way that this data representation resembles the manner in which segmented addresses extended the address space of early 32-bit processors, the components are termed *segment* and *offset*, and the hybrid is called a *far position*. Complete code for the classes and data structures outlined here appears on the companion CD-ROM. For clarity, abbreviated definitions are used here in the text.

```
class FarPosition
{
private:
    FarSegment     m_segment;
    Vector3        m_offset;
    static float   s_segmentSize;
};
```

All positions in space are measured relative to some conceptual fixed point that we call the origin. Because the granularity of floating-point numbers is magnitude dependent, the farther we are from the origin, the greater the granularity. By repositioning the origin so that it is nearer to the position we are measuring, we can reduce the granularity of our measurements. Far positions allow the origin to be repositioned dynamically, maximizing available precision. The segment component of a far position represents an origin in 2D space, which in this case is the XZ plane, assuming a world model in which altitude is represented by the y-axis. The choice was made to limit the segment to the XZ plane because accuracy errors in outdoor rendering environments result from magnitude in horizontal location, not altitude.

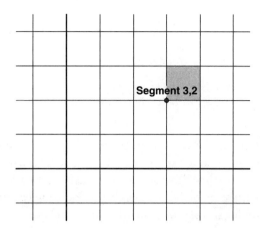

FIGURE 2.3.2 *Example segment layout.*

Figure 2.3.2 illustrates how a particular segment might exist relative to the world origin. The segment space consists of all points relative to the segment origin. Because we are concerned with making the most use of available precision, we normalize positions so that normalized segment space consists of only those offsets within a segment size of the segment origin (shown in gray).

Choosing a Segment Size

The choice of units for segment size is somewhat arbitrary. Since this will be encoded in a global constant, it allows us to balance the accuracy we desire with the maximum expressible range and renormalization overhead. When offsets are renormalized, they are limited to a range of up to one segment size; this allows us to put a clamp on the maximum allowable accuracy error. A value of 1024.0f provides a reasonable range for a unit choice of meters for a typical human avatar based outdoor environment. Different choices for units or scale will affect the choice for segment size.

Since the segment value expresses the origin for the offset in integer units, the choice of 1024.0f for segment size gives quite a large working range. We can express the segment with a signed 16-bit value, giving us a maximum expressible segment range of ±33553408.0f (32767 * 1024.0f); this is more than enough to represent a flat projection of the entire earth's surface.

By packing two 16-bit segment coordinates into a 32-bit value, the size of the FarPosition structure (which includes three floating-point numbers representing offset) totals 16 bytes, a size friendly to structure alignment and packing.

Here is how we define FarSegments:

```
union FarSegment
{
    struct
    {
```

```
        int16    x, z;
    };

    int32          xz;

    matFarSegment() {};
    matFarSegment( ZeroType ) : xz(0) {};
};
```

The union allows us to treat FarSegments as a single 32-bit value, which makes for very simple and fast initializations and comparisons. The ZeroType initializer provides a type-based overload for initializing to a known state, which allows us to conveniently provide both an explicit initializing constructor and an empty constructor (useful for storing in standard container classes).

Renormalization Details

The representation of world positions with far positions is straightforward enough, but we need a means of both encoding traditional positions as far positions and converting back. Converting a far position into a traditional vector representation is fairly straightforward; we simply need to add the offset and the segment scaled appropriately by the segment size.

```
Vector3 FarPosition::GetApproximateVector() const
{
    Vector3 v = m_offset;
    v.x += m_segment.x * s_segmentSize;
    v.z += m_segment.z * s_segmentSize;

    return v;
}
```

There is a catch to this simplicity, however. Performing this operation leaves the result in the range of standard floating-point representations, thus in the realm of reduced precision. Conversion operations should be minimized, and only performed when necessary. This is advertised by the name of the member function: GetApproximateVector().

Converting to far positions from traditional representations involves only slightly more work.

```
void SetFromVector( const Vector3& vector )
{
    m_segment.xz = 0;
    m_offset = vector;
    Normalize();
}
```

When we initially store the vector, the far position is in an unnormalized state. The magnitude of the offset is unknown, and could be far larger than what we have determined is an appropriate segment size. Therefore, we invoke a normalization process on the far position.

```
void FarPosition::Normalize()
{
    if ( fabsf(m_offset.x) >= s_segmentSize )
    {
        m_segment.x += FloatToInt(m_offset.x / s_segmentSize);
        m_offset.x = fmodf(m_offset.x, s_segmentSize);
    }

    if ( fabsf(m_offset.z) >= s_segmentSize )
    {
        m_segment.z += FloatToInt(m_offset.z / s_segmentSize);
        m_offset.z = fmodf(m_offset.z, s_segmentSize);
    }
}
```

After normalization, the offset x and z components will be in the range (-s_segmentSize, + s_segmentSize). Note that the process involves a float-to-integer conversion, so you should use standard optimization tricks for fast conversion.

When converting from Vector3 representations to far positions, the result will only be as accurate as the initial Vector3. To take advantage of the increased accuracy available to us, we need to use far positions for all absolute position representations, not just at render time. This means that object locations should be persisted as far positions, and editors should manipulate objects with far positions. Any time we convert absolute locations to three float vectors, we lose accuracy that cannot be recovered.

Because normalization is based solely on the magnitude of the offset, we can combine it with operations on far positions that might result in unnormalized offsets.

```
void FarPosition::Translate( const Vector3& vector )
{
    m_offset += vector;
    Normalize();
}
```

A key behavior of far positions is the ability to provide their offset relative to a specific segment. This method looks like this:

```
Vector3 FarPosition::GetRelativeVector( const FarSegment& segment )
const
{
    Vector3 r = m_offset;
    r.x += (m_segment.x - segment.x) * s_segmentSize;
    r.z += (m_segment.z - segment.z) * s_segmentSize;
    return r;
}
```

The need for this will become evident when we discuss how far positions fit into the rendering pipeline.

We can measure the distance between two far positions by adding the difference between the offsets and the segments (appropriately scaled).

```
Vector3 operator-( const FarPosition &lhs, const FarPosition &rhs )
{
    matVector3 r = lhs_offset - rhs.m_offset;
    r.x += (lhs.m_segment.x - rhs.m_segment.x) * s_segmentSize;
    r.z += (lhs.m_segment.z - rhs.m_segment.z) * s_segmentSize;
    return r;
}
```

If we want the scalar distance between two far positions, we can simply take the scalar length of the vector returned.

Note that this operation could have been performed by first converting both far positions to world space Vector3 coordinates, and then doing a standard vector subtraction. Doing so, however, could have introduced precision loss, which should be obvious when you consider what happens if the positions are far from the origin.

If the distance between the points is large, a Vector3 might still be incapable of representing the distance vector without accuracy errors. This is probably acceptable, since we are seldom concerned with interactions between objects that are far away from each other. If we need to simply determine the distance between two points, a result with a maximum relative rather than absolute error is usually sufficient.

Render Pipeline Changes

Now that we have a means of representing positions with greatly increased accuracy, how do we make use of it in a rendering pipeline? Rendering engines deal with matrix transformations, not position vectors. How do we create matrices that minimize accuracy errors? The answer turns out to be fairly straightforward: we generate all matrices in the same *segment space*. The devil is in the details, however.

First, let's consider how we represent positions and orientations normally. One natural way of doing this is with a Vector3, representing position, and a quaternion, representing orientation.

```
class Transform
{

private:
    Quaternion          m_quaternion;
    Vector3             m_position;

    mutable Matrix4x4   m_matrix;
};
```

Such a class might also be able to lazily generate a 4 x 4 matrix on demand, caching the results within the object. We can wrap this class in a new one capable of representing a transform with far positions.

```
class FarTransform
{
public:
    void SetBasisSegment( FarSegment segment );
    const matTransform& GetLocalTransform() const;
    mutable bool        m_bPositionDirty;
    mutable FarSegment  m_basisSegment;
};
```

This class combines a local transform with a far position and a *basis segment*. The basis segment is the segment space in which the local transform exists. By generating all rendering transforms, thus all matrices, in the same basis segment or segment space, rendering can proceed as normal. For this to work, all root objects in the scene graph, including the camera, will need to use FarTransforms. Nonroot objects, such as individual bone transforms, can continue to use standard transformation representations, since the offsets they contain relative to their parents are usually minimal. This also avoids any additional performance overhead of far positions except where it is necessary.

Lazy Basis Renormalization

What basis segment should we use? The answer depends somewhat on our usage pattern. If we are rendering, choosing a basis segment based on the camera position is the natural choice. If the camera is in motion (which it invariably is), then the segment from the normalized camera position will change only when the camera has moved a distance greater than the segment size. Because we allow the offset to extend both a positive and negative distance from the segment origin, we avoid changing segments unnecessarily when camera motion is in a pathological case, such as tightly orbiting a segment origin.

If we are not concerned with rendering, but instead with interaction among many objects in a region of space (for example, a server dealing with a region in a continuous large world), then choosing a fixed basis segment at the center of the region of interest makes more sense. All objects within the region can be operated on with local transforms, which minimizes accuracy errors.

What happens when the basis segment changes? The first thing to note is that we must make sure that any object we are rendering has a local transform relative to the current basis segment. This can be done by tracking the last basis segment used for the object, as we do for a FarTransform. Setting a basis segment that is different from the current one invalidates the local transform.

```
void FarTransform::SetBasisSegment( FarSegment segment )
{
    if ( segment != m_basisSegment )
    {
        m_bPositionDirty = true;
        m_basisSegment = segment;
    }
}
```

When we subsequently request the local transform, the dirty flag is checked, and if set, the local transform is repositioned relative to the new basis segment.

```
const Transform& FarTransform::GetLocalTransform() const
{
    if ( m_bPositionDirty )
    {
        // store position
        m_localTransform.SetPosition(
            m_position.GetRelativeVector(m_basisSegment));
        m_bPositionDirty = false;
    }
    return m_localTransform;
}
```

World Space versus Local Space

One of the biggest hurdles in integrating far positions is that we can no longer talk about world space in any meaningful fashion except when dealing specifically with entities incorporating a far position; all other positional representations are relative to the current basis segment. We cannot mix operations on two local transforms unless they are in the same basis segment. If we have a 4 x 4 matrix or a three-float vector, we know we have a local (basis relative) position or transformation, but we don't know *which* basis it is relative to without inspecting the object that contains it. The notion that everything is relative can cause confusion and is a potential source of bugs.

We also need to distinguish between relative position information and absolute positions when doing calculations. We use far positions to represent absolute positions, and Vector3s to represent relative positions (offsets). This definition puts certain operations off limits to us. For example, we don't have an operator to add two far positions together. Besides the fact that the domain of the result doesn't make sense, providing such an operator puts us at risk of segment overflow. Consider the results, for example, if we elected to independently sum the segment coordinates and offsets for several hundred objects. This might be needed to find the average position of the objects. The segment values could easily overflow the available range. The correct way to handle this problem is to choose a segment in which to sum all of the relative offsets.

```
typedef vector<FarPosition> VFP;
FarPosition FindAveragePosition( const VFP &positions )
{
    if ( positions.empty() )
        return FarPosition(Zero);

    FarSegment segment = positions.front().GetSegment();
    Vector3 offset(Zero);
    for ( VFP::iterator it = positions.begin(); it != positions.end();
++it )
    {
        offset += it->GetRelativeVector(segment);
    }
```

```
        FarPosition average;
        average.SetSegment(segment);
        average.SetOffset(offset / positions.size());
        average.Normalize();
        return average;
    }
```

This function uses the segment from the first position in the vector as a reference segment. It then sums the relative positions of each of the positions in that segment space. The result should be precise even for thousands of positions, provided they are fairly local. The pathological case of millions of distant objects will work properly without overflow, but will be subject to the same accuracy restrictions of traditional offsets. This is not a significant limitation, as the need for interactions between such remote positions is almost nonexistent.

Translation into Local Space

Often, we will have some construct in absolute world space and we need to translate it into the local space of a nonroot scene graph node. We might need to do this for a collision intersection test or pick ray intersection. In the case of a pick ray, we would start out with a ray origin expressed as a far position, a ray direction that can be expressed as a normal Vector3, and a scalar maximum pick distance. Transforming this into the local object space represented by a FarTransform consists of two steps: transforming the ray origin, and transforming the ray direction.

Transforming the ray direction is straightforward.

```
// inputs:
// Vector3 vDir = world direction
// FarTransform transform
Transform& localTransform = transform.GetLocalTransform();
Matrix4x4& invMatrix = localTransform.GetInverseMatrix();
Vector3 localDir = invMatrix.TransformVector(vDir);
```

This is identical to the process we would use if we weren't using far positions. Transforming the ray origin involves only a minor change to the normal process.

```
// inputs:
// FarPosition vOrg
Vector3 relOrg = vOrg.GetRelativeVector(transform.GetBasisSegment());
Vector3 localOrg = invMatrix.TransformPoint(relOrg);
```

Before transforming the point by the matrix inverse, we find the position relative to the basis segment of the local transform. It doesn't really matter what this basis segment is; the key thing is that it matches the relative space in which the local transform exists. If we were concerned about maintaining the greatest accuracy in this calculation, we could specifically set the basis segment at the beginning of the operation to the segment from the normalized FarPosition in the FarTransform. This might be important for systems not involved with rendering that couldn't rely on an appropriate basis segment already being set for the FarTransform.

Performance Considerations

There are a few potential pitfalls in implementing far positions. As mentioned previously, maintaining awareness of the relative nature of all transforms is fundamental to avoiding segment-shift bugs. These can be rather insidious, because code that appears to work in simple test cases might fail in the wild when objects, the camera, and the basis segment are all changing.

The performance impact of using far positions is normally quite negligible, for several reasons:

- Normalization tests need only be done on dynamic root node objects, and involve simple floating-point compares.
- For rendering, basis renormalization occurs only when the camera is farther than the segment size along the X- or Z-axis from the origin of the last basis segment used.
- Basis renormalization can be done by simply updating root transform positions. The calculation for this involves just a few integer and floating-point operations.

One potential hitch arises when using multiple cameras to view regions of the world simultaneously. If the cameras are sufficiently remote such that they see completely different sets of objects, the system will work flawlessly. However, if the cameras are near enough to see the same objects, but segments from the camera positions are different, then as each view is rendered, it will update the basis segment in the objects' transforms. The two views will fight over the basis segment to use, and basis renormalization will occur on every render. One case where this might arise is when one camera is used for the user's viewport, and another camera is used to render environment maps for objects within the scene. The solution to this dilemma is to choose a single entity that has control over which basis segment to use for rendering. This could be the primary camera, or it could be based on the position of the player's avatar.

Conclusion

Developers creating large worlds must address problems related to floating-point accuracy. Far positions provide a solution to floating-point accuracy problems that is fast, hardware friendly, and tunable. They don't require higher precision floats or floating-point tricks. They do require a fundamental shift in thinking with regard to what world space means.

References

[Goldberg91] Goldberg, David, "What Every Computer Scientist Should Know About Floating-Point Arithmetic," *ACM Computing Surveys*, March 1991.
[Wilkinson94] Wilkinson, James H., *Rounding Errors in Algebraic Processes*, Dover Publications, 1994.

2.4

Nonuniform Splines

Thomas Lowe, Krome Studios

tomlowe@kromestudios.com

Splines are curved paths, usually defined by a series of points in 3D space called *nodes*. Sometimes more information is required per node to further describe the shape of the curve. Usually splines are evaluated by calling a simple function like `GetPosition(float time)`, where time varies between zero and one.

This article describes three types of nonuniform cubic splines. Nonuniform splines have the useful property that their velocity is not affected by the distance between nodes, making them particularly useful in game development. The three types of splines are:

- **Rounded nonuniform spline:** Approximately constant velocity, useful for trains running along tracks.
- **Smooth nonuniform spline:** C^2 or continuous acceleration, useful for particle effect paths.
- **Timed nonuniform spline:** A variation of the previous spline with specifiable time intervals; for example, for cut-scene cameras.

Types of Splines

The following is a list of commonly used spline types, of which the basic types are compared in Figure 2.4.1 (see [Demidov03] for more information). The notation C^n means that the nth derivative of the spline is continuous.

- **Bezier curves:** These pass through only the start and end nodes and are continuous in all derivatives. Unlike the other spline types, their complexity increases with each extra node added.
- **Catmull-Rom splines:** Pass through each node. C^1 continuous.
- **Kochanek-Bartels splines:** Extension of Catmull-Rom requiring extra parameters per node.
- **Natural cubic splines:** Pass through each node. C^2 continuous.

- **Cubic b-spline:** Do not pass through each node. C^2 continuous.
- **NURBS:** Extension of b-splines, requiring extra parameters per node. Capable of defining exact circles, hyperbolas, and ellipses.

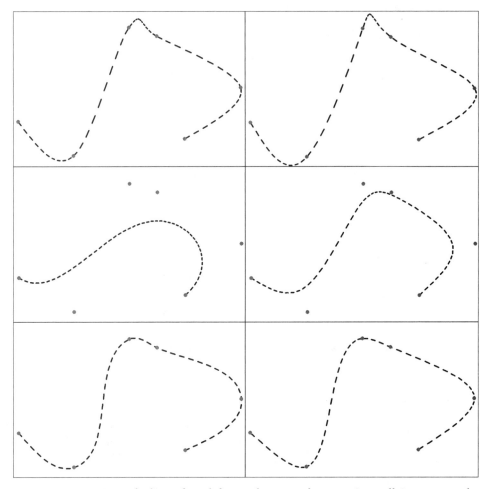

FIGURE 2.4.1 *Types of splines, from left to right, top to bottom. Catmull-Rom, natural, bezier, b-spline, rounded nonuniform, smooth nonuniform.*

Basic Cubic Spline Theory

The nonuniform splines described in this article are very similar to Catmull-Rom and natural cubic splines. They all pass through each node (a useful property giving a high level of control). They are all piecewise; each curve segment between two nodes is a separate function of time. Lastly, they are all cubic, meaning the function is of the form $p(t) = at^3 + bt^2 + ct + d$ where $p(t)$ is position at time t.

Three-dimensional splines are cubic in each dimension, so we can write (in vector notation):

$\mathbf{p}(t) = \mathbf{a}t^3 + \mathbf{b}t^2 + \mathbf{c}t + \mathbf{d}$ or

$\mathbf{p}(t) = [t^3 \quad t^2 \quad t \quad 1]\mathbf{A}$ for some matrix A. $\hspace{2cm}$ (2.4.1)

Looking at a single segment, the curve can be fully described by a start and end position, and a start and end velocity (or by tangents) (see Figure 2.4.2).

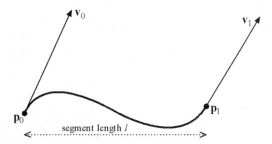

FIGURE 2.4.2 *A cubic curve described by four vectors.*

If we scale t to go from 0 to 1 in this segment, then we can describe these node velocity vectors as the change in position after one time unit if continuing in a straight line. Further, we can fully generate the matrix **A**:

$\mathbf{A} = \mathbf{HG}$ so

$\mathbf{p}(t) = \mathbf{tHG}$ where

$$\mathbf{t} = [t^3 \quad t^2 \quad t \quad 1] \quad \mathbf{H} = \begin{bmatrix} 2 & -2 & 1 & 1 \\ -3 & 3 & -2 & -1 \\ 0 & 0 & 1 & 0 \\ 1 & 0 & 0 & 0 \end{bmatrix} \text{ and } \mathbf{G} = \begin{bmatrix} \mathbf{p}_0 \\ \mathbf{p}_1 \\ \mathbf{v}_0 \\ \mathbf{v}_1 \end{bmatrix} \hspace{1cm} (2.4.2)$$

Here, **t** is the time vector, **H** is a Hermite interpolation matrix, and **G** is the geometry matrix. The Hermite interpolation matrix is the unique matrix that satisfies our description. See [Hermite99] for its derivation. So now we can obtain the position along the segment curve at any time $0 \leq t \leq 1$. Equation 2.4.2 has been implemented in the function GetPositionOnCubic() on the companion CD-ROM.

Catmull-Rom splines and natural cubic splines are both built up from these cubic segments, just with different methods of choosing the node velocity vectors. Since they are uniform, their nodes are equally spaced along the timeline. Returning a position along the spline at some time (between 0 and 1) is simply a case of finding the appropriate segment and its t value, and then applying Equation 2.4.2.

Rounded Nonuniform Spline

Figure 2.4.3 shows a racing path created by a Catmull-Rom spline on the left, and a rounded nonuniform spline on the right. Notice how the unevenly spaced nodes greatly distort the velocity and shape of the left spline, whereas the right spline has a very regular velocity and shape.

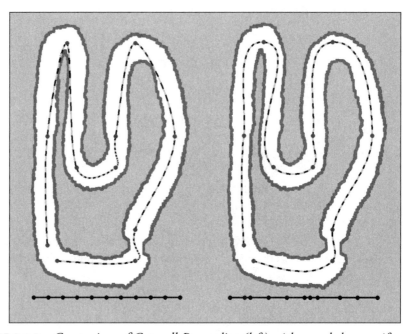

FIGURE 2.4.3   *Comparison of Catmull-Rom spline (left) with rounded nonuniform spline (right). Below each track, we see the nodes placed on timelines.*

The rounded nonuniform spline (RNS) is therefore very useful for describing spatial curves (such as train tracks or rope geometry) or for paths that should be traversed at a constant rate (such as enemy patrol paths or objects on rails). In addition, these splines can be used where rounded corners are required, the traversal speed being controlled externally. The racetrack in Figure 2.4.3 is a good example of this.

Implementation

So, how does one implement an RNS? First, divide the spline's timeline up in proportion to the segment lengths (this is the nonuniform part). One can use the linear distance between nodes here as an approximation to the segment length. This division means that an object traversing the spline evenly (i.e., with a constant time increment) will travel at the same average velocity between each pair of nodes. A simple data structure and lookup function for this is shown in the following pseudocode:

```
struct Node {
    Vector position, velocity;
    float distance; // distance to next node in array
} node[10];

Vector GetPosition(float time)
{
    float distance = time * maxDistance;
    float currentDistance = 0.f;
    int i = 0;
    while (currentDistance + node[i].distance <
           distance && i < 10)
    {
        currentDistance += node[i].distance;
        i++;
    }
    float t = distance - currentDistance;
    // i is segment number, t is time along segment

    // Note: Remainder of function listed below
}
```

Now each segment is a cubic function with a different time range. If we can rescale the cubic to the range $0 \leq t \leq 1$, then we can continue to use Equation 2.4.2 on each segment. This means scaling the node velocities $\mathbf{v}^N$ to get the segment time start and end velocities $\mathbf{v}^S$. First, the time conversion:

$$\Delta t^s = \Delta t^w * \Omega / l \tag{2.4.3}$$

where Ω = traversal speed along spline
= length of spline / time to traverse spline

In English, the segment t value (0 to 1) is scaled from world time by multiplying by the speed that the spline is being traversed, and dividing by the segment length. One can see that a 10-meter segment will take 10 times longer to traverse ($\Delta t^s = 1$) than a 1-meter segment.

From Equation 2.4.3, we get $\mathbf{v}^S = \mathbf{v}^W * l/\Omega$ (2.4.4)

The node velocities are stored as world velocities assuming a traversal speed of one.

So: $\mathbf{v}^S = \mathbf{v}^N * l$ (2.4.5)

In other words, the velocities passed into `GetPositionOnCubic()` must first be multiplied by the segment length so as to be in the correct timescale. We complete the lookup function by appending:

```
t /= node[i].distance; // scale t in range 0 - 1
Vector startVel = node[i].velocity * node[i].distance;
Vector endVel = node[i+1].velocity * node[i].distance;
return GetPositionOnCubic(node[i].position, startVel,
                   node[i+1].position, endVel, t);
```

The second part to implementing an RNS is obtaining the node velocities (here is the rounded part of RNS). We choose them to be unit length (so the velocity at the nodes is equal to the average velocity between nodes), and we split the angle between the previous and the next node in half (see Figure 2.4.4).

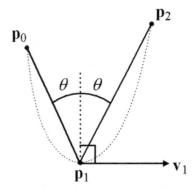

FIGURE 2.4.4   *Choice of node's velocity vector.*

ON THE CD

The complete code for creating and accessing the RNS is on the companion CD-ROM.

Smooth Nonuniform Splines

Figure 2.4.5 compares a smooth nonuniform spline (SNS) with an RNS and a natural cubic spline (smooth uniform spline). Notice how, like the RNS, the velocity is not affected by node spacing, but like the natural spline, the motion appears smooth.

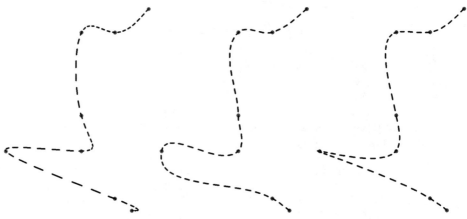

FIGURE 2.4.5   *Natural spline, RNS and SNS.*

The SNS is C^2 continuous, meaning it has a continuous (nonjerky) acceleration as one traverses it, unlike the C^1 RNS. It is a smooth temporal curve and so ideally suited to describing the motion of objects that accelerate and decelerate smoothly and have no turning circle. For example, the motion of a camera, the path of a flying saucer, approximating handwriting, or creating particle effect trails. It's also worth noting that this spline is the "point curve" that 3ds max uses.

Implementation

The SNS works the same way as the RNS; it is just the node velocities that are different, making it C^2 continuous. The complexity here is all in generating these node velocities based on the node positions.

To make this spline C^2 continuous, a velocity vector for each node must be chosen such that the end acceleration of the previous cubic is equal to the start acceleration of the next cubic (see Figure 2.4.6).

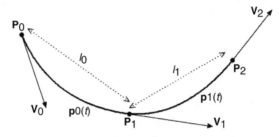

FIGURE 2.4.6 *The SNS is C^2 continuous when*
$$\mathbf{a0}^W(1) = \mathbf{a1}^W(0). \tag{2.4.6}$$

So, what is the formula for acceleration? Examining a single segment and taking derivatives of Equation 2.4.2:

$$\mathbf{p}(t) = (2\mathbf{p}_0 - 2\mathbf{p}_1 + \mathbf{v}_0^S + \mathbf{v}_1^S)t^3 + (-3\mathbf{p}_0 + 3\mathbf{p}_1 - 2\mathbf{v}_0^S - \mathbf{v}_1^S)t^2 + \mathbf{v}_0^S t + \mathbf{p}_0$$

so $\qquad\qquad\qquad\qquad\qquad\qquad\qquad\qquad\qquad\qquad\qquad$ (2.4.7)

$$\mathbf{v}^S(t) = 3(2\mathbf{p}_0 - 2\mathbf{p}_1 + \mathbf{v}_0^S + \mathbf{v}_1^S)t^2 + 2(-3\mathbf{p}_0 + 3\mathbf{p}_1 - 2\mathbf{v}_0^S - \mathbf{v}_1^S)t + \mathbf{v}_0^S \quad (2.4.8)$$

$$\mathbf{a}^S(t) = 6(2\mathbf{p}_0 - 2\mathbf{p}_1 + \mathbf{v}_0^S + \mathbf{v}_1^S)t + 2(-3\mathbf{p}_0 + 3\mathbf{p}_1 - 2\mathbf{v}_0^S - \mathbf{v}_1^S) \quad (2.4.9)$$

However, we are looking for world acceleration. We can derive from Equation 2.4.3 that:

$$\mathbf{a}^W = \mathbf{a}^S * \Omega / l^2 \tag{2.4.10}$$

Converting Equation 2.4.9 and applying to Equation 2.4.6, we get:

$$\frac{6(2\mathbf{p}_0 - 2\mathbf{p}_1 + \mathbf{v}_0^S + \mathbf{v}_1^S) + 2(-3\mathbf{p}_0 + 3\mathbf{p}_1 - 2\mathbf{v}_0^S - \mathbf{v}_1^S)}{l_0^2} = \frac{2(-3\mathbf{p}_1 + 3\mathbf{p}_2 - 2\mathbf{v}_1^S - \mathbf{v}_2^S)}{l_1^2}$$

(2.4.11)

Then, applying Equation 2.4.5 and rearranging in terms of $\mathbf{v}_1$, we get:

$$\mathbf{v}_1^N = \frac{l_1(3(\mathbf{p}_1 - \mathbf{p}_0)/l_0 - \mathbf{v}_0^N) + l_0(3(\mathbf{p}_2 - \mathbf{p}_1)/l_1 - \mathbf{v}_2^N)}{2(l_0 + l_1)}$$

(2.4.12)

We now have each node velocity specified in terms of the velocity of its two neighboring nodes. Given that node velocities can be assigned to the first and last nodes (defined later), there are two methods of solving this system.

First, Equation 2.4.12 forms a tridiagonal system of equations that can be solved in O(n) time. See [RecipesC93] for solving tridiagonal systems.

The second method, and the one implemented in the sample code, is to iteratively apply Equation 2.4.12 to each node. One can think of it as a smoothing filter applied to the spline that reduces the acceleration discontinuities with each pass. In practice, only three or four passes are required to reach an almost exact solution. See the function Smooth() on the companion CD-ROM.

Now that we have this filter, an SNS is simply an RNS that has Smooth() called on it several times after all nodes are added (see Figure 2.4.7).

FIGURE 2.4.7   *Example of an SNS.*

Timed Nonuniform Spline

The timed nonuniform spline (TNS) is an extension of the SNS with an additional parameter per node: the time interval to the next node. It is also C^2 continuous.

Figure 2.4.8 shows three versions of the TNS generated from the same set of points, but with different specified time intervals between each node (shown on the timeline bar at the bottom).

The ability to specify a time schedule for the spline path makes the TNS ideally suited for generating cut-scene camera paths or flythroughs. You can place down points at any location in space and time and the camera will pass through them exactly and smoothly.

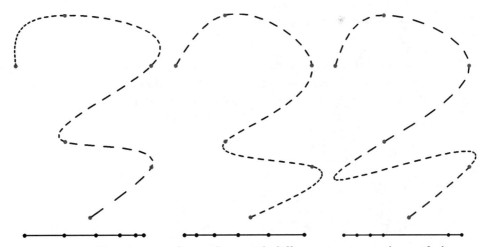

FIGURE 2.4.8   *Timed nonuniform splines with different time intervals specified on the nodes.*

The implementation of this spline is a simple extension of the SNS. One just uses the specified time intervals for each segment in place of the segment length.

In the far right spline in Figure 2.4.8, we see that the large time span allocated to one segment leads to it veering off track quite a bit. This is often undesirable and calls for a modification. A good method of countering the effect is to scale down the node velocity vectors in the more extreme situations after each smooth. The following scaling does this job well and is shown in Figure 2.4.9.

$$\mathbf{v}_1^{N}* = 4r_0 r_1 \big/ (r_0 + r_1)^2 \tag{2.1.13}$$

where $r =$ actual segment length / time interval.

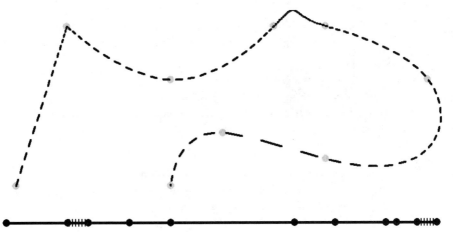

FIGURE 2.4.9   *Constrained TNS. Note how the doubled-up nodes allow the camera to stop and start smoothly.*

Calculating Start and End Node Velocities

This is the last remaining undefined aspect to the splines described previously. Fortunately, there is a fairly standard solution, which is to choose the velocity such that the acceleration is zero at the end (implying that there is no further force on the curve). Visually this means the curve becomes straight at the two end positions.

Taking Equation 2.4.9 at time $t = 0$, we have:

$$\mathbf{a}^S(0) = 2(-3\mathbf{p}_0 + 3\mathbf{p}_1 - 2\mathbf{v}_0^S - \mathbf{v}_1^S) = 0 \text{ So (with Equation 2.4.5):} \qquad (2.4.14\text{a})$$

$$\mathbf{v}_0^N = (3(\mathbf{p}_1 - \mathbf{p}_0) \,/\, l_0 - \mathbf{v}_1^N) \,/\, 2 \qquad (2.4.14\text{b})$$

This is our solution for the spline's start node. The end node velocity is much the same.

$$\mathbf{v}_n^N = (3(\mathbf{p}_n - \mathbf{p}_{n-1}) \,/\, l_{n-1} - \mathbf{v}_{n-1}^N) \,/\, 2 \qquad (2.4.14\text{c})$$

Obtaining the Velocity and Acceleration on the Spline

Examining a single segment, Equations 2.4.8 and 2.4.9 can be written in matrix form and are thus equivalent to Equation 2.4.2 with a different matrix **H**.

$$\mathbf{H}_{velocity} = \begin{bmatrix} 0 & 0 & 0 & 0 \\ 6 & -6 & 3 & 3 \\ -6 & 6 & -4 & -2 \\ 0 & 0 & 1 & 0 \end{bmatrix} \qquad \mathbf{H}_{acceleration} = \begin{bmatrix} 0 & 0 & 0 & 0 \\ 0 & 0 & 0 & 0 \\ 12 & -12 & 6 & 6 \\ -6 & 6 & -4 & -2 \end{bmatrix} \qquad (2.4.15)$$

The standard lookup function can be used, but it returns a value in segment space. To get a world velocity, apply Equation 2.4.4; to get a world acceleration, apply Equation 2.4.10.

These additional quantities can be very useful. The velocity vector can provide an orientation for an object following the spline path. The acceleration is used in measures such as the tilt of the object, the current curvature, or the direction of thrust.

Optimizations

There are opportunities for speeding up the spline access function `GetPosition()`. The function does a linear search of the segments, which, despite being a fast loop, is still $O(n)$. If the segment lengths are stored cumulatively, then one can do a binary search of the segments, which is $O(\log_2 n)$.

In situations where the spline is being traversed, rather than accessed randomly, the current segment and distance from start can be cached, leading to a constant lookup time. Additionally, in such situations the 4 x 4 matrix multiplication **HG** from Equation 2.4.2 can be calculated once and cached, reducing the access code to little more than a vector transform. On architectures with a vector unit, this can be done very quickly in parallel. If the spline is to be traversed with a constant Δt, then we can optimize the evaluation of each cubic even further. The function can be reduced to just three vector additions:

```
acc += jerk;
vel += acc;
pos += vel;
```

where jerk is the third derivative of the cubic (a constant), and acc, vel, and pos are given appropriate initial values.

Conclusion

This article described three types of nonuniform splines that give game developers control over the timing and velocity of a point traversing the spline. This makes them especially useful for objects traveling at constant speed, such as vehicles, or paths with ancillary timing information, like camera paths. Nonuniform splines are more appropriate for these applications than traditional splines, which instead aim for higher order continuity or other goals.

References

[Demidov03] Demidov, Evgeny, "An Interactive Introduction to Splines," available online at *www.people.nnov.ru/fractal/Splines/Intro.htm*.

[Hermite99] "Hermite Splines," available online at *www.siggraph.org/education/materials/HyperGraph/modeling/splines/hermite.htm*.

[RecipesC93] Press, William H., et al., *Numerical Recipes in C, Second Edition*, Cambridge University Press, 1993, available online at *www.library.cornell.edu/nr/bookcpdf.html*.

2.5

Using the Covariance Matrix for Better-Fitting Bounding Objects

Jim Van Verth,

Red Storm Entertainment

jimvv@redstorm.com

When building games, we often use bounding boxes or other simplified forms of an object to speed up intersection checks for graphics and collision. These bounding objects are commonly oriented along the local axes for the model, but doing this does not necessarily give the tightest fitting bounds (that is, bounds with minimum volume). One technique that can help is to create a statistical measure of the object known as the *covariance matrix*. Together with a linear algebra concept known as an *eigenvector*, we can use these to find a coordinate system that aligns along the major and minor axes of an ellipsoid roughly surrounding the object. Finding the minimum and maximum ranges along these axes will give a much better fit than just naively using the model coordinate system.

This article covers the covariance matrix and how to generate it, gives a brief overview of eigenvectors, and then describes how to compute the eigenvectors for the matrix. Finally, it discusses how to use the coordinate axes produced to generate bounding boxes and other bounding objects.

The Covariance Matrix

Suppose we treat our model as a point cloud of n points $\{\mathbf{p}_1, \ldots, \mathbf{p}_n\}$ in 3D space, and we want to take a statistical measure of how spread out the points are, and how they interrelate in the different coordinate axes. For 3D points, these metrics are known as the *variance* within the sets of x, y, and z coordinates, and the *covariance* between the pairs *xy*, *yz*, and *xz*. Variance and covariance are usually used to measure properties of data sets of similar size—for example, a list of patients with age, weight, and medical data. In the case of our model, we will treat the set of *x*, *y*, and *z* values for each point as three equally sized but possibly independent data sets.

The variance of a variable (say the *x* coordinate) measures how a set of data points varies from its mean, and is computed as the normalized sum of squared differences from the mean. For example, we can measure how the set of *x* coordinates $\{x_1, \ldots, x_n\}$ varies from its mean $\bar{x}$.

$$\mathrm{var}_x = \frac{1}{(n-1)} \sum_{i=1}^{n} \left(x_i - \bar{x}\right)^2 \tag{2.5.1}$$

We use $n - 1$ rather than n to correct for bias in our estimate. The overall mean in this case is the centroid of the set of n points, or:

$$\bar{\mathbf{p}} = \frac{1}{n} \sum_{i=1}^{n} \mathbf{p}_i \tag{2.5.2}$$

So in the *x* direction:

$$\bar{x} = \frac{1}{n} \sum_{i=1}^{n} x_i \tag{2.5.3}$$

A high variance means that data is spread out, while low variance is clustered close to the mean. The square root of the variance is the *standard deviation*.

The covariance measures how independent two data sets are. For example, the covariance between the *x* and *y* coordinate sets is computed by:

$$\mathrm{cov}_{xy} = \frac{1}{(n-1)} \sum_{i=1}^{n} \left(x_i - \bar{x}\right)\left(y_i - \bar{y}\right) \tag{2.5.4}$$

Covariance between *x* and *z*, and *y* and *z*, can be computed similarly. A low magnitude covariance means that the data sets vary independently (if zero, they are completely uncorrelated), while a high value means that they vary together. If the covariance is positive, they will in general increase or decrease together. If negative, then as one is increasing, the other will decrease. By the previous definition, the covariance within the same data set is the same as the variance; in other words, $\mathrm{var}_x = \mathrm{cov}_{xx}$.

We can combine the variance and covariance for each coordinate pair into a *covariance matrix* **C** for the set of points.

$$\mathbf{C} = \begin{bmatrix} var_x & cov_{xy} & cov_{xz} \\ cov_{xy} & var_y & cov_{yz} \\ cov_{xz} & cov_{yz} & var_z \end{bmatrix} \tag{2.5.5}$$

Note that this is a symmetric matrix; we will use this fact later.

Why is this useful to us? The covariance matrix gives a measure of variance in a particular direction. If we multiply a unit vector by the matrix, the resulting vector will be longer if it points toward areas of greater variance, and shorter in areas of lower variance. Taking a unit sphere and transforming it by the covariance matrix will produce an ellipsoid. The long axis of this ellipsoid will lie along the direction of greatest variance; in other words, where the points are more spread out. This will roughly align with the long axis of our object. Similarly, the short axis of the ellipsoid will lie along the direction of least variance, where the points are closest together, which will roughly align with the short axis of our object. Therefore, instead of using the local axes to build our bounding objects, we can use the axes of the ellipsoid instead, which in many cases will get us a better fit. These axes are known as the *principal axes* (see Figure 2.5.1).

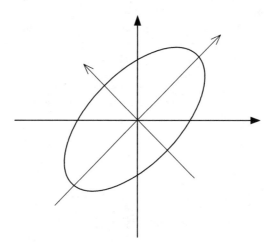

FIGURE 2.5.1 *Ellipsoid of covariant matrix, showing principal axes.*

So, how do we find these principal axes? One simple example is when all the covariance values are zero. In this case, the data is completely independent between the three coordinates. Our principal axes are aligned with the local coordinate axes, and one local axis will point along the direction of longest distance through the point cloud, and one will point along the direction of shortest distance. The resulting matrix will be diagonal:

$$C_{aligned} = \begin{bmatrix} var_x & 0 & 0 \\ 0 & var_y & 0 \\ 0 & 0 & var_z \end{bmatrix} \tag{2.5.6}$$

However, our data won't usually be arranged in this way. In these cases, we can modify our matrix slightly to get a more convenient transformation. We rotate the vector we're transforming to the space of the principal axes, apply the covariance matrix, and then rotate back. Combining this into one matrix gives us a diagonal matrix, similar to the preceding one:

$$\mathbf{D} = \mathbf{R}^T\mathbf{C}\mathbf{R} \tag{2.5.7}$$

This process is known as *diagonalization*.

Since **R** is an orthogonal matrix, the column vectors form an orthonormal basis for a coordinate system. They are also equal to the principal axes for the original covariance matrix, which we can use to build our bounding objects. In the next section, we will see how we can use eigenvectors to find this rotation.

The following code can be used to generate both the mean and the covariance matrix from a set of points. Since the matrix is symmetric, we only compute the upper triangle of values and store them in a one-dimensional array. This is not a problem; as we'll see, we won't need the lower triangular values. We've also chosen to not normalize our matrix by $1/(n-1)$. While this is not a correct covariance matrix, for our calculations the scale factor will not matter and only wastes processing time.

```
void CovarianceMatrix( Vector3* points,
    int numPoints, const Vector3& mean,
    float C[6] )
{
    int i;

    // compute mean
    mean = points[0];
    for (i = 1; i < numPoints; ++i)
    {
        mean += points[i];
    }
    float recip = 1.0f/numPoints;
    mean *= recip;

    // compute each element of matrix
    memset( C, 0, sizeof(float)*6 );
    for (i = 0; i < numPoints; ++i)
    {
        Point diff = points[i] - mean;
        C[0] += diff.x*diff.x;
        C[1] += diff.x*diff.y;
        C[2] += diff.x*diff.z;
        C[3] += diff.y*diff.y;
        C[4] += diff.y*diff.z;
```

```
            C[5] += diff.z*diff.z;
        }
    }
```

Eigenvalues and Eigenvectors

To solve for the principal axes, we need to understand eigenvalues and eigenvectors of a matrix. Suppose we have an $n \times n$ matrix **A**. If there is a nonzero vector **x** such that **Ax** is a scalar multiple of **x**, or

$$\mathbf{Ax} = \lambda\mathbf{x} \tag{2.5.8}$$

then we say that λ is an *eigenvalue* of **A**, and **x** is a corresponding *eigenvector*. In other words, after the transformation, some of the vectors in our vector space remain pointing in the same direction, while their length might have changed.

We can rewrite Equation 2.5.2 as

$$(\mathbf{A} - \lambda\mathbf{I})\mathbf{x} = \mathbf{0} \tag{2.5.9}$$

If, as we've stated, **x** is not **0**, then taking the determinant of both sides gives

$$\det (\mathbf{A} - \lambda\mathbf{I}) = 0 \tag{2.5.10}$$

This is called the *characteristic equation* of **A**. Solving this equation for all values of λ will give us the eigenvalues for **A**. For an $n \times n$ matrix, the characteristic equation expands to a degree n polynomial in λ, called the *characteristic polynomial*. Therefore, for our case we will be trying to solve a cubic equation. While it is possible that a general matrix will have complex eigenvalues, since covariance matrices consist of real values and are symmetric, they only have real-valued eigenvalues.

For a given real eigenvalue, there will be an infinite number of corresponding eigenvectors. We call the vector space encompassing these eigenvectors an *eigenspace*. To solve for the eigenspace for a given eigenvector, we substitute the value of the given eigenvalue for λ into Equation 2.5.2, and solve for **x**.

Eigenvalues also have geometric properties. For some matrices, in particular symmetric matrices, eigenvalues can tell us how the matrix can change the lengths of vectors. [Blinn02] provides a very constructive example of this effect. Figure 2.5.2 shows how the vectors that inscribe the unit circle change when we apply the matrix.

$$\mathbf{A} = \begin{bmatrix} 3 & 1 \\ 1 & 3 \end{bmatrix} \tag{2.5.11}$$

The length of the long axis of the ellipse is 4, which is the first eigenvalue, and the direction of the long axis is the set of corresponding eigenvectors. The same is true of the short axis: its length is 2, or our other eigenvalue, and the direction is the same as the corresponding eigenvector set.

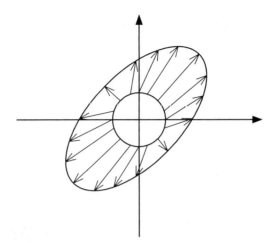

FIGURE 2.5.2   *Effect of matrix on unit circle.*
Vectors along (1,1) and (−1,1) remain pointing
in the same direction.

Figure 2.5.2 should look familiar: it is related to Figure 2.5.1. If we were to over-lay Figure 2.5.1 over Figure 2.5.2, we would see that the eigenvectors are aligned with the principal axes. This gives us the informal notion that perhaps we can find the principal axes by computing eigenvectors for the matrix.

We can state this more formally by noting that symmetric matrices also have other properties. First, they always have a perpendicular set of eigenvectors. Second, they are orthogonally diagonalizable; that is, for a symmetric matrix **A**, we can always find an orthogonal matrix **R** such that $\mathbf{R}^T\mathbf{A}\mathbf{R}$ is diagonal. This should look familiar, as it is just Equation 2.5.7. Therefore, if we can find **R**, we can find our principal axes.

How do we solve for **R**? A further property of symmetric matrices is that the orthogonal eigenvectors for **A**, once normalized, form the columns for **R**. Since in the case of the covariance matrix, these columns are also the principal axes, in order to find the principal axes all we need to do is compute the eigenvectors. Thus, our intuition is correct.

Computing the Eigenvectors of the Covariance Matrix

A number of techniques can be used to compute eigenvalues and eigenvectors for general $n \times n$ matrices (see [Burden93] or [Press93]). A common one is the Householder method, which decomposes the matrix into a tridiagonal matrix, which can be further diagonalized to compute the eigenvalues and eigenvectors. In the case of the 3×3 covariance matrix, this is overkill, as we don't need the kind of generality and precision that such methods afford. Instead, we can compute the characteristic polynomial, which in this case will be a cubic polynomial, and then solve for the roots of the equation directly.

The determinant of the matrix **C- λI** is

$$\begin{vmatrix} c_{11} - \lambda & c_{12} & c_{13} \\ c_{21} & c_{22} - \lambda & c_{23} \\ c_{31} & c_{32} & c_{33} - \lambda \end{vmatrix} = A\lambda^3 + B\lambda^2 + C\lambda + D \qquad (2.5.12)$$

where

$$A = -1$$

$$B = c_{11} + c_{22} + c_{33}$$

$$C = -c_{11}c_{22} + c_{12}^2 - c_{11}c_{33} + c_{13}^2 - c_{22}c_{33} + c_{23}^2 \qquad (2.5.13)$$

$$D = c_{11}c_{22}c_{33} + 2c_{12}c_{13}c_{23} - c_{11}c_{23}^2 - c_{22}c_{13}^2 - c_{33}c_{12}^2$$

We can solve for the roots of this cubic polynomial to give us the eigenvalues, and then compute matrix $\mathbf{M}_I = \mathbf{C} - \lambda_I\mathbf{I}$ for each eigenvalue λ_I. The corresponding eigenvector $\mathbf{v}_i$ can be found by solving the linear system

$$\mathbf{M}_I\mathbf{v}_I = 0 \qquad (2.5.14)$$

After solving the three linear equations, we have our three eigenvectors.

[Eberly02] describes an efficient method for computing the roots of this equation and the corresponding eigenvectors. For this article, this has been implemented in the routine `GetRealSymmetricEigenvectors()`, which can be found on the companion CD-ROM. It sorts the eigenvalues into three different cases, generates the eigenvectors depending on the particular case, and then sorts them into decreasing order of eigenvalue. More detail on the mathematics involved is available in Eberly's article.

ON THE CD

Building Bounding Objects

Now that we have our coordinate basis for our point cloud (the centroid and the eigenvectors), we can compute bounding objects.

To compute a bounding box, we take each point, subtract the centroid from it to get a difference vector, and take the dot product with each normalized eigenvector. This gives the length of the projection of the difference vector against each basis vector. Computing the minimum and maximum of these dot product values will create a bounding box for the point cloud, aligned with the new basis vectors. The corresponding code is:

```
void ComputeBoundingBox(
        const Vector3* points, int nPoints,
        Vector3& centroid, Vector3 basis[3],
        Vector3& min, Vector3& max )
    {
```

```
    float C[6];
    CovarianceMatrix( points, nPoints, centroid, C );

    GetRealSymmetricEigenvectors( C,
        basis[0], basis[1], basis[2] );

    min.Set(MAX_FLT, MAX_FLT, MAX_FLT);
    max.Set(MIN_FLT, MIN_FLT, MIN_FLT);

    // for each point do
    for ( int i = 0; i < nPoints; ++i )
    {
        Vector3 diff = points[i]-centroid;
        for (int j = 0; j < 3; ++j)
        {
            float length = diff.Dot(basis[j]);
            if (length > max[j])
                max[j] = length;
            else if (length < min[j])
                min[j] = length;
        }
    }
}
```

Note that the centroid might not necessarily lie in the center of this box, so minimum and maximum distances might not be the same. This can be adjusted by translating the centroid if desired.

A cylinder is another common example of a bounding volume. To compute it, we begin by finding the long axis of the point cloud, which corresponds to the eigenvector with the largest eigenvalue. The maximal values for the cylinder along the axis can be found in a similar way to the bounding box: we project the difference between each point and the centroid to the cylinder axis and take the dot product with the axis vector. To find the radius of the cylinder, we compute the distance between each point and the axis line formed by the eigenvector and the centroid; the radius is the maximum such distance. The previously projected distance along the axis can be reused for this calculation.

```
void ComputeBoundingCylinder(
        const Vector3* points, int nPoints,
        Vector3& centroid, Vector3& axis,
        float& min, float& max, float& radius )
{
    float C[6];
    CovarianceMatrix( points, nPoints, centroid, C );

    Vector3 v2, v3;
    GetRealSymmetricEigenvectors( C, axis, v2, v3 );

    min = MAX_FLT;
    max = MIN_FLT;
    float maxDistSq = 0.0f;

    // for each point do
```

```
for ( int i = 0; i < nPoints; ++i )
{
    // compute min, max along axis
    Vector3 diff = points[i]-centroid;
    float length = diff.Dot(axis);
    if (length > max)
            max = length;
    else if (length < min)
        min = length;

    // compute radius
    Vector3 proj = (diff.Dot(axis))*axis;
    Vector3 distv = diff - proj;

    float distSq = distv.Dot(distv);
    if (distSq > maxDistSq)
        maxDistSq = distSq;
}

radius = sqrtf(maxDistSq);
}
```

A capsule can be computed similarly, although the hemispherical caps at each end require a little more care to generate. See [Eberly01] or [VanVerth04] for more details.

Note that the bounding shape is in the space defined by the centroid and the eigenvectors. If we need to convert from bounding box space to model space, we can use the matrix

$$
\mathbf{M}_{BM} = \begin{bmatrix} \mathbf{v}_1 & \mathbf{v}_2 & \mathbf{v}_3 & \overline{\mathbf{P}} \\ \hline \mathbf{0}^T & & & 1 \end{bmatrix}
\tag{2.5.15}
$$

Conclusion

This article presented a method for computing better-fitting bounding shapes using the properties of the covariant matrix. While not as fast as naively using the points of a model in their local space, it's reasonably efficient, and if need be can be computed offline.

However, it's not always the most appropriate solution for computing bounding volumes. In some cases, a bounding box aligned with the model space is still the right choice. For example, when using a bounding box to approximate the body of a tank for fast collision, a minimum volume box might lie diagonally to the bottom of the model. This can make testing for ground collision difficult.

In addition, this technique might not compute the best fitting bounding shape; see [O'Rourke85]. Because the covariance matrix is a statistical measure, it is prone to error when the data is too redundant, concave, sparse, or nonuniform. Redundant data can occur if triangle vertices are included more than once in the calculations—for this reason, it is better to work with a triangle mesh. For concave objects, [Gottschalk96] recommends using the convex hull of the object instead of the object data itself, to prevent internal points from throwing off the measurements.

For sparse or nonuniform data, one possible solution is to take uniform samples across the triangle surfaces and use that as the input data. A better solution is to generate the covariant matrix by taking a solid integral through the entire shape, in effect sampling the model at infinite resolution. This is known as the *inertial tensor matrix*, and is useful in physical simulations for computing rotational dynamics. See [Mirtich96] or [Eberly03] for more information on creating inertial tensors from models.

Still, in most cases, using the covariant matrix directly on the model vertex data does produce a very good approximation, much better than the naive method. Using this code or some derivative should create better bounding boxes, and hence tighter collision and culling checks.

References

[Blinn02] Blinn, Jim, "Consider the Lowly 2x2 Matrix," *Notation, Notation, Notation*, Morgan Kaufmann Publishers, 2002.

[Burden93] Burden, Richard L. and J. Douglas Faires, *Numerical Analysis*, PWS Publishing Company, 1993.

[Eberly01] Eberly, David H., *3D Game Engine Design*, Morgan Kaufmann Publishers, 2001.

[Eberly02] Eberly, David H., "Eigensystems for 3×3 Symmetric Matrices," Technical Report, available online at *www.magic-software.com*, 2002.

[Eberly03] Eberly, David H., *Game Physics*, Morgan Kaufmann Publishers, 2003.

[Gottschalk96] Gottschalk, S., M.C. Lin and D. Manocha, "OBB-Tree: A Hierarchical Structure for Rapid Interference Detection," *Proceedings of SIGGRAPH '96*.

[Mirtich96] Mirtich, Brian, "Fast and Accurate Computation of Polyhedral Mass Properties," *Journal of Graphics Tools*, 1(2): pp. 31–50, 1996.

[O'Rourke85] O'Rourke, J., "Finding Minimal Enclosing Boxes," *Internat. J. Comput. Inform. Sci.*, Vol. 14 (June 1985), pp. 183–199.

[Press93] Press, William H., Brian P. Flannery, Saul A. Teukolsky, and William T. Vetterling, *Numerical Recipes in C*, Cambridge University Press, 1993.

[VanVerth04] Van Verth, James M. and Lars M. Bishop, *Essential Mathematics for Games and Interactive Applications*, Morgan Kaufmann Publishers, 2004 (to be published).

2.6

The Jacobian Transpose Method for Inverse Kinematics

Marco Spoerl, KMW

mspoerl@gmx.de

When it comes to goal-oriented movement in games, pre-authored animation data is often inadequate. Haven't we all seen archaeologists, special agents, and other characters trying to grab an object or push a button, only to pick up some imaginary object beyond the real target, or reach into a wall? To fix this, the animation needs to be tweaked at runtime. This is what real-time inverse kinematics is for.

There are plenty of algorithms to solve the inverse kinematics problem. While many of them are good only for offline computations, Chris Welman illustrated two methods suitable for interactive environments in his master's thesis [Welman93]. One of these algorithms, Cyclic Coordinate Descent, or CCD for short, has been explained thoroughly in another article [Weber02]. Our article focuses on the second algorithm from Welman's thesis using the transposed Jacobi matrix. The Jacobian transpose algorithm usually produces better results than the better-known Cyclic Coordinate Descent, as it always manipulates the complete inverse kinematics chain at once, instead of looking at single succeeding links.

Our Test Bed

For the sake of clarity, we won't bother with a full-blown skeletal animation system to demonstrate the Jacobian Transpose in this article. Instead, we will use a single chain made of articulated joints. Each element in this formation is called a *node*. A node is defined by a pointer to its parent, an array of pointers to its children (if any), and of course its transformation (translation and rotation, but no scale) relative to its parent. We use quaternions to represent rotations in our sample implementation.

The first node in the chain is called the *root*, while the last one is called the *effector*. The effector should reach the target with all other nodes down to the root building the inverse kinematics chain, or *manipulator*.

Figure 2.6.1 illustrates the starting configuration of the inverse kinematics chain consisting of five nodes. Note that the effector is only drawn using a simple axis, as it doesn't have a defined length. The axis on the right and the sphere surrounding it denote the target and the threshold allowed to reach its position.

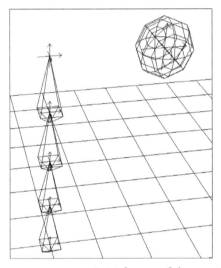

FIGURE 2.6.1   *Initial setup of the manipulator.*

ON THE CD

The complete source code for the application discussed in this article and our own implementation of the CCD for comparison purposes can be found on the companion CD-ROM.

What Is a Jacobian?

With forward kinematics, the position *x* of the effector can be computed using

$$x = f(q) \tag{2.6.1}$$

where *q* denotes a vector of known joint variables (e.g., rotations and translations.) In comparison, when using inverse kinematics, the goal is to reach a known position *x*. Therefore, the inverse of Equation 2.6.1 is needed.

$$q = f^{-1}(x) \tag{2.6.2}$$

The tricky part is that the function f is nonlinear. There's a unique solution from q to x in Equation 2.6.1, but there could be many mappings from a particular x to q in Equation 2.6.2. To solve for this, the problem needs to be linearized. We do so by using the relationship between the joint velocities and the velocity of the effector.

$$\dot{x} = J(q)\dot{q} \qquad (2.6.3)$$

The relationship is given by the Jacobi matrix, or Jacobian for short.

$$J = \frac{\partial f}{\partial q} \qquad (2.6.4)$$

Simply put, the Jacobian J tells us how the effector changes its position and orientation with changes to the joint variables q. It's a $m \times n$ sized matrix, where n denotes the number of joints in the manipulator and m is the size of the effector vector x. In our case, m is 6 for a general-purpose position and orientation task. That is, column i of the Jacobian describes the incremental change of the effector's position and orientation resulting from changes to joint i. A simple iterative method to solve the inverse kinematic problem can be based on the inverted relationship of Equation 2.6.3.

$$\dot{q} = J^{-1}(q)\dot{x} \qquad (2.6.5)$$

In a real-time environment, we want to avoid the expensive inversion required to solve Equation 2.6.5. There is a faster approach using the pseudo-inverse, but that method suffers from problems with singularities [Schreiber98] when J is not a square matrix. Therefore, our algorithm uses the transposed Jacobian.

The Jacobian Transpose Method in a Nutshell

The goal of an inverse kinematics solver is to reach the specified target. To keep track of its "success," some type of error measurement is necessary. Given the current effector position $x_e(t)$ and target position $x_t(t)$, the error measure or distance vector is

$$e(t) = x_e(t) - x_t(t) \qquad (2.6.6)$$

Now consider the error measure e to be a force vector f pulling the effector toward the desired target position. Using that vector f we build a composite force F pulling at our manipulator's tip.

$$F = [f_x, f_y, f_z, 0, 0, 0]^T \qquad (2.6.7)$$

Note that this is different from Welman's version [Welman93].

$$F = [f_x, f_y, f_z, m_x, m_y, m_z]^T \qquad (2.6.8)$$

We ignore the twist m about some axis, as we don't deal with the target's orientation. However, using the principle of virtual work as described in [Paul81], the relationship between the force F and the internal generalized forces τ can be described as

$$\tau = J^T F \tag{2.6.9}$$

So, what does τ represent? Considering an accurate dynamic simulation, τ would be the vector of joint variable accelerations. For our purposes, however, let's think of τ as the vector of joint velocities.

$$\dot{q} = J^T F \tag{2.6.10}$$

Finally, integrating Equation 2.6.10 gives us a new vector q that moves our effector toward the target. In fact, after the integration, q holds rotation angles to be applied to each node. The corresponding axes of rotation are determined while building the Jacobian.

Computing the Jacobi matrix itself is quite simple as well. As we are only using rotational joints (each node's translation is fixed), [Welman93] tells us that the Jacobian column entry for the i'th joint is

$$J_i = \begin{bmatrix} \left[\left(p - j_i \right) \times axis_i \right]^T \\ \left[axis_i \right]^T \end{bmatrix} \tag{2.6.11}$$

where p is the world-position of the effector, j_i is the world-position of joint i, and *axis* is the local axis of rotation of joint i.

Recapping, the Jacobian Transpose works like this.

1. Determine the distance vector and magnitude between effector and target.
2. Skip computation loop if distance falls under a certain threshold.
3. Compute the Jacobian and the axes of rotations.
4. Transpose the Jacobian.
5. Determine force f.
6. Compute joint velocities.
7. Integrate joint velocities to obtain joint rotations and apply rotations.
8. Check for criteria to abort.
9. Apply final result to the manipulator.

Implementing the Algorithm

We start solving the inverse kinematics problem with the Jacobian Transpose method by computing the Jacobi matrix itself. In our implementation, getting p and j_i from Equation 2.6.11 is straightforward. However, what about the *axis*? As the nodes don't have a fixed axis of rotation, we'll simply use the vector perpendicular to the two vectors joint $\rightarrow$ target and joint $\rightarrow$ effector.

```
for( iColumn = 0, iLinkIndex = 1; iColumn < iLevel;   ++iColumn,
++iLinkIndex )
{

    // Position of current node

    m_arrCurrentTM[ iLinkIndex ].GetTranslation( vecLink );

    // Vector current link -> target

    vecLinkTarget = m_vecTargetPosition - vecLink;

    // Vector current link -> current effector position

    vecLinkEnd = vecEnd - vecLink;

    // Compute axis

    m_arrAxis[ iColumn ] = CVector3::CrossProduct( vecLinkTarget,
vecLinkEnd );
    m_arrAxis[ iColumn ] .Normalize();

    // Compute upper part of the Jacobian entry

    vecEntry = CVector3::CrossProduct( vecLinkEnd, m_arrAxis[ iColumn ]
);

    // Set Jacobian entry

    for( iRow = 0; iRow < 3; ++iRow )
    {
      m_arrJacobian[ iRow * iLevel + iColumn ] = vecEntry[ iRow ];
      m_arrJacobian[ ( iRow + 3 ) * iLevel + iColumn ] = m_arrAxis[
iColumn ][ iRow ];
    }
}
```

Note that iLevel denotes the number of links in the manipulator; that is, the number of entries in the Jacobian. Next, of course, the Jacobian has to be transposed.

```
for( iRow = 0; iRow < 6; ++iRow )
   for( iColumn = 0; iColumn < iLevel; ++iColumn )
      m_arrJacobianTransposed[ iColumn * 6 + iRow ] = m_arrJacobian[
iRow * iLevel + iColumn ];
```

The force f from Equation 2.6.7 is the distance between the effector and the target. Note that this vector has a second purpose as well, as its magnitude is used as a criterion to abort the computation loop.

```
// Determine position of effector

m_arrCurrentTM[0].GetTranslation( vecEnd );
```

```
// What do we have to do to reach that?

vecDifference = vecEnd - m_vecTargetPosition;

// How far is that?

fError = vecDifference.GetMagnitude();

// Set force vector

farrForce[0] = vecDifference.GetX();
farrForce[1] = vecDifference.GetY();
farrForce[2] = vecDifference.GetZ();
farrForce[3] = 0.0f;
farrForce[4] = 0.0f;
farrForce[5] = 0.0f;
```

Using Equation 2.6.10, it's easy to get the joint velocities.

```
// Compute q'

for( iRow = 0; iRow < iLevel; ++iRow )
{
    m_arrQDerivate[ iRow ] = 0.0f;

    for( iColumn = 0; iColumn < 6; ++iColumn )
        m_arrQDerivate[ iRow ] += m_arrJacobianTransposed[ iRow * 6 +
iColumn ] * farrForce[ iColumn ];
}
```

Completing the basic computations, we have to integrate the joint velocities and apply the resulting changes.

```
// Integrate and apply changes

for( iIndex = 0, iLinkIndex = 1; iIndex < iLevel; ++iIndex,
++iLinkIndex )
{
    axisAngle.SetAxis( m_arrAxis[iIndex] );
    axisAngle.SetAngle( m_arrQDerivate[iIndex] * 0.01f )
    quatAlign.SetQuaternion( axisAngle );
    quatAlign.Normalize();

    // Store quaternion

    ...

}
```

As you can see, we use a simple Euler integration step. While this is not the best way to integrate, it's certainly the fastest. We leave it to the reader to try a more sophisticated scheme like the Runge-Kutta integrator as proposed by [Welman93].

Finally, the resulting value is used as the rotation angle of the specific joint around the axis computed earlier.

As mentioned earlier, we are using quaternions for rotations. In case of the Jacobian Transpose, the consistent use of an axis-angle representation might be better. In that case, the application of the results from the integration would become simpler, and the conversion illustrated earlier would be unnecessary. In our sample implementation, though, the Jacobian Transpose solver shares a common base class with a generic CCD solver that makes heavy use of quaternions.

ON THE CD

The complete Jacobian Transpose implementation can be found on the companion CD-ROM, in the function `CIKSolverJacobianTranspose::Solve()` in the file CIKSolverJacobianTranspose.cpp.

Results and Comparison

As we are using an Euler integration step to solve Equation 2.6.10, careful consideration has to be taken when choosing the step size. A comparison between several different values using our sample implementation is shown in Figure 2.6.2 (the maximum number of iterations is 100).

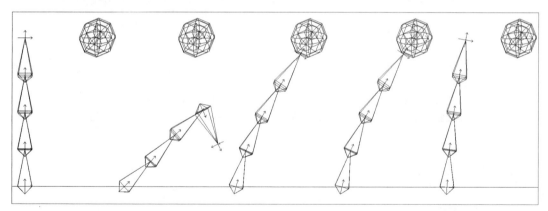

FIGURE 2.6.2 *Euler integration step size comparison. From left to right: initial setup, 0.1, 0.01, 0.001, and 0.0001.*

With a step size of 0.1, the algorithm doesn't converge at all, regardless of any modification to the iteration limit. When using a step size of 0.0001, the number of iterations has to be increased in order to reach the target. Note that a step size of 0.01 is being used for all of the following tests.

First, let's compare the results generated by the Jacobian Transpose (JT) to that from our generic implementation of the CCD.

In the first case, the target is located just to the right and below the effector. The chain consists of seven nodes with no constraints applied to the rotations. The iteration limit is set to 100. Figure 2.6.3 illustrates the main difference between the two

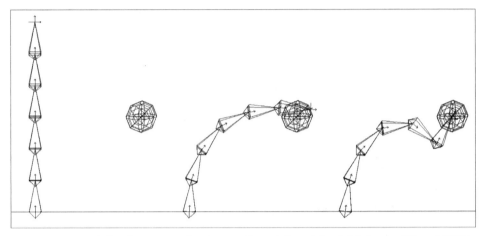

FIGURE 2.6.3   *A simple unconstrained setup. From left to right: initial state, JT, and CCD.*

algorithms. While the Jacobian Transpose distributes rotations evenly across the manipulator, the CCD considers each link independently.

The setup from Figure 2.6.4 is almost identical to the previous one, except that in this case, the rotations around the principal axes are limited to ±50 degrees. We see

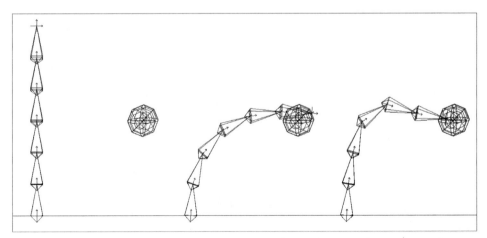

FIGURE 2.6.4   *A simple constrained setup. From left to right: initial state, JT, and CCD.*

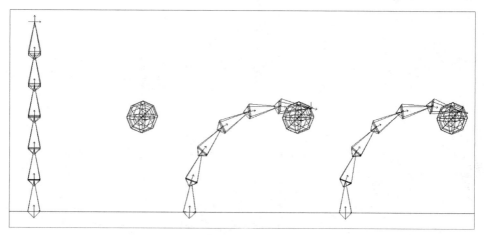

FIGURE 2.6.5 *Another constrained setup with tighter limits. From left to right: initial state, JT, and CCD.*

that the CCD result improves, while the JT appears unchanged. Note that in our sample implementation only a simple Euler angle-clamping scheme is used.

Figure 2.6.5 shows that with tighter limits (±20 degrees), both methods are unable to reach the target and that the CCD's appearance is improved again.

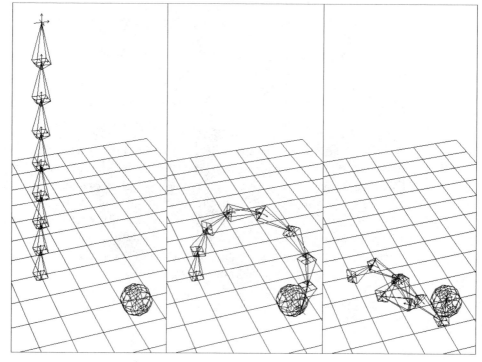

FIGURE 2.6.6 *A complex setup without constraints. From left to right: initial state, JT, and CCD.*

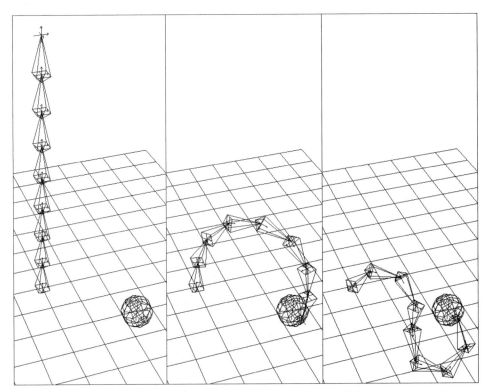

FIGURE 2.6.7 *A complex setup with constraints applied. From left to right: initial state, JT, and CCD.*

Our second test case uses a more sophisticated setup (see Figure 2.6.6). The target is located on the floor away from the effector. The chain consists of nine nodes with no constraints applied to the rotations. Again, the iteration limit is set to 100. While the JT manages to smoothly reach the target, the CCD gives a rather chaotic solution.

As in the two-dimensional test, the rotations are clamped to ±50 degrees. Again, Figure 2.6.7 shows that in this case, the JT still manages to appear smooth while the CCD provides a more precise, yet less satisfying solution.

Finally, the last comparison as seen in Figure 2.6.8 proves that the CCD catches up when using tight rotational limits (±20 degrees).

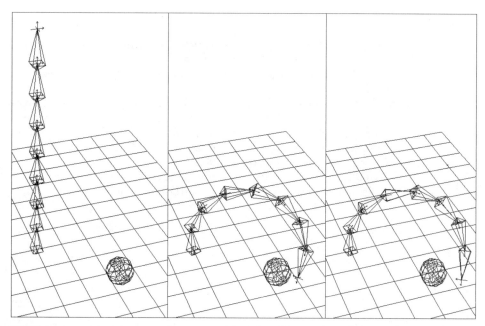

FIGURE 2.6.8 *Another complex setup with tighter limits. From left to right: initial state, JT, and CCD.*

Conclusion

We presented a powerful alternative to the Cyclic Coordinate Descent (CCD) that dominates in unconstrained environments and when using larger rotational limits. Its evenly distributed node rotations provide superior results.

What we haven't dealt with is the way the degrees of freedom are constrained. In our sample implementation, for the sake of clarity, only the quaternion-to-Euler conversion is used to clamp the rotation (using pitch/yaw/roll limits) before storing the resulting quaternion. Note that this doesn't have any noticeable influence on the convergence criteria, as the Jacobian is recomputed for every step. We strongly encourage the reader to look at texts like [Weber02] or [Blow02] for more advanced methods to clamp rotations. Additionally, [Welman93] contains a chapter on incorporating constraints.

Finally, a last word about matching the target's orientation. As mentioned before, we omit the twisting force from Welman's original Equation 2.6.8 in favor of the simplified Equation 2.6.7. To extend the method presented in this article, one could determine a torque to map the orientation of the effector to that of the target, and put the corresponding axis into the force used to pull at the tip of the manipulator.

References

[Blow02] Blow, Jonathan, "Inverse Kinematics with Joint Limits," *Game Developer* Vol. 9, No. 4 (April 2002): pp. 16–18.

[Paul81] Paul, R.P., *Robot Manipulators: Mathematics, Programming, and Control*, MIT Press, 1981.

[Schreiber98] Schreiber, Guenther, and G. Hirzinger, "Singularity Consistent Inverse Kinematics by Enhancing the Jacobian Transpose," German Aerospace Center—DLR, available online at *www.robotic.dlr.de/Guenter.Schreiber/ark1998.pdf*.

[Weber02] Weber, Jason, "Constrained Inverse Kinematics," *Game Programming Gems 3*, Charles River Media, 2002.

[Welman93] Welman, Chris, "Inverse Kinematics and Geometric Constraints for Articulated Figure Manipulation," Master's Thesis, Simon Frasier University, September 1993.

PHYSICS

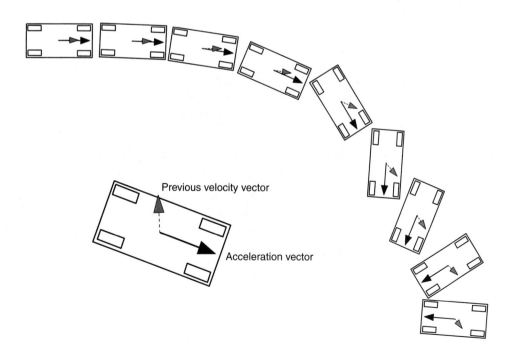

Previous velocity vector

Acceleration vector

Introduction

Graham Rhodes,

Applied Research Associates, Inc.

grhodes@nc.rr.com

I've admired that most curious of physicists, the late Richard Feynman, for many years. Not, as you might be thinking, because of his contributions to our understanding of the physical universe. Beyond physics, Feynman enjoyed every nuance of life, loved to play, and jumped at every opportunity to explore a new experience. His love of games once compelled him to test his inner bloodhound at a party at Caltech, where he delighted the crowd using his very human sense of smell to accurately match individual partygoers with books they had briefly handled away from his sight. He delighted in picking locks and cracking safes during his days at Los Alamos (only to point out design flaws so the contents might be better secured!), and independently translated the Dresden Codex using puzzle-solving techniques. Feynman learned to draw and paint, and was an accomplished bongo drum player.

Game development, more than any other industry I've been involved with, requires this same driving desire to learn, to experiment, and to play. Over the past few years, physics has become one of the many important disciplines of game development. Real-time physics has always been at the core of flight simulators, and to some degree racing games. Today, however, the discipline is proliferating throughout all game genres. To my way of thinking, there are three primary benefits to using real-time physics in games. First (arguably the most important benefit), given the proper pipeline tools, physics can significantly reduce the cost of producing animation for games by reducing the number of animations that must be created by an art team. (In the case of character animation in particular, motion-captured or artist-generated keyframe animation will continue to be necessary in order to apply personality to characters, but these can be blended with physics-based solutions to create an infinity of behaviors.) Second, physics can simulate arbitrary interaction between characters and objects and game worlds, enabling emergent behavior that is not practical using only artist-generated animation.

A third key benefit to using real-time physics is the cool factor. Present-day hardcore gamers regularly discuss the merits of rag doll character physics and interactive water in many Internet forums. Soon enough, the discussion will be about soft body dynamics and full physics-based characters. But eventually, I believe, the cool factor of real-time physics will go away. Use this to your best advantage for now, but continue to use physics to reduce your cost and make better games.

Welcome to the inaugural edition of the Physics Section of the *Game Programming Gems* series! Contained herein you will find a wide variety of topics that will help you to create your game. First up, Roger Smith and Don Stoner provide a set of formulas for estimating the probability that an attack will kill a target, based on live fire military experiments. Use wisely to supercharge your game's killing logic! Marcin Pancewicz and Paul Bragiel describe an elegant model for simplified vehicle physics that is small and fast and suitable for handheld game consoles. Their approach can be adapted to simulate land, sea, and air-based vehicles from a top-down perspective. Next, a trio of chapters can help you develop a complex rigid body dynamics system with sophisticated collision response. First, Nick Porcino presents an object-oriented Verlet integration-based rigid-body engine that can be the foundation for physics-based game worlds. Russ Smith discusses the mathematics of rigid-body constraints in an intuitive manner, removing much of the mystery from the simulation of complex mechanisms and articulating body interactions. Adam Moravanszky and Pierre Terdiman present several approaches to reducing the complexity of contact manifolds during collision detection, which can lead to improved stability (and possibly reduced computation cost) in collision response calculations. For a change of pace, Jerry Tessendorf presents a new method for simulating water waves, dubbed iWave, which readily supports interaction of the waves with objects. Finally, two articles illustrate novel techniques for simulating soft bodies. Thomas Di Giacomo and Nadia Magnenat-Thalmann describe a multilayer approach to simulating soft bodies that can simulate a wide variety of deformations with good speed and stability. Finally, James O'Brien presents the basics of modal analysis, which can be used for the real-time simulation of soft bodies in games, with 100-percent stability regardless of simulation time step or frame rate.

Although authoring tools for physics are improving, they are still difficult to use, and physics engines are not yet as robust as they need to be. My hope is that you will be able to use the articles found here to evolve your game engine and build something new. And perhaps, in the process, you can enable the future of gaming!

3.1

Ten Fingers of Death: Algorithms for Combat Killing

Roger Smith and Don Stoner,

Titan Corporation

roger@fingersofdeath.com,
don@fingersofdeath.com

Good shooting games need good killing algorithms. This article describes a series of "fingers of death," combat algorithms that can be used to improve the realism of combat decisions. Most of the algorithms discussed here were developed for the United States military and have been validated for use in one or more real combat simulations.

First-person shooter killing algorithms are fine, but some situations can be handled more accurately and efficiently by including geometry, statistics, probability, and aggregation. Massively multiplayer and real-time strategy games particularly include a lot of action that does not have to be modeled with individual line-of-sight (LOS) and targeting for a headshot. Other games can also benefit from the inclusion of multiple kill types that are based on real live-fire experiments. First-person shooters can equip enemies with some of these algorithms, while leaving the more detailed LOS algorithms for the avatar controlled by the human player.

Hitting a Ribbon

The first finger of death is a simple method for determining whether a shooter will hit a ribbon target like a road, river, long convoy of vehicles, or a serpentine creature (see Figure 3.1.1). If the target is so long that it is impossible to overshoot or undershoot its length, the probability of hitting the target is dependent only upon the width of the target and the standard deviation of the shot pattern of the weapon. This simple algorithm is also a good way to introduce the logic and mathematics behind several of the attrition algorithms that follow [Parry95].

Deviations in the impact point of the munitions being fired are due to factors such as the quality of the weapon, steadiness and skill of the human operator, variations in the construction of the projectile, and wind conditions.

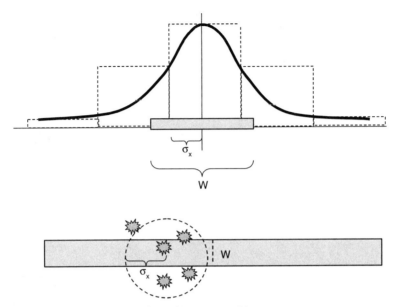

FIGURE 3.1.1   *Probability of hitting a ribbon target.*

The equation for the probability of hit (P_h) for a ribbon target is:

$$P_h = 2W \big/ \sqrt{2\pi}\sigma_x \tag{3.1.1}$$

where

    W is the width of the target

    σ_x is the standard deviation of the dispersion in the x direction

This assumes that the pattern is normally distributed with the same standard deviation in both the x and y dimensions.

ON THE CD

The code for all of these algorithms can be found on the companion CD-ROM.

Hitting the Bull's-Eye

The second finger of death describes the probability of hitting a round target. Like the previous algorithm, this one is based on the fact that all shooters, human and machine alike, have built-in variation in every shot fired.

The algorithm is driven by two very simple variables—the radius of the target, and the standard deviation of the rounds. This deviation is based on a normal distribution in which the mean value is zero, because the shooter is aimed directly at the center of the target [Parry95]. The algorithm determines whether each shot will hit the target, but does not calculate the actual impact point of the round. This simplification eliminates calculations that would have to be done to distribute the round normally in both the x and y direction.

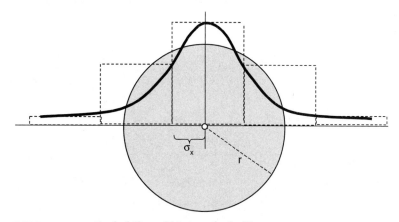

FIGURE 3.1.2   *Probability of hitting the bull's-eye.*

The equation for calculating the probability of hit (P_h) for a round target is:

$$P_h = 1 - e^{-\left(r^2/2\sigma_x^2\right)}$$

(3.1.2)

where

    r is the radius of the target
    σ_x is the standard deviation of the bullet dispersion in the x direction

Hitting a Rectangle

Most targets are not shaped like bull's-eyes, so we need a more flexible algorithm to shoot rectangular targets like the torso of a human or a vehicle. This algorithm includes measures for the length and width of a rectangular target [Parry95] (see Figure 3.1.3).

The equation for the probability of hit (P_h) for a rectangular target is:

$$P_h = \sqrt{A * B}$$

$$A = 1 - e^{-\left(2L^2/\pi\sigma_x^2\right)}$$

(3.1.3)

$$B = 1 - e^{-\left(2W^2/\pi\sigma_y^2\right)}$$

where

    L is the length of the target in the x direction
    W is the width of the target in the y direction
    σ_x is the standard deviation of the bullet dispersion in the x direction
    σ_y is the standard deviation of the bullet dispersion in the y direction

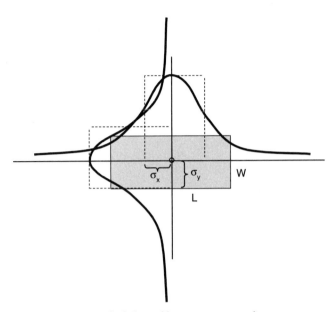

FIGURE 3.1.3   *Probability of hitting a rectangle.*

Weapons often have different standard deviations in the x and y dimensions. For example, when a football quarterback throws a pass, the variation from the aim point along the axis of flight is usually greater than the variation left or right of the aim point. The same is true for missiles being fired at a combat vehicle or rocks being thrown at a dinosaur.

Shotgunning a Small Target

Some weapons unleash a barrage of rockets, bomblets, or explosive munitions all at once in an attempt to totally overwhelm the target and blow it to smithereens. When this happens, there are much faster ways of determining the killing effect of the entire barrage than calculating the impact points and lethality of each rocket individually and then accumulating them.

This algorithm calculates the probability that one of the munitions' lethal areas will overlap with the point target. The size of the target is not considered in these calculations because it is assumed that the lethal blast area can encompass an entire target [Parry95] (see Figure 3.1.4).

$$P_k = 1 - e^{-\left(na/2\pi\sigma_x^2\right)}$$

where

n is the number of rounds in the barrage

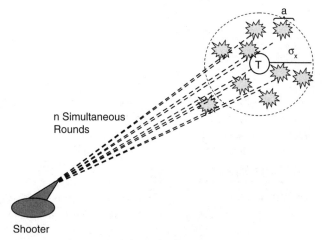

FIGURE 3.1.4   *Probability of killing a target with a simultaneous barrage of munitions.*

a is the lethal area of a single round against this target

σ_x is the standard deviation of the bullet dispersion in the x direction

Death by Walking Artillery

Artillery and catapult rounds are often adjusted by a spotting team that radios corrections back to the firing battery and allows them to place the next round closer to the target. The lethality of such a barrage is higher than the previous shotgunning method. It is calculated through a summation series in the exponent [Parry95] (see Figure 3.1.5).

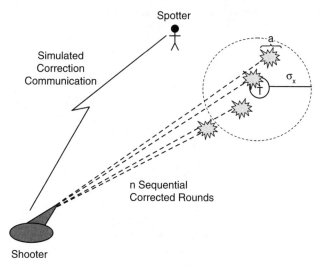

FIGURE 3.1.5   *Lethality of walking artillery with a spotter.*

$$P_k = 1 - e^{-\left(\left(a^2/2\sigma_x^2\right) * \sum_{i=2}^{n} (i-1)/i\right)}$$ (3.1.4)

where

n is the number of rounds fired in the barrage

a is the lethal area of a single round against this target

σ_x is the standard deviation of the bullet dispersion in the x direction

Kills Come in Four Flavors

To paraphrase a famous pig, "All kills are equal, but some are more equal than others." Military simulations usually model four different types of kills that are most often found in real-world combat. The first flavor is a mobility kill, in which the target is no longer able to move, but remains alive enough to fire its weapon or communicate with other vehicles. The second is a firepower kill, in which the weapon is damaged, but the vehicle or person is still able to move. The third is a mobility *and* firepower kill in which the vehicle or person is still alive, but cannot move or use its weapon. This target might still be able to observe enemy operations, communicate, consume supplies, and, in some simulations, trigger a rescue operation. The final kill type is the catastrophic kill or K-kill, often pictured as an aircraft exploding into a million pieces, a flaming tank turret spinning through the air, or a person being turned into fresh chunks of meat.

These four kill types can be pictured as a Venn diagram (see Figure 3.1.6). Although this form clearly communicates the relationships between the kill types, in order to be applied, it has to be separated so that a specific kill type can be determined quickly for each engagement. This separated data is usually represented as a kill thermometer (see Figure 3.1.7). Normalizing the kill types in a single space as represented in the thermometer allows a program to determine the kill type of an engagement by drawing a single random number.

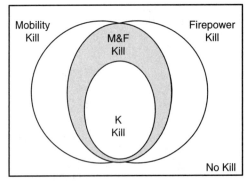

FIGURE 3.1.6   *Standard kill types.*

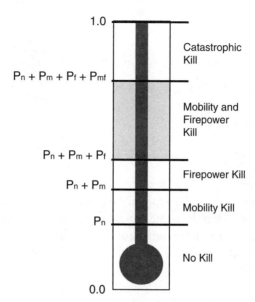

FIGURE 3.1.7 *Kill thermometer.*

Live-fire projects determine the probability of each kill type under different conditions by firing real weapons at real targets and measuring the result. Most simulations and games do not have access to such a rich source of information. Therefore, we have to identify common trends in experimental data and create equations that mimic those, while remaining flexible enough to be applied to new weapon/target pairs. One simulation project noticed a distinct relationship between the mobility, firepower, and catastrophic kill data they had received from live-fire experiments. This relationship allowed them to create simple equations that use the root of a single "probability of mobility or firepower kill" (P_{MoF} is the union of all of the shaded areas in Figure 3.1.7) to calculate all of the other probabilities. The trend they noticed was that a mobility kill occurred 90 percent of the time that damage was done ($P_M = 0.9 * P_{MoF}$); a firepower kill occurred 90 percent of the time ($P_F = 0.9 * P_{MoF}$); and a catastrophic kill occurred 50 percent of the time that damage was done ($P_K = 0.5 * P_{MoF}$).

However, this information cannot be applied directly to the kill thermometer in Figure 3.1.7. P_M does not say that 90 percent of all engagements result in a mobility kill. It says that 90 percent of mobility-or-firepower kills include a mobility kill. Therefore, it has to be separated to make it possible to draw a single random number and determine which kill to apply to the target. These independent kill probabilities can be extracted as shown here:

$$P_n = 1.0 - P_{MoF}$$

$$P_m = P_{MoF} - P_F = 0.1 * P_{MoF}$$

$$P_f = P_{MoF} - P_M = 0.1 * P_{MoF}$$

$$P_k = 0.5 * P_{MoF}$$

$$P_{mf} = P_{MoF} - P_m - P_f - P_k = 0.3 * P_{MoF}$$

(3.1.5)

where the small subscript indicates the probability that only one type of kill occurs. For example, P_m is the probability of *only* getting a mobility kill, but not getting any other form of kill. P_n is the probability of no kill occurring.

ON THE CD

These independent kill probabilities determine where the breakpoints fall in a kill thermometer. A sample implementation is shown in the code on the companion CD-ROM.

Chemicals, Fireballs, and Area Magic

There have been many models of the dispersion of chemicals and other agents. The following simple algorithm calculates the probability of a kill based on the volume of chemical released and the distance that the release occurs from the target. For games, this algorithm could be used for expanding fireballs, area magic, or any other exotic and evil weapon.

$$P_k = \left(\sqrt[3]{nw_r} \bigg/ \sqrt{2\pi} \right) * e^{-0.5*\left(k*d^2/nw_r\right)^2}$$

(3.1.6)

where

n is the number of rounds impacting at a specific point
w_r is the weight of the chemical inside of each round (in kilograms)
d is the distance that the rounds fall from the target location (in meters)
k is a constant representing the dispersion characteristic of the chemical. For these experiments, we recommend beginning with a value of 0.00135.

This equation allows you to deal with each round individually, or to aggregate multiple rounds into a single attack centered at the same impact point. The equation also incorporates the constant k that represents the density and viscosity of a chemical compound. You can adjust this value to create the effect desired.

The Shrapnel Wedge

A missile seldom shoots down an aircraft by flying directly into it. More often, the missile reaches a "point of closest approach" and explodes near the aircraft. The shrapnel from the missile then spreads out in a donut or spherical pattern from the point of explosion and the aircraft is caught in that shrapnel pattern and destroyed [Ball85]. This algorithm can be used with exploding projectiles, fireballs, and magic targeted at aircraft, dragons, and other enemies (see Figure 3.1.8).

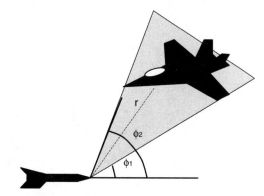

FIGURE 3.1.8 *Probability of killing a target in a shrapnel wedge.*

$$x = nA_v \Big/ \left(2\pi r^2 \left(\cos \phi_1 - \cos \phi_2 \right) \right)$$

$$P_k = 1 - e^{-x}$$

(3.1.7)

where

> n is the number of fragments or projectiles in the missile warhead
> A_v is the vulnerable area of the target presented to the missile, in square meters
> r is the range from the detonation point to the target, in meters
> ϕ_1 is the angle from the trajectory of the missile to the near edge of the vulnerability area of the target
> ϕ_2 is the angle from the trajectory of the missile to the far edge of the vulnerability area of the target

Beating the Bushes

Some engagements involve teams of hunters searching the terrain or bushes for hidden prey [Shubik83]. When a large group of hunters is looking for a large group of prey, it is possible to model the capture or kill of the prey in an aggregate form, rather than representing the individual movement and line-of-sight of every hunter and every prey. As before, this approach is very valuable when the hunting and killing is being conducted by AI-controlled hunters, and especially when it is happening off the player's screen.

The algorithm is structured to calculate the change in the population of the prey based on the number and efficiency of the hunters. It also accounts for different types of prey and hunter animals; for example, small rodents, medium-sized wolves, and large elephants.

To use the algorithm, we must define a probability of detection for each type of hunter against each type of prey under the given conditions (open terrain, forest, city, etc.). We must also select a "hardness" factor that differentiates the ability of the prey to elude, escape, or survive the actions of the hunter. These numbers are usually determined heuristically through experimentation and observation (see Figure 3.1.9).

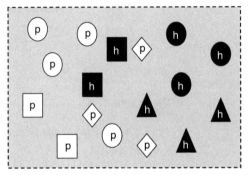

Prey are Light   Hunters are Dark

FIGURE 3.1.9 *Multiple types of hunters searching for multiple types of prey.*

$$x = \left(\left(k_j / p \right) * \sum_{i=1}^{n} D_{i,j} * h_i \right)$$

$$A_j = p_j * (1 - e^{-x})$$

(3.1.8)

where

   A_j is the number of kills of animal type j
   p_j is the number of prey of type j
   k_j is a hardness measure of the prey in the range [0,1]
   p is the total number of prey of all types
   n is the number of prey types
   $D_{i,j}$ is the probability that a hunter of type i can detect a prey of type j
   h_i is the number of hunters of type i

Beating the Bushes with Prey Spacing

The final finger of death is a modification of the previous one. Mathematicians and analysts noticed that the previous algorithm did not account for differences in the density of prey hiding in the bushes. It is clearly much easier to find and kill prey when there are a hundred of them in the search area than when there are just two or three. Therefore, they created a variation known as the Lulejian model [Shubik83] in which the spacing between the prey is an important factor. The visual picture for this algorithm is the same as that shown previously, but the mathematics differ to account for the spacing of prey. The definition of k_j also varies slightly in that Lilejian defines k_j as the average destruction of the hunters on prey type j.

$$x = \left(\sum_{i=1}^{n} k_j * h_i \right) \Big/ \left(s * p \right)$$

(3.1.9)

$$A_j = p_j * (1 - e^{-x})$$

where

A_j is the number of kills of prey type j
p_j is the number of prey of type j
s is the average spacing between the prey in the search area, in meters
p is the total number of prey of all types
n is the number of prey types
k_j is the average destruction of the hunters on prey type j, in the range [0,1]
h_i is the number of hunters of type i

Conclusion

The Ten Fingers of Death described in this article are just a few of the combat killing algorithms that can be applied to computer games. The concepts of geometry, probability, statistics, and physics used in the ten Fingers of Death are good examples of approaches to many problems. Game developers should do what military modelers do to improve these—apply experience, mathematics, creativity, and other sciences to find equations that work well for your game. Don't be afraid to experiment!

References

[Ball85] Ball, Robert E., *The Fundamentals of Aircraft Combat Survivability Analysis and Design*, AIAA Press, 1985.

[Parry95] Parry, Samuel, editor, *Military OR Analyst's Handbook: Conventional Weapons Effects*, Military Operations Research Society, 1995.

[Shubik83] Shubik, Martin, editor, *Mathematics of Conflict*, Elsevier Science Publishers, 1983.

3.2

Vehicle Physics Simulation for CPU-Limited Systems

Marcin Pancewicz, Infinite Dreams, and Paul Bragiel, Paragon Five

highway@idreams.com.pl, paul@paragon5.com

During the development of our first top-down racing game, we faced the problem of creating a fast and flexible physics engine that would work on a CPU-limited system. The engine needed to provide us with the ability to create a broad range of vehicles, ranging from snowmobiles and racing cars to nonland-based vehicles such as helicopters and hovercraft. In this article, we present the details of such an engine. This one was crafted to work on a handheld console with very limited system resources. We hope the algorithms presented here will help you to create your own physics engine based on our solutions.

Assumptions and Overview of the Technique

By carefully observing moving vehicles, you will notice that there are two fundamental elements of the vehicle motion: *acceleration*, due to the throttle and braking, and *steering*. By decoupling the problem to simulate these two elements independently, it is possible to create a very flexible system using a simplified physics rule set that is computationally inexpensive. To simplify calculations, assume that:

- The vehicle throttle causes acceleration only in the current direction. Braking causes acceleration in the opposite direction.
- The time step for each frame is exactly 1.0 so that acceleration can simply be added to the vehicle's previous velocity to determine the updated velocity.
- The vehicle can be freely rotated. This will be presented later, in the section titled *Steering*.

The independent parameters used to simulate the vehicle motion, rotation angle, and acceleration are presented in Figure 3.2.1. The following sections describe the simulation of acceleration and steering.

Vehicle Acceleration/Deceleration along Its Current Orientation Vector

A vehicle's acceleration depends directly on the force acting on it, but to simplify the physics you can assume that the vehicle accelerates in a constrained manner that suits your needs.

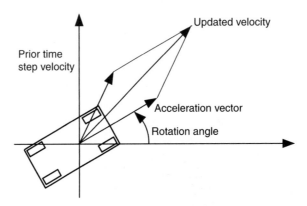

FIGURE 3.2.1 *Simplified parameters of a vehicle's motion.*

As we know, for constant acceleration and zero initial speed, the current speed of motion equals acceleration multiplied by time:

$$v = at \tag{3.2.1}$$

where v represents velocity, a represents acceleration, and t represents running time measured from the time of the initial state.

However, constant acceleration is not very common in games. To allow for variable acceleration, you will need to integrate the following equation to get a value that can be added to the current v for every game iteration.

$$v'(t) = a \tag{3.2.2}$$

(The apostrophe indicates differentiation with respect to time; e.g., the time derivative of velocity is acceleration.) The following equation represents the numerical integration of Equation 3.2.2 using the explicit Euler technique. Recall from the prior section that the time step has been implicitly set to 1.0 for this and all subsequent equations, both for simplicity and to reduce the number of floating-point calculations required. If you want to use a time step other than 1.0, then a must be multiplied by the time step before adding to the previous velocity.

$$v_n = v_{n-1} + a \tag{3.2.3}$$

This equation applies not only to all ideal driving conditions, but also for nonideal conditions in which external forces are applied to the vehicle. You simply need to include the external forces in your calculation of a. Explicit Euler integration isn't the most robust technique, but for the purposes of this simple engine it is adequately precise and very fast. As long as you do not include springlike forces, it also should be fairly stable.

To achieve more realistic motion, we have to take friction into consideration. For our CPU-limited engine, we assume that for each iteration, the previous speed of the object is reduced by a constant factor. While this is not strictly correct in terms of physics, it's a safe enough assumption for our purposes. For our purposes we can call it f for friction, although it doesn't really represent a friction force. The value of f can change depending on current terrain.

This leads our equation to become:

$$v_n = f v_{n-1} + a \tag{3.2.4}$$

In this equation, velocity (v) and acceleration (a) are vectors and the friction factor (f) is a scalar.

Unless you include external forces when calculating a, the acceleration in Equation 3.2.4 represents only the acceleration due to thrust or applied engine torque, or braking, which will be described in the next section. The most convenient way to model the acceleration vector is to use polar coordinates. This way, you can easily direct your car in the desired direction (represented by an angle, *rot*) and represent the force due to acceleration as a single value equal to the vector's length. Conversion from a polar coordinate system to a normal (Cartesian) coordinate system is very easy, as shown in Figure 3.2.2.

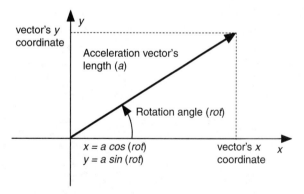

FIGURE 3.2.2   *Conversion from a polar to a Cartesian coordinate system.*

As you can see, the code fragment is very simple.

```
// first we have to multiply the 2D vector Vnm1 —
// described by the Cartesian coordinates x and y —
```

```
// by the scalar fraction factor F:

Vn_x = Vnm1_x*F; // nm1 means n-1
Vn_y = Vnm1_y*F;

// then add to it the acceleration vector, described
// in polar coordinates:

Vn_x += A*cos(rot);
Vn_y += A*sin(rot);
```

Now your car can accelerate when you press down on the acceleration pedal, and come to a slow stop when you release it.

Simulating Input Devices

One small problem is that on most handheld consoles, the acceleration pedal is represented by a single button, which has only two states, on and off. An equivalent real-life situation of this would be a big, blocky Trans Am with only a two-state throttle: fully open and fully closed. In driving such a car, you would suffer some nice neck strain from constantly being thrust into the back of your seat each time you tried to push down the acceleration pedal.

One of the solutions is to change from an on-off acceleration model to an acceleration model that grows over time while the acceleration button is held down and decreases over time when the button is released. You should also impose an initial value and an upper limit to keep the acceleration within a reasonable range. You can tweak the system to get more lifelike results, including making your acceleration grow faster than the deceleration or vice versa. A corresponding diagram is shown in Figure 3.2.3. The behavior indicated in the figure causes the vehicle to moderately slow down when you release the acceleration button.

At times, you will need to push hard on the brake pedal, perhaps to avoid a collision with another player. In such a situation you would need to use the brake button. Its implementation is very simple. When a player depresses the brake button, in

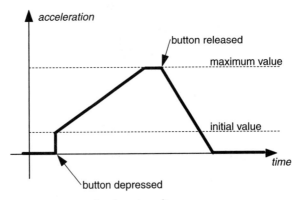

FIGURE 3.2.3   *Acceleration diagram.*

Equation 3.2.4 you shouldn't use the current acceleration a, but the negative value b, which represents the braking acceleration (e.g., deceleration). More precisely, the value of b doesn't represent additional friction acting on the vehicle (as it does in a real car), but rather corresponds to choosing a reverse gear. In your game, the net effect will be similar, and as a bonus, you will be able to use the brake button as a reverse button.

Steering

In most handheld consoles, there is a limited number of buttons with which to work. For example, on the Nintendo GameBoy Advance (GBA) there are only two standard buttons, two shoulder buttons, and a four-way directional pad. In our implementation, we needed to use a few of the buttons for various weapons and turbo. That leaves us with two remaining buttons for steering. Luckily, two buttons are quite enough.

The simplest solution is to assign each button a function that increases or decreases the vehicle's rotation angle. As with the acceleration button, steering buttons have only two states, on and off. That means that for every frame, the rotation angle (rot) will need to be changed by some fixed amount ($drot$).

$$rot_n = rot_{n-1} - drot \qquad\qquad (3.2.5)$$

If you set $drot$ to be a constant, say 5 degrees, the steering model will look unnatural because your vehicle will have the appearance of having a fixed rotation speed, as opposed to real-life vehicles with proportional steering devices. To simulate such devices, you will need to change the rotation speed in response to the duration of the steering button being held down. As with the acceleration pedal, you should use some initial and maximum values. You should also differentiate the rate of change in speed for the depressed and released button states (see Figure 3.2.4).

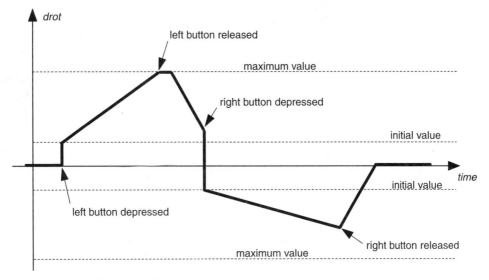

FIGURE 3.2.4 *Changing the rotation factor.*

In our games, we assumed that the vehicle could spin freely. It looks a little bit unnatural, but helps the player to control the vehicle, especially in tough spots. If you want to simulate a more realistic behavior, you can block the user from rotating the vehicle when it is not in motion. You can also move the vehicle's pivot point from its center to its back, simulating steering being done by the front wheels.

Putting It All Together

The two simple mechanisms just described allow the player to drive his or her vehicle following a designed racetrack. Because acceleration has been separated from the steering, some interesting effects are possible, such as skids or simulating a parking brake pull to quickly turn the car 180 degrees. For example, if you're driving at the top speed of your car, while simultaneously depressing and holding one of the steering buttons, you will rotate, but your car will drift to its side. As illustrated in Figure 3.2.5, this can make for some really nice rally car type effects.

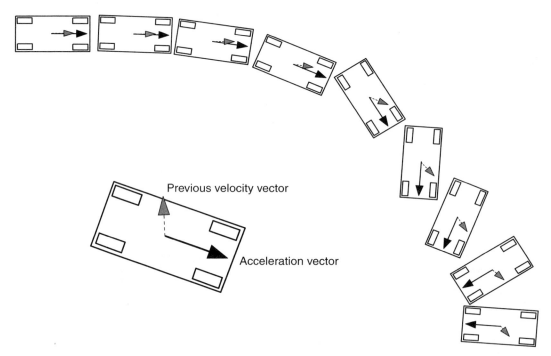

FIGURE 3.2.5 *Vehicle rotation, acceleration, and velocity vector in consecutive frames.*

Influence of Terrain

In each frame, the vehicle probes for the type of terrain it is driving on. Each terrain type has its own set of variables, influencing the acceleration, friction, and rotation of the vehicle. In defining such variables, we can create effects such as oil spilled on the road, an icy bridge, or mud, which can significantly affect driving properties of the vehicle. At the beginning of the simulation's main function, which calculates the cars' physics, you could insert code similar to the code fragment presented here (the fixed-point arithmetic details will be described in the next section):

```
...
// Calculate terrain influences.
// We use them to modify acceleration and steering
// parameters, where:

//   accel       = magnitude of maximum acceleration
//   friction    = friction factor
//   start_drot  = initial value of rotation
//                 changing angle
//   max_drot    = maximum value of rot. changing
//                 angle
//   delta_drot  = increase of rot. changing angle
//   return_drot = decrease of rot. changing angle

char terrain = getMask(car_pos_x, car_pos_y);

switch(terrain){
// standard road surface
case TERR_ROAD :
    // 51 == 0.2*256 = .2 in 8 bit fixed point arithm.
    accel     = 51;
    // 64225 == 0.98 in 16 bit arithmetics
    friction   = 64225;
    // 0x100 == 1 == 1/256 of full circle
    start_drot = 0x100;
    // 0x500 == 5/256 of full circle
    max_drot = 0x500;
    // 0x80 == 0.5/256 of full circle
    delta_drot = 0x80;
    return_drot = 0x80;
    break;
// ice on the road: our vehicle should lose grip
case TERR_ICE :
    accel     = 51;
    friction   = 65208; // 0.995 in 16 bit fp arithm.
    start_drot = 0x40;   // 0.25/256
    max_drot = 0x700;
    delta_drot = 0x20;
    return_drot = 0x20;
    break;
...
```

Implementation Issues

To maximize speed and minimize overhead on platforms that don't have floating-point processors, you should use fixed-point numbers in your calculations. In such

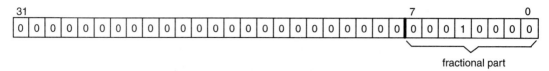

FIGURE 3.2.6   *Fixed-point number with eight digits after the decimal point represented as a 32-bit integer.*

numbers, we assume the fixed position of a decimal point; for example, after the eighth bit of a value, as shown in Figure 3.2.6.

Such values should be treated as divisible by a fixed divisor; in this case the divisor has a value $2^8 = 256$, so we should interpret the presented value (10000_2) as $16/256 = 0.0625$.

The CPU and compiler know nothing about fixed-point values, and instead treat them as plain integer variables. Operations on integer variables are very fast, so addition and subtraction cost us almost nothing, but in the case of multiplication of two fixed-point numbers, the result must be adjusted. After such multiplication you have to downshift the result (e.g., shift it to the right). The shift amount equals the number of fixed-point bits. For example:

$$
\begin{array}{r}
0000\ 0000\ .\ 0001\ 0000 = 16\ /\ 256 = 0.0625 \\
\times\ \underline{0000\ 0000\ .\ 0010\ 0000 = 32\ /\ 256\ =\ 0.125} \\
\\
= 0000\ 0010\ .\ 0000\ 0000 = 512\ /\ 256 = 2.0
\end{array}
$$

As you can see, multiplying 0.0625 by 0.125 gives us a value of 2.0, which is obviously wrong. The result must be shifted eight bits to the right, giving a value of 0. 0000 0010, which equals $2/256 = 0.0078125$, which is exactly $16/256 \times 32/256 = 0.0625 \times 0.125$.

Multiplication of fixed-point numbers by integers requires no adjusting, but adding (or subtracting) integers to (and from) fixed-point numbers requires scaling (shifting left) integers to the fixed-point format. To convert fixed-point numbers to integer values, just drop the fractional part of the fixed-point number by shifting the fixed-point value eight bits to the right.

For cases where division was needed, we decided to not use CPU time in the implementation. You might want to choose the same route, but it depends on how much processor time you have at your disposal. We decided to use a large quotient table instead of using the CPU to divide two numbers. While we lost some precision in the process, we were able to achieve maximum speeds during the calculation process.

Similarly, the trigonometric functions, sine and cosine, are also represented by a table with 32-bit values (with 16-bit fixed-point precision) for every 1/256 of full circle. You can create macros as shown here that perform a lookup into the tables:

```
#define    _SIN16(a) (sincos16[(a)&0xff])
#define    _COS16(a) (sincos16[(((a)&0xff)+64)])
```

Note that the cosine macro uses the same table as the sine macro, but takes values from indices shifted by 64 positions (64/256 represents 90 degrees of full circle). This way, we saved valuable memory.

In the game engine, some parameters (e.g., friction factor) are very sensitive to small changes, so we decided to use 16-bit fixed-point numbers to represent them. This requires a little more caution when scaling is used, but the general principles remain the same.

During development, we noticed some strange things when multiplying small negative fixed-point numbers by positive numbers. In some cases after multiplication, we got results that equaled exactly the multiplicand, although the multiplier was different from the value 1. The culprit ended up being the result of an overflow. To avoid such a situation, we suggest that you check for a negative multiplicand. In this case, negate it while making calculations and then use the negated product.

```
if (value < 0)
    value = -(((-value) * any_factor)>8);
else
    value = (value * any_factor)>8;
```

Potential Improvements

If you would like to use this engine in your own game and would like more accuracy, you can improve the vehicle drivability resulting from the linear simulation of the accelerator or steering wheel. One suggestion is to use a lookup table that defines the behavior of the acceleration pedal or steering wheel after pressing and holding it over a period of time. You can use a 64- or 128-position array with 16-bit fixed-point (including 8 bits for the fraction part) values to hold acceleration parameters for 64 or 128 frames after pressing or releasing the respective buttons. For example, you can fill your array with values from the diagram shown in Figure 3.2.7. This simulates the effect of a violent burst of an afterburner, which then slowly fades out, with the delayed start of the turbo compressor.

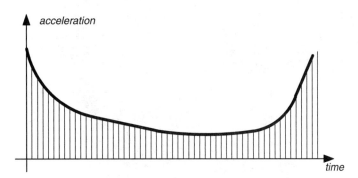

FIGURE 3.2.7 *Simulating complex acceleration changes.*

Conclusion

The algorithm and code snippets presented here are only the basic workings of the skeleton; they must be precisely tuned to give you exactly what you need. To implement this system in a commercial title, you will want to develop production tools, such as an editor with fields allowing precision tuning of every vehicle and terrain parameter. Once you have the tools in place, they can be used to create many types of games, not only vehicle racers, but also shoot-'em-ups, platform games, and any 2D game involving objects moving according to physics rules.

3.3

Writing a Verlet-Based Physics Engine

Nick Porcino, LucasArts

nporcino@lucasarts.com

Games often sport a physical process that needs to be modeled—weather, crates, vehicles, mechanical systems, characters, and so on. If the process can be modeled with equations, an algorithm can be derived to simulate the process. A class of systems of particular interest for games is rigid body dynamics. Such a simulator models systems of rigid bodies that have physical properties, can contact each other, and collide. Soft bodies such as cloth and hair can co-exist in such a simulation. Forces can be input to the system during a frame, making the simulation particularly interesting.

ON THE CD

It can be much easier than you might think to implement a reasonably accurate and sophisticated physics engine. This article describes how it can be done through the description of a simple engine, included on the companion CD-ROM.

About Physics Engines

There are several kinds of simulation: *offline*, wherein the simulation proceeds slower than the real thing; *online*, which runs as fast as the real thing; *interactive*, which runs fast enough that a person can interact with the simulation from within the loop; and *real-time*, which guarantees that a system will be updated at a certain rate. The physics engine presented here is interactive if there are not too many objects in the simulation.

A game has a number of other components besides a physics engine, including rendering, file systems, AI, and so on. A physics engine provides none of those things, and should have no direct interaction with them. In other words, an AI system or rendering system can query the physics engine to retrieve such things as a body's transformation matrix, but the physics engine does not provide AI facilities or rendering functions.

Most of the literature on physics engines for games focuses either on Verlet integration for nonrigid bodies (such as cloth or rag-dolls) modeled as spring systems [Jakobsen03], or the solution of ordinary differential equations for rigid bodies [Hecker96], [Baraff97]. This article shows that with the incorporation of angular effects, the Verlet integrator can also be applied to rigid body simulations.

Furthermore, most presentations of collision within physics engines focus on constraint methods [Smith04], or penalty systems [Jakobsen03]. The engine presented in this article uses the relatively recent technique of impulse-based dynamic simulation and micro-collisions [Mirtich95].

This article does not describe constraint systems, or the simulation of articulated bodies, or the equations of motion. For a grounding in these fundamentals, please refer to Chris Hecker's [Hecker96] or David Baraff's excellent series of articles [Baraff97]. [Smith04] contains a discussion on constraint Jacobians.

Rigid Bodies

A rigid body object is a collection of dynamic and static properties. The dynamic properties of the object are its position and velocity, as well as its orientation, angular velocity, and angular momentum. The static properties of an object are its dimensions, mass, inertia tensor, velocity damping (for friction), and information used for collision calculations. The inertia tensor is a triple integral over the body's volume and mass; it must be recalculated whenever the mass or shape of the body changes. A rigid body object can track other generally useful information such as whether the object can spin, how it participates in collisions, if it is active, and so on.

The dynamic state of the body at the end of the previous time step needs to be tracked while the new dynamic state is built. Forces and torques acting on the body (including friction) are summed into accumulators during a frame for use by the integrator.

The Integrator

There are two major categories of integrators: *implicit* and *explicit*. Implicit integrators must solve a system of equations to determine the present time step, whereas an explicit integrator iterates a system forward using explicit finite differences. The explicit Euler integrator is the simplest of these. The Verlet integrator is a second order explicit difference based integrator that is created by adding two steps of a Taylor series expansion of the equations of motion, one forward and one backward [Verlet67].

$$x(t + d) = x(t) + v(t)dt + F(t)dt^2 / 2m + \ldots \tag{3.3.1}$$
$$x(t - d) = x(t) - v(t)dt + F(t)dt^2 / 2m + \ldots \tag{3.3.2}$$

Adding (3.3.1) and (3.3.2) yields the basic Verlet integrator commonly found in game engines.

$$x(t + dt) = 2x(t) - x(t - dt) + F(t)dt^2 / m + O(dt^4) \tag{3.3.3}$$

Equation 3.3.3 requires only object positions; velocities are approximated at each time step. This integrator uses less memory compared to an integrator that explicitly tracks velocities, and has advantages where the velocities cannot be reliably derived. It is particularly suitable for computationally expensive simulations such as cloth and finite element systems. The primary disadvantage of Equation 3.3.3 is that since accelerations due to the application of force are added directly to position and the approximated velocity, the integrator diverges from an accurate solution very quickly.

In many engines, the divergence of the integrator is reduced through heavy damping, but the resulting simulation can suffer noticeably. In particular, energy will rapidly bleed out of the system, making the simulation feel mushy or sloppy. For some applications, such as cloth simulation, the damping of motion is desirable, and the inexpensive computational cost of the basic Verlet integrator is a perfect match. In simulations involving rigid body dynamics, something more robust is in order.

There are two well-known variations of the Verlet integrator: the Leap Frog integrator, and the velocity-based Verlet integrator. The Leap Frog integrator breaks a single integration step up and evaluates the position at the midpoint of the velocity calculation, and the velocity at the midpoint of the position calculation. The Leap Frog integrator offers better numerical precision, but the velocities are still derived instead of explicitly integrated. The velocity-based Verlet integrator explicitly evaluates the position and velocity at each step. It is the most accurate of the Verlet integrators, although it has the added storage cost of the velocities.

The form of the velocity-based Verlet integrator is reminiscent of high school physics.

$$x(t + dt) = x(t) + v(t)dt + a(t)dt^2 / 2 \qquad (3.3.4)$$

In this equation, x is position, t is time, dt is the time step, v is velocity, and a is acceleration. Acceleration is derived from the sum of all the external forces input during the frame, divided by the mass of the object.

$$a = F / m \qquad (3.3.5)$$

Forces can come from springs, motors, force fields, gravity, friction, viscosity, and so on.

$$F = F_{external} - \sum_{i=springs} d_i k_i x_i \qquad (3.3.6)$$

where the $F_{external}$ term represents externally applied forces except springs, and the rest of the equation describes the springs. The unit length current direction of the spring, d, is measured as pointing away from the mass or object connected to the spring, k is the spring stiffness coefficient, and x is the current length of the spring minus its rest length. If the spring is stretched, it will pull the object in the direction of the spring; if compressed, it will push the object in the opposite direction. A spring damping term, calculated as a per-spring damping constant times the rate at which a spring changed its length during the time step can be subtracted from Equation 3.3.6.

In reality, the integration step is more complicated than simple high school physics; the velocity update equation includes the calculation of the acceleration at the midpoint, and at the end of the time step.

$$v(t + dt) = v(t) + [a(t) + a(t + dt)] \, dt / 2 \qquad (3.3.7)$$

For soft bodies such as cloth, the integrator's work is done. For rigid bodies, however, there are still the angular effects to integrate. Angular velocity is derived from the angular momentum because the integration of angular momentum is much simpler than the integration of angular velocity [Hecker96]. The angular momentum at the new time step is simply the accumulation of torque times the time step into the angular momentum at the previous time step.

$$L(t + dt) = L(t) + [T(t) + T(t + dt)] \, dt / 2 \qquad (3.3.8)$$

where L is the angular momentum, and T is the torque. As in the calculation of forces in Equation 3.3.6, springs must be taken into account in the torque term. The attach points of the springs are used to generate the appropriate torques as shown in Figure 3.3.1.

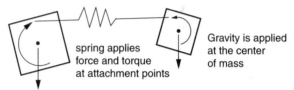

spring applies
force and torque
at attachment points

Gravity is applied
at the center
of mass

FIGURE 3.3.1   *Torques are generated by springs that are not attached at an object's center of mass.*

Remember that given a point on a body where a force is applied, the torque is calculated as the cross product of the distance of the point from the center of mass, and the force vector applied at that point. For a rigorous treatment of spring systems in a physics simulator, see [Kacic03]. The calculation of angular velocity is as follows:

$$\omega = (RIR^T)^{-1}L / m \qquad (3.3.9)$$

ON THE CD

where ω is the angular velocity, R is the orientation matrix, I is the inertia tensor, L is the angular momentum, and m is mass. The matrix multiplication in the parentheses moves the inertia tensor from world space to body space. The matrix inversion can be eliminated by pre-inverting the tensor when the rigid body data structure is created. The mass can be divided out at that stage as well. A further optimization is to recognize that dynamically symmetric objects have a tensor with values only on the diagonal, and that spheres have the same value down the diagonal. If those cases are specialized in the integrator, the calculation of angular effects is greatly simplified. The sample code on the companion CD-ROM shows further specialization for quaternions.

The Physics Engine

The Verlet-based physics engine presented in this article does not support fully general rigid bodies. The following are several simplifications made to improve the system's robustness, minimize the use of system resources, and speed up calculations.

- To simplify the calculation of angular effects, the position of the body corresponds to the center of mass, not the geometric center.
- A full inertia tensor is not maintained; instead, the engine supports only the class of dynamically symmetric bodies (such as boxes, spheres, torii, etc.), for which the inertia tensor is a diagonal matrix. This simplifies the integrator.
- Friction is modeled as a simple opposing force opposite the direction of motion. Surprisingly, Coulomb friction is first-order independent of both speed and area of contact; in Coulomb's model, the force of friction a function of only the normal force between surfaces.

ON THE CD

Referring to the source code on the companion CD-ROM, the physics engine (PhysicsEngine.h) provides the interface to the rigid bodies, runs the simulation, and resolves collisions. It provides access to the transformation matrix of each of the rigid bodies after the simulation step. Although the position, velocity, and orientation of a rigid body are directly exposed to the user, acceleration, angular velocity, and angular acceleration are not. The reason for this is that the unexposed properties are derived by the engine from initial conditions and force and torque inputs during the frame. These values could be exposed, but in practice, the need doesn't seem to arise often. Figure 3.3.2 illustrates the relationships between the classes used to implement the physics engine.

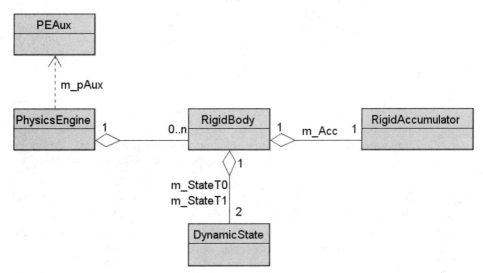

FIGURE 3.3.2 *Physics engine classes.*

PhysicsEngine is the main interface to the physics engine; PEAux is the private implementation. The RigidBody has two DynamicState objects, and a single RigidAccumulator. The static properties of the RigidBody, such as mass, are maintained as members of RigidBody itself. Note that PhysicsEngine does not provide direct access to RigidBody object pointers, but instead returns unique identifiers when rigid bodies are created. The game must track all the unique identifiers returned. These identifiers are used to set and get a RigidBody's properties and to retrieve its transformation matrix. This approach is based on the Manager software design pattern.

The Simulation Loop

After adding and initializing all the rigid bodies to the simulation, the application's main loop calls the PhysicsEngine's Simulate() method once per frame, supplying the elapsed time since the last invocation. The main loop should clamp the time value at a maximum value, such as 1/20 of a second, so that the simulation remains stable. Similarly, zero should not be passed in as the time step, although very small numbers like 1/120 are fine. A discussion of stability criteria is too lengthy to present here; for more information, see [Kačić03].

```
Create rigid bodies and initialize state T1
Simulate
    Copy previous state T1 to state T0
    Velocity += (a * dt) / 2, Equation 3.3.7
    Angular momentum += (T * dt) / 2, Equation 3.3.8
    Calculate position, Equation 3.3.4
    Calculate angular velocity, Equation 3.3.9
    Calculate forces, Equation 3.3.6
    Calculate torques, T, Figure 3.3.1
    Update acceleration, a, Equation 3.3.5
    Velocity += (a * dt) / 2, Equation 3.3.7
    Angular momentum += (T * dt) / 2, Equation 3.3.8
    Collide and Resolve
    Normalize
```

The simulation step is fairly straightforward. First, all internal states are prepared for simulation. Prior to the integration within the Simulate() method, a pre-integration step is performed to copy current values to previous, the new values to current, and so on. Then, the equations of motion are integrated. Note that Equations 3.3.7 and 3.3.8 have been broken apart so that forces can be applied, on average, at the midpoint of the integration. If a constraint system is implemented, constraints should also be applied at the midpoint. Collisions (a very specialized form of constraint) are detected and resolved. Internal values are renormalized if necessary to correct for matrices becoming nonorthogonal due to error accumulation and other similar problems.

Collision Detection and Resolution

The PhysicsEngine handles collision detection and resolution. For clarity, the version presented here deals with elementary geometry only. The algorithm follows the general framework described in [Nettle00]. In short, all objects are initially not in collision with each other. During the simulation, potential collisions are detected by solving equations describing intersections of swept volumes, and resolved through the application of an instantaneous impulse before movement is applied [Mirtich95]. Since the swept volumes determine the exact point and time of contact, illegal situations are prevented from occurring, and no special resolution heuristics are required (such as stepping backward on the motion path until no collision occurs). The equation governing collision resolution is the impulse calculation derived in part three of [Hecker96].

$$j = \frac{-(1 + e)v \cdot n}{n \cdot n(M_A^{-1} + M_B^{-1}) + \left[(I_A^{-1}(r_{AP} \times n)) \times r_{AP} + (I_B^{-1}(r_{BP} \times n)) \times r_{BP}\right] \cdot n} \quad (3.3.10)$$

where j is the impulse resulting from the collision, e is the coefficient of restitution, v is the relative velocity between the two bodies, n is the collision normal, M is the mass of bodies A and B, I is the inertia tensor, and r is the vector from the center of mass of bodies A and B to the collision point P.

Since this physics engine relies on impulse-based collision resolution, the engine does not need to switch modes between static and dynamic friction. The engine treats all collisions as dynamic collisions, and deals with sliding contact via micro-collisions [Mirtich95]. This eliminates the calculation of restoring forces. All modes of contact, including continuous contact, are handled by trains of tiny impulses applied to the object, whether they are resting, sliding, or rolling. Under impulse-based simulation, even objects at rest experience tiny rapid collisions with the supporting surface. These collisions are resolved using only information available at the point of contact. When the micro-collision impulses and object's velocity become small enough, the physics engine puts the objects to sleep and doesn't integrate them again until other objects or forces come into play.

In practice, the micro-collision technique converges on the more traditional dynamic/static model [Mirtich95]. It is more numerically stable and robust because there is no discontinuity when switching between different friction modes. All objects go to sleep when they come to rest; in a simulation of a room full of crates it is possible to have hundreds of crates, as they will consume no CPU time until they are moved.

Collision Handling and Game Logic

An application will need to know when two objects have collided with each other. There is a callback interface class provided for that purpose. The callback provides a few interesting values that can be used by the application to determine things like whether a collision was strong enough to break an object. The callback also returns a value to indicate whether the application should respond to the collision. In practice this is very useful, because some collisions might be conditional. For example, alien blood might pass through wood as if it weren't there, but might stop on steel.

The `PhysicsEngine` will report any collisions via the callback object during the simulation step. The application can handle those in any way deemed appropriate, with one exception: the application cannot invoke any `PhysicsEngine` methods, as invalid conditions can result. Finally, after the simulation step, the application can invoke any of the `Get` functions to retrieve the transformation matrices and other useful information associated with each rigid body.

Complex Geometry—A Brief Word

If the PhysicsEngine is to be extended with more complex geometry than simple spheres, planes, and boxes, a penalty-based collision resolution method such as that described in [Kačić03] is recommended. In such a system, zero-length springs of maximum possible stiffness are introduced at all contact or inter-penetration points, and the system is integrated with small time steps until collisions are resolved to an acceptable degree. These springs are removed when the collision is resolved. The calculation of maximum possible stiffness is related to the stability of the integrator; the reader is referred to [Kačić03] for details. Lagrange-multiplier based techniques also work well, as described in [Smith04].

Platform-Specific Considerations

If possible, vector and quaternion objects can be passed by value, not reference. Many Vector3 and Quaternion implementations are SIMD: SSE on x86 processors, VU0 on PS2, AltiVec on PPC. Passing by value allows the objects to be passed in a single SIMD register. The example code neglects this optimization and simply uses a Real array. Disassembly reveals that on the current crop of Microsoft and Codewarrior compilers, passing SIMD values by pointer or reference in too many cases invokes unnecessary loads and stores, whereas pass by value is more likely to generate fast code, and is also more likely to optimize operations across function calls. Even so, it is still important to check whether const objects passed by value cause the creation of temporaries. Compilers can exhibit better or worse behavior in this regard from version to version.

Extending the Engine

Culling is an important aspect of a physics engine. A typical case that should be dealt with is a portal-based game engine. It doesn't always make sense to iterate physics for an inactive portal region. A unique PhysicsEngine could be instantiated for each region; however, a further problem arises. Objects (such as the player character) will sometimes move between regions and thus between PhysicsEngines. Removing an object from one engine and putting it in another should be done carefully to avoid discontinuities.

Level of detail could also receive some attention. Many excellent tricks can be implemented here. Gravity can be turned off when an object's upward velocity component is approximately zero (such as a hockey puck momentarily sliding along the ice), eliminating a great deal of collision resolution calculation (the check still needs to be done, but since the object will not have been pushed into the floor by gravity, no resolution is required). Collisions can be reverted to sphere or plane checks to make them less accurate but fast. Collision checks can be turned off entirely. The angular integrator can be switched off. The criteria for putting an object to sleep can be relaxed. Sleeping objects can be left sleeping. In all these cases, objects should be snapped to valid states and positions whenever the LOD changes to a higher level.

A next step in the development of the `PhysicsEngine` would be to incorporate a constraint system. This topic is large enough to warrant its own article. Spring mass systems and articulated figures are nicely described in [Jakobsen03]. Constraint systems are explored in depth by [Smith04].

The collision system could be greatly improved, and generalized, by the incorporation of a sophisticated collision handling system such as OPCODE [Terdiman00]. In this volume, [Moravánszky04] discusses the reduction of contacts for faster processing.

Integration with an animation engine is a fascinating extension, and can be used to achieve rag-doll effects and secondary animation. At some point, the animation engine is turned off, and the physics engine takes over. At that moment, a few quantities need to be derived for use by the physics. Velocities are easy to derive given two previous frames of animation and the time step, but angular momentum is a bigger challenge, and beyond the scope of this article. To get started, model a figure's articulated pieces with primitives the physics engine already knows about such as cylinders and cubes. For more information, see [Baraff97].

Conclusion

This article presented a physics engine incorporating a number of interesting techniques. The velocity-based Verlet integrator for both rigid and soft body dynamics was introduced and streamlined for games applications. Impulse-based dynamic simulation with micro-collisions was described. Most of all, the author hopes to have dispelled some of the mystique surrounding physics engines by showing solutions to many common pitfalls, and by showing how easy it really is to write one from scratch, including such difficult aspects as integration of angular movement.

References

[Baraff97] Baraff, David, "Physically Based Modeling, Principles and Practice, Online SIGGRAPH '97 Course Notes," available online at *www-2.cs.cmu.edu/~baraff/sig-course/index.html*, 1997.

[Hecker96] Hecker, Chris, *Game Developer Magazine Physics Series*, available online at *www.d6.com/users/checker/dynamics.htm*, October 1996–June 1997.

[Jakobsen03] Jakobsen, Thomas, "Advanced Character Physics," available online at *www.gamasutra.com/resource_guide/20030121/jacobson_01.shtml*, January 21, 2003.

[Kačić03] Kačić-Alesić, Zoran, Marcus Nordenstam, and David Bullock, "A Practical Dynamics System," *Eurographics/SIGGRAPH Symposium on Computer Animation* (2003).

[Mirtich95] Mirtich, Brian, and John Canny, "Impulse-based Simulation of Rigid Bodies," in *Proceedings of 1995 Symposium on Interactive 3D Graphics*, April 1995, available online at *www.cs.berkeley.edu/~jfc/mirtich/impulse.html*.

[Moravánszky04] Moravánszky, Ádám, and Pierre Terdiman, "Fast Contact Reduction for Dynamics Simulations," *Game Programming Gems 4*, 2004.

[Nettle00] Nettle, Paul, "Generic Collision Detection for Games Using Ellipsoids," available online at *www.fluidstudios.com/publications.html*, October 5, 2000.

[Smith04] Smith, Russell, "Constraints in Rigid Body Dynamics," *Game Programming Gems 4*, 2004.

[Terdiman00] Terdiman, Pierre, "OPCODE, Optimized Collision Detection," available online at *www.codercorner.com/Opcode.htm*, 2000.

[Verlet67] Verlet, L. "Computer experiments on classical fluids. I. Thermodynamical properties of Lennard-Jones molecules," *Phys. Rev.*, 159, 98–103, 1967.

3.4

Constraints in Rigid Body Dynamics

Russ Smith, Author of the Open Dynamics Engine

russ@q12.org

Modern computer games are immersing the player in increasingly realistic virtual worlds. Part of this added realism comes from sophisticated rendering, part of it comes from AI, and part of it comes from more detailed simulation of game object motion. Cars are expected to skid and tumble as they would in real life, bridges must sway when walked on, brick walls must crumble when struck, and game characters must fall convincingly.

A popular technique for creating these motions is rigid body simulation. Rigid body simulation libraries often come with standard joint types that allow the user to connect bodies together with, for example, hinges and ball-and-socket joints. Some libraries allow users to create their own joint types. When this capability is available, it offers many advantages for simulating novel situations. For example, a new joint type could keep the cart of a roller coaster attached to a track, or it could model a particular kind of suspension that connects the wheel of a car to the chassis.

This article shows how to easily build new joints for the popular Cartesian coordinate/Lagrange multiplier-based rigid body simulators (like [Baraff96]) that use velocity constraints. The description is tailored to the Open Dynamic Engine (ODE), an open-source rigid body simulation library [Smith03]. Other simulation techniques, such as the reduced coordinate method [McMillan94], are not covered. We will see how joints can be created from simple parts, without advanced mathematics. This article assumes that the reader is familiar with the basic concepts of rigid body simulation. If not, there are several good places to start, such as [Witkin97] and [Hecker96].

The Basics

In rigid body simulation, each body starts out with six degrees of freedom (three for position and three for orientation). *Constraints* take degrees of freedom away from the system—they are mathematical restrictions on the ways that bodies can move relative to each other. Constraints are enforced by the simulator, for example by having automatically calculated constraint forces applied to each body. Constraints often take the form of joints that can connect pairs of bodies together. The words *constraint* and *joint* are used interchangeably in this article.

Velocity and Acceleration

We define the linear and angular velocity of a body i to be the vectors $[v_{ix}\ v_{iy}\ v_{iz}]$ and $[\omega_{ix}\ \omega_{iy}\ \omega_{iz}]$, respectively. The linear velocity is measured at the body's point of reference (POR), and the angular velocity is the rotation about this point of reference. A vector $\mathbf{p}_i$ gives the location of the POR. Often, a body's POR is its center of mass. Each body also has linear and angular acceleration vectors, which are the time derivatives of the velocity vectors. For convenience, we group these values together into 6-vectors (note that the notation $\dot{x}$ means the time derivative of $\mathbf{x}$).

$$\text{body } i \text{ velocity: } \mathbf{v}_i = \begin{bmatrix} \dot{\mathbf{p}}_i & \Omega_i \end{bmatrix}^{\text{T}} = \begin{bmatrix} v_{ix} & v_{iy} & v_{iz} & \omega_{ix} & \omega_{iy} & \omega_{iz} \end{bmatrix}^{\text{T}}$$

$$\text{body } i \text{ acceleration: } \mathbf{a}_i = \begin{bmatrix} \ddot{\mathbf{p}}_i & \dot{\Omega}_i \end{bmatrix}^{\text{T}} = \begin{bmatrix} \dot{v}_{ix} & \dot{v}_{iy} & \dot{v}_{iz} & \dot{\omega}_{ix} & \dot{\omega}_{iy} & \dot{\omega}_{iz} \end{bmatrix}^{\text{T}} \quad (3.4.1)$$

Equations of Motion

A body i moves under the influence of Newton's law: $\mathbf{f}_i = \mathbf{m}_i\mathbf{a}_i$, where $\mathbf{M}_i$ is the mass matrix and $\mathbf{f}_i$ is the force and torque applied to the body. (From here, the word *force* is used to mean both force and torque). We normally say that $\mathbf{f}_i = \mathbf{f}_{ir} + \mathbf{f}_{ie} + \mathbf{f}_{ic}$, where $\mathbf{f}_{ir}$ is the rotating torque resulting from nonsymmetric rotational inertia, $\mathbf{f}_{ie}$ is some "externally" applied (or user supplied) force, and $\mathbf{f}_{ic}$ is the constraint force. $\mathbf{f}_{ic}$ is computed by the simulator for each time step so that the rigid body motion will satisfy the constraints.

Velocity Constraints

A velocity constraint on a single body is simply a statement that a body's velocity vector is allowed to have some values but not others. An example of a single body constraint is a hinge that connects the body to a fixed point in space. A single body constraint is expressed with the matrix equation $\mathbf{J}_1\mathbf{v}_1 = \mathbf{c}$. Expanded out, this is:

$$\begin{bmatrix} J_{11} & J_{12} & J_{13} & J_{14} & J_{15} & J_{16} \\ \vdots & \vdots & \vdots & \vdots & \vdots & \vdots \\ J_{m1} & J_{m2} & J_{m3} & J_{m4} & J_{m5} & J_{m6} \end{bmatrix} v_1 = \begin{bmatrix} c_1 \\ \vdots \\ c_m \end{bmatrix} \quad (3.4.2)$$

The magic of constraints is that the simulator will compute $\mathbf{f}_{lc}$ such that $\mathbf{v}_1$ always satisfies this equation. $\mathbf{J}$, called the *constraint Jacobian*, has m rows, where m is the *order* of the constraint, or the number of degrees of freedom that are removed from the system. The values inside $\mathbf{J}$ and $\mathbf{c}$ typically change for each time step, as they often depend on the exact position and orientation of the body. Two body constraints have a similar equation: $\mathbf{J}_1\mathbf{v}_1 + \mathbf{J}_2\mathbf{v}_2 = \mathbf{c}$, where $\mathbf{v}_1$ and $\mathbf{v}_2$ are the velocities of the two joined bodies. Constraints that put three or more bodies in a single equation are possible, but they are rarely useful and ODE does not support them.

Constraint Building Blocks

Constraint code computes $\mathbf{J}$ and $\mathbf{c}$ at each time step. $\mathbf{J}$ and $\mathbf{c}$ can be designed row by row, where each row acts independently to control the velocity along a particular axis. The following examples start with very simple single body constraints, and then combine them together to make more complex constraints.

Constraint #1: No Movement along Z (POR in X-Y Plane)

Consider the single body constraint (see Figure 3.4.1 #1):

$$[0 \quad 0 \quad 1 \quad 0 \quad 0 \quad 0]\mathbf{v}_1 = 0 \tag{3.4.3}$$

Expanding the multiplication gives v_{1z}, so this constraint sets the body's POR velocity in the Z direction to zero. Another way of saying this is that the body's POR is limited to move in the X-Y plane only. Note that this constraint says nothing about what the Z position actually is, because it is only the velocity that is constrained, not the position.

Constraint #2: No Rotation about Z

Consider the constraint (see Figure 3.4.1 #2):

$$[0 \quad 0 \quad 0 \quad 0 \quad 0 \quad 1]\mathbf{v}_1 = 0 \tag{3.4.4}$$

This says that $\omega_{1z} = 0$. Therefore, this constraint prevents the body from rotating around the Z-axis. It can still rotate around axes that are perpendicular (i.e., normal) to the Z-axis.

Constraint #3: POR in an Arbitrary Plane

This constraint (see Figure 3.4.1 #3):

$$[a_x \quad a_y \quad a_z \quad 0 \quad 0 \quad 0]\mathbf{v}_1 = 0 \tag{3.4.5}$$

is similar to constraint #1, except that it zeroes POR velocity along the vector $[a_x \ a_y \ a_z]$. Another way of saying this is that POR motion is restricted to the plane that has $[a_x \ a_y \ a_z]$ as its normal vector. Vector $\mathbf{a}$ does not have to be a unit vector.

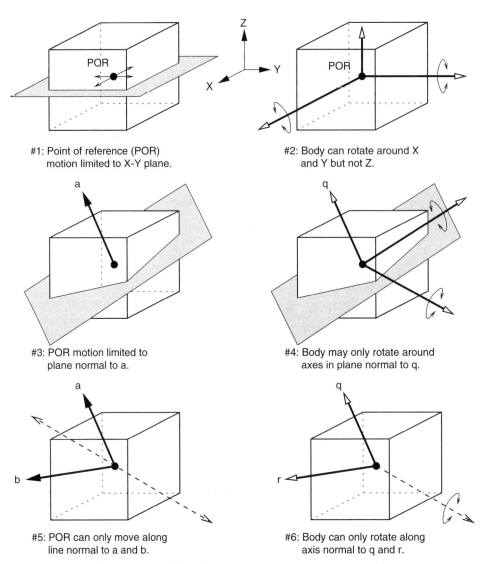

FIGURE 3.4.1   *Constraint building blocks.*

Constraint #4: No Rotation about an Arbitrary Axis

Similar to constraint #3, the following constraint (see Figure 3.4.1 #4) prevents rotation about the axis **q**, allowing rotation around axes in the plane normal to **q**.

$$[0 \quad 0 \quad 0 \quad q_x \quad q_y \quad q_z]\mathbf{v}_1 = 0 \qquad\qquad (3.4.6)$$

Constraint #5: POR Constrained to a Line

To prevent POR motions in two directions simultaneously, we can use two copies of constraint #2, one per row (see Figure 3.4.1 #5).

$$\begin{bmatrix} a_x & a_y & a_z & 0 & 0 & 0 \\ b_x & b_y & b_z & 0 & 0 & 0 \end{bmatrix} \mathbf{v}_1 = \begin{bmatrix} 0 \\ 0 \end{bmatrix} \tag{3.4.7}$$

POR velocity is prevented from having a component in either direction **a** or **b**. The result is that the POR is limited to move along the line $\mathbf{a} \times \mathbf{b}$.

Constraint #6: Rotation about a Fixed Axis

Similar to constraint #5, we can prevent rotation about two axes simultaneously, limiting rotation to the single axis $\ddot{o} = \mathbf{q} \times \mathbf{r}$ (see Figure 3.4.1 #6).

$$\begin{bmatrix} 0 & 0 & 0 & q_x & q_y & q_z \\ 0 & 0 & 0 & r_x & r_y & r_z \end{bmatrix} \mathbf{v}_1 = \begin{bmatrix} 0 \\ 0 \end{bmatrix} \tag{3.4.8}$$

Constraint #7: Fixed POR or Rotation

If we extend constraint #5 to three rows, we can write the following constraint equation:

$$\begin{bmatrix} a_x & a_y & a_z & 0 & 0 & 0 \\ b_x & b_y & b_z & 0 & 0 & 0 \\ d_x & d_y & d_z & 0 & 0 & 0 \end{bmatrix} \mathbf{v}_1 = \begin{bmatrix} 0 \\ 0 \\ 0 \end{bmatrix}, \text{ or } \begin{bmatrix} 1 & 0 & 0 & 0 & 0 & 0 \\ 0 & 1 & 0 & 0 & 0 & 0 \\ 0 & 0 & 1 & 0 & 0 & 0 \end{bmatrix} \mathbf{v}_1 = \begin{bmatrix} 0 \\ 0 \\ 0 \end{bmatrix} \tag{3.4.9}$$

which is an explicit statement that $v_{ix} = v_{iy} = v_{iz} = 0$. The result of applying this constraint is that the body's POR stays fixed in space. If the three vectors are not independent (e.g., one vector is a scaled version of another vector), then the simulation might become unstable, as the simulator will be unable to decide how much force to apply along each constraint direction. A similar principle can be applied to limit all rotational motion. Note also that constraints #7 and #6 can be combined to create a simple single-body hinge.

Creating Useful Game Constraints

The previous examples demonstrated the basic constraint principles. Now let's see how we can put these ideas into action and build constraints that might be useful in a game. Along the way, we'll see how to build two-body constraints, how the vector **c** can be put to use, and how force limits can be used to make hard contacts, motors, and brakes.

A Rope-and-Pulley Constraint

Image a game scenario with two platforms connected by a rope and two pulleys (see Figure 3.4.2). The vectors **a** and **b** point in the directions that the platforms can move. If the player steps on to platform A, the platform will fall under the increased weight and platform B will rise. To be realistic, the rate of fall should be proportional to the player weight, and any extra weight piled onto B should slow the fall. These effects can all be created using simple game logic, but unfortunately, each extra piece of physical realism usually requires an extra piece of code to handle it. If rigid body simulation is used, however, all these physical behaviors (and more) come at no extra cost.

How do we create a constraint to model this situation? Recall that two-body constraints have the form $J_1v_1 + J_2v_2 = c$. If we set $c = 0$, we can say that $J_1v_1 = -J_2v_2$, which illustrates that the velocities of the two bodies along certain directions are traded off against each other. The rope-and-pulley constraint is thus

$$[a_x \quad a_y \quad a_z \quad 0 \quad 0 \quad 0]v_1 + [b_x \quad b_y \quad b_z \quad 0 \quad 0 \quad 0]v_2 = 0$$

This says that the POR velocity of body 1 along direction **a** must match the POR velocity of body 2 along direction **−b** (allowing for the relative lengths of **a** and **b**). Interlocking cogwheels could be simulated using a similar approach, with constraints on the angular rather than linear velocities.

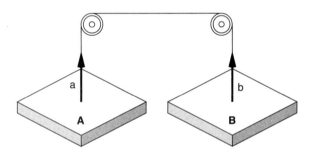

FIGURE 3.4.2   *A rope-and-pulley constraint.*

Screw Constraints

A screw constraint forces a body to rotate as it moves in a particular direction, like a nut moving along the thread of a bolt. This effect is achieved by using a constraint row with both linear and angular parts, so that the linear and angular motions are traded off against each other. For example, the constraint

$$\begin{bmatrix} a_x & a_y & a_z & q_x & q_y & q_z \end{bmatrix} v_1 = \mathbf{a} \cdot \dot{\mathbf{p}}_1 + \mathbf{q} \cdot \omega_1 = 0 \qquad (3.4.10)$$

is split into linear and angular parts to illustrate that the linear velocity along axis **a** must be some multiple of the angular velocity along axis **q**. In the screw constraint, **a** and **q** point in the same direction.

Ball-and-Socket Joints

Ball-and-socket joints have many uses, like connecting together the links of a chain or the limbs of a rag doll. The joint is shown in Figure 3.4.3, where $\mathbf{g}_1$ and $\mathbf{g}_2$ are vectors from the body 1 and 2 PORs to the ball. Looking along each direction $\mathbf{u}_1, \mathbf{u}_2, \mathbf{u}_3$ we want the velocity of the ball to be the same when measured from body 1 or body 2, so for each direction vector we have $\mathbf{u}_i \cdot (\dot{\mathbf{p}}_1 + \dot{\mathbf{g}}_1) = \mathbf{u}_i \cdot (\dot{\mathbf{p}}_2 + \dot{\mathbf{g}}_2)$. This constraint is specified relative to the ball, so we must use the *shifting rule* to make it relative to the body PORs.

The shifting rule says that if a constraint is specified for points $\mathbf{g}_1$ and $\mathbf{g}_2$ relative to bodies 1 and 2, like this:

$$\mathbf{a}_1 \cdot (\dot{\mathbf{p}}_1 + \dot{\mathbf{g}}_1) + \mathbf{q}_1 \cdot \boldsymbol{\omega}_1 + \mathbf{a}_2 \cdot (\dot{\mathbf{p}}_2 + \dot{\mathbf{g}}_2) + \mathbf{q}_2 \cdot \boldsymbol{\omega}_2 = c \qquad (3.4.11)$$

then the equivalent POR-relative constraint is

$$\mathbf{a}_1 \cdot \dot{\mathbf{p}}_1 + \left(\mathbf{q}_1 + \mathbf{g}_1 \times \mathbf{a}_1\right) \cdot \boldsymbol{\omega}_1 + \mathbf{a}_2 \cdot \dot{\mathbf{p}}_2 + \left(\mathbf{q}_2 + \mathbf{g}_2 \times \mathbf{a}_2\right) \cdot \boldsymbol{\omega}_2 = c \qquad (3.4.12)$$

This shifting rule correctly trades off linear and angular velocity at the POR. Applying this to the ball-and-socket joint for each $\mathbf{u}_i$ gives

$$\mathbf{u}_i \cdot \dot{\mathbf{p}}_1 + \left(\mathbf{g}_1 \times \mathbf{u}_i\right) \cdot \boldsymbol{\omega}_1 - \mathbf{u}_i \cdot \dot{\mathbf{p}}_2 - \left(\mathbf{g}_2 \times \mathbf{u}_i\right) \cdot \boldsymbol{\omega}_2 = 0 \qquad (3.4.13)$$

When we evaluate this for $\mathbf{u}_1 \ldots \mathbf{u}_3$ and write all three constraint rows together, we get the ball-and-socket constraint.

$$\begin{bmatrix} 1 & 0 & 0 & 0 & g_{1z} & -g_{1y} \\ 0 & 1 & 0 & -g_{1z} & 0 & g_{1x} \\ 0 & 0 & 1 & g_{1y} & -g_{1x} & 0 \end{bmatrix} \mathbf{v}_1 + \begin{bmatrix} -1 & 0 & 0 & 0 & -g_{2z} & g_{2y} \\ 0 & -1 & 0 & g_{2z} & 0 & -g_{2x} \\ 0 & 0 & -1 & -g_{2y} & g_{2x} & 0 \end{bmatrix} \mathbf{v}_2 = \begin{bmatrix} 0 \\ 0 \\ 0 \end{bmatrix}$$

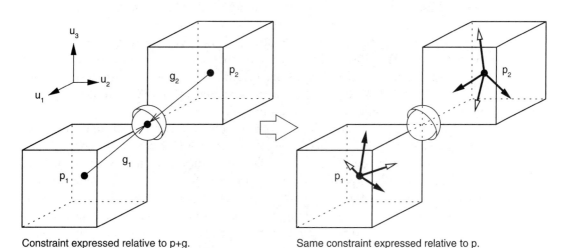

Constraint expressed relative to p+g.   Same constraint expressed relative to p.

FIGURE 3.4.3 *A ball-and-socket joint created using the shifting rule.*

Hinge Joint

A hinge joint is a ball and socket joint with two extra constraint rows that force the bodies to line up along the hinge axis. These extra rows are a generalization of constraint #6 that prevents the bodies from rotating relative to each other along the axes **q** and **r**.

$$\begin{bmatrix} 0 & 0 & 0 & q_x & q_y & q_z \\ 0 & 0 & 0 & r_x & r_y & r_z \end{bmatrix} \mathbf{v}_1 + \begin{bmatrix} 0 & 0 & 0 & -q_x & -q_y & -q_z \\ 0 & 0 & 0 & -r_x & -r_y & -r_z \end{bmatrix} \mathbf{v}_2 = \begin{bmatrix} 0 \\ 0 \end{bmatrix} \quad (3.4.14)$$

Make Stacks of Things with Hard Contacts

Often, a game requires a stack of objects that the player can push over, drive through, or blow up. To stack rigid bodies, we need to model the nonpenetration contact between them. Penalty methods that apply user-calculated restraining forces to each body are difficult to tune and tend to cause instability. What we really want is a hard contact constraint with the following property: when two bodies are pushed together at the contact point, the constraint pushes back with equal force, and when they are pulled apart, the constraint does not resist. This can be achieved with constraint force limits.

First, let's see how force limits work in general. The constraint force vectors $\mathbf{f}_{c1}$ and $\mathbf{f}_{c2}$ that are applied to bodies 1 and 2 are weighted sums of the constraint rows associated with that body. For m rows there are weights $\lambda_1 \ldots \lambda_m$ (the Lagrange multiplier values calculated by the simulator) and

$$\mathbf{f}_{c1} = \mathbf{J}_1^T \lambda \qquad \mathbf{f}_{c2} = \mathbf{J}_2^T \lambda \qquad \text{where } \lambda = \begin{bmatrix} \lambda_1 & \cdots & \lambda_m \end{bmatrix} \quad (3.4.15)$$

In normal unlimited constraints, the solver will allow $\lambda_1 \ldots \lambda_m$ to take any values. In other words, the solver will "do whatever it takes" to make sure that the constraint is satisfied. A force limit restricts the solver so that it only applies constraint forces within a certain range; for example, $\lambda_{iLO} \leq \lambda_i \leq \lambda_{iHI}$. If larger forces would have been necessary, then λ_i will be clamped to one of the limits and the constraint will not be perfectly satisfied. When limits are present, the simulator must solve a Linear Complementary Problem (LCP) at each time step [Murty88]. Simulators such as ODE allow force limits on any constraint row.

To make a contact constraint we can apply the POR shifting rule to the two-body version of constraint #3, so that the bodies experience a force $\lambda\mathbf{a}$ at the contact point. Let's say that if λ is positive, then $\lambda\mathbf{a}$ pushes the bodies apart. If we set $\lambda_{LO} = 0$, $\lambda_{HI} = \infty$ and the *required* λ is positive, then the correct reaction force will be applied to keep the two bodies apart. If the required λ is negative, it will be clamped to zero, allowing the two bodies to come apart without resistance. Often, multiple contact points are required to keep two bodies separated; this depends on the geometry of the bodies.

Here's a neat trick: to "magnetize" the bodies: set $\lambda_{LO} = -M$, $\lambda_{HI} = \infty$. This means that some nonzero force M must be exerted to pull the bodies apart.

Making Motors

Making a car go requires some type of motor. The simplest way to model a motor is to apply a torque between a wheel and the chassis. This does work, but there are problems—in particular, it can cause instability when large torques are applied. An alternative model uses a constraint row that sets a constant angular velocity between the wheel and the chassis, using a nonzero value of **c**. In general, when **c** is nonzero it sets the body velocities along the constrained directions (for example, by setting $\mathbf{c} = c_z$ in constraint #3 we are saying that the POR velocity along **a** must be c_z). Let's take the single body hinge obtained by combining constraints #6 and #7, and add the row:

$$[0 \quad 0 \quad 0 \quad s_x \quad s_y \quad s_z]\mathbf{v}_1 = [c_s]$$

where $s = (q \times r)/|q \times r|$ is the unit length axis of hinge rotation. This is a "powered" hinge that has angular velocity c_s around the hinge axis. However, this is a terrible model for a motor because it is infinitely powerful, as it will achieve its target velocity regardless of any restraining torques.

This problem can be corrected by setting $\lambda_{LO} = -f_{max}$, $\lambda_{HI} = f_{max}$ for the motor constraint row. The motor will now not be able to apply more than $\pm f_{max}$ of torque to achieve its target velocity. If the motor is able to bring the body up to speed within a single time step, it will do so; otherwise, it will apply the maximum possible (clamped) torque to bring the body up to speed over several time steps. Any externally applied torque will now be able to compete with the constraint torque, hindering the motor just as it would in real life. Setting f_{max} to zero disables the motor, effectively removing the influence of the motor constraint row. This motor is much more stable than the equivalent direct-torque motor when f_{max} is large. It is also a reasonable model of an engine with an attached gearbox, where internal friction limits the maximum speed (such as the typical drive train of a car).

Brakes and Dry Friction

Cars need brakes as well as motors. As with motors, the simplest braking solution is a torque applied directly to the wheels. As with motors, this can lead to instability. The braking torque at the disc brake of a wheel is caused by dry friction—a constant torque that resists the angular velocity. Dry friction can be modeled well by using a force-limited motor where the target velocity is set to zero. This constraint will apply a torque not exceeding $\pm f_{max}$ to bring the joint velocity to zero. Here, f_{max} is set according to how much the brake pedal is pressed—if no braking is needed, then f_{max} is zero and the constraint is disabled. If you have a force-limited motor driving the wheel, then you can get braking for free, because the same constraint can be used.

Correcting for Positional Error

If simulators were perfect, we would simply place all the bodies in their starting positions, add some constraints, and the constraints would be enforced perfectly for all time. In practice, simulators are not perfect and numerical errors creep into the body positions and orientations, especially when high rotational speeds are present. A good way to stop this from happening is to allow the constraints themselves to push the bodies back into the correct configuration if they (the bodies) are out of alignment. This is done by using nonzero values in **c**.

A constraint cannot directly affect the position of a body; it can only alter its velocity. However, if the "goal" of a constraint is to maintain a constant position (or to maintain two bodies in a constant position relative to each other), then **c** can be set to force the bodies to move from the incorrect position to the desired one. For example, in constraint #1, if the goal is to keep $p_{1z} = 0$, then we can set $c_z = -kp_{1z}$ so that the correcting velocity is proportional to the positional error. This will exponentially reduce the positional error over time at a rate determined by k. Note that if k is too large, the corrected position will overshoot the mark within one time step, perhaps leading to instability. In general, for each constraint row we set $c = -error/h$, where the error is measured along the direction vector or axis given in the corresponding row of **J**. For example, in the ball-and-socket joint, the error is measured along directions $\mathbf{u}_1 \ldots \mathbf{u}_3$.

What's on the CD-ROM?

ON THE CD

The companion CD-ROM contains example source code for all the constraints mentioned here, implemented using ODE. It also contains a snapshot of the complete source code, documentation, and example programs for ODE itself. Readers interested in creating their own constraints should refer to the source, as there are several practical details that are not covered in this article.

Conclusion

This article showed how new rigid body velocity constraints can be built from various types of simple constraint rows. You can construct almost any constraint from these building blocks plus the shifting rule, an understanding of the **c** vector, and force limits. Simulation libraries such as ODE that allow user-designed constraints to be used alongside standard ones provide the user with a powerful ability to model new situations.

References

[Baraff96] Baraff, David, "Linear-time Dynamics Using Lagrange Multipliers," *Computer Graphics Proceedings, Annual Conference Series*: pp. 137–146, 1996.

[Hecker96] Hecker, Chris, "Rigid Body Dynamics," available online at *www.d6.com/users/checker/dynamics.htm*.

[McMillan94] McMillan, Scott, *Computational Dynamics for Robotic Systems on Land and Under Water*, Ph.D. Thesis, The Ohio State University, Columbus, OH, 1994.

[Murty88] Murty, Katta G., "Linear Complementarity, Linear and Nonlinear Programming," available online at *http://ioe.engin.umich.edu/people/fac/books/murty/ linear_complementarity_webbook/*, 1988.

[Smith03] Smith, Russell, "The Open Dynamics Engine," available online at *http://q12.org/ode/*.

[Witkin97] Witkin, Andrew, and David Baraff, *Physically Based Modeling: Principles and Practice* (Online SIGGRAPH '97 Course notes), available online at *www-2.cs.cmu.edu/~baraff/sigcourse/index.html*.

3.5

Fast Contact Reduction for Dynamics Simulation

Ádám Moravánszky and

Pierre Terdiman,

NovodeX AG

adam.moravanszky@novodex.com,
pierre.terdiman@novodex.com

A typical physics pipeline contains three distinct parts:

- **Collision detection:** Detects collisions between the objects in a scene.
- **Contact generation:** Creates contact points from the collision data.
- **Dynamics simulation:** Enforces the nonpenetration constraints represented by contacts and updates the objects' poses.

To simulate the interaction of bodies in contact, nonpenetration constraints must be expressed in a compact manner that permits efficient simulation of the resulting dynamics. *Contact points* have been introduced and used for this purpose in robotics literature since [Lozano-Perez83], and later in computer graphics literature with [Hahn88] and others. Contact points represent the local nonpenetration constraints between colliding shapes. The number of emitted contact points has a direct influence over the accuracy, stability, and speed of the simulation. Creating a single contact point for each pair of colliding shapes is usually not enough to produce high-quality simulations. Conversely, too many contact points can lead to stability issues or poor performance, depending on how the dynamics part of the pipeline has been implemented. This article presents several *contact reduction* algorithms that diminish the number of emitted contacts and their associated workload: *contact preprocessing, contact clustering,* and *contact persistence.*

Contact Reduction

Collision detection algorithms often work by decomposing meshes into triangles or volume elements. Contact points are then generated independently for each of these elements. In this way, one quickly ends up with too many contact points when the results from the many intersecting elements are combined, especially if the resolution of the elements is high, or the interpenetration of the bodies is great.

Even if the detected contact points succeed in adequately representing the local geometries in contact, generating a large number of contact points has several disadvantages. First, dynamics algorithms that solve for the true contact forces can have difficulty with strongly overdetermined problems imposed by many contacts. These algorithms operate in at least quadratic time in the number of contact points [Baraff92], [Anitescu99]. In this case, having more contact points than absolutely necessary is clearly a bad idea. Furthermore, a matrix representing such an overdetermined system is ill conditioned. Solvers that try to factor this matrix will have a difficult time. Some iterative solvers might also take more iterations to converge than with a problem with the same number of constraints that are linearly independent.

This is becoming less of a practical problem because many approximate algorithms used for interactive dynamics simulation scale linearly with the number of constraints [Jakobsen01]. However, these inexpensive algorithms are often sensitive to the number of contact points used, because they typically apply some penalty force or impulse at each contact, whose effects can become erratic when the number of contacts varies. Solvers based on penalty methods are still commonly used in games. Some of them use various constants and thresholds fine-tuned for the single contact case, such as a sphere rolling on a plane. They work well in that ideal case. However, when the number of simultaneous contacts increases, the simulation becomes less and less stable as it moves away from the fine-tuned case. For example, imagine a torus resting on a plane. If one contact is created at each vertex position, the generated forces will be far from ideal, and also directly depend on tessellation. Reducing the number of contacts helps to solve the stability problem [Kim02]. For these reasons, the number of contact points should be kept at a minimum without sacrificing the realism of the simulation. We tackle this problem in two steps, by preprocessing the colliding shapes, and by clustering contact points.

Overview of Preprocessing

There are at least two different types of contacts:

- Contacts that can be discarded, because they have no influence over the simulation.
- Contacts that can be merged into a single contact, producing a possibly less accurate but still plausible simulation.

Contact preprocessing takes care of the first type of contact. The preprocessing step examines all *potential contacts* of a given shape. This is not always possible, depending on the shape at hand. However, when it is, potential contacts that will not play a significant role in the simulation are marked and discarded in advance.

This is a powerful approach since the best way to get rid of redundant contacts is not to generate them in the first place.

Overview of Clustering

Contact clustering takes care of the second type of contact by reducing a certain set of contact points to a smaller set that is only legitimate when it does not change the nature of the nonpenetration constraints. In the simplest case, such as an object resting on a flat plane, all valid contact normals will be identical and equal to the plane normal, and all the contact points will be on or below the plane. The distance of a contact below a plane is the local penetration depth at that point. Disregarding penetrations, one can show that all contact configurations with the same convex hull in the plane are equivalent for the purpose of rigid body simulation.

Indeed, only three kinds of motions are possible for the body resting on the plane:

- It can be receding from the plane, in which case the contact surface will vanish.
- It can press against the surface, and eventually slide along it.
- It can "fall over" by rolling around any of the edges of the convex hull.

Thus, the contact behavior is only influenced by the common contact normal direction, and the edges of the convex hull of the contact points. All the contact points not on the convex hull can be discarded without changing the nature of the nonpenetration constraints.

It is often desirable to reduce the contact points on the hull even further, especially in cases such as between the cylinder and the floor as in Figure 3.5.1. We have developed an algorithm that removes those hull vertices that cause a minimal decrease in hull area, because in turn this minimizes the probability that the cylinder will fall over when it should not. However, a straight implementation of this rigorous approach is too expensive. Instead, a refined algorithm approximates the convex hull using the axis-aligned bounds of the contact points. This approximate version works fairly well in practice, on both single (see Figure 3.5.1) and composite objects (see Figure 3.5.4).

Overview of Persistence

After reducing the number of contacts, the algorithm makes them persistent. Contact points regenerated from scratch in every simulation frame tend to have strong temporal coherence; in other words, contact points generated in a sequence of frames will be quite similar. Explicitly tracking this similarity over time has several benefits. First, some iterative algorithms solving for the contact forces can be started from an arbitrary *initial guess* force: the closer it is to the solution, the faster the algorithm will converge. This process is called *warm starting*. We warm start the solver with the contact forces of the previous time step, hoping that the contact forces of the current frame will be similar to the forces of the last frame. However, this is only possible if a correspondence can be found between the previous and current contact points.

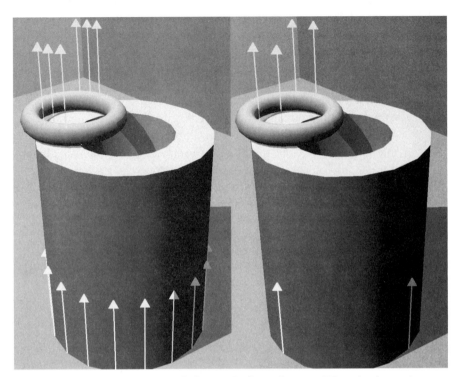

FIGURE 3.5.1   *A set of contacts before and after reduction. The cylinder and torus are handled as meshes, resting on a plane.*

Another application of persistent contacts is to achieve the best possible simulation of static friction between two bodies that must not slide at all relative to each other. We can enforce this no-slip condition by making certain, in each time step, that the relative tangential velocity at the contact points between the bodies is zero. If error accumulates, the bodies slowly drift along the tangent plane of their contacts. The same problem happens when we simulate joints between bodies with Lagrange multiplier-based techniques: pose space error will accumulate at the joint. To combat this error, we must be able to measure it. For joints, it is easy to compute the error, because we know where the joint is supposed to be attached in the local coordinate system of each body. For contacts, it is not possible to do this unless we know where the contact was located when it was created, or when static friction conditions have started to apply. Persistent contacts are a solution to this problem.

Details of Preprocessing

The most efficient way to reduce contact points is not to generate them in the first place. Putting this notion into practice depends on the exact type of collision detection algorithm used, so a single example will be presented: the box-mesh contact generation algorithm used to collide game objects against a mesh representing a static environment.

It is a common desire to perform collision detection with the same data set used for graphics, and one of the most common graphics display formats is an indexed triangle list. The triangles are assumed to be oriented (one of their sides is declared as the front face—the one exposed to the world—while the other is the back face), but must satisfy no other requirement. The efficiency of the method will decrease if the mesh contains many nonmanifold edges or t-intersections.

Given that the collision detection system reports all triangles of the mesh intersecting the box, contact generation is performed between the box shape and each triangle separately. This includes the testing of each of the triangle edges and vertices against the shape. Such a practice can lead to duplicate contacts along edges shared by two triangles that both intersect the colliding shape.

The following types of mesh edges are not worth testing against at all, and can be marked as inactive during preprocessing:

- An interior edge is an edge between two triangles with identical normals. Such an edge only serves to tessellate a planar polygon into triangles; it is not a real geometrical feature, and can be safely ignored.
- A concave edge is an edge between two triangles that form a concave angle with their front faces. This edge cannot be touched by another object in a nondegenerate manner unless it also touches one of the two triangles, and thus it also does not need be tested.

This leaves us with two types of edges that the collision detection system must test: boundary edges (edges not shared by two triangles), and convex edges (nonboundary edges neither interior nor concave) (see Figure 3.5.2). It is sufficient to test convex edges from only one of the triangles that contain them. Nonmanifold edges are treated as convex, because it is assumed that they do not occur frequently enough to demand special attention.

Some vertices can be ignored in a similar manner:

- Declare all vertices connected to a concave edge to be concave, and ignore them. This makes sense for the same reason that concave edges are ignored.
- Declare all vertices connected to only interior edges to be interior, and ignore them.
- Test against all other vertices in one of the potentially several triangles to which they are connected.

Making use of these rules can exempt a significant number of features from collision detection computations, and thus reduce computation times while lowering the number of emitted contact points.

These rules are best implemented in a preprocessing step: first, allocate six bits of additional storage for each triangle. There is one bit for each of the triangle's

vertices and edges, and any vertex or edge will only be involved in contact computations when the corresponding bit is set. Initially, all six bits for all triangles are
cleared. The mesh is traversed and a record is created for each triangle edge. Each
edge record contains two vertex references and a triangle reference. The edges are
then sorted so that two or more edges involving the same two vertices become
adjacent in the list. The sorted list is then traversed. When the system encounters
a run of edges between the same two vertices, only one of the edges is examined: if
it is a convex or boundary edge, set the three bits corresponding to the edge and
its two vertices in the edge's triangle's flag record. If the edge is concave, mark its
record in the sorted edge list as such, but take no other action. Once all edges in
the edge list are processed, perform a second pass: in this pass, look for the concave
edges that were marked, and clear their vertices' flags in all of the triangles in
which they occur. This procedure ensures that no vertex adjacent to a concave edge
ever gets tested.

FIGURE 3.5.2 *Thick black edges are the only ones tested for collision (game level courtesy of Arkane Studios).*

Details on Contact Clustering

The first step in our contact clustering algorithm is to group the contact points according to their contact normals. Some types of collision detection will generate all contact points with an identical normal direction. Two examples are collisions between any types of convex shapes (see Figure 3.5.3), and between a plane and an arbitrary shape (see Figure 3.5.1). In these cases, the normal group generation step is trivial and can be skipped. Otherwise, at least two approaches can be used: a cube map and a k-means based algorithm. The first is suitable for contact sets involving a few distinct normal directions; the second is better for smooth shapes where no two normals tend to be identical.

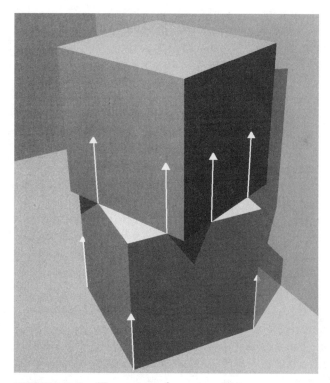

FIGURE 3.5.3 *Two convex shapes in collision generate contacts with similar normal orientation.*

Cube Map Clustering

This algorithm starts from a given set of input contacts and a discrete set of contact clusters. Each cluster represents a group of contacts with similar normals. A cube map lookup maps each contact normal to the corresponding cluster. This lookup is typically faster than normal vector quantization. The six faces of the unit cube are subdivided in a regular N*N grid, resulting in $6N^2$ clusters. This mapping is similar to the one used for normal masks [Zhang-Hoff97]. Contact clusters are never explicitly allocated, in order to save memory. Instead, we compute cluster indices on the fly, and use them to sort recorded contacts by cluster. We then process each cluster in order, reducing them as they are processed.

K-Means Clustering

The cube map-based algorithm performs well if the normals are very tightly clustered. Otherwise, a cluster of normals might fall into different cube map cells, and be split. This can come up during collision detection between round shapes such as spheres, and highly tessellated geometry. This case also leads to many contact points, and is an ideal candidate for reduction. The k-means clustering algorithm is a well-known tool for data analysis. Given a set of input vectors, and k, the number of clusters to be found, it quickly maps the input vectors to k clusters. The cluster centers are also determined. In our application, the contact normals are the input vectors. It is difficult to know ahead of time how many "natural" clusters are formed by the normals, if any. In the case of a sphere versus a high-resolution triangle mesh, three clusters give good results in practice. Asking for a larger number of clusters leads to natural clusters getting split, and increases the running time of the algorithm. Asking for a single cluster is the equivalent of simply averaging all the normals, which can lead to opposing normals canceling out.

In our experience, given input data in natural clusters, k-means converges in just three iterations using arbitrary initial cluster placement. After k-means has identified the three clusters, examine the resulting average normal of each cluster. If two of the three clusters normals are within some small epsilon value of each other, we conclude that there were fewer than three natural clusters, and merge the clusters. Thus, there can be one, two, or three clusters.

Cluster Reduction

For each cluster, whether found using the cube map or k-means, compute a projection plane as the average of all contact planes in this cluster. Then, compute two orthonormal vectors on the plane, forming a basis with the plane's normal vector. Next, project all contacts in the cluster onto the plane using simple dot products, and record extremal values along the two derived basis vectors. In addition, record the contact with greatest penetration depth. You can actually work with contact indices to avoid manipulating the more expensive contact structures.

After all contacts in the cluster have been processed, at most five contacts are left:

- Four contacts located on the 2D AABB around contact projections in the plane.
- One contact with greatest penetration depth.

It sometimes happens that the final list of five contacts actually contains the same contact multiple times. A small $O(n^2)$ loop eventually removes redundant contacts from the list. Remaining contacts are sent to the dynamics engine (see Figure 3.5.4).

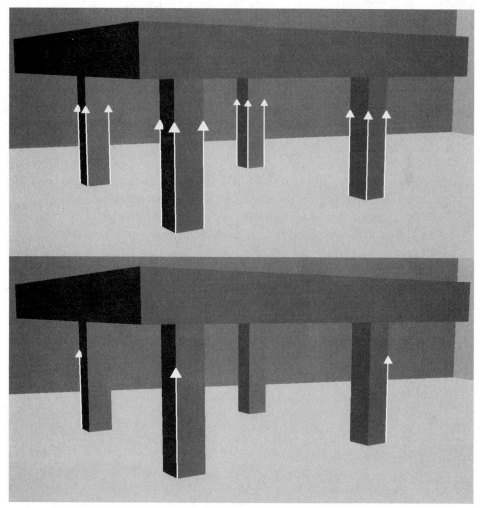

FIGURE 3.5.4 *Composite objects also benefit from contact reduction.*

Details on Persistence

If a physics engine does not already support contact persistence, it can be implemented through hashing. During a simulation step, contacts are recorded in a double-buffered contact vector. Double buffering ensures that contacts from the previous step are still available in the current step. The contact persistence code is then given the two lists of contacts to find correspondences between them.

Contact Identifier

The contact structure originally contains the two bodies in contact (either using handles or actual pointers). To implement contact persistence, a 64-bit *contact ID* is added to the structure. Contact generation routines (i.e., portions of code responsible for filling the contact structure) are now also responsible for creating a unique identifier describing each contact. Typically, this 64-bit ID is composed of two 32-bit parts, each of them encoding an object's *feature* (vertex, edge, face) that was used to create the contact. These identifiers only depend on the contact generation code that created them, and can be set up in any arbitrary way as long as they define a given contact in a nonambiguous way. A feature can actually be more than standard vertices, edges, or faces—for example, a voxel index works as well.

Hashing

First, create hash values for all contacts of the *previous* step, and store them in a hash table. Then, loop through current contacts and hash them into the previous table in search of a similar contact. The key to the algorithm is the use of object *and* contact identifiers in the hash value. The advantages of this approach over one that actually keeps persistent data for each *active pair* (i.e., a pair of colliding objects) are numerous:

- It requires minimal modifications to integrate with an existing physics engine.
- The main hashing part is only about a page of code, plus a few extra lines in each contact routine to generate the IDs.
- It is fast (experiments show an $O(n)$ behavior).
- It is robust, since it does not examine positions or normals to match old contacts to current ones.
- It does not use complex memory management, contrary to a solution where each active pair actually maintains a persistent contact array.

The primary disadvantage is that if a vertex-face contact becomes an edge-edge contact, persistence is lost.

Conclusion

This article presented an approach to reduce contact points by grouping them according to normals before applying an approximate hull computation. Contact points are made persistent using a feature-based identification system. In our own work, friction forces are computed once for each of the resulting reduced groups of contact points, instead of separately at each contact as we did previously. The application of this algorithm did not have a significant negative impact on performance, but managed to reduce contact points when working with high detail geometry, which in turn lead to improved performance and increased stability. The approximate nature of the aggressive contact removal did not lead to a visible drop in simulation accuracy, primarily because the contact points with the greatest penetration are never reduced.

References

[Anitescu99] Anitescu, Mihai, F.A. Potra, and D. Stewart, "Time-Stepping for Three-Dimensional Rigid-Body Dynamics," *Computer Methods in Applied Mechanics and Engineering,* Vol. 177 pp. 183–197, 1999.

[Baraff92] Baraff, David, "Dynamic Simulation of Non-Penetrating Rigid Bodies," Ph.D. thesis, Department of Computer Science, Cornell University, 1992.

[Hahn88] Hahn, J.K., "Realistic Animation of Rigid Bodies," *Computer Graphics (Proc. SIGGRAPH),* Vol. 22, pp. 229–308, 1987.

[Jakobsen01] Jakobsen, Thomas, "Advanced Character Physics," Proceedings of the Game Developer's Conference 2001, San Jose, 2001.

[Kim02] Kim, Young J., Miguel A. Otaduy, Ming C. Lin, and Dinesh Manocha, "Six Degree-of Freedom Haptic Display Using Localized Contact Computations," Tenth Symposium on Haptic Interfaces For Virtual Environment and Teleoperator Systems, March 24–25, 2002.

[Lozano-Perez83] Lozano-Perez, T., "Spatial Planning: A Configuration Space Approach," *IEEE Transaction on Computers,* C-32(2) pp. 108–120, 1983.

[Zhang-Hoff97] Zhang, Hansong, and Kenny Hoff, "Fast Backface Culling Using Normal Masks," *ACM Symposium on Interactive 3D Graphics,* Providence, 1997.

3.6

Interactive Water Surfaces

Jerry Tessendorf,
Rhythm & Hues Studios
jerryt@rhythm.com

Realistic computer-generated ocean surfaces have been used routinely in film features since 1996, in such titles as *Waterworld, Titanic, Fifth Element, The Perfect Storm, X2 XMen United, Finding Nemo,* and many more. For the most part, the algorithms underlying these productions apply Fast Fourier Transforms (FFT) to carefully crafted random noise that evolves over time as a frequency-dependent phase shift [Tessendorf02]. Those same algorithms have found their way into game code [Jensen01], [Arete03] without significant modification, producing beautiful ocean surfaces that evolve at 30 frames per second or more on unexceptional hardware.

What the FFT algorithms do not give, however, is *interactivity* between objects and the water surface. It would be difficult, for example, to have characters wade through a stream and generate a disturbance that depends directly on the motion that the player controls. A jet ski thrashing about in the water would not generate turbulent waves. Waves in a bathtub cannot bounce back and forth using FFT-based simulation. In general, it is not possible in the FFT approach to place an arbitrary object in the water and have it interact in a realistic way with the surface without a substantial loss of frame rate. For practical purposes, wave surfaces are restricted in the ways that the height data can be modified within a frame and between frames.

This article provides a new method, which has been dubbed *iWave*, for computing water surface wave propagation that overcomes this limitation. The three scenarios for the stream, jet ski, and bathtub are handled well with iWave. Objects with any shape can be present on the water surface and generate waves. Waves that approach an object reflect off of it realistically. The entire iWave algorithm amounts to a two-dimensional convolution and some masking operations, both suitable for hardware acceleration. Even without hardware assistance, a software-only implementation is capable of simulating a 128 x 128 water surface height grid at over 30 fps on 1 GHz processors. Larger grids will of course slow the frame rate down, and smaller grids will speed it up; the speed is directly proportional to the number of grid points. Because the method avoids FFTs, it is highly interactive and suitable for a wide range of possible applications.

Linear Waves

Let's begin with a quick review of the equations of motion for water surface waves. An excellent resource for details on the fluid dynamics is [Kinsman84]. The equations that are appropriate here are called the *linearized Bernoulli's equations*. The form of this equation we use here has a very strange operator that will be explained in a moment. The equation is [Tessendorf02]

$$\frac{\partial^2 h(x, y, t)}{\partial t^2} + \alpha \frac{\partial h(x, y, t)}{\partial t} = -g\sqrt{-\nabla^2}\, h(x, y, t)$$

$$(3.6.1)$$

In this equation, $h(x, y, t)$ is the height of the water surface with respect to the mean height at the horizontal position (x, y) at time t. The first term on the left is the vertical acceleration of the wave. The second term on the left side, with the constant α, is a velocity damping term, not normally a part of the surface wave equation, but is useful sometimes to help suppress numerical instabilities that can arise. The term on the right side comes from a combination of mass conservation and the gravitational restoring force. The operator

$$\sqrt{-\nabla^2} \equiv \sqrt{-\frac{\partial^2}{\partial x^2} - \frac{\partial^2}{\partial y^2}}$$

is a mass conservation operator, and we will refer to it as a vertical derivative of the surface. Its effect is to conserve the total water mass being displaced. When the height of the surface rises in one location, it carries with it a mass of water. To conserve mass, there is a region of the surface nearby where the height drops, displacing downward the same amount of water that is displaced upward in the first location.

The next section describes how to evaluate the right-hand side of Equation 3.6.1 by expressing it as a convolution. Throughout the rest of this article, the height is computed on a regular grid, as shown in Figure 3.6.1. The horizontal position (x, y) becomes the grid location (i, j) at positions $x_i = i\Delta$ and $y_j = j\Delta$, with the grid spacing Δ the same in both directions. The indices run $i = 1, \ldots, N$ and $j = 1, \ldots, M$.

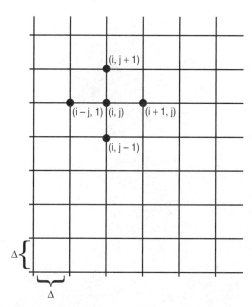

FIGURE 3.6.1 *Layout of the grid for computing wave height.*

Vertical Derivative Operator

Like any linear operator acting on a function, the vertical derivative can be implemented as a convolution on the function to which it is applied. In this section, we build up this convolution, applied to height data on a regular grid. We also determine the best size of the convolution and compute the tap weights.

As a convolution, the vertical derivative operates on the height grid as

$$\sqrt{-\nabla^2}\, h(i,j) = \sum_{k=-P}^{P} \sum_{l=-P}^{P} G(k,l)h(i+k,j+l)$$

(3.6.2)

The convolution kernel is square, with dimensions $(2P+1) \times (2P+1)$, and can be precomputed and stored in a lookup table prior to start of the simulation. The choice of the kernel size P affects both the speed and the visual quality of the simulation. The choice $P=6$ is the smallest value that gives clearly waterlike motion.

Figure 3.6.2 shows the kernel elements $G(k,0)$ as a function of k. The two dashed vertical lines are at the points $k=6$ and $k=-6$. You can see from the plot that at larger values of k, the kernel is mostly zero, and including values of k outside the dashed lines would not contribute much to the convolution. If we stop the convolution at smaller values, say $k=5$ and $k=-5$, evaluating the convolution is faster, but we will miss some small contribution from the $k=6$, $k=-6$ terms. Experience shows that you can get really good-looking waves keeping the terms out to 6, but if you are pressed for computation time, stopping the convolution short of that can work, but it will not be as visually realistic. Terminating the kernel at a value $|\kappa| < 6$ sacrifices significant amounts of oscillation. This analysis is why the choice $P = 6$ is recommended as the best compromise for reasonable wavelike simulation.

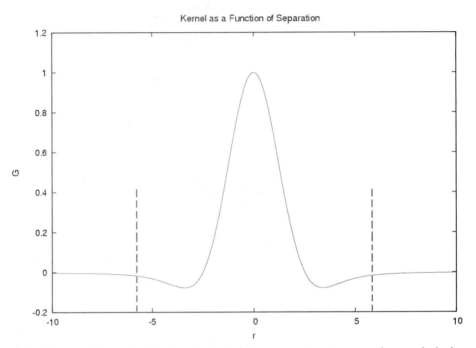

FIGURE 3.6.2   *The vertical derivative kernel in cross section. Between the two dashed lines is the* $|\kappa| < 6$ *region.*

Computing the kernel values and storing them in a lookup table is a relatively straightforward process. The first step is to compute a single number that will scale the kernel so that the center value is one. The number is

$$G_0 = \sum_n q_n^2 \exp\left(-\sigma q_n^2\right)$$

For this sum, $q_n = n\Delta q$ with $\Delta q = 0.001$ being a good choice for accuracy, and n $= 1, \ldots, 10000$. The factor σ makes the sum converge to a reasonable number, and the choice $\sigma = 1$ works well. With this number in hand, the kernel values are

$$G(k, l) = \sum_n q_n^2 \exp\left(-\sigma q_n^2\right) J_0\left(q_n r\right) \Big/ G_0$$

with the parameter $r = \sqrt{k^2 + l^2}$. The computation time for the kernel elements is relatively small, and all of the cost is an initialization; once the elements are computed, they are fixed during the simulation.

One remaining item needed to compute the convolution kernel elements is a formula for the Bessel function $J_0(x)$. This is included in the C standard math library as j0(). If you do not have access to this, a very convenient approximate fit for this function is provided in [Abramowitz72]. Although the formula there is a fitted parametric form, it is accurate to within single precision needs, and works well for the purposes of this simulation.

When you perform the convolution at each time step, there are opportunities to optimize its speed, both for particular hardware configurations and in software. Software optimizations follow because of two symmetries in the convolution kernel: The kernel is rotation symmetric, $G(k,l) = G(l,k)$, and the kernel is reflection symmetric about both axes, $G(k,l) = G(-k,-l) = G(k,-l) = G(-k,l)$. Without applying any symmetries, evaluating the convolution in Equation 3.6.2 directly requires $(2P + 1)^2$ multiplications and additions. Applying these symmetries, the convolution can be rewritten as (using the fact that $G(0,0) = 1$ by construction)

$$h(i, j) + \sum_{k=0}^{P} \sum_{l=k+1}^{P} G(k, l) \left(\begin{array}{c} h(i + k, j + l) + h(i - k, j - l) + h(i + k, j - l) \\ + h(i - k, j + l) \end{array} \right)$$

In this form, there are still $(2P + 1)^2$ additions, but only $(P + 1)P / 2$ multiplications.

This type of convolution can be cast in a form suitable for a SIMD pipeline, so graphics cards and DSPs can execute this convolution efficiently.

Wave Propagation

Now that we are able to evaluate the vertical derivative on the height grid, the propagation of the surface can be computed over time. It is simplest to use an explicit scheme for time stepping. Although implicit methods can be more accurate and stable, they are also slower. Since we are solving a linear equation in this article, an explicit approach is fast and stable in the presence of friction, and time step sizes can be set to whatever is needed for the display frame rate. If necessary, the friction can be kept very low, although for game purposes it might be preferable to have the waves dissipate when they are no longer driven by sources.

To construct the explicit solution, the time derivatives in Equation 3.6.1 must be written as finite differences. The second derivative term can be built as a symmetric difference, and the dissipative friction term as a forward difference. Rearranging the results terms, and assuming a time step Δt, the height grid at the next time step is

$$h(i, j, t + \Delta t) = h(i, j, t) \frac{2 - \alpha \Delta t}{1 + \alpha \Delta t} - h(i, j, t - \Delta t) \frac{1}{1 + \alpha \Delta t}$$

$$- \frac{g \Delta t^2}{1 + \alpha \Delta t} \sum_{k=-P}^{P} \sum_{l=-P}^{P} G(k, l) h(i + k, j + l, t)$$

$$(3.6.3)$$

In terms of data structures, this algorithm for propagation can be run with three copies of the heightfield grid. For this discussion, the grids are held in the float arrays height, vertical_derivative, and previous_height. During the simulation, the array height always holds the new height grid, previous_height holds the height grid from the previous time step, and vertical_derivative holds the vertical derivative of the height grid from the previous time step. Before simulation begins, they should all been initialized to zero for each element. The pseudocode to accomplish the propagation is

```
float height[N*M];
float vertical_derivative[N*M];
float previous_height[N*M];

// ... initialize to zero ...

// ... begin loop over frames ...

// --- This is the propagation code ---
// Convolve height with the kernel
// and put it into vertical_derivative
Convolve( height, vertical_derivative );

float temp;
for(int k=0; k<N*M; k++)
{
    temp  = height[k];
    height[k] = height[k]*(2.0-
                        alpha*dt)/(1.0+alpha*dt)
            - previous_height[k]/(1.0+alpha*dt)
            - vertical_derivative[k]
                *g*dt*dt/(1.0+alpha*dt);
    previous_height[k] = temp;
}
// --- end propagation code ---

// ... end loop over frames ...
```

The quantities in vertical_derivative and previous_height could be useful for embellishing the visual look of the waves. For example, a large value in vertical_derivative indicates strong gravitational attraction of the waves back to the mean position. Comparing the value in previous_height with that in height at the location of strong vertical_derivative can determine roughly whether the wave is at a peak or a trough. If it is at a peak, a foam texture could be used in that area. This is not a concrete algorithm grounded in physics or oceanography, but just a speculation about how peaks of the waves might be found. The point of this is simply that the two additional grids vertical_derivative and previous_height could have some additional benefit in the simulation and rendering of the wave height field beyond just the propagation steps.

Interacting Obstructions and Sources

Up to this point, we have built a method to propagate waves in a water surface simulation. While the propagation involves a relatively fast convolution, everything we have discussed could have been accomplished just as efficiently (possibly more efficiently) with a FFT approach such as the ones mentioned in the introduction. The real power of this convolution method is the ease with which some additional 2D processing can generate highly realistic interactions between objects in the water, and pump disturbances into the water surface.

The fact that we can get away with 2D processing to produce interactivity is, in some ways, a miracle. Normally in a fluid dynamic simulation the fluid velocity on and near a boundary is reset according to the type of boundary condition and requires understanding of geometric information about the boundary, such as its outward normal. Here we get away with effectively none of that analysis, which is critical to the speed of this approach.

Sources

One way of creating motion in the fluid is to have sources of displacement. A source is represented as a 2D grid $s(i,j)$ of the same size and dimensions as the height grid. The source grid should have zero values wherever no additional motion is desired. At locations in which the waves are being "poked" and/or "pulled," the value of the source grid can be positive or negative. Then, just prior to propagation step in Equation 3.6.3, the height grid is updated with $h(i,j) = h(i,j) + s(i,j)$. Since the source is an energy input per frame, it should change over the course of the simulation, unless a constant buildup of energy really is desired. An impulse source generates a ripple.

Obstructions

Obstructions are extremely easy to implement in this scheme. An additional grid for obstructions is filled with float values, primarily with two extreme values. This grid acts as a mask indicating where obstructions are present. At each grid point, if there is no obstruction present, then the value of the obstruction grid at that point is 1.0. If a grid point is occupied by an obstruction, then the obstruction grid value is 0.0. At grid points on the border around an obstruction, the value of the obstruction grid is some intermediate value between 0.0 and 1.0. The intermediate region acts as an anti-aliasing of the edge of the obstruction.

Given this obstruction mask, the obstruction's influence is computed by simply multiplying the height grid by the obstruction mask, so that the wave height is forced to zero in the presence of the obstruction, and left unchanged in areas outside the obstruction. Amazingly, that is all that must be done to properly account for objects on the water surface! This simple step causes waves that propagate to the obstruction to reflect correctly off it. It also produces refraction of waves that pass through a narrow slit channel in an obstruction. In addition, it permits the obstruction to have any shape at all, animating in any way that the user wants it to.

The pseudocode for an application with sources and obstructions is:

```
float source[N*M], obstruction[N*M];
// ... set the source and obstruction grids

for(int k = 0; k < N*M; k++)
{
    height[k] += source[k];
    height[k] *= obstruction[k];
}

// ... now apply propagation
```

Wakes

Wakes from moving objects are naturally produced by the iWave method of interactivity. In this special case, the shape of the obstruction is also the shape of the source. Setting source[k] = 1.0-obstruction[k] works as long as there is an anti-aliased region around the edge of the obstruction. With this choice, moving an obstacle around in the grid produces a wake behind it that includes the V-shaped Kelvin wake. It also produces a type of stern wave and waves running along the side of the obstacle. The details of the shape, timing, and extent of these wake components are sensitive to the shape and motion of the obstacle.

Ambient Waves

The iWave method is not very effective at generating persistent large-scale wave phenomena like open ocean waves. If an application desires these "ambient waves" that are not generated in the iWave method, there is an additional procedure that avoids explicitly simulating the ambient waves.

The ambient waves consist of a height grid that has been generated by some other procedure. For example, FFT methods could be used to generate ocean waves and store them in a height grid. Since we are only trying to compute the interaction of the ambient waves with an obstruction, the ambient waves should not contribute to the simulation outside the region of the obstruction. The pseudocode for modifying the height grid, prior to propagation and just after application of obstructions and sources as done previously, is

```
float ambient[N*M];

// ... set the ambient grid for this time step

// ... just after the source and obstruction, apply:
for (int k = 0; k < N*M; k++)
{
    height[k] -= ambient[k]*(1.0-obstruction[k]);
}
```

```
// ... now apply the propagation
```

With this method, ambient waves of any character can interact with objects of any animating shape.

Grid Boundaries

Up to this point, we have ignored the problem of how to treat the boundaries of the grid. The problem is that the convolution kernel requires data from grid points a distance P in all four directions from the central grid point of the convolution. Therefore, when the central grid point is fewer than P points from a boundary of the grid, missing data must be filled in according to some criterion. There are two types of boundary conditions that are fairly easy to apply: periodic and reflecting boundaries.

Periodic Boundaries

In this situation, a wave encountering a boundary appears to continue to propagate inward from the boundary on the opposite side. In performing the convolution near the boundaries, the grid coordinates in Equation 3.6.3 ($i + k$ and $j + l$) may be outside of the ranges $[0, N - 1]$ and $[0, M - 1]$. Applying the modulus (i+k)%N is guaranteed to be in the range $[-N + 1, N - 1]$. To insure that the result is always positive, a double modulus can be used: ((i+k)%N + N)%N. Doing the same for the $j + l$ coordinate insures that periodic boundary conditions are enforced.

Reflecting Boundaries

Reflecting boundaries turn a wave around and send it back into the grid from the boundary the wave is incident on, much like a wave that reflects off an obstacle in the water. If the coordinate $i + k$ is greater than $N - 1$ then it is changed to $2N-i-k$. If the coordinate is less than zero, it is negated; in other words, it becomes $-i-k$, which is positive. An identical procedure should also be applied to the $j + l$ coordinate.

To efficiently implement either of these two types of boundary treatments, the fastest approach is to divide the grid into nine regions as follows:

1. The inner portion of the grid with the range of coordinates $i \in [P, N-1-P]$ and $j \in [P, M-1-P]$.
2. The right-hand side $i \in [N-P, N-1]$ and $j \in [P, M-1-P]$.
3. The left-hand side $i \in [0, P-1]$ and $j \in [P, M-1-P]$.
4. The top side $i \in [P, N-1-P]$ and $j \in [0, P-1]$.
5. The bottom side $i \in [P, N-1-P]$ and $j \in [M-P, M-1]$.
6. The four corners that remain.

Within each region, the particular boundary treatment required can be coded efficiently without conditionals or extra modulus operations.

Surface Tension

So far, the type of simulation we discussed is the propagation of gravity waves. Gravity waves dominate surface flows on scales of approximately a foot or larger. On smaller scales, the character of the propagation changes to include surface tension. Surface tension causes waves to propagate faster at smaller spatial scales, which tends to make the surface appear to be more rigid than without it. For our purposes, surface tension is characterized by a length scale L_T, which determines the maximum size of the surface tension waves. The only change required of our procedure is a different computation of the convolution kernel. The kernel calculation becomes

$$G(k, l) = \sum_n q_n^2 \sqrt{1 + q_n^2 L_T^2} \, \exp\left(-\sigma q_n^2\right) J_0\left(q_n r\right) \Big/ G_0$$

Other than this change, the entire iWave process is the same.

Conclusion

The iWave method of water surface propagation is a very flexible approach to creating interactive disturbances of water surfaces. Because it is based on 2D convolution and some simple 2D image manipulation, high frame rates can be obtained even in a software-only implementation. Hardware acceleration of the convolution should make iWave suitable for many game platforms. The increased interactivity of the water surface with objects in a game could open new areas of gameplay that previously were not available to the game developer.

References

[Abramowitz72] Abramowitz, Milton, and Irene A. Stegun, *Handbook of Mathematical Functions*, Dover, 1972. Sections 9.4.1 and 9.4.3.

[Arete03] Arete Entertainment, available online at *www.areteis.com*.

[Jensen01] Jensen, Lasse, online tutorial, available online at *www.gamasutra.com/gdce/jensen/jensen_01.htm*, 2001.

[Kinsman84] Kinsman, Blair, *Wind Waves*, Dover, 1984.

[Tessendorf02] Tessendorf, Jerry, "Simulating Ocean Water," *Simulating Nature*, SIGGRAPH Course Notes, available online at *http://users.adelphia.net/~tessendorf*, 2002.

3.7

Fast Deformations with Multilayered Physics

Thomas Di Giacomo and

Nadia Magnenat-Thalmann,

MIRALab, C.U.I.,

University of Geneva

thomas@miralab.unige.ch,
thalmann@miralab.unige.ch

One of the major goals of games is to provide a high level of interaction to players. Deformations, such as convincing animated cloth, facial animation with skinning, soft bodies, and so forth, can enhance the immersion and the gameplay offered to players. However, deformations are expensive to compute, mostly because of the heavy physics required, and because of the processing of collisions. Although recent work has proposed methods to speed up deformation calculations, games still make little use of deformable objects. The cost of combining deformations with other modules and resources involved in a complete game engine is still prohibitive, and the implementation of physically based deformations can still be quite complex.

This article presents a simple yet efficient way to create nice and cheap controllable deformations that can be used to add a bit of life to your game environments. The main idea here is to simplify the mass-spring systems commonly used in soft-body simulation into a two-layer problem that runs much faster. The animation system described herein works well for flexible thin or thick linear deformable bodies (wires with deformable volume, pipes, snakes, etc.) and adapts easily to other objects, such as skin deformations (quite similar to [Jianhua94]) and cloth sleeves, by adjusting the topology of two mass-spring layers in a pre-modeling step.

Integration of such deformable objects into your game environment is quite straightforward. The companion CD-ROM contains sample code that is operable on standard PCs, and some details are given in this article to easily port it to handheld PDAs and programmable GPUs.

Physically Based Animation LOD and Related Work

Similar to level-of-detail (LOD) for rendering geometry, you can use LOD for physics-based animation to manage the expensive CPU and memory costs involved in calculating deformations, providing a controlled tradeoff between speed and realism. Past and ongoing work on LOD for physics should make it more practical to use real-time physics in game engines.

Physics LOD

There are two main ways to increase the speed of physically based animation engines. The first is to optimize the expensive steps, namely collision detection and time integration. The second is the use of LOD for animation. As for rendered geometry, animation is scalable and can be simplified in certain cases; for example, when motions are too fast, too far away, or too numerous for human sight as described in [Berka97], or when motions are of low interest and do not need complex calculations. To simplify or refine motions, you need to create an adaptable animation engine that ensures smooth transitions between LOD levels (to avoid popping animations when switching levels). For example, you can apply this idea to human articulated figures, by decreasing the sampling frequency of motions, and the degrees of freedom of human articulated figure [Granieri95]. By implementing physically based animation for some LOD levels, and procedural animation for other LOD levels, you can create *hybrid models*. Optionally, you can create a single *multiresolution* animation technique that uses the same technique at every LOD level. Using such an animation engine, you can select, at anytime during the game, the appropriate LOD based on a desired visual quality, on available system resources, on target performances, and so forth. For obvious reasons, during transitions, the multiresolution models provide easier continuity of motions than hybrid models do. On the other side, hybrid models give access to a wider range of complexities and behaviors to the animations.

Hybrid Models

Hybrid models combine procedural and physically based animations as the different levels within an animation engine that supports LOD. As an example, refer to [Carlson97], who simulates one-legged robots with three different resolutions, from the most complex and realistic to the fastest: dynamics, kinematics, and single particle motion. Transitions between these levels are possible only at certain times, when the object reaches particular states. If you want animated natural environments in your game, see [Perbet01], "Animating Prairies in Real-Time," or [Di Giacomo03], "Real-

Time Animation of Trees," which uses a similar LOD philosophy. Both of these authors ensured smooth transitions between the levels by cubic or linear blending of motions (depending on the desired smoothness). Some hybrid systems use multilayered mass-spring systems for fast deformations. For example, to simulate wrinkles on cloth, [Kang02] combined two mass-spring systems "loop-linked": one rough mesh for the global physically based deformations, and one dense mesh for the small geometrical deformations, which produce wrinkles. [D'Aulignac99] proposed another example of a multilayered mass-spring network. It is used to simulate the deformation of human meshes.

For hybrid models to be beneficial, the different LOD methods must have resource costs that scale up or down with the LOD as appropriate. Additionally, the different methods should be constrained such that the results between adjacent LODs are matched to ensure smooth transitions.

Multiresolution LOD Models

Existing multiresolution models for physics LOD mainly use mass-spring and finite element networks. Roughly, these models locally refine or simplify the mesh of physical nodes dynamically in time. For example, [Hutchinson96] refines mass-spring systems when certain constraints are forced (e.g., when angles between springs exceed a threshold value). [Brown01] used a simplified mass-spring system to reduce computations. By taking advantage of the locality of deformations in particular applications (such as surgery cuts), physical computations are localized to a few control points and the resulting deformations are propagated to other nodes. For real-time applications, finite element methods are also accelerated by adaptive techniques, such as proposed by [Debunne01] with progressive meshes and an adaptive time step, and by [Capell02] with a multiresolution hierarchical volumetric subdivision to simulate dynamic deformations. With creativity and a bit of time, you can probably integrate all the cited work into your game engines, allowing you to create more dynamic and interactive game worlds.

Fast Deformations with Layered Mass-Spring Physics

The main issue being the running speed, you need to reduce the points that are computed with dynamics. As such, this physically based animation engine has three main features. First, the mesh used for physics contains far fewer vertices and faces than the corresponding rendered mesh does. Second, the deformations are simulated with a bi-layered mass-spring network with the first layer, considered as a backbone structure, controlling global motion, and the second layer being only dynamic in one dimension (to limit computation). The latter layer controls the envelope and overall volumetric deformations of the object; for example, the compression due to some collisions with other objects in the scene. An easy way to understand the combined effect of the two layers is to consider the entire deformable body as a generalized cylinder. The backbone layer computes the stretching, twisting, and turning of the axis of the cylinder.

The second layer computes locally constrained radial deformations. Finally, the use of Verlet integration provides speed and stability to the system. A layered mass-spring system can be computationally very cheap, while providing deformations that are perfect for games.

Representing and Simulating the Backbone Layer

For this method, a stringlike mass-spring network is the backbone structure that moves and provides for stretching, twisting, and turning of an object "skeleton" (see Figure 3.7.1). The axial backbone structure also provides geometrical input and constraints for the volume deformation layer.

The backbone is made of masses linked with linear springs, with each mass having only one parent and one child, except the ones at extremities. At least one mass, called the *root mass*, exists at an end of the network and has no parent.

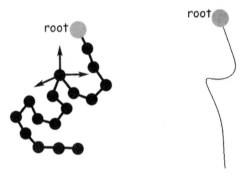

FIGURE 3.7.1   *Backbone spring system (left), and resulting wires with enough masses and appropriate spring lengths (right). The top mass in gray is the root mass. Its motion is user-controlled.*

Simulating the motion of the backbone is straightforward. You must compute a force f^i (in the text, bold is used for vector quantities) for each mass i, using Hooke's law applied to a one-dimensional network:

$$\vec{f}^{i} = -k_s^i \frac{\vec{x}^i - \vec{x}^{i-1} - l_0^i}{\| \vec{x}^i - \vec{x}^{i-1} \|} + k_s^{i+1} \frac{\vec{x}^{i+1} - \vec{x}^i - l_0^{i+1}}{\| \vec{x}^{i+1} - \vec{x}^i \|} \tag{3.7.1}$$

Here, k_s is the stiffness and l_0 the unstretched length (both constant here) of the ith spring; and x_i the position of the ith mass. You can disable external and internal forces on the root mass to make it possible for the user to adjust its position, via mouse interaction for example. In the same manner, the root mass can be geometrically constrained by another object in the scene; for example, bound to the hand of a virtual character. You can add additional fixed nodes similar to the root node, depending on the behavior needed for your game. Once the forces are computed, you update the shape of the backbone using a Verlet integrator to step the motion forward in time.

The Volume Deformation Layer

A second mass-spring layer simulates volume deformations. A series of cross sections, each with four radial masses, comprises this layer. These cross sections represent an envelope for the volume deformation. For the best deformations, you should create a single cross section for every mass of the backbone layer, although it is permissible to use fewer cross sections. The volume envelope masses are connected to the backbone masses with linear constrained elastic springs. Figure 3.7.2 (left) illustrates one of these volume envelope cross sections.

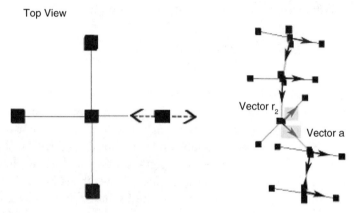

FIGURE 3.7.2 *One-dimensional radial deformations (left), and the reconstruction, at each frame, of the envelope radius depending on the backbone structure (right).*

As illustrated in Figure 3.7.2, each radial mass is constrained to move one-dimensionally along its radius. Simulating the volume deformation requires just slightly more work than the backbone simulation does. Being 1D, the computations of dynamics are highly reduced; however, the resulting motion is also only 1D. To ensure 3D deformations, you need to update the radius as follows. First, during each frame, every cross section radius vector r_i is recomputed to be orthogonal to its corresponding backbone spring direction a, as illustrated by Figure 3.7.2 (right). This computation is done by:

```
void UpdateRadii(vec a, vec* r1, vec* r2, vec* r3, vec* r4)
{
    // Find a vector non-collinear with the axis
    if (a->x!=0)
        r1 = {-a->y, a->x, a->z};
    else if (a->y!=0)
        r1 = {a->y, -a->x, a->z};
    else
        r1 = {a->z, a->x, -a->y};

    // Compute the 3 remaining vectors
    CrossVector(a, r1, r2);
```

```
    // CopyVector(destination, source)
    CopyVector(r3, -r1);    CopyVector(r4, -r2);
    Normalize(r1);          Normalize(r2);
    Normalize(r3);          Normalize(r4);
}
```

The updated radii define the directions along which the cross-section masses are allowed to move. Note that the four vectors, r_i, at each cross section are normalized to simplify the physics update of the cross section masses.

Once you have calculated the new cross section radii, the next step is to compute one-dimensional forces for each cross-section mass using an adapted Hooke's law:

$$f^i = -k_s^i (x^i - l_0^i) \frac{x^i \vec{r}^i}{\| x^i - l_0^i \|} \vec{r}^i \tag{3.7.2}$$

where i, in $[0, 3]$, is the index of the envelope masses for the current cross section, x^i a real number corresponding to the position of mass i on its current radial vector r^i, and l_0 the unstretched position on r. The force f^i does not depend on neighboring envelope masses since envelope nodes are not linked with springs. Note also that this force is applied only to the cross-section masses and not to the corresponding parent axial nodes of the backbone structure. Hence, the volume is not preserved, although one can reduce differences of volume by modifying positions of axial nodes using repositioning within the Verlet integration.

Updating the Deformation Using Verlet Integration

Once the forces are defined, you update the deformation by integrating the backbone and envelope masses over time (Newton's Second Law of Motion) to update their positions. Integration is an important step for physically based engines, as it is determines the stability and for the speed of the simulations. In this case, to compute new positions the application uses explicit Euler or Verlet integration. For detailed considerations on the latter scheme, please refer to the corresponding article by Nick Porcino in this book. The basic Verlet integrator is a velocity-less scheme based on the current and previous positions rather than particles' velocities:

$$\begin{cases} \vec{x}_{t+\Delta t} = \alpha \vec{x}_t - \beta \vec{x}_{t-\Delta t} + \vec{a} \Delta t^2 \\ \vec{x}_{t-\Delta t} = \vec{x}_t \end{cases} \tag{3.7.3}$$

where $x_{t+\Delta t}$ is the next position, x_t the current one, $x_{t-\Delta t}$ the previous one, Δt a constant timestep, a the acceleration, and α and β drag coefficients. For example, one can set $\alpha = 2$ and $\beta = 1$ for a system without drag, or $\alpha = 1.99$ and $\beta = 0.99$, for a system with a small amount of drag. Since this integrator scheme is velocity-less, positions and velocities do not get out of synchronization, ensuring high system stability (see Table 3.7.1 where the stability value is the relative intensity of forces from which the system explodes).

Table 3.7.1   Comparison of Two Explicit Integration Methods, Using the Same Time Step, the Same Number of Masses and Springs, Tested With and Without Collision

Integration Scheme	Speed	Stability
Verlet	36 to 40 fps	$> 10^6$
Explicit Euler	37 to 40 fps	1

Generating Render Meshes from the Physics Model

For games, a physics model for deformation is useless unless it can be tied to a rendered mesh. Ideally, to avoid expensive skinning computations, the rendered geometry and the physics model will be directly related. The envelope masses of the second mass-spring layer can be stitched together to form a coarse mesh for rendering, but the envelope is far too coarse to provide a high-quality visual. You can achieve a higher-quality render mesh while avoiding the need to create a separate artist-generated skin, and an expensive per-frame skinning calculation, by using the coarse physics envelope as a control mesh for a NURBS or subdivision surface. For example, if you consider envelope masses to be control points for NURBS-based interpolation, then you can compute NURBS tessellations offline and update the created vertices on the fly for low cost. The Hermite interpolant is ideal: its inputs are two positions (e.g., envelope mass positions), and two vectors at these positions (e.g., the corresponding radii).

```
void CEnvNod::GeomNodesConstruction()
{
    // Projection of the 1D position on the radius
    vec pos = 3DGlobalPosition();
    vec brosPos = m_Bros->3DGlobalPosition();
    // Derivatives for the interpolation
    vec der = 1.5*brosPos;
    vec brosDer = -1.5*pos;

    CInterp in = CInterp(pos, der, brosPos, brosDer);
    CAlpha alp = CAlpha(0.f, 1.f);
    m_NurbsPts[0] = in(alp(0.f));
    // Interpolation, storage of nodes in m_NurbsPts
    for(int s = 1; s <= Accuracy; s++)
        m_NurbsPts[s] = in(alp((float)s/Accuracy));
}
```

Note that for sake of simplicity, mass positions are projected onto the radii. By specifying the interpolation step, the number of points, and thus the number of polygons, is adjustable and provides a controlled tradeoff between speed and realism for the rendering step (see Figure 3.7.3).

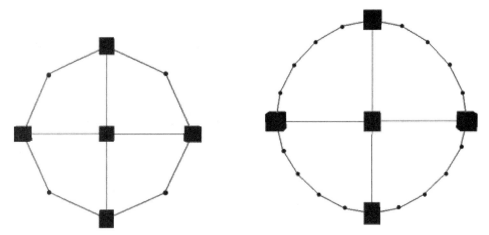

FIGURE 3.7.3   *With the same animation structure, the number of polygons in a mesh can be adapted with a selected accuracy of the NURBS subdivisions (two on the left and five on the right).*

Computing the geometric points in this way enables us to smoothly modify the geometry according to the deformation of the envelope masses; see Figure 3.7.4 (left). The interpolated geometric nodes are then linked to their vertical neighbors along the direction of the backbone layer to build a set of quads, with appropriate normals, for rendering; see Figure 3.7.4 (right).

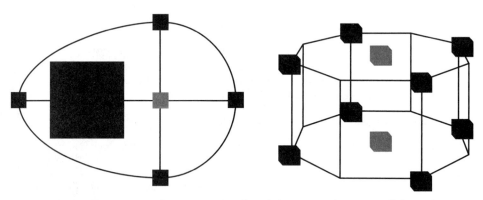

FIGURE 3.7.4   *Illustration of an internal radial deformation due to a colliding object with a spherical bounding box (left), and construction of the mesh, using the NURBS points (right). Axial masses are grayed.*

Sample Implementation

The companion CD-ROM contains a sample PC implementation of this technique. The computations and rendering code are separated to make it straightforward to port the code to different platforms and to use different rendering APIs. Figure 3.7.5 shows several results of using the PC code.

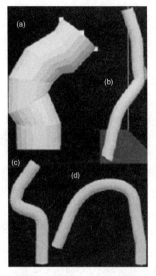 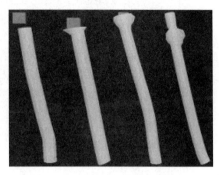

FIGURE 3.7.5 *The picture on the left illustrates the generation of quads and normals (a), an envelope deformation due to collision with a wall (b), and resulting objects (c) and (d). The picture on the right is a sequence that shows how "inside" collisions deform the models. These screenshots are taken from real-time animations of the standard PC implementation.*

This method can even be ported to handheld game consoles and PDAs. To develop graphics on a PDA such as the PocketPC, you should be aware of several facts. First, these devices do not now have external video controllers (at least practical ones). Second, these systems lack a graphics pipeline, and contain no VRAM, thus the main system RAM must be used to store a software framebuffer. Using system memory for both code and framebuffer severely limits the practical complexity of software. Finally, PocketPCs lack a floating-point processor, while most graphical data are floats. Hence, careful choices must be made about how to implement the underlying mathematics on the integer-based hardware. The authors have implemented an implementation of the method for PocketPCs using a naive but straightforward method. The code computes results in a manner similar to the PC version, but uses floating-point emulation. Just before rendering, the coordinates are converted into integers that are scaled to the range of the graphics API (in this case PocketGL 1.2) world.

```
// Function returning a PocketGL integer position
const vec* CIntPGLConversion::ConvertObjPosition()
{
    return ((int) iMaxPocketGL*m_vecPosition/fMaxGL);
}
// Function called at each frame
```

```
void mainLoop()
{
    // Compute with float
    object->CheckWorldCollisions();
    object->ComputeForce();
    object->Integrate();
    // Convert to integer
    convertor->ConvertObjMesh(object->m_Mesh);
}
```

Another possible implementation is the use of GPU hardware shaders to further speed up the animation. Several submodules of this application could be computed directly in hardware: the orthogonality computation of radii, the Verlet integration, and so forth.

Table 3.7.2 illustrates some performance measurements achieved using the PC and PocketPC implementations. The accuracy number is the number of subdivision used for the construction of the geometry.

Table 3.7.2   Performance of the Different Implementations

Number of Mass/NURBS Accuracy	PC Version (fps)	PocketPC Version (fps)
1 axial + 1 * 4 radial/1 accuracy	85	24
10 axial + 10 * 4 radial/2 accuracy	84	23
20 axial + 20 * 4 radial/4 accuracy	83	10
40 axial + 40 * 4 radial/6 accuracy	82	7
100 axial + 100 * 4 radial/6 accuracy	80	3
150 axial + 150 * 4 radial/6 accuracy	76	< 1

Conclusion

While not a very accurate animation in terms of physics, the method described here enables cheap, visually plausible deformations and is easy to implement on a wide range of gaming platforms. Physics computations are reduced mainly by limiting the number of dynamic nodes, and by constraining some of them to be one-dimensional. The method achieves good results thanks to the bi-layered approach, the use of the coarse physics mesh as a control mesh for generating higher resolution meshes for rendering, the constraints between springs, and the stability provided by the Verlet integration scheme. Integrating such deformations in any game engine on different platforms is rather straightforward. Further, the use of CPU and memory remains within acceptable limits.

References

[Berka97] Berka, Roman, "Reduction of Computations in Physic-Based Animation Using Level of Detail," *Proceedings of Spring Conference of Computer Graphics*, 1997.

[Brown01] Brown, Joel, et al., "Real-Time Simulation of Deformable Objects: Tools and Application," *Proceedings of Computer Animation*, 2001.

[Capell02] Capell, Steve, et al., "A Multiresolution Framework for Dynamic Deformations," *Proceedings of Symposium on Computer Animation*, 2002.

[Carlson97] Carlson, Deborah, et al., "Simulation Levels of Detail for Real-Time Animation," *Proceedings of Graphics Interface*, 1997.

[D'Aulignac99] D'Aulignac, Diego, et al., "Modeling the Dynamics of the Human Thigh for a Realistic Echographic Simulator with Force Feedback," *Proceedings of Conference on Medical Image Computing-Assisted Intervention*, 1999.

[Debunne01] Debunne, Gilles, et al., "Dynamic Real-Time Deformations Using Space & Time Adaptive Sampling," *Computer Graphics Proceedings* (SIGGRAPH 2001).

[Di Giacomo03] Di Giacomo, Thomas, et al., "Real-Time Animation of Trees," *Graphics Programming Methods*, Charles River Media, 2003.

[Granieri95] Granieri, John, et al., "Production and Playback of Human Figure Motion for Visual Simulation," *Proceedings of Graphics Interface*, 1995.

[Hutchinson96] Hutchinson, David, et al., "Adaptive Refinement for Mass/Spring Simulations," *Proceedings of Eurographics Workshop on Computer Animation and Simulation*, 1996.

[Jianhua94] Jianhua, Shen, et al., "Human Skin Deformation from Cross Sections," *Proceedings of Computer Graphics International*, 1994.

[Kang02] Kang, Young-Min, et al., "Bilayered Approximate Integration for Rapid and Plausible Animation of Virtual Cloth with Realistic Wrinkles," *Proceedings of Computer Animation*, 2002.

[Perbet01] Perbet, Frank, et al., "Animating Prairies in Real-Time," *Proceedings of Symposium on Interactive 3D Graphics*, 2001.

3.8

Modal Analysis for Fast, Stable Deformation

James F. O'Brien,
University of California, Berkeley

job@eecs.berkeley.edu

Particle systems, rigid-body simulations, and articulated-body simulations have all become relatively common in commercial games. They allow many game objects to demonstrate an essentially unlimited range of realistic behaviors in response to player actions. However, solid objects that bend, twist, stretch, squash, or otherwise change their shape, such as the objects shown in Figure 3.8.1, require some form of deformable object simulation.

FIGURE 3.8.1 *This image sequence shows frames from an animation of a pair of objects colliding with each other. Each object is a hybrid simulation that incorporates a rigid and a deformable component. The deformable component uses modal simulation. Image courtesy of J. O'Brien, C. Shen, and K. Hauser. © Copyright 2003 U.C. Berkeley. Used with permission.*

Simple, low-resolution objects can be easily modeled within a game using, for example, basic spring-and-mass systems, but attempting to use simplistic deformable simulation methods for more interesting, complex objects invariably leads to difficulties caused by lack of realism, excessive computational cost, and/or poor robustness. These systems rely on numerical time integration to compute their behavior, and robust integration schemes can become quite expensive for nontrivial systems. Furthermore, large systems with realistic material parameters can be subject to stability problems that force very small time steps and result in impractically slow simulation times.

This article describes a technique known as *modal analysis* or *modal simulation* that can be used to model certain deformable objects in an extremely effective manner. The basic idea behind the technique is that an existing deformable simulation—for example, a spring-and-mass or finite-element simulation—can be analyzed and then broken apart into distinct mathematical components, called *modes*, that do not interact with each other. Because they do not interact with each other, the modes' behavior can be analyzed independently, and when the behavior of each mode is known, the modes that have undesirable behavior can be discarded. The remaining modes are each simple enough that instead of requiring *numerical* time integration, their behavior can be computed with simple *analytical* solutions. By itself, a modal simulation *cannot go unstable* because it does not use numerical time integration; because stability is not an issue, *large time steps* can be used, and because only a few modes will suffice even for large, complex models, each step is *cheap to compute*. For example, the model shown in Figure 3.8.2 has 871 vertices, but when reduced to a modal simulation using only 40 modes, the simulation can easily run in real-time on a Sony Playstation2 using only a fraction of the CPU.

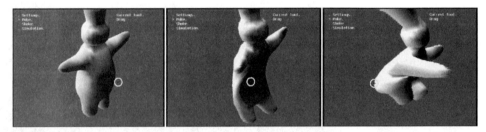

FIGURE 3.8.2   *These images are screen shots from a demo application running natively on a Sony PlayStation2. The circle highlights the cursor that the user is using to poke and pull an elastic figure. Image courtesy of J. O'Brien, C. Shen, and K. Hauser. © Copyright 2003 U.C. Berkeley. Used with permission.*

Working with a modal simulation is fundamentally a two-phase process. The first part, *modal decomposition*, occurs during content development, is computationally expensive, and requires sophisticated software. The second part, the actual *modal simulation*, happens during gameplay, is computationally very cheap, and is easy to implement.

Suitability of Modal Analysis

Although modal simulations can be extremely fast and robust, the technique does have three fundamental limitations of varying significance. The first and most severe limitation requires that the original system be linearized before the modal decomposition can be performed. This puts some fundamental restrictions on the types of object that will work with modal simulation. In particular, large amounts of bending or twisting involve nonlinear deformation, and attempting to model them with a linearized modal simulation will produce visible distortion artifacts. Figure 3.8.3

shows an example of the distortion that results as a straight bar is bent progressively further from its rest shape. As can be seen in the figure, small deformations look acceptable, but large deformations take on an odd exaggerated appearance. Because of these distortions, modal simulation is best suited for compact objects that can squash or stretch but do not bend or twist significantly. Of course, for some situations, for example in a cartoon-like game, one might actually find the distorted exaggeration introduced by the linearization desirable.

The second limitation is that computing a modal decomposition requires a significant amount of work. We will describe the details of computing the decomposition shortly, but essentially it involves computing a partial eigendecomposition for a

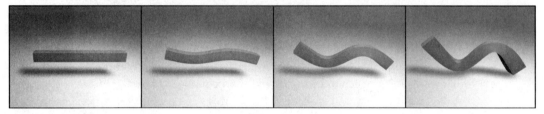

FIGURE 3.8.3 *This figure illustrates the distortion that can be introduced by linearization. The first image shows an undeformed bar. The subsequent images show the result of increasingly larger deformation. Small to moderate amounts of deformation manifest little visible error. However, large amounts of deformation produce noticeable distortion, and the last image shows both noticeable end-flare as well as distortion in its overall length. Image courtesy of J. O'Brien, C. Shen, and K. Hauser. © Copyright 2003 U.C. Berkeley. Used with permission.*

large, but sparse, matrix. Although this process can be quite expensive, the decomposition can be precomputed during game development and the resulting modes stored as part of the object. Thus, as long as the game will not dynamically generate new objects on the fly, this limitation should not pose any particular difficulties.

The final drawback to modal analysis is that it relies on a relatively advanced set of mathematical tools, and so for many people, understanding the concepts involved might at first appear difficult. Happily, it turns out that while the math required to derive the simulation methods can be complex, the final algorithms are actually quite simple.

Modal Decomposition

The first step involved in using a modal simulation requires coming up with a suitable set of modes that describe a given object. This process will consume a fair amount of computation, but as previously discussed, it takes place during content development, not during gameplay. In a very real sense, we are taking computational work that would have been done on the player's machine and precomputing that work ahead of time on the game developer's machine. The fundamentals needed to understand the decomposition are explained here, but you will probably want to use some amount of third-party software (suggestions to follow) rather than implementing it all yourself.

The Original System

We will assume that the equations of motion for the deformable simulation being decomposed can be written as

$$K\left(\mathbf{p}\right) + C\left(\dot{\mathbf{p}}\right) + M\left(\ddot{\mathbf{p}}\right) = \mathbf{f} \tag{3.8.1}$$

The variable $\mathbf{p}$ denotes a vector of parameters that describe the simulation's configuration (for example, the node positions of a mass-and-spring model or of a finite-element model), and an over-dot indicates differentiation with respect to time. K is a nonlinear function that takes as input the positions and returns elastic forces. For example, if we were using a mass-and-spring system, K would be the function that computes the spring forces exerted on all the nodes. C is a nonlinear function that takes as input velocities (possibly positions as well) and returns damping forces. The variable $\mathbf{f}$ denotes a vector of external forces such as collisions or user input. Finally, M takes the accelerations and returns the forces that would be required to generate those accelerations; in other words it is a generalization of Newton's second law, $f = ma$.

We are introducing Equation 3.8.1 in this very generic form because we don't really care what type of simulation method is used to generate the initial set of equations. We will only use Equation 3.8.1 to generate a set of matrices that summarizes how the simulation behaves, and then all subsequent manipulations will make use of those matrices. This does not mean that the results won't depend on the original simulation method: if we use a poor method, then any undesirable anisotropies or inhomogeneities it introduces will show up in the resulting matrices and therefore in the modal simulation as well.

Linearization

Once we have a description of the system to be simulated in the form of Equation 3.8.1, the next step is to linearize the system so that it can be decomposed. This linearization step is where the errors demonstrated in Figure 3.8.3 are introduced.

The process of linearizing Equation 3.8.1 requires finding a suitable linear approximation for each term in the equation. For the first term, $K(\mathbf{p})$, we will form a Taylor series expansion and then throw away all the quadratic and higher terms. This gives us

$$K(\mathbf{p}) = K(\mathbf{p}_0 + \mathbf{d}) \approx K(\mathbf{p}_0) + K(\mathbf{p}_0) \cdot \mathbf{d} \tag{3.8.2}$$

where $\mathbf{p}_0$ is the configuration where we center the expansion, $\mathbf{d} = \mathbf{p} - \mathbf{p}_0$ is the displacement from the expansion point to where one wishes to evaluate the function, and $\mathbf{K}$ is the matrix of first partials called K's Jacobian, given by $K_{ij} = \partial K_i / \partial p_j$. If we choose $\mathbf{p}_0$ to be the rest configuration of the object when no external forces are acting on it then $K(\mathbf{p}_0) = 0$, and the linearization of K is simply:

$$K(\mathbf{p}) \approx \mathbf{K} \cdot \mathbf{d} \tag{3.8.3}$$

where $\mathbf{K}$ is understood to depend on the choice of $\mathbf{p}_0$. This matrix $\mathbf{K}$ is called the system's *stiffness matrix*, and it is the same Jacobian matrix that one requires for most semi-implicit integration schemes.

For finite-element or spring-and-mass systems, K is formed by assembling individual equations, so one easy way to determine $\mathbf{K}$ is to compute a small *element* stiffness matrix for each element or spring in the system and then use those to form the *global* matrix for the entire system. Because these matrices are so frequently used, most finite-element texts will provide the element stiffness matrices for various types of useful elements.

We could proceed in a similar fashion to determine the linearizations of both C and M, but it turns out that they can be arrived at more easily. Because M is just an expression of $f = ma$, it will already be linear for most systems where $\mathbf{p}$ corresponds to position variables. Most finite-element texts will list the element mass matrices alongside the stiffness matrices, or you can use a *lumped* mass matrix where $\mathbf{M}$ is a diagonal matrix and each diagonal entry is the mass of the corresponding node. Because $\mathbf{p}_0$ is constant, $\ddot{\mathbf{d}} = \ddot{\mathbf{p}}$, and we can write $M\!\left(\ddot{\mathbf{p}}\right) \approx \mathbf{M} \cdot \ddot{\mathbf{d}}$. The damping function, C, could be some arbitrary function, but with a technique known as *Raleigh damping*, the damping matrix $\mathbf{C}$ can instead be determined by two coefficients, c_1 and c_2 according to: $\mathbf{C} = c_1 \mathbf{K} + c_2 \mathbf{M}$. With linearizations of K, C, and M, the linearized version of Equation 3.8.1 can be written as

$$\mathbf{K} \cdot \mathbf{d} + \mathbf{C} \cdot \dot{\mathbf{d}} + \mathbf{M} \cdot \ddot{\mathbf{d}} = \mathbf{f} \tag{3.8.4}$$

or, if we substitute the definition of $\mathbf{C}$ using Raleigh damping

$$\mathbf{K} \cdot \mathbf{d} + \left(c_1 \, \mathbf{K} + c_2 \, \mathbf{M}\right) \cdot \dot{\mathbf{d}} + \mathbf{M} \cdot \ddot{\mathbf{d}} = \mathbf{f} \tag{3.8.5}$$

Eigendecomposition

The step where we actually break Equation 3.8.5 apart into its modes is accomplished by solving what is known as a generalized eigenproblem. Due to space considerations, we only summarize the result here, but a more detailed explanation can be found in [O'Brien02], [Maia98], or most texts on the finite-element method.

The matrix $\mathbf{K}$ is symmetric and $\mathbf{M}$ is both symmetric and positive-definite, so we can find an invertible matrix $\mathbf{W}$, and a diagonal matrix $\mathbf{\Lambda}$ such that

$$\mathbf{K} \cdot \mathbf{W} = \mathbf{M} \cdot \mathbf{W} \cdot \mathbf{\Lambda} \tag{3.8.6}$$

The columns of $\mathbf{W}$ are the system's generalized eigenvectors, and the corresponding entries in $\mathbf{\Lambda}$ are their eigenvalues. If we premultiply Equation 3.8.5 by $\mathbf{W}^{\mathrm{T}}$, replace $\mathbf{d}$ and $\mathbf{f}$ respectively with $\mathbf{z}$ and $\mathbf{g}$ using the following substitutions:

$$\mathbf{z} = \mathbf{W}^{-1} \cdot \mathbf{d} \qquad \mathbf{d} = \mathbf{W} \cdot \mathbf{z} \qquad \mathbf{g} = \mathbf{W}^{\mathrm{T}} \cdot \mathbf{f} \qquad \mathbf{f} = \mathbf{W}^{-\mathrm{T}} \cdot \mathbf{g} \tag{3.8.7}$$

and then simplify the result, we obtain the following diagonal equation:

$$\Lambda \cdot \mathbf{z} + \left(c_1 \Lambda + c_2 \mathbf{I}\right) \cdot \dot{\mathbf{z}} + \ddot{\mathbf{z}} = \mathbf{g}$$

(3.8.8)

We will refer to values of $\mathbf{d}$ as values expressed in the original, or *spatial coordinates*, and we will refer to values of $\mathbf{z}$ as being expressed in the *modal coordinates*.

The concept behind this transformation is identical to the idea of switching between 3D coordinate systems: nothing fundamental has changed, we just have a different coordinate system to work with. However, just as some graphics problems become much easier to work with when the proper coordinate system is used, working with a simulation in its modal coordinates instead of its spatial ones will yield substantial benefits. Because Equation 3.8.8 is diagonal, if we have $\mathbf{W}$ and Λ, solving a problem by first transforming from spatial to modal coordinates, using the diagonal equations, and then transforming the solution back to spatial coordinates can be much more efficient than trying to solve the same problem directly in the spatial coordinates. Readers experienced with the Fourier transformation should find this concept very familiar because in some sense, the modal transformation is sort of a generalized Fourier transformation. Of course, computing $\mathbf{W}$ and Λ involves a substantial amount of work (i.e., finding the eigensystem), but because all the matrices are constant, that work only needs to be done once beforehand.

Analytical Solutions

While working with diagonal matrices affords many advantages, the real advantage of this decomposition arises because a diagonal system of equations is actually a set of decoupled equations that do not interact with each other. In other words, each row of Equation 3.8.8 is independent from the other rows, and they can each be written as a scalar second-order differential equation:

$$\lambda_i\, z_i + \left(c_1\, \lambda_i + c_2\right) \dot{z}_i + \ddot{z}_i = g_i$$

(3.8.9)

The homogeneous solution to these types of equations is well known:

$$z_i = a_1 e^{t\omega_i^+} + a_2 e^{t\omega_i^-}$$

(3.8.10)

where t is time, a_1 and a_2 are constants that will be determined later by the initial values of z_i, and the ω are given by:

$$\omega_i^{\pm} = \frac{-\left(c_1\, \lambda_i + c_2\right) \pm \sqrt{\left(c_1\, \lambda_i + c_2\right)^2 - 4\lambda_i}}{2}$$

(3.8.11)

The situation when the quantity under the radical is zero is a special case that we will avoid by testing to see if it is near zero, and if it is, replacing it with some minimal value (e.g., 10^{-4}) with the same sign. It is often useful to be able to evaluate the system's velocity by differentiating Equation 3.8.10, which gives us:

$$\dot{z}_i = a_1\, \omega_i^+ e^{t\omega_i^+} + a_2\, \omega_i^- e^{t\omega_i^-}$$

$$(3.8.12)$$

Understanding and Discarding the Modes

Each of the modes corresponds to one of the columns of **W**, and as we vary one of the z_i, the shape of the object changes by adding a displacement field to the object that is given by the corresponding column of **W**. As shown in Figure 3.8.4, the columns of **W** are basis shapes and any configuration of the object can be generated by some combination of these basis shapes.

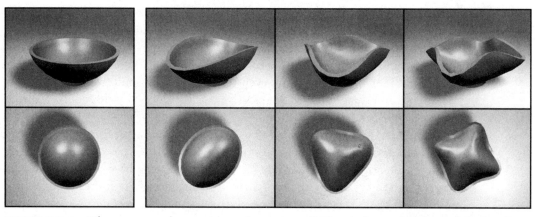

FIGURE 3.8.4 *The two rows show a side and top view of a bowl along with three of the bowl's first (sorted by eigenvalue) vibrational modes. The modes selected for the illustration are the first three nonrigid modes with distinct eigenvalues that are excited by a transverse impulse to the bowl's rim. Image courtesy of J. O'Brien, C. Shen, and K. Hauser. © Copyright 2003 U.C. Berkeley. Used with permission.*

We can also look at Equations 3.8.10 and 3.8.11 to see how each mode will behave. If the quantity in the radical in Equation 3.8.11 is negative, then ω^+ and ω^- will be complex conjugates and Equation 3.8.10 will behave like a decaying sinusoid. This case is referred to as being *underdamped*. The imaginary part of ω determines the mode's frequency in radians per second, and the real part (which will be negative) determines how quickly vibrations of that mode decay. If the quantity in the radical is positive, then $\omega+$ and $\omega-$ will be two distinct negative real numbers. This case is referred to as being *overdamped* and the resulting behavior will be an exponential decay to zero.

Once we can characterize the behavior of each mode, we can derive additional benefit by considering whether each mode is needed. In particular, we can discard modes that will have no significant effect on the phenomena we wish to model. If the eigenvalue, λ_i, associated with a particular mode is large, then the force required to cause discernible displacement of that mode will also be large. We can expect that in a given environment there will be both an upper bound on the magnitude of the forces encountered and a lower limit on the amplitude of observable movement. For example, if modeling an indoor environment, we would not expect to encounter forces in excess of 60,000N (the braking force of a large truck), and we would not be able to observe displacements less than about 0.1mm. Thus, if $\mathbf{w}$ is a column of $\mathbf{W}$ and λ is the corresponding eigenvalue, then if $\|\mathbf{w}\|/\lambda < \texttt{minResolution}/\texttt{maxForce}$, we can omit that mode from the simulation with no noticeable effect. Additionally, underdamped modes that vibrate at more than half the display's update rate will cause ugly temporal aliasing, so omitting them will actually improve the simulation results.

For most objects, nearly all of the modes are either stiff enough or high enough frequency to cause them to be discarded. A typical situation is that an object with several thousand nodes will have around 50 modes that need to be retained. Furthermore, the number of modes that must be retained is nearly independent from the resolution of the model. As a result, even very complicated simulation models can be reduced to just a small number of modes, and this reduction yields enormous computational savings during simulation.

There can also be modes with $\lambda = 0$. These modes are typically the object's rigid body modes, and they will correspond to whatever translational or rotation degrees of freedom the object had. A single free-floating 3D object will have six zero modes that correspond to three translational and three rotational degrees of freedom. Rigid body modes should be discarded as well, as they are handled elsewhere (see the section *Hybrid Simulation*).

Modal Simulation

The solution for each of the modes given by Equation 3.8.10 determines how that mode will behave over time. If we know the appropriate values for coefficients a_1 and a_2, then determining the behavior of the simulation only requires evaluating Equation 3.8.10 for each of the retained modes to determine $\mathbf{z}$, and then using Equation 3.8.7 to map back to the original spatial coordinates.

Updating Modes

Let us assume that at some time, t, we know for each mode the values of a_1 and a_2 that when fed into Equation 3.8.10 returned the current values of z_i for each mode. If we then wanted to compute the new values of z_i for each mode, the most obvious approach would be to update $t = t + \Delta t$ and then re-evaluate Equation 3.8.10. This approach is not ideal for two reasons: first, computing the exponential is relatively expensive, and second, it would complicate the method we will use to apply external forces. Instead, recall that $e^{a+b} = e^a e^b$. When applied to our desired update, we get

$$a_1 e^{(t+\Delta t)\omega_i^+} + a_2 e^{(t+\Delta t)\omega_i^-} = a_1 e^{t\omega_i^+} e^{(\Delta t)\omega_i^+} + a_2 e^{t\omega_i^-} e^{(\Delta t)\omega_i^-}$$

(3.8.13)

That is, we can update each term by simply multiplying them each by some complex values. If the Δt is constant for every frame, as it often is, the values we multiply by will be constant and can be precomputed.

To take advantage of Equation 3.8.13, we will store four values for each mode. The first two, ϕ_i^- and ϕ_i^+, will hold the current values of $a_1 e^{t\omega_i^+}$ and $a_2 e^{t\omega_i^-}$. The second two, φ_i^+ and φ_i^-, will hold the precomputed values of $e^{(\Delta t)\omega_i^+}$ and $e^{(\Delta t)\omega_i^-}$. To update these values for the passage of Δt time requires only a pair of complex multiplies for each mode $\phi_i^+ = \phi_i^+ \varphi_i^+$ and $\phi_i^- = \phi_i^- \varphi_i^-$. Any time the value of z_i is needed, we will simply sum ϕ_i^- and ϕ_i^+. The velocity can be determined by multiplying ϕ_i^- and ϕ_i^+, respectively, by ω_i^+ and ω_i^- and summing the result.

Initial Conditions and External Forces

If a simulation is started with zero velocity and $\mathbf{p} = \mathbf{p}_0$, then the initial values for the ϕ_i^- and ϕ_i^+ are simply zero. However, it is often useful to start a simulation from a state other than its rest state. That is, we might have some initial values for p and $\dot{p}$ that we would like to start the simulation from. The initial values of z and $\dot{z}$ are straightforward to compute.

$$\mathbf{z} = \mathbf{W}^{-1} \cdot (\mathbf{p} - \mathbf{p}_0) \qquad \dot{\mathbf{z}} = \mathbf{W}^{-1} \cdot \dot{\mathbf{p}}$$

(3.8.14)

The appropriate values of ϕ_i^- and ϕ_i^+ for each mode are then given by

$$\phi_i^{\pm} = \frac{z_i}{2} \pm \frac{\left(c_1 \lambda_i + c_2\right) z_i + 2\dot{z}_i}{2\sqrt{\left(c_1 \lambda_i + c_2\right)^2 - 4\lambda_i}}$$

(3.8.15)

To apply some external set of forces, $\mathbf{f}$, to the system, we first assume that the force is constant over some time interval, determine the resulting impulse as $\Delta t\mathbf{f}$, and then transform the impulse to modal coordinates using $\Delta t\mathbf{g} = \mathbf{W}^{\mathrm{T}} \cdot (\Delta t\mathbf{f})$. The impulse will result in a change of the modal velocities $\Delta \dot{\mathbf{z}} = \Delta t\, \mathbf{g}$. Because the entire system is linear, we can compute the changes in the ϕ_i^- and ϕ_i^+ using Equation 3.8.15 with z_i set to zero and $\dot{z}_i$ set to $\Delta \dot{z}_i$, and simply add those values to the existing values of ϕ_i^- and ϕ_i^+.

Hybrid Simulation

Earlier, we discarded the object's rigid-body modes because modal simulation is not the best tool for modeling rigid body behavior; standard rigid body simulation methods work much better. If we want to simulate an object that can both move around and deform, we can model each aspect of the object's motion using the simulation tool that is best suited for that aspect of the motion. Because we know that the rigid body modes are essentially decoupled from the deformation modes, we should expect breaking the simulation up in this way to work well.

The basic idea, known as *hybrid simulation*, was originally proposed in [Terzopoulos88]. A standard rigid body simulation is created for an object with the appropriate mass and with moments of inertia corresponding to the object's rest configuration. The deformable simulation (e.g., a modal simulation) is then embedded in the rigid body's local coordinate frame. Any external forces applied to the object should be applied to *both* the rigid body and the modal simulations.

Putting It All Together

The previous sections were intended to explain the details involved in constructing a basic modal simulation. The following outline summarizes how everything fits together:

I. During content authoring, precompute the object's modal description.
1. Build a spring-mass or FEM simulation for the object you want to model.
2. Based on the model, determine the system matrices ($\mathbf{K}$, $\mathbf{C}$, and $\mathbf{M}$) for a given rest configuration.
3. Compute the corresponding modes and eigenvalues ($\mathbf{W}$, $\mathbf{W}^{-1}$, and $\mathbf{\Lambda}$).
4. Discard the undesirable modes and determine $\omega_i^{\pm}$ for the remaining modes.
5. If the frame rate will be constant, precompute the values of φ_i^+ and φ_i^-.

II. During gameplay, run the simulation.
1. Determine the initial state of the simulation (e.g., initial values of p and $\dot{p}$).
2. Use Equations 3.8.14 and 3.8.15 to compute the initial ϕ_i^- and ϕ_i^+ for each of the modes.
3. For each frame of animation:
   a. Determine $\mathbf{f}$, any external forces acting on the object.
   b. Compute $\Delta \dot{z} = \mathbf{W}^{\mathrm{T}} \cdot \left(\Delta t \, \mathbf{f} \right)$ and use Equation 3.8.15 to determine the increments for each of the ϕ_i^- and ϕ_i^+.
   c. Advance the system forward in time by setting $\phi_i^{\pm} = \phi_i^{\pm} \, \varphi_i^{\pm}$.
   d. Compute new value $\mathbf{z}$ with $z_i = \phi_i^+ + \phi_i^-$.
   e. Update $\mathbf{p} = \mathbf{p}_0 + \mathbf{W} \cdot \mathbf{z}$.
   f. Display object using coordinates in $\mathbf{p}$.

In practice, the most expensive part of the runtime portion of the simulation is the step where $\mathbf{p}$ is reconstructed from $\mathbf{z}$. This operation is essentially computing a weighted blend of basis shapes. It will typically be much cheaper than the original simulation would have been. Remember that only the columns of $\mathbf{W}$ and rows of $\mathbf{W}^{-1}$

corresponding to the retained modes should be used. One can also perform this operation using graphics hardware. (See [James02].)

Conclusion

The code provided with this article implements the runtime simulation portion of the outline presented in the preceding section. It also implements hybrid simulation, constraints, and collisions. Details on the methods used for the constraints and collisions appear in [Hauser03].

There are also some example models that include their modal decomposition. Assuming that you already have some existing code for doing spring-and-mass or FEM simulation, the primary additional tool one needs is a good routine for computing eigendecompositions of sparse symmetric matrices. For small systems there are many options, including Matlab, Numerical Recipes [Press02], or LAPACK. For larger systems, one should use software that is designed specifically for large sparse matrices such as ARPACK or TRLAN. These packages allow you to specify what range of eigenvalues you are interested in, so you can avoid computing the modes that you plan to discard. A good general reference on methods for computing eigendecompositions is [Bai99]. Additionally, many finite-element software packages, such as Nastran, ABAQUS, or ANSYS include tools for computing modal decompositions.

There are many excellent textbooks that discuss modal analysis. The text on modal analysis, [Maia98], provides in-depth details on the mathematical and physical theory behind modal analysis as well as discussing practical applications. Many texts on the finite-element method (e.g., [Cook89]) also include chapters on modal analysis, as well as, of course, significant discussions on the finite-element method. Finally, several papers have been published that discuss using modal simulation for interactive applications [Pentland89], [Stam97], [O'Brien02], [James02], and [Hauser03].

References

[Bai99] Bai, Z., et al., "Templates for the Solution of Algebraic Eigenvalue Problems: A Practical Guide," SIAM, Philadelphia, 1999.

[Cook89] Cook, R. D., D. S. Malkus, and M. E. Plesha, *Concepts and Applications of Finite Element Analysis, Third Edition*, John Wiley & Sons, New York, 1989.

[Hauser03] Hauser, K.K., C. Shen, and J. F. O'Brien, "Interactive Deformation Using Modal Analysis with Constraints," *Graphics Interface 2003*, June 2003, pp. 247–256.

[James02] James, D.L., and D. K. Pai, "DyRT: Dynamic Response Textures for Real Time Deformation Simulation with Graphics Hardware," SIGGRAPH 2002, August 2002, pp. 582–585.

[Maia98] Maia, N., and J. Silva, *Theoretical and Experimental Modal Analysis*, Research Studies Press, Hertfordshire, England, 1998.

[O'Brien02] O'Brien, J. F., C. Shen, and C. M. Gatchalian, "Synthesizing Sounds from Rigid-Body Simulations," *SIGGRAPH 2002 Symposium on Computer Animation*, July 2002, pp. 175–181.

[Pentland89] Pentland, A., and J. Williams, "Good Vibrations: Modal Dynamics for Graphics and Animation," SIGGRAPH 89, July 1989, pp. 215–222.

[Press02] Press, W.H., et al., *Numerical Recipes in C++, Second Edition*, Cambridge University Press, 2002.

[Stam97] Stam, J., "Stochastic Dynamics: Simulating The Effects of Turbulence on Flexible Structures," *Computer Graphics Forum*, 16(3): August 1997, pp. 159–164.

[Terzopoulos88] Terzopoulos, D., and K. Fleischer, "Deformable Models," The Visual Computer, 4(6):1988, pp. 306–331.

ARTIFICIAL INTELLIGENCE

Possible Steering Arcs

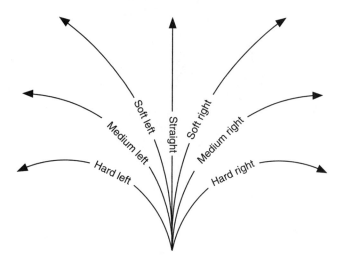

Introduction

Paul Tozour, Retro Studios / Nintendo

ptozour@austin.rr.com

Recently, I've begun offering a lecture called "Introduction to Game AI" at various universities. It's a two-hour talk and I won't try to recap it here, but it boils down to this: artificial intelligence in games is not a single problem. It's a huge set of problems. Not only that, it's a different set of problems for every game. AI depends completely on game design, and every new game design introduces its own problems for AI. It's surprisingly easy to find 50 different games for which the term *AI* means 50 completely different things.

This section illustrates the diversity of game AI quite nicely. John Olsen introduces us to attractors and repulsors. Karén Pivazyan presents a few of the ways we can use dynamic programming to handle randomness. Borut Pfiefer suggests a number of ways to systemically balance the difficulty of our games by programmatically modulating the level of dramatic tension. Jonathan Stone provides us with a thorough introduction to third-person camera navigation techniques.

Boolean logic, discrete if-then rules, and deterministic finite-state machines have been central to game AI for a long time. However, as the industry continues to mature and we raise our standards for game AI development ever higher, we will increasingly need to find ways to move our AI systems closer to "soft computing"— that is, we will require systems that can robustly handle uncertainty, partial truth, and imprecision, and can analyze the output of a large set of rules and combine their results as continuous-valued outputs rather than simply testing a sequence of if-then rules.

To this end, various AI developers have used techniques such as fuzzy logic, Bayesian belief networks, naive Bayesian classifiers, and Dempster-Shafer Theory to move game AI closer to soft computing. In many cases, however, we can do better with even simpler approaches, as long as we fully understand the problem at hand and build a solution exquisitely tailored to the problem. In that vein, John Hancock is my personal hero for his articles on distributed reasoning and utility-based decision architectures.

Finally, whenever I give my "Intro to Game AI" lecture, someone asks the inevitable question: we have hardware accelerators for graphics, so why not AI? In light of the overwhelming success of hardware-accelerated graphics, surely the AI field could benefit from some type of hardware acceleration, too.

My answer has always been "no." Adding more computing power won't help much. It's a software problem. And in the case of game AI in particular, it's also a problem of development costs and industry maturity. Again, we can find 50 different games where the term *artificial intelligence* means 50 completely different things, and it's hard to imagine that we could help more than a handful of those 50 games at once with any type of specialized processor.

Clearly, there's more to the story. I'm not saying "no" because I really believe it. I'm just trying to drive home the point that game AI always needs flexible, general-purpose hardware. As technology progresses, it's inevitable that we will find better ways to use the increasing amounts of power at our disposal for game AI. Programmable hardware in particular opens up numerous possibilities for game AI, and Thomas Rolfes provides an excellent starting point for anyone interested in exploring the current state of the art and is curious as to what the future holds.

4.1

Third-Person Camera Navigation

Jonathan Stone,
Double Fine Productions
jon@doublefine.com

The third-person perspective can be one of the most engaging ways to explore a 3D game world. By maintaining an outside view of the player character, we can create more detailed interactions between the player and the environment than are possible from a first-person view and convey a stronger sense of the player's identity.

For complex scenes, however, we must overcome some significant technical challenges to make a third-person camera interact smoothly with the world. While this problem can be solved by simply limiting the camera to fixed positions or predetermined paths, these solutions restrict the user's ability to explore freely. To allow unrestricted exploration of complex environments, it's necessary to design a dynamic and user-controllable camera.

In this article, we outline a basic set of steps for building a dynamic third-person camera system, and describe a number of solutions for the trickier problems of scene-bounding and occlusion that arise in the camera's navigation of the scene.

Camera Positioning and Motion

The foundation for our third-person camera system will be the *chase camera*, a design that has been used in games from the classic platformers *Zelda 64* and *Rayman 2* through *Jak and Daxter* and *Splinter Cell*. A chase camera generally follows above and behind the player as he makes his way through the game world, but is also responsive to input from the user, allowing him to examine details close up or judge distances by changing the camera perspective.

The first step is to select a target location on the player character that will serve as both the look-at point for camera rotations and a reference point for the camera's position. Typically, this point will be near the top of the player's bounding cylinder, or a short distance directly above.

Next, we need to define an "ideal" spatial relationship between the camera and this location. For example, we might require our camera to stay ρ meters away from the target, and to maintain an altitude of ϕ degrees above it with respect to the horizon.

Spherical Coordinates

A useful notation for describing this relationship is the *spherical coordinate system*, in which every position in 3D space is described by its distance from a target point and its rotation around that point. The three components of a spherical-coordinate vector are ρ, the distance to the origin, θ, the counter-clockwise rotation about the z-axis (or *azimuth*), and ϕ, the signed rotation from the xy-plane (or *altitude*). The altitude coordinate is notated in different ways for different applications, but here we use ϕ to describe the signed angle from the xy-plane as viewed from the origin. Positions above the xy-plane have an altitude between 0 and 90 degrees, and positions below the xy-plane have an altitude between 0 and –90 degrees.

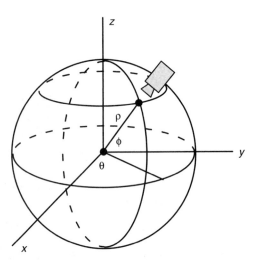

FIGURE 4.1.1　*The chase camera in spherical coordinates.*

In spherical coordinates, we can describe the camera's ideal offset from its target as the vector (ρ, θ, ϕ), and convert this to a position in Cartesian world-space each frame. The equations to convert from spherical coordinates to Cartesian are

$$x = \rho \cos \theta \sin \left(\phi + \frac{\pi}{2} \right) \tag{4.1.1}$$

$$y = \rho \sin \theta \sin \left(\phi + \frac{\pi}{2} \right) \tag{4.1.2}$$

$$z = \rho \cos \left(\phi + \frac{\pi}{2} \right) \tag{4.1.3}$$

To convert from Cartesian coordinates back to spherical, we can use

$$\rho = \sqrt{x^2 + y^2 + z^2} \qquad (4.1.4)$$

$$\theta = \tan^{-1}\left(\frac{y}{x}\right) \qquad (4.1.5)$$

$$\phi = \cos^{-1}\left(\frac{z}{\rho}\right) - \frac{\pi}{2} \qquad (4.1.6)$$

Spring Systems

Once we have defined an ideal position for the camera in world space, we need a method for interpolating the camera toward its ideal. Since the system is completely dynamic—that is, both the target and camera can change position from frame to frame—we cannot simply interpolate the camera over a fixed period of time. Instead, we need a system of accelerations that can be applied to the camera's velocity each frame to maintain continuity even when the target itself is moving. One such model is a *damped spring system*, in which a spring acceleration is applied to an object in the direction opposite from its displacement from a rest position, and a damping acceleration is applied in the direction opposite from its velocity [Treglia00]. This equation can be written as

$$F = m_a = -k_s x - k_d v \qquad (4.1.7)$$

where x is the displacement of the spring, v is the object's velocity, and a is the resulting acceleration. The spring and damping constants, k_s and k_d, are used to control the respective spring and damping components of the acceleration. For a camera system, x represents the camera's distance from its ideal position in world coordinates, and the resulting acceleration, a, drives the camera smoothly toward its ideal position.

When choosing the spring and damping constants for a spring system, it is important to be aware of the system's *damping ratio*, which is written as

$$\xi = \frac{k_d}{2\sqrt{k_s}}$$

When ξ is equal to 1, a spring system is said to be *critically damped*, and the system will return to its rest position in the minimal possible time for the given value of k_s. If ξ is less than 1, the spring system is *underdamped*, and it will oscillate before returning to rest. If ξ is greater than 1, then the system is *overdamped* and it will take longer than is necessary to reach equilibrium. In a camera system, we will generally use critically damped springs, because they give us the most efficient camera motion.

Updating the Camera

We are now ready to create a function to update the camera each frame, and interpolate it toward its ideal offset with respect to the player. We define our simplified chase-camera class as

```
class ChaseCamera
{
    Vec3 m_vPosition;        // Camera position
    Vec3 m_vVelocity;        // Camera velocity
    Vec3 m_vTargetPos;       // Target position
    Vec3 m_vIdealSpherical;  // Ideal spherical coords
    Mat4 m_mView;            // View matrix
};
```

With that in hand, we can create an update function for the camera as follows:

```
void ChaseCamera::Update(float fTime)
{
    // Update the ideal azimuth based on the camera's
    // current position with respect to the target
    m_vIdealSpherical.y = atan2f(
      m_vPosition.y - m_vTargetPos.y,
      m_vPosition.x - m_vTargetPos.x);

    // Calculate the camera's ideal position in
    // world-space
    Vec3 vIdealPos = m_vTargetPos +
      SphericalToCartesian(m_vIdealSpherical);

    // Calculate the spring acceleration toward this
    // ideal position
    Vec3 vDisplace = m_vPosition - vIdealPos;
    Vec3 vSpringAccel = (-m_fSpringK * vDisplace) -
      (m_fDampingK * m_vVelocity);

    // Use Euler integration to update the camera's
    // velocity and position
    m_vVelocity += vSpringAccel * fTime;
    m_vPosition += m_vVelocity * fTime;

    // Build the view matrix
    m_mView = MatrixLookAt(m_vPosition, vTargetPos,
      GetWorldUpVector());
}
```

The first call in this function updates the ideal azimuth each frame to allow the chase camera to auto-rotate about its target. This is the "lazy" rotation that allows the chase camera to remain stationary as the player walks around it in a circle, as in platform-style games such as *Rayman 2*. Without this function call, the camera would instead move in strafe mode, with the azimuth locked to a single value no matter where the player walked. This strafing behavior has been used to good effect in third-person games such as *Splinter Cell*, which require more accurate user aim.

Some degree of user control will be necessary in allowing the player to examine the scene from different vantage points for solving puzzles, or to control the view of the action in real-time. We can add the following code to the beginning of our update function to give the user control over the camera's azimuth.

```
// Calculate the azimuthal acceleration from
// user input and damping
float fAzimuthAccel =
  (GetUserInput(kINPUT_AZIMUTH) * m_fAzDriveK) -
  (m_fAzimuthVel * m_fAzDampingK);

// Update the camera's azimuthal velocity
m_fAzimuthVel += fAzimuthAccel * fTime;

// Apply it to the camera's position
Vec3 vCurSpherical = CartesianToSpherical(
  m_vPosition - m_vTargetPos);
vCurSpherical.y = NormalizeAngle(vCurSpherical.y +
  m_fAzimuthVel * fTime);
m_vPosition = SphericalToCartesian(vCurSpherical);
```

This creates a driven, damped system, with the user's input providing an acceleration to the camera's azimuthal velocity and a damping effect drawing that velocity back to zero. The function GetUserInput() is assumed to return a value from −1 to 1, representing the state of an input device, such as the current left-right position of an analog console joystick. The game designer can then use the constants m_fAzDriveK and m_fAzDampingK to determine the speed and responsiveness of this control. The maximum speed of this system will be m_fAzDriveK / m_vAzDampingK, in radians per unit time, when the controller is held all the way to the left or right.

If we want the user to have control over the camera's altitude as well, which would be useful for looking up toward the sky or down over a sheer cliff wall, we can add a second system to accommodate the additional control.

Camera Scene Boundaries

We've now outlined a chase camera that will follow the player smoothly through a completely open game environment. However, in a more realistic scene, there will be boundaries such as walls and ceilings that we'll need to prevent the camera from passing through. If we were to allow to camera to leave the scene, we would end up rendering the game world from behind its walls, breaking the illusion of a solid environment. To keep the camera within the rendered world, we first need to define what we mean by the scene's *interior* and *exterior*.

Collision Geometry

If our rendered world geometry is of the unrestricted "polygon soup" variety, then we'll need to maintain a separate set of *collision geometry* to demarcate the scene's boundaries. This collision geometry is generally constructed with fewer polygons than the rendered world, and is designed to be *watertight* (or *2-manifold*), in order to optimize our point-in-scene tests. For a triangular mesh, watertightness requires that each triangle has exactly one neighbor along each of its three edges and that the mesh contains no T-junctions or overlapping polygons.

Using a watertight set of collision geometry, we can define the *interior* of the scene as the set of points from which a ray cast in any direction will first hit a collision polygon facing that point (that is, a polygon whose face normal is opposite the ray's direction). Likewise, the *exterior* of the scene is the set of points from which a ray cast in any direction will either hit no polygons or hit one facing away from the given point. We can now quickly determine whether any given location in the world is interior or exterior by using a single ray cast in an arbitrary direction and examining the face normal of the first intersected polygon.

Dynamic Spheres

Up to this point, we have treated the camera as a single point moving through world space, but for scene-bounding, it is desirable to give the camera a volume. If we represent the camera as a sphere of radius r for intersection testing, we can ensure that the viewpoint, at the center of the sphere, maintains a minimum distance of r from the scene boundary. With a sufficiently large value for r, we can prevent the near plane of the camera's view frustum from clipping through rendered polygons at the edges of the scene.

To calculate intersections of a moving camera sphere with the collision geometry, we will need a dynamic sphere-versus-triangle test, which models a sphere moving along a line segment and determines whether the sphere intersects a given triangle at any point along its path. If an intersection is found, the test returns the farthest point along the line-segment the sphere could be swept before the intersection occurred. The swept volume generated by a sphere moving along a line-segment path is referred to as a *line-swept-sphere* [Moller02].

By storing the scene's collision geometry in a hierarchical scene graph, which is designed to give us efficient access to polygons in a specific region of world space, we can extend our collision functionality to a dynamic "sphere-versus-scene" test. This test will be a key component in our camera collision algorithms. It is functionally similar to a ray cast, except that it also allows us to give the ray a "thickness" of radius r (see Figure 4.1.2).

Using these intersection tests, we will now outline two algorithms for camera scene-bounding, which we refer to as the *virtual* and *physical* collision models.

Virtual Camera Collisions

The first approach, which we will refer to as the *virtual* collision model, is one of the simplest to implement. For this method, a camera's collisions are handled as if there were an imaginary beam of light projected from the target toward the camera. Each frame, we sweep a sphere from the target to the camera. If there is an intersection with

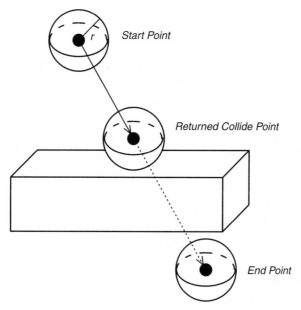

FIGURE 4.1.2 *Dynamic sphere-versus-scene test.*

the scene, we use the returned collide point as the camera's new location. Otherwise, we leave the camera's position alone (see Figure 4.1.3).

Visually, the effect of this algorithm is that the camera jumps forward to avoid all scene obstructions and occlusions. Once the obstruction has passed—in other words, the line-swept-sphere between the target and camera is clear—the camera's spring mechanic interpolates it back to its normal distance ρ. This method effectively keeps the camera within the scene, but it does so at a cost to *frame coherence*. If the player is walking around a cylindrical column in the middle of a room, the

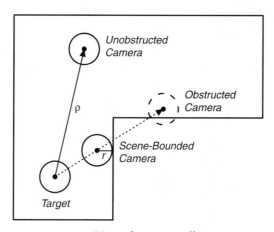

FIGURE 4.1.3 *Virtual camera collision.*

camera will avoid penetrating the geometry by jumping forward to the other side of the column. This forward jump is discontinuous and breaks the smooth motion of the camera for an instant. In a more complex environment, with many smaller camera obstructions, these discontinuities will occur more frequently, potentially disorienting the player.

One improvement we can make is to use a larger value for r in our dynamic sphere tests in order to detect obstructions before the camera actually hits them, and to interpolate the camera forward over time. This doesn't eliminate discontinuities, because the forward-interpolating camera might still be forced to jump when it strikes the actual boundary of the scene—it's not permissible to show the exterior of the scene even for one frame—but it does smooth the camera's motion in many situations. We can also minimize discontinuities by making our ideal spherical-coordinate ρ as small as possible, since the largest jump that can theoretically occur is a forward jump of distance ρ, from the camera's ideal distance to a distance of zero.

Physical Camera Collisions

A second approach is to deal with the camera as if it were a solid object and resolve collisions with sliding behavior. We refer to this approach as the *physical* collision model, because it's based on the algorithms typically used to resolve collisions in player physics [Melax01]. If our camera's bounding sphere is found to intersect the exterior of the scene, we then sweep a sphere from the camera's previous position to the current invalid one. If this test hits a polygon in the collision geometry, we then slide the sphere along the plane of the polygon using the remaining component of the camera's movement. This sliding vector might, in turn, intersect other polygons in the scene geometry, so we will need to repeat the collision query multiple times until the camera's move is complete or a threshold number of queries have executed (see Figure 4.1.4).

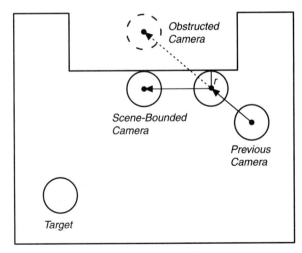

FIGURE 4.1.4 *Physical camera collision.*

Visually, this creates a camera that is "pushed away" by scene boundaries, sliding around small obstructions and slowing to a stop when pushed against large obstructions. The position of the camera in world-space is continuous because the camera is scene-bounded with reference to its position on the last frame. If the player is walking around a cylindrical column as in our earlier example, the camera will avoid intersecting the geometry by sliding smoothly around the edges of the column.

A disadvantage of the physical model is that the sliding calculations can alter the camera's azimuth and altitude, potentially interfering with the user's camera controls. If the user intentionally rotates the camera directly into a large obstruction, he may find that the camera stops at the wall and prevents his intended motion. This can be frustrating in narrow spaces when the player is using the camera controls to look in a particular direction. To minimize these cases, we can allow the camera's ideal radius to temporarily decrease in response to collisions and to increase again as the player moves away from the camera.

Camera Occlusions

Our camera will now stay within the boundaries of the scene, but it is still possible for its view of the player to be obscured by intervening geometry. This is referred to as an *occlusion* of the camera's view. The simple virtual collision model described previously will automatically handle this case by clipping the camera forward to the nearest clear position, but the physical model requires separate handling for occlusions. We will outline our solution to this problem in three steps: detecting the occlusion, finding a new clear view, and pathfinding.

To determine whether the camera is occluded on a given frame, we can use a single dynamic-sphere test from the camera to the target, which will tell us quickly whether there is any collision geometry blocking the view. In practice, however, it is desirable to use a more robust test that determines the overall visibility of the player and ignores small occluding details on the floor and ceiling. For this, we can use two or more dynamic sphere tests from the camera toward positions at varying heights near the target. If any of these tests yields a nonintersection result, we consider the given view to be clear.

Once an occlusion of the current view is detected, we must find a new unoccluded spherical-coordinate *goal* for the camera, ideally situated as close as possible to the original view. The level of detail required for our search method is dependent on the complexity of the environment. If our environment is relatively simple and orthogonal, without inclined floors or sloping surfaces, then we can use a search along a single dimension such as the azimuth component of the camera's spherical coordinate position. If the game situation is more complex, such as a human-sized character walking through rocky terrain with a variety of surface grades, we will require a two-dimensional search pattern in order to take the camera's altitude into account.

For the one-dimensional case, we can efficiently find the smallest change in azimuth that will produce a clear view with a broad-phase/narrow-phase search, as shown in Figure 4.1.5. In the broad-phase portion, we step through azimuth deltas using a large step size to find the nearest one to the original that is clear. Then, in the narrow-phase, we step backward using a smaller step size to fine-tune the results. This produces an accurate goal position for our camera, but the computational expense is great enough that we will need to cache the results and re-use them for as long as they are valid—that is, until the cached goal position has been reached or has been rendered invalid by the player's subsequent motion.

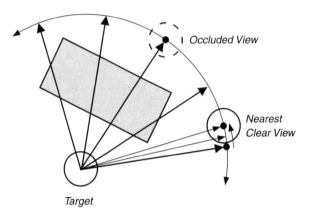

Occluded View

*Nearest
Clear View*

Target

FIGURE 4.1.5 *Searching for a clear view in one dimension.*

In two dimensions, a number of search patterns are possible. A simple extension of our broad-phase/narrow-phase search produces a coarse, expanding grid of test coordinates, starting with an azimuth/altitude delta of (0°, 0°), and proceeding incrementally outward to the maximum angular deltas of (±180°, ±90°). As soon as the broad-phase search finds a clear view, we can then refine the results by stepping backward, first iterating the altitude back toward zero, then the azimuth. Helbing and Strothotte [Helbing00] suggest a spiral search pattern, starting with a delta of (0°, 0°) and spiraling outward with increasing step sizes.

If a clear line of sight exists between the occluded camera and its goal, then we simply use the goal as the camera's new ideal position and allow our engine's spring system to interpolate the camera smoothly to a clear view. In many cases, however, the line of sight will itself be obstructed by intervening geometry, which necessitates the use of pathfinding.

As a solution, we could use a generalized 3D pathfinding approach [Smith02], which divides the game-world into convex sectors and calculates connectivity information offline. A simpler approach that is specific to camera navigation is to use the connectivity information already provided by the player's path through the world. We can maintain a circular buffer of recent player target-sphere positions, and use these as a "trail of breadcrumbs" to lead the camera back to its unoccluded goal position. On any given occluded frame, if the camera's calculated goal is not in view, we instead determine the farthest point along the trail of breadcrumbs that is in the camera's view, and use this intermediate point as the camera's ideal position. Once the goal itself comes into view, the camera can then diverge from the trail and move directly toward the goal.

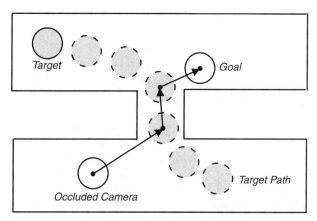

FIGURE 4.1.6 *Breadcrumbs pathfinding.*

This algorithm allows the camera to follow the player through a doorway into another room, as shown in Figure 4.1.6. The resulting path is not as smooth as the path that a full 3D pathfinding algorithm could generate, as such an algorithm can plan out a camera path in advance and smooth the resulting line segments with splines. However, our algorithm is well behaved in dynamic situations in which the player moves rapidly through a complex environment. In some cases, this approach might yield camera positions that are too close to the player target itself, causing a rapid flip in the view direction of the camera. In these situations, it is necessary to push the camera away from the player target to a minimum distance.

Simplifying the Scene

It's important to keep in mind that some camera situations are more effectively solved by simplifying the camera's representation of the scene, or by simplifying the rendered scene itself, rather than relying on navigation logic alone. In a dense playfield with many obstacles, a camera that is frequently adjusting its view can be confusing to the user, so gameplay will be smoother if these situations are avoided.

One way to simplify the camera's environment is to look at potential occluders in the level design phase to determine if they can be moved out of the camera's most common paths. Another approach is to allow the camera to look through certain solid objects by rendering them translucently when they block the camera's view. Rendering objects translucently can be very effective in reducing the complexity of a scene because it removes these objects from consideration when calculating a clear view for the camera. However, it's an effect that's best used sparingly, because it can break the illusion of realism in the game world.

Conclusion

In this article, we presented a number of methods that can provide the foundation for a dynamic, user-controlled third-person camera system. We also described some solutions for the more difficult problems of camera scene-bounding and occlusion. Each game must find its own balance between the smoothness of camera motion, the flexibility of user control, and the navigation of complicated obstructions. However, we hope the ideas presented here can find use in a variety of game designs. The references listed next are intended to provide a thorough background on the mathematics used in this article and a source for further research and inspiration.

References

[Helbing00] Helbing, Ralf, and Thomas Strothotte, "Quick Camera Path Planning for Interactive 3D Environments," available online at *http://isgwww.cs.uni-magdeburg.de/~helbing/publ/quickplanning-sg00.pdf*.

[Melax01] Melax, Stan, "BSP Collision Detection as Used in MDK2 and NeverWinter Nights," available online at *www.gamasutra.com/features/20010324/melax_01.htm*, 2001.

[Moller02] Akenine-Möller, Tomas, and Eric Haines, *Real Time Rendering, Second Edition*, A K Peters, Ltd., 2002.

[Smith02] Smith, Patrick, "Polygon Soup for the Programmer's Soul: 3D Pathfinding," *GDC 2002 Conference Proceedings*, 2002.

[Treglia00] Treglia, Dante, "Camera Control Techniques," *Game Programming Gems*, Mark DeLoura, Editor, Charles River Media, Inc., 2000.

4.2

Narrative Combat: Using AI to Enhance Tension in an Action Game

Borut Pfeifer,
Radical Entertainment
borut_p@yahoo.com

If you are an avid gamer, you have no doubt played games with heavily scripted AI. These games often have incredible moments of gameplay because the player is forced to take each step in a certain way, giving the designer complete control over the pacing of the game. This pacing can seem astounding—the first time you play. With subsequent playing, you know exactly where every enemy is and exactly what each enemy will do next. Such predictability can easily drain the fun out of any gameplay experience. These fully scripted games seldom give the player any significant amount of freedom in gameplay. The only way the designer can maintain the same well-constructed pacing is to script out every potential path.

However, games that create completely systemic worlds can leave the pacing almost entirely in the player's hands. If the player doesn't understand the current goals of the game, he is left to wander through the game aimlessly, making for a lackluster experience. In gaining replayability, the game loses that highly effective pacing.

Ideally, some set of game mechanics could allow designers to adjust the pacing as the player progresses through the game. These mechanics would be driven by the designer but would also take the player's experience and skill level into account, so they would create a more dynamic gameplay environment while increasing and decreasing dramatic tension in an enjoyable fashion.

This article discusses the creation of an AI system that can modulate difficulty and pacing for an action game. In addition to combining strongly paced elements with replayability and more freeform gameplay, it becomes much easier for a designer to create a well-paced level. This is because the system only requires a designer's guidelines for the overall difficulty of a particular area, while in most games, designers must extensively tweak enemy positions, spawn points, weapons, timing issues, and more to accomplish the same task. Adjusting for the player's skill level also avoids the common problem in which designers tune gameplay to their own skill level, rather than the typical user's skill level. As a result, the game becomes much too difficult for the average player. Adjusting for a player's skill allows for more seamless transitions between difficulty levels when the pacing changes.

Dramatic Tension

If you remember your high school English class, you might remember your teacher drawing you a graph like Figure 4.2.1. This graph represents the sequence of rising and falling dramatic tension that broadly defines a pleasurable book, film, video game, or even a basketball game. Dramatic tension can be thought of as the participant's level of involvement in the outcome, but more specifically it is a measure of complication, of what information is known and unknown by the participant. As a mystery novel progresses, for example, more and more questions arise as to who the killer might be, and new information is revealed while also hinting at additional unrevealed information. In a game, this unknown is the uncertainty of the player's success. There is one highest point of the progressing tension, the climax, at which most of the tension created up until that point is resolved. The climax can come at various places, but it is usually most pleasing when it comes shortly before the end, with a small amount of time to decrease the tension. This short period following the climax, where the remaining tension is resolved, is often referred to as *dénouement*.

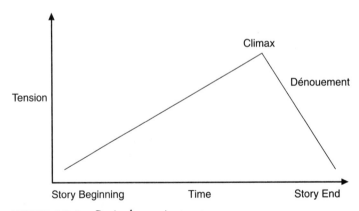

FIGURE 4.2.1 *Basic dramatic structure.*

In reality, the dramatic structure of a story, whether it's a book, movie, or a player's experience in a game, is more varied. The general trend of increasing tension to the point of climax is still valid, but there are many local high and lows. In a game, the local highs could represent difficult challenges such as "boss battles," while local lows would represent periods of particularly low tension, such as the beginning of a new level (see Figure 4.2.2).

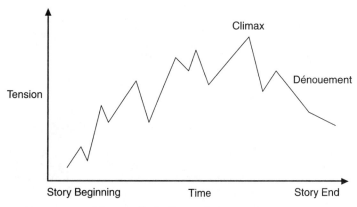

FIGURE 4.2.2   *More realistic dramatic structure.*

In her book *Computers as Theatre*, Brenda Laurel advocates using the dramatic model as a user interface design paradigm [Laurel91]. This is primarily because the dramatic model focuses on action, which also defines interactivity. The action intensifies to condense time, because incidents are selected, arranged, and represented to amplify the emotion involved. The individual incidents that make up the drama are all tied together in the central action or motion.

These characteristics differ from more traditional linear narrative in that narrative typically relies more on description. Individual incidents might expand time, focusing on one brief moment by describing it in great detail, and they might not be causally related, but more episodic in nature.

The concept of dramatic tension in games is not related to the progression of the storyline. It refers to the relationship between the player's skill level and the challenge the game provides the player. In his research on the psychology of optimal experience, or flow, Mihaly Csikszentmihalyi [Csikszentmihalyi90] studies the relationship between a person's skill at a task, the challenge he experiences performing that task, and whether or not the person experiences flow while performing that task. Flow is the state of being in "the zone," being so focused on a task that we lose track of time and our concentration is singularly focused on the task. The characteristics of situations we would describe as "fun" are identical to the characteristics of a flow experience.

Obviously, a player's skill level is typically very low the first time he plays a game. As he plays the game more, his skills increase and he might become bored if the challenge remains constant. The challenge normally increases, but usually at a rate different from the player's skill level. Therefore, the player is constantly in a state of flux between the four points shown in Figure 4.2.3, either growing bored when the challenge doesn't increase in pace with his skills or becoming frustrated when he is slow to learn the necessary skills.

At point A, the player has just begun to play the game. He knows little about it and the challenge is minimal. If the challenge increases drastically at that point, the

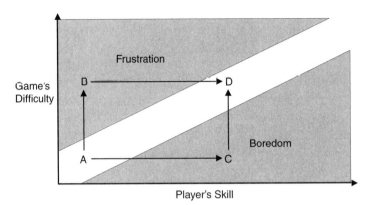

FIGURE 4.2.3   *Flow of the player's game experience.*

player will become frustrated because the game's difficulty exceeds his skill, as indicated by point B. Assuming they do not become frustrated and quit, players will eventually learn the skills they need to succeed at that portion of the game.

If the game's challenge does not increase correspondingly, players will become bored, as the game is too easy (shown by point C). As the challenge level increases, the player will enter the "zone" again and will continue his enjoyment of the game as its difficulty increases to match the player's skill (point D).

The goal of any game's pacing, scripted or otherwise, is to keep the player in the central white zone, where the player's skill matches the game's difficulty within a certain threshold. However, because different players learn at different rates and face different levels of challenge with different tasks, everyone will cycle through boredom or frustration and (hopefully) back into flow.

In Figure 4.2.3, there is no concept of resolution or climax. As long as the player is in a flow state, his skill must be at roughly the same level as the challenge provided. Therefore, the satisfying release of tension that comes with applying learned skills must fall within the same roughly equal zone of skill and challenge.

However, having clear goals is a key characteristic of a flow experience, so providing an effective resolution to the climax is in tune with the notion of meeting the activity's goals. By reducing the tension (and difficulty) toward the end of a section of gameplay and emphasizing the gameplay skills the player has learned, we give the player a stronger sense of accomplishment. Decreasing the difficulty too much can lead to a boring, and therefore unpleasant, conclusion.

A growing subject in AI research is the use of AI to control dramatic structure in interactive narrative, such as the system described in Mateas and Stern's 2003 Game Developers' Conference lecture "Façade: A One Act Interactive Drama" [Mateas03]. While many of these projects involve lofty secondary technological goals such as natural language processing, the basic goal remains the same regardless of the type of interactive environment: using a system to control what events are created in the environment to fine-tune the player's experience. The system acts as a sequencer, mixing in different events to create a sense of pacing that is pleasing to the player, adheres to the general dramatic structure, and adjusts challenge with respect to the skill required so the player maintains an optimal experience at all times.

Overview

There are several steps in the process of creating such a system:

1. Analyze which elements of the game's design can change dynamically as the player progresses through the game. These are the elements that will be used to adjust the level of difficulty the player experiences.
2. Determine a means of describing the difficulty for any one of these dynamically changing elements.
3. Define the means by which designers can control the overall level of difficulty—that is, how the system knows that any given section of the game should be more difficult than another.
4. Define a metric to determine the player's skill level at any point during gameplay.
5. Establish the relationship between the dynamic gameplay elements and the final experienced difficulty. This relationship controls how difficulty is adjusted using these elements—how to combine them in a pleasing fashion with respect to the player's skill.

Designer Control

Designers have two general categories of input to the system. They control the difficulty of each area in the game in relation to other areas, and the difficulty evaluation function for the individual dynamic elements.

Each category has two general approaches. The first and more straightforward approach is to give designers the means of giving hints to the system offline, during the production process. The second approach is to create mechanics to dynamically evaluate how best to define those categories while the game is in progress.

Because most games involve some spatial exploration, it is easy to tie difficulty with particular areas of a level in the game. As the player enters an area of the level, the game uses the attributes of the area to control difficulty adjustment. Each area has a difficulty modification (a range of five values between easiest and hardest is sufficient), which is then used to create a goal difficulty, factoring in the player's skill level. Each area also has associated data about which elements to use in the difficulty adjustment. For example, an area (represented by a trigger volume) could have a list of enemy classes (each with its own difficulty rating) and spawn locations. The game then selects the number of enemies of different classes to create the desired difficulty for the area and selects their spawn locations. Note that if the game can't allow enemies to be created dynamically in view of the player, designers can place the spawn locations outside of the player's view, such as around corners or behind locked doors.

The alternate approach for this category involves determining a relative difficulty level at any one point in the game. One such determination is based on the amount of gameplay the player has remaining in a level. As the player gets close to the end of the level, the game automatically ratchets up the difficulty, decreasing it slightly just before the end. If the player spends too much time in any one area, the difficulty decreases, providing a natural low in the dramatic tension and allowing the player to move past the tough game situation.

The other category of input the designers have into the system is in the evaluation of the difficulty of individual dynamic elements. If the dynamic elements include spawning different numbers and types of enemies, each enemy could have a constant difficulty associated with it. Defining a mechanic for this calculation is usually problematic; a designer's heuristic evaluation will compensate for the variety of potential factors (weapon damage, range, accuracy, movement and attack speeds, AI strategies used) without adding a great deal of complexity to the system. If the difficulty associated with individual elements is changing frequently, then perhaps a mechanic is necessary to define an element's difficulty, but such complexity will also make it harder to tune. A situation in a game where this might occur is when enemies have access to modifications that greatly affect the enemy's strength compared to the player (like changing weapons, speed boosts, or shields). The game might then need to calculate an element's difficulty based on some combination of difficulty factors the designer has given each of these subelements.

Difficulty Calculation

A number of games adjust their difficulty in accordance with some judgment of the player's skill. Racing games, for example, often apply a speed boost to cars following the race leader. To implement difficulty adjustment to control pacing, we must perform a constant reappraisal of the player's skill level. There are several elements that we can factor into the difficulty model for an action- or combat-oriented game.

- **Time to defeat this enemy:** The time between the player's first contact with an opponent and the point where the enemy is neutralized.
- **Enemy difficulty level:** This is defined by the designer as a number from 1 (easiest) to 10 (hardest).
- **Simultaneous enemies:** Number of other enemies engaged in combat with the player at the time this enemy was defeated.

There are usually a number of other associated factors (for example, player accuracy), but it is important to select the fewest, most critical elements of the player's skill level for a simpler measurement. The player's accuracy might be low with a very powerful weapon, but he might still use it to defeat an enemy quickly. By only considering these basic elements, primarily time, whenever a player defeats an enemy, we automatically take these broader factors into account (how well the player can retain powerful weapons, his accuracy, and so forth).

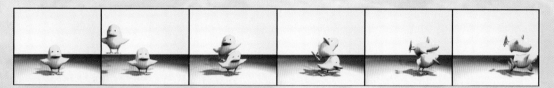

COLOR PLATE 1　This image sequence shows frames from an animation of a pair of objects colliding with each other. Each object is a hybrid simulation that incorporates a rigid and a deformable component. The deformable component uses modal simulation. Image courtesy of J. O'Brien, C. Shen, and K. Hauser. © Copyright 2003 U.C. Berkeley. Used with permission.

COLOR PLATE 2　These images are screen shots from a demo application running natively on a Sony PlayStation2. The yellow circle highlights the cursor that the user is using to poke and pull an elastic figure. Image courtesy of J. O'Brien, C. Shen, and K. Hauser. © Copyright 2003 U.C. Berkeley. Used with permission.

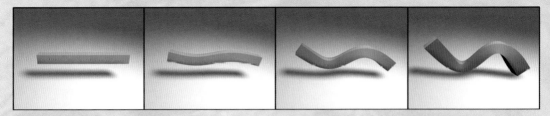

COLOR PLATE 3 This figure illustrates the distortion that can be introduced by linearization. The first image shows an undeformed bar. The subsequent images show the result of increasingly larger deformation. Small to moderate amounts of deformation manifest little visible error. However, large amounts of deformation produce noticeable distortion, and the last image shows both noticeable end-flair as well as distortion in its overall length. Image courtesy of J. O'Brien, C. Shen, and K. Hauser. © Copyright 2003 U.C. Berkeley. Used with permission.

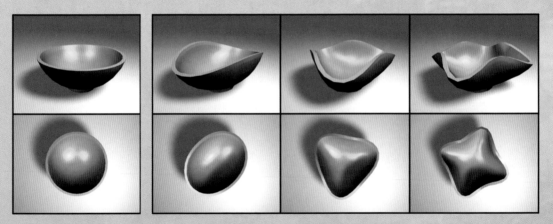

COLOR PLATE 4 The two rows show a side and top view of a bowl along with three of the bowl's first (sorted by eigenvalue) vibrational modes. The modes selected for the illustration are the first three non-rigid modes with distinct eigenvalues that are excited by a transverse impulse to the bowl's rim. Image courtesy of J. O'Brien, C. Shen, and K. Hauser. © Copyright 2003 U.C. Berkeley. Used with permission.

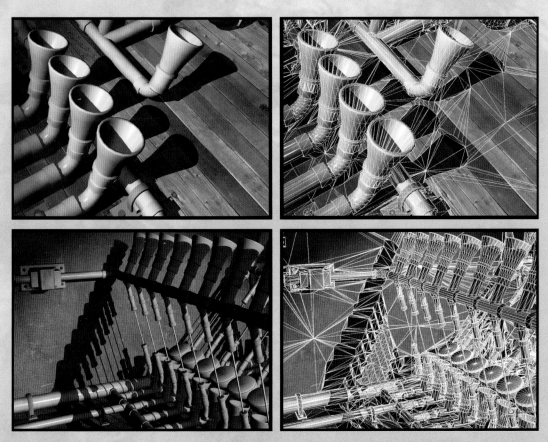

COLOR PLATE 5 White wireframe shows subdivision of geometry for drawing fast, static shadows.
© 2003 ATI Technologies, Inc. Reprinted with permission.

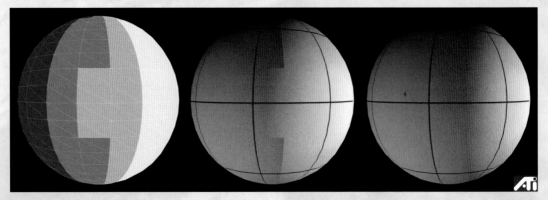

COLOR PLATE 6   [Left] A sphere is separated into multiple meshes depending on the number of scene lights that light its polygons. The brightest shaded mesh has three contributing scene lights while the darkest shade has no contributing scene lights. [Center] Each mesh is then lit using a shader that corresponds to the number of contributing light sources. Light source contribution is determined using face normals during preprocessing, while lighting is calculated using vertex normals during run-time causing a lighting discontinuity. [Right] Diffuse lighting is adjusted so that lights falloff smoothly to compensate for the culling discrepancy. © 2003 ATI Technologies, Inc.

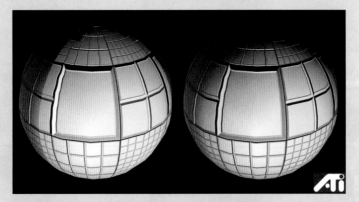

COLOR PLATE 7   [Left] A sphere that has been separated into multiple meshes depending on the number of static scene lights that light its polygons is drawn using a bump map for per-pixel lighting operations. Lighting discontinuities are seen where the per-pixel normal deviates significantly from the face normal. [Right] Diffuse lighting is adjusted to compensate for this discontinuity. © 2003 ATI Technologies, Inc.

COLOR PLATE 8 A conventionally textured and lit level [shown as inset] was converted into a dark comic style by employing real-time halftoning. Note how the shading is depicted by varying the number of strokes displayed. © 2001 Bert Freudenberg, isg. Reprinted with permission.

COLOR PLATE 9 [Left] Texture and alpha maps used for team colors on a military unit. Alpha indicates where team color should be applied. [Center] A red unit. [Right] A blue unit using the same texture. © Copyright 2003 Stainless Steel Studios, Inc. Empires: Dawn of the Modern World™ is a Trademark of Stainless Steel Studios, Inc. Reprinted with permission.

COLOR PLATE 10 A color image converted to sepia tone in real time. Image courtesy of Marwan Y. Ansari. Reprinted with permission.

COLOR PLATE 11   [Left] A typical scene with diffuse lighting. Notice that the image appears washed out even in midday sunlight. [Right] The same scene with gamma adjusted based on sampled scene luminance. © 2003 Dave McCoy/Michael Dougherty. Reprinted with permission.

COLOR PLATE 12   [Left] The heat geometry for a hot gas vent is drawn in wire frame mode. [Center] The distortion values for this vent are scaled by height and to eliminate hard edges. [Right] The final distorted images. © Copyright 2003 ATI Technologies, Inc. Reprinted with permission.

COLOR PLATE 13   Use of a rounded nonuniform spline to generate a "grind rope" as a gameplay element. © Copyright 2003 Krome Studios. Reprinted with permission from Krome Studios.

Ultimately, we want a simple equation to give us a numerical judgment about how difficult the game is for the player at that time. If the number is high, this reflects a high difficulty for the player, while a low number indicates that the player is having an easy time playing the game. Intuitively, the higher the difficulty level of the defeated enemy, the higher the player's skill level, and the longer it took the player to defeat that enemy, the lower the skill level should appear.

Player skill measure = Enemy difficulty/Time to defeat enemy

Ideally, however, this calculation should result in a steady progression of numbers, much like the ranking of an enemy's difficulty. The result should lie within an interval such as the range from 1 to 10, where 1 is a low measure of the player skill and 10 is a high measure. The difficulty adjustment system uses this value to select enemies, so it is necessary to ensure that both sets of numbers share roughly the same relative scale. To accomplish this, we scale the time by a constant. This constant represents a basic unit of difficulty: it is the time it would take a typical novice player (at skill level 1) to defeat a simple enemy (at difficulty level 1), with the simplest available tools (weapon and any other power-ups) the first time he plays the game.

The final consideration is the number of enemies the player is currently fighting. For example, it's typically much more difficult to fight four enemies simultaneously than it is to defeat them individually. This factor acts as a scale, but because the actual difficulty increase caused by fighting multiple enemies is relative to the game's design, you will need to determine how this factor will scale this equation.

For this example, fighting enemies individually results in a constant scale. One additional enemy might result in a scale of 1.125. Two additional enemies provide a scale of 1.25, and three or more additional enemies result in scaling the player's skill measure by 1.5. Therefore, if the player has to defeat three enemies at once, defeating any one of them is harder (by one and a half times) than if the player faced that enemy alone.

These numbers relate to the game's mechanics—how hard does the game make it to fight two enemies at the same time? Many games provide specific weapons and other tools to allow them to damage multiple opponents simultaneously, while others force the player to focus on one enemy at a time. As this can be a subjective decision, it's probably best to determine this number by having several people give you an estimate through a usability test, judging the relative difficulty of fighting one enemy, versus two of enemies of the same difficulty, versus three, and so on. You could take into account the difficulty of the other enemies in the group when using this factor, but in practice this is too much complexity for a very minor gain in a more precise skill measure.

The final measure looks like this:

Player skill measure = (Enemy difficulty * Scale factor for number of simultaneous enemies fought) / (Time to defeat enemy * Basic unit of difficulty)

This formula will give us a good estimate of difficulty measure at any one point. The game must also keep a running tally to account for the player's recent game experience. This aggregate difficulty measure is simply the average of a number of individual skill measures.

Since you steadily measure the player's skill, this list allows you to average the measures for the last few minutes of gameplay. A weighted average where measurements decay over time would not be desirable because it might allow the player to manipulate the system by altering his performance rapidly, cheating the system into lowering the difficulty temporarily. By simply keeping a list of measurements for the last five minutes, you ensure the time period is short enough that the player's skill is not changing much and inhibit that sort of manipulation.

Difficulty Adjustment

Using the approximated player's skill level as a base, the game has to determine the goal difficulty. The method used to define how separate parts of the game vary in difficulty then modifies the player's skill to result in the goal difficulty. This can happen in a number of ways. If the game uses the approach of defining areas with assigned difficulty, the game regularly measures the player's skill while he is inside a particular area, compares it with the goal difficulty, and makes adjustments. If the game uses a mechanic to define how the overall difficulty changes (such as the proportion of a specific part of the game the player has completed or how many out of a set of goals the player has accomplished), the goal difficulty is generated based on that mechanic. However, the methods for selecting and creating the necessary dynamic elements are the same.

Using areas to define difficulty, the designer would assign a difficulty of 1 (easiest) to 5 (hardest) to an area. The player's skill measure is treated as the initial goal difficulty because our measurement has taken into account the input difficulty range to produce a comparable number. For each level of difficulty in an area, a corresponding modifier multiplies this goal difficulty. For a 1, this would reduce the goal by half, while for a 5, it would double.

Alternatively, you could allow the designer to specify the modifier directly, but the indirect approach has two benefits. First, a limited number of discrete difficulty states makes it more intuitive for the designer to understand what type of difficulty should result (very easy, easy, normal, hard, or very hard, in the case of five discrete states). Second, the indirect approach allows you to change the modifiers to result in the described difficulty. If you happen to decide that a multiplier of 2.0 doesn't make the game sufficiently difficult, you can just change the multiplier for the "very hard" difficulty setting instead of potentially having to tweak the difficulty in each area of the game.

While the player is inside an area, the area has to select the appropriate dynamic elements to meet the final goal difficulty. Using a mechanic is fairly similar in that the mechanic determines the modifier—for example, if the player has accomplished half the mission goals, his skill needs to be multiplied by 1.5 to create the goal difficulty.

The game now has a list of dynamic elements it can select from, each with its own difficulty rating, and a goal difficulty. Now we have to consider how the arrangement of elements affects the player's experience. The game can select between different arrangements of enemy classes to create groups of enemies that meet the goal difficulty—for example, one tough enemy and one easy one, two enemies of the same difficulty, or four enemies of weak difficulty. This selection of elements has an aesthetic component to it. You will want to define groupings that accentuate your game's design goals, as just having the game randomly select elements might not result in as pleasing an experience.

Strengths and Weaknesses

There are several design issues that we must consider when using such a system. The relationship between difficulty and the player experience is expressed by arbitrary input parameters (1 to 10 representing relative difficulty, for example), and debugging and tweaking these parameters can be a difficult and time-consuming task. It's generally better to keep the mechanics and relationships as simple as possible. This will still allow you to create a dynamic experience for the player with basic inputs from the designers.

These types of rule-based systems for subtly adjusting an interactive experience must always take care to not expose their mechanics to the player. Interactive music serves as a good illustrative example. If the game adjusts the score based on what the player is doing at any one moment, it can quickly become obvious how to control the system through its mechanics. For example, if dramatic music begins as soon as an enemy is nearby, the player can now use the music to predict gameplay and detect an ambush. This takes him out of the game experience. Similarly, the difficulty adjustment system must take previous game experience into account so the player can't easily "cheat" the system—for example, intentionally taking a long time to kill one enemy immediately changes the difficulty level and makes the game very easy. This is accomplished by determining the player's skill over a larger period of time, and not adjusting difficulty based on one difficulty measurement.

This system was designed to create the feel of a very well-paced game, without having the same pitfalls, such as limited replayability. By controlling difficulty through a small number of inputs, it becomes easy to tweak the game's difficulty and create well-paced gameplay even in dynamic environments. It also creates that well-paced experience without requiring designers to create multiple sets of pacings for user-chosen static difficulty levels (such as "easy," "normal," and "hard"). This helps players in creating their own levels. Bioware's *NeverWinter Nights* and its editing tools allow the player to group and randomize enemy encounters, although since combat is all attribute based (it does not require dexterity on the player's part), the system does not dynamically take into account the player's skill and how difficult recent combat has been, while the system described here adjusts for that.

While this system was created for a combat-oriented action game with specific design goals, the notion of adjusting the player's experience by using the dramatic model is a useful one. The system's goals are similar to features in regular software that try to predict the user's goals to improve their experience; a word processor notes the user typing in a typical letterhead and offers to fill some portions in automatically. Systems such as these can be prone to incorrectly guiding the user's experience (guessing a wrong goal for the user, for example), but when used well they can focus the interactive experience. In the case of games, this means a more consistent and enjoyable experience and fewer moments when the pacing is too slow or too fast.

These principles are not yet in common use, probably because development teams have many more priorities with their short schedules and limited budgets. However, as games advance to a broader market, they will have to deliver a more consistent dramatic experience to keep capturing players' imaginations.

Conclusion

This article described an AI system that uses a player's recent play history to adjust the difficulty of an action game. By adjusting enemy toughness based on the time taken to defeat earlier enemies, designers can provide a consistent difficulty to players of all skill levels.

References

[Mateas03] Mateas, Michael, and Andrew Stern, "Façade: A One Act Interactive Drama," *Game Developer's Conference 2003*.
[Csikszentmihalyi90] Csikszentmihalyi, Mihaly, *Flow: The Psychology of Optimal Experience*, Harper Collins, 1990.
[Laurel91] Laurel, Brenda, *Computers as Theater*, Addison-Wesley, 1991.

4.3

NPC Decision Making: Dealing with Randomness

Karén Pivazyan, Stanford University

pivazyan@stanford.edu

Much effort in game AI is focused on computing actions NPCs should take at every decision point. The examples range from finding a path, to selecting units for construction, to picking an attack behavior. These decisions have effects reaching far into the future—for example, constructing a foot soldier now prevents us from carrying out air attacks in the next turn.

Therefore, it is not enough to compute the best decision now, locally. We must consider how an action will affect our choices in the future, globally. In effect, we are looking for the best possible sequence of decisions starting now and going all the way into the future ending at the goal. In deterministic environments, such as pathfinding with stationary obstacles, we use search algorithms like A*.

However, suppose we have a wild mage who randomly produces one of several possible effects whenever he casts a spell. This randomness breaks A*, at best requiring hacks, and at worst producing completely incorrect decisions. The trouble is that randomness is all pervasive in games: attack rolls, spell effects (duration, area of effect), skill use (hiding, stealing), all have random outcomes. How do we handle these problems?

In this article, we describe an algorithm for solving such multistep decision problems with randomness. The basic algorithm is called *dynamic programming*, or DP. Various versions of DP have been successfully used to build an excellent Tetris player and train a world-class backgammon player.

An Overview

The dynamic programming algorithm finds the shortest path between two points on a stochastic map. A stochastic map can be contrasted with deterministic map. On a deterministic map, any fixed sequence of actions will always reach the same end. On a stochastic map, the outcome of an action is random, and a fixed sequence of actions can reach different ends.

For the sake of simplicity, this article focuses on finding paths on 2D stochastic maps. However, just like A*, the DP algorithm is not limited to pathfinding. We will discuss such uses of DP in the last section of the article. For now, we will present an example of pathfinding in a role-playing game.

In Figure 4.3.1, a drunken halfling must find his way out of a tavern that is partially occupied by a bar. The halfling starts in cell D4 and the door he needs to reach is in A6. The halfling is so inebriated that he does not control his movements very well—any attempt to go straight leads him in the right direction with probability 0.5 and to the right or left with probabilities 0.25. For example, when moving north from D4, the halfling ends up in C4, D3, or D5 with probabilities 0.5, 0.25, and 0.25, respectively. Anytime the halfling bumps into the wall, he is bounced back to the starting cell.

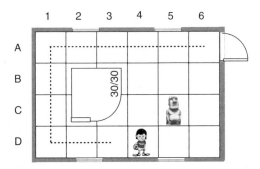

FIGURE 4.3.1   *Maze with a trap.*

We want to compute the shortest path from D4 to A6. We can try to use A* by ignoring the uncertainty and assuming that an action always results in a fixed outcome—for example, we assume that moving west from D4 always brings the halfling to D3. However, when we try to execute the shortest path found by A*, due to the real randomness in actions, the halfling is highly likely to step off the precomputed path. Then we have to recompute the shortest path, wasting memory and cycles, because A* cannot use the still-relevant data from the first search. In fact, for this map, the halfling is likely to visit most of the cells before reaching the goal, and hence A* will result in redundant effort.

Besides the wasted resources, there is an even bigger problem with applying A* to stochastic maps: it generates completely incorrect paths. Imagine that an annoyed giant is enjoying his drink in cell C5 of Figure 4.3.1, and he will gladly eat any halfling that bumps into him. A* would naively assume that the halfling can just skim around the giant, either via C4, B4, B5 or D5, D6, C6, B6. In fact, the halfling is likely to be eaten if he takes either of these paths, with a probability greater than 50 percent. The best path now lies through the left pass (dashed line).

The DP algorithm was designed to handle stochastic maps and can easily find the best path in Figure 4.3.1. The algorithm itself is very simple. Compared to A*, it requires somewhat more data to set up; in particular, it requires us to specify the uncertainty in the map. It also is not as fast as A*: while for deterministic maps it suffices to find the shortest path from the start to the end, for stochastic maps, we really need the best path from every start state to the goal. However, we can introduce various optimizations to speed up the process. These are discussed at the end of this article.

The Dynamic Programming Algorithm

We will now look at the DP algorithm itself. In the process, we will compare DP to A*, so we assume a solid understanding of A*. *AI Game Programming Wisdom* presents several good references for A* ([Matthews02] and [Higgins02]). For rigorous mathematical presentation of DP theory and practice, see [Bertsekas01].

First, we review the concept of path cost. Any algorithm that searches for the shortest path must have some way of comparing the paths. Obviously, we compare paths based on their lengths. It is helpful to think of path length as the sum of individual move lengths. Then, the Euclidean length of the path D4 to A6 in Figure 4.3.1 is $\sqrt{2} + 1 + \sqrt{2} = 3.8$. However, what happens when our map includes different terrain? Crossing over mountains is certainly harder than crossing over plains, so we assign a cost of 10 to the mountain cells and a cost of 1 to the plains cells. Notice how we are no longer comparing paths based on their Euclidean lengths, but rather based on their total cost. In fact, it is no longer correct to speak about shortest paths, and instead we talk about best (least cost) paths.

This is more than a simple linguistic redefinition. Using costs allows us to compare paths based on things completely unrelated to length. In particular, we assign a cost of 100 to the giant's cell in Figure 4.3.1 because we desire a path that avoids it.

The DP algorithm requires the following data:

- The goal cell
- Costs for all cells
- The probability table for the effect of each action

Figure 4.3.2 shows the goal and the costs for our trapped maze. Note that the goal cell has a cost of 0. Moreover, the goal cell is a sink cell—that is, upon reaching it, the NPC is stuck there (has no actions). Because the algorithm searches for the least-cost path, we must be careful in assigning negative costs. If we inadvertently create a loop in the map with a total negative cost, then the algorithm will find it and become stuck in an infinite loop, computing paths with ever-smaller costs.

Also note that there is no starting cell, because the algorithm computes the best paths from all locations to the goal simultaneously. This is necessary because due to uncertainty, the NPC can end up anywhere on the map and must know what to do from that cell (we can introduce some optimizations at this point, which are discussed later).

Finally, Table 4.3.1 shows the probability table for this maze. For this simple map, the probabilities on the outcomes of each action are the same throughout the map. In general they can and do vary depending on location.

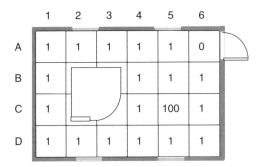

FIGURE 4.3.2   *Cell costs.*

Table 4.3.1 Probability Table for Action Effects

Action	Result	Probability
North	North	0.5
	West	0.25
	East	0.25
East	East	0.5
	North	0.25
	South	0.25
South	South	0.5
	West	0.25
	East	0.25
West	West	0.5
	North	0.25
	South	0.25

The Algorithm

The algorithm maintains a cell value array V, which is the same size as the map itself. The algorithm iteratively updates this array and stores the estimated cumulative cost of reaching the goal from every cell. When the algorithm is finished, the cell value array stores the actual path costs. Now let us look at DP broken down into pseudocode.

1. Initialize the values of all cells in V to the cell costs.
2. For each cell:
   a. For each action possible in that cell:
      Compute action value U.
   b. Choose the smallest action value U_s.
   c. Set the cell's value equal to the smallest action value plus the cell cost:

   $V = U_s + cost.$

3. Repeat.

Figure 4.3.3 shows the cell value array for the first three iterations and after the convergence to the optimal path. Several steps require further explanation. In step 2a, the action value U is computed by summing up the products of the adjacent cell values and the probabilities of going to them. For example, to calculate the action value of going north from D5 we multiply the probability of going to D4 with the value of D4, add the product of going to C5 with the value of C5 and add the product of going to D6 with the value of D6. For the cell value array in Figure 4.3.3, iteration 1, this is equal to 0.25 * 1 + 0.5 * 100 + 0.25 * 1 = 50.5.

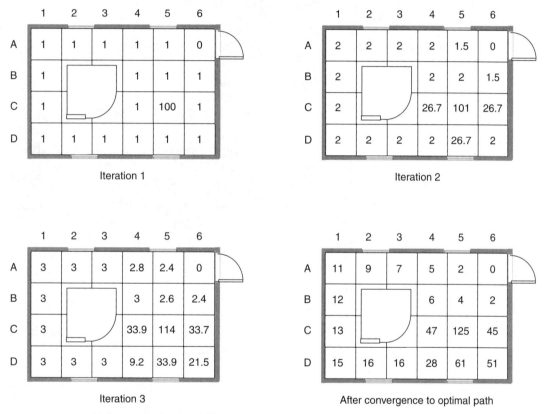

FIGURE 4.3.3   *Value array during different iterations.*

In step 2c, we update the cell value by setting it equal to the cell cost plus the value of the action with the smallest cost. For example, in Figure 4.3.3, iteration 1, D5 has three actions — left, right, and up, with costs 25.75, 25.75, and 50.5 respectively. Hence we set the new cell value for D5 (Figure 4.3.3, iteration 2) equal to the sum of 1 (the cost of D5) and 25.75.

Finally, we need to say a few words about step 3. How many times do we iterate the algorithm? The theory behind DP says that the value array will converge, but this might take a long time. Since we don't care about the exact numbers in the value array and are looking for the best path, we only need a few iterations. *A good rule of thumb is that the algorithm should be iterated at least the number of times equal to the number of moves in the best path.* Of course, a priori we don't know the best path, and this is where the science turns to art. DP is a level-of-detail algorithm (sometimes referred to as an "anytime" algorithm). It produces an approximate solution right away, and with more resources, it outputs better and better paths if better paths exist.

Finally, we consider how to obtain the best path from the cell value array V. The best path is stored in action array A, which is the same size as the size of the map. Here is the pseudocode:

1. Initialize action array A to one of the possible actions.
2. For each cell:
   a. For each action possible in that cell:
      i. Compute action value U using cell value array V.
   b. Store the action with the smallest action value in A (breaking ties in a fixed order or randomly).

Figure 4.3.4 shows the best paths to the goal if we used the cell value array after 1, 2, 3 iterations, as well as after the convergence.

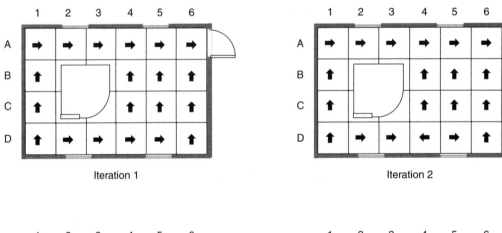

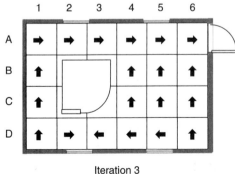

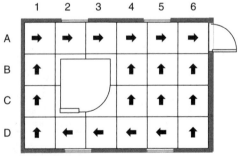

FIGURE 4.3.4 *Best path found so far.*

Code Listing

We start with the data structure for the probability table of action effects.

```
struct CAction {
    float m_probStraight;
    float m_probLeft;
    float m_probRight;
    float m_probBack;
}
```

The map data is stored in class CMap. The array m_walls stores the wall locations, while m_costs stores cell costs.

```
class CMap {
    bool    m_walls[WIDTH][HEIGHT];  //  true if wall
    CAction m_actionProbs;
    float   m_costs[WIDTH][HEIGHT];
}
```

In addition to these member variables, CMap houses various map access functions. We also use an auxiliary class CValue that stores the value function and its access functions. We use both of these helper classes to simplify the presentation of the main algorithm. In production code it would be more efficient (and quite simple) to integrate them into the main code.

The main class that houses data structures and the algorithm itself is CDynamicProgrammingAlg.

```
class CDynamicProgrammingAlg {
private:
    CMap    m_map;
    CValue  m_value;
    char    m_bestAction[WIDTH][HEIGHT];
    int     m_goalRow, m_goalCol;

    float ComputeCostW(int row, int col);
    float ComputeCostE(int row, int col);
    float ComputeCostS(int row, int col);
    float ComputeCostN(int row, int col);

public:
    void Iterate();
}
```

The array m_bestAction stores best action computed from m_value array. The heart of the algorithm is in the method Iterate(), which performs a single iteration of the dynamic programming algorithm.

```
void CDynamicProgrammingAlg::Iterate() {
    float cost, cost_N, cost_S, cost_W, cost_E;

    for (int row = 0; row < WIDTH; row++) {
        for (int col = 0; col < HEIGHT; col++) {
```

For each cell in the map, we compute the cost of each of four actions. Note that the listing for ComputeCostN() is provided later in this section.

```
if (!m_map.isWallN(row, col))
    cost_N = ComputeCostN(row, col);
if (!m_map.isWallS(row, col))
    cost_S = ComputeCostS(row, col);
if (!m_map.isWallW(row, col))
    cost_W = ComputeCostW(row, col);
if (!m_map.isWallE(row, col))
    cost_E = ComputeCostE(row, col);
```

Once we have the costs for all the actions, we check for several special cases, such as the cell being a goal cell or a wall. If none of these special cases applies, we compute the smallest cost action. The action itself is stored in the m_bestAction array, while the smallest cost is used to update the cell value array.

```
 // the cell is a goal
if ((row == m_goalRow) && (col == m_goalCol)) {
    cost = 0;
    m_bestAction[row][col] = GOAL;
}

// the cell is a wall
else if (m_map.isWall(row, col)) {
    cost = 0;
    m_bestAction[row][col] = WALL;
}

// north action has smallest cost
else if (cost_N <=_min(cost_S, cost_W, cost_E)) {
    cost = cost_N;
    m_bestAction[row][col] = NORTH;
}

// south action has smallest cost
else if (cost_S <=_min(cost_N, cost_E, cost_W)) {
    cost = cost_S;
    m_bestAction[row][col] = SOUTH;
}

// west action has smallest cost
else if (cost_W <=_min(cost_N, cost_S, cost_E)) {
    cost = cost_W;
    m_bestAction[row][col] = WEST;
}

// east action has smallest cost
else {
    cost = cost_E;
    m_bestAction[row][col] = EAST;
}

// update cell value array
```

```
m_value.set(row,col)=cost+m_map.getCost(row,col);
} } }
```

We now show how to compute the action cost, using northward movement as an example.

```
float CDynamicProgrammingAlg::ComputeCostN(int row, int col) {
    float prob_north = m_map.getProbStraight(row, col);
    float prob_east = m_map.getProbRight(row, col);
    float prob_west = m_map.getProbLeft(row, col);
```

When we try to go north, we can end up north, east or west. If west or east is blocked by the wall, the halfling bounces back to the starting cell.

```
float prob_N = m_map.getProbStraight(row, col);
float prob_E = m_map.getProbRight(row, col);
float prob_W = m_map.getProbLeft(row, col);

if (m_map.isWallE(row, col))
    prob_E = 0;

if (m_map.isWallW(row, col))
    prob_W = 0;

return prob_N * m_value.getValueNorthOf(row, col) +
       prob_W * m_value.getValueWestOf(row, col) +
       prob_E * m_value.getValueEastOf(row, col) +
       (1 - prob_N - prob_W - prob_E) *
       m_value.getValue(row, col);
```

Optimizations

The algorithm as presented so far can be somewhat inefficient when working on large maps. We introduce several optimizations to speed it up. First, we can set it to work on a small submap that includes the start and the goal cells, but excludes large portions of the map that are farther away. Then, as additional resources become available, we can enlarge the map and use the processing results for the submap as the initial values for the enlarged cell value array. While these first round results certainly will be updated as we keep enlarging the map, they will nonetheless save a lot of processing time.

The second major optimization comes from realizing that DP is a level of detail algorithm. That is, after one iteration, it already produces some paths and consistently improves them given more time. The computation can be split over multiple calls to the algorithm and the NPCs can compute actions as they go.

Other Uses of DP

Now let's take a look at how we can apply DP to other game situations.

Suppose we have an NPC elf mage who is about to engage the player in a spell-casting duel. To use the DP algorithm, we need to set up the goal state, actions, state space, and costs. The goal state is simple—the player dies. The actions are casting an offensive spell that has some chance of harming the player, casting a defensive spell that always heals the elf, and moving to a different (more advantageous) location. The state must describe everything pertinent to the duel: the number of spells left, elf and player hit points, locations. We can write this as a vector of (spells left, elf hit points, player hit points, elf location, player location). The state space that DP searches over is then simply a collection of all possible states. The actions link the states together—for example, casting a healing spell links state (a, b, c, d, e) to state (a – 1, b + 30, c, d, e) with probability 1. The state cost is equal to player hit points remaining.

The value array will now be the size of the state space. The DP algorithm works as before: for each state, for each action within that state, we compute its value, find the smallest cost action, and update the state value array. At convergence, we extract the best actions from the value array.

Note that we have chosen a high-level description of the duel that makes it easy to set up the search. We also could have described the duel at much smaller granularity, with separate actions for spells such as magic missile, sleep, or shield. We could also expand the state to include a character's equipment and various states such as sleeping/awake, or dazed. With a bit of additional effort in setting up the algorithm and a longer search time, we would gain more intricate and interesting strategies.

Conclusion

In this article, we discussed the difficulties of computing best paths on stochastic maps. We investigated the shortcomings of A* when dealing with such maps and went on to present the Dynamic Programming algorithm, which is specifically designed to handle uncertainty. We discussed the details of implementing DP on stochastic maps and showed how to extend it to other game scenarios.

Various extensions to the basic DP algorithm exist that make it applicable to a much wider range of game scenarios. Of particular interest to game developers are learning/sampling extensions of DP that eliminate the need to know the action probabilities or even the whole state space. The algorithm learns the data it requires by playing against itself or human players. In fact, this is how the excellent DP-based Tetris and backgammon players were created. These extensions, called *reinforcement learning* or *Neuro-Dynamic Programming* ([Bertsekas96] [Sutton98]), are beyond the scope of this article.

References

[Bertsekas96] Bertsekas, Dimitri, *Neuro-Dynamic Programming*, Athena Scientific, 1996.

[Bertsekas01] Bertsekas, Dimitri, *Dynamic Programming and Optimal Control: Second Edition*, Athena Scientific, 2001.

[Higgins02] Higgins, Dan, "Generic A* Pathfinding," *AI Game Programming Wisdom*, Charles River Media, 2002.

[Matthews02] Matthews, James, "Basic A* Pathfinding Made Simple," *AI Game Programming Wisdom*, Charles River Media, 2002.

[Sutton98] Sutton, Richard, *Reinforcement Learning: An Introduction*, MIT Press, 1998.

An Object-Oriented Utility-Based Decision Architecture

John Hancock, LucasArts

jhancock93@post.harvard.edu

Artificial intelligence in games is often "sloppy"—it is filled with ad-hoc rules or heuristics for making decisions. There is nothing wrong with heuristics in general. A well-chosen heuristic can save precious CPU cycles. Likewise, in our domain, sloppy or nonoptimal (but fun) results can also be acceptable. Game AI programmers are usually not looking for optimal solutions to problems, except where CPU efficiency is concerned. After all, we are trying to make games fun. If an AI opponent were perfect, it probably would not be fun to play against.

Sloppy architectures, however, are not acceptable. We have all seen (and written) decision tree logic that is a tangled mess of nested if-else rules. Composing logic from a few if-else statements is generally not a problem, but as the number of conditional statements grows, the AI logic can become very difficult to read, maintain, or expand. A poor architecture reduces the flexibility and maintainability of your code and ultimately harms your products. Moreover, game designs often change late in the development process, so adaptable code is extremely valuable.

This article presents an object-oriented utility-based decision architecture that has significant advantages over explicit decision tree architectures in terms of flexibility and maintainability. The principles described in this article derive from decision theory literature and have been applied in many situations, including the weapon selection AI in the real-time strategy game *Star Trek: Armada* and the character AI state machine architecture in *Star Wars: Obi-Wan*. Like traditional AI expert systems, this architecture often derives its intelligence by encoding human knowledge in the form of heuristic rules.

While learning methods might be used to automate decision-making, adapt to design changes, and avoid explicit and messy decision logic, games provide significant challenges to learning methods. Training an AI can be difficult and time-consuming because evaluating AI performance can require minutes or hours to complete the entire game. Moreover, performance evaluation of the AI can be unreliable, as performance metrics such as wins and losses depend as much on the behavior of competing AI or players as on the AI itself. Finally, there is no fitness function for "fun."

If you are fortunate enough to have adequate training data (possibly gathered from human players), you could use neural networks [Champandard02], naive Bayesian classifiers [McCallum98], decision tree generators [Quinlan93], or a host of other methods to save yourself from writing explicit decision logic. Statistical and learned information from these techniques could easily be incorporated and combined with human knowledge in the architecture presented here. However, this article assumes that training data is not available to automatically learn the optimal decision algorithm.

Decision Trees

Finite state machine (FSM) architectures are frequently used as a basis for AI in games, and decision trees are often used to determine state transitions. For example:

```
if (IsInjured())
    RunAway();       //#1 priority: save ourselves
else if (IsEnemyPresent())
    Attack();        //#2 priority: kill enemies
else if (HeardNoise())
    Investigate();  //#3 priority: gather info
else
    Patrol();        //nothing better to do
```

While such decision trees are functional and can be easy to read, explicit decision trees are brittle. That is, they do not scale well as the number of potential decisions grows. A game with 10 similar but fundamentally different AI types might have 10 different explicit decision trees like the preceding one, or perhaps a single large decision tree with additional branches to account for the differences in the various enemies. Using 10 similar but slightly different decision trees is likely to lead to code duplication as well as unintentional duplication of bugs in that code.

However, if we use a single decision tree, this might require us to significantly rewrite the decision code when we need to accommodate an eleventh enemy type or an additional behavior that was not previously accounted for. In either case, maintaining and evolving the decision tree(s) can be time consuming and prone to error. However, we can implement an implicit decision tree using object-oriented design that will ultimately be easier to maintain and more flexible.

Better Architecture through Objects

The State pattern [Gamma95] suggests that we implement AI behaviors or states as objects rather than functions. This allows us to create an implicit decision tree that can accommodate any number of behaviors without change.

Assume that each AI owns a container States of AIState objects. We provide each AIState object with a GetUtility() function that evaluates and returns its own absolute level of importance. This is represented by a floating-point number. Our AI's SelectState() function will look like this:

```
AIState* CharacterAI::SelectState()
{
    AIState* pBest = NULL;
    float bestUtility = 0.0f;
    for (AIStateList::iterator j = States.begin();
        j != States.end(); ++j)
    {
        float utility = (*j)->GetUtility(this);
        if (utility > bestUtility)
    {
            pBest = *j;
            bestUtility = utility;
        }
    }
    return pBest;
}
```

Notice that we can add or remove states from a character or change state functionality without changing SelectState() at all. While AIState subclasses are, in general, dependent on the CharacterAI class, we do not need to muddy the CharacterAI code with state-specific details. In addition, if a character doesn't own or use a particular state/behavior, we expend no effort in calculating its utility.

The concept of *utility* has a strict definition in decision theory, which we describe in detail later in the article. For now, however, we can describe a behavior's utility as the degree to which it can fulfill high-level goals, multiplied by the relative importance of each goal. In a first-person shooter game, the most important high-level goals are staying alive and killing your opponents. Secondary goals might include exploring, acquiring items, and acquiring information. If we rank these goals in order of importance, we can use them as priorities to establish the utility of a corresponding state.

If a state is not currently relevant or cannot achieve its goals, then it should report a value of zero. For example, if there are no enemies for the AI to attack, the Attack state is useless and would have a utility of zero. There is an implied order of importance in the previously listed decision tree, from RunAway (the highest-priority behavior), to Attack, then Investigate, and finally, the lowest-priority behavior, Patrol. It is important to establish a value scale and apply it consistently, especially in the absence of a concrete measure for utility.

To achieve the same behavior as the decision tree, we define the utility functions for our behaviors.

```
float RunAway::GetUtility(CharacterAI *AI) const {
    return AI->IsInjured() ? 0.9f : 0.0f;
}
float Attack::GetUtility(CharacterAI *AI) const {
    return AI->IsEnemyPresent() ? 0.6f : 0.0f;
}
float Investigate::GetUtility(CharacterAI *AI) const {
```

```
        return AI->HeardNoise() ? 0.3f : 0.0f;
    }
    float Patrol::GetUtility(CharacterAI *AI) const {
        return 0.1f;
    }
```

While this solution might seem more complicated than the decision tree, the additional flexibility we gain is well worth the added complexity. We can assemble different AIs from a combination of behaviors without having to write a decision tree for each AI-controlled character. Whenever we implement a new state, we must give it a GetUtility() function that is scaled properly relative to other states.

While this fuzzy concept of utility can be very useful in making an FSM more flexible, it might be difficult to write a large number of utility functions in a cohesive manner without a more concrete means of measuring or defining utility. To more accurately define utility, we first explain the concept of expected value in the context of a weapon selection system.

Expected Value

Decision-makers often have to choose between actions in the presence of uncertain state information. To make matters more complicated, the outcomes of the actions themselves are often uncertain.

In games, it is possible to create AIs that have perfect information about the past and present. However, perfect information can be expensive to compute or store, and might constitute "cheating" if the AI accesses game information it should not be able to access. The AI might be able to predict some future information, but it cannot predict a player's future actions with certainty. Thus, game AI must also make decisions in the presence of uncertainty.

Usually, when humans are faced with a decision, they select a certain course of action because they believe that it will lead to the best outcome among the alternatives. However, how do we define the "best" outcome?

In decision theory, one traditional definition for "best" is *maximum expected value*. The expected value of an action is its average payoff. Mathematically, the expected value of an action is the summation over all possible outcomes i of the probability p_i of an outcome multiplied by the reward r_i of that outcome.

$$E(V) = \sum_i p_i r_i$$

We can use this theory to program an FPS character to equip its best weapon. One way of defining the expected value of the weapon is the predicted damage (or rate of damage) the weapon will cause to a given target, since ultimately the purpose of the weapon is to kill the opponent. We require that each weapon object provide a GetExpectedDamage() function that returns a number indicating how much damage the weapon would likely do if used. The decision function for selecting a weapon is nearly identical to our earlier SelectState() function—we just iterate over the weapons list and find the weapon that returns the highest expected damage.

So far, we have not discussed the function arguments to the GetExpectedDamage() and GetUtility() functions. Assuming damage varies with distance, we write:

```
virtual float GetExpectedDamage(float Distance) const;
```

We also assume that both the weapon damage and the chance of hitting depend on the target distance. In the case of a weapon miss, it inflicts zero damage. Hence:

```
float Weapon::GetExpectedDamage(float Distance) const {
    return HitChance(Distance) * Damage(Distance);
}
```

Every subclass of Weapon can redefine its expected damage by overriding the Get-ExpectedDamage() or HitChance() and Damage() functions.

Planning for Change

A good programmer knows to plan for change. The current function signature for the GetExpectedDamage() function might be sufficient for simple weapons such as shotguns, rifles, and so forth, where it might be reasonable to estimate its expected damage solely on distance, but is unlikely to be sufficient for explosive weapons. For example, we might want to subtract unwanted collateral damage from a grenade's expected damage estimate. However, predicting the quantity and likelihood of unwanted damage would require information such as the number of allies located in the intended area of effect. Adding an additional argument to GetExpectedDamage() during development would require us to change all of its declarations and definitions, so it is a good idea to plan for change and design a more flexible interface from the start.

We make our design more maintainable by using a *helper* struct WeaponContext. A helper struct is used to group frequently needed data together, as in our function arguments.

```
virtual float ExpectedDamage(const WeaponContext& context);
virtual float Damage(const WeaponContext& context);
virtual float HitChance(const WeaponContext& context);
```

By using a structure like WeaponContext, we are free to effectively add function arguments later by adding elements to that structure without having to change existing function definitions. Using a structure also improves efficiency by providing a convenient location to cache contextual information required by multiple weapons in their expected damage calculations.

We used an expected value weapon selection system to great effect in *Star Trek™: Armada*, a real-time strategy game that features more than 40 different weapons [Activision00]. The weapons have diverse effects: some weapons are effective against a single ship, while others are effective against multiple ships. Some weapons can inflict collateral damage to friendly vessels. Some weapons damage shields, while others damage crew, and still others can repair or protect friendly vessels. Because of the variety of effects, it was not possible to simply define the expected value as the expected damage. Instead, expected value also accounted for relative target values, positive effects to allied vessels, collateral damage, and a variety of other effects. Where expected value could not be calculated easily from available information, human experts constructed heuristic measures.

With such a large number of diverse weapons, it would have been nearly impossible to try to select weapons with an explicit decision tree. However. programming ease and flexibility were not the only benefits of the object-oriented architecture: the AI in *Armada* often surprised us with devastating weapon combinations that we never programmed. Instead, the weapon combos were a result of emergent intelligence provided by the weapons' shifts in utility in response to the changing circumstances.

To obtain this intelligence in your systems, your expected value functions should take advantage of human expertise and the specific nature of the object you are evaluating—that is why GetUtility() and GetExpectedDamage() are declared *virtual*. Often, collective intelligence will emerge from very simple rules in the distributed utility functions. However, you should also feel free to "go crazy" in the evaluation functions; if there's any reason to favor or disfavor the object or behavior, it's fair game for inclusion, as long as you do not violate module independence or consume too many CPU cycles. If you discover that you are computing the same value in multiple evaluation functions, calculate it once and cache it in the helper structure instead.

Alternative Decision Criteria

Although expected value is a good criterion for decision-making, it's not the only reasonable one. People often make decisions that do not maximize expected value.

As an example, suppose there is a very unusual lottery that gives you a 50-percent chance of winning $50,000 for an entry price of $20,000. The expected value of such a lottery is $0.5(50,000) + 0.5(0) = \$25,000$. The expected value of not playing that lottery is $20,000—in other words, you keep your money. Expected value theory says that any rational being should play that lottery since playing maximizes the expected value. However, some people would refuse to play such a lottery because they would not risk losing $20,000. Clearly, humans do not always decide based on expected value.

Although it is perfectly reasonable (and intelligent) to maximize expected value, other decision criteria offer us the ability to inject our AIs with a little more personality or human characteristics. The *maximin* criterion, for example, determines the worst outcome for every action (the minimum reward) and chooses the action that maximizes this—that is, it searches for the "best" worst outcome. The maximin criterion is essentially a pessimistic or risk-averse criterion.

The *maximax* criterion determines the best outcome for every action (the maximum reward) and chooses the action that maximizes this—that is, it attempts to discover the "best" best outcome [Winston91]. The maximax criterion is an optimistic criterion. Through utility theory, we can represent both of these criteria, expected value, and more.

Utility Theory

Utility theory provides a way to explain how different people make different (but rational) decisions when faced with the same data. As originally formulated, the utility function is a mathematical representation of an individual's preference or indifference between various lotteries [Winston91]. It is essentially a mathematical description of an individual's attitude toward risk.

Von Neumann-Morgenstern utility theory states that rational beings will choose to maximize expected utility:

$$E(U) = \sum_i p_i u\big(r_i\big)$$

where the utility function $u(x)$ increases over the set of possible rewards ($u'(x) > 0$). Although the utility function does not have to be differentiable, a decision-maker with a differentiable $u(x)$ is:

1) risk-averse if $u(x)$ is strictly concave down; i.e., $u''(x) < 0$
2) risk-neutral if $u(x)$ is linear; i.e., $u''(x) = 0$
3) risk-seeking if $u(x)$ is strictly concave up (convex); i.e., $u''(x) > 0$

Giving different characters unique utility functions will provide them with distinct personalities that will differ in a believable, consistent manner. Since we are not concerned with modeling an actual individual's personality, we are free to choose any utility function that achieves the desired effect. For example, we could choose: $u(x) = x$ for a risk-neutral personality; $u(x) = x^2$ for a risk-seeking personality; $u(x) = \sqrt{x}$ for a risk-averse personality. Alternatively, a piecewise linear function or response curve [Alexander02] could be used to achieve the mixture of risk-seeking behavior (purchasing lottery tickets) and risk-averse behavior (buying insurance) that many people exhibit.

Using maximum utility as our decision criterion for weapon selection leads to this function definition:

```
float Weapon::GetExpectedUtility(const WeaponContext& context) const
{
    return HitChance(Distance) *
           context.Owner->Utility(Damage(Distance));
}
```

The expected utility of the weapon now depends on the `GetUtility()` function of the weapon owner—that is, the AI character itself, which is accessible through the `WeaponContext` object. This architecture allows for varying decisions based on character or personality variations without any changes to the decision logic.

Conclusion

In this article, we presented an object-oriented decision architecture with several alternative decision criteria, including expected utility.

While generating probability estimates might seem like a significant drawback of this method, it is not important to model the world with high fidelity. After all, we do not need optimal results. The needed probabilities will sometimes be available in the game logic. Other times, probabilities might be estimated by hand or gathered through Bayesian reasoning and statistical data collected during gameplay. As long as alternatives have different risk profiles, varying utility functions will produce varying decisions, and thus provide personality to your characters.

Regardless of whether you decide to incorporate utility theory in your AI in favor of another decision criterion, the distributed structure presented here will provide huge benefits to your code in terms of flexibility, maintainability, and opportunities for emergent behavior. If you can use it, however, utility theory provides a way to humanize your AI decision processes for very little cost.

References

[Alexander02] Alexander, Bob, "The Beauty of Response Curves," *AI Game Programming Wisdom*, Charles River Media, 2002.

[Activision00] *Star Trek: Armada*, Activision, Inc., 2000.

[Champandard02] Champandard, Alex, "The Dark Art of Neural Networks," *AI Game Programming Wisdom*, Charles River Media, 2002.

[Gamma95] Gamma, Erich, et al., *Design Patterns: Elements of Reusable Object-Oriented Software*, Addison-Wesley, 1995.

[McCallum98] McCallum, A., Nigam, K., "A Comparison of Event Models for Naive Bayes Text Classification," *AAAI-98 Workshop on Learning for Text Categorization*, 1998.

[Quinlan93] Quinlan, J. R., *C4.5: Programs for Machine Learning*, Morgan Kaufmann, 1993.

[Winston91] Winston, Wayne, Operations Research: Applications and Algorithms, Second Edition, PWS-Kent Publishing Co., 1991.

4.5

A Distributed-Reasoning Voting Architecture

John Hancock, LucasArts

jhancock93@post.harvard.edu

Most behavior-based AI architectures are incapable of obeying multiple behavior modules simultaneously. At any instant, the AI system carries out the active behavior or state and ignores the rest. These systems provide no method to compromise between behaviors or satisfy their goals simultaneously. Unless we specifically design and implement a particular behavior to communicate with other behaviors (an architecture that would introduce regrettable code dependency issues), information provided by the other behaviors is effectively wasted.

This article discusses an alternative AI architecture composed of multiple independent reasoning modules, henceforth called *advisors*, plus an arbiter that performs *command fusion* on the inputs from the advisors. This voting-based architecture is easy to use, easy to implement, and easy to maintain.

We define a "voting space" as the set of options for which each advisor must vote. Developers can implement different advisors independently as long as the advisors output to the same voting space.

The architecture described here can cope with asynchronous modules, with low-level modules running at perhaps 30 Hertz, and with higher-level modules, such as a path planner, running at a lower frequency while maintaining high-frequency output essential for reactive behavior. Asynchronous-friendly operation is useful for CPU-load balancing in games where CPU cycles are at a premium.

Distributed Reasoning

Distributed reasoning spreads cognitive processes and responsibilities among multiple systems or locations. In contrast, centralized architectures might use multiple sources and modules to build a world model, but a single module is responsible for cognition and planning. Game AIs are generally centralized: most of what we term "AI" occurs in a C++ class representing the brain of the actor or the class representing the actor itself.

The distributed voting architecture discussed here is inspired by work by Rosenblatt [Rosenblatt97]. The architecture consists of multiple independent advisors that communicate with a central arbiter (see Figure 4.5.1). Advisors are reasoning modules or behaviors that are responsible for performing a particular task or goal, or reasoning about a specific facet of the problem domain. Each advisor assesses the situation independently, focusing only on its particular task or domain facet, and calculates the utility of each possible course of action.

Advisors are independent; that is, they do not depend on the results of other advisors, and there is no communication between advisors. This independence allows you to add, remove, enable, or disable advisors on the fly without any modifications to the arbiter or other modules. Each advisor can be implemented using whatever techniques are appropriate: one might use Bayesian inference, while another uses heuristic knowledge, and a third uses a neural network for vote generation. This flexibility is a distinct advantage over centralized architectures.

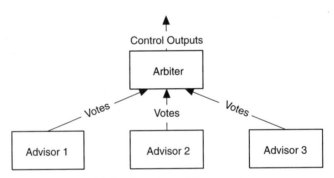

FIGURE 4.5.1   *Multiple active advisors send votes to an arbiter that integrates the votes, selects the best course of action, and then generates control outputs.*

The Wrong Way to Perform Command Fusion

Let us examine the problem of moving a robot toward a goal in the presence of both static obstacles that might be avoided through pathfinding, and dynamic obstacles, such as vehicles, that are not accounted for in the planned path. We will assume that one advisor directs the robot along a planned path toward its goal, and another advisor directs the robot away from dynamic obstacles. A naive solution to the command fusion problem might have each advisor output a single suggested direction vector, and fuse them by outputting the average vector as the desired direction. Figure 4.5.2 illustrates a situation that might lead to disaster.

In fact, this is what potential field methods do. Potential fields average the vectors from all the repulsors and attractors. At any moment, as in Figure 4.5.2, this can cause the robot to head toward an object even though there are better options available. In addition, vector sums can result in local minima that "trap" the AI. Provided the AI does not get trapped in the local minima, it will probably not collide with an obstacle

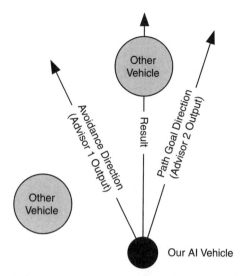

FIGURE 4.5.2 *Averaging vectors from multiple advisors (an avoidance direction and our current path goal direction) can result in an output worse than any of the individual suggested vectors. In this case, the result directs the AI toward one of the obstacles it is supposed to avoid.*

because the repulsion field from an obstacle becomes stronger as the AI approaches it. Nevertheless, we can do better.

Rather than fusing commands, many systems simply prioritize them. The system gives exclusive control to a single behavior either based on state transition logic as in finite-state machines or based on priority as in Brooks' *subsumption* architecture [Brooks91]. In such systems, the vehicle goes into obstacle avoidance mode when in danger of hitting a dynamic obstacle, ignoring the goal-directed behavior. Once the agent is out of danger, the goal-directed (pathfinding) behavior takes over again. While this prioritized behavior is satisfactory when goals are exclusive, these architectures do not provide a way to achieve goals that can and should be achieved concurrently. In our distributed architecture, however, multiple behaviors have concurrent partial control over the AI through the arbiter. Many times, dynamic obstacles can be avoided without significant deviations from the planned path. Other times, deviations from the planned path might force us to replan the path.

Command Fusion through Voting

If we redesign the system such that each advisor outputs votes for multiple actions at once rather than recommending a single action, the arbiter has more information at its disposal, allowing it to make a better decision during command fusion. While a set of advisor votes might have a single "best" action, it is important to know how much better that action is compared to the alternatives, because the best compromise between modules likely includes one of those alternatives.

Advisors communicate to the arbiter by sending analog votes for every possible command in the voting space. A positive vote indicates the action is favored, and a negative vote indicates the action is disfavored. The magnitude of the vote indicates the strength of the (dis)favor. The arbiter examines all the votes from all advisors, selects the best command, and outputs this to the AI controller. The only requirements of the advisors are that they communicate their votes to the arbiter in a format the arbiter can understand, and that the votes are scaled appropriately. Typically, all advisor output is given in the same voting space and votes are normalized between −1 and 1. Using a single voting space (or voting scale) is not absolutely necessary if the arbiter can understand multiple formats and integrate them in a consistent manner.

A Steering Arbiter Example

For illustration purposes, we now assume that we are designing an AI to drive over rough terrain in a vehicular combat game. In particular, we want to design a system that at any instant will choose a steering curvature for the vehicle. Ideally, the AI wants to do any or all of the following simultaneously: avoid enemy fire, avoid obstacles, destroy enemy vehicles by ramming them or driving them into its firing arcs, consider the limitations of vehicle dynamics (avoid tip-over), and drive toward a goal (via a planned path if desired). This type of problem is perfectly suited to our distributed architecture.

Our first step in designing the architecture is to select our voting representation. We do not have to make the voting representation the same as our control output representation, but we do so here to allow the arbiter itself to be knowledge-free or domain-independent (the advisors are not domain-independent). In this case, we want to choose the best steering arc or curvature ρ, defined as the reciprocal of the turn radius. Every advisor generates votes for each of several discrete steering arcs with curvatures from the range $(-1/R_{min}, 1/R_{min})$, where R_{min} is the minimum turn radius of the vehicle (see Figure 4.5.3). How many discrete arcs we choose is a balance between efficiency and adequate resolution from the advisors. We are not necessarily limited to choosing an output matching one of our discrete arcs; we will show later how to achieve analog output despite the discrete number of arcs evaluated.

We then create an advisor responsible for each of the following objectives:

- **Avoid tip-over:** This advisor votes against any turn radii that might tip the vehicle over. At low speeds, all steering arcs are likely valid. At high speeds, the advisor votes against extreme curvatures.
- **Avoid obstacles:** The obstacle avoidance advisor votes against arcs according to their minimum distance from obstacles and the distance along the arc to that obstacle. Arcs that intersect nearby obstacles receive strong negative votes. Arcs that pass near obstacles or intersect far obstacles receive weak negative votes. Note that this advisor only needs to consider local obstacles, as distant obstacles are generally not relevant to the decision.

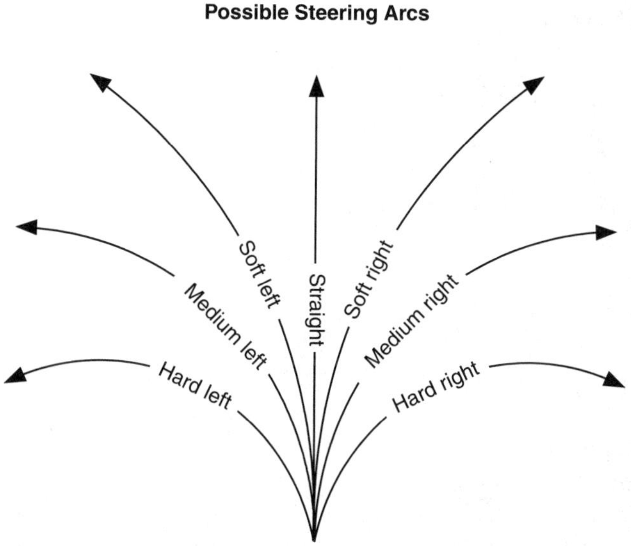

Possible Steering Arcs

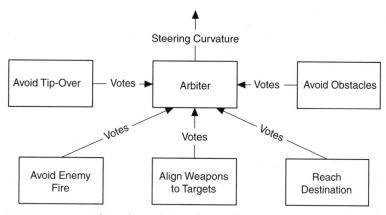

FIGURE 4.5.3 *Every advisor must calculate the utility of following each of several discrete steering arcs.*

- **Avoid enemy fire:** This advisor votes against steering arcs that intersect current enemy lines of fire. The magnitude increases with the length of time the vehicle would stay within the line of fire.
- **Align weapons to target:** This advisor favors steering directions that might allow the AI vehicle to fire upon other vehicles in the near future.
- **Reach destination:** This advisor favors steering directions that best steer it toward the goal. For example, this might output the dot product between the direction to the goal and the resulting vehicle direction, assuming the vehicle continues on the steering arc for a small amount of time.

The resulting architecture appears in Figure 4.5.4.

FIGURE 4.5.4 *This arbiter design chooses the steering curvature for an AI vehicle in a vehicular combat game.*

Arbiter Design

Finally, we must determine how the arbiter selects the "best" steering direction given the input from its advisors. Figure 4.5.5 shows the results of two different methods for vote arbitration given votes from two steering curvature advisors. Note that the advisor votes vary smoothly over the curvature.

In general, if the arbiter is expected to pick an analog output as in our steering arbiter, then the advisors' votes should vary smoothly over the input range. Smooth vote distributions (similar inputs produce similar votes) help to encourage compromise at the arbiter level and better represent true preferences for analog values. For example, if an advisor wants to steer along a certain arc, arcs near the chosen arc should get similar votes, as they are most likely better alternatives than distant arcs. We can generate smooth vote distributions by either using continuous functions in advisor vote generation or by convolving the advisor votes with a Gaussian or other smoothing function—in other words, low-pass filtering the votes [Rosenblatt97].

The first arbiter in Figure 4.5.5 chooses the action that maximizes the sum of the advisor votes. It causes the system to perform a shallow turn to the right. The second arbiter is a "maximin" arbiter—in other words, it chooses the curvature that maximizes the minimum of the advisor votes. In this case, it chooses almost straight ahead. The maximin arbiter is a risk-averse arbiter.

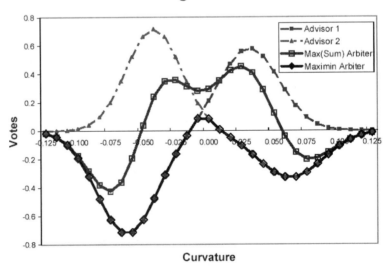

FIGURE 4.5.5   *Voting distributions for a two-advisor system with two different arbiters. The first arbiter, "Max(Sum)," chooses the output that maximizes the sum of votes from the advisors. The maximin arbiter chooses the curvature that maximizes the minimum vote of the two advisors.*

An arbiter that maximizes the weighted sum of advisor votes can also be highly effective. In this case, the most important safety-related advisors are generally given high weights. Allowing advisors to veto actions in a summing arbiter is also an effective way to capture some of the benefits of a risk-averse arbiter. We can implement vetoes with negative votes that are several orders of magnitude greater than the normal vote magnitude [Sukthankar97].

Achieving Analog Output from Discrete Votes

Limiting the output to match one of our discrete arcs might seem a huge drawback to our steering arbiter. Increasing our input resolution significantly in order to increase our output resolution would be computationally expensive. Fortunately, we are not limited to selecting one of our discrete arcs. We can calculate an analog output between our discrete outputs through a quadratic interpolation.

Because three points determine a quadratic, we can solve for parameters a, b, and c in the quadratic curve that passes through the best outcome y_{Max} at ρ_i and its adjacent votes at ρ_{i-1} and ρ_{i+1}.

$$y = a\rho^2 + b\rho + c$$

Then, the best curvature is the one such that:

$$\frac{\partial y}{\partial \rho} = 0 \Rightarrow \rho = \frac{-b}{2a}$$

This determines our new output, which is guaranteed to fall in the interval bracketing the discrete best outcome, (ρ_{i-1}, ρ_{i+1}).

Choosing the Voting Space

For an AI to perform actions, commands must eventually take the form of control outputs. On a physical robot, this might be the set of currents or voltages applied to each motor or actuator in the robot. While additional abstraction layers of programming can provide higher-level controls, we must eventually translate the commands to actuator space. In the context of a game, the programmer has more flexibility in choosing the control outputs: for a vehicle, we do not have to model the engine, the steering linkage, or other factors, because we can control acceleration and direction directly if we desire. In our driving example, we chose the voting and control spaces to be the steering arc curvature ρ (defined as the reciprocal of the steering radius).

For almost any system, there are multiple possibilities for the voting space. First and foremost, you want to select a voting space that is easy and efficient for the advisors to reason about. If the voting space is the same as the output or control space, then no translation is required between the two, and the arbiter module itself can often be "knowledge-free" or domain-independent. However, because there is only one arbiter, it is also acceptable if it requires some work for the arbiter to translate the voting space into control space.

To illustrate the use of a voting space different from the control space, we return to our driving example. Suppose our vehicle advisors vote in terms of discrete map locations instead of steering curvature. The map-based voting space might simplify the obstacle detection advisor since it could simply vote against map grid cells containing obstacles. On the other hand, the voting space would complicate the tip-over advisor since the dynamics are handled more easily in terms of turn radius.

The map-based voting space would require domain-specific knowledge in the arbiter to process the map votes and determine the best steering curvature output (assuming curvature remained our control variable). The map-based approach, however, has advantages with regard to advisor latency since old local maps can be transformed into new local coordinates without an update from the advisor. See [Rosenblatt97] for more discussion on how map-based votes apply to vehicle steering.

Finally, it is important that the chosen voting space provide enough information to the arbiter for it to make intelligent decisions. When the desired arbiter outputs are continuously valued (real) numbers, achieving optimal results might require the sampling resolution of the voting space to be sufficient to fully reconstruct the continuous voting functions used in the advisors. The Nyquist Sampling Theorem states that the sampling frequency must be double the maximum frequency of the signal (function) to allow lossless reconstruction of the signal (function). In practice, optimal results are rarely necessary, so a much lower sampling resolution is likely to be adequate.

A Real-Time Strategy Base-Building Arbiter

To further illustrate map-based voting, we now examine an AI problem from real-time strategy (RTS) games.

A common AI problem in RTS games is base-building. For computer players to conquer their enemies, they need to expand their empire to take advantage of available land and resources to support and grow their army. AIs must be able to construct buildings and occasionally start new bases of operation. Since buildings are generally not movable, it is important to select a good location before building.

There are many factors to consider when choosing a location for a new base or a new building within an existing base. Let us design an arbiter to choose the placement of new buildings. We assume that the AI has already selected the type of building to create.

The control space output is a map location for building placement. We choose our voting space to be the set of possible map locations. Here are some advisors we might create:

- **Free space:** Veto illegal placement locations and favor grid cells that will not block paths through the base.

- **Convenient to resources:** If the building is required for resource gathering (such as a lumber yard in *Warcraft*), strongly favor locations near the relevant resource using a response curve or falloff curve.
- **Avoid enemies:** Vote positively for grid cells far away from enemy bases and negatively for spaces near enemy bases.
- **Needs protection:** If this is a valuable building that cannot defend itself, vote positively for locations near our own bases or defensive structures.
- **Provides defense:** If this is a defensive building such as a guard tower, vote against locations that are already covered by a defensive building and vote positively for locations near buildings or locations of strategic value.

Any of the advisors described, or the arbiter itself, can be implemented as an influence map [Tozour01]. Not all advisors are relevant for all building placements, but our architecture allows us to enable or disable advisors easily depending on the type of building the AI is attempting to create. In addition, different building types might each provide an advisor of its own that encodes building-specific information.

A weighted sum arbiter with vetoes will likely provide us the best results. Different weights can be used to provide different personalities to different AIs. For particularly valuable buildings, we might consider increasing the weights of safety-related advisors, as we want to minimize the risk of losing those buildings to the enemy.

Finding the best weights for the advisors involves some educated guesses and a little trial and error. If you dislike trial and error, a genetic algorithm or other learning method can learn the weights used by the arbiter and tune any internal parameters in the advisors automatically [Baluja97]. Nevertheless, since optimal results are not necessarily "fun" results, some tweaking is inevitable to maximize entertainment value.

Conclusion

In this article, we introduced an architecture that allows multiple behaviors to share concurrent partial control over an AI. The voting architecture has a significant advantage over state or priority-based architectures that have no means to compromise or accomplish multiple tasks at once. Distributed architectures also are more flexible, easier to maintain, and more robust to unexpected circumstances.

Because the voting architecture leads to emergent behavior, it might not be the right architecture when provably correct or optimal behavior is required and possible through centralized planning. Distributed architectures generate output that is difficult to predict compared to centralized architectures, but this is also what makes distributed architectures less brittle and able to cope with unforeseen circumstances. Fortunately, this architecture is perfectly suited to most games, where design flexibility is important, optimal behavior is rarely necessary, and highly dynamic environments can make planning difficult.

References

[Baluja97] Baluja, S., R. Sukthankar, R., and J. Hancock, "Prototyping Intelligent Vehicle Modules Using Evolutionary Algorithms," *Evolutionary Algorithms in Engineering Applications*, Springer-Verlag, 1997.

[Brooks91] Brooks, R.A., "Intelligence without Representation," *Artificial Intelligence* 47 (1991), pp. 139–159.

[Rosenblatt97] Rosenblatt, J., "DAMN: A Distributed Architecture for Mobile Navigation," *Journal of Experimental and Theoretical Artificial Intelligence*, Vol. 9, No. 2 / 3, 1997, pp. 339–360.

[Sukthankar97] Sukthankar, R., "Situation Awareness for Tactical Driving," CMU Technical Report, CMU-RI-TR-97-08.

[Tozour01] Tozour, P., "Influence Mapping," *Game Programming Gems 2*, Charles River Media, 2001.

4.6

Attractors and Repulsors

John M. Olsen, Microsoft

infix@xmission.com

Helping your AI-controlled entities know what to stay close to and what to avoid can go a long way in helping to generate realistic simulated behaviors. A large part of tasks such as walking through a crowd, racing down a track, or flying through space consists of staying close to some objects and avoiding others. Attractors and repulsors can be used for many purposes, including simulating flocking behaviors, collision avoidance for racing, and tracking opponents in 2D or 3D environments. We can build attraction curves—functions that determine the level of push and pull between objects—to influence the movement of our AI-controlled objects. We can also combine simple curves into more complex composite curves to build interesting emergent behaviors.

This technique is most useful as an enhancement to an existing steering or path-finding system. Attractors and repulsors by themselves are not a good choice as your primary path-finding system, since there is no way to tell the AI how to navigate around complex obstacles. As a steering technique, it adds interesting environmental responses, but it encounters problems such as local minima that can capture the AI if there is no underlying path-finding system. This interaction between the various layers of AI control will be addressed after covering the mechanics of the system.

Combining Forces

To move our objects, we need to create a single combined vector that represents the total effect of all attraction and repulsion forces acting on the object. To do this, we will sum up all of the attraction or repulsion forces for objects within an arbitrary cut-off distance. We will then convert this summed force into acceleration using Equation 4.6.1, which is based on simple Newtonian physics. Acceleration is the sum of the forces divided by the mass of the object.

$$a = \frac{\sum f}{m}$$

(4.6.1)

For the purposes of this article, a simple approximation using Euler integration methods is sufficient, as shown in Equations 4.6.2 and 4.6.3. We apply acceleration each frame to the original velocity to determine a new velocity, and then apply this new velocity to the original position to find a new position for the current frame of the simulation. This approximation works fairly well as long as the time steps are small relative to the velocities used.

$$v_f = v_0 + a \times dt \qquad\qquad\qquad\qquad\qquad\qquad (4.6.2)$$

$$p_f = p_0 + v_f \qquad\qquad\qquad\qquad\qquad\qquad\qquad (4.6.3)$$

Sometimes, we will need to use a more rigorous approach to avoid problems with oscillation and other errors that can result from large step sizes or adding damping values into the force system. In such cases, we can use more accurate physical simulation methods, such as Taylor's Theorem [Lander99].

Attraction Curves

Attraction curves are functions that determine force for a given distance. Any function will work as long as there is only one force value for any given distance. Think of it as Y (the amount of force applied, shown along the vertical axis) being a function of X (the distance between the object applying the force and an object subject to that force, shown as the horizontal axis). The curve does not need to be continuous, but continuous curves have some distinct advantages in producing smooth results. Figures 4.6.1 and 4.6.2 show sample attraction curves.

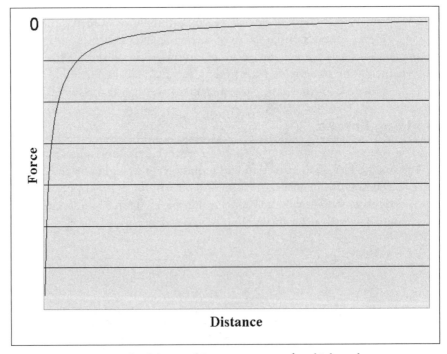

FIGURE 4.6.1   *A graph of the repulsion curve $y = -x^{-1}$, which pushes you away more strongly as you come closer to the repulsor.*

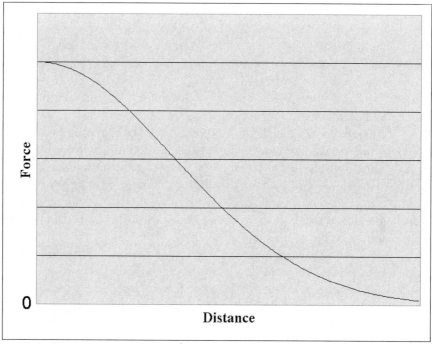

FIGURE 4.6.2 *The attractor* e^{-x^2}. *The positive portion of the bell curve pulls harder as you get closer.*

Note that the curves are cut off to show no negative X values, since the X-axis represents distance from the object rather than a position. We omit negative distances here as they are rarely useful.

We must take particular care to avoid curves that approach infinity at any point. The curve in Figure 4.6.1 reaches infinity at x=0, which means we will have to perform an additional test to avoid attempting to apply infinite or extremely large forces to objects. A simple way to avoid this problem with Figure 4.6.1 would be to shift the curve slightly to the left so it is finite at zero, as shown in Equation 4.6.4.

$$y = \left(\frac{-1}{x + 0.01} \right)$$

(4.6.4)

In practice, approaching the infinite repulsor force is not a large problem because the force will grow as the two objects approach until the system overcomes the force pushing them together, automatically avoiding the condition of having a distance close to zero.

Sums of Curves

We can produce more complex curves by adding the simple curves shown previously. This makes it possible to store a smaller number of simple curves rather than gathering a large collection of purely custom and unique curves. Large collections of curves can become unwieldy, while generating curves based on previously defined curves gives you a more cohesive, interrelated set. We can then automatically update each composite curve whenever one of the lower level curves upon which it is based is altered.

For example, we can represent flocking by applying a sum of multiple attraction and repulsion curves. We can create a primitive flocking algorithm by building a curve that starts out highly repulsive at a range of zero to avoid clumping. Then, at some optimal distance, the force value crosses the zero force line and is attractive for some distance before falling back down into repulsion mode. This combines the "Cohesion" and "Separation" values of standard flocking [Reynolds87] into a single effect curve. A minor difference when merging the cohesion and separation into a single curve is that both are based on the entire flock, rather than limiting the separation test to the nearest neighbors.

The final repulsive force that occurs when the flocking elements are far apart causes stragglers to break off and decide to go their own way. It also limits the flock size, because any flock that becomes too large will start to push away the members at the outer fringes of the flock. We can obtain this behavior with the example curves in Figures 4.6.1 and 4.6.2 by adding them and increasing the scale of the bell curve until it can partially overcome the other curve. This is shown in Figure 4.6.3.

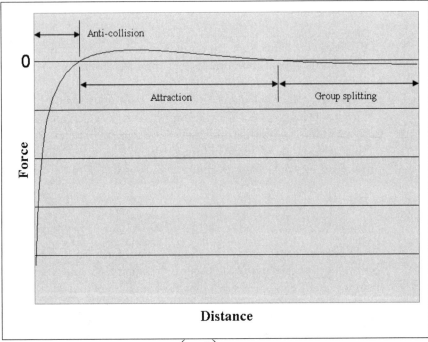

FIGURE 4.6.3 $y = -x^{-1} + 4 \times \left(e^{-x^2} \right)$ *A primitive flocking curve.*

Different Curves for Different Pairings

We can build a more complex system from this humble base by allowing different types of objects to be affected by different attractors and repulsors, and by making certain game objects serve as attractors and repulsors for other objects.

If your game entities consist of wolves and rabbits, for example, you would want the rabbits to draw together into groups, but you would want them to flee from wolves. The wolves will draw together into hunting packs, but unlike a rabbit's fear, which is represented by a repulsive force, the wolves are drawn toward the rabbits with an attraction force representing their hunger.

Dynamic Curves

Up to this point, curve definitions have been constant, but there is no real reason to keep that restriction. Forces can vary over time and be affected by any number of external parameters. Using the wolf and rabbit example, a wolf's hunger varies depending on how many rabbits it has eaten recently, and this could be used to alter how strongly the wolf wants to follow rabbits.

When a wolf is very hungry, it will have a strong attraction toward any rabbits in the neighborhood. When the wolf is completely sated, it will have little or no attraction toward rabbits. We generate this behavior (shown in Figure 4.6.4) by scaling the

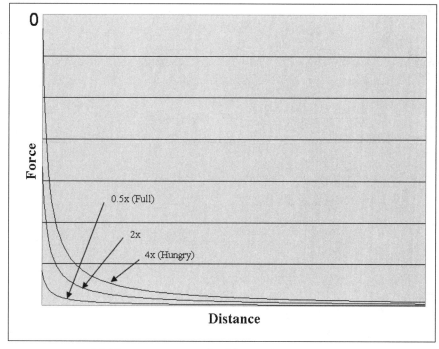

FIGURE 4.6.4 *Wolf attraction toward rabbits.*

entire force curve with a single scaling value based on hunger. It can range anywhere between the top and bottom curves ("–0.5x" and "–4x," respectively), both of which are scaled versions of Figure 4.6.1.

We can also create dynamic force curves by weighting multiple curves rather than adding them. Equation 4.6.5 shows a linear interpolation between two force curves f_1 and f_2, where w is a weight that can vary from zero to one. We can use a similar weighting for any number of force curves as long as the scaling factors of the various curves all sum to one. In this case, $(1-w)$ and w will sum to one automatically in the two-function case shown.

$$y = (1 - w) \times f_1 + w \times f_2 \qquad (4.6.5)$$

Equation 4.6.6 shows a more complex three-function weighted system. The value $(w + x + y)$ must sum to one for the weighting to behave properly.

$$y = w \times f_1 + x \times f_2 + y \times f_3 \qquad (4.6.6)$$

A two-function interpolation performed on scaled versions of the curves from Figures 4.6.1 and 4.6.2 can generate a large number of curves that fit in the space between the two curves, as shown in Figure 4.6.5. A curve mixing the two source curves equally is also shown. If you want to generate a blended curve that goes outside the area between the two curves, you can do that extrapolation by breaking the rule stated previously and making the sum of the scale values exceed one.

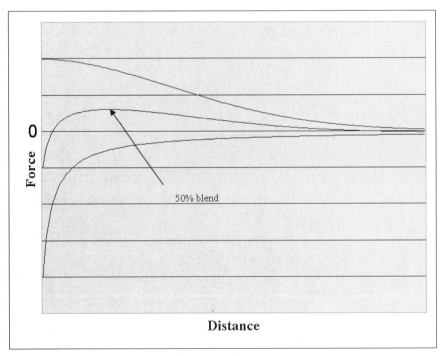

FIGURE 4.6.5   *Curves generated by interpolation.*

It's also possible to blend curves by orientation relative to the repulsor or attractor. This requires adding an orientation to the elements of the system, but in nearly all cases the AI will already have an orientation as part of its basic data. Going back to the wolves and rabbits, a wolf will be attracted more strongly to a rabbit he can see in front of him. The desired effect can be calculated by reducing the scale value for targets that are behind the AI, or otherwise out of its cone of vision.

This same variable effect can be obtained by dynamically switching between multiple curves based on orientation, distance, time of day, or whatever other parameters are available in your game.

Points, Lines, and Planes

Until now, we have described force emitters as points, but we need not be bound to this representation. We can also use more complex objects, such as lines, planes, polygons, and complex geometric objects, to represent attractors and repulsors. The only difference between the various types of emitters is the way we calculate the distance used to determine the force to apply. Instead of simply using the distance to the point in three-dimensional space, we use the distance to the line, plane, or object. For objects, this could be the distance to the center of mass (as in the case of gravity), distance to the surface (as with electrostatic forces), or whatever else is convenient based on the shape of the object and the desired behavior.

One very convenient use for planes is to force objects to remain within a constrained area. A set of infinitely large planes can fully enclose any convex shape, but cubes are likely to be the simplest representation since it is trivial to align a cube to the XYZ axes.

Planar representations impose some additional complexities since it is possible to treat each plane as one-sided or two-sided. With a two-sided plane, the distance to the plane is always positive, just like the distance to a point or line. With a one-sided plane, the distance to the plane can be negative. Since we decided up front to start our force graphs at zero, the easiest way to preserve that constraint is to consider anything on the wrong side of a one-sided plane to be at zero distance from the plane. This is one of the cases where you must be sure to not apply an infinite force at a distance of zero. If you forget, your objects might seem to suddenly vanish, having gained infinite velocity.

The force vector generated by an infinite plane will always be in the direction of the surface normal. The force generated by a line will always be perpendicular to the line in the direction of the object upon which it is exerting a force.

Expanding this concept to include any geometric object as an attractor/repulsor requires the ability to calculate a distance from that object, as mentioned earlier. A good reference for 3D object intersection tests can be found in *Real-Time Rendering* [RTR02]. The Web page for the book [RTRWeb02] also contains a section including many references to intersection methods.

Layers of AI Control

The situation becomes much more complex when we attempt to use attractors and repulsors with AI agents that will attempt to navigate the game world intelligently. There are many components to a movement system that all need to interact cleanly with each other. First is the high-level AI code that decides where to go. This gives us a destination point in world space, and we pass this information on to the path-finding system to determine the overall path to take to get from the current location to the specified destination. Both of these decisions need to be revisited from time to time. A new destination would be chosen whenever a target has moved, or when the high-level goal of the path-finding system changed. The specific path would need to be rebuilt any time the destination has changed, as well as whenever the existing path is found to be blocked.

From there, the steering controls take over as the game proceeds frame to frame. Steering controls include the attractor and repulsor system. They have the responsibility of getting the AI to follow the predetermined path, moving the AI along a reasonably close approximation of the predefined path. Now that the speed and direction are known, we can pass that information through to the animation control system so that the animations are synchronized with the AI character movement. As a final step, the physics engine takes its turn and runs all the necessary collision tests and responses.

Let's consider how this would apply to a racing game. In this case, you would start off with a racetrack that has a beginning and an end to represent the starting point and final destination chosen by the top-level AI path system. Path finding then determines how to follow the road from the starting point to the end. Steering then gets the player down the road one frame at a time while avoiding obstacles and attempting to keep the vehicle on or near the path built by the higher-level path-finding routines. The animation control system steers and rotates the wheels so the vehicle appears correct as it weaves back and forth on the road. The physics system then makes sure the vehicle responds to the ground and any other collisions.

Animation System Interactions

Any alterations to the base navigation system will need to be coordinated with the animation system controlling our AI. In the case of flying or rolling objects this is generally easy to handle because the AI object is either not in contact with the ground, or has simple rules to adjust wheel speeds and angles to match the vehicle speed and direction. A more significant difficulty is where we have walking animation cycles that must be adjusted to compensate for the changes added into the movement system by attractors and repulsors or other steering behaviors.

Attractors and repulsors can modify both the speed and direction of a character, so we must carefully compensate so walk cycles behave properly. It is important to either have dynamic control of the speed of the animation, or have multiple animations at various speeds from which to choose so we can compensate for speed changes imposed by the system. It is also important to have easy control over the direction the AI faces and travels, and to adjust that heading only after the entire movement control system has run each frame. If it is unfeasible to adjust animation playback rates or switch between animations to allow for various speeds, then the attractors and repulsors would be limited to altering just the direction of the AI.

Applying changes to the path finding must also be done in the proper order to get good alignment between the animations and the movement. If we were to apply attractors and repulsors before we advanced down the precalculated path, we would be undoing some of the organic-looking effects added by the forces. If we do any movement from path traversal or steering after checking collisions, we could accidentally move our AI right through a wall.

Steering

This technique is typically best used as an enhancement in combination with other AI steering techniques. A game environment that relies exclusively on attractors and repulsors can easily cause moving objects to get stuck due to local minima that capture objects, so it is usually a good idea to have higher-level steering and path-finding systems generate the higher-level behaviors while attractors and repulsors are used to enhance the realism of those behaviors.

In a racing game, for example, we can add a mutual repulsion force on each car, as an additional influence can help lower the frequency of collisions between the vehicles, yet retain a higher-level control system that moves the cars along the road.

The same mechanism can help make pedestrians leap away from vehicles as they approach, or make vehicles avoid mobile or stationary obstacles. Selectively placed attractors and repulsors can smooth out a racing path that is built from straight-line segments by adding a little pull or push at just the right points in the turns. It cannot be relied upon to make the higher-level decisions of which branch of a road to take, so a higher-level system must be in place to handle those longer-range strategic decisions.

An attractor and repulsor system could also help with some aspects of path finding and navigation under certain circumstances. In a role-playing game, for example, an AI system could use repulsors to help our NPCs avoid trees and other simple obstacles. An attractor and repulsor system could also help AI-controlled characters navigate toward the middle of halls and doorways as the characters move from one room to the next, while appearing to instinctively dodge other players and NPCs in the hallway.

Since games by their nature always seem to need more CPU cycles, it would not work well to consider large numbers of attractors and repulsors within a system when determining responses. You should either use them sparingly, or only consider the closest ones to keep CPU requirements to a minimum. The attractors and repulsors should also be placed within the game's space partitioning system to reuse any culling code that is already in place.

Conclusion

Some select few games might be able to use the techniques described here as the primary method of moving objects in the game world. However, the greatest advantages come from combining this approach with other useful techniques. Once we have defined a set of force curves, we can combine our simple effects to build up a library of more complex behavioral modifiers.

Some systems such as flying or swimming AI will also be easier to influence with attractors and repulsors, while others could be very difficult to represent in this way due to complex interactions with ground-based walking animation cycles. With proper planning, those obstacles can be overcome to lend more realistic and subtle movement to our games.

References

[Lander99] Lander, Jeff, "Lone Game Developer Battles Physics Simulator," *Game Developer Magazine* (April 1999): pp. 15–18.

[Reynolds87] Reynolds, Craig, "Flocks, Herds, and Schools: A Distributed Behavioral Model," *Computer Graphics: ACM SIGGRAPH Conference Proceedings* (1987): pp. 25–34.

[RTR02] Haines and Akenine-Möller, *Real-Time Rendering, Second Edition*, A. K. Peters Ltd., 2002.

[RTRWeb02] Haines and Akenine-Möller, "3D Object Intersection," available online at *www.realtimerendering.com/intl*, September 26, 2002.

4.7

Advanced Wall Building for RTS Games

Mario Grimani,
Sony Online Entertainment
mariogrimani@yahoo.com

Most real-time strategy (RTS) games include walls or similar passive defensive structures that act as barriers against enemy unit movement [Pinter01], [Stout96]. Having an automated wall-building algorithm increases the competitiveness of nonplayer character (NPC) opponents and provides a useful addition to random map generation. The original wall-building article [Grimani03] presented a basic algorithm and discussed a few potential improvements. In this article, we will implement all of the suggested improvements and deal with more advanced issues like walling off cities, reusing existing walls, destructible natural barriers, and walling off shorelines.

The Algorithm

The wall-building algorithm allows us to build walls in an intelligent and controlled manner. Instead of focusing directly on wall placement, it concentrates on territory expansion while keeping track of perimeter locations. The perimeter locations, upon algorithm completion, represent wall placement locations. The shift from building the walls to territory expansion works because there is a one-to-one relationship between walls and the interior areas that they protect.

The algorithm implements territory expansion as a growing list of interior nodes. The interior nodes define the interior area, which expands, one step at a time, by adding one new interior node per step. The new interior nodes are selected from a list of perimeter nodes using a greedy methodology [Cormen01]. This means that at each step, the algorithm looks at perimeter nodes and selects the node ranked by a heuristic function as the cheapest one to add. The use of a greedy methodology implies that the heuristic function has to evaluate nodes based on immediate, locally minimal cost. This approach is fast and easy to implement, but, due to the local nature of the heuristic function evaluation, does not guarantee an optimal solution. The approach does generate near-optimal, high-quality walls that meet given acceptance criteria. Here is the algorithm in pseudocode form:

```
        List PerimeterList  // Nodes bordering the interior
        List InteriorList   // Nodes in the interior
        List OutputList     // The result. On exit, this list
                            // contains nodes to wall off


        WallBuilder(Node StartNode,
                AcceptanceCriteria Criteria)
        {
            Node BestNode, SuccessorNode

            clear PerimeterList, InteriorList and OutputList

            add StartNode to PerimeterList
            while ((PerimeterList is not empty) and
                   (Criteria are not met))
            {
                use heuristic function to find BestNode
                remove BestNode from PerimeterList
                add BestNode to InteriorList

                for each successor SuccessorNode of BestNode
                {
                    if (SuccessorNode is in PerimeterList) or
                       (SuccessorNode is in OutputList)    or
                       (SuccessorNode is in InteriorList)  or
                       (SuccessorNode is a natural barrier)
                         continue

                    if (SuccesorNode is at maximum distance)
                        add SuccessorNode to OutputList
                    else
                        add SuccessorNode to PerimeterList
                }
            }
            move all nodes from PerimeterList to OutputList
        }
```

Algorithm Improvements

As presented, the algorithm solves most common wall-building situations in RTS games. Still, the richness of the RTS environment creates many unique problems. The following sections discuss some of the more interesting ones.

Oceans, Rivers, and Lakes

Many RTS games include maps with bodies of water such as oceans, rivers, and lakes. Walls cannot typically be placed on water surfaces, so water acts as a natural barrier for wall-building purposes. If the game does not support water-based unit movement, water can be treated as an indestructible natural barrier, which is already handled by the algorithm.

A more difficult situation occurs when the game does support water-based unit movement. The problem stems from the fact that, in this case, water surface is a passable terrain type (some units can travel across it), but not a buildable terrain type (no buildings can be placed on it). This is a new combination of terrain properties that requires a different solution: building a wall along the shoreline would stop the units coming across the water.

The simplest way to implement construction of shoreline walls is to change the way the algorithm handles new successor nodes. The new successor nodes, usually automatically added to the perimeter list, are evaluated for adjacency to water. The nodes adjacent to water are added to the output list, and the others are added to the perimeter list. Adding the nodes to the output list guarantees that they will be part of the shoreline wall that will stop the advancing units. Here is the section of pseudocode affected by this change:

```
if (SuccesorNode is at maximum distance) or
   (SuccesorNode is adjacent to water) // Added line
     add SuccessorNode to OutputList
else
     add SuccessorNode to PerimeterList
```

Unfortunately, this solution has two major drawbacks. It introduces a significant performance hit to the algorithm, and it indiscriminately walls off all bodies of water, including the ones that are completely inside the walled-off area.

The performance hit is caused by the water surface adjacency check needed to determine whether a node is a shoreline node. For example, in an eight-way tile map, every perimeter node moved to the interior list generates eight perimeter list candidate checks. Adding a water adjacency check after the candidate check adds eight extra inner loop comparisons per candidate. It's possible to avoid this performance hit by tracking shoreline nodes as a separate terrain type. For games that do not have this feature, we could identify shoreline nodes at startup and tag them for future use.

The second drawback, the walling off of all bodies of water, is a result of an early decision on whether the node adjacent to water should be walled off. Because of the way the algorithm works, the decision to place a wall segment against the water surface must be made as soon as the perimeter node comes in contact with the body of water. At that point, it is impossible to predict whether the body of water in question will end up completely surrounded by interior nodes, so it is walled off just in case. The only solution to this problem is to run a post-processing step on the output list to remove the unnecessary wall segments.

To accomplish this, we begin by identifying all shoreline nodes in the output list. We then use the shoreline nodes we found to generate a list of all water nodes adjacent to them. Next, the list of water nodes is used to detect all bodies of water and associated shoreline nodes using flood fill or a similar algorithm. It is important to note that the shoreline nodes detected this way may or may not be part of the output list. The shoreline nodes in the output list are just a subset of this group of shoreline nodes.

Next, we test the detected bodies of water one at a time to determine whether they are inside the walled-off area. The shoreline nodes associated with each body of water are a crucial piece of information for this test. If every shoreline node for a body of water is either a natural barrier or a node in the output list, the body of water does not need to be walled off, and all shoreline nodes for this body of water that are in the output list need to be tagged as *remove candidates*. Otherwise, the body of water needs to be walled off, and its shoreline nodes that are in the output list need to be tagged as *must keep*.

Once we are finished testing all bodies of water, we can traverse the output list and remove the shoreline nodes that are tagged as *remove candidates* and but not as *must keep*. This extra piece of logic is here to make sure that the nodes that wall off more than one body of water are not accidentally removed. It is important to note that this algorithm improvement is not limited to water barriers. It applies to any terrain type that blocks wall placement but allows unit movement.

Reusing Walls

In the dynamic game environment of an RTS, it is reasonable to expect that objects like walls can be partially destroyed. At the same time, as the strategic situation changes, the requirements for wall placement change as well. In this setting, it is inevitable that, while building a new wall, we will encounter wall segments from previous wall-building efforts. To take advantage of this situation and pick a course of action, we have to evaluate how the existing wall segments compare to the ones we are building. If they are of the same quality or better, we should try to use them and integrate them into the new wall. Conversely, if the existing wall segments are of lower quality than the wall segments we are building, we have to make a decision on whether to keep them. Keeping inferior wall segments introduces a weak spot in the wall, but in some cases, such as when we are trying to build a wall as fast as possible, this approach can be beneficial. To implement wall segment reuse, we need to make a couple of modifications to the algorithm.

First, we need to modify the heuristic function to take advantage of existing wall segments. This modification adjusts the cost of adding perimeter nodes adjacent to nodes with existing wall segments. Usually, this means lowering the cost contribution coming from nodes with existing wall segments. In some undesirable cases, such as wall segments of unacceptable quality, this cost can be increased. Table 4.7.1 gives an example of costs associated with wall segments of varying quality.

Table 4.7.1 An Example of the Heuristic Cost for the Different Obstruction Types

Obstruction Type	Heuristic Cost	Resource Cost
Indestructible natural barrier	0	0
Existing wall segment, better quality	50	0
Existing wall segment, same quality	75	0
New wall segment	100	50
Existing wall segment, lower quality	125	0
Existing wall segment, unacceptable quality	NA or 100	NA, 0, or refund

The indestructible natural barrier is still a perfect obstruction, so we keep its heuristic cost at zero. The heuristic cost of new wall segments is a reference point for other costs, so we choose to set it to a convenient value of 100. The existing wall segments of comparable quality are priced lower to ensure that the algorithm prefers reusing wall segments to building new ones. Better-quality wall segments are priced even lower to make sure they are the first pick after indestructible natural barriers. Finally, to discourage the use of acceptable lower-quality wall segments, we make them more expensive than new wall segments.

Wall segments of unacceptable quality require special handling. We either have to build a wall around them, or remove them and build a new wall on the top of them. The first choice is similar to the way the bodies of water are handled, and it is not very cost effective. In this case, the node with the unacceptable quality wall segment is never considered to be a perimeter node, so it does not have to have a heuristic cost associated with it. This is why the heuristic cost is listed is Not Applicable (NA) in the last row of Table 4.7.1.

The second choice, building a new wall, is a better one, but it requires more work. The removal of existing wall segments requires a new list, the *remove list*, which keeps track of objects that we need to remove prior to placement of new walls. As the algorithm encounters nodes with unacceptable quality wall segments, it treats them as unobstructed nodes that are candidates for new wall segment placement. At the same time, the unacceptable quality wall segments are added to the remove list. The heuristic cost for such nodes is approximately the same as the heuristic cost for new wall segments. If the removal of the existing wall segment is relatively fast and some of the resource cost is refunded, we might want to lower the heuristic cost. Conversely, if the existing wall segments are slow to remove, we might want to slightly raise the heuristic cost.

It is important to remember that while the relative values of the heuristic costs in Table 4.7.1 are accurate, the actual values depend on the situation. As with any heuristic approach, a little experimentation is necessary before we can settle on a particular set of values that produces the desired results. The heuristic cost table can be implemented as a lookup table that maps obstruction types to heuristic cost. Because the table controls the behavior of the algorithm to a large degree, it would be very useful to allow the costs to be set by the code calling the algorithm. This feature would permit the calling code to customize every wall-building request.

Destructible Natural Barriers

We have so far assumed that natural barriers are indestructible, and that their heuristic cost is the lowest. Since some RTS games feature destructible natural barriers, this assumption is not necessarily true in all cases. As one would expect, destructible natural barriers are not as desirable as indestructible ones, and their heuristic cost should reflect this fact. Table 4.7.2 gives an example of costs associated with the different types of natural barriers.

Table 4.7.2 An Example of the Heuristic Costs for Different Natural Barrier Types

Natural Barrier Type	Heuristic Cost	Resource Cost
Indestructible natural barrier	0	0
Destructible natural barrier, strong	20	0
Destructible natural barrier, medium	40	0
Destructible natural barrier, weak	60	0
Destructible natural barrier, unacceptable	NA or 100	NA, 0, or credit

The indestructible natural barriers still need to have the lowest heuristic cost, while the other natural barriers have values inversely proportional to how difficult it is to destroy them. The heuristic costs in Table 4.7.2 are on the same scale as the costs in Table 4.7.1. This is because both tables are used as part of the same heuristic calculation. To demonstrate this cross-dependency, the heuristic cost for weak destructible natural barriers in Table 4.7.2 is intentionally set to a value higher than the heuristic cost for better-quality existing wall segments in Table 4.7.1. This also shows that in some cases, wall segments can be a better choice than destructible natural barriers.

Natural barriers of unacceptable quality need handling similar to handling of wall segments of unacceptable quality. The heuristic cost and the resource cost, listed in the last column of Table 4.7.2, reflect this similarity. Receiving a credit for removal of natural barrier of unacceptable quality is equivalent to getting a refund for removal of a wall segment of unacceptable quality. The credit is earned in the cases when the natural barrier is a resource that is collected by gathering. The actual implementation of the heuristic calculation would store all heuristic values from Table 4.7.1 and Table 4.7.2 in a single lookup table that could be customized prior to each wall-building request.

Walling Off Cities

RTS games typically deal with a large number of buildings and other stationary objects that are clustered together to form villages, towns, and cities. The clusters need to be protected, and expanding the wall-building algorithm to encompass the objects in the cluster would very useful.

We can accomplish this with a simple brute-force approach. Assuming an approximately central location for the starting node, we calculate the distance to the farthest object in a cluster we are walling off. The calculated distance is then passed to the algorithm as the minimum distance, effectively guaranteeing that every object will be inside the wall. This approach definitely works, but it is rather wasteful. It incorrectly assumes that the objects within the city are symmetrically arranged around the starting location, so the minimum distance requirement unnecessarily pushes the walls too far in some directions. As a result, the wall is considerably more expensive than it needs to be, and the interior area is larger than is actually required.

A better, but significantly more complicated approach is to generate the minimum-size interior area that includes and connects all objects required to be inside the wall. This area is then used as a starting point for the wall-building algorithm. Here is the pseudocode for the initial wall creation:

```
List PerimeterList    // Nodes bordering the interior
List InteriorList     // Nodes in the interior
List MinInteriorList  // Nodes that are part of the
                      //   minimum interior area
List OutputList       // Partial result

CreateInitialWall(Node StartNode, List ObjectList)
{
    Node  ObstructedNode, NextNode, SuccessorNode
    Object CurrentObject
    reset PerimeterList, InteriorList,
          MinInteriorList and OutputList

    // Add object footprints to the minimum interior
    for each object CurrentObject in the ObjectList
        for each node ObstructedNode obstructed by
                CurrentObject
            add ObstructedNode to MinInteriorList

    // Add paths between the footprints to the minimum
    //    interior
    for each object CurrentObject in the ObjectList
    {
        find path between StartNode and CurrentObject
        add all path nodes to MinInteriorList
    }

    // Create initial wall
    while (MinInteriorList is not empty)
    {
        remove node NextNode from MinInteriorList
        add NextNode to InteriorList
        for each successor SuccessorNode of NextNode
        {
            if (SuccessorNode is in PerimeterList)  or
               (SuccessorNode is in OutputList)     or
               (SuccessorNode is in InteriorList)   or
               (SuccessorNode is in MinInteriorList)or
               (SuccessorNode is a natural barrier)
                continue

            if (SuccesorNode is at maximum distance)or
               (SuccesorNode is adjacent to water)
                add SuccessorNode to OutputList
            else
                add SuccessorNode to PerimeterList
        }
    }
}
```

Upon exit, the perimeter list, interior list, and output list contain data that must be passed into the main loop of the wall-building algorithm. The main loop must be modified so that these three lists are not reset during initialization. Because the modified main loop starts with the initialized data in the interior list, there is no need for the start node. Even in the initialization code, the start node could be replaced with one of the objects being chosen as the starting point. The initialization code assumes that every object in the object list needs to be directly connected to the start node. If a more optimal set of connections is required, we can generate a minimum spanning tree by using either Kruskal's or Prim's algorithm [Cormen01].

Output List Formatting

In situations where the AI uses the output list to build walls during the game, it is necessary to convert the output list into a usable format. The format needs to be accommodating to the AI issuing the individual build orders. This usually means sorting nodes in the output list by proximity and partitioning the list into smaller, more manageable groups of nodes.

During the game, each group of sorted nodes is used as a part of the build order issued by an NPC player. The formatting and data optimization step is particularly important for RTS games that use builder units. The builder units receive orders and move toward actual wall placement locations, so it is important that they move and work in the most efficient manner possible.

Conclusion

In this article, we explored advanced features and new ideas for a wall-building algorithm. Some of these, like the handling of water surfaces and destructible natural barriers, deal with more complicated terrain features. Others, such as wall segment reuse and walling off cities, improve algorithm efficiency and extend functionality. The material presented should serve as a starting point for writing advanced wall-building algorithms for RTS games.

References

[Cormen01] Cormen, Thomas H., et al., *Introduction to Algorithms, Second Edition,* MIT Press, 2001.

[Grimani03] Grimani, Mario, "Wall Building for RTS Games," *AI Game Programming Wisdom 2,* Charles River Media, 2003.

[Matthews02] Matthews, James, "Basic A* Pathfinding Made Simple," *AI Game Programming Wisdom,* Charles River Media, 2002.

[Pinter01] Pinter, Marco, "Toward More Realistic Pathfinding," *Gamasutra,* available online at *www.gamasutra.com/features/20010314/pinter_01.htm,* March 14, 2001.

[Stout96] Stout, Bryan, "Smart Moves: Intelligent Pathfinding," *Game Developer Magazine,* October 1996, available online at *www.gamasutra.com/features/19970801/pathfinding.htm.*

4.8

Artificial Neural Networks on Programmable Graphics Hardware

Thomas Rolfes

tr@circensis.com

Artificial neural networks mimic biological information processing and are used in a wide range of applications where nonlinear mappings from input to output sets are required. Their evaluation in real-time systems, and the network training involved, are often computationally demanding. Chellapilla and Fogel evolved a small artificial neural network to play checkers at expert level [Chellapilla00]. It took a 400MHz Pentium II over six months to run 840 generations, although no particular effort was made to optimize the program.

The second generation of programmable *graphics processing units* (GPUs) introduced single and half precision floating-point texture formats and floating-point pixel pipelines. Until recently, the simulation of neural networks on consumer graphics hardware was limited to the use of clamped 8-bit blending, and CPU-based implementations were significantly faster. Today, GPUs have taken the vector processing performance lead over standard PC and console CPUs, with instruction and memory throughput being an order of magnitude higher. They are evolving rapidly into fully programmable vector coprocessors with a wide field of applications [GPGPU].

Efficient artificial neural network implementations are often based on numerical linear algebra libraries for scientific computing such as BLAS [Lawson79]. Initial efforts have been made to port subsets of BLAS to GPUs, and further work is in progress. By using GPUs as general-purpose vector processors, programmers can offload vectorizable routines from the CPU, benefit from high GPU performance, and find more opportunities for load balancing.

This article shows how an artificial neural network can be implemented using a GPU-based BLAS level 3 style single-precision general matrix-matrix product (SGEMM) [Dongarra88] and an activation function pixel shader[*] under Direct3D, version 9.

---

[*] "Fragment shader" in OpenGL terminology

CPU and GPU Architectures and Systems

Flynn [Flynn72] introduced a taxonomy based on the number of instruction streams and the number of data streams available. Current console and PC CPUs have partially superscalar SISD cores (single instruction stream, single data stream) and some have floating point SIMD (single instruction stream, multiple data streams) vector extensions, such as Intel SSE on the PC and Xbox CPUs, Altivec on PowerPC (but not on the Gamecube PowerPC 750 CPU), and coprocessor vector units as in the Playstation2. The platforms employ either unified memory architectures (UMA), as on the Xbox, or nonunified (NUMA) with fast DMA paths, as on Gamecube, PS2, and PC in order to link the subsystems.

The programmable components of GPUs are the SIMD vertex and pixel shader units. Vertex shader units read vertex streams and execute vertex programs. Color values, texture coordinates, and other data are then interpolated and passed to pixel shader units, which execute pixel shader programs that can look up texture elements and compute on the other incoming data. Shader programs can be written in assembler and high-level languages. Current high-end GPUs have four vertex shader units and eight pixel shader units, fully working in parallel. The shader units are supported by fast caches and wide buses to the graphics memory.

The Playstation2 vector units can be programmed to work as vector/matrix kernels for artificial neural networks [PS2Neural]. It is also possible to use vertex programs for general-purpose stream processing, and vertex state shaders on the Xbox GPU allow you to persistently modify the constant registers. Future consoles are expected to be well suited for fast general-purpose vector computations.

Artificial Neural Networks

Feed-forward networks, which are also known as *multilayer perceptrons*, are probably the most common architecture for artificial neural networks used in supervised learning. For an introduction to neural networks, see the primer in *Game Programming Gems* [LaMothe00] and the example in *Game Programming Gems 2* [Manslow01].

The evaluation of an *n*-layer feed-forward network with linear basis functions requires the computation of

$$\mathbf{a}_{i+1} = act(\mathbf{a}_i \cdot \mathbf{W}_i) \tag{4.8.1}$$

where *act* is an activation function and the $\mathbf{W}_i$ are weight matrices. The vector $\mathbf{a}_1$ is the input layer and holds the input data nodes and an optional bias node, $\mathbf{a}_2 \ldots \mathbf{a}_{n-1}$ are hidden inner layers, and $\mathbf{a}_n$ is the output layer. The sizes of the vectors and weight matrices are usually different for each layer.

In the case of a parallel computation of *m* input sets, the vector-matrix products become matrix-matrix multiplications

$$\mathbf{A}_{i+1} = act(\mathbf{A}_i \cdot \mathbf{W}_i) \tag{4.8.2}$$

where the $n-1$ matrices $\mathbf{A}_i$ have m rows. The generalized activation function now takes a matrix argument. To archive nonlinear mappings, nonlinear activation functions are used, including:

Gaussian: $\exp(-a^2\sigma^{-2})$
Hardy's multiquadatic: $\sqrt{a^2 + \sigma^2}$
Hyperbolic tangent: $\tanh(a) = (e^a - e^{-a})/(e^a + e^{-a}) = \tanh_2(a/\ln(2))$
Sigmoid: $(1 + \exp(-a/\sigma))^{-1}$

Efficient matrix-matrix kernels such as the optimized BLAS3 routines in ATLAS [Whaley98] use partitioning into submatrices to improve cache reuse. This technique is known as *block matrix multiplication*.

Implementation

A number of authors, including Larsen & McAllister [Larsen01], Moravanszky [Moravanszky03], and Krüger & Westermann [Krüger03], show how to implement GPU-based dense and banded matrix multiplication efficiently. The basic concept is to store matrices as textures and to render quadrilaterals via vertex shaders with appropriately chosen vertex and texture coordinates. The interpolated texture coordinates are then passed to the pixel shader units for performing the actual parallel multiply-accumulate operations on the render target. Some implementations require post pixel shader blending, and this feature is not available on all hardware for floating-point buffers. The blending must then be performed in the pixel shader with two textures as input and a third texture as render target. This can be done repeatedly by rotating sources and targets. Sparse matrix multiplication can be achieved via lookup tables, and GPU implementations can benefit here from the high memory bandwidth and low access latency of the graphics systems.

After computing the matrix multiplication, the resulting render target becomes the input texture for the activation function. Again, a quadrilateral is rendered over the entire matrix-surface, or more than one if the matrix size exceeds the allowed texture size. Matrix multiplication and subsequent activation are repeated for each network layer. The pixel shader assembler code of a straightforward implementation of the hyperbolic tangent activation function looks as follows:

```
ps_2_0                    // shader version
dcl_2d s0                 // texture stage
dcl t0.xy                 // texture coordinate

texld r0, t0, s0          // r0 <- texel.xyzw
mad r0, r0, c0.x, c0.y    // r0 <- r0*scale+bias

// tanh (base 2)
exp r1.x, r0.x            // r1 <- 2^r0
exp r1.y, r0.y
exp r1.z, r0.z
exp r1.w, r0.w
```

```
exp r2.x, -r0.x            // r2 <- 2^(-r0)
exp r2.y, -r0.y
exp r2.z, -r0.z
exp r2.w, -r0.w
add r3, r1, r2             // r3 <- r1+r2
sub r4, r1, r2             // r4 <- r1-r2
rcp r3.x, r3.x             // r3 <- 1/r3
rcp r3.y, r3.y
rcp r3.z, r3.z
rcp r3.w, r3.w
mul r0, r3, r4             // r0 <- r3*r4

// write result to output register
mov oC0, r0
```

While the hyperbolic tangent is naturally bounded to –1 and 1, it can be explicitly clamped by using the min and max instructions of the pixel shader version 2 language

```
max r0, r0, c0.z           // r0 <- maximum(r0, lower)
min r0, r0, c0.w           // r0 <- minimum(r0, upper)
```

or by using the saturate instruction modifier "_sat," which clamps between 0 and 1 and can be used with any arithmetic instruction except the frc and sincos instructions. It costs no additional instruction slots.

```
mul_sat r0, r3, r4
```

The sample code to this article is a GPU implementation of Chellapilla's and Fogel's checkers position-evaluating feed-forward network. The computation is significantly faster on an ATI Radeon 9700 Pro than the version based on a SSE optimized SGEMM on a 3-GHz Pentium4. For large matrices, recursively applied algorithms such as Strassen [Strassen69] and Winograd [Winograd68] might yield further performance gains when combined with the simple submatrix multiplications.

Conclusion

GPU implementations can yield good performance gains over CPU solutions. Current graphics hardware allows the processing of networks with capacities on the order of 10^6 nodes and 10^8 weights for an average connectivity of 100. This is far below the 10^{11} neurons and 10^{15} synapses of a human brain. Simulation hardware is rapidly becoming more powerful, and the true challenges of artificial neural network research will be network organization and learning algorithms.

References

Updated links to online versions of papers are available at *www.circensis.com/gg4.html*.

[Chellapilla00] Chellapilla, K., and D. B. Fogel, "Anaconda Defeats Hoyle 6-0: A Case Study Competing an Evolved Checkers Program against Commercially

Available Software," *Proceedings of the 2000 Congress on Evolutionary Computation*, IEEE Press, Piscataway, NJ, pp. 857–863, available online at *www.natural-selection.com/NSIPublicationsOnline.htm*.

[Dongarra88] Dongarra, J.J., J. Du Croz, S. Hammarling, and R. J. Hanson, "An Extended Set of FORTRAN Basic Linear Algebra Subprograms," *ACM Trans. Math. Soft.*, Vol. 14 (1988), pp. 1–17.

[Flynn72] Flynn, M, "Some Computer Organizations and Their Effectiveness," *IEEE Trans. Computers* Vol. 21, 9 (1972), pp. 984–960.

[GPGPU] "General Purpose Computing Using Graphics Hardware," available online at *www.gpgpu.org*.

[Krüger03] Krüger, J. and R. Westermann, "Linear Algebra Operators for GPU Implementation of Numerical Algorithms," *SIGGRAPH 2003 conference proceedings*, available online at *wwwcg.in.tum.de/Research/Publications/LinAlg*.

[LaMothe00] LaMothe, A., "A Neural-Net Primer," *Game Programming Gems*, Charles River Media, 2000.

[Larsen01] Larsen, E.S. and D. McAllister, "Fast Matrix Multiplies Using Graphics Hardware," *Super Computing 2001 Conference*, Denver, CO, November 2001. Available online at *www.sc2001.org/papers/pap.pap313.pdf*.

[Lawson79] Lawson, C., R. Hanson, D. Kincaid, and F. Krogh, "Basic Linear Algebra Subprograms for FORTRAN Usage," *ACM Trans. Math. Software* Vol. 5 (1979), pp. 308–371.

[Manslow01] Manslow, J., "Using a Neural Network in a Game: A Concrete Example," *Game Programming Gems 2*, Charles River Media, 2001.

[Moravanszky03] Moravanszky, Á., "Dense Matrix Algebra on the GPU," to appear in *ShaderX²*, Wordware Publishing, 2003, available online at *www.shaderx2.com/shaderx.pdf*.

[PS2Neural] "PS2 Neural Network Simulator," project site online at *https://playstation2-linux.com/projects/ps2neural*.

[Strassen69] Strassen, V., "Gaussian Elimination Is Not Optimal," *Numerische Mathematik*, Vol. 13 (1969), pp. 353–356.

[Whaley98] Whaley, R.C., and J. Dongarra, "Automatically Tuned Linear Algebra Software," *Super Computing 1998 Conference*, Orlando, FL, November 1998.

[Winograd68] Winograd, S. "A New Algorithm for Inner Product," *IEEE Trans. Computers*, C-17:693–694, 1968.

GRAPHICS

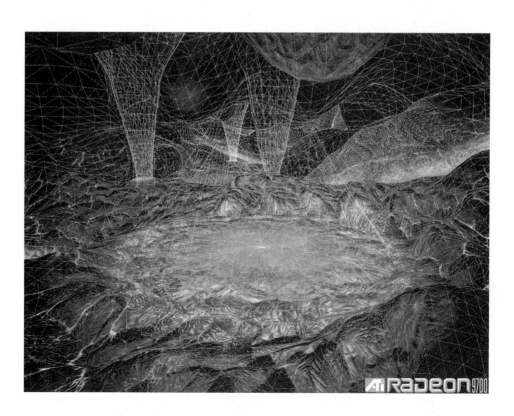

Introduction

Alex Vlachos, ATI Research, Inc.

Alex@Vlachos.com

The quality of graphics in games will continue to improve, as will graphics hardware. It would be naive of us to believe that today's graphics hardware will be interesting to developers just a few years down the road. Since this book might be around for many years to come, the 15 articles chosen for the graphics section aren't tied to current graphics hardware. Although sample source code and shader code is written for today's APIs, you'll find the core of the articles to be useful way beyond the lifespan of current graphics hardware and APIs.

This section begins with "Poster Quality Screenshots," an article that improves upon the methods presented in *Game Programming Gems 2*. Taking high-resolution screenshots is an important part of the production pipeline, and this article provides an excellent method for doing so.

Shadows have always been a hot topic in the graphics industry. The functionality of today's graphics hardware allows developers the freedom to finally experiment with many shadow algorithms that have been explored in literature for so many years. One third of this section, five articles in total, is devoted to shadows. "GPU Shadow Volume Construction for Nonclosed Meshes" provides a great method of generating shadow volumes when there are cracks in the model. "Perspective Shadow Maps" performs the well-known shadow map algorithm in post-perspective space, increasing the relative precision of the shadow map texture. "Combined Depth- and ID-Based Shadow Buffers" explains an optimal method of combining the two forms of shadow maps, depth-based and ID-based. "Carving Static Shadows into Geometry" explains how to preprocess hard shadows by directly cutting the shadows into existing geometry, avoiding the fill overhead of brute-force shadow volumes. The shadow articles end with "Adjusting Real-Time Lighting for Shadow Volumes and Optimized Meshes" where solutions to lighting artifacts introduced by most shadow algorithms are explored.

Post-processing the final rendered image in a game is becoming the norm. Several articles focus on post-processing techniques and related techniques that affect the overall image. "Real-Time Halftoning" shows an interesting nonphotorealistic style. "Fast Sepia Tone Conversion" uses YUV color space to convert regular RGB images to sepia tone, giving the image an antique look. "Dynamic Gamma Using Sampled Scene Luminance" shows an excellent method for simulating the change in perceived light based on the size of your pupils. "Heat and Haze Post-Processing Effects" explores a method for simulating the visual patterns produced by heat.

The remaining articles in this section cover varying topics. "Techniques to Apply Team Color to 3D Models" compares several methods for games to color team members for multiplayer games. "Hardware Skinning with Quaternions" provides an optimal method for computing skinned objects in a vertex shader. "Motion Capture Data Compression" will be extremely valuable to anyone dealing with an unmanageable amount of motion capture data. "Fast Collision Detection" shows a hierarchical approach to bones-based collision detection. "Terrain Occlusion Culling with Horizons" explains a great method for culling geometry hidden behind hills or buildings.

It's been a pleasure editing the articles in this section. The core methods presented here are solid, and I hope you get as much out of them as I have.

5.1

Poster Quality Screenshots

Steve Rabin,
Nintendo of America Inc.

steve@aiwisdom.com

In the promotion of any game, there will come a time when you need screenshots for advertisements, box covers, previews, strategy guides, magazine covers, and full-size posters. Unfortunately, raw screenshots are often inferior for many of these purposes. For example, in print media, typical layouts require 300 dpi, which would make a 640 x 480 console screenshot appear as a mere 2.0 x 1.5 inches. Additionally, console games that look fine on a TV (because of subtle TV blurring) can look strongly aliased when the raw framebuffer is viewed on a computer monitor. Because of these issues, there is a real need to enhance screenshots for many of these promotional purposes.

To render poster quality screenshots, the following two goals must be met:

- Increase the resolution
- Increase the pixel quality (anti-aliasing)

Increased Resolution

There is a very simple way to increase the resolution of a screenshot beyond the size of the framebuffer. Actually, it's the same problem as trying to capture a panoramic shot of the Grand Canyon with a point-and-click camera. The technique involves taking multiple shots side by side and then compositing them together to create a single large shot. For game screenshots, this method can be thought of as stitching several shots together, as shown in Figure 5.1.1. To make this work, each subimage is shot with a unique projection matrix by carefully altering the frustum in places so that the images seamlessly meet at the edges. A detailed account of this technique is covered in [Vlachos01].

While the method in Figure 5.1.1 is an effective way to increase resolution, there is an alternate option that offers some additional advantages. This improved technique also involves taking multiple shots, but each shot shifts its viewport by only a fraction of a pixel (using a standard SetViewport instruction instead of altering the projection matrix). Once all of the slightly shifted shots have been taken, they can be threaded together to create a single high-resolution shot, as illustrated in Figure 5.1.2.

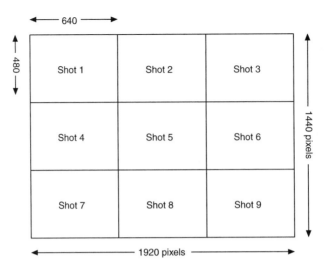

FIGURE 5.1.1 *Stitching method of compositing individual screenshots to increase resolution. In this example, nine shots are taken to increase the resolution from 640 x 480 to 1920 x 1440, thus blowing up the image by nine times.*

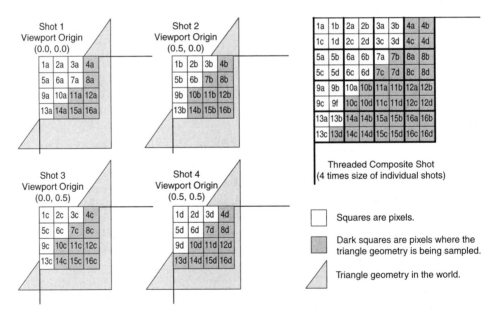

FIGURE 5.1.2 *Four screenshots have been taken, each with its viewport shifted by a fraction of a pixel. The triangle represents geometry in the world that is being sampled and rasterized (samples are taken at the upper-left corner of each square pixel). On the right is the final composite shot, which is quadruple the resolution of the individual shots. Note how each source shot pixel is placed in the composite shot (for example, pixel 13a from the source shot is placed at location 13a in the composite shot).*

This technique of shifting the viewport to sample in-between pixels has three main benefits:

- Relatively simple and unintrusive to the graphics pipeline
- Minimizes clipping problems that arise in the stitching technique
- Allows for arbitrary sampling points for anti-aliasing (discussed in the next section)

An issue that arises in this viewport shifting technique is that the mipmap bias must be adjusted to account for the detailed sampling. Depending on the shot, you might want to bias the mipmap levels to always use the highest resolution texture or simply disable mipmapping altogether.

Increased Pixel Quality

Anti-aliasing is the key to improving pixel quality. However, many games don't feature anti-aliasing, or if they do, they use a very simplistic form. The viewport shifting technique is exciting because it can be used to attain extremely high-quality anti-aliasing. Figure 5.1.3 shows how multiple screenshots, each shifted by a fraction of a pixel (in the same way as Figure 5.1.2), can be combined to create a single image that is anti-aliased. In the case of Figure 5.1.3, four source screenshots are used to create a screenshot of identical size that is anti-aliased at four samples per pixel. This technique can be extrapolated to suit any amount of anti-aliasing, even beyond 1,000 samples per pixel.

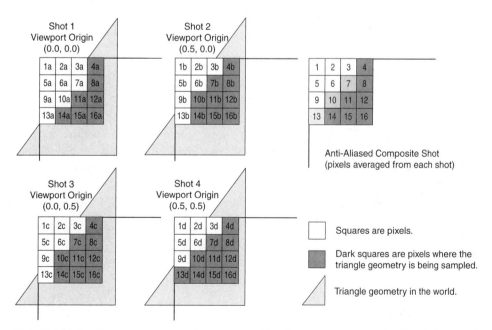

FIGURE 5.1.3 *Four source screenshots are combined to generate an anti-aliased shot with four samples per pixel. Pixels of a given number (for example, pixels 13a, 13b, 13c, 13d) are averaged together into a single pixel (pixel 13) in the final shot.*

The technique shown in Figure 5.1.3 is powerful, but the anti-aliasing is not ideal since the samples are uniformly aligned on a grid. Because of the grid sampling, high-frequency noise can literally fall through the cracks of the samples, resulting in aliasing from detail that is missed. Figure 5.1.4 shows a single pixel that contains high-frequency detail. However, when the grid sampling occurs, the detail is not only lost, it's grossly misrepresented.

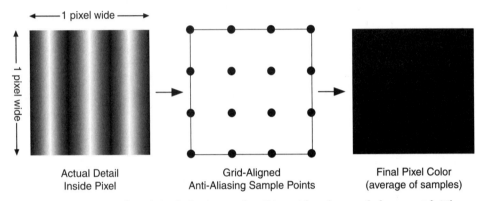

FIGURE 5.1.4   *A pixel with high-frequency detail is uniformly sampled on a grid. The detail falls through the cracks of the sampling, resulting in a misrepresentation of the pixel (which leads to aliasing over many pixels).*

While high-frequency detail can't be captured in a single pixel, it must not be grossly misrepresented, as in Figure 5.1.4. The solution is to convert any high-frequency detail into noise so that on average it represents the actual detail within the pixel. Three stochastic sampling distributions can achieve this: random, jittered, and Poisson disc.

Random Sampling Distribution

The simplest solution is to pick random sample points within a pixel, as shown in Figure 5.1.5b. While this seems reasonable, it generally creates too much noise in the resulting image. Some samples are clustered together while open areas remain unsampled. This is the weakest of the three solutions.

Jittered Sampling Distribution

Ray-tracing algorithms typically use a jittering technique to choose sample points. Figure 5.1.5c shows an example of jittering. This technique divides the pixel into a grid and then a random position is chosen within each grid cell. This reduces cluster-

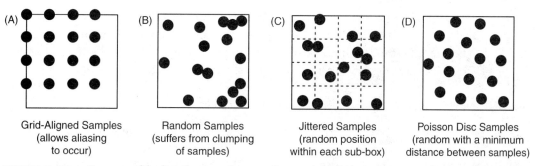

FIGURE 5.1.5 *Four possible distributions for sampling a pixel. (A) represents uniform sampling. (B, C, D) represent different stochastic sampling methods.*

ing and ensures that no large areas remain unsampled. While this performs well, it is an approximation of the ideal solution.

Poisson Disc Sampling Distribution

The ideal solution for picking subpixel samples is to randomly pick locations, but enforce that the samples maintain a minimum distance from each other. An example is shown in Figure 5.1.5d. Interestingly, this is how nature has solved the problem of sampling, since the photoreceptors in your eyes are positioned in a similar manner [Yellott82]. The result is that your eyes tend not to see aliasing, and detail that you can't quite see is turned into subtle noise or fuzziness.

While the Poisson disc sampling produces the best results, it can be very expensive to calculate. This explains why ray-tracing programs tend to favor the jittered algorithm. The algorithm for generating a Poisson disc sampling distribution follows:

1. Pick a random sample point in the pixel.
2. If the point is at least d distance away from every other point, then save the point and go to Step 1.
3. The point was too close to another point—throw it away.
4. If this is the Nth point to fail in a row (where N is something like 100), then return (since it is likely that all possible sample points have been generated).
5. Go to Step 1.

As you can see from the algorithm, the Poisson disc sampling distribution takes $O(n^2)$ time (since each generated point must be compared to every other point) and it is unclear how many points will fill a given space. When you generate the distribution, you must specify the minimum distance (represented by d), but you are unable to specify how many points actually are generated. Trial and error with different d values can give you a feel for how many samples are generated. For example, given a pixel width of 1.0, a minimum distance requirement of 0.08 will give you roughly 100 sample points.

Interestingly, the term *Poisson disc* comes from the fact that the Fourier transform of the Poisson disc distribution resembles a disc. This is important because the Fourier transform of these distributions provides insight into how low and high frequencies are sampled. For more detail and discussion, please see [Watt92], [Watt99].

Using a Poisson Disc Sampling Distribution

As previously mentioned, the Poisson disc sampling distribution is very expensive to calculate. However, this is acceptable because we only need to calculate a distribution once. This single distribution will be used to offset each screenshot that is taken. Figure 5.1.6 shows how a single distribution containing three samples is used to offset three source screenshots. The screenshots are then averaged together similar to Figure 5.1.3, except that each viewport has been shifted according to the Poisson disc sample points, as opposed to the uniform grid shifting shown in Figure 5.1.3.

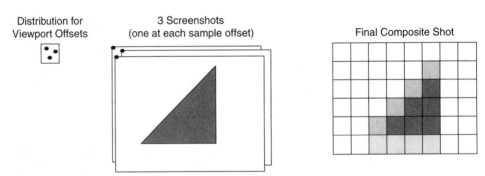

FIGURE 5.1.6   *Three source screenshots are combined to generate an anti-aliased shot with three samples per pixel. Each screenshot viewport has been shifted according to its corresponding sample point in the Poisson disc distribution.*

Adjusting Pixel Sampling Width for Anti-Aliasing

With the goal of better-looking pixels, another improvement is to increase the area of pixel sampling into neighboring pixels. By sampling a tiny bit beyond a pixel's borders, aliasing is further reduced. However, this must be carefully tuned since sampling too far into neighboring pixels will result in a blurry image. In practice, a sampling width of 1.3 pixels works well. Figure 5.1.7 shows how the pixel sampling width for a given Poisson disc distribution can be increased or decreased simply by scaling the generated distribution. Figure 5.1.8 shows the real-world results of changing the pixel width at a close-up range.

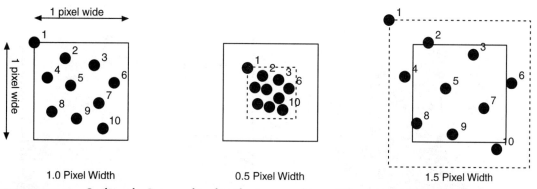

FIGURE 5.1.7 *Scaling the Poisson disc distribution to achieve different sampling widths.*

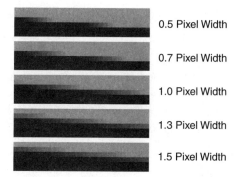

FIGURE 5.1.8 *Anti-aliasing effect of different pixel sampling widths. Small widths result in sharper images, but will show aliasing. Large widths eliminate aliasing, but start to look blurry. In practice, game screenshots look best with a pixel width of roughly 1.3, but this is a subjective result.*

Combining Increased Resolution with Increased Pixel Quality

The previous sections described how to get larger screenshots as well as highly anti-aliased screenshots, but the ultimate goal is to do both at the same time. Figure 5.1.9 shows how a single pixel can be sampled 28 times to create four pixels that are anti-aliased with seven samples per pixel. In Figure 5.1.9, each of the 28 sample points represents a viewport offset for a corresponding shot (similar to Figure 5.1.6). The final image will be made up of these 28 screenshots that have been averaged and threaded together, resulting in an anti-aliased image that is four times larger.

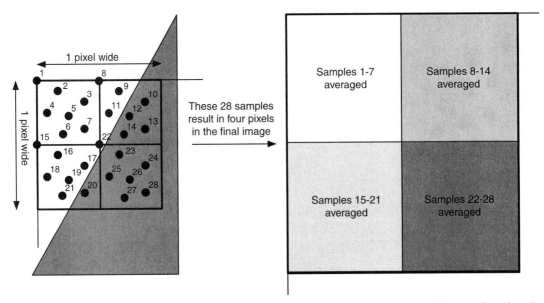

FIGURE 5.1.9 *A single pixel is sampled 28 times to create four pixels that are each anti-aliased with seven samples per pixel. Each dot represents the viewport origin offset for each shot. A Poisson disc distribution of seven samples was initially generated and used in each pixel quadrant. The final screenshot will be four times the original size and anti-aliased with seven samples per pixel.*

Unfortunately, composited screenshots can quickly use up all available memory if you're not careful, especially on video game consoles. The best way to collect the screenshots is to have an extra framebuffer (in CPU-accessible memory) the size of your native screen size that is of type `float` for each red, blue, and green channel. This special framebuffer has more bit-depth and will be used to accumulate the dozens, hundreds, or even thousands of images during the anti-aliasing step. In Figure 5.1.9, images 1 through 7 would be taken and accumulated in the special framebuffer. Then, the framebuffer would be divided by the number of images taken to get the average pixel value for every pixel in the framebuffer. On a game console, that averaged framebuffer would then be sent to a PC to be temporarily stored. This would repeat for images 8 through 14, 15 through 21, and 22 through 28. Then, on the PC, the four stored images would be threaded together as shown in Figure 5.1.2. This method ensures that the minimal amount of console memory is used.

The following pseudocode algorithm describes the steps to take a 4x screenshot (for example, 640 x 480 blown up to 1280 x 960) with seven samples per pixel, as shown in Figure 5.1.9.

```
int group; //Represents each group of images that will
           //be averaged together for anti-aliasing.
           //In Figure 5.1.9 there are 4 groups.
```

```
int size_increase = 4;       // 4 for a 4x screenshot.
int samples_per_pixel = 7;   // For 7 samples per pixel
                             // in the final shot.

// Allocate a float-based framebuffer at the native
// game resolution of 640x480.
Fbuffer* fb = new Fbuffer(640, 480);

// Loop through each group.
for(group=0; group<size_increase; group++)
{
    fb->Zero(); // Zero the framebuffer.

    // Loop through each shot in a group.
    for(int cur=0; cur<samples_per_pixel; cur++)
    {
        // Calculate viewport offset as numbered
        // in Figure 5.1.9.
        int offset = group * samples_per_pixel + cur;

        // Set the viewport to the correct offset
        SetViewportToSubPixelOffset(offset);

        RenderShot(); //Render the 640x480 shot
        AddShotIntoFramebuffer(fb);
    }

    // Divide the framebuffer by the number of shots
    // taken (7 in this case). The resulting image is
    // an anti-aliased group.
    fb->Average(samples_per_pixel);

    // Convert float-based framebuffer to byte-based.
    fb->ConvertToByteBased();

    // Send the byte-based framebuffer data from the
    // game console to a connected PC.
    SendToPC(fb);
}

// All shots taken.
// Composite the sent images on the connected PC
// using the threading technique in Figure 5.1.2.
```

As shown in the preceding algorithm, the anti-aliasing step doesn't require much memory on a game console (~3.5MB) and scales perfectly since multiple shots are accumulated in a special float-based framebuffer. Even if 1,000 samples per pixel were taken, the amount of memory required on the console remains constant. However, the compositing step (performed on a PC connected to the game console) can still require a great deal of memory due to the size of the final image. For example, a 640 x 480 screenshot 625 times larger would be 16,000 x 12,000. A screenshot of this size will require about 550MB (16,000 x 12,000 x 3 bytes = 549.32MB), so very large shots might push the limits of your PC during the compositing step.

Conclusion

This article showed how to improve raw screenshots by making them larger and better looking. The key is to take multiple screenshots, each with its viewport offset by a fraction of a pixel according to a Poisson disc distribution. Through averaging and compositing, thousands of screenshots can come together to create a single truly impressive high-resolution shot.

This technique has been successfully used to generate shots as large as 19,200 x 14,400 at 100 samples per pixel on Nintendo GameCube hardware. A shot of this size requires 90,000 individual screenshots and takes roughly one hour to capture (25 minutes in rendering, 20 minutes in transferring to a PC, and 15 minutes to composite on the PC). In contrast, an impressive 1,920 x 1,440 image at 100 samples per pixel would take a total of about 25 seconds.

Whatever shots you decide to take, the key is having complete control over the size and quality so that you can show your game in its best light and meet all of your promotional needs.

References

[Vlachos01] Vlachos, A., and E. Hart, "Rendering Print Resolution Screenshots," *Game Programming Gems 2*, Charles River Media, 2001.

[Watt92] Watt, A., and M. Watt, *Advanced Animation and Rendering Techniques: Theory and Practice*, Addison-Wesley Publishing Co., 1992.

[Watt99] Watt, A., *3D Computer Graphics, Third Edition*, Addison-Wesley Publishing Co., 1999.

[Yellot82] Yellot, I., "Spectral Analysis of Spatial Sampling by Photoreceptors: Topological Disorder Prevents Aliasing," *Vision Research*, 22, 1982, pp. 1205–1210.

GPU Shadow Volume Construction for Nonclosed Meshes

Warrick Buchanan

warrick@chimeric.co.uk

Shadow volumes [Crow77] have become a popular technique for enhancing lighting quality in games over recent years. This is due to the ability to use the stencil buffer available on most modern graphics hardware to accelerate the technique [Heidmann91], and advances that have been made over the past few years that provide for a robust implementation [Kilgard01].

Current well-publicized techniques for creating shadow volumes on graphics hardware vertex shader units have required the limitation that the subject geometry be a one-sided, closed mesh that has exactly two triangles sharing every edge (a two-manifold mesh) [Brennan02]. While this is not always a major problem, it is desirable to have a technique that is correct given any one-sided mesh topology. In a production environment, closed non-two-manifold meshes are not automatically created without special care. This article presents a method of rendering shadow volumes without requiring a two-manifold, closed mesh.

Back to the Drawing Board

To correctly construct a shadow volume, we have to consider the fact that only the faces visible to the light source determine the shape of the volume, as they are the faces that actually block the light.

The most brute-force approach is simply to construct a shadow volume for each planar face that is visible to the light source, by taking the face itself, the inverted face extruded in the direction of the light source, and the faces constructed from the edges of the original face and the extruded face. From these we can achieve a consistent closed shadow volume for each face that is correct for all meshes. Obviously, this isn't a viable approach, as the fill rate overhead will bring almost any application to its knees.

Although this algorithm works, it is far from efficient, as it does not take into account the information we have regarding the connectivity of mesh faces. As with all shadow volume techniques, we really want to construct the shadow volume sides only from the extrusion of silhouette edges, which are edges between faces that are a boundary between lit and unlit faces. If we then construct our shadow volume sides from the extrusion of silhouette edges and the front and back volume caps as previously stated, we have a technique that works for closed two-manifold meshes, but fails for open meshes and non-two-manifold meshes.

To handle the case of meshes with open edges, we must extend our classification of silhouette edges. A silhouette edge is also an open edge (an edge on a face that is not connected to a neighboring face) whose associated face is visible to the light source. With this new rule, the technique now works for nonclosed two-manifold meshes. However, it still does not deal with the more general case of faces that have more than one neighbor on any edge (a non-two-manifold mesh).

This can be dealt with by pairing the faces that share edges. We start with all faces having all their edges marked as open. Then, for each face we find another face that shares an edge. If the face we find does not already have another face paired with it on this edge, we pair the faces through that edge. If the face we find is already paired with another face, we do not register a connection between them and leave them separate. This process effectively splits the mesh along non-two-manifold edges into separate pieces that individually either have two-manifold connectivity, or become a silhouette edge. Our technique will now work for non-two-manifold meshes.

Implementing the Technique in a Vertex Shader

With the preceding modifications in mind, we can separate the task into three rendering passes: generating the front caps of the shadow volume, generating the back caps of the shadow volume, and generating the sides of the shadow volume. We require three separate rendering passes, as the front and back caps use the same geometry data but different vertex shaders as well as culling order. (Remember that the back caps are formed by flipping the winding order of the front caps in this technique.) The final third pass for the sides of the shadow volume is needed because we again use the same geometry, along with an index buffer that defines our quads, and yet another vertex shader.

Front Caps

The front caps are easy. We simply need to throw away all the triangles that are not facing the light source. If we have the vertex data duplicated (three unique vertices for every triangle), with each vertex containing its face's normal, we can determine whether the vertex is part of a triangle facing the light using a dot product. If it is, we leave the vertex untouched; however, if it isn't, we output the vertex as having a position at the origin. This has the result of creating degenerate, zero-area triangles that will not be drawn by the hardware (see Listing 5.2.1).

Listing 5.2.1 Vertex shader for rendering front caps.

```
; c[0]    0.0, 0.5, 1.0, 2.0
; c[1-4] world*view*projection matrix
; c[5]    light position

vs.1.1

dcl_position v0
dcl_normal   v1
dcl_texcoord v2

; Get vector from vertex to light and normalize
sub r0,c[5],v0
dp3 r0.w, r0, r0
rsq r0.w, r0.w
mul r0, r0, r0.w

dp3 r0,r0,v1
mov oD0,r0

; Make r0 (1, 1, 1, 1) if normal is facing light else (0, 0, 0, 0)
sge r0, r0, c[0].xxxx

; Transform position to clip space
dp4 r1.x, v0, c[1]
dp4 r1.y, v0, c[2]
dp4 r1.z, v0, c[3]
dp4 r1.w, v0, c[4]

mul oPos, r0, r1
```

Back Caps

The back caps are not the same back caps as used in the other well-known methods. They are actually just the front caps projected backwards by some distance along the light direction. Since we want them to act as back cap polygons, they need to face the opposite direction from the front caps. The extrusion is easily done in the vertex shader, but when drawing the back caps, we must remember to reverse the culling order of the triangles. If we simply used the front cap triangles as is, they would have the incorrect winding order (see Listing 5.2.2).

Listing 5.2.2 Vertex shader for rendering back caps.

```
; c[0]    0.0, 0.5, 1.0, 2.0
; c[1-4] world*view*projection matrix
; c[5]    light position

vs.1.1

dcl_position v0
dcl_normal   v1
dcl_texcoord v2
```

```
; Get vector from vertex to light and normalize
sub r0, c[5], v0
dp3 r0.w, r0, r0
rsq r0.w, r0.w
mul r0, r0, r0.w

; Dot light and normal vector
dp3 r1, v1, r0

; Output shading
mov oD0,r1

; Make r2 (1, 1, 1, 1) if normal is facing light else (0, 0, 0, 0)
sge r2, r1, c[0].xxxx

; Extrude vertex
mad r0, c[5].wwww, -r0, v0

; Transform position to clip space
dp4 r1.x, r0, c[1]
dp4 r1.y, r0, c[2]
dp4 r1.z, r0, c[3]
dp4 r1.w, r0, c[4]

mul oPos, r1, r2
```

Extruded Side Polygons

The sides of the volume are somewhat problematic. We start as with the traditional hardware accelerated technique by constructing degenerate quads at each triangle edge [Brennan02]. Note that no new vertices are needed, as an index buffer will suffice to define the quads. Moreover, no quads are needed on edges between triangles that are coplanar. If a vertex faces the light source, we want to leave it where it is; otherwise, we should extrude it along the light source direction as in the other technique.

At this point, we again have an algorithm that is correct only for a closed mesh. To handle the case of an open edge, we first duplicate the edge's vertices and invert the face normal of each new vertex. We can then produce a quad for the edge using the new vertices and the vertices of the original edge. Adding this to our algorithm gives us a correct shadow volume for all cases, except where the light can see the back of a triangle with an open edge.

To fix this case, we have to make sure we don't extrude a quad for silhouette edges originating from an open edge of a back-facing polygon. To do this, we need to be able to flag the vertices we have added due to open edges. By abusing the fact that we know each vertex normal should be approximately of unit length, we can flag these open-edge duplicate vertices with normal vectors that are just slightly larger than one in length (within some epsilon range). This should not affect our triangle/vertex facing light tests noticeably, and it means we do not have to store an extra component per vertex for the flag. Therefore, if we have vertices when we generate the shadow volume sides that are flagged as open-edge duplicate vertices, we always extrude them. If they are not flagged, we only extrude them if their normal faces away from the light. This will now produce the correct behavior for all mesh topologies, as we now create nonvisible degenerate shadow volume sides in the case that previously caused problems (see Listing 5.2.3).

Listing 5.2.3 Vertex shader for rendering extruded sides.

```
; c[0]   0.0, 0.5, 1.0, 2.0
; c[1-4] world*view*projection matrix
; c[5]   light position

vs.1.1

dcl_position v0
dcl_normal   v1
dcl_texcoord v2

; Get vector from vertex to light and normalize
sub r0,c[5],v0
dp3 r0.w, r0, r0
rsq r0.w, r0.w
mul r0, r0, r0.w

; Dot light and normal vector
dp3 r1,v1,r0

; Output shading
mov oD0,r1

; Make r1 (0, 0, 0, 0) if normal is facing light else (1, 1, 1, 1)
slt r1, r1, c[0].xxxx

; Make r2 (1, 1, 1, 1) if normal is not unit length else (0, 0, 0, 0)
mov r2, v1
dp3 r2, r2, r2
sge r2, r2, c[0].w

add r1, r1, r2
min r1, c[0].zzzz, r1

; Extrude vertex if facing away from light
mul r0, r0, r1
mad r0, c[5].wwww, -r0, v0

; Transform position to clip space
dp4 oPos.x, r0, c[1]
dp4 oPos.y, r0, c[2]
dp4 oPos.z, r0, c[3]
dp4 oPos.w, r0, c[4]
```

Considerations

As we submit each of the three parts of the volume separately (front caps, back caps, and sides), we can easily skip individual sections of the volume independently if necessary for any further shadow volume optimizations. Moreover, if we know that our model is closed and has exactly two triangles for each edge, we can use the cheaper traditional technique that relies on closed two-manifold meshes.

As in the original vertex shader generation technique, we are required to duplicate each vertex for each face. Additionally for this technique, we add a further pair of vertices for each open edge. This can result in a large increase in vertex data that has to be sent to the graphics card. Another undesirable consequence of this particular technique is that the geometry must be submitted three times to construct the front caps, the back caps, and the sides of the volume correctly.

Recent hardware has implemented two-sided stencil testing to accelerate shadow volume rendering. This can still be used with this technique; however, the rendering of the back caps must be done with the inverted two-sided stencil logic due to the required flip of their winding order. Thus, if you have front-facing shadow volume faces set to increment the stencil count and back-facing shadow volume faces set to decrement the stencil count for the volume front caps and sides, you must swap the decrement and increment operations when drawing the volume back caps.

The technique presented relies on generating the shadow volume from the faces that are facing the light only, unlike other current techniques. It also requires that open and non-two-manifold edges be identified consistently and correctly.

Conclusion

With this article, developers can provide a more forgiving production workflow for artists, and take full advantage of the possibilities of acceleration that modern graphics cards offer. Moving more elements of the generation of shadow volumes to graphics cards becomes more crucial as triangle counts continue to increase.

References

[Brennan02] Brennan, Chris, "Shadow Volume Extrusion Using a Vertex Shader," in Engel, Wolfgang, ed., *ShaderX*, Wordware, May 2002.

[Crow77] Crow, Frank, "Shadow Algorithms for Computer Graphics," *Proceedings of SIGGRAPH 1977*, pp. 242–248.

[Heidmann91] Heidmann, Tim, "Real Shadows Real Time," *IRIS Universe*, Number 18, 1991, pp. 28–31.

[Kilgard01] Kilgard, Mark, "Robust Stencil Volumes," CEDEC 2001 presentation, Tokyo, September 4, 2001.

5.3

Perspective Shadow Maps

Marc Stamminger,
University of Erlangen-Nuremberg

George Drettakis,
REVES/INRIA Sophia-Antipolis

Carsten Dachsbacher,
University of Erlangen-Nuremberg

stamminger@cs.fau.de,
George.Drettakis@sophia.inria.fr,
dachsbacher@cs.fau.de

Shadow maps are one of the most popular shadow generation algorithms. A shadow map is the depth buffer of a light source view [Williams78], [Reeves87]. The shadow test for a point being shaded maps the point into this shadow map and does a simple depth comparison. Shadow maps are efficient, very general, rather robust, easy to implement, and are supported by current graphics hardware. Their major drawback is shadow aliasing, resulting from the pixelized (discrete) shadow map. This effect is particularly noticeable for large scenes, where the shadow map must cover a large area and has thus generally too low resolution in foreground regions.

Perspective shadow maps (PSMs) are very similar to standard shadow maps, but are distorted such that regions close to the camera have higher resolution than distant regions [Stamminger02]. They are called "perspective" because they account for the observer's perspective distortion. The size of an object in the shadow map corresponds to its size in the final image. In ideal cases, a finite-size PSM can generate shadows on scenes of infinite size (e.g., a procedural terrain), without visible shadow pixelization.

Introduction

The concept of perspective shadow maps can be best understood by thinking in post-perspective space; in other words, in the space after the modelview and projection matrices have been applied. In this space, x- and y-coordinates already correspond to the final position in the image, and the z-coordinate is the depth value. In post-perspective space, the perspective distortion is already applied; that is, objects close to the camera are enlarged, and distant objects are shrunk. A PSM contains the light source view of the scene in this post-perspective space. Consequently, regions close to the viewer occupy more world space resolution than distant regions, resulting in a much better correspondence between sampling densities of the image and the shadow map.

An example is shown in Figure 5.3.1, which shows a simple 2D scene of three characters on a ground plane. A parallel light source illuminates the scene from above. In a standard shadow map, the scene is rendered by parallel projection along the z-axis (Figure 5.3.1 left). In post-perspective space (Figure 5.3.1 right), the scene is distorted according to the viewer's position, and the nearest character is enlarged. The perspective shadow map is a light source view in this post-perspective space, such that the closest character obtains more shadow map resolution than the farther ones. The image also shows the match of resolutions: if we project a single pixel of the shadow map to the ground and then to the image plane, all shadow map pixels cover the same image area.

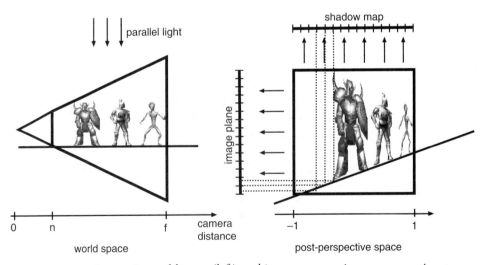

FIGURE 5.3.1   *A scene in world space (left) and its counterpart in post-perspective space with a perspective shadow map (right).*

The previous example is well chosen and shows the case where PSMs work best. For a parallel light source, a PSM is ideal if the light direction is parallel to the camera plane and the shadowed plane is perpendicular to the light direction. If the light source in Figure 5.3.1 is moved to the front (shining toward the viewer), shadows are cast toward the viewer. The shadow is then closer to the viewer and thus larger than the occluder, resulting in pixelization (aliasing). If the light source shines from behind the camera, objects behind the camera frustum must be included. This requires special treatment that also influences shadow resolution negatively. If the light source is moved to the side, the shadows stretch along the ground plane and are thus enlarged, which can also reveal the pixelized structure of the shadow map.

PSMs have been developed for large scenes, usually outdoor scenes, where standard shadow maps fail. Because large scenes are usually lit by a single parallel light source (the sun), we only treat parallel light sources in this article. Point lights in the context of shadow maps are usually not omnidirectional, but only spot lights, which can be well handled by one single shadow map. They normally exhibit distance attenuation, so they have a restricted area of influence and thus don't benefit as much from perspective shadow maps.

In the next section, we first discuss the properties of the scene in post-perspective space. We then show how a PSM is generated and how typical pitfalls can be avoided. For implementation issues we consider OpenGL, although DirectX implementations are very similar. The major difference between the APIs is that in DirectX, the perspective transformation maps the depth range from 0 to 1, instead of −1 to 1 as in OpenGL.

Post-Perspective Space

Since PSMs live in post-perspective space, it is essential to understand the concept of perspective as applied in computer graphics. The perspective transformation is described by a 4 x 4 transformation matrix. In contrast to the usual *affine* modeling transformations composed from translations, rotations, scales, and shears, the perspective transformation uses all entries in the matrix and thus can also create *projective* transformations. We assume that the reader is familiar with the basic concept of homogeneous coordinates and matrices.

Projective transformations map lines to lines. However, in contrast to affine transformations, parallel lines do not remain parallel under projective transformations. Obviously, this is needed for perspective projections, where the rails of a rail track are parallel in world space, but converge in the image. Another interpretation is that projective transformations can map points at infinity to finite points and vice versa, so the infinite intersection point of two parallel lines is simply mapped to a finite intersection point of two nonparallel lines.

The perspective transformation as generated by a `gluPerspective()` call generates such a projective transformation that maps the scene to a space we call *post-perspective space*. In this space, the scene is deformed, such that the following properties hold:

- The observer is moved to infinity $(0,0,-\infty)$, so all lines through the observer become lines parallel to the z-axis.
- The camera frustum is mapped to the unit cube $[-1,1]^3$, where the near plane is mapped to the plane $z = -1$, and the far plane to $z = 1$.
- Points at infinity in world space are mapped to the plane $z = z_\infty = (f + n)/(f - n)$, where f and n are the distances of near and far plane. In a normal setting where f is large, z_∞ is larger than 1, but only slightly. We call $z = z_\infty$ the *infinity plane* (see Figure 5.3.2).

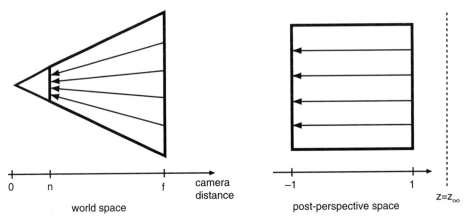

FIGURE 5.3.2   *View frustum and projection rays in world space (left) and post-perspective space (right).*

The final image is obtained by a simple parallel projection of the post-perspective scene to the front side of the unit cube. This means that x and y of a point in post-perspective space are the image coordinates of the point, and z corresponds to its depth. However, note that the depth in post-perspective space does not vary linearly with world space depth.

Less formally, one could say that the perspective transformation squeezes the scene such that distant objects get smaller and objects close to the observer are enlarged (see Figure 5.3.1). When the camera moves, this scaling changes, and objects getting closer are enlarged, whereas objects that move away shrink. A nice property of post-perspective space is that objects have the size that they also have in the final image. This is the key property we will exploit for PSMs.

Lights in Post-Perspective Space

The perspective transformation has surprising effects on light sources. A light source is a bundle of photon rays that are all parallel for a parallel light source or emerge from a finite origin for point light sources. By the projective mapping to post-perspective space, the properties of this ray bundle, and thus the light source type, can change.

Therefore, in general, a parallel light in world space is mapped to a point light in post-perspective space. In the following, we summarize the transformation of a parallel light source in world space to its post-perspective counterpart.

Parallel light sources are point light sources with infinite origin in world space. Now, the projective transformation to post-perspective space can map this infinite origin to a finite one, so that the light source is mapped to a point light in post-perspective space. Equivalently, a point light source (finite origin) in world space can be transformed to a parallel light (infinite origin) post-perspective space. In this article, we will restrict ourselves to parallel light sources in world space, because they are the most interesting application domain for PSMs.

As mentioned previously, a perspective transformation maps points at infinity to points on the infinity plane $z = z_\infty = (f + n)/(f - n)$. Therefore, in general, a parallel light source (origin at infinity) becomes a point light in post-perspective space (origin on the infinity plane). A more thorough analysis gives the following cases, which are also depicted in Figure 5.3.3:

- A parallel light source perpendicular to the viewing direction remains a parallel light in the xy-plane in post-perspective space (Figure 5.3.3 left).
- A parallel light shining toward the observer becomes a point light source on the infinity plane in post-perspective space (Figure 5.3.3 center).
- A parallel light coming from behind the observer becomes a point light *sink* on the infinity plane in post-perspective space. All light rays from the original parallel light source are mapped to light rays that *converge* at a single point. This means that light does not travel from the point on the infinity plane into the scene, but travels toward the light sink on the infinity plane. Such light sources are not very intuitive because they have no real physical counterpart, but in fact they can easily be handled by reversing depth (Figure 5.3.3 right).

The world space origin of a parallel light source is at infinity. If the light shines from direction $(d_x, d_y, d_z)^\mathrm{T}$, its origin can be expressed in homogeneous coordinates as the point $(d_x, d_y, d_z, 0)^\mathrm{T}$. If $\boldsymbol{P}$ is the transformation matrix from world space to post-perspective space, we compute the post-perspective light origin $p = (p_x, p_y, p_z, p_w)^\mathrm{T} = \boldsymbol{P}(d_x, d_y, d_z, 0)^\mathrm{T}$. If $p_w = 0$, the post-perspective origin is also at infinity; in other words, the light source is also a parallel one in post-perspective space (case a from Figure 5.3.3). It can be shown that this only happens if d is perpendicular to the viewing direction and that in this case, p_z is always 0; in other words, the post-perspective light direction is $(p_x, p_y, 0)$. If $p_w \neq 0$, the post-perspective light is at the finite position $(p_x/p_w, p_y/p_w, p_z/p_w)$, where we know that $p_z/p_w = z_\infty$. We then still have to decide whether we have a light source or light sink (cases b or c). One possible criterion is the sign of the dot product between view and light direction, which tells us whether the light shines from the back or from the front. If the standard OpenGL projection matrix obtained from `gluPerspective()` is used, we can also look at the sign of p_w: if $p_w > 0$, we have a light source (case b), if $p_w < 0$, we have a light sink (case c).

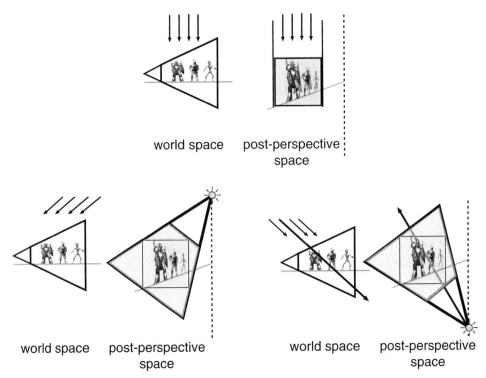

FIGURE 5.3.3   *Light source transformations: a parallel light perpendicular to the view direction is also parallel in post-perspective space (case a, left). Parallel light source from the front of the viewer in world space becomes a point light source at the infinity plane in post-perspective space (case b, center). Parallel light from the back of the viewer becomes a point light sink at the infinity plane (case c, right). Note how the order of the objects along a ray changes in the right case.*

Perspective Shadow Maps

Standard shadow maps are created by rendering the scene from the view of the light source. For a spotlight, the camera is put into the light source position, and its viewing direction and field of view are set to the spot's direction and field of view. For a parallel light source, an orthogonal camera with viewing direction parallel to the light is selected.

In contrast, perspective shadow maps are generated in post-perspective space using the post-perspective light source. The scene and the light source are first transformed to post-perspective space. We then generate a shadow map for the post-perspective light source that sees the scene in post-perspective space.

In post-perspective space, objects close to the viewer are enlarged, and distant objects are shrunk. Objects close to the observer thus obtain higher resolution in the perspective shadow map than distant objects. If we also assume that near shadows result from near objects and far shadows from far objects, we see that near shadows benefit from the increased shadow map resolution, whereas far shadow regions have reduced shadow map resolution.

Construction

Constructing a perspective shadow map means constructing a matrix S that maps a point in world space to shadow map space. After the mapping, x and y are the texture coordinates for the shadow map and z is the light source depth value. Any matrix S is valid, as long as all points along a light ray are mapped to a unique (x,y) position. A point and all its possible shadow casters are mapped to a single point in the shadow map, so that the shadow test becomes a simple depth comparison. The matrix S is used twice: first it is used as projection matrix when rendering the shadow map, then it is used as texture coordinate matrix when applying the shadow map.

In a PSM, S is composed of two matrices: $S = CP$. P maps points from world space to post-perspective space and is defined by the current observer. C maps the points from the post-perspective view frustum (the unit cube) to the PSM. C is defined by a view frustum in post-perspective space, that has the post-perspective light source as origin and that tightly encloses the unit cube (the post-perspective light frusta in Figure 5.3.3).

To compute C, we first transform the parallel light to post-perspective space, determine which of the three cases a, b, or c applies, and then generate C accordingly. Therefore, we first transform the origin of the world space parallel light to post-perspective space: $p = (p_x, p_y, p_z, p_w)^T = P(d_x, d_y, d_z, 0)^T$. We then have to differentiate: if $p_w = 0$, we have a post-perspective parallel light (case a). Thus, C must be a parallel view frustum with view direction $(p_x, p_y, 0)$ that just contains the entire unit cube $[-1,1]^3$. If $p_w > 0$, we have a post-perspective light source (case b). C is then a view frustum with origin $(p_x/p_w, p_y/p_w, z_\infty)$ that encloses the unit cube. Finally, if $p_w < 0$, we have a light sink (case c). In this case, we generate a light frustum as for the previous case, but we invert depth by scaling z by -1. Therefore, C is essentially the matrix that would also be used with a standard shadow map for a scene that is as big as the unit cube.

A first naive implementation as described previously will initially deliver good results. However, it will also quickly turn out that in certain cases, quality degrades massively, or that shadows are missing. In the following, we will describe the pitfalls of PSMs and how they can be circumvented.

Pitfall 1: Close Near Plane

PSMs only work satisfactorily if the near plane of the observer's view frustum is not too close. In general, one can say that if the near plane is at distance n, 50 percent of the shadow map resolution is used for the region that is in the depth range of $[n, 2n]$, and the other 50 percent for the depth range $[2n, \infty]$. If one selects a near plane at 1cm, objects with a view distance of more than 1m will only get 2 percent of the shadow map resolution.

Therefore, it is essential to push the near plane as far out as possible. If this is not possible—for example, because an opponent is very close—the best solution is to virtually extend the view frustum. The observer is virtually moved backward, and the near and far planes are moved forward by the same amount, so they match the near and far planes of the original frustum. This new frustum defines a new post-perspective projection matrix P, which we use for the shadow map construction. The new matrix P wastes some resolution because it covers a larger frustum, but due to its larger near plane distance, it behaves much better.

Pitfall 2: Deep Light Sources

Until now, we assumed that the shadow map covers the entire observer's view frustum (the unit cube in post-perspective space). In general, however, this is already too much, because the view frustum protrudes from the scene and is thus empty in large regions. We can gain resolution if we restrict ourselves to the intersection of the view frustum and a hull of the scene.

The effect is shown in Figure 5.3.4. On the left, we see the view frustum in world space and the scene's bounding box. In the center image, we see the light source frusta in post-perspective space that enclose the view frustum for a high and a deep light source. It can be seen that for the deep light source L2, the frustum (dashed lines) has a very large opening angle and thus degenerates. This can be significantly improved if we fit the light source frustum only around the intersection of view frustum and scene's bounding box. As a result, the opening angle of the deep light source's frustum becomes much smaller and less degenerate. For the high light source L1, the improvement is minor.

For this construction, the intersection between the view frustum and the bounding box must be computed. This requires code to describe a closed convex polyhedron and to cut off half spaces. We start with the scene's bounding box and sequentially cut off the six half spaces defining the view frustum.

Pitfall 3: Shadow Casters Outside the View Frustum

Another remaining problem is that the shadow map must additionally contain all points that can cast a shadow into the view frustum. If, for example, the observer is standing under a tree, he might not see the tree, but the tree can very well cast a visible shadow, so it also must be included in the shadow map. Using the algorithm so far, the tree will be clipped by the near plane of the light frustum.

We can account for this by moving the near plane of the light frustum toward the light, so that all potential shadow casters are included into the shadow map. This can be achieved easily with the previously described intersection computation: instead of cutting off all half spaces of the view frustum as described previously, we only cut off those half spaces that point away from the light source; in other words, we do not cut off regions between the frustum and the light source.

Recent graphics hardware allows for an even more elegant solution. The `NV_DEPTH_CLAMP` extension turns off clipping with respect to the near plane, and

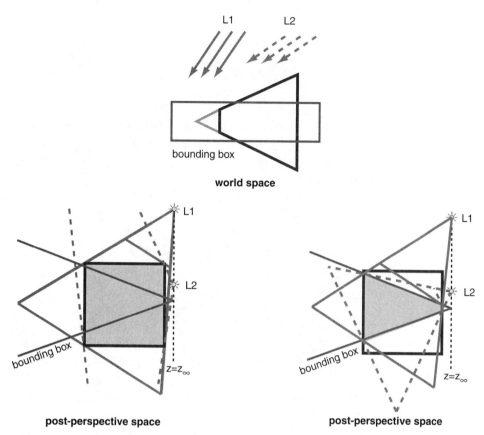

FIGURE 5.3.4 *A view frustum and the scene's bounding box in world space (left). In post-perspective space, a light source frustum that encloses the entire view frustum becomes degenerate for a deep light source, because the post-perspective origin is very close to the unit cube (center). If we compute the intersection between the post-perspective bounding box and view frustum and fit the light source frustum to this intersection, we obtain a less degenerate frustum for the deep light source (right).*

instead projects points in front of the near plane onto the near plane. Using this extension while rendering the shadow map, potential occluders are not clipped, and thus remain visible and can cast correct shadows.

Pitfall 4: Shadow Casters Behind the Viewer

Finally, there is still one remaining, severe pitfall, which arises from a rather unintuitive property of the perspective projection. All points behind the camera are mapped to points beyond the infinity plane, as shown in Figure 5.3.5. The order of points along a ray in world space and in post-perspective space changes, because the infinite point of the ray is mapped to a finite position. For this reason, the inclusion of points beyond the infinity plane is awkward and would, for example, require an additional shadow map. Our solution to this problem is the same as for the close near planes in Pitfall 1: we virtually move the camera backward; in other words, we extend the view frustum backward, until all scene points that need to show up in the shadow map are in front of the viewer. To this end, we cast a ray from the camera toward the light and compute the intersection with the scene's bounding box. This gives us the potential occluding point farthest behind the camera. Then, we virtually extend the view frustum backward, so that this critical point is just in the camera plane. We then generate a perspective shadow map for this extended view frustum, so we can be sure that all necessary points are included.

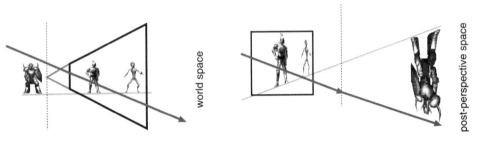

FIGURE 5.3.5   *Objects behind the camera are mapped beyond the infinity plane in post-perspective space (right), thus changing the order of points encountered along a ray.*

Implementation

Perspective shadow maps can be implemented with standard OpenGL functions and a few extensions, as described in this section.

Required and Desired OpenGL Extensions

One of the major advantages of perspective shadow maps is that they can replace standard shadow maps simply by selecting another matrix **S**. Thus, they can be used on every platform that supports standard shadow maps; that is, those that support the extensions ARB_DEPTH_TEXTURE and ARB_SHADOW, which are both part of OpenGL 1.4.

The ARB_SHADOW extension only provides a shadowing value of 0 or 1, which results in completely black shadows. The extension ARB_SHADOW_AMBIENT, which allows you to select a nonzero shadow result value, such that shadows are only dimmed and not completely black, should not be used. Instead, fragment programs (or register combiners) should be used to dim shadow regions: discard specular reflections completely, dim diffuse reflection by a constant factor, and leave ambient reflection unchanged. This is only possible if the three reflection components are provided to the fragment program separately, which in turn requires a tailored vertex program. If vertex programs are used, the generation of the texture coordinates for shadow map access can also be computed by the vertex program, without the awkward glTexGen().

Experiments show that the texture map should have about twice the resolution of the original image, which is only possible using p-buffers (extensions GLX_SGIX_PBUFFER or WGL_ARB_PBUFFER). Furthermore, it must be noted that PSMs are view dependent, so they need to be regenerated for every frame. This is why it is important to optimize texture copy operations. Most shadow map implementations use glCopyTexSubimage() to copy the p-buffer depth map to a shadow map texture. An even better way to completely avoid the costly copy operation is to use WGL_ARB_RENDER_TEXTURE and WGL_NV_RENDER_DEPTH_TEXTURE, which allow us to bind the depth buffer of a p-buffer to a texture, so that the copy can be completely avoided.

The NV_DEPTH_CLAMP extension avoids the loss of occluders outside the view frustum, and makes computation of the relevant region V significantly simpler.

Pseudocode Example

A typical implementation of perspective shadow maps will look as follows:

```
// offset to avoid too close near plane
nearOffset = max(0,zNearMin — zNear)

// offset for light behind viewer
backlightOffset = calcBackOffset();

// generate matrix P
P = frustumWithOffset(max(nearOffset,backLightOffset))

// compute relevant region V
V = intersection(view frustum, scene bounding box)

// compute post-perspective light source frustum C
C = lightFrustumThatSees(postPerspective(V))

// render shadow map
setRenderMatrix(C*P)
setRenderTargetShadowMap()
renderSceneWithDepthClamp()

// render view
setTextureCoordGeneration(C*P)
turnOnShadowMapping()
renderScene()
```

Conclusion

Perspective shadow maps provide higher-quality shadows than the standard shadow map algorithm by using more resolution for shadows in areas near the camera. Because it operates in post-perspective space, the technique introduces some new subtleties in the treatment of lights and shadow casters outside the view frustum. The sample implementation sketched here addresses most of these issues while maintaining high performance.

References

[Reeves87] Reeves, W.T., D.H. Salesin, and R.L. Cook, "Rendering Antialiased Shadows with Depth Maps," *Computer Graphics* (Proc. SIGGRAPH 87), 1987, pp. 283–291.

[Stamminger02] Stamminger, M., and G. Drettakis, "Perspective Shadow Maps," *ACM Transactions on Graphics* 21(3) (Proc. SIGGRAPH 2002), 2002, pp. 557–562.

[Williams78] Williams, L., "Casting Curved Shadows on Curved Surfaces," *Computer Graphics* (Proc. SIGGRAPH 78), 1978, pp. 270–274.

5.4

Combined Depth and ID-Based Shadow Buffers

Kurt Pelzer, Piranha Bytes

kurt.pelzer@gmx.net

Shadows are an important element in our visual perception of an environment. Their location and orientation provide detailed information about object placement and light position. Adding shadows to a scene helps to enhance realism and provide additional depth cues.

For real-time applications, precomputed static light maps that encode shadows were the first step in this direction. However, to correctly handle animated objects and lights, dynamic shadow calculations are necessary. There are currently several well-known real-time techniques for dynamic shadows, including projected shadow textures, stenciled shadow volumes, and shadow mapping. Each method has its advantages and disadvantages.

This article describes a hybrid approach that combines the techniques of both depth and ID-based shadow buffers, exploiting the advantages of both methods. This approach allows for self-shadowing and supports up to 42,875 unique IDs.

Existing Shadow Mapping Techniques

Several methods exist to compute dynamic shadows in real-time. One of the most well-known methods, shadow mapping, requires two render passes per shadow casting light to detect if a pixel is in shadow.

First Pass—Computing the Buffer Values

Computing shadows requires computing visibility from the light source. All objects that fall into the light's frustum are rendered into a texture from the light's point of view. Each pixel of this map stores either pixel depth or ID information of the object closest to the light.

Second Pass—Detecting the Shadows

With respect to the viewer, all scene objects are rendered in the frame buffer. At each pixel, the depth or ID information has to be compared against the value recorded in the shadow map. To be able to run this comparison, the shadow map has to be projected down from the light onto the scene. We want to detect if the fragment can be seen from the light's position. Whatever the light sees is illuminated; what it does not see is in shadow. Therefore, if this test succeeds, then the pixel is lit; otherwise, it is not. Figure 5.4.1 illustrates both cases.

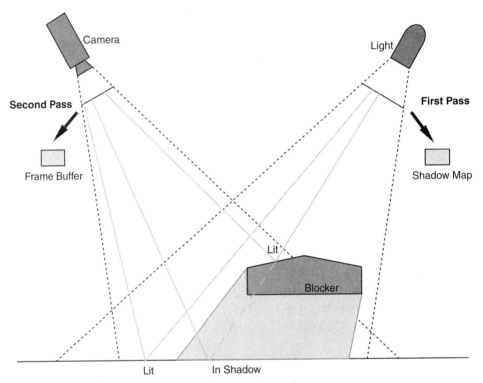

FIGURE 5.4.1   *Shadow mapping techniques in general.*

Depth and ID-Based Shadow Buffers

Let's take a closer look at the most popular shadow mapping techniques: *Depth buffers* [Williams78], and *ID buffers* ([Hourcade85] and [Dietrich01]). Both methods are very similar.

For the *depth buffer* technique, each pixel of the shadow map contains the closest depth value measured from the light. In the shadow detection pass, these depth values are compared to those computed for the viewer's camera (transformed to the light's camera space). If the camera's depth is greater than the shadow map depth, then the pixel is in shadow; otherwise, the pixel is lit. This enables self-shadowing within objects. One disadvantage is that the quality of the shadows depends on the numerical precision of the depth values in the shadow map. While general-purpose hardware

(DX8-level and lower) can perform this method, the z-buffer has to be stored as a color or alpha channel of a texture. This gives only 8 bits of precision, which is not an adequate precision for the general case. DX9-level hardware and later supports rendering to 32-bit floating-point textures. However, even 24 or 32 bits are often not enough precision on its own to differentiate between objects.

ID buffers overcome this precision problem by an exact object differentiation. We assign each object its own ID. These IDs have to be based on the objects' sort order in terms of distance from the light. Instead of comparing z-depths, the IDs are compared. If the current ID is greater than the shadow map ID, then the pixel is in shadow; otherwise, the pixel is lit. However, there are also some disadvantages:

- Limited to IDs with 8 bits of precision, so only 256 different objects are supported.
- An object is defined as something that can't shadow itself. Therefore, individual sections of the object can't shadow each other; we lose self-shadowing.
- The IDs have to be based on a strict sorted order, which is why this technique is sometimes called a *priority buffer*. We have to run an object-sorting pass for each light that casts a shadow.

Combining Depth and ID Buffers

ID-based shadow buffers offer many useful advantages over depth-based shadow buffers, and vice versa. This section outlines each of these advantages and how we propose to use them. In this section, we introduce the *combined shadow buffer*.

Modifying the ID Buffer Technique

One problem with the standard *ID buffer* method is that the objects have to be sorted correctly in terms of distance from the light. We need this sorting, because objects are only going to receive shadows when their IDs are greater than that of the blocker. Therefore, to be able to do our job for the new combined buffers without this sorting, we have to develop an equality test for 8-bit color channels. This means that we can simply detect shadowed objects (those that cannot be seen from the light's position) by failed equality tests (computed ID does not equal projected ID); object sorting is no longer needed.

Another problem with the standard *ID buffer* method is the limited number of IDs. The solution for our combined buffers is to use all three color channels at the same time. Additionally, we have to expand the equality test to cover all three channels. First, in each color channel, the test has to determine a result, and subsequently, these results must be summarized in the alpha channel. Finally, an alpha test is able to detect the pixels in shadow. Later in this article, we take a closer look at the detailed process. As we will see, it is possible to differentiate only 35 IDs per channel. However, combining all three color channels will result in 35*35*35 = 42,875 possible IDs—enough to support all objects with static IDs, even in large scenes.

Adding an Object-Internal Depth Test

Now we want to combine the modified ID buffer technique (running in the color channels) with an additional object-internal depth test ("Is the computed depth greater than the projected depth?") in the alpha channel. This allows us to use 8 bits for object-internal depth (this means that we are able to differentiate 256 object-internal layers)—the same precision that is typically spread across the complete lights' range when running the standard depth buffer technique. Its result will be combined with that of the equality tests and summarized in the alpha channel. Again, a final alpha test detects the pixels in shadow.

Comparison

The combined buffer technique has several advantages in comparison with the standard shadow mapping methods, including higher precision (IDs and object-internal depth), very low CPU work (no more exact object sorting required), and support for self-shadowing. They are summarized in Table 5.4.1.

Table 5.4.1   Comparison of Shadow Mapping Techniques

	ID Buffers	Depth Buffers	Combined Buffers
Precision	**Low** 256 IDs (standard version)	**Low** 8 bits of depth, spread across light's range (standard version)	**High** 42,875 IDs (reduced version) + 8 bits of object-internal depth (complete version)
Self shadowing	**Partial** Only convex pieces	**Yes** Low precision	**Yes** Complete version
Object sorting	**Required** Low CPU work	**Not Required** Very low CPU work	**Not Required** Very low CPU work
Render to texture	**Required**	**Required**	**Required**

An Overview of Combined Shadow Buffers

Taking all these modifications into consideration, let's see how our combined buffer shadows work.

Buffer Creation Phase

```
For each light
  Set combined shadow buffer texture as the render target
  Clear combined shadow buffer texture to 0x00000000
  For each object in light's viewing frustum
    Set object ID as a constant color (RGB) and object's
internal depth as the alpha
```

```
      Render object into texture, using the constant color
```

Shadow Testing Phase
```
      For each light
        Create texture matrix to move vertices from view
         space to light's view space
        For each object in player's viewing frustum
          Set object ID as a constant color (RGB) and object's
   internal depth as the alpha
          Select combined shadow buffer as a texture
          For each vertex
            Calculate the texture coordinates for the projected
   combined shadow buffer
          For each pixel of the object
            Compare constant ID to closest projected ID
            If constant ID != closest projected ID
              Pixel is in shadow
            Else
              Compare constant depth to closest proj. depth
              If constant depth > closest proj. depth
                Pixel is in shadow
              Else
                Pixel is lit
```

In the two following sections, we will take a closer look at both phases (buffer creation and shadow testing) and start to build an implementation based on fixed-function multitexturing methods. This will allow us to use this code with older GPUs (those that are not truly programmable, without pixel shader support). Transferring this implementation to programmable shaders of the first generation (Direct3D ps1.3 and earlier) is easy, since the pixel shader instructions in these versions are fixed-function style and not powerful enough to be considered truly programmable until ps1.4 and later.

First Pass: Rendering from the
Light's Point of View

The first step is to create the shadow map—a render-target texture that contains the scene rendered from the light's point of view. The reduced version of our combined shadow mapping technique writes the IDs of the objects that can be seen from the light source in the RGB color channels of each pixel. The complete version of the combined buffer technique additionally writes the object-internal depths to the alpha channel (see Figure 5.4.2).

Why Do We Need a Special Encoding
for the Object IDs?

Later in the shadow detection pass, we will use the dot product as a color operation in a texture stage to combine the calculated color channel results in the alpha channel. This dot product shifts all inputs (values for the color channels) by half before use to

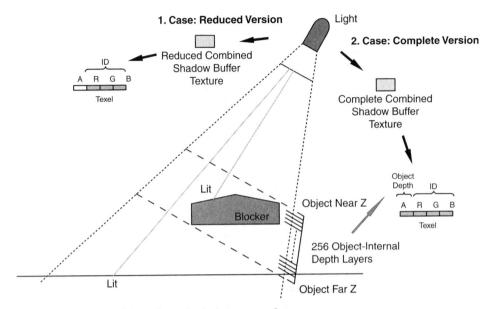

FIGURE 5.4.2   *Rendering from the light's point of view.*

simulate signed data (y = x − 0.5). Therefore, 0x7F will be interpreted as zero. However, because of the limited precision of this calculation, 0x7F isn't the only number that results in zero. There is a small region around this central vector that also generates zero. If the red, green, and blue components of the color are all simultaneously in the interval [0x79, 0x85], the dot product still results in zero. The neighboring values 0x78 and 0x86 (which have a distance of 7 to the central 0x7F) are the first that will cause nonzero results if they appear in at least one color channel. The dot product is a component of our ID equality testing procedure. Therefore, we have to respect its limited precision and guarantee a minimum distance of 7 in at least one color channel to get different IDs. Therefore, it is possible to differentiate only 35 IDs per color channel[*], and 35*35*35 = 42,875 IDs overall, with all three color channels combined.

Reduced Version (without Support for Internal Shadows)

As we have seen, unequal IDs must have a distance of 7 or greater (0, 7, 14, 21, 28, . . .) in at least one of its color channels. Therefore, encoding an object ID i with $0 \le i \le$ 42,874 might look like this:

```
// --- Set Object Data ---
Color.Alpha = 0x00;
Color.Red   = (i/(35*35))*7;
Color.Green = ((i%(35*35))/35)*7;
Color.Blue  = (i%35)*7;
SetColorFactor( Color );
[ i is in [0,42874] ]
```

---

[*] Actually 36 (= 256/7), but adding 0x08 to each channel in the second pass reduces the number again.

For example, $i = 3,487$ will be encoded to 0x000ECB9A (with an A8R8G8B8 format):

Color.Red	= (3,487/1,225)*7	= 2*7	= 14	= 0x0E;
Color.Green	= ((3,487%1,225)/35)*7	= 29*7	= 203	= 0xCB;
Color.Blue	= (3,487%35)*7	= 22*7	= 154	= 0x9A;

and its neighbor 3,488 will be encoded to 0x000ECBA1 (with a distance of 7 in the red color channel).

Transferring this encoded ID from the color factor to the pixels of the shadow map is easy.

```
// --- Texture Stage 0 ---
TexStage0.SetColorCalc(
  TEXOP_SELECTARG1, TEXARG_COLORFACTOR, TEXARG_CURRENT );
TexStage0.SetAlphaCalc(
  TEXOP_SELECTARG1, TEXARG_COLORFACTOR, TEXARG_CURRENT );
```

Complete Version (Supporting Internal Shadows)

The complete version of our technique additionally uses the object-internal depths. Therefore, we have to calculate this depth in a range from 0.0 to 1.0 and use this value as a texture coordinate for addressing a simple depth-to-alpha mapping texture.

```
// --- Initialization ---
[ Depth2AlphaTexture: depth-to-alpha mapping texture
  with Width = 256, Height = 1, Format = A8R8G8B8,
  MipMapLevels = 1 ]
Depth2AlphaTexture.LockLayer( &pBits );
Color.Red = Color.Green = Color.Blue = 0x77;
for( unsigned int i = 0; i<256; i++ )
{
    Color.Alpha = i;
    *((DWORD*)( pBits )+i) = Color;
}
Depth2AlphaTexture.UnlockLayer();

// --- Set Object Data ---
[ set color factor like shown above in the reduced version ]
matTex.m_Elements.m_f31 = 1.0f/(fObjFarZ-fObjNearZ);
matTex.m_Elements.m_f41 = -fObjNearZ/(fObjFarZ-fObjNearZ);
TexStage0.SetTextureMatrix( matTex );
```

Again, we have to transfer the encoded IDs from the color factor to the pixels of the shadow map. Additionally, the object-internal depth must be picked from the depth-to-alpha-texture to write it in the alpha channel of the shadow map.

```
// --- Texture Stage 0 ---
TexStage0.SetColorCalc(
  TEXOP_SELECTARG1, TEXARG_COLORFACTOR, TEXARG_TEXTURE );
TexStage0.SetAlphaCalc(
  TEXOP_SELECTARG2, TEXARG_COLORFACTOR, TEXARG_TEXTURE );
TexStage0.SetTextureCoordinateCalc(
```

```
        TEXCOORDCALC_CAMERASPACEPOSITION );
    TexStage0.SetTextureCoordinateTrafo(
        TEXCOORDTRAFO_COUNT2 );
    TexStage0.SetTextureFiltering(
        TEXFILTER_POINT, TEXFILTER_POINT, TEXFILTER_POINT );
    TexStage0.SetTextureAdressing(
        TEXADDR_CLAMP, TEXADDR_CLAMP, TEXADDR_CLAMP );
    TexStage0.SetTexture( Depth2AlphaTexture );
```

Second Pass: Shadow Detection

Now we are going to compare the values as computed from the camera's point of view against the values recorded in the shadow map. To be able to run this comparison, the shadow map texture has to be projected down from the light onto the scene. Since whatever the light does not see is in shadow, we want to detect if the fragment's computed value equals the projected value (see Figure 5.4.3).

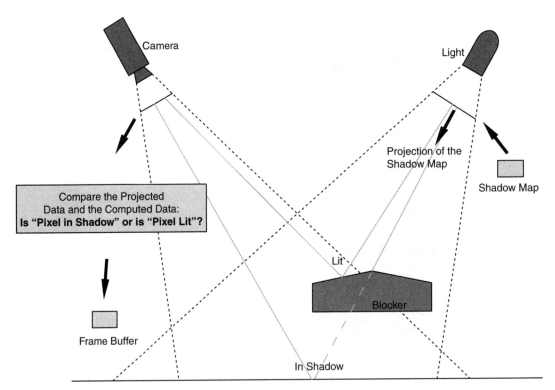

FIGURE 5.4.3 *Shadow detection.*

The next two sections present special setups for the multitexturing pipeline to prepare the shadow detection test. Based on the output of this pipeline, a simple alpha test will enable us to detect the pixels in shadow (e.g., to mark them in the stencil buffer).

Reduced Version

As we saw in the first pass (rendering from the light's point of view), it's easy to encode the object ID in the needed format. This time, however, we have to shift the values in each color channel by adding 0x08.

```
// --- Set Object Data ---
Color.Alpha = 0x77;
Color.Red   = (i/(35*35))*7 + 0x08;
Color.Green = ((i%(35*35))/35)*7 + 0x08;
Color.Blue  = (i%35)*7 + 0x08;
SetColorFactor( Color );
[ i is in [0,42874] ]
```

Adding this shift value is necessary, as can be seen in the setup of the multitexturing pipeline in the next code listing. Without the shift value, the subtraction in stage 0 enables us to differentiate only the following two cases in each color channel:

(Abbreviations: ccIDcc = currently calculated ID color channel; psIDcc = projected stored ID color channel)

- *ccIDcc ≤ psIDcc* (ccIDcc – psIDcc = 0 × 00 because of clamping)
- *ccIDcc > psIDcc* (ccIDcc – psIDcc ≥ 0x07)

By adding the shift vector, we are able to distinguish three cases:

- *ccIDcc = psIDcc* ((ccIDcc+0x08) – psIDcc = 0x08)
- *ccIDcc < psIDcc* ((ccIDcc+0x08) – psIDcc ≤ 0x01)
- *ccIDcc > psIDcc* ((ccIDcc+0x08) – psIDcc ≥ 0x0F)

Only if the subtraction results in 0x08 for each color channel do we have two identical IDs. That's the basis for our equality test.

Finally, we add 0x77 to the calculated differences in each color channel in stage 1 (via the alpha channel of the color factor) and calculate the dot product in stage 2. Only in the case that *ccIDcc* equals *psIDcc* for each color channel, stage 1 generates the color vector (R,G,B) = (0x7F, 0x7F, 0x7F), and stage 2 results in the alpha output dot((R,G,B), (R,G,B)) = 0x00. All other cases will generate alpha values greater than 0x00. That is exactly what our alpha test wants to see: 0x00 indicates lit pixels; all others are in shadow.

```
// --- Pixels In Shadow Will Pass This Test ---
STRUCT_AlphaTestData alphaTestData;
alphaTestData.m_AlphaTestFunc = ENUM_CMPFUNC_NOTEQUAL;
alphaTestData.m_AlphaTestRef  = 0x00;
SetAlphaTesting( ALPHATEST_ENABLE, alphaTestData );
```

The complete workflow is illustrated in Figure 5.4.4. This is the setup for the multitexturing pipeline:

```
// --- Texture Stage 0 ---
TexStage0.SetColorCalc(
```

```
  TEXOP_SUBTRACT, TEXARG_COLORFACTOR, TEXARG_TEXTURE );
TexStage0.SetAlphaCalc(
  TEXOP_SELECTARG1, TEXARG_COLORFACTOR, TEXARG_TEXTURE );
TexStage0.SetTextureCoordinateCalc(
  TEXCOORDCALC_CAMERASPACEPOSITION );
TexStage0.SetTextureCoordinateTrafo(
  TEXCOORDTRAFO_COUNT3|TEXCOORDTRAFO_PROJECTED );
TexStage0.SetTextureFiltering(
  TEXFILTER_POINT, TEXFILTER_POINT, TEXFILTER_POINT );
TexStage0.SetTextureAdressing(
  TEXADDR_CLAMP, TEXADDR_CLAMP, TEXADDR_CLAMP );
[ insert: set the proj. matrix for the shadow map ]
TexStage0.SetTexture( ReducedCombinedBufferTexture );
// --- Texture Stage 1 ---
TexStage1.SetColorCalc(
  TEXOP_ADD, TEXARG_ALPHAREPLICATE|TEXARG_CURRENT,
  TEXARG_CURRENT );
TexStage1.SetAlphaCalc(
  TEXOP_SELECTARG1, TEXARG_CURRENT, TEXARG_CURRENT );
// --- Texture Stage 2 ---
TexStage2.SetColorCalc(
  TEXOP_DOTPRODUCT3, TEXARG_CURRENT, TEXARG_CURRENT );
TexStage2.SetAlphaCalc(
  TEXOP_SELECTARG1, TEXARG_CURRENT, TEXARG_CURRENT );
```

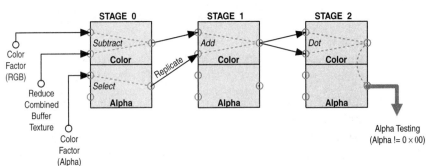

FIGURE 5.4.4   *Workflow for reduced version.*

Complete Version

As shown in the first pass, the object-internal depths are also taken into account. To
be comparable to the depth written in the shadow map, we have to transform the calculated texture matrix (for the depth-to-alpha texture) from the viewer's camera space
to the light's camera space.

```
// --- Set Object Data ---
Color.Alpha = 0x00;
Color.Red   = (i/(35*35))*7 + 0x08;
Color.Green = ((i%(35*35))/35)*7 + 0x08;
Color.Blue  = (i%35)*7 + 0x08;
SetColorFactor( Color );
```

```
[ i is an element of [0,42874] ]
matTex.m_Elements.m_f31 = 1.0f/(fObjFarZ-fObjNearZ);
matTex.m_Elements.m_f41 = -fObjNearZ/(fObjFarZ-fObjNearZ);
[ matVCSpaceToLCSpace: matrix that transforms the
  viewer's camera space to the light's camera space ]
MatrixMultiply( &matTex, &matVCSpaceToLCSpace, &matTex );
TexStage1.SetTextureMatrix( matTex );
```

A modified version of the preparation of the shadow detection test in the multi-texturing pipeline allows us to combine the result of the ID comparison with the depth test in the alpha channel.

```
// --- Texture Stage 0 ---
TexStage0.SetColorCalc(
  TEXOP_SUBTRACT, TEXARG_COLORFACTOR, TEXARG_TEXTURE );
TexStage0.SetAlphaCalc(
  TEXOP_SELECTARG2, TEXARG_COLORFACTOR, TEXARG_TEXTURE );
TexStage0.SetTextureCoordinateCalc(
  TEXCOORDCALC_CAMERASPACEPOSITION );
TexStage0.SetTextureCoordinateTrafo(
  TEXCOORDTRAFO_COUNT3|TEXCOORDTRAFO_PROJECTED );
TexStage0.SetTextureFiltering(
  TEXFILTER_POINT, TEXFILTER_POINT, TEXFILTER_POINT );
TexStage0.SetTextureAdressing(
  TEXADDR_CLAMP, TEXADDR_CLAMP, TEXADDR_CLAMP );
[ insert: set the proj. matrix for the shadow map ]
TexStage0.SetTexture( CompleteCombinedBufferTexture );
// --- Texture Stage 1 ---
TexStage1.SetTextureResultArgument(
  TEXARGUMENT_TEMP );
TexStage1.SetColorCalc(
  TEXOP_ADD, TEXARG_TEXTURE, TEXARG_CURRENT );
TexStage1.SetAlphaCalc(
  TEXOP_SUBTRACT, TEXARG_TEXTURE, TEXARG_CURRENT );
TexStage1.SetTextureCoordinateCalc(
  TEXCOORDCALC_CAMERASPACEPOSITION );
TexStage1.SetTextureCoordinateTrafo(
  TEXCOORDTRAFO_COUNT2 );
TexStage1.SetTextureFiltering(
  TEXFILTER_POINT, TEXFILTER_POINT, TEXFILTER_POINT );
TexStage1.SetTextureAdressing(
  TEXADDR_CLAMP, TEXADDR_CLAMP, TEXADDR_CLAMP );
TexStage1.SetTexture( Depth2AlphaTexture );
// --- Texture Stage 2 ---
TexStage2.SetColorCalc(
  TEXOP_DOTPRODUCT3, TEXARG_TEMP, TEXARG_TEMP );
TexStage2.SetAlphaCalc(
  TEXOP_SELECTARG1, TEXARG_CURRENT, TEXARG_CURRENT );
// --- Texture Stage 3 ---
TexStage3.SetColorCalc(
  TEXOP_SELECTARG1, TEXARG_CURRENT, TEXARG_CURRENT );
TexStage3.SetAlphaCalc(
  TEXOP_MODULATE, TEXARG_COMPLEMENT|TEXARG_CURRENT,
  TEXARG_COMPLEMENT|TEXARG_TEMP );
```

This time, we add 0x77 to each color channel in stage 1 (via the depth-to-alpha mapping texture), and the dot-product calculation is done in stage 2. In stage 3, we combine the results of the ID test and the object-internal depth test (done in the alpha channel of stage 1). See Figure 5.4.5 for an overview.

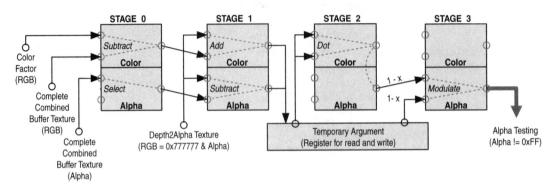

FIGURE 5.4.5   *Workflow for complete version.*

This setup for the multitexturing pipeline means that only in one case we are going to find 0xFF in the alpha output: *calculated ID = projected ID* combined with *calculated depth ≤ projected depth*. That is exactly the case that indicates lit pixels. All other cases indicate pixels in shadow and will generate results lesser than 0xFF. Therefore, our alpha test looks like this:

```
// --- Pixels In Shadow Will Pass This Test ---
STRUCT_AlphaTestData alphaTestData;
alphaTestData.m_AlphaTestFunc = ENUM_CMPFUNC_NOTEQUAL;
alphaTestData.m_AlphaTestRef  = 0xff;
SetAlphaTesting( ALPHATEST_ENABLE, alphaTestData );
```

Implementation in DX9 2.0-Level Shaders

We are able to enhance the precision running the combined shadow buffer technique on DX9-level hardware. In this section, we examine an implementation based on version 2.0 pixel shaders supporting 65,536 unique IDs and full 16-bits for object-internal depth.

We don't have to encode the object IDs any longer, because the equality test will be much simpler in our pixel shader. Using the new pixel format R16G16, the 16-bit precision of the green color channel enables us to support 65,536 unique IDs (instead of 42,875 in our special RGB encoded format). Moreover, this time we are able to support full 16-bit precision for the object-internal depth. We use a depth-to-red mapping texture (instead of depth-to-alpha) containing 2,048 values (that's the maximum width supported by standard DX9-level hardware) representing the interval [0, 65535]. Linear texture filtering then calculates a weighted average of the values that are immediately beside the nearest sample point.

```
// --- Initialization ---
[ Depth2RedTexture: depth-to-red mapping texture
  with Width = 2048, Height = 1, Format = R16G16,
  MipMapLevels = 1 ]
Depth2RedTexture.LockLayer( &pBits );
for( unsigned int i = 0; i<2048; i++ )
{
    ColorR16G16.Red = i*32;
    *((DWORD*)( pBits )+i) = ColorR16G16;
}
Depth2RedTexture.UnlockLayer();
```

First Pass: Rendering from the Light's Point of View

The shadow map must be created with the same pixel format, R16G16. We use a simple pixel shader that transfers the ID and object-internal depth to the red and green color channels in our shadow map.

```
// --- Pixel Shader ---
// c2 Contains the Current Object ID in the green channel
ps_2_0
// Declare used resources
dcl   t0        // Tex-Coords for Depth-to-Red Map
dcl_2 s0        // Sampler for Depth-to-Red Map
// Load the texture
texld r0, t0, s0
// Move the Current Object ID into the green color channel
mov   r0.g, c2.g
// Set the Output Color
mov   oC0, r0
```

Second Pass: Shadow Detection

In this render pass, we use a pixel shader to run a simple equality test for our IDs, and a greater-than test for the object-internal depth values. Again, as in the fixed function version, both results are combined in the alpha channel of the output color (0xFF indicates the lit pixels for the final alpha testing).

```
// --- Pixel Shader ---
// c2 Contains the Current Object ID in the green channel
ps_2_0
// Define c0 and c1
def   c0, 0.0f, 0.0f, 0.0f, 0.0f
def   c1, 1.0f, 1.0f, 1.0f, 1.0f
// Declare used resources
dcl   t0        // Tex-Coords for Depth-to-Red Map
dcl   t1        // Tex-Coords for Shadow Map
dcl_2 s0        // Sampler for Depth-to-Red Map
dcl_2 s1        // Sampler for Shadow Map
// Load the textures
texld r0, t0, s0
texld r1, t1, s1
// Calculate Abs(Calculated ID - Projected ID)
```

```
// and Max(0, Calculated Depth - Projected Depth)
mov   r0.g, c2.g       // r0.r=Calc.Depth & r0.g=Calc.ID
sub   r2, r0, r1       // Calculate ID & Depth Differences
abs   r1, r2           // r1.g=Abs(Calc.ID-Proj.ID)
max   r1.r, c0.r, r2.r // r1.r=Max(0,Calc.Depth-Proj.Depth)
// If( Calc.ID==Proj.ID && Calc.Depth<=Proj.Depth )
// [here: if( r1.g<=0.0f && r1.r<=0.0f )]
//   oC0.a = 1.0f
// Else
//   oC0.a = 0.0f
cmp   r0, -r1, c1, c0  // Run the ID and depth tests
mul   r0.a, r0.g, r0.r // Combine both test results
mov   oC0, r0          // Set the Output Color
```

Conclusion

This article described how to build an advanced shadow mapping technique that is able to handle many object IDs and supports self-shadowing. By running a tricky combination of texture-stage-states, we can overcome some old problems and significantly improve the algorithm's usability. Additionally, the implementation of this technique works on most graphics cards. For the reduced version, we need only three texture stages with one texture, and for the complete version, we need four texture stages with two different textures.

ON THE CD

A complete implementation (including source code) of combined shadow buffers is on the companion CD-ROM. Also included is a simple demo application that uses this technique to compute dynamic shadows.

However, there are several ways to improve and extend upon what we presented in this article. There are some good ideas here: [Woo90], [Vlachos00], [Bloom01], [Haines01] or [Haines02], [Stamminger 02] and [Dietrich03].

References

[Bloom01] Bloom, Charles, and Phil Teschner, "Advanced Techniques in Shadow Mapping," available online at *www.cbloom.com/3d/techdocs/shadowmap_advanced .txt*, June 2001.

[Dietrich01] Dietrich, D. Sim, "Practical Priority Buffer Shadows," *Game Programming Gems 2*, Charles River Media, 2001.

[Dietrich03] Dietrich, D. Sim, "Robust ObjectID Shadows," *ShaderX2*, Wordware Publishing, 2003.

[Haines01] Haines, Eric, and Tomas Moeller, "Real-Time Shadows," GDC 2001 Proceedings, available online at *www.gdconf.com/archives/2001/haines.pdf*, March 2001.

[Haines02] Haines, Eric, and Tomas Moeller, *Real-Time Rendering, Second Edition*, A.K. Peters Ltd., 2002.

[Hourcade85] Hourcade, J.C., and A. Nicolas, "Algorithms for Antialiased Cast Shadows," *Computers and Graphics*, Vol. 9, No. 3, pp. 259–265, 1985.

[Stamminger02] Stamminger, Marc, and George Drettakis, "Perspective Shadow Maps," *Proceedings of ACM SIGGRAPH 2002*, available online at *www-sop.inria. fr/reves/publications/data/2002/SD02/PerspectiveShadowMaps.pdf*, July 2002.

[Vlachos00] Vlachos, Alex, David Gosselin, and Jason L. Mitchell, "Self-Shadowing Characters," *Game Programming Gems*, Charles River Media, 2000.

[Williams78] Williams, Lance, "Casting Curved Shadows on Curved Surfaces," *Computer Graphics (SIGGRAPH '78 Proceedings)*, pp. 270–274, August 1978.

[Woo90] Woo, Andrew, Pierre Poulin, and Alain Fournier, "A Survey of Shadow Algorithms," *IEEE Computer Graphics and Applications*, Vol. 10, No. 6, pp. 13–32, November 1990.

5.5

Carving Static Shadows into Geometry

Alex Vlachos,
ATI Research, Inc.

Alex@Vlachos.com

Stencil shadow volumes provide a robust dynamic shadow solution for animated characters, producing hard shadows. Often, however, game developers choose different methods of rendering shadows for dynamic characters and static scene geometry, leading to an inconsistent look. This article describes a method of carving hard shadows directly into static geometry to create crisp, hard scene shadows that are consistent with the look of the stencil shadows typically used for characters. After the carving process, each resulting polygon is marked as either "in light" or "in shadow" for later rendering. This saves the overhead of rendering full shadow volumes for every detail in a scene, resulting in significant fill-rate savings. Additionally, we will briefly discus how to dynamically cast shadows on moving objects using low-resolution proxy shadow volumes.

Previous Work

A modified Weiler-Atherton algorithm [Weiler77] can provide a similar solution to the method presented here, but the algorithm is susceptible to infinite recursion due to precision errors using 64-bit floating-point variables. Advances based on this approach were published in an article in *Game Programming Gems 3* called "Computing Optimized Shadow Volumes for Complex Data Sets" [Vlachos02] that describes a method for computing just the front cap geometry of a shadow volume.

This article takes a more straightforward approach to carving shadows into geometry, preserving all geometry in and out of light instead of just the polygons visible to the light. The methods presented here deal with numerical precision issues of floating-point variables.

Beam Basics

The technique presented in this article uses beams to carve the shadows. A beam is a pyramid-shaped volume created from a point in space (a light position) and the three edges of a triangle (see Figure 5.5.1). This is represented by three planes.

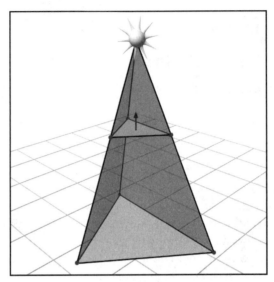

FIGURE 5.5.1   *A full beam generated from a light source and a triangle.*

A beam, as just described, will be referred to as a *full beam*. Two other types of beams will be discussed: *near beam* and *far beam*. A near beam is the volume described by the full beam on the near side of the triangle (see Figure 5.5.2 left). A far beam is the volume described by the full beam on the far side of the triangle (see Figure 5.5.2 right). Each is represented by four planes.

High-Level Algorithm

The ultimate goal is to replace the original mesh with a newer, diced-up one. There are several obvious approaches one can take to attain that goal. For memory storage reasons and simplicity, the most brute-force approach turns out to be the best choice.

The actual carving happens when a polygon occludes another polygon from the light. The closer polygon's far beam tessellates the occluded polygon. Each of the four planes that make up the far beam is used to clip the occluded polygon. After all four planes have sliced the occluded polygon, each resulting polygon that falls inside the far beam is marked as being in shadow. In pseudocode, the algorithm can be described as follows:

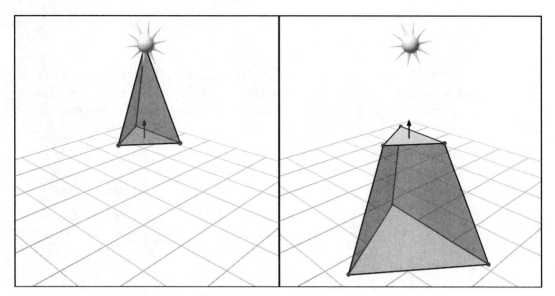

FIGURE 5.5.2 *(Left) Near beam. (Right) Far beam.*

```
For each shadow-casting light in the scene (L)
{
        For each polygon in the light's frustum (A)
        {
                Initialize bin X (array of polygons) with polygon A marked
as in light.
                For each original scene polygon (B) in polygon A's near
beam
                {
                        Use polygon B's far beam to slice all polygons in
bin X, replacing the contents of bin X with the output of the tessella-
tion.
                        If a polygon in bin X is in B's far beam, mark it as
in shadow.
                        Optimize the lit polygons in bin X.
                        Optimize the shadowed polygons in bin X.
                }

                The polygons in bin X are added to the output polygon
array.
        }
}
Resolve t-junctions along original polygon boundaries between polygons
that are in and out of the light frustum.
```

T-Junctions

This shadow-cutting algorithm doesn't create t-junctions within the tessellated polygons, but it does create them along the boundaries of lit and unlit original polygons. For

example, imagine a triangle split directly in half by a shadow, causing two of its edges to be split in half. If that triangle's neighbor is back-facing with respect to the light, its edge won't be tessellated like its immediate neighbor that is facing the light as shown in Figure 5.5.3. The only way to solve this problem is to manually resolve t-junctions at the end. A technique to find and resolve t-junctions can be found in the *Game Programming Gems 3* article "T-Junction Elimination and Retriangulation" [Lengyel02].

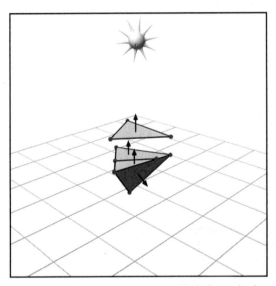

FIGURE 5.5.3 *A t-junction created along the boundary of front-facing and back-facing polygons to the light.*

Mesh Optimization Algorithm

If this algorithm is applied with no optimization, the application will eventually run out of memory for a relatively simple scene. Hence, mesh optimization is a requirement.

It is important to understand where optimization takes place in the earlier pseudocode. Notice that bin X is initialized at each iteration of the middle loop. This means that all polygons in bin X at any given time were generated from the same original polygon. If all polygons in bin X were "glued" back together, they would always make up a single polygon from the original mesh. This allows us to make some key assumptions when attempting to optimize the mesh.

There are two stages to optimizing these meshes: vertex removal and edge collapse. We first apply vertex removal to the entire mesh before moving on to the edge collapse step. Because our polygonal mesh originated from a single triangle, we don't have to bother testing texture coordinates, normals, plane equations, and so forth before running our vertex removal or edge collapse steps. All per-vertex data in the vertices are just linear combinations of the original three vertices of the triangle, and therefore, all share the same face normal.

Because polygons are tagged as *in light* or *in shadow*, they must be optimized separately to preserve the shadow boundaries that we are creating in this process.

Vertex Removal

This method of optimization is only used on vertices that lie on the interior of the original polygon.

1. An edge table that contains edge information for all the edges in the mesh is required. Each entry in the table should contain the two vertices of that edge and the one or two polygons that share that edge.
2. For every unique vertex, choose a starting triangle that contains the vertex, and use the edge table to "walk" clockwise around the vertex to neighboring triangles that also contain the vertex. Continue to walk around the vertex until the original triangle is reached. If it isn't reached, this vertex is not a candidate for vertex removal. Return to Step 2 for the next vertex.
3. Remove the vertex and tessellate the n-gon that is left behind. A robust tessellation algorithm is required to avoid errors. An example method can be found in [deBerg00] (see Figure 5.5.4).

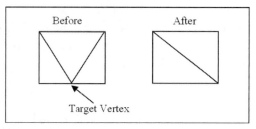

FIGURE 5.5.4 *Results of vertex removal.*

Edge Collapse

This method of optimization is used on all vertices of the mesh.

1. As in the vertex removal step, an edge table that contains edge information for all the edges in the mesh is required. Each entry in the table should contain the two vertices of that edge and the one or two polygons that share that edge.
2. For every unique vertex, choose a starting triangle that contains the vertex, and use the edge table to "walk" clockwise around the vertex to neighboring triangles that also contain the vertex. Continue to walk around the vertex until an edge that is collinear to the first edge is reached. If it isn't reached or you walk around to the starting vertex, this vertex is not a candidate for vertex removal. Return to Step 2 for the next vertex.

3. Remove the vertex and tessellate the n-gon that is left behind. A robust tessellation algorithm is required to avoid errors. An example method can be found in [deBerg00] (see Figure 5.5.5).

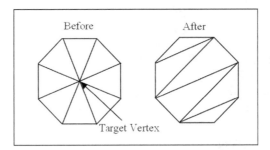

FIGURE 5.5.5   *Results of edge collapse.*

Implementation Details

Although this algorithm is fairly straightforward, implementation can be a nightmare. The most difficult part is getting the optimization code to work flawlessly. Not counting the optimization step, the implementation of the rest of the algorithm shouldn't take more than an afternoon for an experienced programmer to code. Getting the optimization code to work successfully under all conditions requires acknowledging the precision issues of 64-bit floats.

Logical Topology vs. Numerical Precision

The developer must accept the fact that there isn't enough numerical precision in a 64-bit float for this type of algorithm. It isn't uncommon to have triangles with all three vertices in the exact, bit-for-bit positions. It also isn't uncommon for vertices to be different by only the least significant bit of a 64-bit float. In these cases, numerical tests for collinearity or numerical computations of face normals are insufficient. Clipping along these edges will only produce degenerate edges, but this is fine as long as it is assumed beforehand.

Edge IDs

To implement the edge collapse optimization step successfully, numerical tests must be traded for topological tests. Since a numerical colinearity test cannot be trusted, an alternative approach is required. As a polygon is tessellated with the planes of the slicing far beam, all edges produced by a given plane that lie in that plane should share an edge ID. Similarly, edges created by a clipping plane that don't lie in the plane require their own edge IDs. This provides a trivial method for always detecting topological colinearity where numerical tests will ultimately fail. Figure 5.5.6 illustrates this.

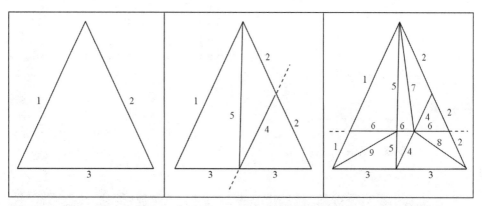

FIGURE 5.5.6 *All numbers in the image represent edge IDs. (Left) A single triangle. (Middle) The resulting polygons after the first clip plane with ID=4 slices through it. (Right) The resulting polygons after the second clip plane with ID=6 slices through it.*

Watertight Meshes and Clipping

Relying on the topology of a mesh requires knowledge of the connectivity properties. The simplest rule to follow is to keep the mesh "watertight." This simply means that no t-junctions should ever be created within the original mesh. This is accomplished in two ways.

The first means of maintaining a watertight mesh is the use of clipping planes. Developers are often tempted to do the most optimal thing and really optimize their clipping algorithm to clip only polygons that absolutely need to be clipped. This can result in t-junctions. Any clipping algorithm that never creates t-junctions is acceptable.

The second means of maintaining a watertight mesh comes for free due to the properties of the algorithm, but it is worth mentioning. After a polygon has been cut, there will be vertices along the shadow boundary that won't be candidates for vertex removal, because lit and shadowed polygons are optimized separately. An edge collapse will happen on the lit side of the edge first, creating a t-junction. This isn't a problem, since the very next step in the algorithm is to optimize the shadowed polygons. Immediately, a similar edge collapse will happen on the shadowed side of the vertex. The edge collapse along a shadow boundary cleans itself up.

Shadowing Dynamic Objects

As mentioned earlier, one of the goals of this technique is to provide a consistent integration of static scene shadows and dynamic stencil shadows. If this offline shadow-cutting algorithm is performed on a scene, the objects in the scene will clearly not cast shadows on dynamic objects in the scene. In many cases, this might be unnoticeable, but we need a solution in the general case.

One of the motivations behind using this method for static shadows is that you can use much lower resolution geometry for the shadow volumes that affect dynamic objects. This can dramatically reduce both the transform load and overdraw in your scene. In addition, the shadow volumes only need to be drawn when a dynamic object is in that light's frustum. Depending on the application, this can win back an enormous amount of performance.

Results

Figure 5.5.7 shows the results of applying the static shadow algorithm to a relatively dense environment. Notice how many interior edges and vertices have been removed from shadows on the floor.

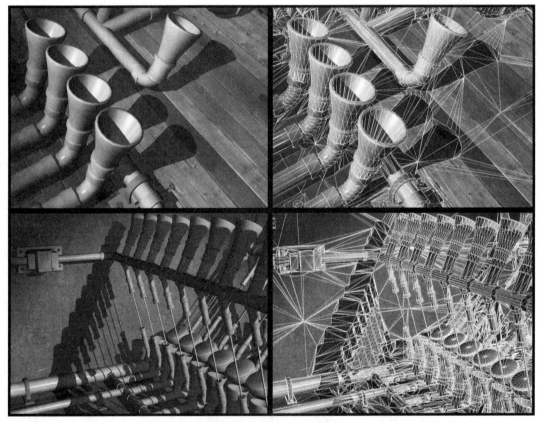

FIGURE 5.5.7 *Two scenes from the ATI RADEON 9700 Pipe Dream demo. (Left) Normal screen shots. (Right) Wireframe showing the results of this article.*

Conclusion

This article discussed a method for cutting hard shadows directly into scene geometry. This provides a consistent look for scenes that use stencil shadow volumes for dynamic characters and objects. This method also reduces the overdraw bottleneck associated with brute-force stencil shadow volumes that games are using today, and ultimately increases frame rates.

References

[deBerg00] de Berg, Mark, et al., "Polygon Triangulation," *Computational Geometry Algorithms and Applications, Second Edition*, pp. 45–61, 2000.

[Lengyel02] Lengyel, E., "T-Junction Elimination and Retriangulation," *Game Programming Gems 3*, Charles River Media, 2002.

[Vlachos02] Vlachos, A., and D. Card, "Computing Optimized Shadow Volumes for Complex Data Sets," *Game Programming Gems 3*, Charles River Media, 2002.

[Weiler77] Weiler, K., and P. Atherton, "Hidden Surface Removal Using Polygon Area Sorting," *Computer Graphics*, Vol. 11, pp. 214–222, 1977 (SIGGRAPH '77).

Figures provided by Eli Turner, ATI Research, Inc.

5.6

Adjusting Real-Time Lighting for Shadow Volumes and Optimized Meshes

Alex Vlachos and Chris Oat, ATI Research, Inc.

Alex@Vlachos.com, coat@ati.com

Lighting an entire mesh is well understood and presents no real, unexpected artifacts. However, when more complex rendering systems optimize the number of polygons being rendered, like backface-culling from the light's point of view, lighting artifacts are introduced. When culling is done based on face normals and lighting is done based on vertex normals, some adjustments are required. The same applies to self-shadowing meshes that use stencil shadow volumes, since the shadow volumes are extruded based on face normals. Additionally, bump mapping needs even further adjustment, because the normal has nothing to do with the geometric shape of the mesh. This article explores these problems and presents a solution that is accomplished entirely in the pixel shader.

The Lighting Problem

Given a mesh that is being lit based on vertex normals, it is important to understand the relationship between the vertex normals and the face normals with respect to lighting. Figure 5.6.1 shows a side view of two bordering polygons and how their interpolated vertex normals are used for lighting. While the face normal gives a negative result for $\vec{N} \cdot \vec{L}$, the interpolated vertex normal across that face yields a positive result. This discrepancy causes problems for several algorithms.

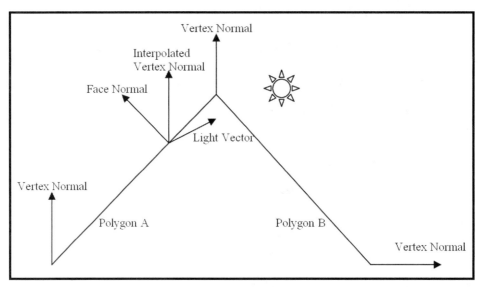

FIGURE 5.6.1   *If the face normal is used to compute light contribution across the face of polygon A, no light contribution will be calculated. Using the interpolated vertex normals will detect light contribution to the polygon. Culling polygon A because it is back-facing to the light would cause a lighting artifact across the boundary of polygons A and B.*

Operations on Face Normals

Certain operations related to lighting can be performed on a mesh prior to rasterization. These operations often require a mesh to be processed or modified based on the face normals, then later lit based on interpolated vertex normals. This discrepancy needs to be compensated for to avoid harsh lighting artifacts.

Shadow Volume Extrusion

Face normals are used to determine how a mesh is extruded for shadow volumes [Brennan02]. Because of this, instead of soft lighting on the silhouette of a mesh, a hard line appearing like a shadow boundary is introduced. As seen in Figure 5.6.1, polygon A would end up inside the shadow volume and receive no light, while polygon B would be well lit. This will cause a harsh lighting boundary between the two polygons. Figure 5.6.2 illustrates this in the rendering of a sphere with a single shadow volume.

Polygon Culling

Contemporary graphics engines that use programmable graphics accelerators might choose to sort geometry based on the number of lights that influence a given polygon. For example, all of the polygons that are influenced by zero lights are drawn using a shader that assumes zero lights, while polygons influenced by a single light are drawn using a shader that assumes a single light. The sphere to the far left in Figure 5.6.3 is an example of static scene geometry that has been preprocessed such that its polygons

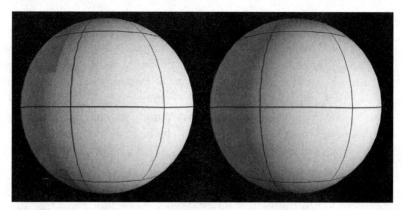

FIGURE 5.6.2   *(Left) A sphere is lit using vertex lighting and shadow volumes. Vertex lighting uses vertex normals to calculate illumination, while shadow volumes rely on polygon face normals. This results in a lighting discontinuity at the shadow border. (Right) Vertex lighting is adjusted so that light falloff transitions smoothly across the shadow volume border.*

have been separated into groups depending on the number of static scene lights that illuminate each polygon. Since, in this case, polygons will be binned according to their face normal and the direction of the light source(s), lighting discontinuities will arise because the face normal does not necessarily correspond to the normal used for calculating diffuse lighting. This lighting discontinuity is visible on the middle sphere in Figure 5.6.3. A hard lighting edge is seen along part of the border that separates the two-light shader and the one-light shader.

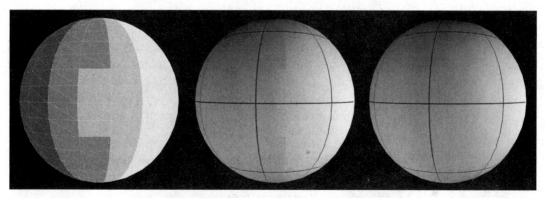

FIGURE 5.6.3   *(Left) A sphere is separated into multiple meshes depending on the number of scene lights that light its polygons. The brightest shaded mesh has three contributing scene lights, while the darkest shade has no contributing scene lights. (Center) Each mesh is then lit using a shader that corresponds to the number of contributing light sources. Light source contribution is determined using face normals during preprocessing, while lighting is calculated using vertex normals during runtime causing a lighting discontinuity. (Right) Diffuse lighting is adjusted so that lights falloff smoothly to compensate for the culling discrepancy.*

Adjusting Diffuse Lighting

There are two logical approaches to solving the problems just discussed. The first is to change our culling algorithm to cull polygons based on all three vertex normals instead of the single face normal. While this works well for the polygon culling problem, it doesn't apply to the shadow volume problem.

The better solution, which is also more general, is to compensate for the lighting discontinuities in the pixel shader. The basic idea is to scale and bias the diffuse term to create a new light falloff angle. Instead of light falling off at 90°, we empirically choose a smaller angle of about 75°. This lighting adjustment can be done for lighting based on interpolated vertex normals or per-pixel normals from a normal map, which are explored in the following two subsections.

Interpolated Vertex Normals

The following example is DirectX 9 HLSL code to scale and bias the diffuse lighting contribution:

```
float ComputeDiffuseAdjustment (float diffuseNdotL)
{
    return saturate ((diffuseNdotL * (5.0f/4.0f)) -
                (1.0f/4.0f));
}
```

The preceding function takes $\vec{N} \cdot \vec{L}$ (in this case, $\vec{N}$ is a vertex normal) as an argument and forces an early falloff. Essentially, the 0.25–1.0 range of the raw $\vec{N} \cdot \vec{L}$ result is scaled to fit the 0–1 range. Once $\vec{N} \cdot \vec{L}$ has been properly adjusted, the returned value can be modulated with the light color, material base color, and so forth.

Per-Pixel Normals from a Normal Map

A normal sampled from a normal map is handled slightly differently, since normal maps can vary wildly from their underlying geometric topology. In this case, we want to implement a similar algorithm to the one for interpolated vertex normals; however, we only want to compute a harsh falloff term to mask the bumped lighting artifacts. The following HLSL function adjusts diffuse lighting when using a normal map:

```
float ComputeDiffuseBumpAdjustment (float diffuseNdotL,
        float diffuseBumpNdotL)
{
    float adjustment =
            ComputeDiffuseAdjustment(diffuseBumpNdotL);
    adjustment *=  1.0f - (pow (1.0f -
            ComputeDiffuseAdjustment(diffuseNdotL), 8.0f));
    return saturate (adjustment);
}
```

This function makes two separate calls into the function from the previous section. The first call is used exactly the same as in the previous section, except we're feeding the function the diffuse lighting based on the per-pixel normal from the normal map, instead of the regular vertex-interpolated diffuse lighting. Since a normal map contains widely varying normals, we also need to introduce a harsh falloff term based on the interpolated vertex normals. Through empirical observation, we find that clamping the inverse of the adjusted diffuse lighting value raised to the eighth power produces acceptable results, as shown in Figure 5.6.4.

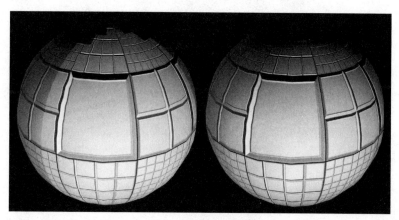

FIGURE 5.6.4 *(Left) A sphere that has been separated into multiple meshes depending on the number of static scene lights that light its polygons is drawn using a bump map for per-pixel lighting operations. Lighting discontinuities are seen where the per-pixel normal deviates significantly from the face normal. (Right) Diffuse lighting is adjusted to compensate for this discontinuity.*

Conclusion

Lighting-related operations are often performed using polygon face normals, either for optimization reasons or because of algorithmic necessity. This article demonstrated a technique for adjusting the diffuse lighting equation to compensate for lighting discontinuities that result from lighting operations dependent on surface normals.

References

[Brennan02] Brennan, Chris, "Shadow Volume Extrusion Using a Vertex Shader," *Direct3D ShaderX: Vertex Shader Tips and Tricks*, Wordware Publishing, Inc., 2002. Images provided by Eli Turner, ATI Research, Inc.

5.7

Real-Time Halftoning: Fast and Simple Stylized Shading

Bert Freudenberg, Maic Masuch, and Thomas Strothotte, University of Magdeburg

bert@isg.cs.uni-magdeburg.de,
masuch@isg.cs.uni-magdeburg.de,
tstr@isg.cs.uni-magdeburg.de

This article introduces halftoning as a way of implementing nonphotorealistic rendering styles for computer games. The technique uses only the conventional multitexturing pipeline on common hardware. We show how to create halftone screens for images that resemble pen-and-ink drawing styles, and how to implement fast halftone rendering with modest pixel shading hardware.

Introduction

In this article, we introduce a technique borrowed and adapted from noninteractive hardcopy to real-time environments. Similar approaches are great resources for inspiration. Some are less flexible [Lake00], [Praun01], while others are more complicated [Webb02].

Halftoning in its original form is the procedure used to print images with gray levels using only black ink. It does so by varying the size of ink dots, and thus, the ratio of paper area to inked area. Viewed from a distance, a certain tone is perceived. A similar effect is used when an artist is drawing a picture with pen and ink, where more lines are put in areas that should appear darker. Yet another variation is employed in engravings or woodcuts, where the width of lines is adjusted to depict variations in shading. All these styles can be recreated by applying real-time halftoning.

Similar to traditional halftoning, when the image intensity changes in a given neighborhood of pixels, pixels are not dimmed. Instead, *more* black pixels are shown while the remaining pixels stay white, so the overall perceived intensity is lower. One interesting difference between halftoning a static image versus an interactive environment is that the halftone screen is not fixed to the screen, but rather attached to the objects in 3D space. Otherwise, the objects would appear to "swim" behind the halftone screen, which is also known as the "shower-door" effect.

Principle

The basic ingredient in halftoning that determines the visual appearance most is the *halftone screen*. This is a grayscale texture containing *threshold* values. To create a halftoned image from a given input image, the intensity of each pixel is compared to the corresponding threshold value in the halftone screen, and a black or white pixel is written depending on the outcome of the comparison (see Figure 5.7.1). If H is the halftone screen threshold value and L is the target intensity, we could write the threshold function in a C-like fashion as

```
H > (1-L) ? 1 : 0.
```

Here, $(1-L)$ represents "darkness," which reflects the subtractive color model of ink on paper.

To make real-time halftoning work, we need a halftone screen texture, and a function to perform the threshold operation. The halftone texture specifies how the image intensity should be mapped into a black-and-white rendering. It can be as simple as the regular dot raster used to print the images in this book, or as complex as the brick texture in Figure 5.7.3.

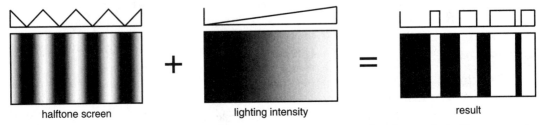

halftone screen   lighting intensity   result

FIGURE 5.7.1 *Traditional halftoning with a threshold function. Each value in the halftone screen is compared to the intensity value. If the halftone value is higher than the darkness (which is 1 minus intensity), a white pixel is generated; otherwise, a black pixel is generated.*

Creating Halftone Screens

Halftone screens can be created either procedurally or manually. The latter is more desirable, as it offers more artistic flexibility. One example of a procedural halftone screen is smooth grayscale stripes, as shown in Figure 5.7.1. This results in lines whose widths depend on the lighting, and resembles a woodcut printing style (see Figure 5.7.2). Other procedural screens can be created for hatching [Lake00], [Praun01].

To create a halftone screen by hand, we developed a layer-based process that yields nice results (see the three leftmost images in Figure 5.7.3). Each layer is drawn in black on transparent layers in Adobe Photoshop. As more layers accumulate, the screen gets darker and darker. This is exactly what we want for halftoning. When all

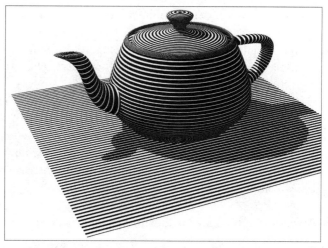

FIGURE 5.7.2 *Halftoning with grayscale stripes like in Figure 5.7.1 creates a woodcut-like style. Shading is conveyed by varying line widths.*

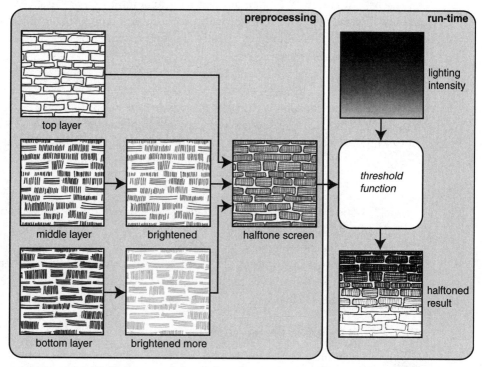

FIGURE 5.7.3 *Halftoning with layered strokes. Several stroke layers are combined into a single halftone texture by encoding the layer's priority in its gray level. At runtime, the lighting intensity is thresholded against this texture to produce a halftoned rendering. In the result, more strokes are displayed in regions of lower intensity.*

layers are painted, they are combined into one halftone screen by changing each layer into a distinct shade of gray. The basic layer remains black, whereas successive layers are assigned lighter grays. The compositing needs to be performed in reverse order, so the black layer is drawn on top of the lighter layers. The resulting image is exported as a single 8-bit grayscale texture.

This layer-based authoring worked well for us, but you can use any method to create the halftone texture. One way to think of the values in the halftone screen is that each pixel encodes a "priority" for drawing strokes—darker strokes have higher priority and get displayed first, even in bright regions. Lower-priority strokes (drawn in light gray) are only displayed in darker areas, whereas white parts of the halftone screen will always remain blank in the rendering, too.

A Threshold Function for Limited Pixel Shaders

For real-time halftoning, the threshold function, which takes a texture and an intensity value as input, has to be evaluated at each pixel. This can be implemented with a conditional operation that outputs black or white fragments depending on a comparison. While more advanced pixel shader versions offer a compare operation that can be used, the least common denominator in OpenGL is support for the `texture_env_combine_ARB` extension. We came up with a formula for a *smooth* threshold function (in contrast to the sharp function normally used for thresholding) that only uses functionality provided by this extension. In the following, H stands for the halftone screen, and L for the lighting intensity:

$$1 - 4(1 - (H + L))$$

Since we are dealing with colors here, every operation implicitly clamps its result to the [0,1] interval. Unfortunately, the straight implementation of this formula would need three texturing stages (sum, invert and scale, invert again), while some common graphics boards only provide two. With a little rearrangement, though, we get

$$1 - 4((1 - H) - L)$$

which can be implemented in two stages (scaled difference of inverted operand and inversion). When we experimented with higher values than the constant 4 in this equation, we lost one nice advantage of the smooth threshold function, which is that it produces anti-aliased images. This is a form of shader anti-aliasing that removes high image frequencies introduced by a shader (a sharp step function essentially has unlimited frequency and will alias at any resolution). (See Figure 5.7.4.)

Threshold Function Implementation

To implement the threshold function described in the previous section, two multitexturing stages need to be set up in the following way to perform the thresholding function:

```
// macro to keep lines short
#define TexEnv(pname, param) \
```

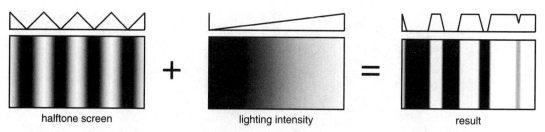

halftone screen   lighting intensity   result

FIGURE 5.7.4 *With a smooth threshold function, the resulting image is not only black and white; some gray levels are preserved. This reduces shader aliasing artifacts.*

```
glTexEnvi(GL_TEXTURE_ENV, pname, param)

// stage 0: smooth threshold function 4*((1-L)-H)
glActiveTexture(GL_TEXTURE0);
TexEnv(GL_TEXTURE_ENV_MODE, GL_COMBINE);
TexEnv(GL_COMBINE_RGB, GL_SUBTRACT);
TexEnv(GL_SOURCE0_RGB, GL_PREVIOUS);
TexEnv(GL_SOURCE1_RGB, GL_TEXTURE);
TexEnv(GL_OPERAND0_RGB, GL_ONE_MINUS_SRC_COLOR);
TexEnv(GL_OPERAND1_RGB, GL_SRC_COLOR);
TexEnv(GL_RGB_SCALE,  4);

// stage 1: invert function (1-previous)
glActiveTexture(GL_TEXTURE1);
TexEnv(GL_TEXTURE_ENV_MODE, GL_COMBINE);
TexEnv(GL_COMBINE_RGB,GL_REPLACE);
TexEnv(GL_SOURCE0_RGB,GL_PREVIOUS);
TexEnv(GL_OPERAND0_RGB, GL_ONE_MINUS_SRC_COLOR);
```

The first texture stage gets the per-vertex lighting value as SOURCE0 and the halftone texture as SOURCE1. The first operand is subtracted from one using the ONE_MINUS_SRC_COLOR input mapping, and the overall operation is set to SUBTRACT. Finally, the result is multiplied by four. The second texture stage only uses one operand and replaces its input with the inverse, again using the input mapping.

Note that you can perform all of this in the alpha portion of the texture combiners as well. This would free up the RGB portion for other uses. This equation can also be implemented in a shader program if the graphics hardware supports pixel shaders.

Example Implementation

To demonstrate how easy it is to integrate real-time halftoning into a traditional game engine [Shark3D], we converted a conventionally textured demo level [Requiem00] to a pen-and-ink comic style. In Figure 5.7.5, you can see the scene before and after our modification.

First, the textures were converted to grayscale. Similarly, the colored light sources were changed to grayscale. Some of the textures, like in the ceiling or the colored glass

FIGURE 5.7.5 *A conventionally textured and lit level (shown as inset) was converted into a dark comic style by employing real-time halftoning. Note how the shading is depicted by varying the number of strokes displayed.*

windows, looked good enough after the grayscale conversion even without further touchup. Others, most notably the walls and floor, were drawn in a pen-and-ink-like hatching style using the layer drawing technique described previously. Other changes include new textures for the candles' glow effects, and the adjustment of lighting intensity to create harder shadows. On the programming side, only the shaders had to be rewritten to implement the threshold function.

Conclusion

This article presented real-time halftoning, a simple and fast technique for nonphotorealistic shading suitable for games. It can provide a distinct look for an entire game, or for special sequences. One can imagine an introduction for a game where the main character reads a comic novel and gets drawn right into it. There are many nonphotorealistic visual styles yet to be explored in real-time graphics.

References

[Lake00] Lake, Adam, Carl Marshall, Mark Harris, and Marc Blackstein, "Stylized Rendering Techniques for Scalable Real-Time 3D Animation," *Proceedings of*

NPAR 2000, Symposium on Non-Photorealistic Animation and Rendering, pp. 13–20.

[Praun01] Praun, Emil, Hughes Hoppe, Matthew Webb, and Adam Finkelstein, "Real-Time Hatching," *Proceedings of SIGGRAPH 2001*, pp. 581–586.

[Requiem00] Punkt im Raum, "Requiem: A Technology Study for the Shark 3D Engine," available online at *www.punkt-im-raum.com/eng/projekte_requiem.shtml*.

[Shark3D] Spinor GmbH, "Renderer and Shader Architecture," Shark3D engine technology white papers, available online at *www.shark3d.com/goto/technology_render.html*.

[Webb02] Webb, Matthew, Emil Praun, Adam Finkelstein, and Hugues Hoppe, "Fine Tone Control in Hardware Hatching," *Proceedings of NPAR 2002, International Symposium on Non Photorealistic Animation and Rendering*, pp. 53–58.

5.8

Techniques to Apply Team Colors to 3D Models

Greg Seegert, Stainless Steel Studios

gseegert@alum.wpi.edu

Applying visually appealing team color to 3D models is an important technique in any game with multiple players, whether AI or human controlled. This article explores several techniques for applying team color to arbitrary 3D models. The implementation of each technique is carefully explained, and the benefits and drawbacks of each method are discussed.

The different methods to apply team color to 3D models could affect how the art team creates assets for your game. Thus, it is important to make an informed decision regarding the appropriate team color technique as early in a project as possible. Deciding on the technique that best meets your project's goals could save countless hours of art time.

What Is Team Color?

Team color is a commonly used technique in many genres of games. The primary usefulness of team color is to quickly distinguish between teams in a 3D game. It is also helpful in avoiding unnecessary strain on the art schedule and the memory waste of creating custom models or textures for each supported team in a game. For example, most real-time strategy games use this technique to distinguish between troops and property owned by different players. The techniques discussed are not limited to distinguishing teams; they can easily be adapted for other purposes, such as customizing player vehicles in a racing or spaceship simulation game.

Team Color Algorithms

There are several algorithms to apply team color to 3D models, each with its own set of advantages and disadvantages. We will look at the following algorithms: using unique textures for each team color, tinting model polygons to the appropriate team color, texture masking using multitexturing, texture masking using multiple passes, and advanced pixel shader effects.

Unique Textures

This technique is the most brute-force implementation covered. It involves simply creating a unique texture for every team color you want to support in your game. As such, it requires almost no programming, while affording the highest level of artistic control. The major disadvantage of this technique is the large amount of memory that is required.

Advantages
- Almost no programming time to implement.
- Highest level of artistic control over the resulting textures.

Disadvantages
- Large amounts of texture memory wasted.
- Difficult for the art team to maintain changes to the textures.
- Potentially lower quality textures if texture resolution is sacrificed to alleviate memory constraints.

Implementation
- None.

Polygon Tinting

Polygon tinting is the method whereby artist-designated polygons on the mesh are tinted the color of the player's team. This is a fairly common method used in many games, but has several serious limitations.

Advantages
- No additional texture memory required for any number of teams.

Disadvantages
- *Limited artistic control.* The artists are forced to designate large polygonal areas as team color polygons, which can result in a less attractive model. This technique further impacts art asset creation, as the artists must avoid using color on these polygons, so that the proper team color can be displayed.
- *Rendering performance.* The mesh must be drawn in two separate draw calls with a render state change in between them, which can limit opportunities for batching and potentially affect rendering performance. However, it is possible to avoid this through the clever use of vertex shaders.

DirectX Implementation

```
/* Set material to pure white. */
D3DMATERIAL9   theMaterial;
theMaterial.Diffuse.r = theMaterial.Ambient.r = 1.0F;
```

```
theMaterial.Diffuse.g = theMaterial.Ambient.g = 1.0F;
theMaterial.Diffuse.b = theMaterial.Ambient.b = 1.0F;
theMaterial.Diffuse.a = theMaterial.Ambient.a = 1.0F;
mD3DDevice->SetMaterial(&theMaterial);

/* Texture Stage 0: Setup the texture normally. */
mD3DDevice->SetTextureStageState(0, D3DTSS_COLOROP,   D3DTOP_MODU-
LATE);
mD3DDevice->SetTextureStageState(0, D3DTSS_COLORARG1, D3DTA_TEXTURE);
mD3DDevice->SetTextureStageState(0, D3DTSS_COLORARG2, D3DTA_DIFFUSE);
mD3DDevice->SetTextureStageState(0, D3DTSS_ALPHAOP,   D3DTOP_MODU-
LATE);
mD3DDevice->SetTextureStageState(0, D3DTSS_ALPHAARG1, D3DTA_TEXTURE);
mD3DDevice->SetTextureStageState(0, D3DTSS_ALPHAARG2, D3DTA_DIFFUSE);

/* Texture Stage 1: Disabled. */
mD3DDevice->SetTextureStageState(1, D3DTSS_COLOROP,   D3DTOP_DISABLE);
mD3DDevice->SetTextureStageState(1, D3DTSS_ALPHAOP,   D3DTOP_DISABLE);

/* Draw only the non-team color polygons of the model. */
mD3DDevice->DrawIndexedPrimitive(D3DPT_TRIANGLELIST ...

/* Set the team color to the material (this example uses yellow). */
theMaterial.Diffuse.r = theMaterial.Ambient.r = 1.0F;
theMaterial.Diffuse.g = theMaterial.Ambient.g = 1.0F;
theMaterial.Diffuse.b = theMaterial.Ambient.b = 0.0F;
theMaterial.Diffuse.a = theMaterial.Ambient.a = 1.0F;
mD3DDevice->SetMaterial(&theMaterial);

/* Draw only the team color polygons. */
mD3DDevice->DrawIndexedPrimitive(D3DPT_TRIANGLELIST ...
```

Texture Masks, Multitexturing

This technique involves using the alpha channel of the model's texture to allow the artist to essentially "paint" areas of team color in the texture. This technique offers excellent freedom to the artists, low texture memory costs, and high performance on supporting hardware.

Advantages

- *High level of artistic control.* The artist will be able to essentially paint areas of team color in the alpha channel of the texture. This will allow the artist to create intricate designs, patterns, and to fully integrate team color into the model. For example, a military vehicle could have faded and scratched numeric paint designations smoothly blended in with the camouflage paint scheme, all in team color.
- *Less texture memory required.* As this technique makes use of the alpha channel of the texture, no additional textures will be needed to specify any number of team colors. If high-resolution team color is not a requirement for the model, the use

of a 1-bit alpha channel, coupled with various texture compression algorithms capable of compressing 1-bit alpha channels, provides further advantages to memory consumption.

- *Improved performance.* On models that do not require the use of the alpha channel for transparency, the entire model can be rendered in one draw call. Additionally, hardware that supports the required multitexturing techniques will benefit from high performance.

Disadvantages

- *Hardware compatibility.* Certain graphics hardware might not be able to support the required texture stages and operations. This causes the technique to be unusable on these systems, which could be a severe problem if team colors are a gameplay critical feature.
- *Precludes use of the alpha channel for transparency.* Using the alpha channel to specify team colors means that the alpha channel cannot be used for transparency as well. One workaround to this issue is to have the artist designate which polygons use this technique, and which polygons on the mesh do not. The required polygons can then be rendered with the technique, while the other polygons can be rendered normally. This could impact performance, however, as the model must now be drawn in multiple draw calls. It is possible to limit the negative impact this would have on performance by only using texture specified transparency when absolutely necessary. On more recent hardware that supports many multi-texture stages or pixel shaders, this isn't an issue.

DirectX Implementation

```
/* Put the team color in TFACTOR (this example uses yellow). */
mD3DDevice->SetRenderState(D3DRS_TEXTUREFACTOR,
D3DCOLOR_COLORVALUE(1.0F, 1.0F, 0.0F, 1.0F));

/* Texture Stage 0: Blend between the texture color
 * and TFACTOR based on the textures alpha. We use
 * only the diffuse for alpha. */
mD3DDevice->SetTextureStageState(0, D3DTSS_COLOROP,   D3DTOP_BLENDTEX-
TUREALPHA);
mD3DDevice->SetTextureStageState(0, D3DTSS_COLORARG1, D3DTA_TEXTURE);
mD3DDevice->SetTextureStageState(0, D3DTSS_COLORARG2, D3DTA_TFACTOR);
mD3DDevice->SetTextureStageState(0, D3DTSS_ALPHAOP,   D3DTOP_SELEC-
TARG1);
mD3DDevice->SetTextureStageState(0, D3DTSS_ALPHAARG1, D3DTA_DIFFUSE);
mD3DDevice->SetTextureStageState(0, D3DTSS_ALPHAARG2, D3DTA_DIFFUSE);

/* Texture Stage 1: Modulate current with diffuse to get lighting.
 * Do nothing with alpha. */
mD3DDevice->SetTextureStageState(1, D3DTSS_COLOROP,   D3DTOP_MODU-
LATE);
mD3DDevice->SetTextureStageState(1, D3DTSS_COLORARG1, D3DTA_CURRENT);
```

```
mD3DDevice->SetTextureStageState(1, D3DTSS_COLORARG2, D3DTA_DIFFUSE);
mD3DDevice->SetTextureStageState(1, D3DTSS_ALPHAOP,  D3DTOP_SELEC-
TARG1);
mD3DDevice->SetTextureStageState(1, D3DTSS_ALPHAARG1, D3DTA_CURRENT);
mD3DDevice->SetTextureStageState(1, D3DTSS_ALPHAARG2, D3DTA_CURRENT);

/* Texture Stage 2: Disabled. */
mD3DDevice->SetTextureStageState(2, D3DTSS_COLOROP,  D3DTOP_DISABLE);
mD3DDevice->SetTextureStageState(2, D3DTSS_ALPHAOP,  D3DTOP_DISABLE);

/* Render model. */
mD3DDevice->DrawIndexedPrimitive(D3DPT_TRIANGLELIST ...
```

Texture Masks, Multipass

It is possible to achieve identical results to the multitexturing technique by using a multipass solution. This technique requires parts of the mesh to be rendered twice. The first time, the mesh is rendered normally. During the second pass, the mesh is tinted the desired team color and the blend modes are inverted so that the mesh is only rendered where there is transparency in the alpha channel of the texture.

Advantages

- *Good hardware compatibility.* The advantages of this technique are identical to those of the multitexture solution, with the added benefit of being very compatible with a wide range of graphics hardware.

Disadvantages

- *Performance concerns.* This technique introduces performance concerns, as the number of polygons rendered in the mesh could double. Moreover, the change of the render state requires the complete mesh to be rendered in two passes. The number of additional polygons rendered can be minimized if the artist is able to specify the minimum polygons that need to be team color enabled.

DirectX Implementation

```
/* Set material to pure white. */
D3DMATERIAL9  theMaterial;
theMaterial.Diffuse.r = theMaterial.Ambient.r = 1.0f;
theMaterial.Diffuse.g = theMaterial.Ambient.g = 1.0f;
theMaterial.Diffuse.b = theMaterial.Ambient.b = 1.0f;
theMaterial.Diffuse.a = theMaterial.Ambient.a = 1.0f;
mD3DDevice->SetMaterial(&theMaterial);

/* Setup normal blending. */
mD3DDevice->SetRenderState(D3DRS_SRCBLEND, D3DBLEND_SRCALPHA);
mD3DDevice->SetRenderState(D3DRS_DESTBLEND,D3DBLEND_INVSRCALPHA);

/* Texture Stage 0: Setup the texture normally, letting
```

```
 * just the diffuse alpha through. */
mD3DDevice->SetTextureStageState(0, D3DTSS_COLOROP,   D3DTOP_MODU-
LATE);
mD3DDevice->SetTextureStageState(0, D3DTSS_COLORARG1, D3DTA_TEXTURE);
mD3DDevice->SetTextureStageState(0, D3DTSS_COLORARG2, D3DTA_DIFFUSE);
mD3DDevice->SetTextureStageState(0, D3DTSS_ALPHAOP,   D3DTOP_SELEC-
TARG2);
mD3DDevice->SetTextureStageState(0, D3DTSS_ALPHAARG1, D3DTA_TEXTURE);
mD3DDevice->SetTextureStageState(0, D3DTSS_ALPHAARG2, D3DTA_DIFFUSE);

/* Texture Stage 1: Disabled. */
mD3DDevice->SetTextureStageState(1, D3DTSS_COLOROP,   D3DTOP_DISABLE);
mD3DDevice->SetTextureStageState(1, D3DTSS_ALPHAOP,   D3DTOP_DISABLE);

/* Draw all the model's polygons. */
mD3DDevice->DrawIndexedPrimitive(D3DPT_TRIANGLELIST ...

/* Invert blend modes. */
mD3DDevice->SetRenderState(D3DRS_SRCBLEND,   D3DBLEND_INVSRCALPHA);
mD3DDevice->SetRenderState(D3DRS_DESTBLEND, D3DBLEND_SRCALPHA);

/* Set the team color to the material (this example uses yellow). */
theMaterial.Diffuse.r = theMaterial.Ambient.r = 1.0f;
theMaterial.Diffuse.g = theMaterial.Ambient.g = 1.0f;
theMaterial.Diffuse.b = theMaterial.Ambient.b = 0.0f;
theMaterial.Diffuse.a = theMaterial.Ambient.a = 1.0f;
mD3DDevice->SetMaterial(&theMaterial);

/* Texture Stage 0: Use just the diffuse for color, and texture for
alpha. */
mD3DDevice->SetTextureStageState(0, D3DTSS_COLOROP,   D3DTOP_SELEC-
TARG2);
mD3DDevice->SetTextureStageState(0, D3DTSS_COLORARG1, D3DTA_TEXTURE);
mD3DDevice->SetTextureStageState(0, D3DTSS_COLORARG2, D3DTA_DIFFUSE);
mD3DDevice->SetTextureStageState(0, D3DTSS_ALPHAOP,   D3DTOP_SELEC-
TARG1);
mD3DDevice->SetTextureStageState(0, D3DTSS_ALPHAARG1, D3DTA_TEXTURE);
mD3DDevice->SetTextureStageState(0, D3DTSS_ALPHAARG2, D3DTA_DIFFUSE);

/* Texture Stage 1: Disabled. */
mD3DDevice->SetTextureStageState(1, D3DTSS_COLOROP,   D3DTOP_DISABLE);
mD3DDevice->SetTextureStageState(1, D3DTSS_ALPHAOP,   D3DTOP_DISABLE);

/* Draw only the team color polygons again. */
mD3DDevice->DrawIndexedPrimitive(D3DPT_TRIANGLELIST ...
```

Advanced Texture Mask, Pixel Shader Implementation

The use of pixel shaders in rendering team color affords many opportunities to improve on the team color technique. It is relatively simple to emulate the texture masking techniques in a pixel shader, but pixel shaders also offer many opportunities to enhance the effect. Potential areas of improvement include using multiple team colors or subtle hue shifts per model, a different lighting model applied to the team color areas, view-dependent special effects, and more flexibility in the application of multiple textures. The sample code on the companion CD-ROM includes a technique where two team colors are blended via a second texture whose UV coordinates are altered based on an anisotropic reflectance. A specular term is also added to the team color areas to increase the perceived "shininess" of the team color, and to demonstrate different lighting.

Advantages

- Maximum implementation flexibility and the ability to apply special effects that would be extremely difficult or impossible to implement using the fixed function pipeline.

Disadvantages

- *Hardware compatibility.* If some of the target graphics hardware does not support pixel shaders, an alternate technique will need to be used.

ON THE CD

Implementation

- Please see the companion CD-ROM for the full vertex and pixel shader listings.

A Practical Example

At Stainless Steel Studios, we decided to improve upon the team color technique used in our first title, *Empire Earth*. *Empire Earth* used the polygon tinting algorithm, which suited the low polygon models and the target platform. However, during the development of our next title, *Empires: Dawn of the Modern World*, it quickly became apparent that the archaic polygon tinting technique would be insufficient for many of our high detail models. The lack of artistic control caused frustration among the art staff, and degraded the overall quality of the new models. Rapidly prototyping several algorithms to remedy this situation resulted in some of the techniques discussed in this article. However, our solution was more complex than simply adopting one algorithm.

Support for the Polygon Tinting Technique

Despite its disadvantages, it was important for us to continue to support the polygon tinting technique. While new art assets came online, existing assets needed a method to render team color. Moreover, the polygon tinting technique proved to be completely adequate for certain models, such as buildings and some vehicles, as their blocky form did not necessarily require the intricate detail of the other methods.

Support for the Multitexturing Texture Mask Technique

The texture masking technique proved to be the ideal technique for *Empires: Dawn of the Modern World*. Although this technique afforded the art team excellent artistic control, we discovered potential problems. The additional alpha channel caused an increase in the texture size. This problem was addressed through the use of 1-bit alpha channels and DXTC (DirectX texture compression format) where appropriate. Another obstacle included the use of a multitexturing technique. Multitexturing precluded this technique from working on every graphics card we wanted to support. The hardware compatibility issue was successfully addressed using the multipass technique.

Support for the Multipass Texture Mask Technique

To support the gameplay critical team color technique, it became imperative to address the incompatibilities exposed by the multitexturing technique. Simulating the effects of the multitexture technique through multiple passes proved to be a sufficient workaround. On graphics hardware unable to support the multitexturing technique, the rendering engine would fall back to the multipass solution.

Performance Concerns

We took several steps to address performance concerns. As mentioned previously, the art team was encouraged to use 1-bit alpha whenever possible to reduce the impact of the texture memory footprint. Moreover, the multitexturing technique lends itself to the best performance possible when rendering the model in a single draw call. However, this could require the model to be rendered twice on graphics hardware unable to support the necessary multitexturing stages. Thus, we decided that team color polygons would be limited to a fixed percentage of the total number of polygons in the model. This required us to render all models with team color in two separate draw calls, but at the same time reduced the performance impact of the multipass fallback algorithm.

On the CD-ROM

ON THE CD

The accompanying code includes a DirectX 9.0 application that showcases each of the techniques discussed here on models from Stainless Steel Studios' game, *Empires: Dawn of the Modern World*. The sample code also includes an advanced technique using vertex and pixel shaders.

Conclusion

In this article, we explored various techniques that can be used to render 3D models with team colors. Each technique has its own strengths and weaknesses, which can be evaluated early in a project to determine the best solution for a particular game. A carefully chosen method of team color can save countless hours of art and programming time, while increasing the overall quality of the models in your game and supporting a large number of players with a much smaller set of models.

Fast Sepia Tone Conversion

Marwan Y. Ansari,
ATI Research, Inc.
mansari@ati.com

Achieving a stylized look via post-processing is becoming increasingly prevalent in gaming. One such technique is converting an image from RGB space to sepia tone. Sepia tone is a color space that is used to give images an aged or antique feel. Color conversion from RGB to sepia has usually been performed by mapping an RGB color into a lookup table. Although this technique is simple and effective, we have found a simpler and faster way to perform the same conversion with just a few pixel shader instructions and no table lookup.

To perform the conversion, we need to transform our RGB sample from the input image into YIQ space, process it, and then transform it back to RGB space. This article describes both the general approach to the conversion and an optimized method.

Background

YIQ space is similar to YUV space and is sometimes used in television broadcasts [Jack93]. It is defined as a linear combination of the R, G, and B values. Colors can be converted to and from YIQ space via a simple matrix multiply, as shown in [Foley96].

The matrix to convert an RGB sample into YIQ is

$$M = \begin{matrix} 0.299 & 0.587 & 0.114 \\ 0.596 & -0.275 & -0.321 \\ 0.212 & -0.523 & 0.311 \end{matrix}$$

The first row of M computes the luminance of the input RGB sample—the Y component in YIQ—while the second and third rows encode the chromaticity into I and Q [Foley96].

The matrix to convert YIQ back to RGB is M's inverse:

$$M' = \begin{matrix} 1.0 & 0.956 & 0.620 \\ 1.0 & -0.272 & -0.647 \\ 1.0 & -1.108 & 1.705 \end{matrix}$$

General Approach

First let's discuss the brute-force method of this conversion before we discuss optimizations.

1. Convert the RGB sample to YIQ via a matrix multiply with M.
2. Replace the I and Q components with 0.2 and 0.0, respectively.
3. Convert the YIQ value back to RGB via a matrix multiply with M'.

The interesting part of this operation is the replacement of I and Q with 0.2 and 0.0. To really understand what is happening here, let's take a look at the conversion from YIQ to RGB. The operation $M'[YIQ]^T$ is expanded to

$$R' = I + 0.956 * I + 0.620 * Q$$
$$G' = I - 0.272 * I - 0.647 * Q$$
$$B' = I - 1.108 * I + 1.705 * Q$$

Replacing I with 0.2 and Q with 0.0, the equations can be simplified and rewritten as

$$R' = Y + 0.191$$
$$G' = Y - 0.054$$
$$B' = Y - 0.221$$

We can see here that this operation simply replaces the color channels with offsets of the computed luminance, resulting in a sepia tone image.

The values 0.2 and 0.0 were determined by experimentation, and other values might look better in different applications. It is up to the programmer or artist to find the right constants that look best for their application.

Clearly, this method can also be used to convert grayscale images directly to sepia tone. Since the important input into this process is just luminance, this method is ideal for such a conversion.

Optimization

Having rewritten the preceding color-space conversion as simple offsets from the computed luminance, it is easy to see how to optimize this algorithm to just a few instructions. Since the only work required is computing the luminance value of the RGB sample and then adding a constant, we can reduce the work to just two operations: a dot product and an addition. This is much more efficient than performing the matrix multiplies to and from YIQ space or storing a lookup table for the conversion.

This optimized algorithm is implemented here in the DirectX 9 High-Level Shading Language (HLSL):

```
sampler inputImage;

float4 Sepia_Optimized(float2 tc : TEXCOORD0) : COLOR
{
```

```
float  Y;
float4 c, currFrameSample;
float3 IntensityConverter= {0.299, 0.587, 0.114};
float4 sepiaConvert = {0.191, -0.054, -0.221, 0.0};

// get sample
currFrameSample = tex2D(inputImage, tc);

// get intensity value (Y part of YIQ)
Y  = dot(IntensityConverter, currFrameSample);

// Convert to Sepia Tone by adding constant
c =  Y + sepiaConvert;

return c;
}
```

As expected, this HLSL code compiles to just two arithmetic operations.

```
ps_1_1
def c0, 0.299, 0.587, 0.114, 0
def c1, 0.191, -0.054, -0.221, 0
tex t0
dp3 r0, c0, t0
add r0, r0, c1
```

Conclusion

In this article, we showed that conversion of a color image to sepia tone does not require a lookup table, since the conversion can be performed in real-time using just two pixel shader operations. Using this method will save memory and time while still giving acceptable results.

References

[Foley96] Foley, James, Andries van Dam, et al., *Computer Graphics: Principles and Practice, Second Edition*, Addison-Wesley, 1996.
[Jack93] Jack, Keith, *Video Demystified: A Handbook for the Digital Engineer*, High-Text, 1993.

5.10

Dynamic Gamma Using Sampled Scene Luminance

Michael Dougherty
and Dave McCoy

mdougher@hotmail.com,
david.mccoy@comcast.net

The human eye constantly samples the brightness of available light and dilates the pupil in response. This variable sensitivity allows it to operate under a much wider range of lighting conditions from dark to bright. By sampling the frame buffer and adjusting the output gamma based on analysis of the data, the technique outlined in this article is able to simulate this type of variable sensitivity and make much better use of video's limited dynamic range. The same technique also allows the simulation of a number of visual phenomena that occur as the eye responds to changing, high dynamic range lighting.

Modulus Lighting

Because diffuse modulus lighting is multiplicative (Light Color ∗ Material Color), white or even bright pixels tend to be rare in game images. Anything other than a pure white light source shining on a pure white material will result in a shade darker than white. No matter how bright the light source, a gray material will never be drawn any lighter than it starts. This is because real-time lighting calculations are performed at the same precision as our displays. The latest generation of real-time graphics hardware allows for higher precision shading calculations, but the ubiquitous diffuse modulation based lighting on current fixed precision 24-bit hardware doesn't allow for the expression of light sources brighter than 1.0.

The upshot of all this is that most games fail to use the full range of video's already limited dynamic range, and output is often darker and lower contrast than ideal. Our article shows how to compensate for this deficiency by simulating the eye's response to changing lighting conditions in real-time.

Limited Dynamic Range

Figure 5.10.1 is a screen capture with a fairly typical brightness distribution. Figure 5.10.2, a histogram of the image's luminance (brightness), shows that the image does not fully exploit the available dynamic range and is distinctly biased toward darker values. As in many current games, the output is rather dingy in appearance, as if a dull film had formed on our monitor screen. Supposedly bright sunlit scenes look as dreary as an all-too-common rainy Redmond, Washington day.

FIGURE 5.10.1   *A typical outdoor scene using modulus lighting.*

FIGURE 5.10.2   *Luminance histogram of Figure 5.10.1.*

If video monitors were about 10,000 times brighter, our games could replicate the full range of light our eyes can detect, and our eyes would react to game graphics more like they react to reality. Unfortunately, video monitors aren't up to the challenge. The brightest light a video screen can produce is only about 100 times brighter than the darkest, and we have to simulate the eye's reaction to diverse lighting conditions with output that's dimmer than a 50-watt light bulb.

Optimization of Images

Generally speaking, if the eye observes little or no bright light, it opens the pupil wider to admit more light. Analogously, we can analyze an image, and if we find that it contains few or no bright pixels, we can appropriately expand the brightness of the output. This gives us the ability to respond to varying brightness levels in the game with output optimized to the dynamic range of our display. Interestingly enough, this actually frees artists and designers to develop environments with darker and brighter levels with less concern about the suitability of the output. In addition to creating more pleasingly balanced, saturated, and higher-contrast images, this post-processing step also results in the brightest pixels in the image being boosted to very high brightness levels. This results in realistic over-saturation that is typical of what we see when bright lights illuminate light-colored surfaces. Figure 5.10.3 shows the same image data as Figure 5.10.1 after dynamic range expansion. The histogram of the expanded image is shown in Figure 5.10.4.

FIGURE 5.10.3 *Modulus lit scene after adjustment using dynamic gamma.*

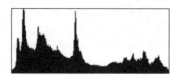

FIGURE 5.10.4 *Luminance histogram of Figure 5.10.3.*

Just as our eyes can never admit enough light to make a moonless night as bright as day, the amount of the adjustment our algorithm executes can be arbitrarily limited to avoid undesirable results. Extreme brightening of very dark images can lead to quantization artifacts due to the precision limitations of 24-bit color. The addition of some high-frequency detail to textures can greatly mitigate any quantizing that occurs.

Variable Sensitivity to Light

Beyond producing images with the best possible dynamic range under widely varying lighting conditions, the eye's variable sensitivity results in a number of interesting phenomena. For example, our perception of light sources is quite different under different overall lighting conditions. A flashlight that is blinding at night is only barely perceivable in full daylight. Our algorithm produces similar effects. Brighter pixels are boosted in brightness far more in a predominantly dark image than they are in a generally light one. This is shown in Figures 5.10.5 and 5.10.6.

FIGURE 5.10.5   *Already bright pixels are not significantly boosted in a generally bright image.*

FIGURE 5.10.6   *Identically bright lens flares and brightly lit surfaces are biased much brighter in a predominantly dark image.*

Transitions

Since it takes time for the pupil to dilate, transitions between dark and bright lighting conditions can result in our perceiving lighting changes more dramatically. Walking from a darkened movie theatre into the full daylight, one is bathed in blinding brilliance. Moving from a bright environment into a darker one similarly produces a plunge into darkness until our eyes adjust. The speed of adjustment of our technique can be regulated to produce similar effects. This is shown in Figures 5.10.7 through 5.10.11. In each case, the left frame shows the unaltered picture, and the right frame shows the image after gamma adjustment.

FIGURE 5.10.7 *In the darker interior, the algorithm expands the dynamic range, effectively brightening the image.*

FIGURE 5.10.8 *Still adjusted to the dark interior, the outdoor sun appears brilliant.*

FIGURE 5.10.9 *The algorithm begins adjustment to the brighter exterior scene.*

FIGURE 5.10.10   *The algorithm has now adjusted to the brighter exterior.*

FIGURE 5.10.11   *With gamma levels biased for exterior brightness levels, the interior now appears dark.*

Beyond producing more realistic imagery, this can enhance gameplay. For example, it takes a moment to scan for enemies when entering a dark environment from the bright outside. Enemies who approach with the sun behind them can be obscured by the glare. Flash-bang grenades can momentarily blind the opponent.

Algorithm

The algorithm to perform dynamic gamma is quite simple and can be broken into discrete steps. The CPU and GPU overhead is extremely low. Not all of the steps need to be done every frame, further reducing the effective performance overhead. The overall steps of the algorithm are outlined in Figure 5.10.12.

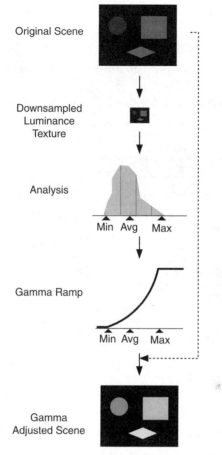

FIGURE 5.10.12   *Dynamic gamma step by step.*

Step 1: Downsample the Scene While Applying a Luminance Transform

First, the scene is downsampled using the GPU while a luminance transform is applied. The final rendered image is used as a texture, and a much smaller 8-bit-per-channel texture is set as the render target. We have found that a target size of the original scene size divided by 10 is sufficient. For example, a 640 x 480 scene would only require a 64 x 48 8-bit luminance texture. Moreover, since we are interested in the minimum and maximum luminance of a scene, we have found that point sampling is preferred over bilinear filtering to avoid artificial brightening of the dimmest pixel and artificial dimming of the brightest pixel. The luminance transform is done in a pixel shader.

$$Luminance = 0.30 * R + 0.59 * G + 0.11 * B$$

Step 2: Distribution Analysis of Luminance Texture

Next, the luminance texture is analyzed using the CPU. On PC systems, the small texture must be copied from GPU memory to CPU memory. On systems with a unified memory architecture, the video-memory to system-memory copy is not required.

The luminance distribution is generated by stepping though the small texture and counting the number of pixels per luminance value. The luminance distribution is then analyzed to determine the instantaneous minimum, maximum, and average luminance values of the scene. To eliminate outliers, lower and upper percentages are used to calculate the minimum and maximum. The average is defined to be at the fiftieth percentile.

```
struct Histogram
{
    float Lum[255];   // Lum[i] = fraction of pixels at the
                      //    ith luminance value
    float Min;        // smallest luminance value
    float Max;        // largest luminance value
    float Avg;        // average luminance value
};

struct LuminanceImage
{
    uint NumPixels;
    byte* pPixels;    // Each pixel is one byte since it
                      // only holds luminance data.
};

void BuildNormalizedHistogram( const LuminanceImage* pImg,
                               Histogram* pHG )
{
    // percentages used to remove outliers
    const float LowerPercent = 0.05f;
    const float UpperPercent = 0.95f;

    // 50th percentile
    const float AveragePercent = 0.50f;

    // Build the normalized histogram by summing the
    // fraction of pixels per luminance value.
    memset( &pHG->Lum, 0, 255 * sizeof(float) );
    float InvNumPixels = 1.0f/pImg->NumPixels;
    for( uint i = 0; i < pImg->NumPixels; i++ )
        pHG->Lum[pImg->pPixels[i]] += InvNumPixels;

    // find the histogram min, max, and average
    float Sum = 0.0f;
    for( byte c = 0; c < 255; c++ )
    {
        Sum += pHG->Lum[c];
        if( Sum <= LowerPercent )
```

```
                        pHG->Min = c/255.0f;
                else if( Sum <= AveragePercent )
                        pHG->Avg = c/255.0f;
                else if ( Sum <= UpperPercent )
                        pHG->Max = c/255.0f;
                else
                        break;
        }
}
```

Step 3: Update the Current Gamma Ramp

Next, the minimum, maximum, and average values that are used to build the gamma ramp are adjusted over time to simulate the eye's response to brightness and darkness.

```
struct GammaRamp
{
    byte Ramp[255];  // current ramp values
    float Min;        // current min
    float Max;        // current max
    float Avg;        // current average
};

void UpdateGammaRamp( const Histogram* pHG,
                      float Dt,
                      GammaRamp* pGR )
{
    // The current value is updated if the change is
    // greater than delta.
    const float Delta = 0.01f;

    // The following values can be updating dynamically to
    // affect the time it takes to adjust to varying scene
    // luminance.
    const float DMinDt = 0.1f;  // change in min over time
    const float DMaxDt = 0.1f;  // change in max over time
    const float DAvgDt = 0.1f;  // change in average over
                                //   time

    // Update the current min, max, and average over time.
    float Change;
    Change = pHG->Min - pGR->Min;
    if( fabsf( Change ) > Delta )
        pGR->Min += sign(Change)*DMinDt*Dt;
    Change = pHG->Avg - pGR->Avg;
    if( fabsf( Change ) > Delta )
        pGR->Avg += sign(Change)*DAvgDt*Dt;
    Change = pHG->Max - pGR->Max;
    if( fabsf( Change ) > Delta )
        pGR->Max += sign(Change)*DMaxDt*Dt;

    // Clamp the values for min, max, and average to
    // prevent overcompensation due to extremely dark or
```

```
// bright scenes.
const float LargestMin = 0.25f;
const float SmallestMax = 0.50f;
clamp( &pGR->Min, 0.0f, LargestMin );
clamp( &pGR->Max, SmallestMax, 1.0f );
clamp( &pGR->Avg, pGR->Min, pGR->Max );

// Bias is used to slightly saturate the visible color
// values to keep them from appearing washed out.
const float BiasMax = 0.5f;
float Diff = ( pGR->Avg - pGR->Min ) /
             ( pGR->Max - pGR->Min );
float Bias = 1.0f + Diff * BiasMax;

// discretize min and max
byte Min = (byte) roundf( pGR->Min * 255.0f );
byte Max = (byte) roundf( pGR->Max * 255.0f );

// Set the gamma ramp based on the new min, max
// and bias.
// All values less that min are set to 0.
// All values between min and max set along a curve
//    determined by the bias value.
// All values greater that max are set to 255.
byte c = 0;
for( ; c < Min; c++ )
    pGR->Ramp[c] = 0;
for( ; c < Max; c++ )
    pGR->Ramp[c] = (byte) ( powf( (float)( c - Min ) /
                         ( Max - Min ), Bias ) * 255.0f );
for( ; c < 255; c++ )
    pGR->Ramp[c] = 255;
}
```

Step 4: Apply the Current Gamma Ramp to the Scene

Finally, the gamma ramp is used to update the final scene. This can be done in hardware either by using a pixel shader, or by setting the hardware gamma ramp directly. Either approach has pros and cons. Setting the hardware gamma ramp does not require another full screen pass on the scene to apply the gamma ramp, but elements that should not be affected by scene lighting (such as a HUDs and other overlay graphics) will need to be adjusted with an inverse gamma ramp applied in a pixel shader (details are in the code on the companion CD-ROM). Using a pixel shader is more costly, but the image can be drawn to the back buffer before HUD elements are drawn, and other post-processing techniques such as blooming and depth of field can be added to the pass.

Conclusion

Newer hardware supports higher precision render target formats. This technique becomes even more exciting with these higher precision formats, as scenes can be adjusted dramatically with less banding, and color values beyond the chosen luminance maximum can be bloomed out. Since this is a post-processing technique, it should be fairly easy to integrate into existing engines. All source code for the technique is available on the companion CD-ROM.

5.11

Heat and Haze Post-Processing Effects

Chris Oat and Natalya Tatarchuk,

ATI Research, Inc.

Coat@ati.com, Natasha@ati.com

T he current generation of hardware graphics accelerators allows programmers a huge amount of fill rate compared to the accelerators of just a few years ago. Too often, this bandwidth goes unused, as game programmers strive to reach the broadest "lowest common denominator" market. One simple way of taking advantage of powerful graphics hardware without butchering your game's rendering pipeline is to add post-processing effects. These effects can be easily included at the end of just about any rendering pipeline, and can significantly enhance the final output by creating stunning visual effects with relatively little effort on the part of the programmer.

Heat and Haze Shimmering

Anyone who has been outside on a hot summer day has probably observed the heat shimmering effect visible above a hot surface such as the sun-baked asphalt along the highway. This shimmering is technically known as an *inferior mirage* [Berger90] and is the result of light rays bending as they pass between the layers of dense cool air far above the asphalt and the hot expanding air directly above the asphalt. Because gases exhibit different indices of refraction as their densities change, light refracts differently as it passes through air of different temperatures. A heat source, such as a pool of lava, with massive, quickly moving convection currents, exhibits a very pronounced and animated heat shimmering effect.

High-Level Algorithm

A highly accurate physical simulation of heat shimmering is unnecessary overkill for the purposes of most game engines. Instead, this article focuses on reproducing the visual phenomenon of gaseous convection by approximating an image such that it looks visually convincing. Figure 5.11.1 shows a screenshot of the ATI Caves demo illustrating the heat haze effect described in this article. The basic algorithm is as follows:

1. Create a renderable RGBA texture that is the same size as the back buffer.
2. Clear renderable texture to (0.0, 0.0, 0.0, 1.0).
3. Render the entire scene into the renderable texture, writing the color to RGB and a depth/distortion scalar to alpha.
4. Bind the renderable texture to one of the texture units and render a screen-aligned quad to the back buffer. Use the normalized device coordinates (NDC) as texture coordinates into the texture to fetch the distortion scalar stored in the alpha channel. Offset the NDC coordinates according to the distortion scalar, and resample the texture to get the distorted RGB values, and output these to the back buffer.

FIGURE 5.11.1 *Heat haze effect in the Caves demo.*

Computing Distortion Values

A per-pixel distortion value is needed to determine how much distortion should be applied to a given pixel. Three different methods for generating distortion values are presented here. The first method uses a per-pixel scene depth value to determine the distortion weight. This method is simple to implement and produces relatively nice results on its own. More complex implementations will benefit from the use of heat geometry and heat textures in conjunction with scene depth. While any one of these methods can be used on its own to generate distortion values, a combination of the three is ideal.

Scene Depth

As light passes through the layers of the atmosphere, it encounters multiple pockets of gases with varying densities. The more pockets of gases the light ray intersects, the higher the probability of the light ray being refracted. Therefore, the scene depth has to play a significant part in the simulation of the heat haze effect. The distance from the eye can be easily calculated on a per-vertex basis by projecting the vertex into eye space and extracting the z-component of the vertex's position. This per-vertex depth value can then be passed down to the pixel shader. It is important to first clear the destination buffer using an alpha that represents maximum distortion, so that any pixels in the frame that are not written will be regarded as infinitely far away (this is only strictly necessary if you aren't drawing to every pixel in the frame buffer). A simple implementation can stop here by writing this depth value to destination alpha; however, this simplistic method only provides a constant distortion for the entire image.

Heat Geometry

To render a distortion value into the alpha channel of an off-screen buffer, some geometry must be drawn. For example, a hot pool of lava might have some domelike mesh above it. Figure 5.11.2 shows the wireframe dome mesh for the center pool of lava. This mesh acts as our "heat geometry" since its only purpose is to draw heat distortion values to the alpha channel.

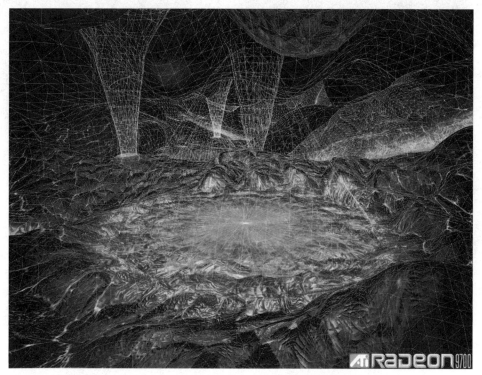

FIGURE 5.11.2 *Distortion geometry wireframe for a hot pool of lava.*

When drawing heat geometry, special care must be taken to avoid drawing sharp edges into the alpha channel of the off-screen buffer. Since the simulated heat geometry encloses a volume of gas, hard edges create visually disturbing artifacts, as uncontained gases expand to fill their environment and don't display any visible edges. If we look at the example of heat shimmering above a hot asphalt surface, there is no distinct line where the shimmering begins and ends. Thus, to maintain visual integrity for this effect, we need to avoid these hard edges; the alpha value generated by heat geometry should fade slowly toward its silhouette edges. For domes and vents, this can be achieved by scaling alpha by $N \bullet V$, such that alpha fades as the surface normal deviates from the eye vector. Figure 5.11.3 shows a heat vent that uses heat geometry to model the hot gas that it is emitting.

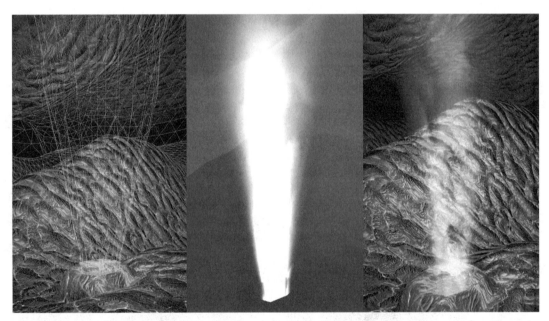

FIGURE 5.11.3   *(Left) The heat geometry for a hot gas vent is drawn in wire frame mode. (Center) The distortion values for this vent are scaled by height and $N \bullet V$ to eliminate hard edges. (Right) The final distorted images.*

Heat Textures

Heat geometry works nicely for enclosing a homogeneous volume of gas. When a volume of gas needs a more random density distribution, heat geometry can be enhanced by using heat textures, such as the one shown in Figure 5.11.4. Heat textures scroll across the surface of the heat geometry and are modulated per pixel with the distortion values contributed by depth and the heat geometry itself. The direction that these textures scroll is important, and depends on the type of heat geometry to which they are being applied. Heat rising off a hot highway should scroll upward in world-space to simulate convection currents, while the heat streaming for a jet engine should scroll outward, consistent with the engine's output vent. Figure 5.11.5 shows the combined contributions of the scene depth, heat geometry, and heat textures.

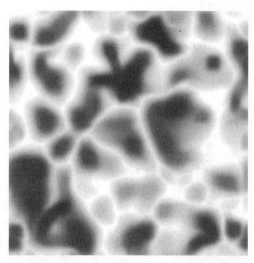

FIGURE 5.11.4 *An example of a heat texture used in the lava demo.*

FIGURE 5.11.5 *Scene depth, heat geometry, and heat textures all contribute to the final distortion value.*

Interpreting Distortion Values

So far, we've covered different ways to render distortion values to the alpha channel of an off-screen buffer. The next step is to bind the off-screen buffer as a texture, and then draw a full-screen quad to the back-buffer that interprets the per-pixel distortion values in alpha and modifies the RGB channels accordingly.

Per-Pixel Perturbation

A perturbation map can be used to simulate the way light bends as it refracts through various density layers of atmosphere. A perturbation map is a texture that contains per-pixel texture offsets. This is similar to a normal map used for bump mapping, but the normals need only be 2D since we're perturbing in image space. This single map can effectively be scrolled in two different directions in the vertex shader and sampled twice per pixel in the pixel shader to obtain two perturbation vectors (see Figure 5.11.6). These vectors are then averaged and scaled by the distortion value stored in the alpha channel of our off-screen render target. This scaled vector is then summed with the normalized device coordinate and used for a dependent texture fetch into the off-screen render target to recover a perturbed RGB scene pixel.

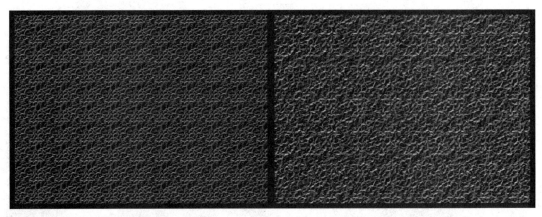

FIGURE 5.11.6   *(Left) The perturbation map. (Right) The result of scrolling the perturbation map in two different directions and averaging the results.*

Per-Pixel Blurring

Simply perturbing the pixels achieves a suitable shimmering effect, but it ignores the overall blurring effect resulting from the light refracting in to or out of the observer's eye. Ultimately, we need a way to blur our perturbed pixel based on the distortion value. One way to achieve a per-pixel blurring effect is by using a *Growable Poisson Disc sampling* approach [Riguer03]. A group of sample points arranged according to a Poisson distribution is scaled according to the distortion value, and these scaled sampling points are averaged to obtain a single blurred sample.

The following DirectX 9 HLSL pixel shader code performs *Growable Poisson Disc blurring*.

```
//================================================================
// Growable Poisson Disc Filter (13 tap)
//
// sampler tSource = source texture being filtered.
// float2 texCoord = texture coordinate for destination texel.
// float2 pixelSize = size of a texel in the source and
//                    destination image. usually this will be a
//                    vector like: <1/width, 1/height>
// float discRadius = size to grow circle of confusion (0 will
//                    only sample from texel at texCoordDest,
//                    1.0 will sample from up to a pixel
//                    away in any direction, etc).
//================================================================
float3 SiGrowablePoissonDisc13FilterRGB (sampler tSource, float2
texCoord, float2 pixelSize, float discRadius)
{
    float3 cOut;
    float2 poissonDisc[12] = {float2(-0.326212f, -0.40581f),
                              float2(-0.840144f, -0.07358f),
                              float2(-0.695914f, 0.457137f),
                              float2(-0.203345f, 0.620716f),
                              float2(0.96234f, -0.194983f),
                              float2(0.473434f, -0.480026f),
                              float2(0.519456f, 0.767022f),
                              float2(0.185461f, -0.893124f),
                              float2(0.507431f, 0.064425f),
                              float2(0.89642f, 0.412458f),
                              float2(-0.32194f, -0.932615f),
                              float2(-0.791559f, -0.59771f)};

    // center tap
    cOut = tex2D (tSource, texCoord);

    for (int tap = 0; tap < 12; tap++)
    {
        float2 offset = (pixelSize*poissonDisc[tap]*discRadius);
        float2 coord = texCoord.xy + offset;

        // Sample pixel
        cOut += tex2D (tSource, coord);
    }

    // average and return
    return (cOut / 13.0f);
}
```

This form of per-pixel blurring might prove too expensive for some older graphics accelerators. A less expensive way to achieve a similar effect is to perform a separable Gaussian blur to a down-sampled copy of the off-screen buffer and then linearly interpolate between the blurred and unblurred buffers based on the distortion value.

The following is the full HLSL pixel shader for this effect.

```
sampler tRBFullRes; // off-screen buffer (distortion in alpha)
sampler tNormalMap; // perturbation map

float  fBumpStrength;

struct PsInput
{
   float2 texCoord0   : TEXCOORD0;  // static screen quad coords
   float2 texCoord1   : TEXCOORD1;  // scrolling coords
   float2 texCoord2   : TEXCOORD2;  // more scrolling coords
};

float4 main (PsInput i) : COLOR
{
    // fetch from perturbation map with scrolling coords
    float3 vNormal0 = tex2D (tNormalMap, i.texCoord1);
    float3 vNormal1 = tex2D (tNormalMap, i.texCoord2);

    // scale and bias
    vNormal0 = SiConvertColorToVector(vNormal0);
    vNormal1 = SiConvertColorToVector(vNormal1);

    // sum and scale
    float2 offset = (vNormal0.xy + vNormal1.xy) * fBumpStrength;

    // get color and distortion info from renderable texture
    float4 cScene = tex2D (tRBFullRes, i.texCoord0);

    // square distortion value
    cScene.a *= cScene.a;

    // compute perturbed texture coords
    offset.xy = ((offset.xy * cScene.a) * fBumpScale);
    float2 newCoord = i.texCoord0 + offset.xy;

    // pixel size assuming an off-screen buffer of 1600x1200
    float2 pixelSize = float2(1.0f/1600.0f, 1.0f/1200.0f);

    // fetch the distorted color
    float4 o;

    // max disc radius is 5.0 pixels
    o.rgb = SiGrowablePoissonDisc13FilterRGB(tRBFullRes,
            newCoord, pixelSize, 5.0f * cScene.a * cScene.a);

    o.a = 1.0f;

    return o;
}
```

Conclusion

This article demonstrated a method for adding heat and haze shimmering as a post-processing step. This effect is presented as a set of steps that scales with graphics complexity; simple perturbation distortions can be done on older legacy graphics accelerators, while more powerful hardware can also add extra heat geometry, heat textures, and per-pixel blurring. One further extension of this article is the inclusion of particle systems to add more complex gas/object interactions. Special thanks to Eli Turner for providing the art for the images used in this article.

References

[Berger90] Berger, M., T. Trout, and N. Levit, *IEEE Computer Graphics and Applications*, pp. 36–41, May 1990, Vol. 10, Issue 3.

[Riguer03] Riguer, G., N. Tatarchuk, and J. Isidoro, "Real-Time Depth of Field Simulation," *ShaderX2: Shader Programming Tips & Tricks with DirectX 9*, Wordware Publishing, Inc., 2003.

5.12

Hardware Skinning with Quaternions

Jim Hejl, Electronic Arts Tiburon

jhejl@ea.com

Given an existing detailed skin mesh, and an associated animation hierarchy, the goal is to come up with a means of deforming the mesh automatically when the underlying skeleton structure is animated. This process is called *skinning*.

Currently, most video game character skinning is done using a linear blending technique called *vertex blending* (also known as *skeletal-subspace deformation*, *matrix palette skinning*, and *smooth skinning* in Maya). Although popular, vertex blending is notorious for its shortcomings. The most severe artifact, a direct consequence of the linear approach, will cause a joint to physically collapse as the deflection angle increases. As a dramatic demonstration, simply twisting a joint will produce the characteristic *candy wrapper* deformation. Figure 5.12.1 illustrates this effect, showing a joint that is simultaneously twisted and rotated.

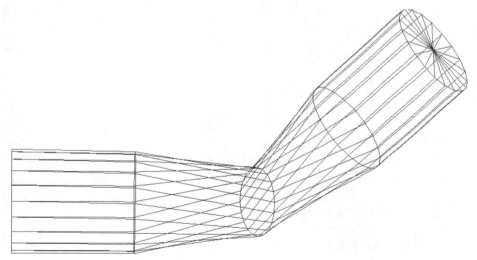

FIGURE 5.12.1 *Linear vertex blending.*

Such problematic side effects are usually tolerated in exchange for the relative simplicity and efficiency of the basic algorithm. Indeed, the entire solution is easily implemented in hardware using consumer-grade programmable vertex processing [Domine03].

Vertex blending performs badly because it lacks the notion of spherical interpolation. This article introduces *spherical joint blending*, an alternative skinning algorithm that is free from linear artifacts. Spherical joint blending is implemented using quaternions, and executed *entirely* in a vertex shader. As we will see, the final implementation uses fewer instructions and far less GPU memory than the comparable vertex blending solution.

Figure 5.12.2 shows the improved deformation using the same deflection angles.

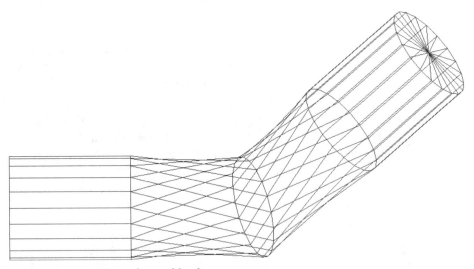

FIGURE 5.12.2   *Spherical joint blending.*

Skinning Concepts

The basic skinning algorithm works by first placing a hierarchical skeleton inside a static model of a character, and then "binding" the two together. The skeleton and mesh are carefully aligned, and typically bound in some neutral pose. Then, each vertex in the mesh is assigned a set of influencing joints and a blending weight for each influence. As the underlying skeleton is animated, the mesh is deformed by the moving skeleton. This deformation, the influence of moving bones on the vertices, is the task of the skinning algorithm.

Skeleton Overview

The skeleton can be seen as a tree structure with the bones represented as nodes. The highest node of the tree is the root node, which corresponds to the root object of the hierarchy. The translation and rotation of the root node is known as the "root rotation," and the transformation of all other nodes in the hierarchy will be relative to this node. A node *higher* in the hierarchy is a node closer to the root node, while a descendant node is a node farther away from the root node. When comparing nodes connected to each other, the one higher up in the hierarchy is referred to as the *parent* node, and the descendant node is referred to as the *child* node. The descendants from the root of the skeleton form an articulated chain, where the coordinate frame of the child is always relative to the coordinate frame of the parent.

A node in the skeleton is a *joint*, and is a rigid-body rotation. The segment connecting two joints is a *bone displacement*, and is a rigid-body translation. The complete transform of a joint rotation followed by the bone displacement is a *bone*.

Vertex Blending Overview

The vertex-blending algorithm transforms a vertex multiple times, once for each bone of influence, and blends the results together using the corresponding blend weights stored in the vertex. For this interpolation to work, it is necessary to *localize* the vertex to each target bone before transformation. See [Domine03] for details. This localization has the effect of skinning the vertex multiple times in a single coordinate system. These results are weighted and accumulated into a final vertex.

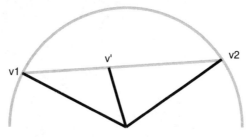

FIGURE 5.12.3   *Vertex blending.*

Notice the subspace created by the line between $\mathbf{v}_1$ and $\mathbf{v}_2$. The first major shortcoming of vertex blending results directly from the fact that the deformation of $\mathbf{v}$ is restricted to this subspace. This subspace will continue to collapse as the deflection angle increases, eventually falling into a singularity at 180 degrees. It is quite unlikely that the *desired* deformation lies in this subspace; hence, no amount of adjusting the blend weight will produce the desired result.

Linear blending of vertices is essentially the same as directly interpolating between bone matrices. That is to say, a point transformed by a weighted sum of matrices equals the weighted sum of the transformed points [Shoemake92]. This is a useful insight, as most graphics engineers are familiar with the consequences of attempting to interpolate matrices. One can imagine interpolated basis vectors of the matrix becoming denormalized, like the vectors in Figure 5.12.3. Additionally, the interpolated basis vectors might not be mutually perpendicular, introducing skew into the transform. Forensic science on direct matrix interpolation increases our understanding of why vertex blending fails.

It is not immediately obvious how to interpolate between multiple weighted rotations. Indeed, the space of three-dimensional rotations is not a simple vector-space, but a closed three-dimensional manifold. Don't worry if you are not familiar with the terms; the concepts are simple. A closed manifold is just something that *locally* looks like Euclidean space (a plane) but actually curves back on itself. This is why the Earth appears flat and why vertex blending *seems* to work for small angles. The notation for this three-dimensional manifold of rotation-space is *SO(3)*, for special orthogonal. (*Special orthogonal* is the set of "proper rotations," or orthogonal matrices with determinant 1.)

As mentioned, because of the topology of SO(3), vertex blending appears to work for small angles. Previous works in *Game Programming Gems 3* [Weber02] and at SIG-GRAPH 2003 [Mohr03] suggest adding extra joints to the skeleton to break up large deflection angles. Picture a rotation divided into small angles, like Figure 5.12.4. Linearly interpolating between these angles will create piecewise-linear approximation that begins to converge on what we are really after: a spherical interpolation.

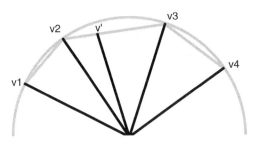

FIGURE 5.12.4   *Piecewise-linear approximation*

Introducing Joint Blending

Rather than averaging transformed vertices, suppose we move the interpolation down to the joints. That is, rather than synthesizing a skinned vector, consider synthesizing the *transform* that properly skins the vector.

Each vertex in the mesh is rigidly bound to a single bone, but the rotation at the joint is an average over several joints. In other words, we are synthesizing a new coordinate frame by averaging several other coordinate frames. The position of this new coordinate frame is given by the hierarchical position of the attached bone. (As bones typically do not change length during animation, they are assumed to be a series of constant displacements down the articulated chain). The synthesized coordinate frame, $\mathbf{M}'$, is rotationally influenced by multiple joints. As shown in Figure 5.12.5, coordinate frame $\mathbf{M}'$ will transform vertex $\mathbf{v}$ directly to skinned position $\mathbf{v}'$.

So, how is $\mathbf{M}'$ synthesized? We have seen that interpolating between rotation matrices does not work. In fact, joint blending with matrix interpolation would produce vertex-blending results. A new parameterization of rotations is needed.

FIGURE 5.12.5 *Spherical joint blending.*

Quaternion Parameterization

Recall that quaternions are hyper-complex numbers constituting a four-dimensional vector space. The set of unit quaternions forms a four-dimensional sphere, known as S^3. If you are not familiar with the notation, the exponent "3" refers to the topological, not geometric, definition. Geometers refer to the number of coordinates in the underlying space, and topologists refer to the dimension of the surface itself [Coxeter73]. Think of S^3 as two *solid spheres* (or balls) glued together. Just as an ordinary sphere is the union of two discs glued along their boundary circles, two solid spheres can be so joined to create a hypersphere.

This is all especially interesting because S^3 happens to be the "double cover" of SO(3). That is, unit quaternions are the double cover of the three-dimensional rotation group. Technically known as the *universal covering*, this allows unit quaternions to capture all of the geometry and topology of three-dimensional rotations in the simplest possible form [Shoemake94]. The details of this relationship are fascinating, but are well beyond the scope of this article.

Spherical Interpolation

As we have seen, unit quaternions represent a rotation with a vector on the S^3 sphere. Thus, quaternions *linearize* the rotation group, without approximating it. Interpolating a rotation is now as straightforward as interpolating a single vector.

Interpolating between two rotations should give points on the great circle arc between two points on S^3. This interpolation across the surface of the hypersphere is known as *spherical linear interpolation*, or SLERP. Given quaternions p and q with acute angle θ between them, SLERP at position w is defined as [Shoemake85].

$$\mathrm{slerp}\big(w; p, q\big) = \frac{\sin\big((1 - w)\theta\big)p + \sin\big(w\theta\big)\, q}{\sin\big(\theta\big)} \tag{5.12.1}$$

As a performance optimization, we can approximate the SLERP with

$$\text{slerp}(w; p, q) = \left\| (1 - w)p + wq \right\|$$

(5.12.2)

This approximation will produce orientations that can be viewed as four-dimensional points on a straight line in quaternion space. The interpolated quaternion will not maintain unit length during the interpolation, so the result is projected back onto the hypersphere. The cheap approximation traces out the *exact* same curve as the SLERP, but the shortcut across the sphere will result in nonconstant speed across the arc. We will accept this tradeoff for the simpler math.

After synthesizing an interpolated quaternion, it needs to be converted to matrix form before transforming vectors. Fortunately, this conversion is a simple chain of polynomials, with no trig required. Thus, interpolating a quaternion and converting it to a rotation matrix can be implemented on vector hardware with simple arithmetic instructions.

Antipodal Quaternions

We mentioned earlier that S^3 is the double cover of SO(3). Let's take a deeper look at this. Suppose we have two points A and B on a sphere. There is a short arc connecting the A to B (the geodesic), and a long arc connecting B to A. Because there are two classes of paths for every rotation, the universal covering group S^3 has twice as many elements as SO(3). This means two different unit quaternions can represent the same rotation in SO(3). It might be helpful to view SO(3) as a *projection* of S^3, where each pair of antipodal points in S^3 projects to a single point in SO(3).

This double cover has interpolation consequences. When interpolating between two unit quaternions, we are always interested in the geodesic on the sphere, never the "long way" around. To achieve this, we select the quaternions such that the dot product between the two is nonnegative. This has the effect of selecting the short path. With skinning, this means that all the quaternions for a skeleton must be forced into the same (4D) hemisphere. The algorithm is simple: test each joint in the skeleton against the first joint. If the dot product between the two is negative, invert the quaternion at the selected joint. This will guarantee that all rotations in the skeleton point into the hemisphere defined by the orientation of the first joint resulting in the correct interpolation. This operation should happen on the CPU before uploading the quaternions to the constant store. Skipping this step will produce unexpected results.

Hardware Implementation

To prepare for hardware skinning, the CPU will upload joint transforms to vertex shader constant registers: one quaternion rotation and one bone translation per joint in the skeleton. This uses seven elements of two quad registers. (The unused eighth element could be used to store a uniform scale, as the quaternions cannot include a scale.) Therefore, a 28-bone character would use 56 vertex shader registers.

In the microcode, the GPU will interpolate between multiple joint rotations using corresponding blend weights stored in each vertex. The blended quaternion will be converted to a 3 x 3 rotation matrix. This rotation matrix will be used to skin vectors (position, normal, bi-normal, tangent, etc.) as needed. The vertex is assumed to be rigidly bound to the first bone of influence, and will be translated by its bone displacement.

Spherical Interpolation Approximation

In Microsoft's DirectX vertex assembly shader language, each quaternion is weighted and blended.

```
; four-bone interpolation
mov     a0.x, v[BONE].x
mul     r0, c[a0.x], v[WGT].x      ; quat 1
mov     a0.x, v[BONE].y
mad     r0, c[a0.x], v[WGT].y, r0  ; quat 2
mov     a0.x, v[BONE].z
mad     r0, c[a0.x], v[WGT].z, r0  ; quat 3
mov     a0.x, v[BONE].w
mad     r0, c[a0.x], v[WGT].w, r0  ; quat 4
```

As discussed, it is necessary to renormalize the blended quaternion to push it back onto the 4D sphere.

```
; normalize quaternion
dp4     r1.w, r0, r0
rsq     r1.w, r1.w
mul     r0, r0, r1.w
```

This produces blended quaternion in *r0* that approximates a weighted spherical interpolation over four joints.

Quaternion to Matrix

To transform vectors, we need to convert our interpolated quaternion to matrix form. This rotation is expressed as

$$R = \begin{bmatrix} 1 - 2y^2 - 2z^2 & 2xy + 2wz & 2xz - 2wy \\ 2xy - 2wz & 1 - 2x^2 - 2z^2 & 2yz + 2wx \\ 2xz + 2wy & 2yz - 2wx & 1 - 2x^2 - 2y^2 \end{bmatrix} \text{ where } \begin{bmatrix} A & B & C \\ D & E & F \\ G & H & I \end{bmatrix} \quad (5.12.3)$$

As (naive) C code, this looks like

```
Mat[A]  = 1.0 - (2.0 * Quat.y * Quat.y);
Mat[A] -= 2.0 * Quat.z * Quat.z;
Mat[B]  = 2.0 * Quat.x * Quat.y;
Mat[B] += 2.0 * Quat.z * Quat.w;
Mat[C]  = 2.0 * Quat.x * Quat.z;
Mat[C] -= 2.0 * Quat.y * Quat.w;
Mat[D]  = 2.0 * Quat.x * Quat.y;
Mat[D] -= 2.0 * Quat.z * Quat.w;
Mat[E]  = 1.0 - (2.0 * Quat.x * Quat.x);
Mat[E] -= 2.0 * Quat.z * Quat.z;
```

```
Mat[F]  = 2.0 * Quat.y * Quat.z;
Mat[F]  + 2.0 * Quat.x * Quat.w;
Mat[G]  = 2.0 * Quat.x * Quat.z;
Mat[G] += 2.0 * Quat.y * Quat.w;
Mat[H]  = 2.0 * Quat.y * Quat.z;
Mat[H] -= 2.0 * Quat.x * Quat.w;
Mat[I]  = 1.0f - (2.0 * Quat.x * Quat.x);
Mat[I] -= 2.0 * Quat.y * Quat.y;
```

Running this through a basic compiler produces a 25-instruction conversion (the generated code is omitted for space). In this case, the compiler failed to exploit the shared products, or to vectorize a single operation. This gives us a general starting point for optimization.

Quaternion to Matrix Optimization

We know that the matrix produced by the quaternion conversion is orthogonal, and thus has an orthonormal basis (vectors are unit length and mutually perpendicular). Therefore, any single row (or column) can be derived with the cross product of the other two. The cross product has two solutions, depending on the order of the cross. The handedness of the coordinate system determines the correct order of the cross; one solution is always correct for a right-handed coordinate system, the other is correct for left.

We'll derive GHI by crossing basis vectors ABC and DEF. Or,

```
; ABC in r8, DEF in r9
mul    r10, r8.yzxw, r9.zxyw     ;GHI with a cross
mad    r10, -r9.yzxw, r8.zxyw, r10
```

The next step is an aggressive combination of shared products and shared sums.

```
; Quat (r5) to rotation matrix (r8,r9,r10)
def    c[CONST],0.0,1.0,2.0,0.5
add    r6, r5, r5                ; 2x, 2y, 2z, 2w
mul    r1, r6.xyyy, r5.xyzw      ; 2xx, 2yy, 2yz, 2yw
mul    r2, r6.xxzz, r5.ywzw      ; 2xy, 2xw, 2zz, 2zw
add    r3, r1.xxyy, r2.zzzz      ;(2xx+2zz),(2xx+2zz)
add    r8.x, c[CONST].y, -r3.z   ;A = 1 - (2yy + 2zz)
add    r8.y, r2.x, r2.w          ;B = 2xy + 2zw
mad    r8.z, r6.x, r5.z, -r1.w   ;C = 2xz - 2yw
add    r9.y, r2.x, -r2.w         ;D = 2xy - 2zw
add    r9.y, c[CONST].y, -r3.x   ;E = 1 - (2xx + 2zz)
add    r9.z, r1.z, r2.y          ;F = 2yz + 2xw
mul    r10, r8.yzxw, r9.zxyw     ;GHI with a cross
mad    r10, -r9.yzxw, r8.zxyw, r10
```

This quaternion-to-matrix conversion is 12 instructions in the vertex shader.

The final shader blends four arbitrary joints, converts the quaternion to a matrix, skins a vertex, and rotates a normal. The shader is 31 instructions long, and uses 56 quad-registers of GPU memory for a 28-bone character. This can be compared with the vertex blending implementation of 40 instructions and 84 registers for the same character [Domine03].

Conclusion

In this article, we demonstrated that spherical joint blending with quaternions is a fast, accurate, and compact skinning solution.

References

[Coxeter73] Coxeter, H. S. M., *Regular Polytopes, Third Edition*, New York: Dover, 1973.

[Domine03] Domine, Sebastien, "Mesh Skinning," available online at *http://developer.nvidia.com/object/skinning.html*, July 1, 2003.

[Mohr03] Mohr, Alex, and Michael Gleicher, "Building Efficient, Accurate Character Skins from Examples," ACM SIGGRAPH 2003.

[Shoemake85] Shoemake, Ken, "Animating Rotations with Quaternion Curves," ACM SIGGRAPH 1985.

[Shoemake92] Shoemake, Ken, and Tom Duff, "Matrix Animation and Polar Decomposition," *Proceedings of the 1992 Graphics Interface Conference*, pp. 245–254, 1992.

[Shoemake94] Shoemake, Ken, *Quaternions*, May 1994, available online at *ftp://ftp.cis.upenn.edu/pub/graphics/shoemake/quatut.ps.Z*, July 1, 2003.

[Weber02] Weber, Jason, "Improved Deformation of Bones," *Game Programming Gems 3*, Charles River Media, 2002.

5.13

Motion Capture Data Compression

Søren Hannibal,
Shiny Entertainment

sorenhan@yahoo.com

In the video game industry, the stakes increase every year, and budgets can surpass tens of millions of dollars. Often, a large amount is reserved for motion capture sessions, which result in gigabytes of raw key frame data. However, with console memory still one of the scarcest resources in game development, tradeoffs often result in some of the more interesting animations being cut, leaving only the bare minimum.

This article demonstrates a lossy compression system that was developed to improve memory usage for motion capture data. While the system has some features that take advantage of bone hierarchies, a more general solution can be used on any keyframed animation, such as prerecorded camera movements and hand-animated physics objects.

This article focuses on the compression and decompression of animation data, and does not rely on how models are rendered, how animations are blended together, or how curves are interpolated. The techniques presented here can easily be implemented in existing animation systems.

Memory savings depend on how aggressively compression is applied. Animation size can be compressed to below 500 bytes per second for a hierarchical model with 16 bones, compared with over 15,000 bytes per second for uncompressed data. The performance cost for decompression is negligible. Compression is processor-intensive, and requires a small amount of user interaction for optimal results.

Plan of Attack

The compression scheme has a three-step approach:

1. Organize the data so the smallest number of data channels is stored.
2. Reduce the number of keys by removing those that have little or no impact on the animation.
3. Pack the remaining keys by reducing precision.

Each step has several settings available to the animator. With a little experience, the animator will be able to choose settings that will yield good results with minimal tweaking. It is important to keep the number of settings low, so as not to overwhelm the animator.

Organizing the Data Channels

The first step is to figure out which data channels are necessary. For the purposes of this system, a data channel is defined as a series of keys for rotating, moving, or scaling a single bone. For a standard human body, you typically need to store the position of the root and the orientation of every bone. However, when the system has to support facial animation, hand animation, squash-and-stretch animation, or has to render other types of articulated models such as cars or weapons, flexibility in choosing which channels are used becomes more important.

Similarly, if the system has to play multiple animations on a character at the same time, you might not want to calculate all bones for all animations. An example is a character that is running and aiming a weapon at the same time. The character would use a standard running animation for the legs and the torso, and an animation for gripping the weapon for the arms and the shoulders.

Some channels can be further optimized if full freedom of rotation about all three axes is not required. For example, the jawbone, the eyelids, and some finger bones might only rotate around a single axis. You can save a lot of space by storing only a single axis, as you then need only store one-third of the data. Speed is also improved, since creating a local matrix from a single axis is much faster than reconstructing it from three axes or converting it from a quaternion. A single-axis interpolation is also much simpler and faster than a quaternion slerp (spherical linear interpolation) when interpolating between keyframes or blending between animations.

Note that for some animations, some joints might change from single to multi-axis. For example, an animation that shows a character moving her jaw from side to side would not be possible if the jaw were limited to only rotate about a single axis.

Reducing the Number of Stored Keys

Once you have all the data organized, it has to be optimized so keys that have little or no visual impact are removed.

The algorithm itself is simple:

1. Measure the significance of each key.
2. Remove more keys based on some criteria.
3. Remove the least significant key.
4. Recalculate the significance of the two neighbor keys around the removed key.

While the algorithm is simple, it will run very slowly if the data is not organized with the following two questions in mind: which key is the least important, and, for each remaining key, which two keys are its neighbors? This turns out to be easy.

For each channel, an array of keys is stored sorted by frame number. Those keys should also be linked together in a linked list. Whenever a key is removed, it should be taken out of the linked list; thus, knowing which keys are valid and which have been discarded is trivial. You can also quickly find the neighbor keys for each removed key, which is useful when finding the keys that need to be recalculated.

It also helps to have a balanced binary tree sorted by significance of the keys in all channels. This will substantially reduce the amount of time it takes to find the least significant key, and to reposition keys within the binary tree after their significance is recalculated.

Measuring the Significance of Each Key

The one thing that can make or break the compression system is the heuristic for measuring the significance of each key. The heuristic does not matter as much for smaller levels of compression, but becomes increasingly important when higher compression ratios are used. This can mean the difference between a 3D model waving its limbs around unnaturally, and a living, breathing human being.

The animator should be able to tweak the number of keys removed for each animation individually. This can, for example, be input as a target number of keys per second of animation. The optimal amount of compression that can be used varies for each animation, but with a good heuristic, 5 to 10 keys per second can produce natural animations.

The simplest heuristic is simulating the removal of each key from the optimized dataset and comparing the datasets before and after the removal. The simulation is done by decompressing the frames in both datasets and making comparisons between them.

It is not acceptable to find the importance of the key based on the original dataset, because many keys are collinear. The problem collinearity causes is that if any of the collinear keys is removed, the other keys will control the curve through the same path as before. However, if all collinear keys are removed, the curve will change its path.

It is important to use the same interpolation scheme for calculating the significance of the keys and decompressing the frames in the game. Linear interpolation gives the worst results and is not recommended. Animation often looks robotic and unnatural with linear interpolation. Spline interpolation produces much better results by smoothing the animation.

Finding the Right Criteria for Key Removal

Many different removal criteria are possible. The most obvious criterion is to measure how far apart the keys would be in the two datasets. This could be done by using Pythagoras' method, for example. When using this criterion, all the decompressed frames will closely resemble the frames of the original animation.

However, for the animations to seem realistic, the individual frames do not matter as much as the overall feeling of the final animation. If the heuristic looks only at absolute values, each frame will look correct, but when watched in motion, it might deviate too far from the original animation. Two equally important criteria are speed and acceleration, the first and second derivatives of the curve. For example, a punch animation needs to have the correct acceleration and deceleration to feel fast, yet controlled. Video game players do not know where a punch landed in the original motion capture session, but they do notice if the animation doesn't feel right when they are playing the game.

When dealing with hierarchical animation, the position of each bone matters significantly. Rotational movement affects the extents of an object much more than the center of the object. A one-degree discrepancy in a hand joint would be less noticeable than a one-degree discrepancy on a shoulder joint, because the number of bones between the shoulder and the fingertips is much higher than the number of bones between the hand and the fingertips. This is one area that should not be determined automatically, because in some cases, the animators want the focus to be on certain parts of the body. For example, if there is a close-up of a hand, it is important that all of the bones between the hand bone and the root bone are stored at high quality, but the opposite arm and the legs do not matter as much. Therefore, an easy way to achieve better results is to give the animator control over which groups of the body require more detail.

Finally, if a bone has stored a key on a certain frame, then the child bone and the parent bones should store a key on the same frame. This tends to create a calmer and more precise animation, especially when using linear interpolation.

Recalculating the Importance of the Neighbor Keys

The removal of a key has an impact on its neighbor keys, and they need to have their importance recalculated to eliminate problems with collinearity. If you use spline interpolation, then two remaining neighbor keys on each side of the removed key are affected. With linear interpolation, only one neighbor key on each side is impacted.

If the heuristic takes parent or child bones into consideration, the keys that could be affected for those bones also need to have their importance recalculated.

Packing the Remaining Keys

The hard part is over. Now that you have found which keys you need to store, it's time to think about how to pack the data. Instead of storing everything in 32-bit floating point, significant memory savings can be achieved by storing the final values with less precision.

Quaternions can be packed down to 4 bytes with reasonably good results [Zarb-Adami02]. Similar methods can be developed for positional animation. This type of technique works especially well on fast-moving animations, but on slow animations where the player can pay attention to the details of the character more easily, this can make the animation jittery.

In a hierarchical system, the bones near the root of the character create the majority of the jitter. Therefore, the animations can benefit if you pack the different channels with different levels of precision. Keys for bones near the root should be stored with 8 or 12 bytes of precision, while keys for arms and legs can be stored with only 4 bytes of precision.

Each animation can obviously have a different packing level. If you know that one animation is used in a close-up, or an animation does not look good enough, you can use the highest quality packing. Again, this is something that the animator should be able to control. An easy way to allow the animator to tweak this value is to have a number of predefined settings.

With the key data packed, the only thing left in the compression process is to store the data in a logical format. For each channel, you need to store the remaining keys and their frame numbers. To minimize memory usage, you can store the frame number for each key as an offset from the previous remaining key, in multibyte format. This means that either one or two bytes are used, where the top bit of the first byte will indicate whether a second byte is used. This method works for animations of fewer than 32,768 (2^{15}) frames.

Runtime Decompression

There are two steps required for decompression for each frame rendered:

1. Update the decompression buffers so the keys are in the right frame ranges
2. Interpolate between the keys in the decompression buffers to get the animation for that frame

At the start of each animation, the animation player must allocate a decompression buffer for each data channel. The buffers are used to store the unpacked keys that the interpolation routine uses to get the current frame. Each decompression buffer should be large enough for either two or four uncompressed keys per data channel, depending on the type of interpolation that was used during compression. These buffers are kept in memory over the duration of the animation, and each buffer is continuously updated whenever it is not valid for the current animation frame.

The final step is to interpolate between the keys. This is done with the same interpolation routines used during compression. After this step, you are done; you have successfully decompressed a frame of the animation. All that is left is to render the model.

Future Improvements

If you follow the steps in the previous sections, you will have a complete compression system, perfectly capable of delivering good compressed animations. However, as with everything else, there are plenty of ways to improve this system. You can probably come up with some good ideas yourself, but here are a few suggestions and tips:

- **Curve fitting.** After many keys are removed, the curves might no longer be optimal. The curve passes through the values at the frames where a key is stored, but between keys, the curve will be off. By trying to fit the curve to the best result for all keys combined, you will be able to get the overall animation closer to the original, while still keeping the timing unchanged.

- **Storing channels interleaved.** If animation channels are stored interleaved, it might be possible to stream in animations a small piece at a time. This is useful for cut-scenes, as there is no need to have a full animation in memory at once. Regular animations can also benefit, because it will keep random memory access down, as there is only one location in memory that will be read, instead of one location for each channel.

- **Separating key removal from key packing.** Key removal is the slowest part of the system, but it is only one of the parts that animators will need to adjust. By storing an intermediate result between key removal and key packing, animators might be able to tweak the packing parameters and see the result much more quickly than if the system has to recompress the animation from the start.

Conclusion

Every game has memory constraints. Compressing animation data is one path you can take to reclaim some memory. Compression can be a simple process, simply removing keys that are not important for the look and feel of the animation, and packing the remaining keys as much as possible.

The heuristic for measuring a key's significance is the most important, and can be the toughest component to get right. However, even less refined heuristics can result in significant memory savings. Packing the remaining keys is also important, and with high compression levels, the jitter introduced by having packed keys disappears, making the result look better than uncompressed animation with packed keys.

The results vary from animation to animation; there is not one good set of options that can be applied universally. It is therefore important to give animators freedom to tweak compression levels for each animation. However, for the animators to process a large number of animations quickly, it is important to keep the number of options down to a minimum.

While it might seem complicated before you start, making a compression routine is straightforward. Remember that the rules here are not set in stone, but are meant as a guideline—feel free to experiment.

References

[Zarb-Adami02] Zarb-Adami, Mark, "Quaternion Compression," *Game Programming Gems 3*, Charles River Media, 2002.

5.14

Fast Collision Detection for 3D Bones-Based Articulated Characters

Oliver Heim, Carl S. Marshall, and Adam Lake, Intel Corporation

oliver.heim@intel.com,
carl.s.marshall@intel.com,
adam.t.lake@intel.com

Simulation is a vital component of any game engine aiming to achieve the realism needed to immerse a user in a virtual world. This quest for realistic virtual experiences drives the need for higher performing CPUs, graphics cards, bandwidth, and memory. One of the most computationally intensive areas driving this increase in performance is the application of accurate and efficient collision detection. Gone are the days that a rectangle surrounding a sprite is sufficient approximation of a model. We require collisions that look and feel accurate, and that occur in 3D space. This article aims to give a practical, efficient implementation for a modern 3D game engine that offers several advantages over techniques common in today's engines.

Collision Detection vs. Collision Resolution

We define *collision detection* as finding the exact moment when two objects in a scene collide with one another, and we define *collision resolution* as the task of resolving a collision by applying some reaction to the objects associated with the collision. Moving the objects so that their triangles do not intersect, applying physically based forces to the objects, or selecting one of the two objects to apply a reaction on are just a few means of resolving a collision. Collision resolution is a large enough topic by itself; this article primarily focuses on collision detection.

Terminology

Bone: Each individual bone of a skeletal character is associated with a series of vertices. When the bones are transformed, the vertices move along with the bone. In collision detection we exploit the same bones to provide input to the collision detection subsystem. Typically, a vertex might be associated with several bones and have a weighting factor per bone. Moreover, the bones are connected via a parent-child relationship that forms the model's bones hierarchy, or skeleton.

AABB: Axis-aligned bounding box. Each face of the box is aligned with one of the main axes.

OBB: Oriented bounding box [Gottschalk96]. OBBs are a generalization of AABBs that can be rotated arbitrarily in 3D space. Because rotations of the box are affine, these boxes do not stretch or shrink under rotation. Each OBB is represented relative to a bone; thus, when the bone transforms, we do not need to recalculate the position and orientation of the OBB (see Figure 5.14.1).

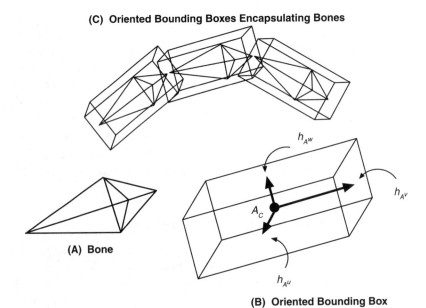

(C) Oriented Bounding Boxes Encapsulating Bones

(A) Bone

(B) Oriented Bounding Box

FIGURE 5.14.1   *A bone, an oriented bounding box, and oriented bounding boxes surrounding three connected bones. A_c refers to the centroid (approximate center) of the box, and $\{h^A{}_u, h^A{}_v, h^A{}_w\}$ refer to the positive half-widths of the box.*

Skinning: The process by which mesh information, such as vertices, triangles, and vertex weights, are mapped to the underlying skeleton of a bones-based model. Each vertex can be mapped to one or more bones in the skeleton, and corresponding weights determine how much a vertex will be shifted when its underlying bone is moved. Therefore, once the skeleton has been skinned, the mesh can be deformed in a natural way when the skeleton's orientation changes. While skinning is not directly related to the runtime of the fast collision detection algorithm, we apply a skinning operation during the pre-process phase to determine which vertices/triangles are associated with each bone.

Integration of Collision Detection into a 3D Game Engine

Collision detection for bones-based characters is a computationally intensive problem because two distinct phases of transformation are involved. During the *simulation* phase, we transform all the vertices into the coordinate system of the collision detection engine. During *rendering*, all of the vertices are transformed for the skinning algorithm. The inefficiency here involves the requirement of a complete transform during collision detection. It would be desirable to reduce this computational requirement.

Before we dive into the details of the proposed solution, let's look at what typically must happen in a game on a per-frame basis. Further, let's assume that our game engine is written as a loop that runs per frame.

```
For each frame:
    While simulation time remains:
        Advance system to current time
            For each model:
                Transform model to world space
                Transform bones in bones-based models
        DetectCollisions();
        ResolveCollisions();
    SkinBonesBasedModels();
    RenderScene();
```

From the preceding pseudocode, one can see that there are several disjoint steps involved in generating the final displayed image. For example, it's not advisable to render the frame before collision detection, just as it is ill advised to do collision detection before the next series of world space transforms have been applied to each model.

Traditional Collision Detection Solutions

A straightforward solution would be to use separate mesh topologies, one for collision detection and a separate one for rendering. In this case, the collision mesh is generally at a much lower resolution than the rendered mesh. This solution works, but is subject to inaccurate collision results given the different topologies. More importantly, although the mesh might be smaller, the entire mesh is still transformed. The collision area might, however, be only a small subset of the total number of polygons in the mesh.

Another solution is to use *proxy* or *impostor* geometry, like a bounding volume hierarchy, which approximates the model's geometry for collision detection. A bounding volume hierarchy organizes the geometry into a treelike structure in which each lower level splits the parent into a predetermined number of subvolumes. Once fully populated, the tree for a model with N polygons contains a single root volume encapsulating the entire model, multiple internal levels, and N leaf nodes at the lowest level. At each leaf node, a single triangle is enclosed within a bounding volume. Given the tree structure, the bounding volume hierarchy yields much faster collision detection, because many of the bounding volumes within the tree do not require intersection testing during any given collision detection test. Because the hierarchy is quite costly to compute, it is only ideally suited for static models where it is created once and reused for the lifetime of the model. It is very poorly suited for dynamic models, such as bones-based characters, because it must be recomputed each time the orientation or pose of the model changes.

Fast Bones-Based Collision Detection Algorithm

Our algorithm uses the bones of a model to provide fast collision detection with an object. We do this by calculating simple bounding volumes per bone of an articulated model, instead of providing a complete bounding volume hierarchy for the entire model. Each bone within the bones list has a set of associated vertices; therefore, we can quickly determine where a collision occurs and only transform the vertices associated with the bounding volumes involved in the collision. Next, we describe the data structures, pre-processing steps, and runtime of our algorithm.

Advantages over previous collision detection algorithms include:

- Transforms are applied to vertices only as needed.
- OBBs do not require recomputation unless bone sizes change.
- No need to recompute a bounding volume hierarchy on a per-frame basis because volumes are static per bone.
- No need to have different simulation vs. rendering topology.

Collision Detection Using Oriented Bounding Boxes

The core of our algorithm is based on Stephan Gottschalk's oriented bounding box intersection test [Gottschalk96]. This algorithm uses the *separating axis theorem*, which states that it is sufficient to find a single axis between OBB_A and OBB_B to prove they are disjoint. A maximum of 15 axes tests are required: 3 axes from the faces of OBB_A, 3 axes from the faces of OBB_B, and 9 axes from a combination of edges from OBB_A and OBB_B. All tests involve projecting the sum of each box's radii onto the axis being tested. An intersection occurs only if the projections overlap on all 15 axis tests. Figure 5.14.2 presents a 2D version of a single projection that shows these OBBs are disjoint. For more information on these operations, see [Gottschalk96].

Data Structures

Before diving into the core algorithm, it's important to understand how our data structures are defined. Because we chose oriented bounding boxes as proxy geometry, the

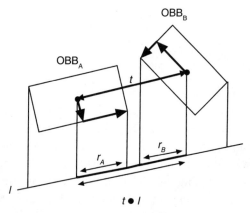

FIGURE 5.14.2 *Separating axis illustration—the figure shows that OBB$_A$ and OBB$_B$ are disjoint because the projection of the radii, r_A and r_B onto the axis, L, do not overlap.*

data structures will reflect this. The following is a partial listing of the most essential data structures that our algorithm employs.

```
class OrientedBone
{
    // Bone Information
    Matrix4x4      m_mReferenceTransform;  // Bone xform
    int            m_iID;                  // Bone id
    TriList*       m_pTriangleList;        // Triangles per
                                           // bone
    Vector3*       m_pVertexList;          // Vertex
                                           // indices

    // Oriented Bounding Box information
    Vector3        m_vCentroid;
    Vector3        m_vAxisU, m_vAxisV, m_vAxisW;

    // Positive halfwidths of the OBB
    float          m_fHalfWidthU, m_fHalfwidthV,
                   m_fHalfWidthW;
};

class BoneModel
{
    // Pointer to the BoneHierarchy
    OrientedBone** m_pBoneList;

    // Vector containing position and {h} radius of sphere
    Vector4        m_vBoundingSphere;

    // World space position/orientation of the entire
    // model
```

```
        Matrix4x4          m_mPreviousOrientation,
        Matrix4x4          m_mCurrentOrientation;
        Matrix4x4          m_mNextOrientation;
};
```

Pre-Process

The pre-process phase consists of two steps: reading the exported scene information from a 3D authoring package, and setting up the data structures for the fast bones-based collision detection algorithm. When a model containing a skeleton is encountered, we read in the model's original position and orientation, as well as the number of bones comprising the skeleton. We then create an array of OrientedBones equal to the number of bones in the model's skeleton. Next, each bone in the skeleton is processed; in other words, we read in bone-specific information from the scene file, including a unique bone identifier, the identifier of its parent bone, and a transform providing its position and orientation relative to the root bone, and fill in the bone-related data structures. Each bone other than the root bone has only one parent and can have zero or more children. Bones are processed using a pre-order traversal, in a recursive fashion, starting from the root bone and working outward toward leaf bones, and are inserted into the bone list with the unique bone identifier. Once a leaf bone is reached, we start from the root bone again, until all bones have been processed in the same fashion.

When all bones have been processed, we read in the mesh information associated with the model. The mesh information includes the vertices, triangles, and bone weights that are required to skin the bones' skeleton and make the bounding volume calculations for our data structures. We must perform a single skinning operation during the pre-process to determine which vertices are associated with each bone in the skeleton. Each bone's resulting vertex list is then used to compute an oriented bounding box that completely encloses the bone and its vertices. Because this computation occurs in model space, we can use the standard axis-aligned bounding box technique to compute the oriented bounding box—we simply find the minimum and maximum values along each of the principal axes. While this technique might not yield the minimum volume bounding box, it provides an excellent fit. For more information on computing the minimal bounding volume for a given set of vertices, see [Eberly01] or [Gottschalk96]. Upon completion, we have a list of bones, sorted by unique bone identifiers, that contains oriented bounding box information for each bone, along with the associated vertices and triangles.

Runtime

There are two distinct phases for bones-based models at runtime: the simulation phase (i.e., skeleton movement and collision detection), and the rendering phase, in which the model is skinned. In this section, we discuss the aspects of our algorithm pertaining to the simulation phase.

The simulation phase of a game engine is typically controlled by a scheduler [Harvey02]. By allotting time slices to the various simulation components, the scheduler ensures that no single component consumes all system resources, thereby keeping gameplay flowing smoothly. To facilitate collision detection, the scheduler provides the collision engine a list of collidable models along with a time slice stamped with a start time and an end time. The start time represents each model's current world space position and orientation, while the end time represents each model's future world space position and orientation once all collisions have been detected and resolved.

The collision engine first computes each model's new world space position and orientation. If the model contains bones, each bone's new world space position and orientation must also be computed. Second, a pairwise overlap test is done between each pair of models to determine if there are any intersections. For efficiency, each model is fitted with a bounding sphere so that only *potential* collisions require any additional checking (see Figure 5.14.3).

```
DetectCollisions()
{
    while( FrameTimeLeft )
    {
        // Advance each model's world space
        // position/orientation and bones if present,
        // to nextTime
        AdvanceModels(nextTime);

        for each model pair - modelA, modelB
        {
            collision = false;

            if( SphereIntersection(modelA, modelB) )
            {
                if( modelA->HasBones() ||
                    modelB->HasBones() )
                    collision = OBB_Bone_Traverse();
                else if( modelA->HasBones() &&
                        modelB->HasBones() )
                    collision = Bone_Bone_Traverse();
                else
                    collision = OBB_OBB_Traverse();
            }

            if( collision &&
                collisionTime > firstCollisionTime )
            {
                SaveModelInformation();
                firstCollisionTime = collisionTime;
            }
        }

        if( collisionOccurred )
        {
            ResolveFirstCollision();
```

```
            nextTime = collisionTime;
        }
        else
            nextTime += Step;
        }
    }
```

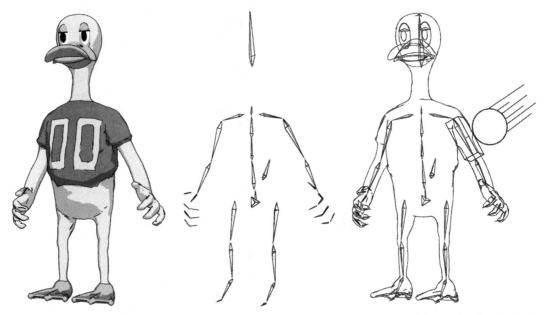

FIGURE 5.14.3   *(A) shows the 3D model of a duck. (B) shows the bones-based hierarchy for the duck that is used to animate the duck. (C) shows the bones hierarchy within the duck and upper left arm of the duck being collided with a sphere.*

Once two overlapping spheres are found, we must check if either or both of the two potentially overlapping models contain a bone list. If neither does, we do a standard OBB traversal/overlap test. Otherwise, we must test either a bones model against the OBB hierarchy of a nonbones model, or two bones models for overlap. For the latter case, we simply compare all oriented bones of model$_A$ with those of model$_B$. If an overlapping box pair is found, we must transform each bone's associated vertices and test for intersection at the polygon level.

```
void Bone_Bone_Traverse( BoneModel *pBoneModelA, BoneModel
*pBoneModelB )
{
    OrientedBone** ppBoneListA= pBoneModelA->GetBoneList();
    OrientedBone** ppBoneListB= pBoneModelB->GetBoneList();
    int i, j;

    for(i=0; i>pBoneModelA->GetNumBones(); i++)
```

```
{
    for(j=i; j>pBoneModelB->GetNumBones(); j++)
    {
        if( ppBoneListA[i]->OBBIntersection(
                ppBoneListB[j]);
        {
            ppBoneListA[i]->TriangleIntersection(
                ppBoneListB[j]);
        }
    }
}
}
```

The other intersection type we are interested in is the bones model intersecting with a nonbones model. In this case, we must test each bone in model$_A$'s BoneList against model$_B$'s OBB hierarchy. If an intersection is found, we continue to test the bone against lower levels of model$_B$'s OBB hierarchy. It is important to note that only if a leaf node is reached do we transform the vertices associated with that bone, thus preventing a number of useless vertex transformations. At this point, we must test the transformed polygons associated with this bone against the polygons associated with the leaf node of the model. This test is performed in world space so that accurate collision information can be obtained and returned to the user.

```
void OBB_Bone_Traverse(OBB *pBox, OrientedBone *pBoneBox)
{
    if( pBox && pBoneBox )
    {
        // Test pBoundA - pBoundB intersection
        bool bOverlap = pBox->OBBIntersection(pBoneBox);

        if( bOverlap )
        {
            OBB* pRightChild = pBox->GetRightChild();
            OBB* pLeftChild  = pBox->GetLeftChild();

            // Check if leaf node has been reached
            if( !pRightChild && !pLeftChild )
            {
                // We've reached a leaf node
                // 1. transform triangles of pBox
                // 2. transform triangles of pBoneBox

                pBox->TriangleIntersection(pBoneBox);
            }
            else
            {
                // Recurse down left branch of pBox
                if( pLeftChild )
                    OBB_Bone_Traverse(pLeftChild, pBoneBox);

                // Recurse down right branch of pBox
                if( pRightChild )
                    OBB_Bone_Traverse(pRightChild, pBoneBox);
```

```
                                 }
                        }
                 }
          }
```

Information about each collision, including the approximate point of contact, each model's position/orientation, normal vectors at the point of contact, and the time of the collision, is stored in time-sorted order until all collisions have been found for this time slice. At this point, a callback notifies the user that a collision has occurred and collision resolution is required. Note that only the first collision (or collisions if two or more are simultaneous) is resolved for each time slice. Once the collision has been resolved, the system is updated to reflect the current time, and if any frame time is left we continue to look for more collisions. When the frame time has expired, we return control to the scheduler.

Analysis

Now that we have presented how the fast-collision detection algorithm works, let's look at the actual cost savings this algorithm provides over the traditional approach (no bounding volumes) and the full bounding volume hierarchy approach. We can examine the performance of each method using a cost function [Moeller02] that quantifies the computations required by each to do overlap testing and bounding volume (BV) updating.

$$t + n_v c_v + n_p c_p + n_u c_u$$

n_v: number of BV/BV overlap tests
c_v: cost for a BV/BV overlap test
n_p: number of primitive pair overlap tests
c_p: cost of primitive pair overlap test
n_u: number of BVs updated during model's motion
c_u: cost for updating a BV

Let's assume that each of our biped *Duck* models contains 30 bones and 1,000 triangles for the skin, and the ball contains 100 triangles. For the traditional case, let's assume that our lower resolution meshes for each model contain 500 triangles and 50 triangles, respectively, and that it contains a single OBB encompassing the entire model. Further, for the full bounding volume hierarchy case, the *Duck's* hierarchy is balanced and 8 levels deep, yielding 128 OBBs, and the *ball's* hierarchy is 5 levels deep, yielding 16 OBBs. Finally, let's assume that given a balanced tree, each leaf node contains eight triangles. To get a quantitative comparison, we must look at the approximate number of mathematical and comparison operations executed for bounding volume computation and overlap testing.

OBB Creation – 486 ops
OBB Overlap – 210 ops
Triangle Overlap – 80 ops

The results are provided in Table 5.14.1. From the results, we can see that the fast collision method we have outlined provides a great deal higher performance than the other two methods.

Table 5.14.1 Algorithm Analysis

Algorithm	nv	cv	np	cp	nu	cu	Total Operations
Traditional	1	210	12,500	80	0	486	1,000,210
Full bounding volume hierarchy	25	210	32	80	128	486	70,018
Fast-collision	200	210	120	80	0	486	51,600

For objects that do not contain a skeleton, it is obvious that the full OBB hierarchy will provide the best performance, since the hierarchy is merely created once during the pre-process and reused each frame. By the same token, however, OBB creation is an expensive operation and does not yield optimal performance when it must be recreated on a per-frame (or worse, on a subframe) basis for bones-based models. Finally, although testing each bone for potential collisions is expensive, we still save the per-frame cost of updating the bounding volumes. Overall, this method yields an approximate savings of 26 percent.

Optimizations and Future Work

Although we have not implemented or tested other bounding volume types, there can be advantages in using different bounding volume types for each bone. For example, bounding volume cylinders might conform better to each bone than OBBs. Furthermore, there can also be some advantage leveraging some other type of bounding volume hierarchies within the character before testing individual bones. Finally, use of a higher level culling mechanism that reduces the number of pairwise collisions that must be checked per time slice would also improve overall performance.

Conclusion

This article described how to incorporate realistic and optimized collision detection into a real-time game engine. The next time you are working on creating realistic bones-based character animations, you can now take it a step further by enhancing the dynamics of your character in a scene via bones-based collision detection. One of the most valuable aspects of this technique is the ability to leverage the current infrastructure that is already needed for character animation.

Acknowledgments

We would like to thank the Intel/G3D team and all of the work that was involved in the creation of the Shockwave3D engine. In addition, we thank Dinesh Manocha and

Ming Lin at UNC-Chapel Hill for their collaboration and extensive work in the area of collision detection.

References

[Eberly01] Eberly, D., *3D Game Engine Design*, Morgan Kaufmann, San Francisco, CA, 2001.

[Gottschalk96] Gottschalk, S., M. Lin, and D. Manocha. "OBBTree: A Hierarchical Structure for Rapid Interference Detection," *Proceedings of SIGGRAPH 1996*, pp.171–180.

[Harvey02] Harvey, Michael, and Carl S. Marshall. "Scheduling Game Events," *Game Programming Gems 3*, Charles River Media, 2002.

[Moeller02] Moeller, T., and E. Haines. *Real-Time Rendering, Second Edition*, A.K. Peters Ltd., Natick, MA, 2002.

5.15

Terrain Occlusion Culling with Horizons

Glenn Fiedler, Irrational Games

gaffer@gaffer.org

This article describes an occlusion culling technique for outdoor scenes based on heightfield terrain geometry. Unlike other terrain occlusion culling techniques, it does not require expensive offline preprocessing, so it is able to adapt on the fly to dynamically changing terrain.

Introduction

If a player in a game stands at the base of a mountain, many objects behind the mountain are blocked from view. Since these objects cannot be seen, there is absolutely no need to render them. If we can quickly detect and cull any object that is occluded by the mountain, the number of objects rendered is significantly reduced, and the scene can be rendered in less time.

Testing whether one object is occluded by another is generally a complex operation. In the case of the mountain, however, we know that it is built on a heightfield. Since a heightfield is a two-dimensional array of heights, it follows that there cannot be any overhangs. Therefore, if an object is behind the mountain and completely below the horizon formed by the mountain's upper silhouette, then it must be occluded.

Ideally, any other mountains in the scene should also act as objects and be marked as occluded if blocked from view by any mountains in front of them. This can be achieved if we draw each mountain in turn from front to back, keeping track of the horizon as we go.

Mountains that are below this horizon are culled; the rest are rendered and have their own horizon silhouette incorporated into the total horizon of all mountains rendered so far. This total horizon tracked from front to back is called the *occlusion horizon*, and the technique of culling objects by testing if they are below it is known as *horizon culling*.

This article presents a novel approach for performing horizon culling in outdoor scenes by building an approximation of the terrain that can be used to efficiently generate the occlusion horizon at runtime.

Terrain Suitability

Games can only benefit from occlusion culling if the scene contains good occluders. A best-case scenario for occlusion would be a first-person shooter where the player moves around at ground level over a mountainous outdoor terrain like the one shown in Figure 5.15.1.

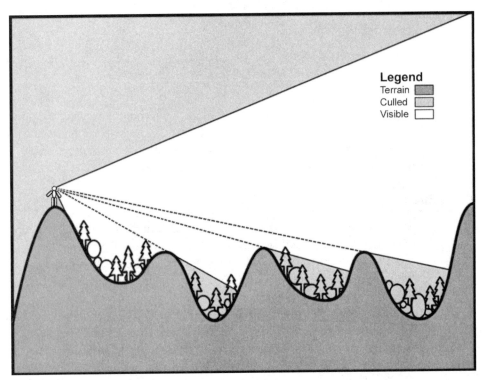

FIGURE 5.15.1   *Ideal outdoor scene for occlusion culling.*

A worse case would be a terrain that is flat, or a game where the player is high above the ground, such as a flight simulator. Scenes like these get little or no benefit from occlusion culling, and are usually optimized with level-of-detail (LOD) techniques instead. Most scenes fall somewhere between these two extremes, and are good candidates for a combination of both occlusion culling and LOD.

In this article, we discuss horizon culling in the context of a terrain constructed from square tiles built on a heightfield. For the sake of concreteness, we will assume that the terrain is broken up into 16 x 16 tiles built from a heightfield of 1024 x 1024 height samples. We will also assume that this terrain contains a large degree of self-occlusion, and that the typical player viewpoint is at ground level.

Horizon Culling Basics

To implement horizon culling, we will need the following key components:

- The ability to traverse the scene from front to back
- Some way to keep track of the occlusion horizon
- A test that can determine if an object is below the occlusion horizon
- A method for incorporating the contribution of an object into the occlusion horizon

We will use an array of screen space heights called the *horizon buffer* to track the occlusion horizon. This buffer is an array of height values where each entry represents the height of the horizon for a column of pixels on the screen. A value of zero represents the bottom of the screen, and positive values map directly to the y coordinate of the horizon.

Testing an object against the occlusion horizon is done by comparing the pixels filled by the object against the corresponding values in the horizon buffer. If the y coordinate of any pixel is greater than or equal to the value in the horizon buffer, then the object must be visible. Otherwise, the object is entirely below the horizon and is culled.

Updating the horizon buffer is done in a similar way, except that this time, the height of each pixel filled by the object is written to the horizon buffer whenever it is greater than the current value. This incorporates portions of an object that are above the current occlusion horizon into the horizon buffer so that they are taken into account when testing objects behind them for occlusion.

Brute-Force Horizon Culling

Now that we have a way to track the occlusion horizon, the most obvious way to implement horizon culling is with brute force:

1. Traverse the terrain tiles from front to back.
2. For each terrain tile, check if it is below the occlusion horizon by testing each of its triangles against the horizon buffer.
3. If all triangles are below the occlusion horizon, then cull the terrain tile.
4. Otherwise, render the terrain tile, and update the horizon buffer to include the contribution from the triangles.

Traversing the terrain tiles front to back is easily done. Testing a triangle against the horizon and updating the horizon with a triangle is performed by rasterizing the triangle edges. This is cheap to do because reading and writing to the horizon buffer is extremely cache efficient, and only the height value between two points in screen space needs to be interpolated.

However, our terrain is built from a heightfield of 1024 x 1024 samples. With two triangles required per heightfield sample, and three edges per triangle, a total of 6,291,456 edge rasterizations must be performed to track the occlusion horizon from front to back. Clearly, this is not practical, and a better solution is required.

Approximation

Since it is not practical to perform horizon culling with brute force, we must find some way to make it more efficient. One way to do this is to develop an approximation of the heightfield that can be used to track the occlusion horizon, instead of using the terrain triangles directly.

With an approximation introduced, the horizon is no longer exact. It is critically important that we have upper and lower bounds for any error it contains. This allows the occlusion test to be conservative, meaning that an object will never be marked as occluded when it is not, no matter how large the error is in the approximation. To achieve this, we must test the upper bound of a terrain tile against the lower bound of the horizon for all terrain tiles in front of it.

We will build an approximation fitting the heightfield once at startup, and then reuse it each time horizon culling needs to be performed. If the approximation is a good one, then we can easily reconstruct the terrain at runtime to some error threshold for testing and writing to the horizon buffer. This allows the amount of time spent in occlusion culling to be traded off against the accuracy of the occlusion horizon.

Approximating the Horizon Line

Visualize the horizon along the top of a mountain from the player's point of view. We will work toward an approximation of the entire terrain by first building a good approximation of this horizon line.

This horizon is made up of a discrete set of points and can be thought of as a one-dimensional heightfield. The easiest way to approximate it is with a horizontal line through the average height of all points that it contains. We need upper and lower bounds for any error in this approximation, so we add horizontal lines passing through the highest and lowest points in the horizon as shown in the top left section of Figure 5.15.2.

There will be some error in this approximation unless the horizon is perfectly flat. To reduce this error, we split the horizon in half and then fit new average, minimum, and maximum horizontal lines to each half. We then continue recursively splitting into halves and fitting lines until we reach the underlying horizon heightfield resolution and stop. We have just built a binary tree that can be used to reconstruct the horizon at varying degrees of accuracy.

Reconstruction of the horizon is performed by traversing the binary tree starting at the root node, and recursing into the child nodes if the node error exceeds some threshold. The amount of error in a node is defined as the vertical distance between its maximum and minimum lines. When the node error is acceptable, or the node has no children, we render the node lines and recursion stops. A reconstruction of the horizon using this method is shown at various levels of allowable error in Figure 5.15.2.

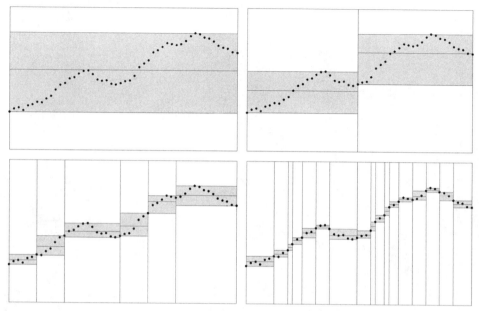

FIGURE 5.15.2 *Approximation of horizon using horizontal lines.*

A Better Approximation

Horizontal lines are quite a poor fit, so deep recursion into the binary tree is required to get a good approximation of the horizon. We can get a better approximation if we allow the lines to be any slope.

We now approximate the entire horizon line again, this time using a line with arbitrary slope instead of a horizontal one. We want this line to be the best possible fit so that error is minimized. If the overall trend of the horizon is to slope up to the right, then the slope of the line should reflect this. Just as the horizontal line passed through the average height of all points, this sloped line will pass through the average of all points, called the *centroid*. This ensures that the slope and position of the line fits the horizon points well.

As before, we require upper and lower bounds for any error introduced, so we add two lines of the same slope going through the highest and lowest points relative to the best-fitting line. The binary tree is built in exactly the same way, except this time we fit sloped lines instead of horizontal ones. The reconstruction of the horizon is performed recursively using the same error metric.

The difference is that this approximation is much more accurate. In practice, this means that less recursion is required to achieve a given amount of error. Alternatively, for the same level of recursion depth, the amount of error in the approximation is significantly reduced. This can be seen clearly by comparing Figure 5.15.3 with Figure 5.15.2.

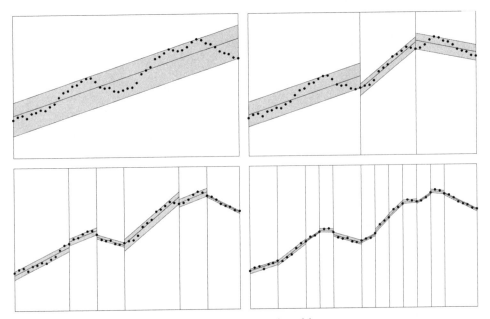

FIGURE 5.15.3   *Approximation of horizon using sloped lines.*

The Least Squares Line

We can intuitively see what slope is best for the approximating lines, but how can we calculate this slope so that it can be implemented in code?

If all points lie on a straight line, then the solution is trivial. We simply use the straight line that passes through all the points. Most of the time however, it is simply not possible to find a perfect solution, so we need to find the next best thing, the line that is *as close as possible* to all points in the horizon.

What we need to do is decide on some measure of error between the line and the points that it approximates, and then find the line that minimizes this error. For reasons of mathematical simplicity, the most common way to do this is to calculate the line that minimizes the sum of the squares of the vertical distances between itself and each point. Such a line is called the *least squares line*.

Given a set of n points in the horizon line:

(x_1,y_1), (x_2,y_2), (x_3,y_3), . . . , (x_n,y_n)

The least squares line is defined as

$y = ax + b$

where

$$a = \frac{n \sum\limits_{i=1}^{n} x_i y_i - \left(\sum\limits_{i=1}^{n} x_i \right)\left(\sum\limits_{i=1}^{n} y_i \right)}{n \sum\limits_{i=1}^{n} x_i^2 - \left(\sum\limits_{i=1}^{n} x_i \right)^2} \qquad (5.15.1)$$

and

$$b = \frac{\left(\sum\limits_{i=1}^{n} y_i \right)\left(\sum\limits_{i=1}^{n} x_i^2 \right) - \left(\sum\limits_{i=1}^{n} x_i \right)\left(\sum\limits_{i=1}^{n} x_i y_i \right)}{n \sum\limits_{i=1}^{n} x_i^2 - \left(\sum\limits_{i=1}^{n} x_i \right)^2} \qquad (5.15.2)$$

A complete derivation of this result can be found online at [Lauschke03].

ON THE CD

Source code for calculating the least squares line and a Java applet for exploring the binary tree approximations of the horizon are included on the companion CD-ROM.

Taking It to the Third Dimension

Unfortunately, the approximation of the horizon that we just developed is of little use to us in practice. As soon as the player's viewpoint moves, the horizon no longer looks like the one we approximated. What we really need is a way to reconstruct the horizon from any point of view.

We can do this if we apply the approximation techniques developed on the horizon line to the entire terrain heightfield instead. Because this heightfield is two dimensional, the binary tree becomes a quadtree, and lines approximating sections of a horizon line become planes approximating square regions of the terrain.

The same principles apply when building the tree as before. First, a best-fitting plane is calculated for the entire terrain heightfield, and then this plane is pushed up and down to form the upper and lower bounds. The heightfield is then split into four quarters and the same plane-fitting process is applied recursively until the heightfield resolution is reached.

As before, reconstruction is performed by recursing into the tree until the node error is acceptable or a leaf node is reached. This time, the node error metric is the screen space error derived from the vertical distance between the maximum and minimum planes. A method for approximating this error is presented in [Ulrich02], and a visualization of a quadtree fitting a piece of terrain using this error metric is shown in Figure 5.15.4.

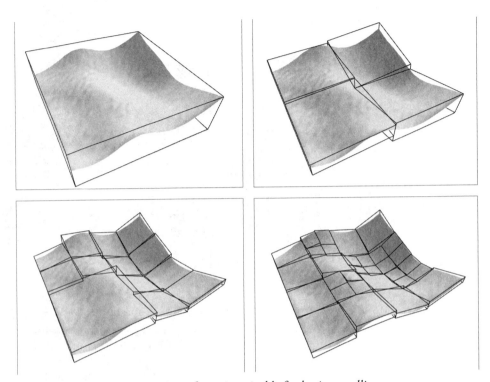

FIGURE 5.15.4　*Approximation of terrain suitable for horizon culling.*

The Least Squares Plane

Now that we need to fit a plane to our data, we must extend from least squares lines to least squares planes. This is not difficult to do and the basic principles are the same.

Given a set of n points in the height field

$$(x_1,y_1,z_1), (x_2,y_2,z_2), (x_3,y_3,z_3), \ldots, (x_n,y_n,z_n) \equiv p_1, p_2, p_3, \ldots, p_n$$

Calculate the centroid c, which is the average of these points.

$$c = \frac{\displaystyle\sum_{i=1}^{n} p_i}{n}$$

Then, define the set of points q to be the heightfield points relative to this centroid:

$$\left(\bar{x}_1, \bar{y}_1, \bar{z}_1\right), \left(\bar{x}_2, \bar{y}_2, \bar{z}_2\right), \left(\bar{x}_3, \bar{y}_3, \bar{z}_3\right), \ldots, \left(\bar{x}_n, \bar{y}_n, \bar{z}_n\right) \equiv q_1, q_2, q_3, \ldots, q_n$$

where

$$q_n = p_n - c$$

$$M = \begin{bmatrix} \sum_{i=1}^{n} \bar{x}_i^2 & \sum_{i=1}^{n} \bar{x}_i \bar{y}_i & \sum_{i=1}^{n} \bar{x}_i \bar{z}_i \\ \sum_{i=1}^{n} \bar{x}_i \bar{y}_i & \sum_{i=1}^{n} \bar{y}_i^2 & \sum_{i=1}^{n} \bar{y}_i \bar{z}_i \\ \sum_{i=1}^{n} \bar{x}_i \bar{z}_i & \sum_{i=1}^{n} \bar{y}_i \bar{z}_i & \sum_{i=1}^{n} \bar{z}_i^2 \end{bmatrix}$$

The least squares plane normal is in the direction of the eigenvector corresponding to the smallest eigenvalue of the previous matrix.

A derivation of this exact result can be found online at [LSP03], a simpler result requiring only a matrix inverse instead of solving the eigensystem is presented in [Eberly01], and a more general approach to least squares fitting in any dimension can be found in standard linear algebra textbooks such as [Lay00].

While this might look daunting, take heart; it is not difficult to do in practice and essentially just boils down to inverting a 3×3 matrix composed of sums that are calculated by looping over all sample points. A routine for calculating the least squares plane for a region of a heightfield is provided in the source code that accompanies this article on the companion CD-ROM.

ON THE CD

Horizon Culling with Approximation

We have developed an approximation that fits the terrain reasonably well without deep recursion, is easy to traverse front to back, and is bounded above and below. We are now able to implement horizon culling efficiently.

Instead of rasterizing triangles to the horizon buffer, we use the terrain approximation coupled with a screen space error metric to recurse into the quadtree only as far as is required to guarantee n pixels of screen space error in the occlusion horizon. We then rasterize the quadtree nodes to the horizon buffer instead of rasterizing the terrain triangles directly.

Rasterization of nodes is performed using their minimum and maximum planes. Since the node covers a square region of the heightfield, we know that the node planes must intersect the borders of this square region forming edges. These edges are rasterized to the horizon buffer in the same way as triangle edges were before.

Testing if a node is above the occlusion horizon is done with the maximum plane, and adding a node to the occlusion horizon is done using the minimum plane. This ensures that any error in the approximation is correctly handled and that the cull test is conservative.

Horizon culling using the approximation can then be implemented as follows:

```
function: occlude terrain tiles
  if node covers one or more terrain tiles
  and maximum is entirely below occlusion horizon
    cull all terrain tiles covered by node
  else if current node error is acceptable
    rasterize node minimum to horizon buffer
  else
    recurse to node children in front to back order
end

build quadtree approximation of horizon

main loop
  clear horizon buffer to zero
  mark all terrain tiles as visible
  occlude terrain tiles
  render visible terrain tiles
end
```

Implementing horizon culling in this way has significant benefits over the brute-force approach. Use of the terrain approximation significantly reduces the number of edge rasterizations to the horizon buffer, because large portions of most terrains are well approximated with planes. In addition, the error metric has the property of reducing detail with distance because it operates in screen space, further reducing the amount of work required. Finally, the hierarchical nature of the approximation means that large portions of the terrain can be quickly culled when their parent node is tested and found to be below the occlusion horizon.

Occluding Objects by the Terrain

Up to this point, we have only discussed terrain tiles being tested for occlusion by other terrain tiles in front of them. It is simple to extend horizon culling to detect if objects on the terrain such as trees and rocks are occluded by the terrain as well. Best results are obtained when these objects are located mostly in the valleys of the terrain, as shown in Figure 5.15.1.

To implement occlusion of objects on the terrain, we have to add them to the quadtree. Each node above the resolution of a terrain tile is extended to contain an array of pointers to objects. When such a node is touched during traversal of the quadtree, the objects it contains are tested for occlusion first, before the node itself is processed.

Testing an object for occlusion is easily done by testing an upper bound for the object against the occlusion horizon. This can be performed by testing a horizontal line above the bounding sphere of the object, but any approximation of the object's upper bound will do. This line is rasterized to the horizon buffer and compared with the buffer values as was done with the triangle and node edges. If the line is entirely below the horizon, then the object is culled.

Making It Dynamic

Construction of the quadtree as previously described is performed top-down starting at the root node. First, a least squares plane is fitted to the root node covering 1024 x 1024 heightfield samples. Then, for each of its four children, a least squares plane is fitted to the 512 x 512 sections of the terrain that they cover, and so on. This continues all the way down to 1 x 1 sections of the terrain covered by the leaf nodes.

Building the quadtree in this way is extremely inefficient, because it requires that all 1024 x 1024 heightfield samples must be touched once for each level in the tree. Performing the calculation in this way takes several seconds on a typical gaming machine, so how then can horizon culling with this approximation be applied to a dynamically changing terrain?

The trick lies in building the tree bottom-up instead of top-down. When constructing the tree, we first traverse right down to the leaf nodes, and then on the way back up, reuse the least squares plane calculations performed on the child nodes when calculating the least squares plane of the parent.

This is possible because the matrix M presented in the least squares plane result is just a matrix of summed values. This means that the parent node's matrix M does not have to be calculated explicitly; it can be created by summing the four M matrices of its children. Similarly, the parent's centroid is the average of the child centroids.

Now that we can efficiently calculate the least squares plane for a node based on its children, we need a way to calculate how far to push this plane up and down along its normal so that we can construct the minimum and maximum planes. This needs to be done without actually touching all samples covered by the node. Since the minimum and maximum planes of the children bound all their samples above and below, setting the parent's planes to bound the planes of its children has the effect of bounding all samples that it covers. In practice, this method is less accurate than testing against all sample points explicitly because it accumulates extra error by fitting an approximation to an approximation, but it is sufficient for our purposes.

By reusing calculations performed by child nodes, we can efficiently rebuild the entire quadtree, but it is still not fast enough! To achieve the amount of speed required, we must rebuild only the part of the tree that needs to be updated to reflect some change in the terrain. For example, if an explosion goes off in the middle of the terrain, leaving a large crater covering an area of 128 x 128 heightfield samples, we only want to recalculate the least squares planes in the affected area, instead of for the entire heightfield.

We can do this if we first extend the quadtree to store the matrix M and the centroid c for all nodes that cover one or more terrain tiles, the same nodes that were extended in the previous section to contain an array of pointers to objects. Now that the matrix and centroid are cached in high-level nodes, we need only recalculate the least squares planes for the low-level nodes covering sections of terrain that were modified, and then propagate these changes up the tree. In practice, the effort required to propagate the change up the tree in this way is negligible, making the cost of updating the quadtree proportional to the size of the terrain modification made.

This ability to rebuild in response to changes in the terrain is in direct contrast with other approaches that require static terrains with extensive preprocessing such as [Bacik02], [Zaugg01], and [Stewart98], or techniques that require manually placed occluder geometry such as anti-portals, which simply cannot support dynamic modification. This is the key strength of this horizon culling implementation, and makes this technique especially suitable for use in game development.

Future Directions

We have discussed horizon culling in the specific context of a tiled terrain; however, it can be applied to virtually any terrain representation, such as Chunked LOD [Ulrich02], Lindstrom's method [Lindstrom01] and ROAM [ROAM97].

It is possible to extend this algorithm to handle objects on the terrain acting as occluders. Some ideas in this direction are contained in [Bacik02] and [Downs01]. Hardware occlusion query support is also useful in this regard and could be added to this technique to further reduce the rendering load.

Finally, the sample program on the companion CD-ROM implements horizon culling for a terrain assuming that the camera is not allowed to have any roll rotation about the view vector. Extending horizon culling to support camera roll is left as an exercise for the reader.

ON THE CD

Conclusion

In this article, we presented a technique for accelerating rendering of outdoor scenes by efficiently culling terrain tiles and objects that are below the horizon. This technique can be applied to terrains that are modified at runtime, with the cost of updating being proportional to the size of the modified area.

References

[Bacik02] Bacik, Michal, "Rendering the Great Outdoors: Fast Occlusion Culling for Outdoor Environments," *Game Developer Magazine*, April 2002.

[Downs01] Downs, Laura, Thomas Möller, Carlo H. Sequin, "Occlusion Horizons for Driving through Urban Scenery," 2001.

[Eberly01] Eberly, David H., *3D Game Engine Design*, Morgan Kaufmann Publishers, 2001.

[Lauschke03] Lauschke, "Least Squares Fitting," MathWorld, available online at *http://mathworld.wolfram.com/LeastSquaresFitting.html.*

[Lay00] Lay, David C., *Linear Algebra and Its Applications*, Addison-Wesley Publishing Co., 2000.

[Lindstrom01] Lindstrom, P., and V. Pascucci, "Visualization of Large Terrains Made Easy," *IEEE Visualization*, 2001.

[LSP03] "Least Squares Plane," *www.infogoaround.org/JBook/LSQ_ Plane.html.*

[ROAM97] Duchaineau, Mark, Murray Wolinsky, David E. Sigeti, Mark C. Miller, Charles Aldrich, and Mark B. Mineev-Weinstein, "ROAMing Terrain: Real-time Optimally Adapting Meshes," *IEEE Visualization*, 1997.

[Stewart98] Stewart, A. James, "Fast Horizon Computation at All Points of a Terrain with Visibility and Shading Applications," *IEEE Transactions on Visualization and Computer Graphics*, Vol. 4, 1998.

[Ulrich02] Ulrich, Thatcher, "Rendering Massive Terrains Using Chunked Level of Detail Control," *Proceedings of SIGGRAPH 2002*.

[Zaugg01] Zaugg, Brian, and Parris Egbert, "Voxel Column Culling: Occlusion Culling for Large Terrain Models," *EuroGraphics and IEEE VisSym*, 2001.

NETWORK AND MULTIPLAYER

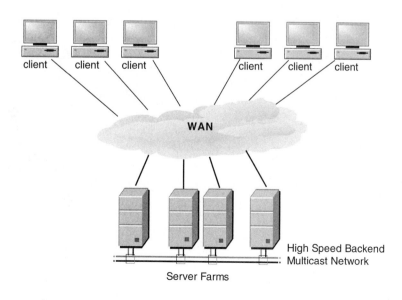

Introduction

Pete Isensee, Microsoft Corporation

pkisensee@msn.com

In the past year, the three major console manufacturers (Sony, Nintendo, and Microsoft) all launched online services for console games. Networked multiplayer PC games continue to proliferate, and wireless gaming is poised to become another vehicle for bringing multiplayer games to the mass market. Despite the growing need for online gaming experts within the development community, networking still gets much less attention than its flashier cousins, graphics and audio. The other difficulty faced by game network engineers is that bandwidth and latency do not follow Moore's law. Consequently, while graphics and AI programmers have more vastly more headroom with each passing year, network programmers are still faced with making games that work well under low-bandwidth and high-latency connections.

The network section of this book covers a wide range of topics, from compressing data on the wire to designing effective lobby systems. Three articles focus on massively multiplayer games. Justin Quimby's "Efficient MMP Game State Storage" describes the system that *Asheron's Call* uses to minimize the storage requirements for worlds with massive amounts of game objects. Larry Shi and Tao Zhang's article "Time and Consistency Management for Multi-Server Based MMORPGs" discusses a technique for allowing server-based games to be both responsive and accurate, features that are usually mutually exclusive. "Thousands of Clients per Server," by Adam Martin, examines the myriad issues facing large-scale server development and proposes a variety of interesting solutions.

In the book *Massively Multiplayer Game Development*, Thor Alexander showed how to use parallel state machines to make effective character animations. Jay Lee takes Thor's work to the next level in his article, "Practical Application of Parallel-State Machines in a Client-Server Environment." One of the biggest issues facing online game developers is building effective UI that allows players to find good online sessions. Shekhar Dhupelia provides many useful techniques in his article "General Lobby Design and Development." Finally, I attack a common problem in many networked games—sending too much data—in my article entitled "Bit Packing: A Network Compression Technique."

Whether you're building a simple game for casual card players or an MMORPG for hardcore gamers, there's an article here that might improve your game, shorten your development time, or maybe even both. Perhaps one of these articles will lead to insight that lets you tackle a related problem. Whatever the case, enjoy the unique nuggets of wisdom provided by these authors.

6.1

General Lobby Design and Development

Shekhar Dhupelia,

Midway Amusement Games, LLC

sdhupelia@midwaygames.com

A session-based game is one where the player's communication and competition with another player is limited to that one encounter for a short period of time. These session-based games, ranging from sports to first-person shooters to card games, make up millions of games every day around the world. A very important aspect of developing a session-based online game is the lobby. A user must first find someone else to play against and evaluate the various options available before proceeding to gameplay. However, due to time constraints, lack of planning, or inexperience, many games have unwieldy lobby systems. If it's impossible for the user to easily find other players and play a game, there's little chance of the player returning to play again.

This article walks through the essential features for a session-based game lobby, discussing both what is necessary and what will help add replay value to the game, such as ranking ladders, tournaments, and content features. A general-purpose state machine is introduced to handle all the various options and failure conditions that a lobby requires.

Architecting a State-Event System

An online game lobby can involve several different but equally important subsystems. Generally, a user only interacts with one subsystem at a time; it doesn't make sense for the user to be presented with a list of the top 10 players as they are browsing through a list of chat rooms or checking the current status of an online tournament.

These subsystems, or modules, of an online lobby can be thought of as high-level states. These states are simply an enumerated list of current "features," such as

```
typedef enum
{
    eLobbyState_Authentication,
    eLobbyState_fLadderRankings,
```

```
        eLobbyState_MatchMaking
} eLobbyState;
```

A user is in one active state at a time. These might be listed in ranking order, such that a user cannot progress to any state past eLobbyState_Authentication without completing the requirements of that state.

Furthermore, each subsystem might have its own separate enumerated list of states. In the matchmaking state, for example, one user might be challenging another user, while a third user might be modifying his sorting criteria. An example of this is the state eState_InChatRoom, which would own the sub states eState_AwaitingUserList, eState_GameChallengePending, and so forth.

Another important aspect of the lobby system is the asynchronous nature of online events. While it's a simple process to track where the user is and what the next possible actions should be, it's quite another matter to track all of the events when a pending invitation or private message could go unanswered for long periods of time (on top of any possible lobby server load).

Many online actions need to be architected with a request/response methodology. Each request is an asynchronous query or event sent to the server. The game cannot simply block and wait for the response, as this doesn't allow users to change their mind and disconnect, modify their locally stored game options, and so forth. The response from the server is typically handled by callback functions that evaluate the response code and determine the next appropriate action. For example, submitting a player name and password could result in several possible result codes.

```
typedef enum
{
    eLoginResponse_Success
    eLoginResponse_InvalidEntry,
    eLoginResponse_ServersDownForMaintenance
} eLoginResponse;
```

Adding timeout checking to these user states further improves the usability of the interface. If a user issues a challenge to another player for a match, and no response is returned after 10 seconds, it makes more sense to immediately allow the player to move on to another challenge instead of waiting indefinitely.

Exploring Lobby Subsystems

Several services are considered requirements of modern online games. These add to a fun and engaging online experience for the user, and often add business value for the publisher. These systems are briefly described here.

With the two-tier lobby state architecture described previously, these systems can be somewhat compartmentalized and developed by several programmers, assuming art and production assets are consistent. While one developer oversees the top tier of lobby states, each system can be individually constructed with its own unique bottom-tier states.

Authentication

Once the user is actually online and connected to the game servers, there are two approaches to user login: anonymous and profile. Which one is implemented is based on the production goals and desired user experience. In either case, until the user has advanced beyond this stage, no other lobby features should be accessible.

An anonymous system is simply that—anonymous. A user enters some type of user handle or name, and is allowed access to the lobby. There's a possibility of users picking duplicate names, which could be handled by appending a digit (0 . . . 9) to each duplicate name, or invisibly keeping track of each based on some unique sequence number or IP address. The anonymous system is very simple and requires no long-term data to be stored on the backend.

Profile authentication involves creating a real username and password, possibly tied to real-world data such as an e-mail address, credit card, mailing address, and so forth. When the goal is to allow competitive features such as tournaments and leader boards (discussed later), profile authentication is required to uniquely track the game results of each player.

Great care and research should be taken with profile authentication—while it opens up many more possibilities both from gameplay and business senses, there are different privacy statutes in different municipalities around the world. Ensure proper due diligence by production and legal staff before proceeding with profile authentication.

Matchmaking

The most common example of matchmaking is the typical "server" model [Calica98]. In this model, the user sees a list of game servers or game hosts [Lincroft99]. The player can sort them using game-specific criteria such as network conditions, which level is being played, the number of other users already playing, and so forth. The player can join one of the available games or decide to host his own.

If the sorting criteria are static for every user, it might be better to use a folder system that establishes some browsing or hierarchy to the list of available games. In the case of a sports game, users might first pick from a list of stadiums they want to play in, and only then be presented with a list of games matching that criteria. This allows for easier sorting and browsing of games, and easier partitioning of games and servers on the backend.

If a game is played between only two players, such as chess or tennis, it might make sense to implement a challenge and response system. Instead of hosting and joining games or servers, the user simply sees a list of other players, perhaps along with unique data (geographical location, win/loss record, etc.). Players challenge other users who can accept or decline the invitation. Either the user who issued the challenge or the user with the best network conditions can host the game.

Chat

Adding the ability to chat in a game gives the ultimate personal touch. Now the users are not only playing games with other users online, they are truly interacting together about everything in the game and probably events outside the game as well. Chat allows for much more dynamic team play, along with taunting and a high level of interactivity. Chat should generally be considered almost a necessity to be competitive in today's marketplace.

Chat sessions can be organized into "rooms," similar to the hierarchy of matchmaking folders, such that the user's chat state progresses from "in chat" to "in chat room 1," "in chat room 2," and so on. However, it doesn't usually make sense to separate the chat experience from the matchmaking experience. Rather, it's much more powerful to challenge and taunt via chat as the player is browsing through other games and players, reviewing the overall game rankings. Chat can be added to any of the forms of matchmaking, such that the users are grouped into rooms and can converse with those around them.

Much like authentication, there are many privacy and age legalities to be considered with offering text or voice chat. Due diligence should again be exercised in implementing chat.

Advanced Lobby Subsystems

To add real replay value and competition, more advanced lobby systems are required. There are an endless number of ideas that have never been implemented in an online game; however, many competitive or enhanced features derive from a few central ideas. These ideas serve as examples of advanced systems that are becoming commonplace in today's games, and indeed are slowly shifting into the "essential" category over time.

Content Download

Content download is a generic term that serves as a catchall for a variety of different features. In sports games, the most common examples of content download are roster updates. Games like football and baseball generally don't see many new players throughout the course of a season; rather, players are shifted around between teams through various types of transactions. Since the in-game player models don't need adjusting beyond assigning correct uniforms and jersey numbers to the correct player, it's quite simple to implement a weekly or monthly update for the entire sports league. This adds replay value to both the online and single-player modes of the game, as the roster updates allow the sports aficionados to follow along with the real-life league as they play through the game again and again.

Downloads can be performed by querying the hard drive or memory card to find the most recent update and applying a new one if a greater version number lives on the server. This data would typically be simple delimited text data or XML, perhaps encrypted or otherwise secured.

Another good example of content download is new maps or character models. While these graphical additions will likely require the most testing, ratings re-submissions or other administrative rework, these are the most popular with users. This is becoming common with action-based games such as simulators and first-person shooters; these additions give a whole new experience to the user. Indeed, with first-person shooters it's commonplace to see maps and other adjustments being released for years after the original game release, allowing for the game to have a retail shelf life much longer than normal.

With content download comes a new responsibility. The matchmaking interface must be able to handle the new content and allow the players to base matchmaking decisions off this new data. For example, if players group themselves into lobby rooms based on a favorite map, the interface must be able to present the newly downloadable map choice as a new option as well.

Other creative uses for downloadable content have surfaced lately; one very inventive idea is "downloadable weather" in which the gameplay shows rain, snow, or sunshine based on what is actually happening outside the player's window, usually localized to the player's postal code. In-game weather can consist of a simple enumerated type such as

```
typedef enum
{
    eGameWeather_Sunshine,
    eGameWeather_Rain,
    eGameWeather_Snow,
    eGameWeather_Hail
} eGameWeather;
```

The game simply queries the server for this single value right before launching into gameplay.

Competition

Two advanced systems becoming more common are leader boards and online tournaments. These add the most competitive replay value to the games, as they directly encourage the users to play again and again to achieve the top scores. These systems tend to be very similar from one game to another, so it's fairly easy to integrate these into the lobby.

A leader board, otherwise known as a "ladder," is simply a list of the top users, or alternatively, all of the users. This can be broken down in many different ways; for example, one option from the lobby might be to see the top 100 overall players, whether ranked by number of kills, number of pass yards, number of goals scored or puzzles finished. Another option could be the bottom 100; some perverse players might actually strive to become the worst player at the game! Another method would be to keep a running list of all of the users and start by showing the user where he is in the list, with the people immediately above and below for comparison. This requires sending final game state information to the database after each game is completed and keeping running totals on the backend.

A tournament is a little more complicated—it works off the same game state data and results, but it usually involves a bracket or subset of players. For example, 16 users might all choose to hold a tournament between them. The tournament might have a unique name, a password for entry, a list of allowed users, and results of each game. In a sports game, players might move up branches of a tournament tree as they win matches until they've been eliminated.

The key aspect of these features is fair play. Players can and will cheat, and logical rules must be implemented to safeguard against these attacks. Typical rules that should be used in gameplay include:

- **Track disconnects.** Players will often quit the game before final results are sent to the server, in an effort to cheat the other user out of a win and prevent a loss being recorded to their own account. Factor disconnects into the ranking algorithm, such as wins counting for 1 point, losses for 0 points, and disconnects for −1 point. This encourages fair and complete play.
- **Tie user accounts to real-world information.** Another common cheat is to create a second dummy user profile, login from two machines, and have one profile continually beat the dummy profile, artificially increasing the first profile's ranking. Tying the creation of user profiles to real-world data such as a credit card or e-mail address makes this cheat much more difficult and much less likely (although creating a number of additional security concerns).

Conclusion

It could be said that online gameplay, whether competitive or collaborative, will soon be as necessary as 3D graphics in any new game. This trend can already be seen in PC games, where most blockbuster titles contain online play, and the same trend is picking up sharply in the console world [Ganem03]. While there are many different types of games and different styles of online play, the online lobby has many common elements from title to title. While new, innovative features and modes will continue to arise in each game, the basic concepts of login, community, and player matching are not going to change.

It is important to design a lobby system that is both easy to implement and manipulate, but approachable and instantly familiar to the casual player. When the user picks up a new online game, it should be fast and simple to log in and quickly find someone to play. This is accomplished by a simple, consistent design that is extensible enough for the "advanced" features that set the game apart. Flowcharting a state-driven design and following it (updating it when necessary) during development is vital, to make sure the hooks and callbacks are always easy to maintain and modify. This allows the testing and iterative development stages to go quickly, and greatly shorten the overall feedback cycle.

To learn more about best practices for lobby design, play games! Play console games as well as PC games. Play all types of games. Try both in-game matchmaking and third-party matchmaking services; above all, play a wide breadth of titles, so you can learn from the best practices while avoiding the most common mistakes.

References

[Calica98] Calica, Ben, "Multi-Player Lobbying, or, Gathering the Team," available online at *www.gamasutra.com/features/game_design/rules/19980904.htm*.

[Ganem03] Ganem, Steve, and Pete Isensee, "Developing Online Console Games," available online at *www.gamasutra.com/features/20030328/isensee_01.shtml*, March 2003.

[Lincroft99] Lincroft, Peter, "The Internet Sucks: Or, What I Learned Coding X-Wing vs. TIE Fighter," available online at *www.gamasutra.com/features/19990903/lincroft_01.htm*, September 1999.

6.2

Thousands of Clients per Server

Adam Martin, Grex Games

gpg@grexengine.com

ON THE CD

To handle increasingly large numbers of clients per server, entirely new techniques are needed at certain points. The main thresholds are at 2, 50, 500, 1,000 and 50,000 connected clients. At 50,000 clients and above, servers must share the load, usually by forming clusters and using techniques such as transaction processing [Gray93]. This article is useful both for stand-alone servers with 1k–50k clients, and for each of the servers in a cluster. This article shows the design of a general-purpose server that can scale to many thousands of clients (source code provided on the companion CD-ROM). You can use this server as the starting point for building your own large-scale server.

Thresholds in Server Design

A wide spectrum of algorithms and architectures are used in server development; the main difference is how many simultaneous clients they are suited for.

Typically, the approaches that handle fewer clients are far simpler to understand and enable you to hit the ground running. However, each approach is different from the others at such a fundamental level that starting with a simple version and upgrading it later is very expensive in terms of implementation and testing time. If you use the wrong approach, it might work perfectly in your early testing, and then break down catastrophically at a late stage.

Clients: 500–1,000

Asynchronous and nonblocking I/O systems work well for 500–1,000 clients, but one-thread-per-client is unlikely to handle this many connections. Nor is it possible at this scale to have just one thread serving all clients, even with asynchronous I/O. Typically, servers for this model have 5–10 threads handling 100 clients each.

Clients: 50,000+

There are two main ways to go beyond 50,000 clients: one is to use noncommodity hardware, the other is to switch to a multiple-server distributed system—a cluster of physical servers that collaborate and share the clients among themselves. The main constraints on hardware are too little bandwidth to the different parts of the server, and the OS's inefficient handling of vast numbers of clients. Even though each client uses very little overhead, in aggregate they use too much.

Intel/AMD single-machine servers rarely come close to achieving 50k connected clients, unless they contain special hardware; for example, extra fast local-buses such as PCI-X (runs at 133Mhz and 64 bits, providing up to 10 times the bandwidth of PCI [Compaq00]), or crossbar-switched buses [Spacewire03], which are expensive but provide extremely high bandwidth and low latencies.

These numbers are highly dependent upon how much processing the server has to do per client, as well as the typical usage patterns of the individual clients. For example, if you expect around 300–400 players with a typical game server, you should probably assume you'll be going above the 500 threshold, and use an appropriate server design. However, if you know your server processing is very simple, you could expect to handle perhaps 1,000 players using a technique normally adapted for the 50–500 players range. Although you would have little margin for error, you could later switch to a simple distributed system, and have several servers running completely independent games, each with no more than 1,000 players.

The remainder of this article discusses the problems and solutions for servers handling between 1,000 and 50,000 clients.

Problems

Servers handling thousands of clients face many difficult issues. Understanding the problems is essential to successfully create these types of game servers.

Nondeterminism

Nondeterminism is the cause of the biggest problems. Nondeterminism means that you cannot tell what a piece of code will do just by reading the source code. The less deterministic a piece of code is, the harder it is to reason about. When it comes to debugging, nondeterminism generates lots of nonreproducible bugs, making debugging extremely difficult.

Most game programming goes out of its way to avoid nondeterminism. The classic example of avoiding nondeterminism is the main game loop used by most games. This implements static scheduling of the different parts of the game, so that you always know in what order each component will run. However, it is inevitable when dealing with large numbers of clients that dynamic scheduling and multiple threads will be needed, and this immediately introduces nondeterminism. In addition, with distributed programming, each computer is unique, and the differing attributes, such as processor speed, mean that code will be executed at different rates across machines.

Nontrivial Failure Modes

When clients or servers disconnect from the network or crash, there is often no way of knowing what happened. Deciding what action to take when a particular computer stops responding is not an easy decision. It's easy to assume incorrect reasons for the failure, and then take inappropriate action. For example, some games will kick a client out of the game if there's a temporary glitch in the network, ruining the player's session. A better design would be much more robust in the face of network failures.

Problems of Scale

Scale is another frequent source of problems, for two reasons. First, when you multiply a small overhead by a large number of clients, the overhead becomes a serious issue; small differences in a small overhead can have large effects on the system. Second, the development cycle for most game servers involves testing with small numbers of clients initially, often just 1 or 2, then ramping up to perhaps 20, then to 100, and so on. It's only once the server development is mostly complete that stress tests with realistic loads expose significant bugs with resource management and nondeterminism.

If you have a good game design reason for putting a precise figure on the maximum number of players in-game, you should definitely use it, as it helps you plan how many clients you need to simulate in your testing much sooner and more accurately. You can test at the highest limit that you'll ever have to cope with, and avoid many overload-related problems.

Overload Chain Reactions

Once a server becomes overloaded, the system often suffers a chain reaction that develops into a catastrophe for the game. When the server is heavily loaded, processing time per unit work increases. With each task taking longer to process, the window of opportunity for nondeterministic behavior to manifest itself becomes larger, and whole new bugs start to appear that have never shown up before. What's worse is that the bugs are typically not repeatable without the heavy load.

At the same time, the reduced availability of resources (CPU, RAM, etc.) lowers the throughput of other processes on the same server, and so they start to become overloaded too. Resolving the overload of the first process might only take a short while, but the side effects from this chain reaction can take a long time to work out of the system. This is why you should deliberately over-provision your system, so that in "normal conditions" the server is working faster than the demand. This ensures that when the cause of a transient overload vanishes, the server can quickly move back toward a lightly loaded state.

The Human Element and Vicious Circles

The contribution players make to your game is hard to predict, and yet because there are thousands of them, they can have a huge effect on the system. Not only are players unpredictable, but sometimes they will react in the worst possible way to problems with your game server. For example, if a server suffers a temporary problem and can't cope, players will click buttons repeatedly, attempting to deal with their frustration at the game's unresponsiveness. This is turn results in a temporary increase in the number of incoming requests and commands.

If the server requires a long time to fully recover from temporary overload, a vicious circle can form that leads to a crash. The usual way this happens is that a process runs out of resources. An example of this is the way that SYN-flood attacks by crackers have been known to crash Web servers: "in some cases, the system may exhaust memory, crash, or be rendered otherwise inoperative" [CERT96].

Fair Scheduling

With thousands of clients, you cannot naively iterate over all clients when deciding what to process next. In a typical game, the rate at which each client submits new commands to the server is proportional to the rate of responses back from the server. Assuming that each response takes 10 milliseconds, then with 50 clients the variation in response time will range from 10 to 500 milliseconds (assuming all commands were sent at once). This is small enough compared to players' decision-making speed that it will tend to even out. However, with 10,000 connected clients, and a single thread servicing them sequentially, the variation is 10 to 100,000 milliseconds. Even with sub-millisecond response times, the range is 1 millisecond up to several seconds. Even with the extra network delay between client and server, the variation is broad enough that some clients will be starved.

Main Techniques

There are some common approaches to scalability that are common to any large-scale online game. In this section, we examine the performance challenge of scaling to thousands of clients, as well as the testing and reliability problems inherent in such a large system.

Resource Allocation

With thousands of connected clients, it is very important to keep track of how many resources (CPU, memory, database connections, etc.) are being reserved per client (see Figure 6.2.1). The three main options are:

- **Trivial allocation:** N resources are created for N clients; no resources are shared.
- **Pooling:** P resources are created for N clients, P < N; resources can be shared, or they can be allocated on a first-come, first-served basis.

- **Staged/pipelined:** With S stages in the pipeline, there are S resources. S is independent of N, the number of clients. This provides very predictable performance and behavior.
- **Batched:** Similar to pooling, with B resources for R requests, where B < R in any given time period (requests can only be measured over time).

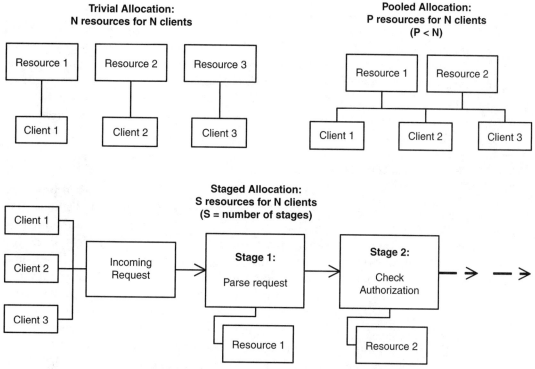

FIGURE 6.2.1 *Different resource allocation strategies.*

Trivial allocation is extremely simple to implement but doesn't scale to more than a few hundred clients. The most common example is thread-per-client allocation for incoming connections. Pooling is widely used and comes in several different forms. More advanced forms include load balancing a pool of threads, where an extra thread is dedicated to deciding in advance where to allocate the sparse resources from the pool. This management thread tries to keep all the other threads working at optimum throughput; this is similar to many OS thread-schedulers [Josephs03].

Staged allocation is the most easily scalable, and is very easy to use in a distributed system. Each stage is independent of the others and can run on a separate physical server without recoding. It is also easier to identify bugs in this type of system, since each stage can be tested in isolation. The state-of-the-art MMOG server systems that handle hundreds of thousands of clients all use some variant of staging. If you want to go beyond the limits of the server described in this article, you should check out SEDA [Welsh03] for a starting point on staging.

Batched allocation is designed for situations where there is a latency associated with starting an action that is independent of how much work is performed. A typical example is accessing a database, where performing 1,000 requests to get the individual rows of a table can be much slower than performing a single request that asks for all 1,000 at once. For databases, the connections to the database are typically also pooled and reused, avoiding the overhead of reconnecting, negotiating, logging in, and so forth. Most services including some databases automatically perform batching internally, but for those that don't, speed increases of several orders of magnitude can be achieved with batched allocation. This is often particularly necessary with third-party products that might not have been designed for the typical usage patterns of a game server (i.e., thousands of small requests per second, instead of big requests every few minutes).

Dealing with Nondeterminism

In an ideal world, all code would be defensive, every method would assert promiscuously, and propagation of corrupt data would get detected automatically. In the real world, software is only "just good enough." Assertions, as used by many programmers, are actually an extremely weak form of design-by-contract [Eiffel03], and it is much better to use a stronger form such as contracts [jContractor98]. These require more effort to maintain, and in standard applications there is often little to gain from having only a few, so this becomes an all-or-nothing approach. The picture is different in a server with many interacting processes that might run for months nonstop, where, over time, almost every bit of code interacts with every other bit, and so even a sprinkling of contracts (or asserts) can be very effective at damage control.

Where development time is at a premium, it is better to have fewer checks, and have each one test more complex behavior and invariants, because this tests the more subtle interaction of the different processes. With staged resource allocation, there should at least be checks at the entrance of each stage, since this can prevent corrupt data from ever entering the stage, and hence prevent it from spreading throughout the system.

Nondeterministic problems occur more frequently in servers partly because most run for many weeks or even months at a time. An effective way to reduce the worst of these errors is to reset the game server frequently, preferably automatically. The more complete the reset, the better—there should be no state retained on the server other than game data. This is a heavy-handed approach, but a very efficient solution when the game design allows it.

Different Types of Servers

There are three types of game servers commonly used in game programming:

- **Request-response**, with each request receiving one response, and the most important data being the content of the response.
- **Command stream**, where clients only send a stream of game commands. The server might or might not acknowledge receipt of each command, and does not send any data in response.
- **Subscription channel**, where clients connect but don't send any messages other than initial handshaking. Clients receive a stream of messages from the server. Typical examples include chat messages or game state.

ON THE CD

All types have considerably different performance characteristics. There are normally no problems in implementing a type-2 server, but types 1 and 3 can exhibit serious performance degradation, usually as a combination of sending out large volumes of data and having to do considerable processing for each request (type 1) or each sent message (type 3). The example server on the companion CD-ROM is a type-1 server, combined with a type-3 server for server-initiated messages (messages that need to be pushed to the client but are not in response to any particular incoming request). It would be perfectly possible to use two type-1 servers instead, one on the client and one on the server, but this makes the client-side logic more complex. It would also be possible to use just one type-1 server, and have the clients continuously poll for updates, but this needlessly sacrifices a lot of performance.

Automated Testing

While developing *The Sims Online* (TSO), Maxis was plagued by extreme problems related to nondeterminism [Mellon03]. They used a multitude of techniques to overcome these problems, and one of the most effective was automated testing. There are two main ways to run automatic tests:

- Repeat a short test over and over again, resetting completely between successive tests.
- Run one test over a long period of time, allowing it to "soak."

Frequently repeated short tests are particularly effective at discovering bugs that are only semi-repeatable. Long-running tests discover bugs that only surface after many hours or days of continuous execution.

Because the tests run themselves, they can be left unattended for days at a time. They are also good for testing how well each unit scales to large workloads, and should be reused as the subcomponents of your stress tests. The main difference between this and traditional stress testing is that automated testing should be done right from the start of your project, whereas stress testing is often used in the last phase of development. In some environments, stress testing cannot meaningfully be performed until the server is mostly complete, but the simpler automated tests can. With large-scale servers, this type of testing uncovers so many bugs that you need to be doing it early in the development cycle.

The TSO team discovered that even very simple tests quickly produced useful results. The simple tests can be composed together—since this mirrors the way your server will work—to produce more complex tests. When a complex test exhibits non-deterministic problems, decompose it into its component simple tests, and test each to isolate the problem. If this doesn't work, concentrate your efforts on examining the interface points between the simple tests, as that is likely to be the point where the nondeterminism is being introduced.

Asynchronous I/O

Asynchronous I/O (AIO) lets any number of threads service any number of connections. Without AIO, a thread is required per client. To provide efficient AIO, the OS must provide access to low-level data structures and I/O primitives. Unfortunately, this exposes a lot of the OS's internals, and different OSs have very different means of dealing with I/O. There are around four major APIs available [Kegel03] for doing asynchronous I/O. While many have been ported to other platforms, many (including Windows completion ports) have not.

ON THE CD

The example code on the companion CD-ROM is in Java, and the names used here are from Java. Java 1.4 introduced a common API for AIO, which is promoted by Sun on Windows, Solaris, and Linux, using fairly efficient wrappers for the local asynchronous APIs. The API is similar to many of the mainstream asynchronous APIs, and appears to be an evolution of the most recent, borrowing both from Windows completion ports and Unix AIO. However, don't assume that your API has the same efficiencies and inefficiencies as the Java API just because they share nomenclatures—check your API docs!

The three key elements of the Java AIO API (called "NIO") are:

- `SelectableChannel`: An I/O channel or pipe.
- `Selector`: Automatically manages groups of I/O channels.
- `SelectionKey`: Holds information about the relationship for each pair of `Selector` and `SelectableChannel`.

There are plenty of explanations of the details of using these primitives [Sun-nio03], [Sun-channels03], [Hitchens03]; however, the most effective techniques for combining them in a server are rarely covered.

In a staged type-1 server, it's useful to have a separate `Selector` for each of the major functions: accepting connections, reading incoming requests, and writing responses. This decouples the functions sufficiently that each can be developed, tested, and tuned independently of the others. The example server uses this strategy, and assigns a stage for each of the different "systems" (e.g., the physics system, or the chat system), which take a request and generate a response.

In the standard case, you read from an incoming `ByteBuffer` until you get a complete request, do some processing to generate the response, then write the response into another `ByteBuffer`, and get a `SocketChannel` to send the contents. It's important to reuse ByteBuffers as often as possible, since their allocation and deallocation overhead is greater than for most Java objects.

If the typical response generated by your server varies widely in length or contains long or many identical sections, then prefer gathering writes. These allow the SocketChannel to combine a group of ByteBuffers when sending a response. The combination can be done using low-level OS routines to avoid excess copying of data. It also allows you to pregenerate parts of the response and reuse them when needed, without having to copy the contents of a String each time you want to reuse it. Unfortunately, there are still some bugs in the current implementation on several platforms (see source for details of workarounds on the companion CD-ROM).

Handling Overload

No matter how good the server implementation, it will probably become overloaded at some point. The most important thing is deciding what to do in this situation, and then coding the various components of your server with this strategy in mind. Spikes in the server load can be caused by a spike in the number of players, or internal delays causing requests/responses to bunch up. The worst-case scenario is not handling the overload. When overload occurs, the game will rapidly degrade to an unplayable state. New players attempting to connect will find that the game "hangs." They will assume it's crashed, when in fact the client is just waiting a very long time for the server to get around to processing it. Every additional player stuck waiting to get in causes the game to slow even more.

Aside from improving the efficiency of your server, so that overloading occurs more rarely, the first two steps are to stop any further increases in load, and then to start shedding the load. Some servers do these two steps in the wrong order, hastily disconnecting clients, only to have those clients immediately attempt to reconnect.

Any new clients that attempt to use the overloaded server need to be given the highest priority. The aim is to get them out of the way as rapidly as possible, and to prevent them from coming back soon. A special message should be sent that causes the client to refuse to retry for a given period. The back-off period should be randomized; otherwise, a new form of overload can occur where a large number of clients all try to reconnect at the same time, causing the server to oscillate between underloaded and overloaded.

Shedding existing load can be done using in-game decisions (logging out hyperactive players) or a variant on the algorithms for improving throughput, given in the next section. Disconnecting the least-desirable 10 percent of clients, as rated by those algorithms, can be used in extreme cases. An overloaded server is usually no good to anyone, and in most situations having some disconnected players is better than not having a playable game at all.

Improving Throughput: SRPT and FCF

The Shortest Remaining Processing Time (SRPT) and Fastest Connection First (FCF) are scheduling algorithms adapted from traditional OS schedulers and now used quite widely in HTTP servers. They are well suited to servers where the responses contain the most data (types 1 and 3).

With SRPT, each candidate is examined—either an outstanding request or pending response—and given a processing rating. A lower rating means that less processing is required to fulfil the task. For example, if the response is in a cache, it is given +0. A response not in the cache is given a +2. If the request involves a complex calculation, it is given +3. Then, all the candidates are sorted, and the lowest rated ones processed first. Counterintuitively, starvation is not necessarily a problem [Bansal01], but it is wise to decrement the rating on each candidate whenever it is rejected, to ensure that all candidates get processed in a reasonable amount of time.

FCF is based on the observation that you can lower the response time for outgoing messages by processing the lowest-latency connections first [FCF02]. This is usually done with protocol- or OS-specific knowledge (e.g., in the kernel) for performance. However, most type-3 servers can implement this in software quite easily. Usually, these servers send identical data to many clients; instead of maintaining a "bytes to send" buffer for each connected client, the server maintains a single queue for each group receiving the same response, and each client maintains a pointer to how far through that queue it has transmitted already. The fastest connection will be whichever one has the pointer that is deepest into the buffer. The duplicate() method on a typical Buffer class supports this scheme very well, since it conserves memory, but maintains separate "current position" pointers for each duplicate.

Application-Level Caching

Client cache programming is all about making the best use of hardware caches that already exist, whereas in network/server ("application-level") caching, you have to build the caches in software. Caching is often the most effective way to increase performance, but because it is not automatic you have to actually decide to implement it. Although it might seem that caching is worthless for your game, even just caching something for one second might significantly reduce CPU load. Where caching seems impossible because no two requests generate the same response, it is sometimes worth splitting requests into subrequests, where some of these are cacheable. This process needs to be directed by benchmarking and knowledge of the CPU bottlenecks. Like other forms of optimization, caching should not be implemented until the main server is complete. If you implement your cache as being transparent to the surrounding classes, then it can be very easily added even at a late stage.

Server Design

Figure 6.2.2 is a UML activity diagram, showing the four main stages in the server. Each column represents the actions taking place inside a particular class.

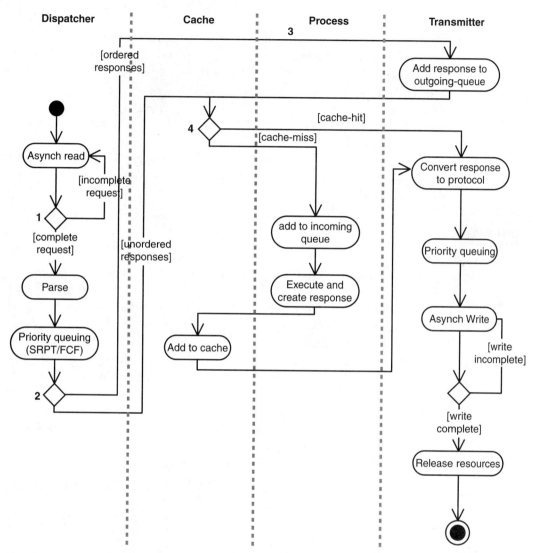

FIGURE 6.2.2 *Overview of the server design.*

Key Points

- The pre-parse stage needs to be able to very quickly decide if a Buffer contains a complete request. Although this could be achieved by attempting to parse and stopping on the first failure, in an asynchronous server, reparsing can happen many many times for a single request. This is a very good reason for having explicit MSG_START and MSG_END strings in your client-server protocol.
- Some protocols, like HTTP [RFC2616], require that a single client send a stream of requests, and that the response arrive precisely in the same order the requests

were made. In HTTP this is necessary because there is no other way of knowing which response is for which request. For these protocols, the server must create a "response object" *before* processing the request, and insert that response object into the outgoing queue, to guarantee in-order responses. Getting this wrong leads to hard-to-trace bugs.

- The Process column represents any of many processing stages you might have. Typical examples including having one processing stage for movement, world-view, and configuration.
- Commands are diverted to the appropriate stage by the cache, using a simple hash table for "command-name" mapped to "processing stage that handles that command."

Conclusion

Server development for large numbers of clients is difficult, unpredictable, and full of traps for the unwary. The many sources of nondeterminism can lead to the creation of servers that appear to work perfectly in all your tests, yet fail spectacularly in live deployment. The most effective techniques are sometimes those that are lacking in finesse (e.g., rebooting the server every 24 hours), but even these can save huge amounts of frustration. For the rest, it's necessary to pick and mix techniques for your particular game, while keeping an eye on the bigger picture: how well each works with thousands of clients, and how fragile it is in a highly nondeterministic environment.

Rather than attempting to deal with the difficult problems one by one, use the techniques from this article to start from a decent base. You can also use the knowledge to make intelligent guesses about how best to expand or improve your server.

Additional references and corrections are available at [Martin03].

Special thanks to D. Blake, G. van den Driessche, J. Fowlston, and J.C. Lawrence for their help in producing this article.

References

[CERT96] CERT, "CERT Alert CA-96.21," available online at *www.mycert.org.my/network-abuse/dos.htm.*

[Compaq00] Compaq/HP, "PCI-X Frequently Asked Questions," available online at *http://h18000.www1.hp.com/products/servers/technology/pci-x-qa.html.*

[Eiffel03] Eiffel Software Inc., "An Introduction to Design by Contract," available online at *http://archive.eiffel.com/doc/manuals/technology/contract/*, 2003.

[FCF02] Murta, C., and T. Corlassoli, "Fastest Connection First: A New Scheduling Policy for Web Servers," available online at *www2002.org/CDROM/poster/110/*, 2002.

[Gray93] Gray, Jim, and Andreas Reuter, *Transaction Processing: Concepts and Techniques*, Morgan Kaufmann Publishers, 1993.

[Hitchens03] Hitchens, Ron, *Java NIO*, O'Reilly, August 2002 .

[jContractor98] Karaorman, Holzle, Bruno, "jContractor: a Reflective Java Library to Support Design by Contract," available online at *www.cs.ucsb.edu/labs/oocsb/papers/TRCS98-31.pdf*, December 1998.

[Josephs03] Josephs, Mark, "Scheduling Algorithms," available online at *www.scism. sbu.ac.uk/ccsv/josephmb/CS-L2-OS/oss/week9.html#Scheduling Algorithms*, June 2003.

[Kegel03] Kegel, Dan, "The C10K Problem," available online at *www.kegel.com/ c10k.html*, June 2003.

[Martin03] Martin, Adam, "Supporting Material for GPG4," available online at *www.grexengine.com/sections/people/adam/gpg4/*, July 2003.

[Mellon03] Mellon, Larry, "Automated Testing of Massively Multiplayer Games," *GDC 2003*, available online at *www.gdconf.com/archives/2003/Mellon_Larry-AutomatedTesting.ppt*, March 2003.

[RFC2616] Fielding, R., et al., "Hypertext Transfer Protocol—HTTP/1.1," available online at *www.w3.org/Protocols/rfc2616/rfc2616.html*, November 7, 2002.

[Spacewire03] Spacewire, "Spacewire Crossbar Switch," available online at *www.mrcmicroe.com/SpaCroSwit.htm*.

[Sun-channels03] Sun Microsystems, "java.nio.channels: Java 2 SDK SE Developer Documentation," available online at *http://java.sun.com/j2se/1.4.2/docs/api/java/ nio/channels/package-summary.html*.

[Sun-nio03] Sun Microsystems, "java.nio: Java 2 SDK SE Developer Documentation," available online at *http://java.sun.com/j2se/1.4.2/docs/api/java/nio/package-summary.html*.

[Welsh03] Welsh, Matt, "SEDA: An Architecture for Highly Concurrent Server Applications," available online at *www.eecs.harvard.edu/~mdw/proj/seda/*, March 2003.

6.3

Efficient MMP Game State Storage

Justin Quimby,
Turbine Entertainment Software

Justin@TurbineGames.com

Massively multiplayer (MMP) games are online games in which thousands of people inhabit and adventure in the same virtual world. MMPs have a unique technical hurdle to overcome: massive scalability. The server code must handle thousands of players finding, killing, collecting, using, and triggering tens of thousands of game objects, each of which has dozens of variables that are used by the game servers. It is these values that pose a scalability threat to both runtime memory usage and game state size. This article introduces a programming pattern to address the issue of game state bloat.

The Problems of MMPs

Every game object has state that makes it unique compared to other objects in the game world, such as the hit points of a giant spider, the rounds left in a railgun, or the number of times a barkeep has sold rotgut beer in the last five minutes. Despite the vast differences between objects, many objects have state that rarely changes from item to item. For example, all orcs have a maximum carrying capacity of four items, and all doors automatically close after 14 seconds. The simplest and least memory efficient implementation would store the full data set for each copy of every object. This approach works for small data sets, but begins to break down when the number of objects increases dramatically.

At the extreme end of the scale, picture a game that supports 1 million users in the same world space. If every player has an inventory of 100 items, where each item has a memory footprint of 1 kilobyte, then the server farm will require 100 gigabytes of disk space just to keep track of players' inventories. From the perspective of running the game service, this means that data backups take longer, the risk of data corruption increases, and the length of server downtime during game state rollbacks grows.

The other drawback to the raw storage of game state relates to runtime memory usage. In the aforementioned 1-million player game, 10,000 concurrent players will require the server farm to use 10 gigabytes of RAM just to track the players' inventories. Obviously, this is an untenable situation.

As with many problems in computer science, it pays to be lazy and not reinvent the wheel. These MMP scalability problems echo issues that operating system designers have been grappling with for decades. In multithreaded operating systems, there are situations where a program will fork, creating a separate copy of the thread. A naive forking implementation simply creates a new copy of the address space for every forked process. However, copying an address space is an expensive task. Sometimes the forked process will not actually modify the address space, meaning that the child process could actually share the address space with its parent and save the cost of the copy.

Modern operating systems optimize for this situation by having forked processes only generate a unique address space when the new process needs to modify its address space. This technique is called "copy-on-write." A more formal definition for copy-on-write is "a technique for maintaining a point-in-time copy of a collection of data by copying only data that is modified after the instant of replicate initiation. The original source data is used to satisfy read requests for both the source data and for the unmodified portion of the point in time copy" [SNIA03].

Copy-on-write provides an approach to mitigate the scalability issues of runtime memory usage and game state storage for games with extremely large data sets. *Qualities* is a copy-on-write data structure that encapsulates the copy-on-write mechanic for the storage of object game state.

Qualities Theory

Qualities is a Turbine-designed mechanism for storing object game data in key-value pairs. Integers, floating-point numbers, and Booleans are among the simple data types that Qualities can store. For each of these types, each data value is referenced by a unique key. This key is used to index the value associated with it inside Qualities. A list of examples is shown in Figure 6.3.1. Complex data types can be storied in Qualities, but the resulting issues are beyond the scope of this article.

Index keys can be allocated in a variety of ways. The implementation of how keys are assigned does not particularly matter, as long as there are no collisions in the key namespace. The elimination of namespace collision results in the ability to access any given data member in $O(1)$ time via a hash lookup. The implementation that the Turbine Engine uses is to typedef keys for each of the values to be stored. The downside is that this list of typedefs must be included in every class that wants to use the Qualities API. As a result, every time a new key is added, every file #including the header file will need to be recompiled. This forced recompilation can be avoided by breaking the typedefs into separate headers by logical groupings.

Qualities for a Game Object	
Key	**Data Value**
Health_Max_IntStat	100 (integer)
Health_Current_IntStat	100 (integer)
XP_Value_IntStat	1700 (integer)
AttackDelay_FloatStat	5.5 (float)
UsesMagic_BoolStat	true (boolean)

FIGURE 6.3.1 *Examples of key-value pairs stored in Qualities.*

Another problem with this implementation is that typedefs are weak [Wilson03], providing no type safety. Despite these potential weaknesses, Turbine has not had significant problems with typedef'd keys.

```
// IntStat.H

typedef int IntStat;
IntStat Undef_IntStat = 0;

// IntStatList.H

#include "IntStat.H"

IntStat Health_Current_IntStat = 1;
IntStat Health_Max_IntStat = 2;
// etc.
```

Given the definition of both the key and data types, the next issue to address is where the data is stored. Qualities are comprised of two parts: per-object type default data and per-object instance data (see Figure 6.3.2). The default values for a given world object are kept in the "defaults" Qualities object. Each object maintains a "local" Qualities that serves as a repository of all data members that vary from the default values. Any data that has not changed is not stored locally on an object. The storage of only modified data members is the lynchpin of the Qualities pattern, enabling Qualities to minimize object state memory overhead.

The default Qualities for objects are defined by the content designers and are pre-processed into the back-end data storage mechanism. At runtime, these values are loaded on-demand by a per-server global object that operates as a singleton [Gamma95]. The default Qualities object provides access to the default data members for game objects. Operating as a singleton means that the global default Qualities

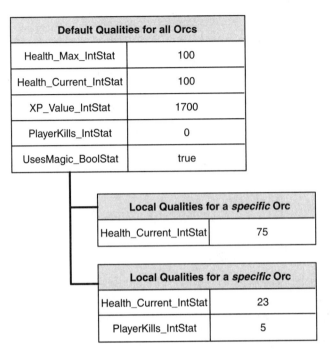

Default Qualities for all Orcs	
Health_Max_IntStat	100
Health_Current_IntStat	100
XP_Value_IntStat	1700
PlayerKills_IntStat	0
UsesMagic_BoolStat	true

Local Qualities for a *specific* Orc	
Health_Current_IntStat	75

Local Qualities for a *specific* Orc	
Health_Current_IntStat	23
PlayerKills_IntStat	5

FIGURE 6.3.2 *An illustration of the Qualities structures for two orcs.*

object minimizes memory overhead by delaying the loading of an object's default state until it is requested. Once loaded, only one copy is needed in memory, as every request will route to the loaded version.

Qualities APIs

All the data in the world is useless without a means to access and modify it. The Qualities APIs can be broken into two categories: value queries and value adjustments. Queries allow game logic to gather the current value of a stat. Value adjustments are broken into further subcategories: value sets and value resets. Value sets are the modification of the stat to a particular value that adds the new value to the object's local Qualities, while resets revert the stat's value back to the object's default by removing the value from local Qualities.

When game logic wants to know a given data value, the query first checks the object's local Qualities. If a value is stored locally, then that value is returned; otherwise, the object's default Qualities are queried. The APIs for accessing Qualities are stored at the top of the game object hierarchy. These APIs provide simple wrappers around Qualities' interfaces for the entire gameplay codebase. API placement is very engine-architecture specific, so for other game engines the API might make more sense in another location.

```
class BaseGameObject
{
public:
    bool GetInt(IntStat intStat, int32& val) const {
        return m_qual.GetInt( intStat, val );
    }
    bool SetInt(IntStat intStat, int32 val) {
        return m_qual.SetInt( intStat, val );
    }

private:
    Qualities m_qual;
};
```

The internals of Qualities are straightforward. For each data type, a hash table linking the key typedef to the data type is stored along with the ID of the base values for this object. This value is initialized when the object is created, ensuring that every instance of an orc has a data link to the default orc Qualities.

The default Qualities use the same class as local Qualities, the primary difference being the initialization of the data members. Local Qualities are created by gameplay code, while default Qualities are initialized from the game's content database.

```
typedef hash_table< IntStat, int32 > IntStorage;
// repeat for each data type

class Qualities
{
public:

    // the main accessors
    bool GetInt(IntStat intStat, int32& val) const;
    bool SetInt(IntStat intStat, int32 val);
    // repeated for each data type

    // is this a default Qualities structure?
    inline bool IsDefaultQualities() const {
        return (m_BaseQual == INVALID_DATABASEID);
    }

private:

    // the ID of our default values
    DatabaseID    m_BaseQual;

    // data type specific storage
    IntStorage*    m_IntStore;
    FloatStorage* m_FloatStore;
    BoolStorage*  m_BoolStore;
};
```

When querying a value, Qualities first check the local Qualities. If no value is found locally, then the default Qualities for the object are inquired.

```
bool
Qualities::GetInt(IntStat intStat, int32& val) const
{
    // Check if we have a local hash table for the
    // datatype. If so, then check for a local version
    // of the value.
    if (m_IntStore != NULL &&
        (m_IntStore->Lookup(intStat,val))) {
        return true;
    }

    // If we are the default qualities, then stop
    // since the value requested is not stored
    if (IsDefaultQualities()) {
        // assert, log error and abort
        return false;
    }

    // Now we need to check the default Qualities
    // The call to Database:: should be replaced with
    // whatever your codebase's singleton access
    // method is
    Qualities* baseQualities =
    Database::GetBaseQual(m_BaseQual);
    if (!baseQualities) {
        // assert, log error and abort
        return false;
    }

    // return the value in the default Qualities
    return baseQualities->GetInt(intStat,val);
}
```

Setting a value in Qualities during runtime is simple. If no existing local storage exists, then one must be allocated. Then a call to the hash table adds the key-value pair.

```
bool
Qualities::SetInt(IntStat intStat, int32 val)
{
    // make sure that we are a local Qualities copy
    // and not a default Qualities
    if (IsDefaultQualities()) {
        // assert, log error and abort
        return false;
    }

    // create a new local storage if one is needed
    if (m_IntStore == NULL) {
        m_IntStore = new IntStorage();
    }

    // actually store the value locally
    return m_IntStore->AddValue(intStat,val);
}
```

Benefits of Using Qualities

There are numerous benefits to using the Qualities pattern. The just-in-time memory allocation inherent in the copy-on-write approach means that the memory footprint of multiple identical objects is significantly reduced. Each game object only stores data locally that is unique to the object. When the world state needs to be saved, the most efficient way to save an object's state is to save only the state that differs from the default values. Storing the local Qualities of each game object automatically stores only the differences from the default object values. Qualities obviates the need to iterate over the object's state to determine the difference from the default object.

Qualities provides a clean interface between gameplay logic and gameplay state. This leads to cleaner gameplay code, as only a narrow interface is exposed to gameplay systems. By separating the two, the data structures and internal code paths of Qualities can be modified without requiring the modification of the code using those APIs. This separation also reduces compile times when the structure of Qualities is modified.

By storing the default values for an object separate from the object, Qualities allows for the simple modification of every instantiated object in the game world. By updating the data values in global Qualities, every object in the world automatically will reference the new value, since the value is not stored with each object instance. This means that to update the default damage of every long sword in the game, the designers can just update a single entry in the game content database, rather than running a script to iterate over the entire stored game state and update every object instance. This reduces the downtime of servers when game data changes, which is always appreciated by players.

Conclusion

As games continue to support more and more players, new challenges present themselves. Memory usage and the size of game state storage are two important factors to consider when planning a large-scale game. The Qualities framework provides a copy-on-write mechanism to address some of these scaling-related issues. Turbine has had great success using Qualities in the Turbine Engine.

References

[Gamma95] Gamma, Erich, et al., *Design Patterns: Element of Reusable Object-Oriented Software*, Addison-Wesley Publishing Co., 1995.

[SNIA03] Storage Networking Industry Association, "A Dictionary of Storage Networking Terminology: Common Storage Networking-Related Terms and the Definitions Applied to Them," available online at *www.snia.org/education/dictionary/c/#copy_on_write*, 2003.

[Wilson03] Wilson, Matthew, "True typedefs," March 2003, *C/C++ Users Journal* (March 2003), pp. 35–38.

6.4

Practical Application of Parallel-State Machines in a Client-Server Environment

Jay Lee, NCsoft Corporation

jlee@ncaustin.com

In [Alexander03], the author provides an introduction to the concept of parallel-state machines (PSM) and their use in creating more believable and engaging game characters. By coordinating several simple state machines in parallel, the PSM concept allows the modeling of character behavior far more complex than any single state machine can represent on its own.

The PSM described in [Alexander03] contains three layers or state machines to describe character behavior, one each for Posture, Movement, and Action. That approach is mirrored here. The Posture state machine handles how a character appears visually when in the world, including stances such as standing upright, swimming, hovering, or riding a mount. The Movement layer handles the motion of a character in the game world. This would include a state for each distinct movement direction: forward, backward, left, and right, plus the stopped state for when the character is at rest. The Action layer deals with the various in-game behaviors a character can perform. These can potentially occur independently of the states in the other two layers. For example, a character could be swimming while attacking a creature with a weapon.

PSM can be reused by various game subsystems, such as artificial intelligence (AI), the user interface, spell effects, and animation systems. Interestingly, each subsystem need only rely on the states in the PSM to ensure they are consistent with each other. The need to carry state flags or complex conditional code in these subsystems is eliminated.

This article demonstrates the use of PSM in a client-server environment, where PSM drives the visual behavior of characters controlled by both AI and players while maintaining synchronicity between the clients and server. The code is presented in Python, but the concepts should be easy to apply in your language of choice.

Individual States

The basic building block of PSM is the state. States are modeled after the concepts in the State pattern introduced in [Gamma95].

563

Each state shares the following interface:

```
def GetStateId():
    # returns a unique value for the state

def GetStateTypeId():
    # returns the layer the state belongs to

def OnEnterState(actor):
    # setup code executed when entering this state

def OnExitState(actor):
    # teardown code executed when exiting this state
```

The process of transitioning between states is demonstrated in the following code snippet.

```
def Transition(self, actor, newState):
    self.currentState.OnExitState(actor)
    self.currentState = newState
    self.currentState.OnEnterState(actor)
```

On every transition, each outgoing state does the appropriate teardown, is replaced with the new incoming state, and executes its setup code. For example, if the act of a character changing its posture to sitting down renders it unable to move, then the Sitting state should implement that characteristic in its entry method.

One of guidelines of the State pattern is that each state should be implemented using the Singleton pattern [Gamma95] to minimize memory usage. Any given state should only exist as a single instance, with clients of the state holding a reference to the singleton to indicate being in that state. Python provides a convenient mechanism for the implementation of singletons—the module. A module is an encapsulation scoped to a Python file. Each place where a state needs to be referenced will do so by holding a reference to the given module.

The following is an example of a state implemented as a module:

```
# dead.py

import shared
import shared.characterstatedata as _csd

# register this state for convenient lookup
# from id value to state module
shared.RegisterState(__name__)

def GetStateId():
    return _csd.DEAD

def GetStateTypeId():
    return _csd.POSTURE

def OnEnterState(actor):
```

```
    # when dead, block movement
    actor.BlockMovement()

def OnExitState(actor):
    # moving out of dead, unblock movement
    actor.UnblockMovement()
```

While states are singletons and hold no instance data, they derive their context for operation through the arguments they are passed. The OnEnterState and OnExit-State methods take a reference to the actor being operated on. This allows a state to operate on the specific instance of a character. In this example, when a character enters the dead state in the Posture layer, any transitions in the Movement layer on that character are blocked. When exiting the dead state, transitions in the Movement layer for that character are subsequently unblocked. It is the responsibility of each state to implement the desired game rules upon entry, and to undo them on exit.

Adding new states is easy as the system evolves, and doesn't require any changes in understanding of PSM. Simply choose the appropriate layer to add to and ensure that the new state is distinctly named from the other states in the chosen layer. Be suspicious of a new state that doesn't fit nicely with the others, especially ones with names that sound like a combination of other states.

Note that the assignment of a unique ID for each state has an ulterior motive. Doing so provides the foundation for a data-driven approach to various clients of the PSM, to be demonstrated later in the article.

Character State Manager

CharacterStateMgr is the manager class that brings each of the states together as distinct, coordinated state machines or layers.

When constructed, a CharacterStateMgr initializes as follows:

```
self.__stateMachine = {}
self.__stateMachine[_csd.POSTURE]  = _standing
self.__stateMachine[_csd.MOVEMENT] = _stopped
self.__stateMachine[_csd.ACTION]   = _idle
self.__blockedState = {}
```

The first dictionary, self.__stateMachine, represents each layer or distinct state machine as a key-value pair of layer to current state. Each state machine is initialized to the appropriate initial states.

The second dictionary, self.__blockedState, manages which states are currently blocked for transitions. Significantly, blocking of state transitions is implemented via a reference counting mechanism where the key is the state reference and the value is the number of blocks currently on the given state. This allows for multiple subsystems to issue Block() and Unblock)_ calls while retaining the correct overall desired effect.

To illustrate: Two spells of different duration are cast on a character, and both have the effect of blocking the character from transitioning to the Fighting state in the

Posture layer. When both are present, the character cannot fight. When the spell with the shorter duration wears off, the character is still unable to fight because of the block still in place from the other spell. Only when the second spell wears off is the transition to Fight allowed, which is exactly the expected behavior.

The CharacterStateMgr class offers methods for the following functionality:

- Transitioning to a state honoring the blocking mechanism
- Transitioning to a state without checking blocking
- Accessing the various state layers and their values
- Blocking and unblocking individual states
- Blocking and unblocking groups of states

ON THE CD

Refer to the source in characterstatemgr.py on the companion CD-ROM for further details.

Using CharacterStateMgr

CharacterStateMgr is a "mixin" class, designed to "mix into" any class that requires the services of a character state manager through inheritance. Given a class called Actor designed to represent the base class of player characters and nonplayer characters in the game, one would derive Actor from CharacterStateMgr. Thus, every Actor is a kind of CharacterStateMgr, and the PSM interface can be accessed directly through each Actor instance. Actors on both the client and server inherit from CharacterStateMgr in the same manner.

Keeping the Client and Server Synchronized

Note that the entire source of CharacterStateMgr and the associated states are platform independent. That is, no client- or server-specific code exists in the source. It is left up to systems outside the PSM to implement the platform-specific code while using the CharacterStateMgr API.

It is critical that client and server stay in sync with respect to the current values of each Actor's CharacterStateMgr data. This is achieved with the following approach.

The client uses the RequestTransition() method on CharacterStateMgr to request entering a state. On a client machine, this code honors its current known states and will react accordingly. Once the client starts moving, it sends the same request for the server to process. It also calls UpdateStateDependentSystems(), which is the method that notifies every subsystem dependent on the actor's PSM (such as the animation system) to allow the subsystem to handle the state change appropriately. The following code demonstrates handling a request to move forward on the originating client.

```
def HandleMoveForward():
    if actor.RequestTransition(_moveforward):
        actor.MoveForward()
        SendServerRequest("StateChangeRequest",
            actor.GetId(), _moveforward.GetStateId())
        UpdateStateDependentSystems(actorId)
```

```
    else:
        DisplayMessage("Unable to move at this time")
```

On the server, the request is received and processed. The server determines if the transition is valid, honoring any known prohibitions that have been applied using the transition blocking mechanism. If the transition is allowed, the RequestTransition() method calls TransitionTo() to transition to the specified state. Outside CharacterStateMgr(), the state change is also broadcast to all interested clients except the originator. The requesting client is left out because it is already in the desired state, and we gladly accept any opportunity for bandwidth savings.

Only the originator of the request is notified if the request is denied. For example, if the server determines that the actor is in fact dead and cannot move, then it will send a state correction back to the originating client. The other interested clients already match the server state, so we again avoid unnecessary notification and save bandwidth. The following code segment illustrates the server handling the state change request.

```
def StateChangeRequest(clientId, actorId, stateId):
    actor = GetActorInstance(actorId)
    state = characterstatemgr.GetState(stateId)
    if actor.RequestTransition(state):
        BroadcastToAllButSender("StateChange",
            actorId, stateId)
    else:
        # send client correction
        SendClientMessage("StateCorrection",
            clientId,actorId,actor.GetAllStateIds())
```

Upon receipt of a state correction, the client immediately synchronizes to the specified set of states. No checking is done when corrected by the server; each state is transitioned into without question on the specified actor. The call to UpdateStateDependentSystems() allows subsystems to handle the correction appropriately. This is shown in the following code snippet.

```
def StateCorrection(self, actorId, stateList):
    actor = GetActorInstance(actorId)
    for stateId in stateList:
        state = GetStateModuleById(stateId)
        actor.TransitionTo(state)
        UpdateStateDependentSystems(actorId)
```

Should the transition be valid when checked on the server, every client except the originator of the transition receives and processes the state change. Once the actor is updated, a call is made to UpdateStateDependentSystems() to allow the other subsystems to respond appropriately. The following code shows the StateChange handler on interested clients.

```
def StateChange(actorId, stateId):
    actor = _GetActorInstance(actorId)
    state = _characterstatemgr.GetState(stateId)
```

```
actor.TransitionTo(state)
UpdateStateDependentSystems(actorId)
```

States will also change on actors because of server-initiated activity or server-determined outcomes of activity from other clients. For example, NPCs are controlled by the server and should look correct on interested clients. The next section of code shows an example of a creature deciding to move toward another actor that is not yet in attack range. The state change is broadcast to all interested clients and handled by the `StateChange()` method shown previously. Since the server is solely in control of the creatures' states, there is no need to check whether the transition is valid on the client. Any time state is transmitted from the server to the client, we consider the server to be the authority, and perform the transition(s). In doing so, we are assured that the only client that is out of sync would be one where tampering has occurred. As long as every other client observes a tampered client in the correct state, we don't care what the experience is for the hacker.

```
def Attack(self, actorId):
    actor = _GetActorInstance(actorId)
    if InRange(self.GetPos(), actor.GetPos()):
        # attack with weapon
    else:
        if self.RequestTransition(_moveforward):
            BroadcastToAll("StateChange",
                self.GetId(),
                _moveforward.GetStateId())
```

State-Dependent Subsystems

As states change in an actor, each state-dependent system is notified for an appropriate response. In an animation system, the response would likely be to trigger the `UpdateAnimation()` method, as shown here:

```
def UpdateAnimation(actorId):
    actor = _GetActorInstance(actorId)
    if actor.GetMovementState() == _stopped:
        baseAnimName = GetIdleAnim(actor)
    else:
        baseAnimName = GetMovementAnim(actor)

    actionAnim = None
    if actor.GetActionState() != _idle:
        actionAnim = GetActionAnim(actor)

    PlayAnimations(baseAnimName, actionAnimName)
```

This animation system always plays a base animation, based on the combination of the current movement and posture states. If the character is at rest, it will return an appropriate at-rest animation. If the character is moving, then a suitable moving animation is returned. This system also allows for the prioritization of bones within an animation. If an action animation is played with an idle animation, the action is shown across the entire character. For example, a character swinging a weapon will be seen in a swing stance, feet planted appropriately. However, if the character is moving, the action will be played on the upper portion of the body, while the lower portion of the body will reflect movement. This supports the ability to have a character able to move while attacking with the weapon.

The following shows how the animation system might implement the methods for retrieving animations of the various types based on current state values in the PSM.

```
idleAnims = {_standing : 'fidget.ani',
             _swimming : 'tread_water.ani'}

moveAnims = {
    (_standing,_moveforward) : 'runforward.ani',
    (_hover, _moveright)     : 'hover_right.ani'}

actionAnims = {_crafting  : 'crafting.ani',
               _fighting  : 'fighting.ani'}

def GetIdleAnim(actor):
    # return idle based on posture state
    stateId = actor.GetPostureState().GetStateId()
    return idleAnims[stateId]

def GetMovementAnim(actor):
    # return movement anim based on posture and
    # movement states
    posStateId = actor.GetPostureState().GetStateId()
    movStateId = actor.GetMovementState().GetStateId()
    return moveAnims[posStateId, movStateId]

def GetActionAnim(actor):
    # return anim based on current action state
    stateId = actor.GetActionState().GetStateId()
    return actionAnims[stateId]
```

The code illustrates an important concept. The nature of changing behavior based on the states in `CharacterStateMgr` can be completely data driven. Because each state has an associated unique identifier, the code can look up the result via a simple data structure—in our case, dictionaries that map one or more state identifiers to an animation filename. Note that while they are hand generated here, the values could be in an external text file, or even better, automatically generated from a centralized repository such as a relational database. Further exploration of this concept can be found in [Lee03].

It is not difficult to imagine other subsystems leveraging the PSM data—for example, a set of sounds that are driven off the current states of a character. Regardless of the application of PSM, it provides consistent results to both clients and servers.

Conclusion

This article demonstrated that parallel-state machines are a simple yet powerful concept that significantly eases the burden of complex character state management and synchronization in a client-server environment.

The basic source for implementing states and `CharacterStateMgr` is the same on client and server, making it easier to grasp and maintain. Game systems on both the client and server can leverage `CharacterStateMgr` to implement their desired functionality and do so in a manner that will be in sync across multiple clients on a shared server. As needs grow and new features are added, adding to the architecture is straightforward and does not result in exponential growth or management issues.

References

[Alexander03] Alexander, Thor, "Parallel State Machines for Believable Characters," *Massively Multiplayer Game Development*, Charles River Media, 2003.

[Gamma95] Gamma, et al., *Design Patterns*, Addison-Wesley Longman, Inc., 1995.

[Lee03] Lee, Jay, "Leveraging Relational Database Management Systems to Data-Drive MMP Gameplay," *Massively Multiplayer Game Development*, Charles River Media, 2003.

6.5

Bit Packing: A Network Compression Technique

Pete Isensee, Microsoft Corporation

pkisensee@msn.com

Network games often send structures of data containing position, velocity, acceleration, status flags, and other important game state information. Often, many bits of transmitted information do not contain important data. For example, a game might send positions that range from 0 to 100,000 using 32-bit integers. Each position occupies 17 bits, but the remaining 15 bits are wasted. Those unused bits can add up quickly for large data structures.

One of the mantras of the network game developer is to limit the amount of data on the wire. This article shows a bit packing technique that compresses individual elements of a network data structure into a binary stream where every bit of the stream contains relevant data. This technique can significantly reduce the size of network packets. A secondary advantage of this approach is that elements in the network data structure can be range-checked in debugging versions to verify that they fall within a developer-specified tolerance. Similar packing techniques have been used in existing online games [Frohnmayer00].

An Example

This technique is designed to integrate easily into existing C structs or C++ classes sent on standard sockets. Here's a simplified example of game networking code:

```
struct NetData
{
    unsigned char  MsgType;    // 0 - 28
    unsigned long  Time;       // 0 - 0xFFFFFFFF
    unsigned short Element;     // 148 to 1153
    int            XPosition;   // -100,000 to 100,000
    int            Yposition;   // -100,000 to 100,000
};

NetData nd;
send( s, (const char*)( &nd ), sizeof(nd), 0 );
```

On a 32-bit platform, the amount of data being sent and received is at least 17 bytes. If the structure is not byte-aligned, the amount of data could be upwards of 20 bytes. If the sender and receiver are on different platforms, there can also be byte ordering issues that require the sender to convert each item to network order before sending and the receiver to convert each item back to host order.

Here's the same structure defined using the bit packing technique:

```
struct NetData : public BitPackCodec< 5 >
{
    PkUint<unsigned char,5>              MsgType;
    PkUint<unsigned long>                Time;
    PkUintRange<unsigned short,148,1153> Element;
    PkInt<int,-100000,100000>            XPos;
    PkInt<int,-100000,100000>            YPos;
};
```

The raw data items are replaced with "packable" data items. Users of these data items can treat them exactly the same as their raw integer counterparts. They can be assigned, read, and written exactly like normal integers. The advantage of a packable item is that it also knows how to pack itself into a bit stream. Moreover, the range of values that an integer can take is now known by the compiler. Because the range consists of template parameters, there's no additional memory overhead, but the compiler can be put to good use doing range checking.

The NetData struct derives from a mixin class called BitPackCodec, which supports two key functions, Pack() and Unpack(), along with a registration function that informs the codec which items will be inserted into the stream and in what order they will appear.

Now, rather than sending the raw NetData structure, the structure is packed into a bit stream first. The size of the bit stream buffer in this particular example is only 83 bits, versus 136 bits for the original struct, a savings of 40 percent.

```
NetData nd;
int size = nd.GetPackedBytes();
char* pBitStream = new char [ size ];
send( s, nd.Pack( pBitStream ), size, 0 );
```

The target, upon receiving the bit stream, decompresses it back to the original struct format by unpacking it.

```
nd.Unpack( pBitStream );
```

The packing functions automatically handle all the dirty details, including byte swapping. The new NetData structure can consist of whatever integer types are most efficient, rather than having to resort to bit fields or other methods of in-memory compression.

Hurdles

There are three tricky issues about this particular technique. The hardest part is the bit packing itself. Although a simple function that packs one bit at a time can be written in a few lines of code, packing bits one by one is inefficient. Writing an algorithm that packs bytes at a time is much more complex. The second difficult part is minimizing the memory footprint of the technique, since it requires a separate buffer for the bit stream, lists to keep track of what to pack, and so forth. The third thorny problem is making the technique flexible enough that it can be easily incorporated into existing game code. The next sections discuss each issue in detail.

Packing the Bits

The algorithm used in this article is based on lining up the source integer and destination bit buffer so that the next available bit in the destination and the first significant bit in the source are aligned. The source bits are copied into the bit buffer one section at a time, where each section is defined by the next nearest byte boundary of either the source or destination. Figure 6.5.1 shows an example. The first available bit in the destination buffer is bit 6. There are 13 bits to copy. Lining up the bits to be copied (the shaded areas), it's clear there will be four copy operations, defined by A, B, C, and D. For example, section B is defined by the first byte boundary at bit 8 in the bit buffer, and the next byte boundary is at bit 8 in the source integer.

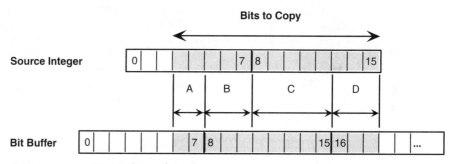

FIGURE 6.5.1 *Bit packing algorithm.*

If the byte boundaries of the source integer and the bit buffer happen to be aligned, then up to 8 bits can be copied at a time. If they're not aligned, then each byte is copied in two chunks totaling 8 bits. Unpacking works exactly the same way, but the source and destination are reversed. Prior to copying the bits of an integer to the bit buffer, the integer is converted to network format (big endian). During the unpacking phase, the restored integer is converted back to host format.

The packing algorithm is implemented using a single C++ template function that packs any unsigned integer type from 8-bit to 64-bit integers. The prototype for the function follows. To maintain compatibility with standard socket functions, the bit buffer is a regular char pointer instead of an unsigned char pointer, and the size is an int instead of an unsigned.

```
template< typename T > // T is any integer type
```

```
void Pack( const T& tSrc, int nSrcBits,
          char* pDestBitBuffer, int nDestStartBit );
```

The byte swapping is also implemented using template functions, avoiding unnatural switch statements to determine whether to use htonl() or htons(). The byte swapping functionality is shown next. It takes advantage of the STL reverse function. An efficient compiler can optimize away the call to IsPlatformLittleEndian() and completely inline the reversing algorithm, making these functions highly efficient.

```
inline bool IsPlatformLittleEndian()
{
    const int n = 1;
    return( *((char*)( &n ) ) ? true : false );
}

template< typename T >
T ReverseBytes( T n )
{
    unsigned char* p = (unsigned char*)( &n );
    std::reverse( p, p + sizeof( T ) );
    return n;
}

template< typename T >
T HostToNetworkOrder( T n )
{
    if( IsPlatformLittleEndian() )
        return ReverseBytes( n );
    return n;
};
```

A Generic Interface for a Packable Data Type

Integers are not the only data type that can be efficiently packed. For example, IEEE floating-point values can also be packed by stripping off bits from the mantissa. Strings can be packed using a variety of compression techniques. The approach shown here focuses on integers of various flavors, but is designed to allow the bit packing of any data type. The best way to abstract the notion of packing is via an abstract base class.

```
class Packable
{
public:
    virtual ~Packable() = 0;
    virtual int GetBits() const;
    virtual void Pack( char*, int* StartBit ) const;
    virtual void Unpack( const char*, int* StartBit );
};
```

The Packable class includes other helper functions, but the three shown here are the key methods. GetBits() returns the number of significant bits in the Packable object. These are the bits that will be packed and unpacked by the object. `Pack()` copies `GetBits()` of the `Packable` object into the incoming input buffer starting at the bit specified. It increments the incoming start bit by `GetBits()`. `Unpack()` generates a new `Packable` object from the incoming bit buffer starting at the bit specified. It also increments the incoming start bit by `GetBits()`. The `Packable` interface is designed to be compatible with the socket interface, which uses plain old char pointers.

A Concrete Interface for a Packable Data Type

This article packs integers. Rather than creating a specific class for each integer type (e.g., unsigned char, short, long, etc.), the code is template-based. All integers are supported via one of three different interfaces.

```
template< typename T, int Bits >
class PkUint : public Packable

template< typename T, uint64 Min, uint64 Max >
class PkUintRange : public Packable

template< typename T, int64 Min, int64 Max >
class PkInt : public Packable
```

The `PkUint` class is designed for unsigned integers that hold a specific number of bits. The caller specifies the number of bits as a template parameter. For example, a network message type might be stored using 5 bits (values 0 through 31, or a bitmask with 5 important bits). The `PkUintRange` class is designed for unsigned integers that hold a specific range of values. The range can be zero-based, or it can have a positive minimum value. In either case, the `PkUintRange` class is smart enough to normalize the number before it's packed and denormalize upon unpacking. For example, if the range were 1000–1127, only 7 bits would be used to store the value in the bit buffer. The `PkInt` class is designed for signed integers that hold a specific range of values. This class also normalizes the number and converts the number to an unsigned value before it's packed.

Each of these three concrete classes derives from the `Packable` class and implements the appropriate `Packable` functions. The constructors and conversion operators ensure that users of packable integers can treat them exactly as they would treat normal integers. Because these classes use template parameters, no additional storage is required to hold the bits or range values. The only overhead to these classes is `sizeof(T)` plus the virtual function table pointer required by the `Packable` class.

The Codec

Now all we need is a way to easily pack structs and classes or lists of `Packable` objects. The design goals require that the method be transparent and take as little memory as possible. Enter the `BitPackCodec`. All the `BitPackCodec` needs to know is how many items to pack, the order in which to pack them, and a bit buffer to pack them into. Although the bit buffer could be maintained internally by the class, that would be costly in terms of performance and efficiency. It makes more sense in a game to preal-locate a single bit buffer that's large enough to handle the largest network packet and pass that buffer to the codec as needed.

When it comes to maintaining a list of the items to pack, flexible list data types like std::vector or std::list have memory allocation overhead we'd like to avoid. The solution used in this article is to store the list of Packable objects in a C-style array. For maximum flexibility and performance, the array size is a template parameter. The advantages of this solution are that it uses minimal memory, requires no heap allocations, and is very fast. In debug builds, the class can check to ensure that the bounds of the array are not exceeded.

```
template< int N >
class BitPackCodec
{
private:
    Packable* mPackList[ N ];

public:
    void  Register( Packable& );
    char* Pack( char* ) const;
    void  Unpack( const char* ) const;
    int   GetPackedBytes() const;
};
```

BitPackCodec is designed as a mixin class. For any struct X containing multiple Packable objects, derive X from BitPackCodec. Register() adds items to the list of packable items. Register() is designed to be called by X's constructor. Here's an example using the NetData structure:

```
NetData() // NetData ctor
{
    Register( MsgType );
    Register( Time );
    Register( Element );
    Register( XPos );
    Register( YPos );
}
```

Pack() and Unpack() do all the work. They expect an external buffer allocated by the caller that's at least GetPackedBytes() in size. Here's the implementation of the Pack() function:

```
char* Pack( char* pPackBuffer )
{
    memset( pPackBuffer, 0, GetPackedBytes() );
    int nCurrBit = 0;
    for( int i = 0; i < N; ++i )
        mPackList[i]->Pack( pPackBuffer, &nCurrBit );
    return pPackBuffer;
}
```

Pack() clears the bit buffer, and then packs each registered Packable item into the bit buffer by calling Packable::Pack(). Any object that implements the Packable interface can be used by the codec object. This design flexibility allows new data types to become packable as needed.

Evaluating the Tradeoffs

By far the biggest advantage of packing bits is the reduction of network bandwidth. There are a few side benefits, too. Network data structs don't need special alignment, bit fields, or unusually sized data types. There's additional range checking on packed values in debug mode. Finally, packing also helps obfuscate network messages to casual observers.

The cost of packing bits is threefold: readability, performance, and memory. Sending a network struct is simple and easy to understand; packing a struct into a bit stream adds complexity and makes debugging network packets more difficult. In terms of performance, packing and unpacking bits is an $O(N)$ operation, where N is the number of items being packed. In terms of CPU cost, it's quite low considering the relatively small size of network packets sent by most modern games. The classes shown previously have a negligible memory impact. A packable integer is sizeof(T) plus a pointer for the Packable virtual function pointer table. The codec class introduces an array of size N, and the game must support a bit buffer the size of the largest network packet. All in all, this is not a bad set of tradeoffs for eliminating a significant amount of bandwidth.

Improvements

This article includes code for packing integers from 8- to 64-bit values. The basic technique can be extended to all types of other game data, including floats and strings. Bit packing is a fine lossless compression technique that works well for network data. However, it's not the best you can do. If you're interested in even better methods, check out the arithmetic coders from [Blow03] and [Nelson96] as well as other compression techniques [Bloom].

Conclusion

Bit packing accomplishes the following goals:

* Packs data structures into streams that only contain the "important" bits. All nonessential bits are discarded. The resulting bandwidth savings can be significant.
* Integrates easily into existing code. Existing network data structures can be treated as if they contain the original raw data.
* Allows network data structures to be aligned for speed rather than size.
* Is as transparent as possible.

- Has minimal performance impact.
- Has minimal memory overhead.

References

[Bloom] Bloom, Charles, "Compression Algorithms," available online at *www.cbloom .com/algs/index.html*.

[Blow02] Blow, Jonathan, "Packing Integers," *Game Developer Magazine* (May 2002): pp. 16–19.

[Blow03] Blow, Jonathan, "Using an Arithmetic Coder: Part 1," *Game Developer Magazine* (August 2003): pp. 14–18.

[Frohnmayer00] Frohnmayer, Mark, and Tim Gift, "The TRIBES Engine Networking Model," available online at *www.gdconf.com/archives/2000/frohnmayer.doc*.

[Nelson96] Nelson, Mark, and Jean-Loup Gilly, *The Data Compression Book, Second Edition*, M & T Books, 1996.

6.6

Time and Consistency Management for Multiserver-Based MMORPGs

Larry Shi and Tao Zhang,
Georgia Institute of Technology

shiw@cc.gatech.edu, zhangtao@cc.gatech.edu

MMORPGs (massively multiplayer online role-playing games) have become increasingly popular since the commercial success of *Ultima Online*. Today, almost every commercial MMORPG uses a client-server architecture. In most cases, a multi-client, single-server based approach is adopted because of its simplicity. To support massive numbers of players, developers often divide a persistent world into many isolated regions, so that each is small enough to be managed by a single server. There is often no synchronization or interaction between regions. However, problems arise when one cannot partition the virtual world into sufficiently fine regions so that there are not too many players residing within a single region. To achieve scalability, a single region might have to be handled by multiple servers. Multiserver design introduces two new challenges: time management and consistency management. The focus of this article is to show how to design solutions to time and consistency management problems for multiserver-based MMORPG. The goal is to provide sufficient detail so that these solutions can be easily implemented in new games.

Why Time and Consistency Management?

In a multiserver-based MMORPG, servers are typically connected via a data distribution network. Each game server simulates a set of entities using an event-driven simulation. An entity can be a monster, a playable character, a building, a piece of treasure, and so forth. If we can guarantee that there are no interactions between entities belonging to different servers, we can avoid time and consistency management problems because each server can compute the correct state of an entity locally without interacting with other servers. If this requirement cannot be guaranteed, disturbing and annoying anomalies might occur in the game, like "dead man shooting" [Mauve02]. The problem results from inconsistent views of game state across different servers due to network delays when transmitting events between servers. Consistency can be maintained if all the servers process events strictly in timestamped order. Time management provides the principal service for meeting this constraint.

Clock Synchronization

To perform time management, first we need to synchronize clocks among servers and clients to maintain a globally consistent notion of wall clock time. There are several ways to synchronize clocks, including the Network Time Protocol (NTP) [Mills92]. Clock synchronization is not the main focus of this article. For this discussion, we will assume that servers and clients are globally synchronized to within a certain specified clock skew.

Consistency vs. Responsiveness

Responsiveness is a feature that many game designers desire in their games. However, it is important to realize that responsiveness and consistency are often contradictory and cannot normally be achieved on the Internet due to unpredictable network delays. To achieve a high level of responsiveness, each client or server can immediately update its local state based on local player's actions. This maximizes responsiveness, but the results might be incorrect and might lead to inconsistency. To maintain strong consistency, each client or server must not process an event unless it is guaranteed to be safe to do so. However, consistency will almost inevitably result in low responsiveness if network delays are large.

Achieving Both Consistency and Responsiveness with Multitime Management

Different consistency and responsiveness requirements lead to different approaches to time and consistency management. Existing time and consistency management schemes can be categorized as conservative or optimistic methods. A conservative method can achieve absolute consistency, but is often unsuitable for real-time applications because it does not guarantee responsiveness. Conservative methods can be found in some peer-to-peer RPG games where consistency is given high priority [Bettner01]. However, optimistic methods use techniques such as rollback to achieve consistency of the game state, but transitory inconsistent states might not be acceptable for gameplay. A related technique (which one might regard as a form of optimistic computing, although it is generally not regarded as such) is the use of predictive contracts such as dead reckoning [Aronson97]. These techniques can be used to achieve real-time performance, but do not by themselves guarantee strong consistency.

This article handles the problem by categorizing entity attributes based on their consistency requirements. Attributes such as entity position are often considered as only requiring a relaxed form of consistency where some inconsistencies can be tolerated, while attributes such as entity experience and aliveness can require a stricter form of consistency to be maintained. For attributes requiring only a relaxed consistency, predictive contracts can be applied. A client can update those attributes immediately using any prediction technique [Aronson97] based on inputs from the local player. The controlling server for the entity computes another official state update and sends it back to the client some time later. If these two states differ by more than a specified threshold value, the official update might simply overwrite the client's local state, or the client might try to gradually converge to the official update; for example, using a smoothing technique to avoid abrupt changes in visual displays. For attributes requiring a stricter consistency, conservative time management is used to ensure timestamp-order processing of events. It might take longer for the servers to compute the correct states, but they are guaranteed to be safe. Such an approach is called *multitime management* because both predictive contracts and a conservative time management mechanism are employed. Multitime simulation uses multitime management to achieve a suitable tradeoff between responsiveness and consistency. It uses predictive contracts to achieve responsiveness, and conservative simulation to ensure consistency.

Multitime Management Implementation

In this section, we present an implementation of multitime management. The implementation assumes:

- The virtual world is divided into multiple disjoint regions. Each region is simulated by a set of servers belonging to one server farm (see Figure 6.6.1).
- Servers in a server farm are connected through a high-speed local network with multicast enabled.
- Each event from a local player is timestamped on the client side. Timestamps could be generated on the server side to simplify time and consistency management, but that will lead to reduced fairness among clients and low responsiveness due to network delay. It is preferable to do timestamping on the client side.
- There are reliable connections between clients and their connecting servers, as well as between any two connected servers. We could choose TCP connections or a customized implementation of reliable UDP.

The pseudocode for the implementation is shown next. The code is multithreaded. A threaded implementation is not a requirement but does make the code easier to understand. In each client and server, there are two threads. One is the main thread; the other is devoted to time management and communication. On the client side, the main thread implements user input handling, entity prediction, scene rendering, and so forth. On the server side, the main thread implements game logic and entity simulation.

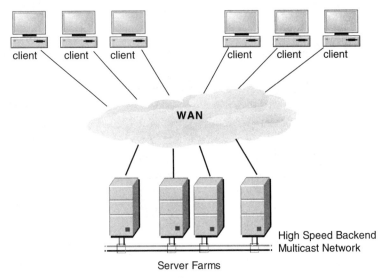

FIGURE 6.6.1   *Multiserver architecture.*

The message structure is defined as follows:

```
typedef MSG_t struct
{
    DWORD type;        //type of the message
    DWORD client_id; //id of the client machine
    DWORD server_id; //id of the server machine
    struct time_t timestamp; //timestamp of the
                             //message
    struct time_t safe_time; //client/server safe time
    struct user_input_t user_input; //user
                                    //input/command
    ...
} MSG_t;
```

The possible message types and their purposes are shown in Table 6.6.1.

Table 6.6.1   Message Types and Explanation

Type	Purpose
SERVER_SAFE_TIME	Server safe time
CLIENT_SAFE_TIME	Client safe time
CLIENT_INPUT	Client timestamped input/command
PREDICTIVE_STATE_UPDATE	State update computed by predictive simulation
CONSERVATIVE_STATE_UPDATE	State update computed by conservative simulation

Client/server safe time messages are necessary for conservative time management to progress. Conservative time management requires that each timestamped event be processed only after no other events whose timestamp is less than the processed event will arrive. The safe time message is a promise sent by a client/server that it will not send a message whose timestamp is less than the value indicated in the promise message. It enables the servers to decide when it is safe to process an event. Safe time messages are similar to null messages used in [Chandy78].

The Client

The client side code is shown in this section. A client repeatedly checks whether there is a client safe time message sent in the last MAX_NOTIFY_INTERVAL milliseconds. If not, the client will create a dedicated local safe time message and send it to the connecting server. Each timestamped message sent by the client is a guaranteed lower bound concerning the timestamp of messages it might later send. This is because the client never rolls back its clock and the messages will arrive in order (guaranteed by the assumed reliable connection). Normally, we do not need such a dedicated message because each timestamped user input/command message sent by the client already acts as a safe time message. Dedicated safe time messages are only sent when the local player is idling.

The client also implements a popular latency-hiding technique that adds a small look-ahead time (DELAY_COMPENSATION in the pseudocode) to each player's input/command so that the event's timestamp will be some time in the future. Thus, its processing will be delayed correspondingly on the client side and the server side. The look-ahead time can be used to overlap some amount of network latency and is useful to reduce the impact of network delays. It is a known fact that a look-ahead value around or less than 100ms often causes no noticeable effects for human players [DIS94]. Since Internet delay is often in the range from 100ms to 600ms, this technique alone cannot solve time and consistency management problems. Table 6.6.2 describes the timing parameters the client uses to remain in sync with the server.

Table 6.6.2 Constants Used in the Pseudocode and Their Meanings

Name	Meaning
MAX_NOTIFY_INTERVAL	Maximal interval between two succeeding promises sent by a client
DELAY_COMPENSATION	Processing of a client input/command is delayed by this amount
MAX_SAFE_TIME_UPDATE_INTERVAL	Maximum interval between two computations of the global safe time in a server
SERVER_LOOKAHEAD_TIME	Small positive value added to the timestamp of every new event generated by conservative simulation

Here's the client time management/communication thread:

```
while (1)
{
    //timestamp messages in the output FIFO
    //and sent them out
     MSG_t* msg;
    msg = out_msg_FIFO->pop_front();
    while (msg)
    {
        msg->timestamp  = now + DELAY_COMPENSATION;
        msg->safe_time  = msg->timestamp;
        send_msg(msg);
        last_safe_time  = msg->safe_time;
        //timestamp ordered work queue
        work_queue->enqueue(msg);
        msg = out_msg_FIFO->pop_front();
    }

    if (now + DELAY_COMPENSATION - last_safe_time >
        MAX_NOTIFY_INTERVAL)
    {
        msg            = new_msg();
        msg->type      = CLIENT_SAFE_TIME;
        msg->client_id = self_id;
        msg->safe_time = now + DELAY_COMPENSATION;
        send_msg(msg);
        last_safe_time = msg->safe_time;
    }
    //receiving possible server updates
    MSG_t* msg;
    while(msg = nonblocking_receive_from_server())
    {
        work_queue->enqueue(msg);
    }
    // ...
}
```

Here's the client main thread:

```
while (1)
{
    UserInput* new_input  = collect_user_input();
    MSG_t* input_msg      = new_message();
    input_msg->type       = CLIENT_INPUT;
    input_msg->user_input = *new_input;
    //push the message into an output FIFO
    out_msg_FIFO->push_back(input_msg);

    //return the earliest message whose timestamp is
    //less than now, otherwise return null
    MSG* cur_msg = work_queue->dequeue(now);
    //process user inputs and server updates
    while (cur_msg)
```

```
    {
        if(cur_msg->type == CLIENT_INPUT)
            client_predictive_simulation(cur_msg);
        else
            process_server_updates(cur_msg);
        cur_msg = work_queue->dequeue(now);
    }
    // ...
}
```

The Server

Now let us consider the server side. It implements multitime management. There are two timestamp-ordered event queues on each server, a predictive queue (for predictive contract messages) and a conservative queue. The predictive queue uses the current server clock as its processing time. Any received events whose timestamp is less than the current server clock will be processed. The conservative queue is different. Its event processing time is based on the global minimum safe time received by the server. The global minimum safe time is the minimum of all the promises received from the clients and other servers. If the server is responsible for simulating any objects, its local time will also be taken into account in the global safe time calculation. At each moment, all the events and inputs in the conservative queue whose timestamp is less than the global safe time can be processed safely without causing an inconsistency. It is important to keep in mind that for the conservative simulation, the simulation clock is the conservative time, not the real server clock.

One tricky issue is that conservative simulation might spawn some new timestamped events. For example, a hit event might be generated when the conservative simulation decides that an arrow hits a monster. The timestamp value of such an event should be set to the current conservative time plus a small constant lookahead (SERVER_LOOKAHEAD_TIME). This small constant lookahead is necessary to avoid a deadlock in conservative simulation. Moreover, lookahead is a very important technique for improving the performance of conservative simulation. Interested readers are referred to [Fujimoto98]. Another subtle issue is that a server can only remove a message from the conservative queue after the message is processed and the new events (if any) are generated. Otherwise, other servers might receive out-of-order new event messages from this server because conservative simulation can be context-switched in the middle. Predictive simulation in the server side does not have such a problem because it never generates new events.

Here is the server time management/communication thread:

```
while (1)
{
    MSG_t* msg;
    if (now - last_safe_time_update >
        MAX_SAFE_TIME_UPDATE_INTERVAL)
    {
        //conservative_queue->get_minimum() returns
```

```
                    //the minimal timestamp in queue if the
                    //queue is not empty, otherwise it returns a
                    //maximum timestamp value
                    local_safe_time = MIN(client_safe_time_array->
                      get_minimum(), now, conservative_queue->
                      get_minimum()) + SERVER_LOOKAHEAD_TIME;
                    server_local_safe_time_array[self_id] =
                      local_safe_time;
                    global_safe_time =
                      server_local_safe_time_array->get_minimum();
                    last_safe_time_update = now;
                    if (local_safe_time != old_local_safe_time)
                    {
                        msg                   = new_msg();
                        msg->type             = SERVER_SAFE_TIME;
                        msg->server_id        = self_id;
                        msg->safe_time        = local_safe_time;
                        reliable_multicast_to_other_servers(msg);
                        old_local_safe_time = local_safe_time;
                    }
                }
                //process all kinds of messages here
                while (msg = nonblocking_receive_msg())
                {
                    if (msg->type == SERVER_SAFE_TIME)
                    {
                        server_local_safe_time_array
                            [msg->server_id] = msg->safe_time;
                    }
                    else if (msg->type == CLIENT_SAFE_TIME)
                    {
                        client_safe_time_array [msg->client_id] =
                            msg->safe_time;
                    }
                    else if (msg->type == CLIENT_INPUT)
                    {
                        client_safe_time_array [msg->client_id] =
                            msg->safe_time;
                        //timestamp ordered work queue
                        predictive_queue->enqueue(msg);
                        conservative_queue->enqueue(msg);
                    }
                    else if (msg->type == PREDICTIVE_STATE_UPDATE)
                    {
                        predictive_queue->enqueue(msg);
                    }
                    else if (msg->type ==
                            CONSERVATIVE_STATE_UPDATE)
                          conservative_queue->enqueue(msg);
                }
            }
```

Here's the server main thread:

```
while (1)
{
    MSG_t* cur_msg;
    cur_msg = predictive_queue->dequeue(now);
    while (cur_msg)
    {
        server_side_predictive_simulation(cur_msg);
        cur_msg = predictive_queue->dequeue(now);
    }
    //similar to dequeue but no removal of the message
    cur_msg = conservative_queue->
            peek(global_safe_time);
    while (cur_msg)
    {
        server_side_conservative_simulation(cur_msg);
        conservative_queue->dequeue(global_safe_time);
        cur_msg = conservative_queue->
                peek(global_safe_time);
    }
    // ...
}
```

Note that the difference between predictive contract and conservative simulation messages is not shown in the preceding pseudocode. Both predictive simulation and conservative simulation process all user inputs, and both simulations generate their updates to the game state during the processing. However, predictive simulation can only generate state updates to the entity attributes requiring relaxed consistency, while conservative simulation can generate state updates to all entity attributes. In this way, the attributes requiring strong consistency are always safely updated. Another important difference is that only the conservative simulation can generate a new event. Very complex rollback is required if we allow predictive simulation to generate new events. It can lead to annoying gameplay if not handled properly [Mauve02], so we simply prohibit it here.

One issue that needs to be addressed is the problem of a client crash or occasional long retransmission delay. Will the entire conservative simulation freeze if a single client fails? The answer is no. Each server can expect a promise from each of its clients within a time limit (not shown in the pseudocode). If a client fails to deliver a safe time message within that limit, the client is considered dead. The server ignores the client and the client must resynchronize with the server to "rejoin" the game. Any event received from a dead client with an out-of-order timestamp is simply discarded.

When to Use Multitime Management

Which multitime management solution to choose depends on many factors, such as network topology and game design. Table 6.6.3 lists several types of MMORPG architectures and suitable time management approaches for each.

Table 6.6.3   MMORPG Architectures and Suitable Time Management Approaches

	Client performs prediction locally and player commands/inputs are timestamped at client side	Player commands/inputs are timestamped at server side (client might or might not use prediction technique)
Single server	Server side rollback Delay compensation [Bernier01]	No need for special time/consistency management at server side
Server farm	Multitime management	Conservative time management at server side No need for multitime management

Conclusion

This article illustrated how to solve time and consistency management problems for multiserver-based MMORPGs. This solution properly handles the tradeoffs of responsiveness and consistency.

Acknowledgments

The authors are deeply grateful to Dr. Richard Fijimoto for his constructive suggestions and careful polishing of this article.

References

[Aronson97] Aronson, "Dead Reckoning: Latency Hiding for Networked Games," Gamasutra, 1997, available online at *www.gamasutra.com/features/19970919/ aronson_01.htm*.

[Bernier09] Bernier, "Latency Compensating Methods in Client/Server In-game Protocol Design and Optimization," GDC Proceedings, available online at *www.gdconf.com/archives/2001/bernier.doc*, 2001.

[Bettner01] Bettner, Terrano, "1,500 Archers on a 28.8: Network Programming in Age of Empires and Beyond," in the 2001 GDC Proceedings, available online at *www.gdconf.com/archives/2001/terrano_1500arch.doc*.

[Chandy78] Chandy, Misra, "Distributed Simulation: A Case Study in Design and Verification of Distributed Programs," IEEE Transactions on Software Engineering, SE-5(5): pp. 440–452, 1978.

[DIS94] DIS Steering Committee, "The DIS Vision: A Map to the Future of Distributed Simulation," Institute for Simulation and Training, 1994.

[Fujimoto98] Fujimoto, "Time Management in the High Level Architecture," Simulation, Vol. 71, No. 6, pp. 388–400, December 1998, available online at *www.cc.gatech.edu/computing/pads/PAPERS/Time_mgmt_High_Level_Arch.pdf*.

[Mauve02] Mauve, "How to Keep a Dead Man from Shooting," in the Proceedings of 7th International Workshop on Interactive Distributed Multimedia Systems and

Telecommunication Services, October 2002, available online at *www.infor-matik.uni-mannheim.de/informatik/pi4/publications/library/Mauve2000a.pdf.*

[Mills92] Mills, David L., "Network Time Protocol (version 3) Specification, Implementation and Analysis," RFC1305, 1992, available online at *www.faqs.org/rfcs/rfc1305 .html.*

AUDIO

Introduction

Eddie Edwards,
Sony Computer Entertainment Europe
eddie@tinyted.net

It seems that audio has taken a back seat in game development over the last decade. I cut my teeth on the British Acorn Archimedes computer (the first 32-bit RISC desktop machine). In those days (circa 1988), it was quite normal for a computer game to use up to 20 percent of the CPU to create music and audio effects for the game. These days, every ounce of CPU is required for AI, physics, and graphics, and audio has been given short shrift in all but a few exceptional cases. Even the game creation process often treats the provision of music and sound effects as an afterthought. It is rare, now, to find a programmer who calls himself or herself an "audio specialist," and the field of game audio often seems somewhat slow moving. However, we've been able to round up some excellent new techniques from experts in the field.

In this section, you will find six articles on the subject of game audio. James Boer and Jake Simpson describe specific programming techniques—the former explains a set of C++ classes that aid in audio sequencing, while the latter reveals a very simple yet effective method for automatic "lip-synching" between sound and animations. Borut Pfeifer and Frank Luchs then talk about more systemwide issues—creating a sound scripting system, and connecting sound synthesis with game physics. Finally, Scott Velasquez and Joe Valenzuela both talk about specific audio programming APIs—EAX and ZoomFX for environmental audio, and OpenAL for open, cross-platform access to sound hardware.

It is my hope that these articles inspire you, the reader, to push more machine and development resources toward audio, so that we might rekindle the flame of audio programming, push the envelope, and create new articles!

7.1

A Brief Introduction to OpenAL

Joe Valenzuela, Treyarch

jvalenzu@infinite-monkeys.org

OpenAL is a 3D positional audio library. It presents a simple and concise alternative to the bigger, object-oriented libraries more commonly used for games today. This article serves as a short introduction to a small library.

A Short History

OpenAL was started informally. The initial versions were little more than a header file and a mailing list. Infused with the energy and insight of talented programmers such as Terry Sikes, Jonathan Blow, and Sean Palmer, OpenAL's unique focus started to take form: to provide spatialized audio with an API that complemented modern graphics libraries.

The early design was strongly influenced by OpenGL [Kreimeier02]. This influence extended from the emphasis on simplicity and orthogonal use to the most basic decisions on namespaces: if OpenGL did it one way, OpenAL would too. An important aspect of the early evolution of OpenAL was the fact that it was being used in commercial application development almost immediately upon development of the initial implementation. This led to immediate feedback from application programmers and an almost frenetic pace of early development. Of course, this early enthusiasm was not without problems, as evidenced by the fact that the token to specify a looping source was changed four times in the course of one year!

Implementation simplicity was a hallmark of that initial design, and serves as a touchstone for all proposed features and extensions today. There is a very high standard to be met by any features put into the core library. As a consequence, for example, the application (not OpenAL) is given the responsibility for most scene management. Since most 3D audio applications already have sophisticated scene management for their graphical portions, this has not proven to be a burdensome requirement, and serves to simplify the library.

The OpenAL API

This section describes the OpenAL interface, from the basic concepts through optional extensions.

A Gentle API Introduction

It's been joked that the necessary OpenAL library functions would fit on the back of a matchbook. That's not far from the truth. It embodies the spirit that simple things should be simple, and that hard things are someone else's problem! While neophytes don't need a lot of code to be productive, good understanding of the vocabulary of the API goes a long way to avoid initial confusion.

OpenAL is at its heart an audio scene graph library. It describes a series of relationships between objects. Most of the objects embody a discrete concept. The important ones are devices, contexts, listeners, sources, and buffers. Most OpenAL entry points are related to creating, destroying, or changing the attributes of one of these types of objects [Kreimeier02].

Generally speaking, the relationships are as follows: A *device* is the hardware that ultimately outputs PCM data. A *listener* belongs to exactly one *context*, and each context has exactly one listener. Thus, a context is an instance of something listening to sound in a scene. Usually, one listener is present per scene, and it corresponds to the position and other attributes of the user of the application. *Buffers* are raw PCM samples, and cannot be played directly: only by associating a *source* with a buffer, and playing the source, can sound be rendered. Sources can have multiple buffers associated with them, in which case we say they possess a *buffer queue*.

Sources and buffers are generally referred to using *names*, which are integer IDs (unique for each object type). For example, no two source names will be the same, although they might use the same numerical IDs as a set of buffers.

Objects are instantiated, and have names bound to them, using the `alGen{Object}` syntax. They are destroyed with a corresponding `alDelete{Object}` call. For example, sources are created and destroyed with `alGenSources()` and `alDeleteSources()`. Contexts and devices are created using a different set of calls, which are discussed later in this article.

Sources are context-specific. The source names valid in one context will not be valid in another. Buffers are context-independent, and are created without reference to any active context. Buffers can be associated with multiple sources in multiple contexts simultaneously.

Most of these objects have attributes that can be explicitly set and queried. Attributes have a specific type as well as default values. The most common are source attributes, which enable you to associate buffers with sources, set a source position, and so forth. Listeners and sources share a similar syntax for setting and querying attributes, `al{Object}{n}{if}{v}`. This syntax specification should be familiar to those accustomed to reading OpenGL documentation. Most attribute accessors are available in either numeric (n) or vector (v) form, and the types of the parameters passed or accepted are specified by i for integer, or f for floating point. For example, a source's position is set using the AL_POSITION token in conjunction with either alSource3f() or alSourcefv().

The most important buffer attribute, the set of PCM samples that constitute a sound, is set with alBufferData().

Here's an example of a small OpenAL program:

```
// open device, create context
ALCdevice *dev = alcOpenDevice(NULL);
ALCcontext *cc = alcCreateContext(dev, NULL);

alcMakeContextCurrent(cc);

// create source and buffer
ALuint bid, sid;
alGenSources( 1, &sid );
alGenBuffers( 1, &bid );

// get pcm data, associate it with buffer
ALvoid *data;
ALsizei size, bits, freq;
ALenum format;
ALboolean loop;

alutLoadWAVFile("boom.wav", &format, &data, &size,
&freq, &loop);
alBufferData(bid, format, data, size, freq);

// associate buffer with source
alSourcei( sid, AL_BUFFER, bid );

// play source and wait until it's done,
// then destroy it
alSourcePlay(sid);
ALint state;
do {
    alGetSourcei(sid, AL_SOURCE_STATE, &state);
} while(state == AL_PLAYING);

alDeleteSources(1, &sid);
alDeleteBuffers(1, &bid);

alcMakeContextCurrent(NULL);
alcDestroyContext(cc);
alcCloseDevice(dev);
```

As illustrated, devices are opened with alcOpenDevice(), which takes an optional device specifier string. The syntax and meaning of the string is implementation-dependent. It is meant to allow applications to specify alternative backends or device-specific configuration parameters. In the GNU/Linux reference implementation, the device string is interpreted as a LISP-like token that can specify multiple backends, as well as attributes like sampling rates and backend-specific features.

Contexts are created with `alcCreateContext()`, and require a device that will serve as the rendering target for sound mixed in the context. It takes an optional context attribute list, in the form of integer pairs terminated with 0. Context attributes required to be supported by an implementation are `ALC_SYNC`, `ALC_REFRESH`, and `ALC_FREQUENCY`. `ALC_FREQUENCY` and `ALC_REFRESH` affect the performance and fidelity of the context's rendering, while `ALC_SYNC` requires that the context defer mixing until explicitly refreshed with `alcProcessContext()`. Since it's possible to have multiple contexts, `alcMakeContextCurrent()` is required to specify a current context.

As the preceding example illustrates, OpenAL's syntax, coding style, and conventions were designed to mimic OpenGL. This was a decision designed partly to comfort developers already familiar with the popular graphics library, and to emulate the sensible design principles pioneered by the OpenGL ARB.

Digging Deeper

Source attributes are set via the `alSource{n}{if}{v}` entry point.

They can be split into three groups: those that affect a source's physical placement in the OpenAL world, like `AL_POSITION` and `AL_VELOCITY`; those that represent "knobs and dials" on how a source is played, like `AL_PITCH`; and state attributes useful for high-level management of sources, like `AL_LOOPING` and `AL_SOURCE_STATE` [Kreimeier02].

The positions set using the `AL_POSITION` attribute are in world space. The only exceptions are sources with the additional attribute `AL_SOURCE_RELATIVE`, which informs the implementation that the source is positioned with its context's listener as its origin. This is useful for head-relative sounds such as might emanate from a helmet, or "2D" sounds, like music, that don't require positioning. Nonpositional sounds are often used with the `internalFormat` (multichannel) extension, which will be addressed later.

The `AL_PITCH` source attribute controls the relative pitch of a sound. At 1.0, there is no shift in the rendered source. Each reduction by 50 percent results in a pitch change of one octave (−12 semitones) [Kreimeier02]. In the GNU/Linux implementation, the Doppler filter computes the Doppler effect as a factor with which the existing pitch attribute is scaled. This is a great effect, and can be used dramatically within an application. Software implementations of pitched sources can be expensive, however, so some judgment is necessary in their usage.

The Doppler effect illustrates some finer points about the OpenAL API. To use the Doppler effect, some attributes both on the listener and source must be set.

```
ALfloat l_pos[] = { 0, 0, 5 };
ALfloat s_pos[] = { 0, 0, -5}, s_vel[] = {0,0,1};
ALfloat zeros[] = { 0, 0, 0 };

alListenerfv(AL_POSITION, l_pos);
alListenerfv(AL_VELOCITY, zeros);
```

```
alSourcefv(sid, AL_POSITION, s_pos);
alSourcefv(sid, AL_VELOCITY, s_vel);

alSourcePlay(sid);
ALint state;
do {
    s_vel[2] += 0.001;
    s_pos[2] += 0.001;

    alSourcefv(sid, AL_VELOCITY, s_vel);
    alSourcefv(sid, AL_POSITION, s_pos);

    alGetSourcei(sid, AL_SOURCE_STATE, &state);
} while(state != AL_PLAYING);
```

The important thing to notice in this example is that evaluation of the source's position is not derived—it is explicitly set by the application. All positions and velocities are assumed instantaneous.

OpenAL supports streaming sounds through the buffer queuing facility. Buffer queuing is a mechanism that associates multiple buffers with a single source. When the source is played, each buffer is rendered in succession, as if the buffers composed one contiguous sound. These are managed via a set of special functions.

Streaming sources usually work in the following way. A source is queued with a set of buffers via `alSourceQueueBuffers()`, then the source is played, and at some point queried with AL_BUFFERS_PROCESSED. This attribute gives the number of buffers already processed, which allows the application to remove these processed buffers with `alSourceUnqueueBuffers()`, which removes buffers in order from the beginning of the queue. Then, additional buffers are queued on the source [Creative03]. It is an error to remove buffers while they are playing.

```
// attach first set of buffers using queuing mechanism
alSourceQueueBuffers(sid, NUMBUFFERS, Buffers);

alSourcePlay(sid);

ALuint count = 0;
ALuint buffers_returned = 0;
ALint processed = 0;
ALboolean bFinished = AL_FALSE;
ALuint buffers_in_queue = NUMBUFFERS;

while (!bFinished)
{
    // get status
    alGetSourceiv(sid, AL_BUFFER_PROCESSED, &processed);

    // if some buffers have been played, unqueue them
    // then load new audio into them, then add them to
    // the queue
```

```
if (processed > 0)
{
    buffers_returned += processed;

    while(processed)
    {
        ALuint bid;
        alSourceUnqueueBuffers(sid, 1, &bid);

        if(!bFinished)
        {
            DataToRead = (DataSize > BSIZE) ? BSIZE : DataSize;
            if (DataToRead == DataSize)
                bFinished = AL_TRUE;

            // code to read DataToRead bytes from audio source into
data elided
            // ...

            DataSize -= DataToRead;

            if (bFinished == AL_TRUE)
                memset(data + DataToRead, 0, BSIZE - DataToRead);


            alBufferData (bid, format, data, DataToRead, wave.Sam-
plesPerSec);

            // Queue buffer
            alSourceQueueBuffers(sid, 1, &bid);
            processed--;
        }
        else
        {
            processed--;
            if (buffers_in_queue-- == 0)
            {
                bFinished = AL_TRUE;
                break;
            }
        }
    }
}
```

Spatialization

The heart of OpenAL is the attenuation of sound as a function of distance. OpenAL has a set of distance models that are runtime selectable and differ in level of compatibility with Direct3D, ease of application support, and conformance to physical formulas.

Distance models are selected via `alDistanceModel()`. The default distance model, `AL_INVERSE_DISTANCE`, conforms to the equation

$$G\_db = \text{clamp}(GAIN - 20 \times \log_{10}(1 + Rf \times (dist - Rd) / Rd, MinG, MaxG)$$

Rf and Rd in this equation correspond to the source attributes `AL_ROLLOFF_FACTOR` and `AL_REFERENCE_DISTANCE`. `MinG` and `MaxG` correspond to `AL_MIN_GAIN` and `AL_MAX_GAIN`, which are also source attributes. The reference distance is the distance at which the listener will experience `GAIN`. The source specific rolloff factor can be used to alter the range of a source, in the inverse direction of a change to the factor. A rolloff factor of 0 indicates no attenuation applied to a source [Kreimeier02].

OpenAL also provides an IASIG I3DL2 compatible distance model that might be more familiar to users of DS3D. This distance model is modeled by the equation

$$G\_db = \text{clamp}(GAIN - 20 \times \log_{10}(1 + Rf \times \text{clamp}(dist, Rd, Md) / Rd, MinG, MaxG)$$

Added to the previous equation is the clamping of the source distance between the reference distance and source specific `AL_MAX_DISTANCE`. Additional distance models under consideration for future simplifications are simplified linear models, which allow gain to fall to 0.

Extensions and the alut Library

OpenAL is extendible in a manner similar to OpenGL. Applications first query the implementation using the call `alGetString(AL_EXTENSIONS)`. This returns an extension string that can be searched for specific tokens. Alternatively, `alIsExtensionPresent()` will confirm or deny the existence of specific extensions. Once sure of the presence of an extension, applications can retrieve specific functions and enumeration tokens using `alGetProcAddress()` and `alGetEnumValue()`.

Extensions are implementation dependent, and their presence or necessity is highly volatile. The most commonly used in the GNU/Linux implementation are the Ogg Vorbis and MP3 extensions, which provide functions for playing common compressed file formats. Also important is the quadraphonic extension, which supplies four-channel sound, and the `internalFormat` extension, which allows the use of multichannel audio sample formats (e.g., stereo sources).

The most common addition in the Creative implementation is the EAX set of functions, which allow manipulation of EAX properties. EAX is used to add advanced features to the core library, such as reverberation, reflection, and occlusion between the listener and individual sources. Garin Hiebert of Creative Labs notes that the latest versions of EAX "incorporates more control . . . panning of effects around the listener, filtering depending on variable-size openings between the listener and the source," and so forth. EAX properties are manipulated using the `EAXGet()` and `EAXSet()`. Both are of the form:

```
ALenum EAX{Get,Set}(const struct* propertySetID,
ALuint property, ALuint source,
ALvoid* value, ALuint size);
```

Here's an example of some sample code to set up EAX properties:

```
// code to allocate source and buffer, set their
// properties omitted
ALuint Env = EAX_ENVIRONMENT_HANGAR;
eaxSet(&DSPROPSETID_EAX20_ListenerProperties,
        DSPROPERTY_EAXLISTENER_ENVIRONMENT |
        DSPROPERTY_EAXLISTENER_DEFERRED, NULL, &Env,
        sizeof(ALuint));
```

In general, EAX presents a set of room-oriented effects that can be used to add a realistic (if not actually physically modeled) feeling to an application [EAX02].

Missing from the core library is any provision to handle file formats. This functionality is provided, where available, through the alut auxiliary library. Different versions of the WAV file format can be loaded via `alutLoadWavFile()` and `alutLoadWavMemory()`. As well as providing convenience functions for loading audio, alut has the simplified initialization and finalization routines `alutInit` and `alutExit`. These hide the details of context and device initialization, with the cost of reduced flexibility.

OpenAL Implementations

Because OpenAL is a specification, and not an implementation, users must be aware of how different implementations can vary. Without some understanding of how most implementations work, loss of sound quality or performance is possible

Common Mistakes

New users of OpenAL tend to run into the same set of problems. This section describes some of the most common.

Multichannel Audio

Data associated with a buffer name via `alBufferData()` is copied by the library and, if necessary, converted to a more suitable format. The precise format that the implementation chooses is not defined. This is a performance concession, as different back-ends or drivers have special requirements for their data formats. A large portion of spatialized sound is the application of channel-independent effects. With this in mind, it should be clear that multichannel audio represents "pre-spatialized" sound, and the purpose when used in the context of positional audio is unclear. The most common usage of multichannel audio in games is for music, in which case spatialization can be ignored and the source played as an ambient sound.

However, because the application has no special insight into the internal format of the implementation, it risks losing the multichannel quality of the sound if the implementation uses a mono format. To circumvent this problem, some implementations provide the internalFormat extension, which provides a hint to the implementation that it is important to preserve the multichannel attribute of the data. This extension provides an additional function

```
alBufferWriteData_LOKI(ALuint buffer, ALenum format,
    ALvoid *data, ALsizei size,
    ALsizei freq, ALenum internalFormat);
```

This function has the same semantics and syntax as `alBufferData()`, except for the additional `internalFormat` parameter [Kreimeier02].

Ambient Sounds

There is no attribute to inform the driver that a source is ambient, and not meant to be positional. To create the effect of an ambient sound, applications are encouraged to ensure that their audio is positioned about the head by using the `AL_SOURCE_RELATIVE` attribute and using the `internalFormat` extension if necessary.

Enumerated Values

Enumerated token values, with the exception of `AL_TRUE` and `AL_FALSE`, are not guaranteed to have the same numeric value across implementations. In situations where drivers are expected to change without recompilation, the application should query the value of required tokens with `alGetEnumValue()`.

Common Performance Problems

In addition to conformance or fidelity problems, neophytes sometimes encounter performance problems. These are more pronounced in software implementations (for example, the GNU/Linux reference implementation), but all applications have a limited budget for sound processing. While more and more processing is being moved onto silicon, many sophisticated effects are still done on the CPU [Kreimeier01]. This is true even for hardware-accelerated implementations. For this reason, some of the common problems for software implementations are applicable in varying degrees to all drivers.

As one would suspect, the more data is touched, the more CPU time it takes to touch it. Applications should always use the lowest sampling rate acceptable. To minimize internal conversions, the same sampling rate for the device and rendering context should be used. This is a common use for the implementation-dependent device specifier argument to `alcOpenDevice()`. In the GNU/Linux implementation this is specified as follows:

```
int attrlist[] = { ALC_FREQUENCY, 22050, 0 };
ALCdevice* dev = alcOpenDevice("'((sampling-rate 22050))";
ALCcontext* cc = alcCreateContext(dev, attrlist);

alcMakeContextCurrent(cc);
```

The most expensive filters on sources are the ones that affect pitch. In the GNU/Linux implementation, these are AL_PITCH and the Doppler filter. Using a pitch value of 1.0 allows the implementation to disable pitch processing. Applications can disable Doppler processing for all sources by calling alDopplerFactor() with a parameter of 0. There is no official method for disabling Doppler effects for individual sources, although applications can do so by specifying a source as listener-relative with AL_SOURCE_RELATIVE and setting the velocity to 0.

Road Map for Implementation Solidarity

Ambitious programmers aim for cross-platform and cross-implementation compatibility. Often, zeal turns to frustration when they must spend time differentiating bugs from implementation-dependent behavior. To reduce confusion and promote interoperability, many areas where implementations needlessly differ either from one another or from the 1.0 API specification are planned to converge. This will be accomplished through several steps:

- More shared code and common enumeration values
- Speaker placement
- Standardized extensions

More Shared Code and Common Enumeration Values

A good deal of code (even in hardware-accelerated implementations) deals with the traditional responsibilities of a sound library. Tasks like object bookkeeping, loading audio files, and conversion to and from different internal formats are similar on all platforms. These are the "low hanging fruit" where any developer can easily attain similar results. The generous license terms in the Creative and GNU/Linux implementations are intended to encourage code reuse.

As mentioned previously, enumeration token values are not defined in the 1.0 specification. In spite of the fact that there is no requirement for binary compatibility between implementations, this is another case where small changes are planned to increase user convenience.

Speaker Placement

There is no interface for speaker placement in the OpenAL API, and there is a reason for this: end users configure speaker placement, not application developers. Speaker placement is therefore best handled at the operating environment level. Sound card manufacturers routinely bundle utilities to allow users to specify their speaker placement. While a comprehensive API for speaker configuration is unlikely to find its way into the core library, some facility to either complement or supplement operating system features is planned.

Standardized Extensions

Many of the existing extensions on each platform are intended eventually to find themselves either in the core AL section or in an auxiliary library. Many of the file format extensions for loading compressed audio have been adopted by more than one implementation, as well as extensions relating to additional distance models. In the future, sharing of common extensions can only lead to more conformant code.

The OpenAL Roadmap—Future Plans

To paraphrase Woody Allen, library development is like a shark. If it stops moving, it dies. The continued well being of OpenAL depends on planning for future growth, keeping pace with technology developments, and contributions from the community. Without organizational growth, development efforts would become frustrated. Without technological advancement, professional interest would atrophy. Moreover, without contributions from the community, a "grass roots" effort like OpenAL would have no basis to compete with industry standards like DirectSound.

Future organizational plans include the formation of an architectural review board (ARB) to organize future development of the OpenAL specification. Previously, this role was the informal responsibility of a small set of capable Loki and Creative engineers. In the future, choices about the structure and composition of the libraries will be decided (or codified) by this professional organization. Specifically, the ARB will decide not only general API trends, but also which features to require in the core library, as well as what behavior can be standardized and what must be left to the discretion of the implementer. As a model, the OpenGL ARB has provided a foundation that has required little major change in spite of the continual integration of new features. This is a major accomplishment indeed.

However, what good would this organization be without a technology worth advocating? OpenAL has been designed to offer a somewhat sane alternative to a world where audio APIs are more about the API and less about the audio. With an interface designed to be simple and complete, it competes for the hearts and minds of programmers who want a small, cross-platform audio library capable of positional 3D audio.

The real difference between OpenAL and other libraries, though, is you. Users have been vital in contributing source code, writing auxiliary documentation, and providing support in informal forums. More than any other positional audio library, OpenAL not only benefits from developers who use it, but also requires them to take an active role in its development.

For more information about OpenAL, visit *www.openal.org*, and the OpenAL section of *http://developer.creative.com*. These sites contain information about installing, using, and distributing OpenAL, as well as instructions for the mailing list and contributing. Join in—it really is your library!

Conclusion

OpenAL is a cross-platform audio interface that attempts to do for audio what OpenGL does for graphics. As the interface continues to evolve, audio programmers can spend more of their time improving actual game audio, and less time struggling with differences in hardware.

References

[Creative03] Creative Labs, *OpenAL Programmers Guide*, available online at *http://developer.creative.com*.

[EAX02] Creative Labs, *Environmental Audio Extensions: EAX 2.0*, available online at *http://developer.creative.com*.

[Kreimeier01] Kreimeier, Bernd, "The Story of OpenAL," *Linux Journal* (January 2001): pp. 102–107.

[Kreimeier02] Kreimeier, Bernd, et al., *OpenAL Specification and Reference, Snapshot*, available online at *www.openal.org*.

7.2

A Simple Real-Time Lip-Synching System

Jake Simpson, Maxis
jmsimpson@maxis.com

As you speak, your mouth and tongue form configurations that create sounds as air moves through them. These individual sounds are called *phonemes*. The English language has approximately 40 phonemes—from vowel sounds to nasals, approximants, and plosives. Forty is an approximate number due to regional accents and local dialects.

Our simple lip-synching system is not going to try to emulate phonemes. There are plenty of expensive commercial systems out there that will enable you to do that; they use a variety of techniques and produce varying levels of quality.

Phonemes are actually how lip readers are trained to watch for words, but most untrained people cannot notice (at a conscious level) exactly how mouth shapes correspond to sounds. However, they *do* recognize when they are not made in conjunction with the sounds being generated. For example, when we see a movie with the sound out of synch, we recognize it immediately—our brains "see" that the sound and lip and mouth movements aren't matched, at a seemingly instinctive level.

This idea is what we are trading on with our simple lip-synching system. We aren't going to try to emulate the correct phonemes, because that's just too much work for some situations. We are going to just make sure that the mouth changes positions at appropriate times, and that it does it in synchronization with the sounds being generated. This system has been used in several shipping titles, and each time players have mentioned how cool it was to see exact lip-synching, when the software was doing no such thing!

Implementation

At the simplest level, all our implementation does is to calculate, frame by frame, the average amplitude of a range of samples around the current "play position" of the current sound file. It then uses this result to decide which of a predefined set of mouth poses should be displayed.

More specifically, as you're playing a sample, on each frame you look ahead about 100 milliseconds and average the sample values. You then use that average amplitude to determine which mouth poses to use. Some parts of the sample will be silent, with an average amplitude of zero, which equates to a closed mouth. (A value of –1 might indicate that the sample has in fact finished, so the face is done speaking at the moment.)

The effectiveness of this system relies highly on your modeler (or animator or texture artist) supplying you with a set of radically different mouth poses that you can quickly blend between to give the illusion of the mouth moving as someone speaks.

To make this look good, you'll have to guarantee a decent frame rate, but any lip-synching solution will need a decent frame rate, so that's a given. The rate at which you'll want to actually set the mouth pose to the new amplitude value varies, and depends on what you feel comfortable with when viewing the results. Generally, you need enough time for the animation to blend to the new position and for the eye to recognize it. Change poses too quickly and your blends look weird and you get "flappy lips"; too slowly, and sometimes the mouth will be open (or closed) when it should be the opposite, which defeats the point of what we are trying to accomplish. Past experience indicates that a sample rate of around 10 Hz, or possibly just a bit less, is optimal. This is something you will need to tune until it looks right.

If you are able to use high sample-rate sounds, then instead of reading every sample value for your volume approximation, you can read every other one, or every third—whatever gives you a decent result.

Animation Notes

One of the things that can bring the most effective lip-synching system to its knees is what you do with the lip pose data after you've gotten it. Actually showing the animation or texture requires a little finesse.

Some games don't do anything to the mesh at all, but just replace a mouth texture with another one of the mouth in a different position, or just closed. This can be surprisingly effective—look at Raven Software's *Star Trek Voyager: Elite Force* for an example of this. However, care must be taken to make sure the texture in question is only of the mouth area; if you do the entire face you effectively lose the ability to blend together upper-face emotion textures with your speech animation.

If you do want to move the mesh, take a hint from Ritual Entertainment's *F.A.K.K. 2* and don't just stick a bone in the jaw and wiggle that up and down. Real humans don't do that, and everyone ends up looking like some kind of Muppet if you do. On a game currently in development, we're using a mixture of boned animation and morph targets, and the result is quite satisfactory. We use a bunch of mouth positions and do a fast blend between them per frame.

Experience has shown that, on average, five or six mouth positions will give you enough variety to make it look acceptable. Figure 7.2.1 has some examples of what might work for you in terms of mouth shapes.

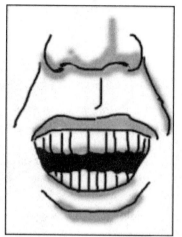
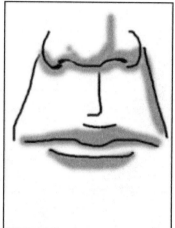
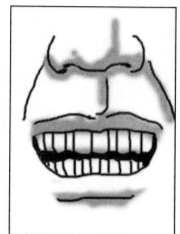

FIGURE 7.2.1 *Mouths in a variety of different poses, from closed to completely open.*

If your artists build the faces correctly (by placing the morph targets where real muscles are) you can actually blend in speech with an "emotion set" on the face. This enables, for example, your character's eyes to blink, or go wide or cross, to emphasize the speech. Emotional reaction while speaking is a powerful effect; if you can do it, you should.

When constructing the mouth poses, you don't want to just create grades of an open mouth. That has the effect of making the character look like it's are saying "ooooooooooo" at various volumes. Go for specifically different phoneme mouth shapes, with perhaps a wide-open pose for the one used with the highest volume. The shapes don't match the speech, but that doesn't really matter. It's the overall effect that we're after.

Watermarks

If you set your amplitude percentages for each of your five (arbitrary) mouth shapes to, say, 12 percent, 26 percent, 47 percent, 58 percent, and 80 percent, then the question gets raised, exactly what shape does 47 percent correspond to?

Some speech samples will doubtless be louder than others. Situations can arise with a lip-synching system where a character whispers, and because his average volume is so low, the system picks the same mouth pose for the entire sample.

One way to fix this is to spin through the speech samples and assign them watermark volume values based on percentages of the highest volume in the sample. You need to ascertain exactly what the maximum volume of any given sample is, so you can assign actual values to those percentages. This can be done at load time (although this is not a good idea if you are streaming, since it just adds to load times), or as a pre-processing step.

It might be argued that having set watermark percentages (on the order of 20 percent, 40 percent, 60 percent, etc.) would work well, but experience has proven that this is not necessarily the case. If 80 percent of your speech sample falls in the 60-percent to 80-percent range, then you'll end up with the mouth being in the same shape for a fair amount of the animation. The whole idea here is to mix it up a little, to not have the same mouth shape appear too frequently. You might think that you should regenerate the percentages per sample, but that's generally overkill. Some experimentation is required to find what ranges look best for you. Don't go with purely random ones—it's possible to get this to look right, but there's a lot of tweaking that goes into getting the possible random ranges correct. Usually, it's just not worth the time.

It's worth noting that a possible enhancement of the system is to check the maximum volume and to use slightly different watermark percentages (or even remove the top level entirely) if a sample is very quiet. If you use a big open-mouth pose for the highest volume level, it can look a bit strange when a character is whispering and his mouth is wide open!

Caveats

This system requires you to have the *uncompressed* sample data available to you. If you are using hardware that works on compressed data, this approach isn't going to work. You also need to be able to get a current pointer to where the mixer is in the sound sample at any given millisecond. Some hardware, when doing internal mixing, won't give you this information. In this case, you can get away with using absolute timing, but it's a little more error prone.

Another potential drawback is that this system requires at least 100 milliseconds of raw waveform data laid out in front of it per frame. This could be a problem if, for example, you are streaming MP3s and don't pre-decompress the sample. Another slight challenge with MP3s is that since they are decompressed in 4K chunks, you sometimes need two buffers available to do the calculations properly.

Conclusion

This article presented a system that is cheap and simple to implement. One of the biggest advantages is that it works for *all languages* with no other work.

You might be unconvinced. It does not sound like this method would give satisfactory results. However, you would be surprised at what people will persuade themselves that they've seen! Try this system and see what it can do for you. Additionally, try using sound inputs that aren't voices. The results are quite fun to watch.

Thanks to BJ West for the mouth shape images.

7.3

Dynamic Variables and Audio Programming

James Boer

james.boer@gte.net

In audio and music programming, one of the most common tasks is changing a variable, such as the volume of a playing sound, from one value to another over a specified period of time. This type of basic interpolation is trivial to implement, but it can be a bit tedious to write the same code over and over again. One way to solve this problem is to use C++ operator overloading to create a "smart" variable that knows how to interpolate its own value over time [Boer02].

What Is a Dynamic Variable?

A dynamic variable is a C++ object designed to act like a normal variable (typically a floating-point value), except that it can automatically interpolate between two given values over a specified duration. It's a very simple class, but ends up saving quite a bit of tedium when putting together more complex interpolation scenarios. Because C++ allows overloading of basic operators, a class can mimic a built-in data type, which often leads to much more intuitive usage and cleaner-looking code [Meyers96], [Meyers98].

The Dynamic Variable Class

A basic dynamic variable class is shown in Listing 7.3.1.

Listing 7.3.1 The DynamicVar class tracks the value of a variable over time.

```
class DynamicVar
{
public:
    DynamicVar()
    {
```

```
        m_fVar       = 0.0f;
        m_fTime      = 0.0f;
        m_fTimeTarget = 0.0f;
    }

    void setVar(float fVal, float fTime)
    {
        m_fTime      = 0.0f;
        m_fTarget    = fVal;
        m_fDelta     = m_fTarget — m_fVar;
        m_fTimeTarget = fTime;
    }

    void update(float fDeltaTime)
    {
        m_fTime += fDeltaTime;

        if (hasReachedTarget())
            m_fVar = m_fTarget;
        else
            m_fVar += (m_fDeltaTime / mfTimeTarget) * m_fDelta;
    }

    operator float()
    {   return m_fVar;  }

    void operator = (float fVal)
    {
        m_fVar       = fVal;
        m_fTarget    = fVal;
        m_fTime      = 0.0f;
        m_fTimeTarget = 0.0f;
    }

    bool hasReachedTarget()
    {   return (m_fTime >= m_fTimeTarget);  }

private:
    float   m_fVar;         // current value
    float   m_fTarget;      // target value
    float   m_fDelta;       // delta value (slope)
    float   m_fTime;        // current time
    float   m_fTimeTarget;  // target time
};
```

The basic components of the class consist of an assignment operator to set the "variable" represented by the object, an initialization function to tell the variable how to interpolate over how much time, an update function to perform the actual work of interpolation, an overloaded float operator used to retrieve the variable value from the object, and a query function hasReachedTarget(), which is used to tell when the interpolation has reached its target value.

Using Dynamic Variables in Audio Programming

ON THE CD

There are literally dozens of places where simple interpolation can be used in audio programming. A basic fade of a music stream is a simple example. When playing a sound of organic origin, such as a loop representing a howling wind, you might try varying the pitch, volume, and pan (or position for 3D sounds) over time to create an even more dynamic experience for the user. This use of dynamic interpolation can help avoid problems inherent in repetitive ambience tracks—namely, that the user quickly recognizes the sound as a repeating loop. For a simple example of this type of use of dynamic variables with ambient soundscapes, you can examine the sample program SoundscapeTest.exe that comes on the companion CD-ROM.

We'll demonstrate one of the more interesting applications of our dynamic variables—implementing an envelope control class using the same principles and basic mechanisms as the `DynamicVar` class.

You can see in Figure 7.3.1 that an audio envelope is nothing more than a series of basic linear interpolations over time. Often, the sustain time is an unknown variable that will be resolved at runtime. This might be a car engine, an elevator, or any other device a player might control in real-time; anything that produces a repeating in-game sound. However, we can easily create the control to handle both pre-programmed sustain times and sustains that are controlled in real-time. In our demonstration class, passing a positive value as the sustain time parameter means a fixed time, where passing a negative value means the sustain time will be controlled at runtime.

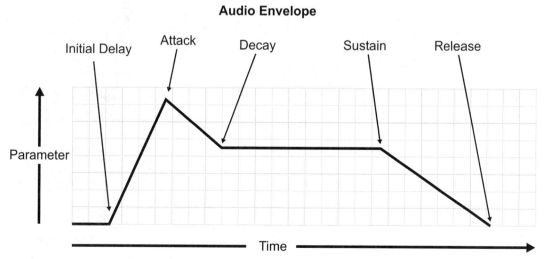

FIGURE 7.3.1 *An audio envelope.*

Keep in mind that this envelope control can represent not only volume, but other parameters such as pitch. For example, an elevator loop can pitch from low to high at the beginning of the run, and then pitch back down as the loop ends.

In Listing 7.3.2, we can see the fully developed envelope class, EnvelopeVar. Like the DymamicVar class, EnvelopeVar is designed to mimic a single variable that interpolates its value over time, only this time the interpolation is much more complex, and so uses a DynamicVar internally to perform its job.

Listing 7.3.2 The EnvelopeVar class builds on DynamicVar to perform more Interesting Interpolation of a value over time.

```
struct SoundEnvelope
{
public:
    SoundEnvelope()
    {  clear();  }

    void clear()
    {
        m_fInitialTime  = 0.0f;
        m_fAttackTime   = 0.0f;
        m_fAttackLevel  = 0.0f;
        m_fDecayTime    = 0.0f;
        m_fDecayLevel   = 0.0f;
        m_fSustainTime  = 0.0f;
        m_fSustainLevel = 0.0f;
        m_fReleaseTime  = 0.0f;
        m_fReleaseLevel = 0.0f;
    }

    float m_fInitialTime;
    float m_fAttackTime;
    float m_fAttackLevel;
    float m_fDecayTime;
    float m_fDecayLevel;
    float m_fSustainTime;
    float m_fSustainLevel;
    float m_fReleaseTime;
    float m_fReleaseLevel;
};


class EnvelopeVar
{
public:

    enum Progression
    {
        ENV_FLOOR,
        ENV_INITIAL,
```

```
            ENV_ATTACK,
            ENV_RELEASE,
            ENV_SUSTAIN,
            ENV_DECAY
    };
    EnvelopeVar()
    {  clear();  }

    void clear()
    {
        m_Envelope.clear();
        m_Level  = 0.0f;
        m_eState = ENV_FLOOR;
    }

    void setVar(const SoundEnvelope& env)
    {
        m_Envelope = env;
        m_eState   = ENV_INITIAL;
        m_Level.setVar(
            m_Level, m_Envelope.m_fInitialTime);
    }

    operator float()
    {  return m_Level;  }

    void update(float fDeltaTime)
    {
        m_Level.update(fDeltaTime);
        if(m_Level.hasReachedTarget())
        {
            switch(m_eState)
            {
            case ENV_FLOOR:
                break;
            case ENV_INITIAL:
                m_eState = ENV_ATTACK;
                m_Level.setVar(
                    m_Envelope.m_fAttackLevel,
                    m_Envelope.m_fAttackTime);
                break;
            case ENV_ATTACK:
                m_eState = ENV_DECAY;
                m_Level.setVar(
                    m_Envelope.m_fDecayLevel,
                    m_Envelope.m_fDecayTime);
                break;
            case ENV_DECAY:
                m_eState = ENV_SUSTAIN;
                m_Level.setVar(
                    m_Envelope.m_fSustainLevel,
                    m_Envelope.m_fSustainTime);
                break;
```

```
                        case ENV_SUSTAIN:
                            m_eState = ENV_RELEASE;
                            m_Level.setVar(
                                m_Envelope.m_fReleaseLevel,
                                m_Envelope.m_fReleaseTime);
                            break;
                        case ENV_RELEASE:
                            m_eState = ENV_FLOOR;
                            break;
                        };
                    }
                }

                private:
                    SoundEnvelope   m_Envelope;
                    DynamicVar      m_Level;
                    Progression     m_eState;
                };
```

ON THE CD

The `EnvelopeVar::update()` function simply cycles through the list of states via the `Progression` enumeration, and uses the data stored in the `SoundEnvelope` struct to move from interpolation to interpolation. It's now a simple matter to take complete control over a sound's entire aural envelope using a single object representing a variable you want to interpolate over time, such as volume, pitch, or pan. To see how this class works, you can try the SoundEnvelope demo program on the companion CD-ROM and listen to the results.

Additional Enhancements

Depending on your specific game engine and circumstances, you might want to approach the code to these classes in a different manner. If, for example, you are writing for video game consoles and your engine has a fixed simulation (nonrendering) update rate of 60 cycles per second, you can optimize a good portion of the `DynamicVar` class to perform its updates using nothing but simple integer math by precalculating some of the variables. The sample code is more appropriate for most PC-style engines that typically have a variable update rate.

For some applications, it might be desirable to allow the program to trigger the progression of various states of the envelope within the `EnvelopeVar` class, such as when playing dynamic sequences whose length cannot be easily predicted. In this case, it would be a simple matter to add a method that prevents the envelope from advancing beyond a specific state (typically *sustain*). Additionally, it should be noted that this code was written with clarity in mind to demonstrate the concepts of this article. There is obviously some room for optimization, which would be advisable if you are planning to implement envelope control on every voice playing in a musical sequencer, or if you plan to use a large number of these objects simultaneously.

Conclusion

The basic concept of creating a custom data type that can dynamically interpolate on its own is a simple concept, and almost as simple to implement. Yet the practical application of this concept in audio programming is something that might not be quite as obvious. By creating programming tools and utilities that enable us to more easily create organic and naturally flowing audio output programmatically, we give audio designers a way to squeeze more out of existing hardware.

References

[Boer02] Boer, James, *Game Audio Programming*, Charles River Media, Inc., 2002.
[Meyers96] Meyers, Scott, *More Effective C++*, Addison-Wesley Longman, Inc., 1996.
[Meyers98] Meyers, Scott, *Effective C++, Second Edition*, Addison Wesley Longman, Inc., 1998.

Creating an Audio Scripting System

Borut Pfeifer, Radical Entertainment

borut_p@yahoo.com

Audio has had an increasing emphasis in games in the past few years. For a long time, technology didn't support high-quality sound. Even as it improved, audio continued for some time to be ignored as a tool for immersing the player in the game. Now there are a variety of tools available to help create a compelling audio experience for your game; however, it can be tough, especially for the novice audio programmer, to determine exactly what functionality is necessary to create that experience. Fortunately, there is a relatively simple set of functionality that, when exposed to the composer or sound designer through a scripting system, you can use to create interesting audio for your game.

This article describes a scripting system that controls elements of playback and randomization to help immerse the player in the game using audio. It uses an XML-based audio dictionary that ties audio tag IDs with control parameters affecting how each sound is played back. There are three basic types of audio: effects, music, and ambient audio, each with its own issues in using it effectively. The system also allows for randomization of playback of a group of audio pieces. With players playing a game for hours on end, frequent repetition can detract from even the best audio.

Game audio has several goals. The first is to convey simple information about what is going on in the world to players—what items they are using, what kind of area they are in, and what is about to happen to them. Second, dialog is mainly used to convey story elements, but dialog in the middle of gameplay can also provide flavor and tone. The final goal, which is somewhat more difficult to realize, is to affect the player's mood in the way the game desires. There are exciting points, quiet points, aggressive, somber—any number of adjectives that might describe the feelings a game wants the player to have at a given time.

Several techniques are used to achieve this last goal. Using music to control the player's mood can be very powerful. Ambient audio immerses the player in the narrative situation the game wants to convey; every moment of our lives is filled with small sounds we rarely notice consciously, but their presence continually informs us of our location.

A good audio scripting system should enable a sound designer to convey audio information (including story) and set the mood of the game in a straightforward manner.

Game Audio Categories

There are several categories of audio used in games, each with its own technical requirements, design issues, and scripting needs. The system controls the playback of these different categories of audio through a database consisting of audio files and parameters associated with them.

This database consists of an XML file, in which each tag corresponds to a piece of audio you'd want to play back in the game. A tag could be as simple as specifying a .wav file, or it can specify groups of files that can be looped, each with a random probability of being selected. Each tag has a number of parameters to control and randomize playback of audio files, to create a more diverse and unique sound experience for the player.

Each piece of audio, regardless of category, has a few basic control or scripting needs. For example, to deal with a limited number of audio buffers, each piece of audio needs to have a priority level so we can determine which sound will be interrupted when all buffers are full and a new sound is requested. If the requested sound has the lowest priority, it will not replace any of the currently playing sounds and will go unplayed. Other basic parameters include a volume adjustment range (to produce sounds randomly slightly louder or quieter), and the ability to loop at a random interval.

Effects

Effects are responses to changes in the game; they are typically very short in duration. Examples of these dynamic sounds are gunshots, grunts, and footsteps. Because these effects are based on what is currently happening in the game, they must be very responsive, so that the player receives visual and audio feedback in perfect sync, regardless of other processing.

Because the majority of effect files are short and played frequently, they can be read into memory once from disk and then played back by the audio engine as the demand for the sound comes up. (If the game has longer response sounds that are less repetitive, you might want to stream some sounds from the disk, and only store the most common sounds in memory.) Each sound in memory is then loaded into a separate sound buffer when played, so the sound library can perform processing on it to spatialize the sound. This is because two instances of the same sound that are at different distances from the player should sound slightly different.

When an effect is played multiple times in quick succession, so that several copies are being played back at once, an unpleasant audio artifact known as *flanging* can occur. This is distortion resulting from the same sound being played out of phase. In a game, this is a common scenario, such as a number of opponents all firing similar guns. To prevent this, each effect might have a secondary sound that is played when it has been requested to play a specific number of times. This effect can cascade, such that the new sound effect can have its own secondary sound. This also applies to more general game situations. For example, playing the sound of a small glass breaking multiple times does not adequately simulate a pane of glass breaking. Therefore, when a number of small glass-breaking sound effects are requested, a larger glass-breaking sound effect replaces them all. Then, when a number of the larger glass-breaking sounds are requested, an even larger glass-breaking sound replaces them all. This also helps cut down on the number of hardware sound buffers you take up for this group of related sounds.

Music

Interactive music is of increasing interest to the game industry. Functionality provided by tools like DirectMusic allows for fully layered soundtracks, even dynamically adjusting the amount one instrument adds to the final score. This level of complexity can seem fairly daunting, but *Halo* [O'Donnell02], well known for its excellent interactive score, used a fairly straightforward system to control the music played back during the game.

Each musical composition is made up of three subpieces: the music to play at the beginning of the composition, the music to loop for the desired duration of the composition, and a final piece of music that is played when the loop is over. Each individual piece of music can take advantage of control and randomization tags, allowing for a wider variety of music experience when playing back one composition. The scripting system need only specify the music composition to play back, providing a very simple interface. Additionally, each composition needs to specify how the transition between the loop music and the exit music is to be handled. The system can cross fade between the two individual pieces for a specific period of time, or it can transition immediately. The system in [O'Donnell02] used an additional set of loop and exit tags, which could be requested separately from the scripting system, although some of this functionality can be recreated using another similar composition tag.

One of the keys to creating a successful interactive score is to make sure that the music fits the mood of the player's actions without giving the player direct control over the music that is playing. Giving the player too much control has the effect of taking the player out of the game, as he starts to play around with your rules for creating the interactive score. For example, if the music becomes very dramatic as the player takes a step down a creepy hallway, but immediately shifts back to less dramatic when the player turns around, it jars the player's immersion. The composer needs to be able to help define the player's overall emotional mood, not adjust every moment based on the player's whim.

Another key issue to consider is the fact that most games play over 20 hours, while they rarely have much more than 1 hour of unique soundtrack. This can result in a very repetitive musical experience if music is used constantly throughout the game. If the goal for the game's music is to heighten the player's mood, it must be used sparingly during gameplay to keep its emotional punch.

Ambient Audio

Ambient effects are similar to other more general sound effects in that they are typically spatialized. Ambient audio is used to create a sound space for the game; little detail sounds like crickets chirping in a swamp or background chatter on a city street add a lot to immerse the player in the game. Ambient audio does not have the same responsiveness requirements as other effects, and because the length of individual ambient pieces might be longer, they are better suited for streaming at runtime.

To create an ambient audio space for the game, script tags will need to allow for easy randomization and grouping. For example, a tag for jungle-related ambient audio might include crickets chirping, wind rustling, and other assorted animal noises. These individual elements could then loop at different, randomized rates, and move their random 3D position. This would help ensure that the ambient audio does not repeat in the same sequence, which players would easily detect.

Dialog

Dialog falls into two main categories: dialog in cut-scenes, and automatic responses between characters in the game. The control of cut-scene dialog is straightforward. The dialog doesn't have to be stored in memory like other effects, however, and most likely it does not need to use 3D audio. Cut-scene dialog should almost always come from the center channel. If it was processed to make the sound seem 3D with respect to the user's position, the cut-scene dialog might not be very audible if the player happens to trigger the cut-scene from a slightly more distant location. You might still want to process environmental effects (like reverb and echo) based on the location in which the cut-scene is taking place. The main goal for this dialog is just to communicate the story to the player.

In-game dialog also helps to communicate story, but more commonly through setting or mood. It helps to express characters' anger through taunts and responses, or fear if they decide they should be running away. This helps opponents and teammates seem more alive by giving them a greater range of communication or expression, even if there is not much actual story detail delivered in the dialog. It especially helps to communicate AI decision making, so players can understand and strategize about the world they are playing in. This type of dialog is conditional upon the type of game. *Halo* used a system that had a limited number of recorded voices for marines. Each marine had different sayings for different situations; if one marine died, the voices might be chosen to ensure using the lowest number of duplicates at any point during gameplay. Your game could easily have different requirements for in-game dialog, such as different categories of responses, so some of the requirements of in-game dialog need to be analyzed with respect to your game's design.

Tools

ON THE CD

The example implementation on the accompanying CD-ROM uses DirectSound [DirectX]. It offers a wide range of functionality, including DirectMusic, but we will use it for basic low-level sound playback and 3D audio. There are a number of similar libraries (free and commercial) available on various platforms that implement similar functionality, if your needs are not met by DirectSound. However, you must port the code yourself.

XML is used to define the audio tag database. It's very simple to define and load the necessary audio parameters. Another article previously discussed using XML for other areas in game development [Seegert02], and there are a number of resources online, so its usage is not elaborated on in this article.

The Ogg Vorbis SDK is used for music playback ([Moffit02], [OggVorbis]). Support for other formats is easy to add into the architecture of the example (it only involves deriving a new C++ class, using the Ogg Vorbis functionality as an example). The audio is of comparable quality to MPEG Layer 3 (mp3) encoding, but there is no licensing fee for implementing a decoder. This makes Ogg Vorbis an attractive solution for music playback, especially for independent developers on tight budgets.

XML Audio Tag Database

The tag database file contains a list of audio tags that the game can reference. An audio tag represents any logical piece of audio the sound designer might want to play at any one point (even if it's made up of a number or different physical sound files). The list of tags is surrounded by the following:

```
<?xml version="1.0"?>
<AudioTagDatabase>
...
</AudioTagDatabase>
```

There are six types of tags: EFFECT, AMBIENT, MUSIC, COMPOSITION, GROUP, and RANDOM. Here is an example of a tag's format to show some of the common attributes available to every tag:

```
<TAG_TYPE_NAME  ID="FOO"  PRIORITY="0"
    VOLUME_ADJUST="5.0"  VOLUME_ADJUST_RANGE="3.0"
    LOOP_DELAY="10.0"  LOOP_DELAY_RANGE="5.0"/>
```

Table 7.4.1 XML Attributes Available on All Tags

ID	The string the game code or script will use to tell the audio engine to play the desired sound.
PRIORITY	An integer reflecting the importance of this audio tag (how likely it is to be replaced by another sound when all buffers are being used). The higher the priority value, the fewer the sounds will be able to interrupt it. The default priority is zero.
VOLUME_ADJUST	The number of decibels to adjust the sound playback over the game's default volume. This adjustment is limited to the maximum volume, and to no volume. A positive number increases the volume, and a negative number decreases it.
VOLUME_ADJUST_RANGE	The range in decibels to randomly add or subtract to the volume adjust amount. For example, if the VOLUME_ADJUST is 3.0, and the VOLUME_ADJUST_RANGE is 1.0; every time the effect is played, the volume will be adjusted somewhere between 2 and 4 decibels up or down.
LOOP_DELAY	The number of seconds to repeat this sound. If this parameter is not specified, or is less than zero, the sound is not repeated.
LOOP_DELAY_RANGE	The number of seconds to randomly adjust the delay in repeated playback.
LOOP_TIMES	The number of times the sound file should be looped. If this value is 0, and there is a LOOP_DELAY specified, this means to always loop the audio.

Effect

An effect tag has additional parameters, as listed in Table 7.4.2.

Table 7.4.2 XML Attributes on the Effect Tag

FILE	The .wav file to play for this effect.
MINDIST	If the player is within this distance of the sound, the sound will not be audible.
MAXDIST	If the player is farther than this distance from the sound, it will not be audible.
CASCADENUM	The number of times this sound has to be simultaneously requesting before the cascade tag is played instead.
CASCADETAG	The audio tag to play when the audio manager has the specified number of occurrences of this tag currently playing.

Ambient

An ambient audio tag is also an effect, so it might have any of the effect tag parameters. It might also have the following parameters, as shown in Table 7.4.3.

Table 7.4.3   XML Attributes on the Ambient Tag

X	The X coordinate used to place the sound in the world.
Y	The Y coordinate used to place the sound in the world.
Z	The Z coordinate used to place the sound in the world.
XRANGE	The amount to randomly adjust the X coordinate of the sound's position on each playback. For example, if an ambient tag has an X position of 5.0 and an XRANGE of 10.0, the x coordinate of the sound's position will vary from –5.0 to 15.0. The numbers are specified in whatever units the game uses.
YRANGE	The amount to randomly adjust the Y coordinate of the sound's position on each playback.
ZRANGE	The amount to randomly adjust the Z coordinate of the sound's position on each playback.

Music

The music tag has only a single parameter, the name of the file to play (see Table 7.4.4).

Table 7.4.4   The XML Attribute Available on the Music Tag

FILE	The .ogg file to stream in for this piece of music.

Composition

The composition tag describes a piece of looping music. It consists of an opening audio stream, a loop, and a closing audio stream (see Table 7.4.5).

Table 7.4.5   XML Attributes on the Composition Tag

IN	The audio tag to play first, when the composition is requested.
LOOP	This tag is played after the IN tag finishes, for the duration requested of the composition's playback.
OUT	This tag is played after the LOOP tag finishes playing.
CROSS_FADE_TO_OUT_TIME	This is the number of seconds to cross fade between the ending of the LOOP tag's playback and the beginning of the out tag's playback. If this parameter is 0 or is not specified, there is no cross fade, and the OUT tag begins playback immediately after the LOOP tag finishes.

Group

This tag doesn't have any attributes in the tag itself, but instead can have any number of subtags of the format

```
<ITEM TAG="TAGNAME" DELAY="delay time" DELAY_RANGE="delay range"/>
```

When the group tag is played, every tag name specified by its subtags is played back. If a DELAY parameter is specified, the system waits to play this individual element while playing the others. The DELAY_RANGE parameter adjusts the delay by a random amount. All times are in seconds.

Random

Similar to the GROUP tag, this tag has no attributes. Instead, it has any number of subtags of the format:

```
<ITEM TAG="TAGNAME" PROB="percentage 0-100">
```

While there can be any number of subtags, the total sum of all the subtags' PROB attributes cannot be over 100. These values represent the percentage likelihood that the subtag will be played back when the RANDOM tag is requested; hence, a sum greater than 100 percent does not make sense.

Components

ON THE CD

There are a few basic pieces to the sample implementation provided on the companion CD-ROM. The example code was compiled with Microsoft Visual C++ 6.0.

The AudioManager **Class**

This is a singleton class that serves as the game's main interface to the audio engine. It is responsible for allocating the hardware sound buffers, and updating them periodically with the currently playing sounds. Because there is limited memory for sound buffers, a fixed number of them are allocated, and then they are filled with the sound as it continues to play (looping through the buffer if the sound is longer than the buffer). Some important functions are shown in Table 7.4.6.

Table 7.4.6   The Primary Interface to the AudioManager **Class**

LoadAudioTags	Takes as a parameter the name of the audio XML setup file.
Play	Takes the audio tag name, a pointer to a WorldObject (used for sounds that are to be spatialized; can be NULL), the duration of the playback, in milliseconds (0 for the normal duration of the sound file), and the delay (milliseconds to wait before playing back the sound), and an IAudioListener (can be NULL; receives notification when sound is finished).
Update	Requires the number of milliseconds that have passed since the last update. Advances the sound buffers so the next portions of each playing sound are loaded into them.

SetOverallVolume	Adjust parameters away from their default values. SetDistanceFactor SetDopplerFactor SetRolloffFactor
SetListenerCamera	Takes a pointer to a Camera object as a parameter; this allows the AudioManager to update the 3D listening position for certain sounds to be spatialized.

Audio Classes

The Audio class represents a specific type of audio that knows how to load its data into a buffer owned by the AudioManager. It does this through its virtual function Fill-Buffer(), which interprets the audio data into a format usable by the AudioManager (in this implementation, PCM data used by DirectSound). It also lets the AudioManager know if there's more of the audio left to play.

There are several Audio subclasses. The Sound class implements .wav file loading through the FillBuffer() interface. Its subclass, Sound3D, specifies an object in the world with a position to attach the sound. The MusicOggVorbis class implements an audio object that uses a streamed .ogg file. It inherits from the Music subclass of Audio, which is the base class for any additional music file types.

The IAudioListener Interface

Any class that wants to be notified when a particular piece of audio is done playing should inherit from this abstract class. It has one virtual function, shown in Table 7.4.7.

Table 7.4.7   The Pure Virtual Interface of the IAudioListener Class

AudioFinished	The AudioManager calls this function when the desired piece of audio is finished playing. It takes one argument, a pointer to the Audio object that finished playing (in case the IAudioListener is waiting for multiple Audio objects to finish).

The AudioTag Class

AudioTag is the base class for any audio tag to be defined in the XML dictionary. Each object of this class has three attributes: a priority that affects which sounds are interrupted when there aren't enough sound buffers to play an incoming piece of audio, and two parameters to define how the volume should be adjusted for any audio the tag creates. It has three functions that can be overridden by subclasses, listed in Table 7.4.8.

Table 7.4.8   The Interface of the AudioTag **Class**

LoadTag	This function loads the tag's data from an XML document element.
CreateAudio	This function creates an object of the appropriate subclass of Audio (for example, the AudioEffectTag creates a Sound3D object). The memory allocated by this function is cleaned up by the AudioManager when the Audio object is finished playing. Each subclass must implement this function.
AudioFinished	AudioTag inherits this class from the IAudioListener interface, and it uses it to create another instance of the sound when done in case it requires looping. Subclasses can override this behavior.

Each subclass of AudioTag (AudioEffectTag, AudioAmbientTag, AudioMusicTag, AudioCompositionTag, AudioGroupTag, and AudioRandomTag) has its own data members that correspond to the parameters for each tag in the audio dictionary XML file.

The WaveFile **Class**

The WaveFile class is a simpler version of the class with the same name in the Direct-Sound SDK samples. The WaveFileFactory class handles the memory management of the WaveFile objects. The factory's management of memory could be more complex—in the example, it allocates memory for any requested .wav file. You might want it to keep only a certain number of files in memory, based on their playback frequency and memory required.

The OggVorbisFile **Class**

The OggVorbisFile class is derived from documented Ogg Vorbis examples ([OggVorbis], [Moffit02]). It serves as a thin wrapper around the Ogg Vorbis SDK (specifically, the vorbisfile library, which does most of the work of reading the .ogg files).

The Camera **Class**

This class represents the object the game uses to keep track of the player's view. It consists of the camera's position, a vector describing its look direction, and a vector describing the vertical orientation of the camera. The AudioManager uses this information to update DirectSound's 3D Listener for 3D audio spatialization.

The WorldObject **Class**

This class represents a game object that has a position in the 3D game world. Spatialized sounds have corresponding WorldObjects to update their 3D position and velocity. The GetPosition(), SetPosition(), GetVelocity(), and SetVelocity() functions are used to set this data.

Scripting Control

Any audio tag can be called in scripts, or attached to objects, animations, particle systems, characters, locations, and so forth. The only interface that is required is the `Play()` method of the `AudioManager` class.

Sample Application

ON THE CD

The sample application on the companion CD-ROM is a very simple GUI that allows you to control audio parameters you might find in a game. You can select from any of the audio tags in the database to play, adjust the listener's position, and the overall volume. Experiment with the different ambient, music and effect tags to see how the different tag types and parameters interact to create an immersive sound space.

Further Work

This XML scripting system is very extensible. Requirements for dialog are not addressed, such as adjusting cut-scene dialog to not be spatialized, and in-game dialog, whose requirements would be based on a specific game design. It would be easy to add different types of tags or parameters for such functionality, such as a 2D-only parameter for effects, or a special dialog tag that includes a matrix of dialog lines for response categories like getting hit, dying, and so forth.

Some types of games also require sounds that adjust to the game's environment dynamically while playing (for example, a car's engine changing pitch with acceleration); this could easily be implemented as another specialized audio tag. Additional 3D effects, such as echo and reverb, could be added as EFFECT tag parameters, with additional parameters to randomize how the sound is affected.

Conclusion

A simple collection of scriptable sound attributes can allow you to quickly develop more interactive sound for your game. Existing technologies like XML work well for providing this data definition, along with tools for editing those attributes.

References

[DirectX]   DirectX 9.0 SDK DirectSound examples, available online at *www.msdn.com/directx*.

[Moffitt02] Moffitt, Jack, "Audio Compression with Ogg Vorbis," *Game Programming Gems 3*, Charles River Media, 2002.

[O'Donnell02] O'Donnell, Marty, "Producing Audio for *Halo*," available online at *www.gamasutra.com/resource_guide/20020520/odonnell_01.htm*, May 20, 2002.

[OggVorbis] Ogg Vorbis SDK, available online at *www.vorbis.com*.

[Seegert02] Seegert, Greg, "Real-Time Input and UI in 3D Games," *Game Programming Gems 3*, Charles River Media, 2002.

7.5

Implementing an Environmental Audio Solution Using EAX and ZoomFX

Scott Velasquez, Gearbox Software

scottv@gearboxsoftware.com

If you are reading this article, then you are probably one of many first time audio programmers who have been assigned the daunting task of adding environmental audio to your current project. Or, perhaps you are an audio veteran, but only have experience in the world of 2D audio. In either case, this is the article for you!

This article covers ideas and suggestions for implementing environmental audio in your game. The code examples are demonstrated in C++ on a Windows platform using DirectSound. The author assumes that the reader has some experience with DirectSound and DirectSound3D, as teaching DirectSound basics is beyond the scope of this article. The code samples could be rewritten in another language or to a different audio library if the reader is experienced in both, although the ZoomFX extension is only available for DirectSound.

What Is Environmental Audio?

After correctly positioning sounds in 3D space, the most important thing you can do to create a completely immersive world is to create an aural environment with environmental properties, affecting the sounds in your game. James Boer makes a very good comparison: environmental audio is as critical to sound as lighting is to rendering [Boer03].

When a sound travels from a source to a listener, the audio is modified due to the environments that the sound travels through on the way. Sound energy has possibly been reflected or absorbed by objects in its path.

Environmental audio is the simulation of these effects in software. These modifications of the original audio sample are created by applying various environmental effects such as echo, reverb, and frequency filtering. Echo and reverberation (also known as "early" and "late" reflections, respectively) give the player's brain a cue about how far away a sound source is and what type of environment it is coming from. Sound that reaches the listener directly (without any obstructions) is known as "direct path sound" (see Figure 7.5.1).

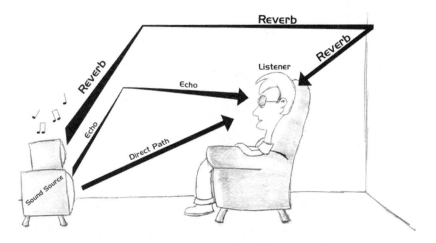

FIGURE 7.5.1   *Demonstration of direct path, echo, and reverb.*

Frequency filtering is used to create a muffling effect on sounds that are obstructed by objects in your game by removing a percentage of the sample's high frequency component. The amount of filtering is determined by the composition of what is occluding the sounds. Material properties can give good hints for this (see Figure 7.5.2).

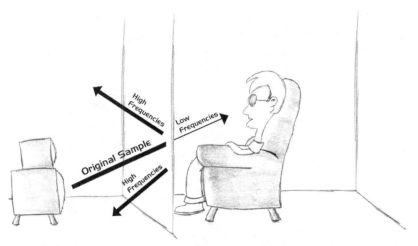

FIGURE 7.5.2   *Demonstration of obstruction/occlusion.*

Filtering is also applied to sounds with directivity information such as a character speaking. The speaker's voice is projected in a forward direction so that when standing next to or behind him you will hear less of the original high frequencies. These effects work together to create what's known as a *reverberation model*, which we discuss in more detail later when we introduce Creative Labs' EAX (Environmental Audio Extensions).

Most of the audio cards produced today have the capability of mixing these effects in hardware. Unfortunately, some on-board chips (such as the SoundMAX, which is found in most new tDell PCs) can't even perform basic 3D spatialization in hardware, let alone calculate full environmental effects. Therefore, when planning audio features, keep in mind that even today, environmental effects should be considered an advanced effect and should not break your gameplay if a user's hardware doesn't support it.

Audio Engine Requirements

Perhaps the most difficult piece of software required for your environmental audio system is the efficient storage and fast retrieval of spatial data. Creating believable and dynamic aural environments based on highly detailed geometry is not cheap in either processing or storage requirements. Audio programmers now are in the same predicament that graphics programmers were in before the adoption of BSP (binary space partitioning) trees, which most people use today to store and retrieve graphics data efficiently.

The amount of difficulty implementing this part of your audio engine depends on your experience with spatial sorting (which is beyond the scope of this article), what spatial sorting is already in your game engine (most likely for rendering or AI), and how much control you have over affecting your artists' content creation path.

Storing and Retrieving Data

There are a great many ways to store your environmental data. Basically, any 3D graphics data storage system is a candidate for storing audio spatial data: this includes such systems as a BSP tree, a quad tree (a two-dimensional tree where each parent has four children), or an octree (a three-dimensional tree where each parent has eight children). There is also an application created by Creative Labs called EAGLE (Environmental Audio Graphical Librarian Editor). EAGLE uses simplified geometry to store environmental data (retrieval in your game is done through an external DLL).

There are basically three things you need to store and have accessible each frame:

- The sound environment data (the player's current environment and last frame's environment needed for morphing)
- The potentially audible set (the sounds that are potentially audible by the player)
- The material data needed when calculating obstruction and occlusion

Storing EAX Environment Data

There needs to be a way to store the environmental data that you will give to EAX when describing the listener's and sound source's environments. In our last project we handled this by creating portals that contained environmental properties. This worked very well and used rendering systems already present in the game. The approach you should take depends on your game. A racing game, for example, could get away with using a quad tree or a gridlike structure for most of the track and use a 3D structure to represent tunnels and other special case structures. When making your choice, obviously you want the fastest method requiring the least memory, but you should also consider how it will impact the person (level or sound designer) who is required to input the data.

Potentially Audible Set (PAS)

You might have heard of a potentially visible set (PVS), which describes the potentially visible objects for rendering. PAS is the same idea, but for audio sources. *Quake* engine games called it the PHS (potentially hearable set). It defines the set of sounds that could possibly reach the listener at each given position.

This functionality is probably already built into your sound engine. If not, it should be noted that there is no magic formula or industry-standard way of calculating the PAS. PAS calculation is a topic in its own right. The engines we've been involved with use the renderer's PVS data. There are quite a few people researching this topic, though, as 3D audio is now becoming important in video games. Reducing expensive runtime calculations and creating a more realistic experience is what we all are shooting for.

Implementing a True PAS

A few games create true PAS structures that take into account wave bounces and other acoustic properties when building its list of potentially audible sounds. Implementing a PAS structure will require a bit of work and requires extra memory storage, which might or might not be possible considering your target platform. However, it more accurately represents the potentially audible sounds because it takes into account the acoustic properties of waves bouncing and materials absorbing different amounts of energy. A true PAS should also create a simplified version of the geometry to decrease memory storage and increase ray-casting calculations, which are required to detect obstruction.

Using the Renderer's PVS

Others have opted for a slightly less realistic approach and a lower amount of work (because of time or memory constraints) by using their rendering engine's PVS. *Quake 2*'s PAS, for example, combines the current PVS with the second-order PVSs of portal nodes seen from the current PVS. This makes the data set include much more area then just the standard PVS. It wouldn't be the first time this structure was used by other systems, since AI and physics simulations both require it as well. Using the PVS to detect potentially audible sounds produces great results, but will more than likely be something we eventually move away from, as advances are made in 3D audio. The only other downside to using the PVS is that you are forced to ray cast against all the highly detailed level geometry. This would be much faster if you had a simplified set.

Calculating Sound Obstruction

The PAS implementation you choose will determine how you calculate obstruction. If you decided to use Creative Labs' EAGLE application, then this work is already taken care of for you, so all you need to do is make a call to EAX Manager passing it the listener position and the sound source position.

Otherwise, the process is essentially the same no matter which PAS implementation you choose. Basically, you will simply check to see if the sound source is in the PAS. If it is not, then the sound source is occluded. You could take the easy way out and just assign a default occlusion value, but we won't settle for that. It will feel more realistic to the player if materials are used to calculate occlusion. For example, a brick room should occlude differently than a room made of drywall.

There are several things you can do to make the occlusion sound more realistic. You can figure out what objects (composition-wise) are occluding the path to the listener. This can be as simple as doing a ray cast toward the listener and a ray cast from the listener to the sound source. Then, you figure out which material preset (or texture) is used on the first object they both hit. (Material presets are discussed later, when EAX is introduced.) Depending on your preference, you can combine the two, or just prioritize materials as more important than others. Another thing you could do is factor in the encoded distance required for the source to reach the listener. Either way, the occlusion effect will sound more convincing than just having the sound always occluded by the same amount.

If the sound source *is* in the PAS, you must now ray trace to determine if the source gets to the listener without colliding with anything. If a collision occurs, the source is obstructed. Using materials to calculate obstruction is useful, but only for acoustically transmissive objects. The best way to calculate obstruction (and unfortunately the most time consuming) is to determine the angle needed to get past the obstruction. This is probably too expensive in most games, so firing off one or two ray traces to the listener is the method you will most likely use to check for collisions.

Creative Labs' EAGLE

As mentioned in the *Storing and Retrieving Data* section, EAGLE is one option you have to allow content creators to set up the game for EAX. Using EAGLE should require little programming support unless your world creation tool is unable to export to an EAGLE supported format: 3D Studio MAX (.ase), LightWave (.lwo), or DirectX Mesh (.x). EAGLE also includes an SDK for writing a custom importer should you need one. The only real downside is that each level will now have a separate process, which depends on level geometry. Thus, any substantial change in world geometry will require opening EAGLE and modifying the environment settings. EAGLE will create a BSP file, which is used by EAX Manager to calculate environment properties during the game.

Sound/Level Designer Tools

As with any feature that requires content, you will need to create an interface for sound and level designers to create and place environments and material presets and volumes to be used by ZoomFX. This interface should streamline as much as possible into their current art path.

If the decision were left up to the artists, they would more than likely prefer that you add functionality to their world creation tool rather than add a tool to their art path. If your game happens to use portals for rendering, you can tie the environment settings into them. Otherwise, you will need to create some system for sectioning off your world to represent environments. Material presets should be the easiest to add, since your game should already have some way of assigning textures to faces or brushes.

Introducing EAX

EAX is a set of audio extensions from Creative Labs. This section describes its interface, and how it is accessed through DirectSound.

DirectSound Basics

Before you can begin coding your new environmentally aware audio engine, you must first understand how EAX interfaces with DirectSound. Although DirectSound hasn't changed much since DirectX 5 (with the exception of the addition of software-based I3DL2), Direct3D engineers envy us audio engineers because of one feature that DirectSound provides that isn't available in Direct3D: property sets.

Property sets are COM interfaces exposed by DirectSound that provide access to hardware features not part of the DirectSound API, such as EAX and ZoomFX effects. This ability makes DirectSound extensible by allowing hardware manufacturers to create a new property set containing new features. Each property set is identified by a unique GUID (Globally Unique Identifier) created by the hardware manufacturer. You will soon learn how everything we do will travel through these interfaces directly to the audio hardware.

EAX Basics

EAX property sets provide adjustable parameters, which internally build the acoustic model used by the EAX reverberation engine when creating your environmental audio effects. The main difference between EAX 1.0 and EAX 2.0 is not the reverberation engine, but the properties exposed through the EAX interface. EAX 2.0 gives sound engineers and designers more knobs to turn.

There are two basic property sets you will be using with when working with EAX: the listener and source property sets. There is at most one listener property and one source property for each 3D sound buffer in your sound engine. When designing your system, be sure to keep in mind your minimum sound card requirements. If you are supporting non-EAX hardware, you will want to structure your objects in such a way that you are not storing EAX objects that will never be used.

There are a few things you should do when using EAX properties. Like DS3D, EAX provides a deferred mechanism, which allows you to change EAX properties and postpone executing their changes. Setting deferred properties is highly recommended because committing each setting individually will make multiple system calls to the sound driver and cause unnecessary work to happen multiple times per buffer. Another thing you should handle is checking the range of a property before you set it. If you set a property to a value out of its range, the EAX call will fail, and depending on the driver will either clamp the value or not set it at all.

EAX Listener Property Set

Like DirectSound's IDirectSoundListener object, the EAX listener property set is responsible for describing the player's environment in the game world. In Direct-Sound, there is one primary buffer, representing the listener. When 3D mode is enabled, this primary buffer contains properties such as position, orientation, velocity, and so on. EAX builds on this concept and adds extra listener properties, which help describe the listener's environment. This can be used to great effect as it provides the ability to describe the size of the room the listener is in, the reflection and reverberation qualities of the room, and morphing between environments. The listener (in both DirectSound and EAX) represents the global effect, which is applied to the final mix. Each version of EAX is a bit different, but they all support at least a few properties to describe the listener's environment.

Once you have created the standard DirectSound interfaces, you can obtain the EAX listener property set interface from one of your DS3D secondary buffers. You might find it a bit strange to have to use one of the secondary buffers to retrieve the listener property set, but this is because of a DirectSound quirk that prevents using the primary buffer. To get the listener property set interface (IKsPropertySet), you will need to call QueryInterface() on one of your 3D secondary buffers.

```
LPKSPROPERTYSET pEAXListener = NULL;
if ( FAILED(hr = p3DBuffer[0]->QueryInterface(
    IID_IKsPropertySet, (void**)&pEAXListener))
    || pListener == NULL )
{
    printf("QueryInterface failed to obtain EAXListener property set
interface!");
}
```

Querying for Listener Support

Before you can start setting EAX listener properties, you need to make sure the user's card supports the EAX listener property set.

```
ULONG support = 0;

if( FAILED(pEAXListener->QuerySupport(
    DSPROPSETID_EAX_ListenerProperties,
    DSPROPERTY_EAXLISTENER_ALLPARAMETERS,
    &support)) )
{
    // EAX listener properties are not supported
}

if( (support &
    (KSPROPERTY_SUPPORT_GET|KSPROPERTY_SUPPORT_SET)) !=
    (KSPROPERTY_SUPPORT_GET|KSPROPERTY_SUPPORT_SET) )
{
    // EAX listener properties are not supported
}
```

Setting and Manipulating the Listener Environment

If EAX listener is supported, now you can set a property:.

```
EAXLISTENERPROPERTIES environment = EAX30_PRESET_AUDITORIUM;
if ( FAILED(pEAXListener->Set(
    DSPROPSETID_EAX_ListenerProperties,
    DSPROPERTY_EAXLISTENER_ALLPARAMETERS, NULL, 0,
    &environment, sizeof(EAXLISTENERPROPERTIES)) )
{
    // Failed to set EAX listener preset
}
```

EAX provides environmental presets, which are a predefined group of properties used to represent the listener's environment. This feature has been available since EAX 1.0 and is very easy to use, as it requires very little programming. However, you might want to stay away from using the presets if your game will consist of more than one environment. This is because it's impossible to morph between two preset environments if you are using EAX 2.0 or earlier. A better way is to create your own presets that consist of individual properties so that you can interpolate the settings yourself. Since you are doing it yourself, you could interpolate different settings by different times so that, say, reverb is interpolated last (ask your sound designer). Performing the interpolation of multiple environments yourself guarantees that this will always work, no matter the version of EAX. In some situations, morphing shouldn't be used, such as when a player is going underwater. In this case, you should immediately switch the environment.

To perform manual environment morphing, you can do something like the following (written for readability), where t represents the percent of morphing time that has passed.

```
/*
[Each frame]
1) Find best sound environment containing player.
2) If moving into or out of water environment, skip
   interpolation and instantly assign new environment.
3) Otherwise, linearly interpolate each environmental
   property of current environment moving
   towards best environment.
*/
// Get the best and current environment using the
// method you chose to store this data.
best_environment = get_sound_environment();
current_environment = &sound_globals.environment;
new_environment->decay_time = t * best_envrionment->decay_time +
(old_environment->decay_time + (1 - t));
```

EAX Source Property Set

EAX source property sets build upon DirectSound secondary buffer objects by adding environmental properties to describe the sound source's environment and how it relates to the listener's environment. For example, in EAX 2.0 and later, the occlusion property represents the amount of attenuation and filtering that will be applied to a sound source depending on the characteristics of the occluding object.

Each sound source has its own properties, so the output mix could contain quite a few different environmental effects. This also means that you will need to store EAX source properties for each 3D sound channel in your game. To get and set EAX source properties on a buffer, the DS3D secondary buffer must have been created in hardware and with the DSBCAPS_CTRL3D flag set; otherwise, all property set calls will fail. You will most likely run into this situation if your voice allocation code fails to create a buffer in hardware, but then tries to set the EAX defaults for that buffer.

You need to obtain an EAX source property set interface from each DS3D buffer that you want to control. To get the property set interface (IID_IksPropertySet), you will need to call QueryInterface() on each of your 3D secondary buffers.

```
LPKSPROPERTYSET pEAXSource[n] = NULL;
if ( SUCCEEDED(hr = p3DBuffer[i]->QueryInterface(
    IID_IKsPropertySet, (void**)&pEAXSource[i])) &&
    pEAXSource[i] != NULL )
{
    // Successfully obtained interface
}
```

Querying for Source Support

Just as we did with the EAX listener object, you need to verify that the user's card supports EAX source properties before using them.

```
ULONG support = 0;

if( FAILED(pEAXListener->QuerySupport(
    DSPROPSETID_EAX_BufferProperties,
    DSPROPERTY_EAXBUFFER_ALLPARAMETERS, &support)) )
{
    // EAX listener properties are not supported
}

if( (support &
    (KSPROPERTY_SUPPORT_GET|KSPROPERTY_SUPPORT_SET))
!=  (KSPROPERTY_SUPPORT_GET|KSPROPERTY_SUPPORT_SET) )
{
    // EAX listener properties are not supported
}
```

Two Levels of Control

All versions of EAX provide a high level and a low level of control for source property sets. The high level is meant to decrease the complexity of adding EAX to your system by allowing the EAX reverberation engine to handle the source properties internally. This might be acceptable for some games, but for most you will want to support source properties as well so sounds can be obstructed and occluded properly. The low level of control allows you to set environmental properties on each 3D sound source. This requires a bit more work setting up, since it will require a method of tracking or requesting which environment each sound source occupies, but the 3D experience will more closely resemble that of what the player sees in the game.

You will need to make a decision about which version(s) of EAX you will be supporting. The current version as of this writing is EAX 3.0, also known as EAX Advanced HD [EAX01]. However, the most popular version with the greatest hardware saturation is EAX 2.0 [EAX00]. The most common choice is to try to support all versions, which means you have two choices: translate the EAX version calls yourself, or use Creative Labs' EAX Unified DLL, which handles this for you. In the former case, you must create separate EAX effects objects, which translate your engine's EAX settings (probably stored as EAX 3.0) into settings available for that version of EAX. In the latter case, the library automatically translates EAX 3.0 calls into calls for the correct version (or none at all if the hardware doesn't support EAX). Creative Labs recommends that you use the EAX Unified interface, as it removes the hassle of supporting each version, but this decision is totally up to you.

To use the EAX Unified interface, all you need to do is change the way you create your DirectSound interface object. Instead of calling DirectSound's `DirectSoundCre-`

ate function, you will call EAX's version, EAXDirectSoundCreate8. The following code sample shows how you can statically link against EAX.lib.

```
HRESULT hr;
LPDIRECTSOUND8 lpDS8 = NULL;  // DirectX 7 app would
                             // use LPDIRECTSOUND
// DirectX 7 app would use EAXDirectSoundCreate
if ( FAILED(hr = EAXDirectSoundCreate8(NULL,
        &lpDS8, NULL)) )
{
    printf("EAXDirectSoundCreate8 failed!");
    return hr;
}
```

After creating the DirectSound object through the EAX Unified interface, you can call DirectSound functions exactly as you would with a standard Direct-Sound object.

You should download and read the EAX Unified documentation on Creative Labs' Web site for further explanation.

Table 7.5.1 lists the different listener and source property sets available in each version of EAX.

Table 7.5.1   Comparison of Features Available in Different Versions of EAX

Listener	EAX 1.0	EAX 2.0	EAX 3.0	Source	EAX 1.0	EAX 2.0	EAX 3.0
Environment Preset	Yes	Yes	Yes	Direct	No	Yes	Yes
Volume	Yes	No	No	Direct HF	No	Yes	Yes
Damping	Yes	No	No	Room	No	Yes	Yes
Room	No	Yes	Yes	Room HF	No	Yes	Yes
Room HF	No	Yes	Yes	Room Roll-off Factor	No	Yes	Yes
Room LF	No	No	Yes	Obstruction	No	Yes	Yes
Room Roll-off Factor	No	Yes	Yes	Obstruction LF Ratio	No	Yes	Yes
Decay Time	Yes	Yes	Yes	Occlusion	No	Yes	Yes
Decay HF Ratio	No	Yes	Yes	Occlusion LF Ratio	No	Yes	Yes
Decay LF Ratio	No	No	Yes	Occlusion Room Ratio	No	Yes	Yes
Reflections	No	Yes	Yes	Outside Volume HF	No	Yes	Yes
Reflections Delay	No	Yes	Yes	Air Absorption Factor	No	Yes	Yes
Reflections Pan	No	No	Yes	Exclusion	No	No	Yes
Environment Size	No	Yes	Yes	Exclusion LF Ratio	No	No	Yes
Environment Diffusion	No	Yes	Yes	Doppler Factor	No	No	Yes
Air Absorption HF	No	Yes	Yes	Roll-off Factor	No	No	Yes
Reverb	No	No	Yes	Modulation Time	No	No	Yes
Reverb Delay	No	No	Yes	Modulation Depth	No	No	Yes
Reverb Pan	No	No	Yes	HF Reference	No	No	Yes
Echo Time	No	No	Yes	LF Reference	No	No	Yes
Echo Depth	No	No	Yes				

Material Presets

As it was mentioned in the *Calculating Sound Obstruction* section, material presets, either created by you or by EAX, can be used to help you set occlusion properties or obstruction properties if the obstructing object is acoustically transmissive. Thankfully, Creative uses the same range for their occlusion and obstruction properties, so only one material needs to be created to represent occlusion and obstruction.

A material preset consists of four values (two of which are discarded if used for obstruction):

- **Occlusion/Obstruction:** Attenuation at high frequencies
- **Occlusion/Obstruction LF Ratio:** Low frequency level
- **Occlusion Room:** Room effect control
- **Occlusion Direct Ratio:** Direct path control (usually 1.0)

To apply a material preset, simply use the EAX source property set and pass either DSPROPERTY_EAXBUFFER_OCCLUSIONPARAMETERS for occlusion or DSPROPERTY_EAXBUFFER _OBSTRUCTIONPARAMETERS for obstruction and the material preset array.

EAX 3.0 comes with eight predefined material presets: single window, double window, thin door, thick door, wood wall, brick wall, stone wall, and curtain. This will more than likely not be enough to cover your entire game, but you can easily create more from scratch or use one of the predefined materials as a base and modify it.

ON THE CD

On the companion CD-ROM you will find an EAX demo containing a very simple environment that demonstrates the effects of obstruction and occlusion as well as different EAX environments.

ZoomFX

One feature that is missing from EAX and DS3D (and one that was available in A3D) is the ability to represent sound sources as a 3D volume. Currently, EAX and DS3D both use 3D point sources in their positioning algorithms. This makes representing large or odd-shaped sound emitters a bit tough. Objects such as a chirping cricket or a bunch of dirt chunks flying in a racing game are fine to represent as point sources, since their area is small when compared to the size of the player. (Of course, if the player is a small ant in an insect fighting game, then the much larger cricket should have its musical legs represented as an area!)

From a distance, it's more practical to represent objects as point sources. However, when the listener is close to the object, the area from which the sound is emanating consumes a great deal of area around the listener's head, the same way it fills the listener's field of view. Thus, a number of virtual sources are required to produce a realistic effect (see Figure 7.5.3).

Consider this situation encountered while creating a sound engine for a 3D platform game very early in development. Our 3D engine programmer had just finished our water technology, which gave artists the ability to add water to levels, and our audio producer was eager to add water environment effects. One thing we quickly

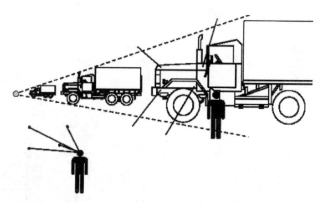

FIGURE 7.5.3 *ZoomFX dynamic decorrelation.*

realized was that representing the long, twisting stream that ran through the entire level with only point sources required a large amount of sounds to cover its area. Not only were we using too many sound sources, but we were also forced to crank up the minimum distance of each source so that they overlapped with the next sound source. Because DS3D's minimum and maximum distances are measured with spherical volumes, there was unnecessary coverage outside of the stream. This caused the stream sound effects to be played at full volume even when the player was not standing very close to the stream (see Figures 7.5.4 and 7.5.5).

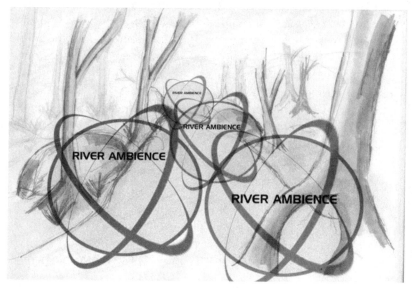

FIGURE 7.5.4 *River represented by point sources.*

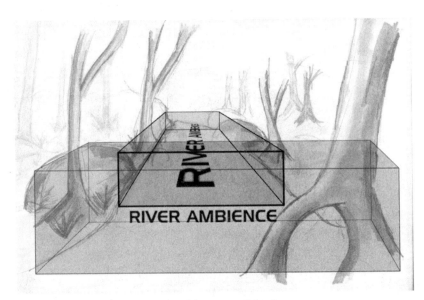

FIGURE 7.5.5 *River represented by ZoomFX volumes.*

Enter Sensuara's ZoomFX API [Zoom02]. ZoomFX is an open-standard API that bridges the gap by allowing sound designers to represent an acoustic size for sound-emitting objects. Like EAX, the ZoomFX API is accessible through DirectSound property sets on supported audio hardware. ZoomFX is a source buffer only extension; it doesn't use DS3D's listener interface.

Adding ZoomFX to your audio engine is straightforward. For each sound source that will receive ZoomFX effects, you will need to store an axis-aligned bounding box, a forward vector, and an up vector. These properties will be passed to the Sensuara hardware to create a volumetric 3D sound source. Once the bounding box representing the sound source has been set, you are free to rotate the bounding box by changing the forward and up vectors.

The implementation of ZoomFX is much like EAX; all properties are accessed through DS3D property sets. Here is the structure definition for the bounding box used by ZoomFX:

```
typedef struct
{
    D3DVECTOR vMin;
    D3DVECTOR vMax;
} ZOOMFX_BOX, *LPZOOMFX_BOX;


#define ZOOMFXBUFFER_BOX_DEFAULT \
    { {0.0f, 0.0f, 0.0f}, {0.0f, 0.0f, 0.0f} }
```

And the orientation structure:

```
typedef struct
{
    D3DVECTOR vFront;
    D3DVECTOR vTop;
} ZOOMFX_ORIENTATION, *LPZOOMFX_ORIENTATION;
#define ZOOMFXBUFFER_ORIENTATION_DEFAULT \
    { {0.0f, 0.0f, 0.0f}, {0.0f, 0.0f, 0.0f} }
```

ON THE CD

That's about it for ZoomFX. You will find a demo on the companion CD-ROM that demonstrates getting and setting properties as they are very much like EAX.

Conclusion

This article described the DirectSound, EAX, and ZoomFX interfaces for creating realistic environmental audio. The creation of Potentially Audible Sets for use with these APIs is an excellent topic for further investigation.

References

[Boer03] Boer, James, *Game Audio Programming.* Charles River Media, 2003.
[EAX00] Creative.com, "EAX 2.0 Application Programming Interface," available online at *http://developer.creative.com*, November 30, 2000.
[EAX01] Creative.com, "EAX 3.0 Application Programming Interface," available online at *http://developer.creative.com*, November 30, 2001.
[Zoom02] Sibbald, Alastair, "ZoomFX for 3D-sound," available online at *www.sensaura.com/whitepapers/pdfs/devpc012.pdf.*

7.6

Controlling Real-Time Sound Synthesis from Game Physics

Frank Luchs,

Visiomedia Software Corporation

gameprogramminggems@visiomedia.com

In this article, we describe how you can integrate your engine's physics and audio subsystems. With audio synchronized to your physics, you can avoid the tedious manual process of audio dubbing—your spatial environment will always be in perfect sync with your animation. Rather than present a general solution, we will concentrate on a specific example of a car (or other vehicle) driving around a virtual world.

Our main aim is to find a way to produce dynamic and evolving sounds where parameterization and timing is taken care of automatically. We just want to take advantage of the scene we already have, letting game physics and geometric environment drive the audio in an interactive way. With this method, we can automatically produce accurately synchronized sounds with time-varying spectral content for complex situations that would be very difficult to achieve by other means, especially with static audio samples.

This article makes use of the DirectScene engine. This combines the Sphinx Modular Media system, SphinxMM [Luchs02] with the Open Dynamics Engine (ODE) [Smith00].

We begin with a look at the main elements of our engine, and then describe the synthesis methods and the influences of audible object properties, and finally the demo. The demo is a vehicle simulation inspired by Brown's BuggyDemo [Brown03] that shows a concrete implementation of our model within a living environment.

Game Engine

Discrete objects in our game are represented by *entities*. An entity is a generic node in our main data structure, the scene graph. The entity manages a container for attributes of specialized objects defined by our subsystems. These are graphics objects, physics objects, and audio objects, corresponding to the game's graphics, physics, and audio engines. Figure 7.6.1 depicts a high-level overview of the DirectScene system.

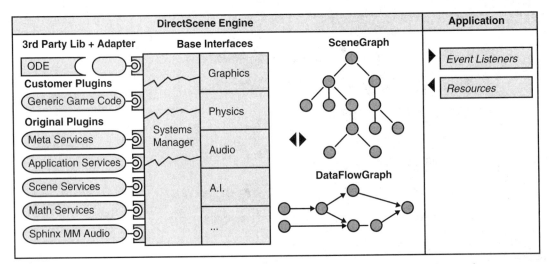

FIGURE 7.6.1   *Engine overview including scene graph, graphics, physics, and audio rendering subsystems.*

For example, each possible obstacle in our scene is associated with a graphical mesh, a collision mesh, and a collision sound.

While the renderable mesh for a wall might consist of hundreds of polygons, the audio system needs only a simple reduced version. In our scene graph, an object has references to versions with different levels-of-detail (LODs). Most engines will implement simplified geometries for collision testing; these detail-reduced objects can also be used for audio purposes.

The engine creates dynamic sound sources through object instantiation. Some sources are predefined by the game logic, while others are created in response to events generated by the subsystems.

We can illustrate this with our vehicle example. At game start, we create a sound source for the background music, which requires no further processing and has no spatial information. We also create the engine sound as part of our vehicle. The audio patch responsible for the synthesis of the motor sound has modulation inputs, which are dynamically updated by both the velocity, taken from the physics system, and the positional information from our graphics system. In the case of a squeaking tire or a collision with another object, we create and destroy a sound source based on the contact time and set the modulation parameters according to the physical status of the objects involved.

In a complex environment, we have a potentially large number of contacts occurring simultaneously. For efficiency, we limit the number of concurrent sound sources that can be active at the same time to those related to foreground events. We also precreate audio patches for later use to prevent the unnecessary and resource-intensive process of object creation and destruction.

Audio Patches

A synthesis method is defined by an audio patch, which describes the dataflow between the individual sound processing units, and contains all the state needed for sound generation and modulation. A typical audio patch has a generator followed by one or more processing filters. Generators play prerecorded audio samples or operate as oscillators to synthesize audio based on a specific algorithm. The information described in a sound patch is similar to the texture and material scripts in the graphics world, where surface attributes are mapped to the specified object. Sample sounds are real-world elements, analogous to using digitized photographic images as textures in the graphics system. Synthesized sounds are artificial elements, analogous to procedural textures like fire and water effects on the graphics side. Audio patches can be shared by several entities for efficiency.

Synchronization

Synchronous processing of virtual objects is achieved by providing event listeners from individual subsystems to the application. For synchronization we use a timer-based loop, which allows us to specify an exact frame rate. Audio buffer processing is done blockwise, with a typical buffer size (and thus latency) on the order of 20 ms, to match the typical graphics rendering frame rate of 50 Hz.

Hybrid Sound Synthesis

Our particular approach is a hybrid synthesis based on modeling sounds by mixing a stochastic noise component and a deterministic quasi-sinusoidal component. This provides an alternative to explicit physical modeling, permitting a simple control through a small number of parameters taken directly from the other subsystems. These parameters are related either to the resonating objects or to the interaction force.

Rather than doing a vibrational analysis based on strict physical laws, we concentrate on sound rendering methods with a high computational efficiency at the cost of losing some accuracy and realism. Often, an exaggeration of certain acoustic aspects, while losing less important ones, is preferable.

We implement only two different synthesis methods, but despite this simplicity we will achieve a wide range of natural collision sounds simulating the audio response of everyday objects made out of stone, metal, or wood. The two methods work in opposition and complement each other.

The first sound we synthesize is a fractal-type noise-based sound, which is achieved by overlapping and adding multiple independent sound producing particles. This PhISEM synthesis is described in [Cook02], where it is used to simulate unpitched percussion instruments like maracas, tambourine, and guiro. The raw noise is a mix of random amplitudes and phases with an exponential decay that runs through a single two-pole resonance filter.

This method is fine for less pronounced timbres of wood and plastic, and is the ideal basic sound for continuous contacts such as scraping, sliding, and rolling, where it simulates the random series of micro-impacts between two resonating shapes.

Scraping noise is the sound most frequently used in our simulation; therefore, the synthesis algorithm must be efficient. Our multiparticle noise is an extremely simple model and only requires two random number calculations, two exponential decays, and one resonant filter calculation per source. This method can even simulate the sound generated by the tire/ground contact. A nice challenge here is to model the grain size depending on the terrain's texture (e.g., asphalt, gravel). This would bring us one step further in our quest for automatic parameterization. This feature currently is under development.

The second sound is a synthesis based on damped oscillations (modes). Modes of vibration are the latent spectral patterns of vibration of a given object. We only take relatively few exponentially decaying and weakly coupled sinusoids. The decay coefficient of the wave equation to damp the sounds depends on the object's properties (mass, size, material, etc.) and the impact energy, and is proportional to the frequency. A higher mode has a stronger damping factor. The friction coefficient also is material dependent and approximately invariant over the object's surface. Both model parameters respond linearly to the input force.

This method is fine for pitched sounds needed for collisions with resonating objects made of glass and metal. The addition of sines with integer ratios results in harmonic sounds; using noninteger relationships leads to inharmonic sounds. Modulation input parameters are the frequencies corresponding to the natural modes of the vibrating object, the sinusoid's initial amplitude, and the damping coefficients that describe the spectrum's evolution in time domain.

In the case of two colliding bodies, our audio system performs the following steps, based on the assigned sound material.

1. We start the fractal noise as the basic sonic element. This is the multiparticle synthesis that models the sound generated by two objects with rough surfaces rubbing against each other. The resonance of the single two-pole filter is tuned to a value suitable to the volume of the object touched. For fast repeated impulses, our system does not reset the attack with each new collision. This is similar to legato articulation on a synthesizer: playing the next note while still holding a key down does not retrigger the note.

2. If the collision energy is high enough to cause shape resonances, we add the sinusoid-based signal.

3. If we have an assigned sample, it will be triggered in accordance with the peaks of the noise envelope.

Audible Object Properties

Dynamic sound control is straightforward if we have access to the attributes of the various objects in our scene graph. We can take the physical and geometric characteristics, such as size, elasticity, mass, and shape, and assign their attributes to audio controllers. These controllers are responsible for the mapping process between values. They do all the calculations we need: normalization, scaling, limiting, summing, and so forth.

In our sonic environment, we typically have two types of objects: static meshes and dynamic meshes. Static meshes are used for the terrain and nondynamic elements, while dynamic meshes are used for animating objects. In most cases, the multiparticle noise alone is sufficient for static elements, while dynamic meshes are more affected by the physics system, and need individual audio attributes to balance the visual experience with the "expected" sound.

Influence of Shape

The shape of an object determines a characteristic frequency spectrum. Let's look at some basic geometries and see what set of modes we need to create a credible sound.

- A simple string has only harmonic ratios.
- A rigid bar has these modes: 1.0, 2.765, 5.404, and 8.933. A metal bar, for example, rings with a sparse nonharmonic spectrum, with the higher modes decaying rapidly.
- A rectangular membrane has an extremely dense sound spectrum, giving a rich, complex sound.
- A circular membrane has resonances (eigenfunctions) that are Bessel functions.
- A circulate plate has a much less dense spectrum than a circular membrane does.
- Open or closed tubes have harmonic modes; a tube closed on one side has odd multiples of the fundamental.
- A box resonator has a frequency response that is the superposition of harmonic combs, each having a fundamental frequency as calculated by

$$f_0, l, m, n = \frac{c}{2} \sqrt{\left(l \,/\, x\right)^2 + \left(m \,/\, y\right)^2 + \left(n \,/\, z\right)^2} \tag{7.6.1}$$

where c is the speed of sound; l, m, n is a triple of positive integers with no common divisor; and x, y, and z are the edge lengths of the box.

The sphere resonator has a frequency response that is the superposition of inharmonic combs each having peaks at the extreme points of spherical Bessel functions:

$$fns = \frac{c}{2\pi r} * zns \tag{7.6.2}$$

where fns is the resonance frequency, c is the speed of sound, r is the radius of the sphere, and zns is the sth root of the derivative of the nth Bessel function.

You can find detailed information about the preceding formulas in [Avanzini01], [O'Brien02], and [Riegel00].

Some rules will help us to modify the synthesis in real-time:

- Generated sounds depend on the location of impact on an affected object. Higher frequencies become relatively more excited for collision points near the boundary of the shape. In other words, the tone sounds dull near the center and bright near the boundary.

- For large forces, nonlinear effects will come into play.
- An exact decay rate for the individual partials plays a much larger role than the center pitch of the resonating material [Avanzini01].
- A long period of contact damps those high frequency modes of vibration of the surface whose periods are shorter than the time of contact itself.
- The contact time t_0 (i.e., the time after which the objects move apart from another) has a major role in defining the spectral characteristics of the initial transient. A short t_0 corresponds to an impulselike transient with a rich spectrum, and thus provides a bright attack; similarly, a long t_0 corresponds to a smoother transient with little energy in the high-frequency region.

Influence of Material

Acoustic properties of materials can be characterized using the coefficient of internal friction. This parameter measures the degree of elasticity and defines the decay time of vibration and the bandwidth of spectral components. When we categorize materials by internal friction, we get two groups: a soft group containing plastic and wood, and a hard group with glass and metal. In going from plastic to metal spectra we have progressively increasing decay times and progressively decreasing bandwidths [Avanzini01]. This is only true for free vibrating shapes; damped glass sounds similar to plastic.

Impact and Collisions

In principle, we don't use different synthesis methods for a single impact and multiple continuous contacts, because they have a flowing transition. Complex sounds like bouncing, scraping, rolling, and breaking can be simulated by repeating simple impact sounds on different time scales.

Most collisions have a "skid" component where the surfaces slide past each other for a short time during the impact. For example, a bouncing ball will skid more the faster it spins. In the case of a high contact frequency, the sound mix amplifies the noise portion.

The main problem is keeping track of when a contact is created and destroyed and when it is sufficient to start and stop the related audio patch.

Our physics system, ODE, requires us to supply the NearCallback() function where we handle our collisions. The system provides a list of "contact joints," which are pairs of objects that are in collision at that specific moment in time. This is unfortunately not very convenient for doing single sound triggering, because the list includes not only collisions that have just occurred, but also objects simply resting on one another, staying continuously in contact. Most of these contacts do not make a sound, so we should suppress them; otherwise, we would hear a horrible series of machine-gun like sounds! One way to fix this is to compare the collision list of the current frame with that of the previous frame. When an object pair comes into contact for the first time, we trigger a collision sound.

A related problem is that, rather than staying in permanent contact, objects might "bounce" and collide frequently. In this case, we don't want to retrigger the sound every time. Especially if the sound has a fast "attack" phase, we would again end up with a "machine gun" noise. A way to cause more natural sounds is to control the amplitude of the sound, especially its attack phase, depending on the frequency of contacts. We sum up the impulses over time, and gradually increase the level of the already playing sound.

The Demo

In the demo, you steer a vehicle through an environment with different obstacles. A collision with an obstacle will create the appropriate sound. The engine sound is controlled by the vehicle's velocity. Additional effects are the tire/ground noise, which varies depending on the ground type, and a squeaking tire sound. A hall with a machine shows the concept of occlusion, audio portals, and pre-calculated reverb. The demo is available at *www.directscene.com*.

Sound Source

It is straightforward to calculate the speed of our vehicle given its velocity vector. In the 2D case, we calculate $\sqrt{v.x^2 + v.z^2}$. For a simple model, we would just map this value to the sound source's pitch modulation, and we are done. In a more complex model, we would control a synthesized engine sound, which would change in a more complex way according to the input speed parameter.

Rolling

Ground textures with different roughness demonstrate different rolling sounds using the filtered noise part alone. Some ground surfaces contain more or less regular patterns, which cannot be suitably simulated using our filtered fractal noise. Such irregularities on the surface are modeled by adding amplitude modulation to the basic noise sound.

Slipping

In our example, we also simulate "squeaking" when the wheels slip on the ground (e.g., due to a skid). For an automatic squeak sound we compare the current angular velocity of the wheels with the nonslipping value. We know that a free-rolling wheel with zero slip has an angular velocity of

$$\omega = v\Big/2\pi r$$

where r is the radius of the wheel, and v is the longitudinal velocity.

We use the absolute difference of both velocities to control the level of our squeak generator. (Of course, we only enable this sound when the wheels are in contact with the surface!)

Conclusion

Rendering realistic object sounds in real-time directly from physical models will become increasingly important. The DirectScene graph implements known paradigms from 3D graphics APIs and enables the creation of detailed aural environments based on known geometric and physical information. The complex and time-intensive process of manual sound creation and synchronization is eliminated by using audio controllers that listen in real-time to physical and geometric properties and map them to useful synthesis parameters.

The audio patch based architecture can easily be extended for describing new synthesis methods for environmental sounds.

References

[Avanzini01] Avanzini, Frederico, and Davide Rocchesso, "Controlling Material Properties in Physical Models of Sounding Objects," available online at *www.soundobject.org/papers/avaroc_icmc2001.pdf*, 2001.

[Brown03] Brown, Si, "BuggyDemo," available online at *http://freefall.freehosting.net/downloads/buggydemo.html*, 2002.

[Cook02] Cook, Perry R., *Real Sound Synthesis for Interactive Applications*, AK Peters LTD, 2002.

[Luchs02] Luchs, Frank, "Real-Time Modular Audio," *Game Programming Gems 3*, Charles River Media, 2002.

[O'Brien02] O'Brien, James F., Chen Shen, and Christine M. Gatchalian. "Synthesizing Sounds from Rigid-Body Simulations," available online at *http://citeseer.nj.nec.com/518076.html*, 2002.

[Riegel00] Edward Riegelsberger, Micah Mason, and Suneil Mishra, "Advancing 3D Audio through an Acoustic Geometry Interface," available online at *www.gdconf.com/archives/2000/riegelsb.pdf*, 2000.

[Smith2000] Smith, Russell, "Open Dynamics Engine," available online at *http://opende.sourceforge.net*, 2000.

APPENDIX

About the CD-ROM

The book's CD-ROM contains all of the code mentioned in the articles. The following articles have accompanying code:

- 1.2: An HTML-Based Logging and Debugging System
- 1.3: The Clock: Keeping Your Finger on the Pulse of the Game
- 1.5: Fight Memory Fragmentation with Templated Freelists
- 1.6: A Generic Tree Container in C++
- 1.7: The Beauty of Weak References and Null Objects
- 1.8: A System for Managing Game Entities
- 1.9: Address-Space Managed Dynamic Arrays for Windows and the Xbox
- 1.10: Critically Damped Ease-In/Ease-Out Smoothing
- 1.11: A Flexible, On-the-Fly Object Manager
- 1.12: Using Custom RTTI Properties to Stream and Edit Objects
- 1.13: Using XML without Sacrificing Speed
- 2.1: Zobrist Hash Using the Mersenne Twister
- 2.2: Extracting Frustum and Camera Information
- 2.3: Solving Accuracy Problems in Large World Coordinates
- 2.4: Nonuniform Splines
- 2.5: Using the Covariance Matrix for Better-Fitting Bounding Objects
- 2.6: The Jacobian Transpose Method for Inverse Kinematics
- 3.1: Ten Fingers of Death: Algorithms for Combat Killing
- 3.3: Writing a Verlet-Based Physics Engine
- 3.4: Constraints in Rigid Body Dynamics
- 3.5: Fast Contact Reduction for Dynamics Simulation
- 3.6: Interactive Water Surfaces
- 3.7: Fast Deformations with Multilayered Physics
- 3.8: Modal Analysis for Fast, Stable Deformation
- 4.3: NPC Decision Making: Dealing with Randomness
- 5.2: GPU Shadow Volume Construction for Nonclosed Meshes
- 5.3: Perspective Shadow Maps
- 5.4: Combined Depth and ID-Based Shadow Buffers
- 5.7: Real-Time Halftoning: Fast and Simple Stylized Shading
- 5.8: Techniques to Apply Team Color to 3D Models
- 5.10: Dynamic Gamma Using Sampled Scene Luminance
- 5.15: Terrain Occlusion Culling with Horizons
- 6.2: Thousands of Clients per Server
- 6.4: Practical Application of Parallel-State Machines in a Client-Server Environment
- 6.5: Bit Packing: A Network Compression Technique

- 7.3: Dynamic Variables and Audio Programming
- 7.4: Creating an Audio Scripting System
- 7.5: Implementing an Environmental Audio Solution Using EAX and ZoomFX

We've also included copies of the third-party libraries that are required to link code from the articles.

More information about this book, including errata and updates, is available online at *www.GameProgrammingGems.com*.

System Requirements

Windows: Intel® Pentium®-series, AMD Athlon or newer processor recommended. Windows 98 (64MB RAM) or Windows 2000 (128MB RAM) or later required. 3D graphics card recommended for optimal performance. DirectX 9 and GLUT 3.7 or newer are also required.

Linux: Intel® Pentium®-series, AMD Athlon or newer processor recommended. Linux kernel 2.4.x or later required. 32MB RAM recommended. 3D graphics card recommended for optimal performance. XFree86 4.0, GLUT 3.7, OpenGL driver, glibc 2.1 or newer are also required. Mesa can be used in place of 3D hardware support.

INDEX

A

A* algorithm, GPG2: 250
  aesthetic optimizations, GPG1: 264–271
  costs, GPG3: 295–296, 298–300, 304–305
  Master Node List and Priority Queue Open List implementation, GPG1: 285–286
  navigation meshes and, GPG1: 294–295
  pathfinding and, GPG1: 294, GPG2: 315, 325
  path planning with, GPG1: 254–262
  performance, GPG3: 301–302
  priority queues for speed, GPG1: 281–282, 283–286
  speed optimizations for, GPG1: 272–287
  A Star Explorer program, A* tool, GPG3: 305
  stochastic maps and, 325–326
  tactical pathfinding, GPG3: 294–305
  waypoints and, GPG2: 315
  weaknesses of, GPG1: 261–262
Abstract interfaces
  described and defined, GPG2: 20–22
  disadvantages of, GPG2: 26–27
  factories, GPG2: 22–23
  as traits, GPG2: 23–26
  virtual destructors, GPG2: 23
Abstract syntax trees (AST), for programmable vertex shader compiler, GPG3: 410
Acceleration, 221–225
  lookup tables and, 229
  and velocity on splines, 180
Accidental complexity, GPG2: 258–259
Accuracy
  far position (hybrid between fixed-point and floating-point numbers), 162–166
  large world coordinates and, 162–166
ActionState class
  GoCap, GPG3: 231–232, 233–234
  for MMPs, GPG3: 509
Actor class
  GoCap, GPG3: 232
  for MMPs, GPG3: 512–513
ActorProxy class for massively multiplayer games, GPG3: 513
Address-space management of dynamic arrays, 85–93
ADPCM audio compression format, GPG3: 589, 620–621
Ahmad, Anis
  article by, GPG1: 581–583
  contact information, GPG1: *xxv*
AI. *See* Artificial Intelligence (AI)
AIControlStates, for massively multiplayer games (MMPs), GPG3: 509–510
Aiming, tactical pathfinding and, GPG3: 298

Air, cellular automata to model currents and pressure, GPG3: 200, 206
Alexander, Thor
  articles by, GPG3: 231–239, 506–519
  contact and bio info, GPG3: *xxiii*
Algorithms
  for authentication, GPG3: 555
  bit packing algorithm, 573–574
  Bloom Filter algorithm, GPG2: 133
  bones-based collision detection algorithm, 506–513
  brute-force comparison algorithm, GPG2: 228
  collision detection, GPG2: 228–238
  combinatorial search algorithms, GPG2: 354
  contact reduction algorithms, 253–263
  cPLP algorithm, GPG3: 355–358
  curvature simulation, GPG3: 425–426
  Cylinder-frustum intersection test, GPG1: 382–384
  data key evaluation algorithm, 498–500
  for decals, GPG2: 411–413
  Diamond-square algorithm, GPG1: 505–507
  Dijkstra's algorithm, GPG1: 294
  DP (dynamic programming) algorithm, 325–335
  dynamic gamma algorithm, 470–474
  for encryption, GPG3: 555
  Fast Fourier Transforms (FFT) and, 265
  Goertzel's algorithm, GPG3: 172–174
  Graham's algorithm, GPG3: 276
  group finding with, GPG2: 229
  for heat shimmer or haze distortion, 477–478
  Heuristic costs algorithm, GPG1: 276–278
  for infinite universes, GPG1: 136–139
  killing algorithms and real physics, 209–219
  for landscaping, GPG1: 485–490
  LCA (linear congruential algorithm), GPG3: 623–624
  learning algorithms, GPG1: 345–350
  levels of detail (LOD) selection, GPG1: 435–437
  Linear congruential algorithm (LCA), GPG3: 623–624
  line / line intersection, GPG2: 191
  Marching Cubes algorithm, GPG2: 229
  mazes, GPG1: 492–493
  Metaball clusters and, GPG2: 229
  name generation, GPG1: 493–498
  negamax algorithm and game trees, GPG1: 250–251
  occlusion, GPG3: 354–358
  Perlin noise algorithms, GPG3: 453
  PLP algorithm, GPG3: 354–355, 356–358
  pseudo-random number generation, GPG3: 623–624
  randomness, GPG1: 135–136, GPG3: 453, 623–624
  random number generator algorithm, GPG2: 130
  RDC algorithm, GPG2: 229